BUTLER'S
LIVES OF THE SAINTS

Concise Edition

BUTLER'S
LIVES OF THE SAINTS
Concise Edition

EDITED BY MICHAEL WALSH

Foreword by Cardinal Basil Hume, O.S.B.
Archbishop of Westminster

1817

HARPER & ROW, PUBLISHERS, San Francisco

Cambridge, Hagerstown, New York, Philadelphia
London, Mexico City, São Paulo, Singapore, Sydney

NIHIL OBSTAT: ANTON COWAN CENSOR
IMPRIMATUR: MONSIGNOR JOHN CROWLEY, V.G.
WESTMINSTER: 15th August 1984
FEAST OF THE ASSUMPTION B.V.M.

Library of Congress Cataloging in Publication Data 84–48781

ISBN 0·06–069251–0

85 86 87 88 89 10 9 8 7 6 5 4 3 2 1

FOREWORD

We live in a sophisticated, if not cynical, age in which the former 'certainties' of faith, which brought comfort to so many, are now widely questioned. But surely a living faith can have no absolute certainties? Which of us has matured in religious belief without having experienced any intellectual difficulty? Faith, by very definition, grows through a constant, indeed daily, process, whereby doubts, old and new, must ever be conquered afresh.

This growth in faith can be helped by stories and legends of the saints. Some of these members of the Church in glory who were commemorated liturgically in former days are rather forgotten today. Yet they may have much to teach us. Furthermore, the lives of good men and women can be, and often are, an inspiration to us. Happily, their memory is recorded in one of the great classic works on Christian sainthood, *Butler's Lives of the Saints*.

The heroic men and women described and speculated upon in this book have bequeathed to us an inspiration that transcends ordinary history. It is not surprising then, that there should be a demand today for a 'concise edition' of *Butler's Lives*, to form both an introduction to and a foretaste of the complete work. For this present generation seems to be seeking not the letter which kills, but the spirit which awakens.

This 'concise edition' then, is welcome, not least because of the curiously attractive echoes of its original eighteenth-century style. The modern re-editing, moreover, tends to belie the modest comment of Father Herbert Thurston, who edited the first edition of *Butler's Lives* in this century, that 'This book is not intended for scholars'. I hope that many people will find inspiration in reading it.

Archbishop of Westminster

Editor's Introduction

On the shelves of the library in which this Introduction is being written is a much-prized copy of *The Lives of the Fathers, Martyrs and other Principal Saints: Compiled from Original Monuments and other authentick records: Illustrated with the Remarks of judicious modern criticks and historians*. It was published in four volumes, though in rather more parts, in London between 1756 and 1759. It appeared anonymously, but its author was no secret. Alban Butler's *Lives of the Saints*, as it has come to be known, must surely rank with the Douai Bible and the *Garden of the Soul* as one of the most influential works of piety produced within the English Catholic community.

Butler was born at Appletree in Northamptonshire on October 24, 1710. He seems to have attended a school in Lancashire before being sent overseas in June 1724 to continue his education at the English college at Douai. There he was ordained priest ten years later, and there for a time he taught philosophy and theology to other candidates for the priesthood. The middle years of his life he spent on the mission in England, working chiefly in Staffordshire, and in Norwich as chaplain to the family of the Duke of Norfolk. In 1766 he was appointed President of the English College at St Omer, from which the English Jesuits had recently been expelled, and he died in that office on May 15, 1773. In the midst of a very busy life he had found time to copy manuscripts for Bishop Challoner's *Memoirs of Missionary Priests*, and to write a number of learned works of his own. *Butler's Lives of the Saints*, however, has remained his masterpiece.

For well over a century and a half Butler's Gibbonesque prose survived unscathed through a variety of editions—the British Library catalogue lists at least a dozen. In 1926 Father Herbert Thurston, S.J., was engaged to produce a thorough revision and, with the help first of Miss Norah Leeson and later of Donald Attwater, this he did. The final volume appeared in 1938, a year before he died. Fr Thurston commented that he doubted whether more than half a dozen consecutive sentences survived from the original, but this was not because he or his fellow revisors doubted Butler's ability. Quite the contrary. As Attwater wrote later, Butler's 'manner of writing is tiresome, but it does not obscure his sound sense and the solid traditional teaching of his exhortation. Credulous and uncritical he is not. He is as critical a hagiographer as the state of knowledge and available materials of his age would allow'.

Attwater himself produced a further, four-volume, revised edition in 1956, and there was yet another revision ten years later, though the changes in this printing were very few. A book that in the mid-eighteenth century had contained just under 1500 entries, by the mid-twentieth had grown to well over 2500. It is upon this last revision that the present work has been based.

Massive though the expansion may have been, the Thurston-Attwater edition can lay no claims to completeness. An authority on the sociology of sainthood has pointed out that while the 1926 edition of the January volume of *Butler's Lives* has 258 entries, the equivalent French version for the same month, produced by the Paris Benedictines, has well over 509. Yet even those figures pale into insignificance beside the scholarly *Bibliotheca Sanctorum*, published by Rome's Lateran University in 1970, which for January notes almost a thousand names. Part of the problem lies in deciding who is, and who is not, a saint (or 'blessed', for they are generally included as well, though not in this Concise Edition). Mere inclusion in a martyrology, or calendar of saints, is not enough. Dr David Farmer remarks in the introduction to his *Oxford Dictionary of Saints* that the Irish martyrologies list some three hundred saints all called Colman. He includes a representative four in his own compilation, while the *Bibliotheca Sanctorum* notes twenty and Thurston-Attwater has five. This book has one. How much, if any, local veneration, or cult, was ever paid to these many saints whose names have been handed down to us, it is now often impossible to determine. It is accordingly difficult to determine whether someone who is, and despite all efforts remains, totally unknown apart from the name, should be included in modern listings of the saints.

The number of the formally recognized saints is regularly added to, in the Roman Catholic Church, by the process of canonization. Only rarely is the number reduced. In 1961 St Philomena disappeared and in 1969, by a decree of the Sacred Congregation of Rites, a few others followed her. In the words of the Congregation, they posed 'serious historical problems', a phrase which may reasonably be interpreted as 'probably never existed'. St Catherine of Alexandria, for instance, she of the catherine wheel, was one such. Another was St Cecilia, but so great was the veneration shown her as the patron saint of music that she was allowed to remain in the calendar. Also allowed to remain, but only just, were a number of others whose existence was probable but of whose lives little but legends survives. St George, patron saint of England, was one of these. This group was, as it were, demoted in rank, and celebration of their feasts moved from the Church's universal calendar to the particular calendars of dioceses or countries. Finally, the 1969 revision re-scheduled many of the feast-days of saints. The traditional practice had been to celebrate the memory of a saint on the day of his or her death, the saint's 'birthday' into heaven. Down the centuries other feasts have supervened, and feast-days have been changed. Now, for the most part, the day of death has been restored as the principal occasion for liturgical observance of a saint's life, work, and virtue.

All these changes have been noted in what follows. They have also been incorporated in the general index, which lists all surviving saints, and all those blesseds who have been promoted to the rank of saint, included in the 1956 index to Thurston-Attwater. The volume itself contains one saint's life for each day. The new calendar has been adhered to, with the result that some outstanding individuals have had to be excluded in favour of someone else sharing the same feast day, while other, distinctly less memorable, saints have found a place because there was less competition on their day.

The selection has been made in such a way that this 'Concise Butler' is, it is hoped, a faithful reflection of the whole work. The choice has been world-wide, but if there is a slight bias in favour of Anglo-Saxon saints, that is also in fidelity to Butler. The New World has not been forgotten, however, and the only two wholly new lives in this edition are both of saints from the United States. There are very long entries, and some extremely short ones. There are well-known saints, and some who are very little known. Legends are recounted, again in fidelity to the original, but they are generally recognized for what they are. Fr Thurston's fascination with psychic phenomena is well represented, but so also is his healthy scepticism. Occasionally entries have had to be up-dated and language modified. Pious exhortations have been deleted. The saints, with all their achievements and all their eccentricities, should be allowed to stand up for themselves. They do not need apologists to commend them to our devotion.

The labour of putting this book together would have been much greater had I not been able to rely upon the help of Ms Jenny Hansford. In the midst of looking after Clare (two entries) and Alexandra (alas, none) she applied scissors and paste with care and rapidity. I am most grateful.

Feast of St Vincent of Lérins
May 24, 1984

MICHAEL J. WALSH
Heythrop College

Contents

March

1	St David	17	St Patrick
2	St Chad	18	St Cyril of Jerusalem
3	St Cunegund	19	St Joseph
4	St Casimir of Poland	20	St Cuthbert
5	St John Joseph-of-the-Cross	21	St Enda
6	St Colette	22	St Nicholas Owen
7	St Drausius	23	St Turibius
8	St John of God	24	St Irenaeus of Sirmium
9	St Frances of Rome	25	St Lucy Filippini
10	St John Ogilvie	26	St Braulio
11	St Oengus	27	St John of Egypt
12	St Theophanes the Chronicler	28	St Tutilo
13	St Euphrasia	29	St Rupert (of Salzburg)
14	St Leobinus	30	St Zosimus of Syracuse
15	St Louise de Marillac	31	St Guy of Pomposa
16	St Abraham Kidunaia		

April

1	St Hugh (of Grenoble)	16	St Bernadette
2	St Francis of Paola	17	St Stephen Harding
3	St Richard of Wyche	18	St Galdinus
4	St Isidore (of Seville)	19	St Alphege (of Canterbury)
5	St Vincent Ferrer	20	St Agnes of Montepulciano
6	St William of Eskilsoë	21	St Anselm (of Canterbury)
7	St John Baptist de la Salle	22	St Theodore of Sykeon
8	St Julia Billiart	23	St George
9	St Waldetrudis, or Waudru	24	St Fidelis of Sigmaringen
10	St Fulbert	25	St Mark
11	St Stanislaus (of Cracow)	26	St Stephen
12	St Alferius	27	St Zita
13	St Hermenegild	28	St Peter Mary Chanel
14	St Bénezet	29	St Catherine of Siena
15	St Hunna	30	St Pius V

May

1	St Marculf	11	St Francis di Girolamo
2	St Athanasius	12	St Germanus (of
3	SS. Philip and James		Constantinople)
4	St Godehard	13	St John the Silent
5	St Hilary	14	St Michael Garicoïts
6	St Petronax	15	St Isidore the Farmer
7	St John of Beverley	16	St Brendan
8	St Peter of Tarentaise	17	St Paschal Baylon
9	St Pachomius	18	St Eric of Sweden
10	St Antoninus (of Florence)	19	St Dunstan

June

July

August

1	St Peter Julian Eymard	17	St Clare of Montefalco
2	St Eusebius	18	St Helen
3	St Waltheof, or Walthen	19	St John Eudes
4	St John Vianney	20	St Bernard of Clairvaux
5	SS. Addai and Mari	21	St Pius X
6	St Hormisdas	22	St Sigfrid (of Wearmouth)
7	St Cajetan	23	St Rose of Lima
8	St Dominic	24	St Audoenus
9	St Oswald of Northumbria	25	St Louis of France
10	St Laurence	26	St Elizabeth Bichier des Ages
11	St Clare (of Assisi)	27	St Caesarius
12	SS. Porcarius and companions	28	St Augustine (of Hippo)
13	St Maximus the Confessor	29	St Medericus, or Merry
14	St Marcellus	30	St Pammachius
15	The Blessed Virgin Mary	31	St Aidan
16	St Stephen of Hungary		

September

1	St Drithelm	17	St Hildegard
2	St William (of Roskilde)	18	St Joseph of Cupertino
3	St Gregory the Great	19	St Emily de Rodat
4	St Rose of Viterbo	20	St Vincent Madelgarius
5	St Laurence of Giustiniani	21	SS. Michael of Chernigov and
6	St Bega, or Bee		St Theodore
7	St Clodoald, or Cloud	22	St Thomas of Villanova
8	St Corbinian	23	St Adamnan of Iona
9	St Peter Claver	24	St Gerard (of Csanad)
10	St Nicholas of Tolentino	25	St Albert (of Jerusalem)
11	St Paphnutius	26	St Teresa Couderc
12	St Guy of Anderlecht	27	St Vincent de Paul
13	St John Chrysostom	28	St Wenceslaus of Bohemia
14	St Notburga	29	SS. Rhipsime, Gaiana and
15	St Catherine of Genoa		companions
16	St Cyprian	30	St Jerome

October

1	St Teresa of Lisieux	11	St Mary Soledad
2	The Guardian Angels	12	St Wilfrid
3	St Thomas Cantelupe	13	St Edward the Confessor
4	St Francis of Assisi	14	St Callistus, or Calixtus, I
5	St Flora of Beaulieu	15	St Teresa of Avila
6	St Bruno	16	St Margaret-Mary
7	St Osith	17	St Ignatius (of Antioch)
8	St Keyne	18	St Luke
9	St Louis Bertrand	19	The Martyrs of North America
10	St Francis Borgia	20	St Bertilla Boscardin

November

December

BUTLER'S
LIVES OF THE SAINTS

Concise Edition

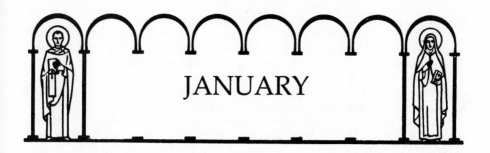

JANUARY

1 : ST PETER OF ATROA, ABBOT (A.D. 837)

ST PETER of Atroa, who was born in 773 near Ephesus, was the eldest of three children, and was christened Theophylact. Nobody was surprised when, at the age of eighteen, he decided to be a monk. Directed, it is said, by the All-holy Mother of God, he joined St Paul the Hesychast (Recluse) at his hermitage at Crypta in Phrygia, who clothed Theophylact with the holy habit and gave him the name of Peter. Immediately after his ordination to the priesthood at Zygos some years later, at the very door of the church, there happened the first wonder recorded of him, when he cured a man possessed by an unclean spirit.

Shortly afterwards St Peter accompanied his spiritual father on his first pilgrimage, when they directed their steps towards Jerusalem; but God in a vision turned them aside, telling them to go to the Bithynian Olympus, where St Paul was to establish a monastery at the chapel of St Zachary on the edge of the Atroa. This accordingly was done, the monastery flourished, and before his death in 805 Paul named Peter as his successor: he was then thirty-two years old.

The monastery continued to flourish for another ten years, when St Peter decided to disperse his community in the face of the persecution by the Emperor Leo the Armenian of those who upheld the orthodox doctrine concerning the veneration of images. Peter himself went first to Ephesus and then to Cyprus; on his return, at a conference of some of his refugèe brethren, he escaped arrest by imperial troops only by making himself invisible. Then, with one companion, Brother John, he continued his wanderings and visited his home, where his brother Christopher and his widowed mother received the monastic habit at his hands. He tried to settle down as a recluse in several places, one of which was Kalonoros, The Beautiful Mountain, at the end of the Hellespont; but so great was his reputation as a wonder-worker and reader of consciences that he was never left in peace for long. He remained at Kalonoros for some years, making journeys about western Asia Minor from time to time, each of which was starred with miracles.

He then undertook the restoration of St Zachary's and the reorganization of two other monasteries that he had established, taking up his own residence in a hermitage at Atroa. But a few years later the Iconoclast troubles began again and, the local bishop being an opponent of images, Peter judged it wise once more to disperse his monks to more remote houses. He was only just in time, for soon after the bishop came to St Zachary's with the intention of driving them out and arresting those who resisted. St Peter, meanwhile, having seen his community safely housed elsewhere, stayed for a period with a famous recluse called James, near the Monastery of the Eunuchs on Mount Olympus.

Persecution becoming more envenomed in Lydia, Peter and James retired to the monastery of St Porphyrios on the Hellespont, but soon after St Peter decided to go back to Olympus to visit his friend St Joannicius at Balea, from whence he returned to his hermitage at St Zachary's. A few weeks later St Joannicius had a vision: he seemed to be talking with Peter of Atroa, at the foot of a mountain whose crest reached to the heavenly courts; and as they talked, two shining figures appeared who, taking Peter one by each arm, bore him away upwards in a halo of glory. At the same moment, in the church of St Zachary's, while the monks were singing the night office with their abbot on a bed of sickness in the choir, death came to St Peter of Atroa, after he had lovingly addressed his brethren for the last time. It was January 1, 837.

2 : ST CASPAR DEL BUFALO, FOUNDER OF THE MISSIONERS OF THE PRECIOUS BLOOD (A.D. 1837)

CASPAR; who was born in Rome, the son of a chef, in 1786, received his education at the Collegio Romano and was ordained priest in 1808. Shortly after this Rome was taken by Napoleon's army, and he, with most of the clergy, was exiled for refusing to abjure his allegiance to the Holy See. He returned after the fall of Napoleon to find a wide scope for work, as Rome had for nearly five years been almost entirely without priests and sacraments.

In 1814 he conducted a mission at Giano, in the diocese of Spoleto, and there the idea of the Congregation of the Most Precious Blood first came to him. He found a house at Giano suitable for his purpose, and with the help of Cardinal Cristaldi, and the approval of Pope Pius VII, the new congregation was formally approved in 1815. The house and adjoining church of San Felice in Giano were given him by the pope. The second foundation was made in 1819 and the third shortly afterwards at Albano. His wish was to have a house in every diocese, the most neglected and wicked town or district being chosen.

Grave difficulties arose under Pope Leo XII; but these were cleared up, and in 1824, the houses of the congregation were opened to young clergy who wished to be trained specially as missioners. A missioner, the founder said, must be ready for anything. He required not only devotion, but also hard study. To evangelize the whole world, which was their aim, they must learn foreign languages besides theology and Holy Scripture. In his life-time their work covered the whole of Italy.

Del Bufalo's biographer gives us a graphic account of a mission, describing its successive stages. Some of his methods were distinctly dramatic, e.g. the missioners took the discipline in the public piazza, which always resulted in many conversions. On the last day forbidden firearms, obscene books, and anything else that might offend Almighty God were publicly burnt. A cross was erected *in memoriam*, a solemn *Te Deum* sung, and the missioners went away quietly. Caspar founded works of charity in Rome for young and old, rich and poor of both sexes.

His last mission was preached in Rome at the Chiesa Nuova during the cholera outbreak of 1836. Feeling his strength failing, he returned at once to Albano, and made every preparation for death. He asked to be left alone as much as possible, that his prayer might be less interrupted. After the feast of St Francis Xavier he went to Rome to die. On December 19 the doctor forbade him to say Mass; he received the last sacraments on December 28, and he died the same day.

3 : ST GENEVIEVE, OR GENOVEFA, VIRGIN (*c*. A.D. 500)

GENEVIEVE'S father's name was Severus, and her mother's Gerontia; she was born about the year 422 at Nanterre, a small village four miles from Paris, near Mont Valérien. When St Germanus, Bishop of Auxerre, went with St Lupus into Britain to oppose the Pelagian heresy, he spent a night at Nanterre on his way. The inhabitants flocked about them to receive their blessing, and St Germanus gave an address, during which he took particular notice of Genevieve, though she was only seven years of age. After his sermon he inquired for her parents, and foretold their daughter's future sanctity. He then asked Genevieve whether it was not her desire to serve God only and to be naught else but a spouse of Jesus Christ. She answered that this was what she desired, and begged that by his blessing she might be from that moment consecrated to God. The holy prelate went to the church, followed by the people, and during the long singing of psalms and prayers, says Constantius, 'he laid his hand upon the maiden's head.'

When she was about fifteen years of age, Genevieve was presented to the bishop of Paris to receive the religious veil, together with two other girls. From that time she frequently ate only twice in the week, on Sundays and Thursdays, and her food was barley bread with a few beans. After the death of her parents she left Nanterre, and settled with her godmother in Paris, but sometimes undertook journeys for motives of charity.

The Franks had at this time gained possession of the better part of Gaùl, and Childeric, their king, took Paris. During the long blockade of that city, the citizens being reduced to extremities by famine, St Genevieve, as the author of her life relates, went out at the head of a company who were sent to procure provisions, and brought back from Arcis-sur-Aube and Troyes several boats laden with corn. Childeric, when he had made himself master of Paris, though always a pagan, respected St Genevieve, and upon her intercession spared the lives of many prisoners and did other generous acts. She also awakened the zeal of many persons to build a church in honour of St Denis of Paris, which King Dagobert I afterwards rebuilt with a monastery in 629. St Genevieve likewise undertook many pilgrimages, in company with other maidens, to the shrine of St Martin at Tours, and the reputation of her holiness is said to have been so great that her fame even reached St Simeon Stylites in Syria.

King Clovis, who embraced the faith in 496, often listened with deference to St Genevieve, and more than once granted liberty to captives at her request. Upon the report of the march of Attila with his army of Huns the Parisians were preparing to abandon their city, but St Genevieve encouraged them to avert the scourge by fasting and prayer. Many of her own sex passed whole days with her in prayer in the baptistery; from whence the particular devotion to St Genevieve, formerly practised at S.-Jean-le-Rond, the ancient public baptistery of the church of Paris, seems to have taken rise. She assured the people of the protection of Heaven, and though she was treated by many as an impostor, the event verified the prediction, for the barbarous invader suddenly changed the course of his march. Attributed to St Genevieve was the first suggestion of the church which Clovis began to build in honour of SS. Peter and Paul, in deference to the wishes of his wife, St Clotilda, in which church the body of St Genevieve herself was enshrined after her death about the year 500.

4 : ST ELIZABETH BAYLEY SETON, WIDOW, FOUNDRESS OF THE DAUGHTERS OF CHARITY OF ST JOSEPH (A.D. 1821)

ELIZABETH was born in New York of a very distinguished family on August 28, 1774. Her mother Catherine Charlton was the daughter of the Episcopalian Rector of St Andrew's church, Staten Island, while her father Dr Richard Bayley was not only a noted physician, but also professor of anatomy at King's College, an institution later to develop into Columbia University. It was her father who undertook in a somewhat unorthodox fashion, though with remarkable success, Elizabeth's education, for her mother died when she was only three years old.

In 1794 Elizabeth married a young merchant of ample means, William Magee Seton, and she bore him two sons and three daughters. But their happiness was short-lived. William Seton lost his fortune, and with it his health, and though they went to Italy in an attempt to effect a cure, William died there in December 1803. His widow remained on in Italy, staying with friends, until the May of the following year, and during that time her natural piety was strongly attracted to Roman Catholicism. When, upon her return to the United States, this attraction became apparent, she met a good deal of opposition from her family and her friends. Nonetheless she persevered, and on March 14, 1805 she was received into the Catholic Church.

This step, which estranged her from her family, left her in some financial difficulty. She therefore welcomed the invitation from a priest to establish a school for girls in Baltimore. The school opened in June 1808. Even while her husband had been alive, Elizabeth had devoted much time to the care of the poor in New York, and had founded the Society for the Relief of Poor Widows with Small Children. So active had she and her friends been, that Elizabeth became known in the city as 'the Protestant Sister of Charity'. Now in Baltimore she again gathered around her a group of like-minded women, and there was the possibility of establishing formally a congregation of nuns. In the Spring of 1809 the community based on the school in Baltimore formed a community, the Sisters of St Joseph, and from that time onwards Elizabeth, as their superior, was known as Mother Seton.

In the June of that same year Mother Seton and her community moved to the town of Emmitsburg in north-west Maryland and there, with some modifications and adaptations, the Sisters took over the rule of the Daughters of Charity of St Vincent de Paul. The congregation from 1812 onwards was therefore known as the Daughters of Charity of St Joseph. It spread rapidly. The sisters established orphanages and hospitals, but they gained most renown for their commitment to the then burgeoning parochial school system, which became one of the glories of the Catholic Church in the United States. In moments caught from running her congregation, Mother Seton not only herself worked with the poor and with the sick, but found time to compose music, write hymns and prepare spiritual discourses, many of which have since been published.

It was at Emmitsburg that Elizabeth died, on January 4, 1821, by which date her congregation, the first to be founded in America, numbered some twenty communities spread right across the United States. Her cause was introduced in 1907 by Cardinal Gibbons, himself the successor in the see of Baltimore of Archbishop James Roosevelt Bayley, a nephew of Mother Seton, and she was canonized in 1975. She is the first native-born North American to be raised to the altars.

5 : ST JOHN NEPOMUCENE NEUMANN, BISHOP (A.D. 1860)

BORN at Prachitz in Bohemia on March 28, 1811, John was the third of the six children of Philip, a German, and of Agnes, a Czech. He early showed signs of considerable intellectual ability, coupled to a wish to become a religious. He went to school in Budweis, and then to the diocesan seminary in 1831. He continued his theological studies at the Charles Ferdinand University in Prague, whither he went in 1833, but on completion of his studies he was not ordained to serve his home diocese because of the great number of clergy already at work there.

For this reason he determined to leave Europe and to set out for the New World as a missionary. Soon after his arrival in New York he was accepted for ordination and was promptly ordained by Bishop James Dubois on June 25, 1836. He spent four years of pastoral work in and around Buffalo before joining the Redemptorists. For a short time he was in charge of the American vice-province of the order, though for most of the time he returned to parish work where his chief care was for the establishment of schools.

In 1852 Pope Pius IX appointed him Bishop of Philadelphia, and this office gave him yet great scope for his efforts to increase the system of parochial schools. To staff them he attracted to the diocese a number of orders of teaching brothers and nuns, so that in a short time the population of his schools increased twenty-fold. He also erected a large number of new parishes, introduced the devotion of the Forty Hours, and began the building of the cathedral. Despite all this activity he still found time to write, including, usually anonymously, articles for newspapers. His most important works, however, he composed in German, his preferred language for composition even though he had a thorough grasp of seven other modern languages. The two catechisms he produced were, in 1852, given the approval of the entire American hierarchy, and continued in wide use in the United States for most of the rest of the century.

He died, renowned for his sanctity and for his pastoral work, on January 5, 1860, on a street in Philadelphia. He was canonized by Pope Paul VI in 1977.

6 : ST JOHN DE RIBERA, ARCHBISHOP OF VALENCIA (A.D. 1611)

PETER DE RIBERA, the father of Don John, was one of the highest grandees in Spain; he was created duke of Alcalá, but already held many other titles and important charges. Among the rest, he governed Naples for fourteen years as viceroy. But above all, he was a most upright and devout Christian. His son, therefore, was admirably brought up, and in 1557, at the age of twenty-five, Don John was ordained priest. After teaching theology at Salamanca for a while, he was appointed bishop of Badajoz, much to his dismay, by St Pius V in 1562. His duties as bishop were discharged with scrupulous fidelity and zeal, and six years later, by the desire both of Philip II and the same holy pontiff, he was reluctantly constrained to accept the dignity of archbishop of Valencia. A few months later, filled with consternation at the languid faith and relaxed morals of this province, which was the great stronghold of the Moriscos, he wrote begging to be allowed to resign, but the pope would not consent; and for forty-two years, down to his death in 1611, St John struggled to support cheerfully a load of responsibility which almost crushed him. In his old age the burden was increased by the office of viceroy of the province of Valencia, which was imposed upon him by Philip III.

The archbishop viewed with intense alarm what he regarded as the dangerous activities of the Moriscos. He was one of the advisers who were mainly responsible for the edict of 1609 which enforced their deportation from Valencia. We can only bear in mind that a decree of beatification pronounces only upon the personal virtues and miracles of the servant of God so honoured, and that it does not constitute an approbation of all his public acts or of his political views. The archbishop did not long survive the tragedy of the deportation. He died, after a long illness most patiently borne, at the College of Corpus Christi, which he himself had founded and endowed, on January 6, 1611. Many miracles were attributed to his intercession. He was beatified in 1796 and canonized in 1960.

7 : ST RAYMUND OF PEÑAFORT, (A.D. 1275)

THE family of Peñafort claimed descent from the counts of Barcelona, and was allied to the kings of Aragon. Raymund was born in 1175, at Peñafort in Catalonia, and made such rapid progress in his studies that at the age of twenty he taught philosophy at Barcelona. This he did gratis, and with great reputation. When he was about thirty he went to Bologna to perfect himself in canon and civil law. He took the degree of doctor, and taught with the same disinterestedness and charity as he had done in his own country. In 1219 Berengarius, Bishop of Barcelona, made Raymund his archdeacon and 'official'. He was a perfect model to the clergy by his zeal, devotion and boundless liberalities to the poor. In 1222 he assumed the habit of St Dominic at Barcelona, eight months after the death of the holy founder, and in the forty-seventh year of his age. He begged his superiors that they would enjoin some severe penance to expiate the complacency which he said he had sometimes taken in his teaching. They, indeed, imposed on him a penance, but not quite such as he expected: it was to write a collection of cases of conscience for the convenience of confessors and moralists. This led to the compilation of the *Summa de casibus poenitentialibus*, the first work of its kind.

Pope Gregory IX, having called St Raymund to Rome in 1230, nominated him to various offices and took him for his confessor, in which capacity Raymund enjoined the pope, for a penance, to receive, hear and expedite immediately all petitions presented by the poor. Gregory also ordered the saint to gather into one body all the scattered decrees of popes and councils since the collection made by Gratian in 1150. In three years Raymund completed his task, and the five books of the 'Decretals' were confirmed by the same Pope Gregory in 1234.

For his health St Raymund returned to his native country, and was received with as much joy as if the safety of the kingdom depended on his presence. Being restored again to his dear solitude at Barcelona he continued his former contemplation, preaching and work in the confession-al. He was frequently employed in important commissions, both by the Holy See and by the king. In 1238, however, he was thunderstruck by the arrival of deputies from the general chapter of his order at Bologna with the news that he had been chosen third master general, Bd Jordan of Saxony having lately died. He wept and entreated, but at length acquiesced in obedience. He made the visitation of his order on foot without discontinuing any of his austerities or religious exercises. He instilled into his spiritual children a love of regularity, solitude, studies and the work of the ministry, and reduced the constitutions of his order into a clearer method, with notes on the doubtful passages. The code which he drew up was approved in three general chapters. In one held at Paris in 1239 he procured that the voluntary resignation of a superior, founded upon just reasons, should be accepted: the year following he resigned the generalship which he had held only two years. He grounded his action on the fact that he was now sixty-five years old.

But St Raymund still had thirty-four years to live, and he spent them in the main opposing heresy and working for the conversion of the Moors in Spain. With this end in view, he engaged St Thomas to write his work *Against the Gentiles;* he contrived to have Arabic and Hebrew taught in several convents of his order; and he established friaries, one at Tunis, and another at Murcia, among the Moors. In 1256 he wrote to his general that ten thousand Saracens had received baptism. He was active in getting the Inquisition established in Catalonia; and once he was accused—not without some reason—of compromising a Jewish rabbi by a trick.

During the saint's last illness, Alphonsus, King of Castile, and James of Aragon visited him, and received his final blessing. St Raymund gave up his soul to God on January 6 in the year 1275, the hundredth of his age.

8 : ST THORFINN, BISHOP OF HAMAR (A.D. 1285)

IN the year 1285 there died in the Cistercian monastery at Ter Doest, near Bruges, a Norwegian bishop named Thorfinn. He had never attracted particular attention and was soon forgotten. But over fifty years later, in the course of some building operations, his tomb in the church was opened and it was reported that the remains gave a strong and pleasing smell. The abbot made enquiries and found that one of his monks, an aged man named Walter de Muda, remembered Bishop Thorfinn staying in the monastery and the impression he had made of gentle goodness combined with strength. Father Walter had in fact written a poem about him after his death and hung it up over his tomb. It was then found that the parchment was still there, none the worse for the passage of time. This was taken as a direction from on high that the bishop's memory was to be perpetuated, and Father Walter was instructed to write down his recollections of him.

For all that, there is little enough known about St Thorfinn. He was a Trondhjem man and perhaps was a canon of the cathedral of Nidaros, since there was such a one named Thorfinn among those who witnessed the Agreement of Tönsberg in 1277. This was an agreement between King Magnus VI and the Archbishop of Nidaros confirming certain privileges of the clergy, the freedom of episcopal elections and similar matters. Some years later King Eric repudiated this agreement, and a fierce dispute between church and state ensued. Eventually the king outlawed the archbishop, John, and his two chief supporters, Bishop Andrew of Oslo and Bishop Thorfinn of Hamar.

The last-named, after many hardships, including shipwreck, made his way to the abbey of Ter Doest in Flanders, which had a number of contacts with the Norwegian church. It is possible that he had been there before, and there is some reason to suppose he was himself a Cistercian of the abbey of Tautra, near Nidaros.

After a visit to Rome he went back to Ter Doest, in bad health. Indeed, though probably still a youngish man, he saw death approaching and so made his will; he had little to leave, but what there was he divided between his mother, his brothers and sisters, and certain monasteries, churches and charities in his diocese. He died shortly after, on January 8, 1285.

9 : ST ADRIAN, ABBOT OF CANTERBURY (A.D. 710)

ADRIAN was an African by birth, and was abbot of Nerida, not far from Naples, when Pope St Vitalian, upon the death of St Deusdedit, the archbishop of Canterbury, judged him for his learning and virtue to be the most suitable person to be the teacher of a nation still young in the faith. The humble servant of God found means to decline that dignity by recommending St Theodore in his place, but was willing to share in the more laborious part of the ministry. The pope therefore enjoined him to be the assistant and adviser of the archbishop, to which Adrian readily agreed.

St Theodore made him abbot of the monastery of SS. Peter and Paul, afterwards called St Augustine's, at Canterbury, where he taught Greek and Latin, the learning of the fathers, and, above all, virtue. Under Adrian and

Theodore this monastic school at Canterbury had a far-reaching influence—St Aldhelm came there from Wessex, Oftfor from Whitby, and even students from Ireland. Roman law could be studied as well as the ecclesiastical sciences; and Bede says that there were pupils of St Adrian who had a good knowledge of Greek and spoke Latin as well as they did English. St Adrian had illuminated this island by his doctrine and the example of his holy life, for the space of thirty-nine years, when he departed to Our Lord on January 9 in the year 710.

10 : ST PETER ORSEOLO, (A.D. 987)

BORN in 928 of a distinguished Venetian family, Peter seems at the age of twenty to have been appointed to the command of the fleet of the city of the lagoons, in which office he conducted a successful campaign against the Dalmatian pirates who infested the Adriatic. How far he was personally involved in the popular outbreak of 976, which ended in the violent death of the Doge Peter Candiani IV, and in the destruction by fire of a large part of the city, cannot be clearly determined. The testimony of St Peter Damian which attributes the responsibility to Orseolo can only be accepted with reserve. It was, however, Orseolo who was chosen doge in place of the murdered Candiani, and the best modern authorities pay a high tribute to his energy and tact during his brief administration.

On the night of September 1, 978, Peter Orseolo secretly left Venice and took refuge in the Benedictine abbey of Cuxa, in Roussillon on the borders of France and Spain. His wife, to whom he had been married for thirty-two years, and his only son, who was himself destined to become one of the greatest of the Venetian doges, were apparently for a long time in entire ignorance of the place of his retreat. Still, Peter's apparently sudden resolution may not have been so entirely unpremeditated as it seems. There is early evidence for the belief that he and his wife had lived as brother and sister ever since the birth of their only child, and it has also been suggested that a letter of Ratherius, addressed to him possibly as early as 968, shows that Peter had already entertained the idea of becoming a monk. There is in any case no doubt that at Cuxa Orseolo led for a while a life of the strictest asceticism and self-effacement under the holy Abbot Guarinus; and then, desirous of still greater solitude, he built a hermitage for himself, probably at the urging of St Romuald, whom he met at Cuxa, and who was the great propagator of this particular development of the Benedictine vocation. St Peter died in 987, and many miracles were said to have taken place at his tomb.

11 : ST THEODOSIUS THE CENOBIARCH, (A.D. 529)

ST THEODOSIUS was born at Garissus, 'Cappadocia' in 423. He was ordained reader, but being moved by Abraham's example in quitting his country and friends, he resolved to do likewise. He accordingly started for Jerusalem, but went out of his road to visit the famous St Simeon Stylites on his pillar.

Having satisfied his devotion in visiting the holy places in Jerusalem, he put himself under the direction of a holy man named Longinus, who soon conceived a warm affection for his disciple. A lady having built a church on the high road to Bethlehem, Longinus could not well refuse her request that his pupil should undertake the charge of it; but Theodosius could not easily be induced to consent: absolute commands were necessary before he would undertake the charge. Nor did he govern long; instead he retired to a cave at the top of a neighbouring mountain.

The sanctity and miracles of St Theodosius attracting numbers who desired to serve God under his direction, the available space proved too small for their reception. Accordingly he built a spacious monastery at a place called Cathismus, not far from Bethlehem, and it was soon filled with monks.

The monastery itself was like a city of saints in the midst of a desert, and in it reigned regularity, silence, charity and peace. There were four churches belonging to it, one for each of the three several nations of which his community was chiefly composed, each speaking a different language; the fourth was for the use of such as were in a state of penance. Sallust, Patriarch of Jerusalem, appointed St Sabas head of all the hermits, and our saint of the cenobites, or men living in community, throughout Palestine, whence he was styled 'the Cenobiarch'.

The Emperor Anastasius patronized the Eutychian heresy, and used all possible means to win our saint over to his own views. In 513 he deposed Elias, Patriarch of Jerusalem, just as he had previously banished Flavian II of Antioch, and intruded Severus into that see. Theodosius and Sabas maintained the rights of Elias, and of John his successor; whereupon the imperial officers thought it advisable to connive at their proceedings, considering the great authority they had acquired by their sanctity. Soon after, the emperor sent Theodosius a considerable sum of money, for charitable uses in appearance, but in reality to engage him in his interest. The saint accepted it, and distributed it all among the poor.

Anastasius, now persuading himself that Theodosius was as good as gained over to his cause, sent him a heretical profession of faith, in which the divine and human natures in Christ were confounded into one, and desired him to sign it. The saint wrote him an answer full of apostolic spirit, and for a time the emperor was more peaceable. But he soon renewed his persecuting edicts against the orthodox, despatching troops everywhere to have them put into execution. On intelligence of this, Theodosius travelled through Palestine, exhorting all to stand firm in the faith of the four general councils. The emperor sent an order for his banishment, which was executed; but dying soon after, Theodosius was recalled by his successor, Justin.

During the last year of his life St Theodosius was afflicted with a painful infirmity, in which he gave proof of heroic patience and submission to the will of God. He went to his reward in 529, in the one hundred and fifth year of his age. Peter, Patriarch of Jerusalem, and the whole country were present at his funeral, which was honoured by miracles. He was buried in his first cell, called the cave of the Magi, because the wise men who came to find Christ soon after his birth were said to have lodged in it.

12 : ST BENEDICT, OR BENET, BISCOP, ABBOT OF WEARMOUTH AND JARROW (A.D. 690)

BENEDICT BISCOP, a man of noble birth at the court of Oswy, king of the Northumbrians, at the age of twenty-five made a journey to Rome, and at his return devoted himself wholly to the study of the Bible and other holy exercises. Some time after he travelled there a second time, he went to the great monastery of Lérins, took the monastic habit, and spent two years in exact observance of the Rule. After this he returned to Rome, where he received an order from Pope St Vitalian to accompany St Theodore, the new archbishop of Canterbury, and St Adrian, to England. When he arrived at Canterbury, St Theodore committed to Benedict the care of the monastery of SS. Peter and Paul at that city.

He stayed two years in Kent, and then he took a fourth journey to Rome, with the view of perfecting himself in the rules and practice of a monastic life. For this purpose he made a considerable stay in Rome and other places, and he brought home with him a choice library, with relics and sacred pictures. When he returned to Northumberland, King Egfrid bestowed on him seventy hides of land for building a monastery: this the saint founded in 674 at the mouth of the river Wear, whence it was called Wearmouth. St Benedict went over to France, and brought back with him skilful masons, who built the church for this monastery of stone and after the Roman fashion; St Benedict also brought over glaziers from France, for the art of making glass was then unknown in England.

His first monastery of Wearmouth was dedicated in honour of St Peter; and such was the edification which it gave that the king added a second donation of land, on which Biscop built another monastery in 685, at Jarrow on the Tyne, six miles distant from the former, this latter being called St Paul's. These two monasteries were almost looked upon as one, and St Benedict governed them both, though he placed in each a superior, who continued subject to him, his long journeys to Rome and other absences making this substitution necessary.

St Benedict on his last voyage brought back with him from Rome the abbot of St Martin's, who was the precentor of St Peter's. This abbot, John by name, was expert in music, and our saint persuaded Pope St Agatho to send him in order that he might instruct the English monks in the Gregorian chant and in the Roman ceremonial for singing the divine office. These two monasteries thus became the best-equipped in England, and St Benedict's purchase of books was of special significance, for it made possible the work of the Venerable Bede.

About the year 686 St Benedict was stricken with paralysis in his lower limbs. He lay three years crippled and suffering, and for a considerable time was entirely confined to his bed. During this long illness, not being able to raise his voice or make much effort, at every canonical hour some of his monks came to him, and whilst they sang the psalms appointed, he endeavoured as well as he could to join not only his heart but also his voice with theirs. He died on January 12, 690.

13 : ST HILARY, BISHOP OF POITIERS, DOCTOR OF THE CHURCH (c. A.D. 368)

ST HILARY was born at Poitiers, and his family was illustrious in Gaul. He himself testifies that he was brought up in idolatry, and gives us a detailed account of the steps by which God conducted him to a knowledge of the faith when somewhat advanced in years.

The Emperor Constantius and a synod at Milan in 355 required all bishops to sign the condemnation of St Athanasius: such as refused to comply were banished. St Hilary wrote on that occasion his 'First Book to Constantius', in which he entreated him to restore peace to the Church.

Hilary had been married before his conversion, and his wife, by whom he had a daughter named Apra, was yet living when he was chosen bishop of Poitiers, about the year 350. He did all in his power to escape this promotion; but his humility only made the people more earnest in their choice; and, indeed, their expectations were not disappointed, for his eminent qualities shone forth so brilliantly as to attract the attention not only of Gaul, but of the whole Church. Soon after he was raised to the episcopal dignity he composed, before his exile, a commentary on the Gospel of St Matthew, which is still extant. That on the Psalms he compiled after his banishment. From that time on the Arian controversy chiefly employed his pen.

St Hilary went into exile about the middle of the year 356, and remained there for some years, which time he employed in composing several learned works. The principal and most esteemed of these is that *On the Trinity*. The earliest Latin hymn-writing is associated with the name of Hilary of Poitiers.

The emperor, again interfering in the affairs of the Church, assembled a council of Arians, at Seleucia in Isauria, to neutralize the decrees of the Council of Nicaea. St Hilary, who had then passed three years in Phrygia, was invited by the semi-Arians, who hoped that he would be useful to their party in crushing those who adhered strictly to the doctrine of Arius. But he boldly defended the decrees of Nicaea, till at last, tired out with controversy, he withdrew to Constantinople and presented to the emperor a request, called his 'Second Book to Constantius', begging permission to hold a public disputation about religion with Saturninus, the author of his banishment. The issue of this challenge was that the Arians, dreading such a trial, persuaded the emperor to rid the East of a man who never ceased to disturb its peace. Constantius accordingly sent him back into Gaul in 360.

St Hilary returned through Illyricum and Italy to confirm the weak. He was received at Poitiers with great demonstrations of joy. A synod in Gaul, convoked at the instance of Hilary, condemned that of Rimini in 359; and Saturninus, proving obstinate, was excommunicated and desposed. Scandals were removed, discipline, peace and purity of faith were restored. The death of Constantius in 361 put an end to the Arian persecution. Hilary undertook a journey to Milan in 364 to confute Auxentius, the Arian usurper of that see, and in a public disputation obliged him to confess Christ to be the true God, of the same substance and divinity with the Father. St Hilary, indeed, saw through his hypocrisy; but Auxentius so far imposed on the Emperor Valentinian as to pass for orthodox. Hilary died at Poitiers, probably in the year 368, but neither the year nor the day can be determined with certainty.

St Hilary was proclaimed a doctor of the Church by Pope Pius IX in 1851.

14 : ST SAVA OR SABAS, ARCHBISHOP OF THE SERBS (A.D. 1237)

SAVA, born in 1174, was the youngest of the three sons of Stephen I, founder of the dynasty of the Nemanydes and of the independent Serbian state. At the age of seventeen he became a monk on the Greek peninsula of Mount Athos, where he was joined by his father when that prince abdicated in 1196. Together they established a monastery for Serbian monks, with the name of Khilandari, which is still in existence as one of the seventeen 'ruling monasteries' of the Holy Mountain. As abbot, Sava was noted for his light and effective touch in training young monks; it was remarked, too, that his influence was always on the side of gentleness and leniency. He began the work of translating books into the Serbian language, and there are still treasured at Khilandari a psalter and ritual written out by himself, and signed, 'I, the unworthy lazy monk Sava'.

In the meanwhile his brothers, Stephen II and Vulkan, had fallen out over their inheritance, and in 1207 St Sava returned home. Religiously as well as civilly he found his country in a bad way. The Serbs had been Christians for some time, but much of it was a nominal Christianity, quite uninstructed and mixed up with heathenism. The clergy were few and mostly unedu-cated, for the church had been ruled from Constantinople or Okhrida in Bulgaria, whose hierarchs had shown little care or sympathy for those whom they regarded as barbarians. So St Sava utilized the monks who had accompanied him from Khilandari for pastoral and missionary work. He established himself at the monastery of Studenitsa, from where he founded a number of small monasteries in places convenient for travelling around and getting to the people.

It remained desirable (and politically advantageous also) that the Serbs should have their own bishops. So Stephen II sent his brother to Nicaea, where the Eastern emperor and patriarch had taken refuge from the Frankish intruders at Constantinople. Sava won over the emperor, Theo-dore II Laskaris (who was related to the Nemanya family), and he designated Sava as the first metropolitan of the new hierarchy. The patriarch, Manuel I, was unwilling, but in the circumstances dared not oppose obstinately and he ordained Sava bishop in 1219. Sava returned by way of Mount Athos, bringing with him more monks and many books that had been translated at Khilandari, and straightway set about the organiza-tion of his church. It seems that already Stephen II, 'the First-Crowned', had asked to be recognized as king by Pope Honorius III and had been duly crowned by a papal legate in 1217. But in 1222 he was again crowned by his brother as archbishop, and one source asserts that it was on this occasion that Honorius sent a crown in response to a request from Sava, who had informed the Holy See of his own episcopal ordination.

Thus the retiring young prince, who had left home as a youth to be a monk, succeeded before he was fifty years of age in consolidating the state founded by his father by reforming the religious life of the people, giving them bishops of their own race, and sealing the sovereign dignity of his brother: St Sava is regarded as the patron-saint of Serbia.

The later years of St Sava's life were marked by two voyages to Palestine and the Near East; the first seems to have been a pilgrimage of devotion, the second an ecclesiastical mission. On his way back he was taken ill at Tirnovo in Bulgaria and died there, with a smile on his face, on January 14, 1237.

15 : ST ITA, VIRGIN (c. A.D. 570)

AMONG the women saints of Ireland, St Ita (also called Ida and Mida, with other variant spellings) holds the foremost place after St Brigid. Although her life has been overlaid with a multitude of mythical and extravagant miracles, there is no reason to doubt her historical existence. She is said to have been of royal descent, to have been born in one of the baronies of Decies, near Drum, Co. Waterford, and to have been originally called Deirdre. A noble suitor presented himself, but by fasting and praying for three days Ita, with angelic help, won her father's consent to her leading a life of virginity. She accordingly migrated to Hy Conaill, in the western part of the present county of Limerick. There at Killeedy she gathered round her a community of maidens and there, after long years given to the service of God and her neighbour, she eventually died, probably in the year 570.

It appears that St Ita conducted a school for small boys, and we are told that the bishop St Ere committed to her care one who was afterwards destined to be famous as abbot and missionary, the child Brendan, who for five years was trained by her.

16 : ST HONORATUS, BISHOP OF ARLES (A.D. 429)

HONORATUS was of a consular Roman family settled in Gaul, and was well versed in the liberal arts. In his youth he renounced the worship of idols and gained to Christ his elder brother Venantius, whom he also inspired with a contempt for the world. They desired to forsake it entirely, but their father put continual obstacles in their way. At length they took with them St Caprasius, a holy hermit, to act as their instructor, and sailed from Marseilles to Greece, intending to live there unknown in some desert. Venantius soon died at Modon; and Honoratus, having also fallen ill, was obliged to return with his conductor. He first led an eremitical life in the mountains near Fréjus. Two small islands lie in the sea near that coast: one larger and nearer the continent, called Lero, now St Margaret's; the other smaller and more remote, two leagues from Antibes, named Lérins, at present Saint-Honorat, from our saint. There he settled; and being followed by others he founded the famous monastery of Lérins about the year 400. Some he appointed to live in community; others in separate cells as anchorets. His rule was chiefly borrowed from that of St Pachomius. Nothing can be more attractive than the description St Hilary of Arles has given of the virtues of this company of saints, especially of the charity and devotion which reigned amongst them.

Honoratus was by compulsion consecrated archbishop of Arles in 426, and died exhausted with austerities and apostolic labours in 429.

17 : ST ANTONY THE ABBOT, (A.D. 356)

ST ANTONY was born at a village south of Memphis in Upper Egypt in 251. His parents, who were Christians, kept him always at home, so that he grew up in ignorance of what was then regarded as polite literature, and could read no language but his own. At their death he found himself possessed of a considerable estate and charged with the care of a younger sister, before he was twenty years of age. Some six months afterwards he heard read in the church those words of Christ to the rich young man: 'Go, sell what thou hast, and give it to the poor, and thou shalt have treasure in Heaven'. Considering these words as addressed to himself, he went home and made over to his neighbours his best land, and the rest of his estate he sold and gave the price to the poor, except what he thought necessary for himself and his sister. Soon after, hearing in the church those other words of Christ, 'Be not solicitous for tomorrow', he also distributed in alms the moveables which he had reserved, and placed his sister in a house of maidens, which is commonly assumed to be the first recorded mention of a nunnery. Antony himself retired into solitude, in imitation of a certain old man who led the life of a hermit in the neighbourhood.

He soon became a model of humility, charity, prayerfulness and many more virtues. The saint's food was only bread, with a little salt, and he drank nothing but water; he never ate before sunset, and sometimes only once in three or four days. When he took his rest he lay on a rush mat or the bare floor. In quest of a more remote solitude he withdrew to an old burial-place, to which a friend brought him bread from time to time. Satan was permitted to assault him in a visible manner, and to terrify him with gruesome noises; indeed, on one occasion he so grievously beat him that he lay almost dead, and in this condition was found by his friend.

Hitherto Antony, ever since he turned his back on the world in 272, had lived in solitary places not very far from his village of Koman. About the year 285, however, at the age of thirty-five, he crossed the eastern branch of the Nile and took up his abode in some ruins on the top of a mountain, in which solitude he lived almost twenty years, rarely seeing any man except one who brought him bread every six months.

To satisfy the importunities of others, about the year 305, the fifty-fourth of his age, he came down from his mountain and founded his first monastery, in the Fayum. This originally consisted of scattered cells, but we cannot be sure that the various colonies of ascetics which he planted out in this way were all arranged upon the same plan. He did not stay permanently with any such community, but he visited them occasionally.

In the year 311, when the persecution was renewed under Maximinus, St Antony went to Alexandria in order to give courage to the martyrs. He publicly wore his white tunic of sheep-skin and appeared in the sight of the governor, yet took care never presumptuously to provoke the judges or impeach himself, as some rashly did. The persecution having abated, he returned to his monastery, and some time after organized another, called Pispir, near the Nile; but he chose for the most part to shut himself up in a cell upon a mountain difficult of access with Macarius, a disciple whose duty it was to interview visitors. St Antony cultivated a little garden on his desert mountain, but this tillage was not the only manual labour in which he employed himself. St Athanasius speaks of his making mats as an ordinary occupation.

At the request of the bishops, about the year 355, he took a journey to Alexandria to confute the Arians, preaching that God the Son is not a creature, but of the same substance with the Father; and that the Arians, who called him a creature, did not differ from the heathen themselves, 'who worshipped and served the creature rather than the Creator'. All the people ran to see him, and rejoiced to hear him; even the pagans, struck with the dignity of his character, flocked around him. He converted many, and even worked miracles. St Athanasius conducted him back as far as the gates of the city, where he cured a girl possessed by an evil spirit.

St Jerome relates that at Alexandria Antony met the famous Didymus, the blind head of the catechetical school there, and exhorted him not to regret overmuch the loss of eyes, which were common even to insects, but to rejoice in the treasure of that inner light which the apostles enjoyed, by which we see God and kindle the fire of His love in our souls. Heathen philosophers and others often went to discuss with him, and returned astonished at his meekness and wisdom. About the year 337 Constantine the Great and his two sons, Constantius and Constans, wrote a letter to the saint, recommending themselves to his prayers. St Antony, seeing his monks surprised, said, 'Do not wonder that the emperor writes to us, a man even as I am; rather be astounded that God should have written to us, and that He has spoken to us by His Son'. He said he knew not how to answer it; but at last, through the importunity of his disciples, he penned a letter to the emperor and his sons, which St Athanasius has preserved, in which he exhorts them to constant remembrance of the judgement to come. St Jerome mentions seven other letters of St Antony to divers monasteries. A maxim which he frequently repeats is, that the knowledge of ourselves is the necessary and only step by which we can ascend to the knowledge and love of God.

St Antony made a visitation of his monks a little before his death, which he foretold, but no tears could move him to die among them. He gave orders that he should be buried in the earth beside his mountain cell by his two disciples, Macarius and Amathas. Hastening back to his solitude on Mount Kolzim near the Red Sea, he some time after fell ill; whereupon he repeated to these disciples his orders that they should bury his body secretly in that place. He ordered them to give one of his sheep-skins, with the cloak upon which he lay, to the bishop Athanasius, as a public testimony of his being united in faith and communion with that holy prelate; to give his other sheep-skin to the bishop Serapion; and to keep for themselves his sackcloth. 'Farewell, my children. Antony is departing, and will no longer be with you.' At these words they embraced him, and he, stretching out his feet, without any other sign, calmly ceased to breathe. His death occurred in the year 356, probably on January 17, on which day the most ancient martyrologies commemorate him. He was one hundred and five years old.

18 : ST DEICOLUS, or DESLE, ABBOT (c. A.D. 625)

HE quitted Ireland, his native country, with St Columban and lived with him at Luxeuil; but when his master left France, he founded the abbey of Lure, in the diocese of Besançon, where he ended his days as a hermit. Amidst his austerities the joy and peace of his soul appeared in his countenance. St Columban once said to him in his youth, 'Deicolus, why are you always smiling?' He answered in simplicity, 'Because no one can take God from me'. He died probably in the year 625.

19 : ST WULFSTAN, BISHOP OF WORCESTER (A.D. 1095)

WULFSTAN (Wulstan) was a native of Long Itchington, in Warwickshire. He made his studies in the monastery of Evesham and afterwards at Peterborough, and put himself under the direction of Brihtheah, Bishop of Worcester, by whom he was advanced to the priesthood. Having been distracted while celebrating Mass by the smell of meat roasting in the kitchen, he bound himself never to eat of it again. Not long after he became a novice in the great monastery at Worcester, where he was remarkable for the innocence and sanctity of his life. The first charge with which he was entrusted was instructing the children. He was afterwards made precentor, and then treasurer of the church, but he continued to devote himself to prayer, and watched whole nights in the church. It was only in despite of his strenuous resistance that he was made prior of Worcester and, in 1062, bishop of that see. Though not very learned, he delivered the word of God so impressively and feelingly as often to move his audience to tears. To his energy in particular is attributed the suppression of a scandalous practice which prevailed among the citizens of Bristol of kidnapping men into slavery and shipping them over to Ireland. He always recited the psalter whilst he travelled, and never passed by any church or chapel without going in to pray before the altar.

After an initial uncertainty King William the Conqueror recognized Wulfstan's worth and treated him with respect and trust. Lanfranc even commissioned him to make the visitation of the diocese of Chester as his deputy. When any English complained of the oppression of the Normans, Wulfstan used to tell them, 'This is a scourge of God for our sins, which we must bear with patience'. He caused young gentlemen who were brought up under his care to carry in the dishes and wait on the poor at table, to teach them the true spirit of humility, in which he himself set an example. Wulfstan rebuilt his cathedral at Worcester, c. 1086, but he loved the old edifice which had to be demolished. 'The men of old', he said, 'if they had not stately buildings were themselves a sacrifice to God, whereas we pile up stones, and neglect souls.' He died in 1095, having sat as bishop thirty-two years, and lived about eighty-seven. He was canonized in 1203.

20 : ST EUTHYMIUS THE GREAT, ABBOT (A.D. 473)

THE birth of this saint was the fruit of the prayers of his parents through the intercession of the martyr Polyeuctus. His father was a wealthy citizen of Melitene in Armenia, and Euthymius was educated in sacred learning under the care of the bishop of that city, who ordained him priest and made him his deputy in the supervision of the monasteries. The saint often visited that of St Polyeuctus, and spent whole nights in prayer on a neighbouring mountain, as he also did continuously from the octave of the Epiphany till towards the end of Lent. The love of solitude daily growing stronger, he secretly left his own country at twenty-nine years of age; and, after offering up his prayers at the holy places in Jerusalem, chose a cell six miles from that city, near the *laura* of Pharan. He made baskets, and earned enough by selling them to provide a living for himself and alms for the poor. After five years he retired with one Theoctistus ten miles farther towards Jericho, where they both lived in a cave. In this place he began to receive disciples about the year 411. He entrusted the care of his community to Theoctistus, and himself retired to a remote hermitage, only meeting on Saturdays and Sundays those who desired spiritual advice.

By making the sign of the cross and a short prayer, St Euthymius cured a young Arab, one half of whose body had been paralysed. His father, who had vainly invoked the much-boasted arts of physic and magic among the Persians to procure some relief for his son, at the sight of this miracle asked to be baptized. So many Arabs followed his example that Juvenal, Patriarch of Jerusalem, consecrated Euthymius bishop to provide for the spiritual needs of these converts, and in that capacity he assisted at the Council of Ephesus in 431. Juvenal built St Euthymius a laura on the road from Jerusalem to Jericho in the year 420. Euthymius could never be prevailed upon to depart from his rule of strict solitude, but governed his monks by vicars, to whom he gave directions on Sundays. His humility and charity won the hearts of all who spoke to him. He seemed to surpass the great Arsenius in the gift of perpetual tears, and Cyril of Scythopolis relates many miracles which he wrought, usually by the sign of the cross.

When the heretical Empress Eudoxia, widow of Theodosius II, frightened by the afflictions of her family, consulted St Simeon Stylites he referred her to St Euthymius. As Euthymius would allow no woman to enter his laura she built a lodge some distance away, and asked him to come and see her there. His advice to her was to forsake the Eutychians and to receive the Council of Chalcedon. She followed his counsel as the command of God, returned to orthodox communion, and many followed her example.

In the year 473, on January 13, Martyrius and Elias, to both of whom St Euthymius had foretold that they would be patriarchs of Jerusalem, came with several others to visit him and accompany him to his Lenten retreat. But he said he would stay with them all that week, and leave on the Saturday following, giving them to understand that his death was near at hand. He appointed Elias his successor, and foretold to Domitian, a beloved disciple, that he would follow him out of this world on the seventh day, which happened exactly as he had prophesied. Euthymius died on Saturday, January 20, being ninety-five years old, of which he had spent sixty-eight in the desert.

21 : ST MEINRAD, MARTYR (A.D. 861)

A S the patron and in some sense the founder of the famous abbey of Einsiedeln in Switzerland, one of the few which have preserved unbroken continuity since Carolingian times, St Meinrad (Meginrat) cannot be passed over. By birth he is supposed to have been connected with the family of the Hohenzollerns. He became a priest, entered the Benedictine abbey at Reichenau, and later on was given some teaching work beside the upper Lake of Zurich. His soul, however, pined for solitude, and for the opportunity of devoting himself entirely to contemplation. He consequently sought out a spot in a forest, and there, with the permission of his superiors, he settled about the year 829. The fame of his sanctity, however, brought him many visitors, and seven years later he found it necessary to move still farther. The place where he finally took up his abode is now called Einsiedeln (*i.e.* Hermitage). There he lived for twenty-five years.

On January 21, 861, he was visited by two ruffians who had the idea he had treasure stored away. Though he knew their purpose, he courteously offered them food and hospitality. In the evening they smashed his skull with clubs, but finding no valuables, took to flight.

The body of the saint was conveyed to Reichenau and there preserved with great veneration. Some forty years later Bd Benno, a priest of noble Swabian family, went to take up his abode in St Meinrad's hermitage at Einsiedeln. Though forced, much against his inclination, in 927 to accept the archbishopric of Metz, he returned to Einsiedeln later on, gathering round him a body of followers who eventually became the founders of the present Benedictine abbey.

22 : ST VINCENT PALLOTTI, FOUNDER OF THE SOCIETY OF CATHOLIC APOSTOLATE (A.D. 1850)

V INCENT PALLOTTI was born in Rome, son of a well-to-do grocer, in 1795, and his vocation to the priesthood was foreshadowed at an early age. His beginnings at school were disappointing: 'He's a little saint', said his master, Don Ferri, 'but a bit thick-headed'. However, he soon picked up, and was ordained priest when he was only twenty-three. He took his doctorate in theology soon after, and became an assistant professor at the University of Rome. Pallotti's close friendship with St Caspar del Bufalo increased his apostolic zeal, and he eventually resigned his post to devote himself to active pastoral work.

Don Pallotti was in very great repute as a confessor, and filled this office at several Roman colleges, including the Scots, the Irish and the English, where he became a friend of the rector, Nicholas Wiseman. But he was not appreciated everywhere. When he was appointed to the Neapolitan church in Rome he endured persecution from the other clergy there of which the particulars pass belief. Equally astonishing is it that this went on for ten years before the authorities took official notice and brought the scandal to an end. Vincent's most implacable tormentor, the vice-rector of the church, lived to give evidence for him at the informative process of his beatification. 'Don Pallotti never gave the least ground for the ill-treatment to which he was subjected', he declared. 'He always treated me with the greatest respect; he bared his head when he spoke to me, he even several times tried to kiss my hand.'

St Vincent began his organized work for conversion and social justice with a group of clergy and lay people, from whom the Society of Catholic Apostolate developed in 1835. He wrote to a young professor: 'You are not cut out for the silence and austerities of Trappists and hermits. Be holy in the world, in your social relationships, in your work and your leisure, in your teaching duties and your contacts with publicans and sinners. Holiness is simply to do God's will, always and everywhere'. Pallotti himself organized schools for shoemakers, tailors, coachmen, joiners and market-gardeners, to improve their general education and pride in their trade; he started evening classes for young workers, and an institute to teach better methods to young agriculturalists. But he never lost sight of the wider aspects of his mission. In 1836 he inaugurated the observance of the Epiphany octave by the celebration of the Mysteries each day with a different rite, in special supplication for the reunion of Eastern dissidents: this was settled at the church of Sant' Andrea delle Valle in 1847, and has continued there annually ever since.

It was well said that in Don Pallotti Rome had a second Philip Neri. How many times he came home half naked because he had given his clothes away; how many sinners did he reconcile, on one occasion dressing up as an old woman to get to the bedside of a man who threatened—and meant it—to shoot the first priest who came near him; he was in demand as an exorcist, he had knowledge beyond this world's means, he healed the sick with an encouragement or a blessing. St Vincent foresaw all Catholic Action, even its name, said Pius XI; and Cardinal Pellegrinetti added, 'He did all that he could; as for what he couldn't do—well, he did that too'. St Vincent Pallotti died when he was only fifty-five, on January 22, 1850.

He was beatified one hundred years later to the day, and canonized in 1963 during the Second Vatican Council.

23 : ST JOHN THE ALMSGIVER, PATRIARCH OF ALEXANDRIA (A.D. 619?)

ST JOHN was of noble family, rich, and a widower, at Amathus in Cyprus where, having buried all his children, he employed his income in the relief of the poor, and won the respect of all by his personal holiness. His reputation raised him to the patriarchal chair of Alexandria, about the year 608, at which time he was upwards of fifty years of age. On his arrival St John ordered an exact list to be taken of his 'masters'. Being asked who these were, he explained that he meant the poor, because they had such power in the court of Heaven to help those who had been good to them on earth. Their number amounted to 7500, and all these he took under his special protection. He published severe ordinances, but in the most humble terms, commanding all to use just weights and measures, in order to protect the poor from a very cruel form of oppression. He rigorously forbade all his officers and servants to take presents, seeing that these are no better than bribes, which bias the most impartial. Every Wednesday and Friday he sat the whole day on a bench before the church, that all might have free access to lay their grievances before him, and make known their necessities.

One of his first actions at Alexandria was to distribute the eighty thousand pieces of gold which he found in the treasury of his church among the hospitals and monasteries. He consecrated to the service of the poor the great revenues of his see, then the first in all the East both in riches and dignity. Besides these, a continual stream of contributions flowed through his hands representing the alms of those who were kindled by his example.

When the Persians plundered Syria, and sacked Jerusalem, St John entertained the refugees who fled terror-stricken into Egypt, and sent to Jerusalem for the poor there, besides a large sum of money, corn, pulse, iron, fish, wine, and Egyptian workmen to assist in rebuilding the churches; adding, in his letter to Modestus the bishop, that he wished it had been in his power to come in person and contribute by the labour of his hands to the carrying on of that work.

The patriarch lived himself in the greatest austerity and poverty. A person of distinction being informed that he had but one blanket on his bed, and this a sorry one, sent him a valuable rug, asking that he would make use of it for the sake of the donor. He accepted it and put it to the intended use, but it was only for one night, and this he passed in great uneasiness, with self-reproach for reposing in luxury while so many of his 'masters' were miserably lodged. The next morning he sold it and gave the price to the poor. The friend, learning what had happened, bought it and gave it him a second and a third time, for the saint always disposed of it in the same way, saying with a smile, 'We shall see who will get tired first'.

Nicetas, the governor, projected a new tax, which bore very harshly upon the poor. The patriarch modestly spoke in their defence. The governor in a passion left him abruptly. St John sent him this message towards evening, 'The sun is going to set,' putting him in mind of the advice of the apostle, 'Let not the sun go down upon your anger'. This admonition had its intended effect. The governor came at once to the patriarch, asked his pardon, and by way of atonement promised never more to give ear to informers and tale-bearers. St John confirmed him in that resolution, adding that he never believed any man whatever against another till he himself had examined the party accused, and that he made it a rule to punish all calumniators with such severity as would serve as a warning to others.

Nicetas persuaded the saint to accompany him to Constantinople to visit the Emperor Heraclius on the approach of the Persians in 619. At Rhodes, while on their way, St John was admonished from Heaven that his death was near at hand, and he said to Nicetas, 'You invite me to the emperor of the earth; but the King of Heaven calls me to Himself'. He therefore sailed back to his native Cyprus, and soon after died happily at Amathus, in 619 or 620.

24 : ST FRANCIS DE SALES, BISHOP OF GENEVA AND DOCTOR OF THE CHURCH, CO-FOUNDER OF THE ORDER OF THE VISITATION (A.D.1622)

ST FRANCIS DE SALES was born at the Château de Sales in Savoy on August 21, 1567, and on the following day was baptized in the parish church of Thorens under the name of Francis Bonaventure. His patron saint in after-life was the *Poverello* of Assisi, and the room in which he was born was known as 'St Francis's room', from a painting of the saint preaching to the birds and fishes. During his first years he was very frail and delicate, owing to his premature birth, but with care he gradually grew stronger, and, though never robust, he was singularly active and energetic throughout his career. His mother kept his early education in her own hands, aided by the Abbé Déage, who afterwards, as his tutor, accompanied Francis everywhere during his youth.

At the age of eight Francis went to the College of Annecy. There he made his first communion in the church of St Dominic (now known as St Maurice), there he also received confirmation, and a year later he received the tonsure. Francis had a great wish to consecrate himself to God, and regarded this as the first outward step. His father (who at his marriage had taken the name of de Boisy) seems to have attached little importance to it, and destined his eldest son for a secular career. In his fourteenth year Francis was sent to the University of Paris, which at that time, with its 54 colleges, was one of the great centres of learning. He was intended for the Collège de Navarre, as it was frequented by the sons of the noble families of Savoy, but Francis, fearing for his vocation in such surroundings, implored to be allowed to go to the Collège de Clermont, which was under Jesuit direction and renowned for piety as well as for learning. Having obtained his father's consent to this, and accompanied by the Abbé Déage, he took up his abode in the Hôtel de la Rose Blanche, Rue St Jacques, which was close to the Collège de Clermont.

Francis soon made his mark, especially in rhetoric and philosophy, and he ardently devoted himself to the study of theology. To satisfy his father he took lessons in riding, dancing and fencing, but cared for none of them. His heart was more and more set upon giving himself wholly to God.

He was twenty-four when he took his final degree, became a doctor of law at Padua, and rejoined his family at the Château de Thuille on the Lake of Annecy. Francis had so far only confided to his mother, to his cousin Canon Louis de Sales, and to a few intimate friends his earnest desire of devoting his life to the service of God. An explanation with his father, however, became inevitable. The death of the provost of the chapter of Geneva suggested to Canon Louis de Sales the possibility that Francis might be appointed to this post, and that in this way his father's opposition might relax. Francis put on ecclesiastical dress the very day his father gave his consent, and six months afterwards, on December 18, 1593, he was ordained priest. He took up his duties with an ardour which never abated.

At this time the religious condition of the people of the Chablais, on the south shore of the Lake of Geneva, was deplorable, and the Duke of Savoy applied to Bishop de Granier to send missioners who might win back his subjects to the Church. The bishop, summoning his chapter, put the whole matter before them, disguising none of the difficulties and dangers. The provost stood up and offered himself for the work. The bishop accepted at once, to Francis's great joy. But M. de Boisy took a different view of the matter and Francis had the disappointment of starting on his mission without his father's blessing. It was on September 14, 1594, Holy Cross day, that, travelling on foot and accompanied only by his cousin, Canon Louis de Sales, he set forth to win back the Chablais.

The missionaries worked and preached daily in Thonon, gradually extending their efforts to the villages of the surrounding country. One evening Francis was attacked by wolves, and only escaped by spending the night in a tree. Twice in January 1595 he was waylaid by assassins who had sworn to take his life, but on both these occasions, as also several times later, he was preserved seemingly by miracle. Time went by with little apparent result to reward the labours of the two missioners, and all the while M. de Boisy was sending letters to his son, alternately commanding and imploring him to give up so hopeless a task. Francis was constantly seeking new ways to reach the hearts and minds of the people, and he began writing leaflets setting forth the teaching of the Church. In every spare moment of his arduous day he wrote these little papers, which were copied many times by hand and distributed widely by all available means. These sheets, composed under such stress and difficulty, were later to form both the volume of 'Controversies', and the beginning of his activities as a writer.

In the summer of 1595, going up the mountain of Voiron to restore an oratory of our Lady which had been destroyed by the Bernese, he was attacked by a hostile crowd, who insulted and beat him. Soon afterwards his sermons at Thonon began to be more numerously attended. The tracts too had been silently doing their work, and his patient perseverance under every form of persecution and hardship had not been without its effect. Conversions became more and more frequent, and before very long there was a steady stream of lapsed Catholics seeking reconciliation with the Church. After three or four years, when Bishop de Granier came to visit the mission, the fruits of Francis's self-sacrificing work and untiring zeal were unmistakable. The bishop was made welcome, and was able to administer confirmation. He even presided at the 'Forty Hours', a possibility which had seemed unthinkable in Thonon.

Mgr de Granier, who had long been considering Francis in the light of a possible coadjutor and successor, felt that the moment had now come to give effect to this. When the proposal was made Francis was at first unwilling, but in the end he yielded to the persistence of the bishop, submitting to what he ultimately felt was a manifestation of the Divine Will. Soon he fell dangerously ill with a fever which kept him for a time hovering between life and death. When sufficiently recovered he proceeded to Rome, where Pope Clement VIII, having heard much in praise of the virtue and ability of the young provost, desired that he should be examined in his presence. The pope himself, Baronius, Bellarmine, Cardinal Frederick Borromeo (a cousin of St Charles) and others put no less than thirty-five abstruse questions of theology to Francis, all of which he answered with simplicity and modesty, but in a way which proved his learning. His appointment as coadjutor of Geneva was confirmed, and Francis returned to take up his work with fresh zeal and energy.

Francis succeeded to the see of Geneva on the death of Claud de Granier in the autumn of 1602, and took up his residence at Annecy, with a household organized on lines of the strictest economy. To the fulfilment of his episcopal duties he gave himself with unstinted generosity and devotion. He organized the teaching of the catechism throughout the diocese, and at Annecy gave the instructions himself, with such glowing interest and fervour that years after his death the 'Bishop's Catechisms' were still vividly remembered. Children loved him and followed him about. His unselfishness and charity, his humility and clemency, could not have been surpassed. In dealing with souls, though always gentle, he was never weak, and he could be very firm when kindness did not prevail.

A prominent place in this work of spiritual direction was held by St Jane Frances de Chantal, who first became known to him in 1604, when he was preaching Lenten sermons at Dijon. The foundation of the Order of the Visitation in 1610 was the result that evolved from this meeting of the two saints. His most famous book, the *Introduction to the Devout Life*, grew out of the casual notes of instruction and advice which he wrote to Mme de Chamoisy, a cousin by marriage, who had placed herself under his guidance. He was persuaded to publish them in a little volume which, with some additions, first appeared in 1608. The book was at once acclaimed a spiritual masterpiece, and soon translated into many languages.

In 1622, the Duke of Savoy, going to meet Louis XIII at Avignon, invited St Francis to join them there. Anxious to obtain from Louis certain privileges for the French part of his diocese, Francis readily consented, although he was in no state of health to risk the long winter journey. But he seems to have had a premonition that his end was not far off. Before quitting Annecy he put all his affairs in order, and took his leave as if he had no expectation of seeing people again. At Avignon he led as far as possible his usual austere life. But he was greatly sought after—crowds were eager to see him, and the different religious houses all wanted the saintly bishop to preach to them. On the return journey he stayed at Lyons, where he lodged in a gardener's cottage belonging to the convent of the Visitation. Here for a whole month, though sorely in need of rest, he spared himself no labour for souls. In bitterly cold weather, through Advent and over Christmas, he continued his preaching and ministrations, refusing no demand upon his strength and time. On St John's day he was taken seriously ill with some sort of paralytic seizure. He recovered speech and consciousness, and endured with touching patience the torturing remedies used in the hope of prolonging his life, but which only hastened the end. After receiving the last sacraments he lay murmuring words from the Bible expressive of his humble and serene trust in God's mercy. The last word he was heard to utter was the name of 'Jesus'. While those kneeling around his bed said the litany for the dying, and were invoking the Holy Innocents, whose feast it was, St Francis gently breathed his last, in the fifty-sixth year of his age.

The beatification of St Francis de Sales in 1662 was the first solemn beatification to take place in St Peter's at Rome, where he was canonized three years later. He was declared a doctor of the Church in 1877, and Pope Pius XI named him the patron-saint of journalists.

25 : THE CONVERSION OF ST PAUL, (A.D. 34)

THE Apostle of the Gentiles was a Jew of the tribe of Benjamin. At his circumcision on the eighth day after his birth he received the name of Saul, and being born at Tarsus in Cilicia he was by privilege a Roman citizen. His parents sent him when young to Jerusalem, and there he was instructed in the law of Moses by Gamaliel, a learned and noble Pharisee. Thus Saul became a scrupulous observer of the law, and he appeals even to his enemies to bear witness how conformable to it his life had always been. He too embraced the party of the Pharisees, which was of all others the most severe, even while it was, in some of its members, the most opposed to the humility of the gospel. It is probable that Saul learned in his youth the trade which he practised even after his apostleship—namely, that of making tents. Later on Saul, surpassing his fellows in zeal for the Jewish law and traditions, which he thought the cause of God, became a persecutor and enemy of Christ: he was one of those who took part in the murder of St Stephen. In the fury of his zeal he applied to the high priest for a commission to arrest all Jews at Damascus who confessed Jesus Christ, and bring them bound to Jerusalem.

Saul was almost at the end of his journey to Damascus when, about noon, he and his company were on a sudden surrounded by a great light from Heaven. They all saw this light, and being struck with amazement fell to the ground. Then Saul heard a voice which to him was articulate and distinct, though not understood by the rest: 'Saul, Saul, why dost thou persecute me?' Saul answered, 'Who art thou, Lord?' Christ said, 'Jesus of Nazareth, whom thou persecutest. It is hard for thee to kick against the goad.' Christ told him to arise and proceed on his journey to his destination, where he would learn what was expected of him. When he got up from the ground Saul found that though his eyes were open he could see nothing.

There was a Christian in Damascus much respected for his life and virtue, whose name was Ananias. Christ appeared to this disciple and commanded him to go to Saul, who was then in the house of Judas at prayer. Ananias trembled at the name of Saul, being no stranger to the mischief he had done in Jerusalem, or to the errand on which he had travelled to Damascus. But he went to Saul, and laying his hands upon him said, 'Brother Saul, the Lord Jesus, who appeared to thee on thy journey, hath sent me that thou mayest receive thy sight, and be filled with the Holy Ghost'. Immediately something like scales fell from his eyes, and he recovered his sight.

Saul arose, was baptized, and ate. He stayed some days with the disciples at Damascus, and began immediately to preach in the synagogues that Jesus was the Son of God, to the great astonishment of all that heard him, who said, 'Is not this he who at Jerusalem persecuted those who called on the name of Jesus, and who is come hither to carry them away prisoners?' Thus a blasphemer and a persecutor was made an apostle, and chosen to be one of the principal instruments of God in the conversion of the world.

26 : ST EYSTEIN, ARCHBISHOP OF NIDAROS (A.D. 1188)

IN the year 1152 an English cardinal, Nicholas Breakspeare (afterwards to be pope as Adrian IV), visited Norway as legate of the Holy See, and gave a new organization to the Church in that country, consisting of a metropolitan see at Nidaros (Trondhjem) with ten bishoprics. Five years later the second archbishop of Nidaros was appointed, Eystein Erlandsson, chaplain to King Inge, an appointment which violated the regulations for canonical appointments laid down by Cardinal Breakspeare. But it proved to be the life work of the new archbishop to maintain the Church's right of conducting its affairs without interference and to bring the Norwegian church into the general pattern of the west European Christendom of that day. After his appointment Eystein made his way to Rome, but it is not known exactly when or where he was consecrated bishop by Pope Alexander III and received the *pallium*. In any case he did not get back home till late in 1161, and then he came as papal legate *a latere*. One of his first interests was to finish the enlargement of the cathedral, Christ Church, of Nidaros, and some of his building still remains.

After the death of King Haakon II, Jarl Erling Skakke wanted to get his own eight-year-old son Magnus recognized as king of Norway. And in 1164, probably in return for concessions touching ecclesiastical revenue, Archbishop Eystein anointed and crowned the child at Bergen, the first royal coronation in Norwegian history. Relations between the archbishop and the king's father continued to be close, and St Eystein was able to get accepted a code of laws some of which were of great importance for the discipline and good order of the Church. But one matter which he does not seem to have tackled, at any rate directly, was clerical celibacy, which was not observed in the Scandinavian churches at that time. It was perhaps for this reason that St Eystein founded communities of Augustinian canons regular, to set an example to the parochial clergy.

Most of St Eystein's activities as they have come down to us are matters of the general history of his country and were directed towards the free action of the spiritual power among a unified people. This brought him into collision with Magnus's rival for the throne, Sverre, and in 1181 the archbishop fled to England; whence he is said to have excommunicated Sverre. St Eystein had a strong devotion for St Thomas Becket, which later became common in the Norwegian church, and it seems that it was in England that he wrote *The Passion and Miracles of the Blessed Olaf.*

Eystein returned to Norway in 1183, and he was in his ship in Bergen harbour when Sverre attacked Magnus's ships there and forced the king to flee to Denmark. In the following year Magnus lost his life in a renewal of the struggle, and it may be assumed that the archbishop was reconciled with King Sverre.

St Eystein died on January 26, 1188, and in 1229 a synod at Nidaros declared his sanctity.

27 : ST ANGELA MERICI, VIRGIN, FOUNDRESS OF THE COMPANY OF ST URSULA (A.D. 1540)

THE foundress of the Ursulines—the first teaching order of women to be established in the Church—was born on March 21, 1470 or 1474, at the little town of Desenzano, on the south-western shore of Lake Garda in Lombardy. Her parents both died when Angela was ten years old, leaving their two daughters and a son to the care of a well-to-do uncle living at Salo.

The death of her elder sister came as a great shock to Angela when she was thirteen; for the young girl had passed away before she could receive the last sacraments. Angela's first vision—she was to have many in after years—seems to have been granted to her at this time, in order to set her mind completely at rest as to her sister's salvation. In gratitude she consecrated herself more completely to God and soon afterwards was admitted as a Franciscan tertiary. Her life became one of extreme austerity. Striving to emulate St Francis, she wished to possess nothing of her own—not even a bed—and lived almost entirely on bread, water and a few vegetables.

After the death of her uncle, when she was about twenty-two, Angela returned to Desenzano. There, as she went about amongst her neighbours, she was appalled by the ignorance which prevailed amongst the poorer children whose parents could not or would not teach them the simplest elements of religion. She talked the matter over with her friends. They were mostly fellow tertiaries or young women of her own class with little money and less influence, but they were eager to help her if she would show them the way. Though very small of stature, Angela had all the necessary qualifications for leadership, including charm of manner and good looks. At her suggestion they set to work to gather together the little girls of the neighbourhood, to whom they gave regular and systematic instruction. The work so humbly begun prospered and developed. Angela was invited to go to Brescia to begin a similar school in that city. There she was brought into touch with the leading families of Brescia and became the centre of a circle of devout women and men whom she inspired with her great ideals. From time to time we find her making pilgrimages to various shrines. Thus she visited the tomb of Bd Osanna at Mantua and eagerly seized an opportunity which presented itself of going to the Holy Land with a young relative.

In the holy year of 1525 Angela went to Rome to obtain the jubilee indulgence, and had the privilege of at least one private audience with the pope. Clement VII suggested that she should stay in Rome to take charge of a congregation of nursing sisters, but a sense of her true vocation as well as a shrinking from publicity led her to decline the offer. She accordingly returned to Brescia from whence, however, she was soon obliged to withdraw, for war had broken out again in Italy, and when Charles V was on the point of making himself master of Brescia it became essential that as many non-combatants as possible should leave the city. St Angela with some of her friends went to Cremona, where they remained until peace was concluded. Her return to Brescia was greeted with joy by the citizens who, besides appreciating her charity, venerated her as a prophetess and a saint.

About the year 1533 she seems to have begun to train a select few of her companions in a kind of informal novitiate. Twelve of them came to live with her in a house she took near the church of St Afra, but the greater number continued to live with parents or other relations. Two years later twenty-eight young women consecrated themselves with her to the service of God. She placed them under the protection of St Ursula, the patroness of medieval universities who was popularly venerated as a leader of women: hence the name of Ursulines which her daughters have always borne. This date—November 25, 1535—is reckoned as that of the foundation of the Ursuline Order. It was, however, during the lifetime of its foundress more in the nature of an association; no habit was worn, although a black dress was recommended; no vows were taken, and the sisters were not enclosed, nor did they lead a community life. They met together for classes and worship, carried out such duties as were allotted to them, and lived a holy life in the midst of their families. The idea of a teaching order of women was so novel that time was required in which to let it develop.

At the first election St Angela was unanimously chosen superioress, and she continued to fill that office for the last five years of her life. She was taken ill early in January 1540 and died on the twenty-seventh of the same month. In 1544 Pope Paul III issued a bull confirming the Company of St Ursula and declaring it to be a recognized congregation, and in 1807 its foundress was canonized.

28 : ST THOMAS AQUINAS, DOCTOR OF THE CHURCH (A.D. 1274)

THE family of the counts of Aquino was of noble lineage, tracing its descent back for several centuries to the Lombards. St Thomas's father was a knight, Landulf, and his mother Theodora was of Norman descent. There seems something more northern than southern about Thomas's physique, his imposing stature, massive build and fresh complexion. The precise year of his birth is uncertain, but it was about 1225 and took place in the castle of Rocca Secca, the ruins of which are still to be seen on a mountain crag dominating the fertile plain of Campagna Felice and the little town of Aquino.

A few miles to the south of Rocca Secca, on a high plateau, stands the abbey of Monte Cassino, whose abbot at this time was a kinsman of the Aquino family, Landulf Sinibaldo. As a child of five Thomas was taken here as an oblate and he remained till he was about thirteen, living in the monastery and getting his schooling there. He was taken away probably because of the disturbed state of the times, and about 1239 was sent to the University of Naples, where for five years he studied the arts and sciences. He became attracted by the Order of Preachers, whose church he loved to frequent and with some of whose members he soon became intimate. At the age of about nineteen, he was received and clothed in the habit of the order.

News of this was soon carried to Rocca Secca, where it aroused great indignation—not because he had joined a religious community, for his mother was quite content that he should become a Benedictine, and indeed probably saw in him the destined abbot of Monte Cassino, but because he had entered a mendicant order. Theodora herself set out for Naples to persuade her son to return home. The friars, however, hurried him off to their convent of Santa Sabina in Rome, and when the angry lady followed in pursuit, the young man was no longer to be found there. The master general of the Dominicans, who was on his way to Bologna, had decided to take Thomas with him, and the little party of friars had already set out on foot together. Theodora, not to be baulked, sent word to the saint's elder brothers, who were serving with the emperor's army in Tuscany, desiring them to waylay and capture the fugitive. As Thomas was resting by the roadside at Aquapendente near Siena, he was overtaken by his brothers at the head of a troop of soldiers, and after a vain attempt to take his habit from him by force, was brought back, first to Rocca Secca and then to the castle of Monte San Giovanni, two miles distant, where he was kept in close confinement, only his worldly-minded sister Marotta being allowed to visit him. During his captivity Thomas studied the *Sentences* of Peter Lombard, learned by heart a great part of the Bible, and is said to have written a treatise on the fallacies of Aristotle.

This captivity lasted two years before Thomas's family gave up and in 1245 permitted him to return to his order. It was now determined to send him to complete his studies under St Albert the Great, and he set out in company with the master general, John the Teutonic, who was on his way to Paris; from thence Thomas went on to Cologne. The schools there were full of young clerics from various parts of Europe eager to learn and equally eager to discuss, and the humble reserved new-comer was not immediately appreciated either by his fellow students or by his professors. His silence at disputations as well as his bulky figure led to his receiving the nickname of 'the dumb Sicilian ox'.

There are chronological difficulties about these years of St Thomas's life, but certainly in 1252, at the instance of St Albert and Cardinal Hugh of Saint-Cher, he was ordered to Paris to teach as a bachelor in the university. Academical degrees were then very different from what they are now, and were conferred only in view of the actual work of teaching. In Paris Thomas expounded the Holy Scriptures and the *Liber sententiarum* of Peter Lombard; he also wrote a commentary on these same Sentences, and others on Isaias and St Matthew's Gospel. Four years later he delivered his inaugural lecture as master and received his doctor's chair, his duties being to lecture, to discuss and to preach; and towards the end of the time he began the *Summa contra Gentiles*. From 1259 to 1268 he was in Italy. Here he was made a preacher general, and was called upon to teach in the school of selected scholars attached to the papal court, and, as it followed the pope in his movements, St Thomas lectured and preached in many of the Italian towns. About 1266 he began the most famous of all his written works, the *Summa theologiae*.

In 1269 he was back again in Paris. St Louis IX held him in such esteem that he constantly consulted him on important matters of state, but perhaps a greater testimony to his reputation was the resolution of the university to refer to his decision a question upon which they were divided, *viz.* whether in the Blessed Sacrament of the altar the accidents remained really or only in appearance. St Thomas, after fervent prayer, wrote his answer in the form of a treatise which is still extant, and laid it on the altar before making it public. His decision was accepted by the university first and afterwards by the whole Church.

In 1272 there was a sort of 'general strike' among the faculties, in the midst of which St Thomas was recalled to Italy and appointed regent of the study-house at Naples. It was to prove the last scene of his labours. On the feast of St Nicholas the following year he was celebrating Mass when he received a revelation which so affected him that he wrote and dictated no more, leaving his great work, the *Summa theologiae*, unfinished. To Brother Reginald's expostulations he replied, 'The end of my labours is come. All that I have written appears to be as so much straw after the things that have been revealed to me'.

He was ill when he was bidden by Pope Gregory X to attend the general council at Lyons for the reunion of the Greek and Latin churches and to bring with him his treatise 'Against the Errors of the Greeks'. He became so much worse on the journey that he was taken to the Cistercian abbey of Fossa Nuova near Terracina, where he was lodged in the abbot's room and waited on by the monks. In compliance with their entreaties he began to expound to them the Canticle of Canticles, but he did not live to finish his exposition. His soul passed to God in the early hours of March 7, 1274, when he was only about fifty years of age.

St Thomas was canonized in 1323, but it was not until 1368 that the Dominicans succeeded in obtaining possession of his body, which was translated with great pomp to Toulouse, where it still lies in the cathedral of Saint-Sernin. St Pius V conferred upon him the title of doctor of the Church, and in 1880 Leo XIII declared him the patron of all universities, colleges and schools.

29 : ST GILDAS THE WISE, ABBOT (c. A.D. 570)

THIS famous man seems to have been born about the year 500, in the lower valley of the Clyde. He must have travelled south at a somewhat early age, and we may reasonably trust the tradition which describes him as practising asceticism at Llaniltud in South Wales. He was no doubt younger than either St Samson or St Paul Aurelian, but all three, either simultaneously or successively, lived under St Illtud, we are told. How long Gildas remained in Britain cannot be determined, but the terrible indictment of the scandalous lives of his contemporaries, both ecclesiastics and laymen, which he left in his *De excidio Britanniae* was written probably on British soil somewhere about the year 540. Severely as this work has been criticized as a mere jeremiad (even Bede calls it *sermo flebilis*, a pitiful tale) and as an often incoherent patchwork of the most denunciatory texts to be found in both the Testaments, it should be remembered that there is no reason to suppose that the author's object was to write a history. On the contrary, he tells us himself that his main purpose was to make known 'the miseries, the errors and the ruin of Britain', and he certainly manifests an acquaintance with Holy Scripture which must be deemed highly creditable in any writer during this period of barbarism; nor was he ignorant of Vergil and St Ignatius of Antioch. Moreover, there can be no question that Gildas, in spite of his querulous tone, was animated by a real zeal for morality and religion.

Little can be affirmed with confidence regarding the life of Gildas himself. He seems to have lived for a time on the island of Flatholm in the Bristol Channel, where he copied a missal for St Cadoc and perhaps wrote the *De excidio*. The last years of his life, however, were certainly spent in Britanny, where he lived for some time as a hermit on a tiny island near Rhuys, in Morbihan bay. Here disciples gathered around him, and in spite of his desire for solitude he does not seem to have cut himself off entirely from the world, for we hear of his travelling to other places in Brittany.

There has been much difference of opinion regarding the date of St

Gildas's death. Some put it as early as 554, but the majority of recent critics incline to *c*. 570.

30 : ST HYACINTHA MARISCOTTI, VIRGIN (A.D. 1640)

CLARICE MARISCOTTI, born of a noble family at Vignarello in 1585, was educated in the Franciscan convent at Viterbo, where one of her sisters was already a nun. She is said in her childhood to have shown little inclination for piety, and when a marriage was arranged between her youngest sister and the Marquis Cassizucchi, she herself being passed over, her pique and morose ill-humour seem to have made her almost unendurable in the family circle. As a result they, according to the evil custom of the times, practically forced her to enter a convent. She went back to the Franciscans, a community of the third order regular, at Viterbo, where she became Sister Hyacintha (Giacinta) and was admitted in due course to profession.

At the same time she let it be known that though she wore the habit of a nun she intended to claim every indulgence which she could secure for herself in virtue of her rank and the wealth of her family. For ten years she scandalized the community by leading a life in which she confined herself without disguise to conformity with certain external observances, while disregarding altogether the spirit of the religious rule. At last, when she was suffering from some slight indisposition, a worthy Franciscan priest came to hear her confession in her cell, who, seeing the comforts she had accumulated around her, spoke to her severely on the subject of her tepidity and the danger she ran. Hyacintha seems to have taken the rebuke to heart and to have set about a reform with almost exaggerated fervour. This sudden conversion, however, showed every sign of breaking down, and she was beginning to slip back into her bad old ways, when God sent her a much more serious illness. This grace was effectual, and from that date she gave herself to a life in which cruel disciplines, constant fasts, deprivation of sleep and long hours of prayer all played their part.

What was perhaps most remarkable in such a character as hers was the fact that, becoming in time mistress of novices, she seems to have shown the most healthy common sense in the guidance of others, restraining their devotional and penitential excesses and giving very practical advice to the many who wrote to seek her counsel. Hyacintha's charity was also remarkable, and it was not limited to those of her own community. Through her influence two confraternities were established in Viterbo which devoted themselves to the relief of the sick, the aged, decayed gentry and the poor, Hyacintha herself helping largely to provide the necessary funds by her own begging. She died at the age of fifty-five, on January 30, 1640, and was canonized in 1807.

31 : ST JOHN BOSCO, FOUNDER OF THE SALESIANS OF DON BOSCO (A.D. 1888)

BORN in 1815, the youngest son of a peasant-farmer in a Piedmontese village, John Melchior Bosco lost his father at the age of two and was brought up by his mother, a saintly and industrious woman who had a hard struggle to keep the home together. A dream which he had when he was nine showed him the vocation from which he never swerved. He seemed to be surrounded by a crowd of fighting and blaspheming children whom he strove in vain to pacify, at first by argument and then with his fists. Suddenly there appeared a mysterious lady who said to him: 'Softly, softly . . . if you wish to win them! Take your shepherd's staff and lead them to pasture'. As she spoke, the children were transformed into wild beasts and then into lambs. From that moment John recognized that his duty was to help poor boys, and he began with those of his own village, teaching them the catechism and bringing them to church. As an encouragement, he would often delight them with acrobatic and conjuring tricks, at which he became very proficient. One Sunday morning, when a perambulating juggler and gymnast was detaining the youngsters with his performances, the little lad challenged him to a competition, beat him at his own job, and triumphantly bore off his audience to Mass.

He was sixteen when he entered the seminary at Chieri and so poor that his maintenance money and his very clothes had to be provided by charity, the mayor contributing his hat, the parish priest his cloak, one parishioner his cassock, and another a pair of shoes. After his ordination to the diaconate he passed to the theological college of Turin and, during his residence there, he began, with the approbation of his superiors, to gather together on Sundays a number of the neglected apprentices and waifs of the city. St Joseph Cafasso, then rector of a parish church and the annexed sacerdotal institute in Turin, persuaded Don Bosco that he was not cut out to be a missionary abroad: 'Go and unpack that trunk you've got ready, and carry on with your work for the boys. That, and nothing else, is God's will for you'. Don Cafasso introduced him, on the one hand, to those moneyed people of the city who were in time to come to be the generous benefactors of his work, and on the other hand to the prisons and slums whence were to come the beneficiaries of that work.

His first appointment was to the assistant chaplaincy of a refuge for girls founded by the Marchesa di Barola, the wealthy and philanthropic woman who had taken care of Silvio Pellico after his release. This post left him free on Sundays to look after his boys, to whom he devoted the whole day and for whom he devised a sort of combined Sunday-school and recreation centre which he called a 'festive oratory'. When the marchesa, who with all her generosity was somewhat of an autocrat, delivered an ultimatum offering him the alternative of giving up the boys or resigning his post at her refuge, he chose the latter.

In the midst of his anxiety, the holy man was prostrated by a severe attack of pneumonia with complications which nearly cost him his life. He had hardly recovered when he went to live in some miserable rooms adjoining his new oratory, and with his mother installed as his housekeeper he applied himself to consolidating and extending his work. A night-school started the previous year took permanent shape, and as the oratory was overcrowded, he opened two more centres in other quarters of Turin. It was about this time that he began to take in and house a few destitute children. In a short time some thirty or forty neglected boys, most of them apprentices in the city, were living with Don Bosco and his devoted mother, 'Mamma Margaret', in the Valdocco quarter, going out daily to work. He soon realized that any good he could do them was counterbalanced by outside influences, and he eventually determined to train the apprentices at home. He opened his first two workshops, for shoemakers and tailors, in 1853.

The next step was to construct for his flock a church, which he placed under the patronage of his favourite saint, Francis de Sales, and when that was finished he set to work to build a home for his increasing family. At first they attended classes outside, but, as more help became available, technical courses and grammar classes were started in the house and all were taught at home. By 1856 there were 150 resident boys, with four workshops including a printing-press, and also four Latin classes, with ten young priests, besides the oratories with their 500 children.

For years St John Bosco's great problem was that of help. Enthusiastic young priests would offer their services, but sooner or later would give up, because they could not master Don Bosco's methods or had not his patience with often vicious young ruffians or were put off by his scheme for schools and workshops when he had not a penny. Some even were disappointed because he would not turn the oratory into a political club in the interests of 'Young Italy'. By 1850 he had only one assistant left, and he resolved to train young men himself for the work. In any case something in the nature of a religious order had long been in his mind and, after several disappointments, the time came when he felt that he had at last the nucleus he desired. 'On the night of January 26, 1854, we were assembled in Don Bosco's room,' writes one of those present. 'Besides Don Bosco there were Cagliero, Rocchetti, Artiglia and Rua. It was suggested that with God's help we should enter upon a period of practical works of charity to help our neighbours. At the close of that period we might bind ourselves by a promise, which could subsequently be transformed into a vow. From that evening, the name of Salesian was given to all who embarked upon that form of apostolate.' The name, of course, came from the great Bishop of Geneva.

In December 1859, with twenty-two companions, he finally determined to proceed with the organization of a religious congregation, whose rules had received the general approval of Pope Pius IX; but it was not until fifteen years later that the constitutions received their final approbation, with leave to present candidates for holy orders. The new society grew apace: in 1863 there were 39 Salesians, at the founder's death 768, and today they are numbered by thousands, all over the world. Don Bosco lived to see twenty-six houses started in the New World and thirty-eight in the Old.

His next great work was the foundation of an order of women to do for poor girls what the Salesians were doing for boys. This was inaugurated in 1872 with the clothing of twenty-seven young women to whom he gave the name of Daughters of Our Lady, Help of Christians. This community increased almost as fast as the other, with elementary schools in Italy, Brazil and the Argentine, and other activities.

Any account of Don Bosco's life would be incomplete without some mention of his work as a church-builder. His first little church soon proving insufficient for its increasing congregation, the founder proceeded to the construction of a much larger one which was completed in 1868. This was followed by another spacious and much-needed basilica in a poor quarter of Turin, which he placed under the patronage of St John the Evangelist. The effort to raise the necessary money had been immense, and the holy man was out of health and very weary, but his labours were not yet over. During the last years of Pius IX, the project had been formed of building in Rome a church in honour of the Sacred Heart, and Pius had given the money to buy the site. His successor was equally anxious for the work to proceed, but it seemed impossible to obtain funds to raise it above the foundations. The task was proposed to Don Bosco and he undertook it.

When he could obtain no more funds from Italy he betook himself to France, the land where devotion to the Sacred Heart has always flourished pre-eminently. Everywhere he was acclaimed as a saint and a wonder-worker, and the money came pouring in. The completion of the new church was assured, but, as the time for the consecration approached, Don Bosco was sometimes heard to say that if it were long delayed he would not be alive to witness it. It took place on May 14, 1887, and he offered Mass in the church once shortly after; but as the year drew on it became evident that his days were numbered. Two years earlier the doctors had declared that he had worn himself out and that complete rest was his only chance, but rest for him was out of the question. At the end of the year his strength gave way altogether, and he became gradually weaker until at last he passed away on January 31, 1888, so early in the morning that his death has been described, not quite correctly, as occurring on the morrow of the feast of St Francis de Sales. Forty thousand persons visited his body as it lay in the church, and his funeral resembled a triumph, for the whole city of Turin turned out to do him honour when his mortal remains were borne to their last resting-place. St John Bosco was canonized in 1934.

FEBRUARY

1 : ST HENRY MORSE, MARTYR (A.D. 1645)

HENRY MORSE was born in 1595 at Brome in Suffolk, and was brought up in the Protestant faith of his parents, who were of the country gentry. While reading law in London he decided to become a Catholic, and at the age of twenty-three went abroad and was received into the Church at Douai. He began his studies for the priesthood there, but finished them in the Venerabile at Rome, where he was ordained. Soon after landing at Newcastle in 1624 he was arrested and imprisoned in the castle at York. Before leaving Rome he had obtained the agreement of the father general of the Society of Jesus that he should be admitted to the Society in England, and it so happened that a Jesuit, Father John Robinson, was a fellow prisoner at York. Accordingly, the three years that Henry Morse spent in prison there were passed as a novitiate, and he there made his simple vows. Eventually he was released and banished, whereupon he went to Flanders and for a time was chaplain and missioner to the English soldiers serving the king of Spain there.

At the end of 1633 Father Morse came back to England and, under the name of Cuthbert Claxton, ministered in London. He was particularly active during the plague epidemic of 1636–7. He had a list of four hundred infected families, Protestant as well as Catholic, which he visited regularly with physical and spiritual help. This made so great an impression that in one year nearly a hundred families were reconciled with the Church. He himself caught the disease three times, but each time recovered; and he had to be warned by his superiors to moderate his zeal. At this very time the authorities deemed it suitable to arrest Father Morse, and charge him with being a priest and with 'perverting' 560 of his Majesty's Protestant subjects 'in and about the parish of St Giles in the Fields'. On the second charge he was found not guilty, but on the first guilty; however, Queen Henrietta Maria intervened and he was released on a bail of 10,000 florins. When the royal proclamation was made ordering all priests to leave the country by April 7, 1641, Father Morse obeyed it in order not to involve his sureties; and he again took up his work with the English troops abroad.

From Ghent he was in 1643 sent back to England, and laboured in the north for eighteen months, till he was apprehended on suspicion while making a sick-call on the borders of Cumberland. He was taken off towards

Durham, but on the way the Catholic wife of one of his captors, at whose house they were spending the night, enabled him to escape. But about six weeks later he was arrested (through his guide to a certain house losing his memory), and after some weeks in jail at Durham he was shipped from Newcastle to London. Here he was brought to the bar of the Old Bailey and sentenced to death on the strength of his conviction nine years before.

On the day of execution Father Morse celebrated a votive Mass of the Most Holy Trinity, and was drawn on a hurdle by four horses to Tyburn, where, as well as the usual crowd of sightseers and others, the French, Spanish and Portuguese ambassadors were present with their suites to do honour to the martyr. He told the people that he was dying for his religion, that he had worked only for the welfare of his countrymen, and that he knew nothing of plots against the king; and after he had prayed aloud for himself and for his persecutors and for the kingdom of England, the cart was drawn away. This was on February 1, 1645.

He was canonized as one of the Forty Martyrs in 1970.

2 : ST JOAN DE LESTONNAC, WIDOW, FOUNDRESS OF THE ⸴RELIGIOUS OF NOTRE DAME OF BORDEAUX (A.D. 1640)

JOAN DE LESTONNAC'S father belonged to a distinguished Bordelais family and, at a time when Calvinism was flourishing in Bordeaux, was a good Catholic—her mother, Joan Eyquem de Montaigne, sister of the famous Michael de Montaigne, apostatized. She tried to tamper with her child's faith, and when her endeavours failed Joan was ill-treated. These troubles turned her heart to God and made her long for a life of prayer and mortification. However, when she was seventeen she married Gaston de Montferrant, who was related to the royal houses of France, Aragon and Navarre. The marriage was a very happy one, but her husband died in 1597, leaving her with four children to whom she devoted herself till they were old enough to do without her. Two daughters eventually became nuns. At the age of forty-seven Joan de Lestonnac entered the Cistercian monastery of Les Feuillantes at Toulouse. This step was violently opposed by her son, and she herself was heartbroken at leaving her youngest daughter.

Mme de Lestonnac, now become Sister Joan, spent six months in the Cistercian novitiate, giving great edification. But the life was too hard for her, and at the end of that time her health completely broke down; though she implored to be allowed to remain in the convent to die, her superiors decided that such a valuable life must be preserved for the service of God.

Her health recovered almost miraculously as soon as she left Les Feuillantes. She returned to Bordeaux and visited Périgord, where she gathered round her several young girls who were eventually to be her first novices. She then spent two quiet years in her country place, La Mothe, preparing for her great work. We find her again in Bordeaux, where her directors advised her to content herself with an ordinary life devoted to works of charity. Bordeaux being visited by the plague, Mme de Lestonnac and a band of brave women gave themselves to nursing the victims. She now came under the influence of two Jesuits, Father de Bordes and Father Raymond, who fully realized the devastation which Calvinism was working amongst young girls of all classes who were deprived of Catholic education. To both these priests the assurance was given simultaneously, whilst they were celebrating Mass, that it was the will of God they should assist in founding an order to counteract the evils of the surrounding heresy and that Mme de Lestonnac should be the first superior. Thus the work began, and it grew rapidly. The infant congregation was affiliated to the Order of St Benedict, though its rule and constitutions were founded on those of St Ignatius, and the first house was opened in the old priory of the Holy Ghost at Bordeaux.

Mme de Lestonnac and her companions received the habit from Cardinal de Sourdis, Archbishop of Bordeaux, in 1608. After Mme de Lestonnac had been elected superior in 1610, subjects came rapidly. They were carefully taught the religious life—their aim and object being the training and teaching of young girls of all classes. The schools prospered beyond all expectation. Foundations were made in many towns, Périgueux being the earliest. The nuns lived lives of great poverty and mortification, and all seemed peaceful and happy when suddenly cruel trials fell on the foundress. One of her nuns, Blanche Hervé, and the director of one of the houses conspired against her, and for a time their ill-considered designs succeeded. They invented discreditable stories about her and, most surprising of all, Cardinal de Sourdis believed them. Mother de Lestonnac was deposed and Blanche Hervé elected superior. Blanche then treated Mother de Lestonnac most cruelly, insulting her in every possible way— even ill-treating her with physical violence. This state of things lasted for some time, but at last Blanche's heart was touched by St Joan's unalterable patience and she repented. As Mother de Lestonnac was now an old woman she did not wish to be reinstated as superior, and Mother de Badiffe was elected.

The last few years of the foundress were spent in retirement and preparation for death. She passed away just after her nuns had renewed their vows, on the feast of the Purification 1640. Joan de Lestonnac was eventually canonized in 1949.

3 : ST BLAISE, Bishop of Sebastea, martyr (A.D. 316?)

THERE seems to be no evidence earlier than the eighth century for the cult of St Blaise, but the accounts furnished at a later date agree in stating that he was bishop of Sebastea in Armenia and that he was crowned with martyrdom in the persecution of Licinius by command of Agricolaus, governor of Cappadocia and Lesser Armenia. It is mentioned in the legendary acts of St Eustratius, who is said to have perished in the reign of Diocletian, that St Blaise honourably received his relics, deposited them with those of St Orestes, and punctually executed every article of the last will and testament of St Eustratius.

This is all which can be affirmed with any faint probability concerning St Blaise, but according to his 'legendary acts' he was born of rich and noble parents, receiving a Christian education and being made a bishop while still quite young. When persecution arose, he withdrew by divine direction to a cave in the mountains which was frequented only by wild beasts. These he healed when they were sick or wounded, and they used to come round him to receive his blessing. Hunters, who had been sent to secure animals for the amphitheatre, found the saint surrounded by the beasts, and, though greatly amazed, they seized him and took him to Argricolaus. On their way they met a poor woman whose pig had been carried off by a wolf; at the command of St Blaise, the wolf restored the pig unhurt. The incident is worth mentioning because of a ceremony which arose in connection with it. On another occasion a woman brought to him a little boy who was at the point of death owing to a fishbone in his throat, and the saint healed him. On account of this and other similar cures St Blaise has been invoked during many centuries past for all kinds of throat trouble. The governor ordered him to be scourged and deprived of food, but the woman whose pig had been restored brought provisions to him and also tapers to dispel the darkness of his gloomy prison. Then Licinius tortured him by tearing his flesh with iron combs, and afterwards had him beheaded.

4 : ST JOHN DE BRITTO, MARTYR (A.D. 1693)

IT is stated that when John de Britto as a child fell grievously ill, his mother, a lady of noble family connected with the court of Lisbon, invoked the aid of St Francis Xavier and dedicated her son to him. Be this as it may, John, though he was the favourite companion of the Infante Don Pedro, who eventually succeeded to the throne of Portugal, aspired only to wear the habit of the great missionary and to devote his life to the conversion of the infidel. Born in March 1647, he made application at the age of fifteen to be received into the Society of Jesus, and in spite of much opposition he accomplished his purpose. His success in his studies was so remarkable that great efforts were made after his ordination to keep him in Portugal, but grace triumphed, and in 1673 he set sail for Goa with sixteen of his fellow Jesuits; the rest of his life, except for a brief interval, was spent amid incredible hardships and hindrances of all kinds in evangelizing southern India. He was made superior of the Madura mission and travelled most painfully on foot through all that vast region, only ten degrees north of the equator. Those who worked with him in their letters to Europe speak in glowing terms of his courage and devotion, of the extraordinary austerity of his life, and of the rich harvest of conversions which were the fruit of his labours.

From the beginning Father de Britto realized the wisdom of the method previously adopted by the missionary Father de Nobili, viz. of living a life identical with that of the natives of the country, adopting their dress, abstaining from animal food, and respecting in all things lawful the ineradicable prejudices of caste. To describe in detail the terrible odds against which de Britto had to contend would be impossible here, not the least handicap being the delicacy of his constitution which, in the fevers to which he was subject, repeatedly brought him face to face with death.

Many times Father de Britto and his Indian catechists were subjected to brutal violence. On one occasion in 1686, after preaching in the Marava country, he and a handful of devoted Indians were seized, and upon their refusal to pay honour to the god Siva, were subjected for several days in succession to excruciating tortures. They were hung up by chains from trees, and at another time by means of a rope attached to an arm or foot and passing over a pulley, were dipped repeatedly in stagnant water, with other indescribable outrages.

Father de Britto's recovery was deemed miraculous, and not long after he was set at liberty he was summoned back to Lisbon. Great efforts were made by King Pedro II and by the papal nuncio to induce him to remain in Europe, but he pleaded so strongly that duty called him back to Madura that he was allowed to have his way. For three years more he returned to his mission to lead the same life of heroic self-sacrifice; he was arrested and eventually put to death at Oriur, near Ramuad, by order of the Rajah Raghunatha. Father de Britto sent two letters from his prison the day before his execution. 'I await death', he writes to the father superior, 'and I await it with impatience. It has always been the object of my prayers. It forms today the most precious reward of my labours and my sufferings.' The next morning, February 4, 1693, a large crowd gathered to see the end of this teacher (*guru*) who was sentenced to die because he had taught things subversive of the worship of the gods of the country. After a long delay, for the local prince was nervous about the whole business, St John's head was struck from his body. When the news reached Lisbon, King Pedro ordered a solemn service of thanksgiving; and the martyr's mother was there, dressed not in mourning but in a festal gown. St John de Britto was canonized in 1947.

5 : ST ADELAIDE OF BELLICH, VIRGIN (A.D. 1015)

SHE was the daughter of Megengose, Count of Guelder, and ruled over the nunnery of Bellich on the Rhine, near Bonn, but died in 1015 as abbess of St Mary's in Cologne, both convents having been founded by her father and both being under her rule at the time of her death. Her festival is kept at Bellich, where the nunnery she instituted under the Benedictine rule was subsequently converted into a church of canonesses. She used to make it a great point that her nuns should know Latin so that they might follow the choir offices properly. She showed great prudence in other matters too, notably in the way in which she provided for the poor during a severe famine. St Heribert, Archbishop of Cologne, had the greatest respect for her and consulted her in all his difficulties.

6 : ST PAUL MIKI AND COMPANIONS, 'THE MARTYRS OF JAPAN' (A.D. 1597)

ST FRANCIS XAVIER planted Christianity in Japan where he arrived in 1549. He himself converted and baptized a considerable number and eventually whole provinces received the faith. It is said that by 1587 there were in Japan over two hundred thousand Christians. In that year the regent Hideyoshi ordered that all missionaries should leave his dominions within six months; some obeyed, but many remained behind in disguise. In 1596 he was roused to fury by the boast of the captain of a Spanish ship that the object of the missionaries was to facilitate the conquest of Japan by the

Portuguese or Spaniards, and three Jesuits and six Franciscans were crucified on a hill near Nagasaki in 1597.

The Franciscans were PETER BAPTIST, commissary of the friars in Japan, ST MARTIN DE AGUIRRE, ST FRANCIS BLANCO, ST FRANCIS-OF-ST-MICHAEL (a lay-brother), all Spaniards; ST PHILIP DE LAS CASAS, born in Mexico City and not yet ordained, and ST GONSALO GARCIA. The nationality of the last named, also a lay-brother, has been a subject of discussion. He was born at Bassein, near Bombay, it is generally said of Portuguese parents; but others claim that his parents were Indian converts who took Portuguese names. Of the Jesuits, one was ST PAUL MIKI, a high-born Japanese and an eminent preacher; the other two, ST JOHN GOTO and ST JAMES KISAI, were admitted to the order as lay-brothers shortly before they suffered. The remaining seventeen martyrs were also all Japanese; several of them were catechists and interpreters, and all were Franciscan tertiaries. They included a soldier, ST CAIUS FRANCIS, a physician, ST FRANCIS OF MIAKO, a native of Korea, ST LEO KARASUMA, and three boys of about thirteen who used to serve the friars at Mass, SS. LOUIS IBARKI, ANTONY DEYNAN and THOMAS KASAKI, whose father also suffered.

Twenty-four of the martyrs, after part of their left ears had been cut off, were led through various towns, their cheeks stained with blood, as a terror to others. Upon their arrival at the place of execution near Nagasaki, they were allowed to make their confession to two Jesuits and, after being fastened to crosses by cords and chains about their arms and legs and with an iron collar round their necks, they were raised into the air, the foot of each cross falling into a hole in the ground prepared for it. The crosses were planted in a row, about four feet apart, and each martyr had an executioner near him with a spear ready to pierce his side—according to the Japanese method of crucifixion. As soon as all the crosses had been planted, the executioners raised their lances at a given signal, and the martyrs were killed almost at the same instant. Their blood and garments were treasured by their fellow Christians and miracles were ascribed to them. These twenty-six witnesses to Christ were canonized in 1862.

7 : ST LUKE THE YOUNGER, (*c.* A.D. 946)

ST LUKE THE YOUNGER, also surnamed Thaumaturgus or the Wonder-worker, was a Greek. His family came from the island of Aegina, but were obliged to leave on account of the attacks of the Saracens, and came eventually to settle in Thessaly where they were small farmers or peasant proprietors. His father, Stephen, and his mother, Euphrosyne, had seven children, of whom he was the third. He was a pious and obedient boy, and was at an early age set to mind the sheep and cultivate the fields. From a child he often went without a meal in order to feed the hungry, and sometimes he would strip himself of his clothes that he might give them to beggars. When he went forth to sow, he was wont to scatter half the seed over the land of the poor, and it was noticed that the Lord used to bless his father's crops with abundant increase.

After the death of Stephen, the boy left the work of the fields and gave himself for a time to contemplation. He felt called to the religious life, and on one occasion he started off from Thessaly, meaning to seek a monastery, but was captured by soldiers who took him to be a runaway slave. They questioned him; but when he said that he was a servant of Christ and had undertaken the journey out of devotion, they refused to believe him and shut him up in prison, treating him very cruelly. After a time they discovered his identity and released him, but upon returning home he was received with gibes and was jeered at for running away.

Although he still desired to consecrate himself to God, Luke's relations were unwilling to let him go, but two monks who, on their way from Rome to the Holy Land, were hospitably entertained by Euphrosyne, managed to persuade her to let her son travel with them as far as Athens. There he entered a monastery, but was not suffered to remain there long. One day the superior sent for him and gave the young man to understand that his (Luke's) mother had appeared to him in a vision and that, as she was needing him, he had better go home again to help her. So Luke returned once more and was received with joy and surprise; but, after four months, Euphrosyne herself became convinced that her son had a real call to the religious life and she no longer opposed it. He built himself a hermitage on Mount Joannitsa near Corinth, and there he went to live, being at that time in his eighteenth year.

He is one of the early saints of whom a circumstantial story is told that he was seen raised from the ground in prayer. St Luke's cell was converted into an oratory after his death and was named Soterion or Sterion—the Place of Healing.

8 : ST JEROME EMILIANI, FOUNDER OF THE SOMASCHI (A.D.1537)

JEROME was born at Venice in 1481, the son of Angelo Emiliani (*vulgo* Miani) and Eleanor Mauroceni, and served in the armies of the republic during the troubled times of the beginning of the sixteenth century. When the League of Cambrai was formed to resist the Venetians, he was appointed to the command of the fortress of Castelnuovo, in the mountains near Treviso; at the fall of the town he was taken prisoner and chained in a dungeon. Hitherto he had led a careless and irreligious life, but now he sanctified his sufferings by prayer and turning to God, and, in circumstances which appeared to be miraculous, he was enabled to make his escape. He made his way at once to a church in Treviso and, probably later, hung up his fetters as votive offerings before the altar of our Lady, to whom he had vowed himself; and was given the post of mayor in the town. But he shortly after returned to Venice to take charge of the education of his nephews and to pursue his own sacerdotal studies, and in 1518 he was ordained.

Famine and plague having reduced many to the greatest distress, St Jerome devoted himself to relieving all, but particularly abandoned orphans. These he gathered in a house which he hired; clothed and fed them at his own expense, and instructed them himself in Christian doctrine and virtue. After himself recovering from the plague, he resolved in 1531 to devote himself and his property solely to others, and founded orphanages at Brescia, Bergamo, and Como, a shelter for penitent prostitutes, and a hospital at Verona. About 1532 Jerome with two other priests established a congregation of men, and at Somascha, between Bergamo and Milan, he founded a house which he destined for the exercises of those whom he received into his congregation. From this house it took its name, the Clerks Regular of Somascha, and its principal work was the care of orphans. The instruction of youth and young clerics became also an object of his foundation, and continues still to be. It is claimed for St Jerome Emiliani that he was the first to introduce the practice of teaching Christian doctrine to children by means of a set catechism drawn up in the form of questions and answers.

While attending the sick in 1537 he caught an infectious disease of which he died on February 8. He was canonized in 1767, and in 1928 was named patron-saint of orphans and abandoned children by Pope Pius XI.

9 : ST TEILO, BISHOP (SIXTH CENTURY)

THERE is ample evidence from the manuscript Book of St Chad, church-dedications and the like that St Teilo was a very important man in South Wales in his time, but there are no extant writings about his life till some five hundred years after his death. Around the year 1130 Geoffrey (Galfridus), a priest of Llandaff, composed a life of Teilo in the form of a sermon; and what seems to be a longer version of this life, altered to add glory to the see of Llandaff, is contained in the *Liber Landavensis*.

Stripped of obvious accretions and borrowings from the lives of other saints, we are told that Teilo was born near Penally, hard by Tenby in Pembrokeshire, and the earlier form of his name was Eliud. He was the pupil first of St Dubricius and then of one Paulinus (possibly St Paul Aurelian is meant), with whom he met St David. Teilo is then made to accompany David on his mythical visit to Jerusalem. During the yellow plague, so called 'because it made everyone it attacked yellow and bloodless', Teilo with others went abroad, the Book of Llandaff says to Brittany, where he stayed with St Samson at Dol; and they 'planted a big orchard of fruit-trees, three miles long, reaching from Dol to Cai, which is still called after their names'.

After seven years St Teilo returned to Wales, and died eventually at Llandeilo Fawr in Carmarthenshire, where (and not at Llandaff) was certainly his chief monastery and the centre of his ministry. Traces of the *cultus* of St Teilo in place-names and church-dedications are abundant all over South Wales, and are also found in Brittany, especially at Landeleau in the diocese of Quimper. His feast is still observed in the archdiocese of Cardiff and on Caldey island. Teilo is one of the four saints in whose honour the cathedral of Llandaff is dedicated.

10 : ST SCHOLASTICA, VIRGIN (A.D. 543)

THIS saint, who was St Benedict's sister, traditionally his twin, consecrated herself to God from her earliest years, as we learn from St Gregory. It is not known where she lived, whether at home or in a community; but after her brother had moved to Monte Cassino, she settled at Plombariola in that same neighbourhood, probably founding and ruling a nunnery about five miles to the south of St Benedict's monastery. St Gregory tells us that St Benedict governed nuns as well as monks, and it seems clear that St Scholastica must have been their abbess, under his direction. She used to visit her brother once a year and, since she was not allowed to enter his monastery, he used to go with some of his monks to meet her at a house a little way off. They spent these visits in praising God and in conferring together on spiritual matters.

St Gregory gives a remarkable description of the last of these visits. After they had passed the day as usual they sat down in the evening to have supper. When it was finished, Scholastica, possibly foreseeing that it would be their last interview in this world, begged her brother to delay his return till the next day that they might spend the time discoursing of the joys of Heaven. Benedict, who was unwilling to transgress his rule, told her that he could not pass a night away from his monastery. When Scholastica found that she could not move him, she laid her head upon her hands which were clasped together on the table and besought God to interpose on her behalf. Her prayer was scarcely ended when there arose such a violent storm of rain with thunder and lightning that St Benedict and his companions were unable to set foot outside the door. He exclaimed, 'God forgive you sister; what have you done?' Whereupon she answered, 'I asked a favour of you and you refused it. I asked it of God, and He has granted it.' Benedict was therefore forced to comply with her request, and they spent the night talking about holy things. The next morning they parted, and three days later St Scholastica died.

11 : ST BENEDICT OF ANIANE, ABBOT (A.D. 821)

BENEDICT was the son of Aigulf of Maguelone and served King Pepin and his son, Charlemagne, as cupbearer. At the age of twenty he made a resolution to seek the kingdom of God with his whole heart. He took part in the campaign in Lombardy, but, after having been nearly drowned in the Tesino, near Pavia, in endeavouring to save his brother, he made a vow to quit the world entirely. Upon his return to Languedoc he was confirmed in his determination by the advice of a hermit called Widmar, and he went to the abbey of Saint-Seine, fifteen miles from Dijon, where he was admitted as a monk. He spent two and a half years here learning the monastic life and bringing himself under control by severe austerities. Not satisfied with observing the Rule of St Benedict, he practised those other points of perfection which he found prescribed in the Rules of St Pachomius and St Basil. When the abbot died, the brethren were disposed to elect him to fill the post, but he was unwilling to accept the charge because he knew that the monks were opposed to anything in the shape of systematic reform.

Benedict accordingly quitted Saint-Seine and, returning to Languedoc, built a small hermitage beside the brook Aniane upon his own estate. Here he lived for some years in self-imposed destitution, praying continually that God would teach him to do His will. Some solitaries, of whom the holy man Widmar was one, placed themselves under his direction, and they earned their livelihood by manual labour, living on bread and water except on Sundays and great festivals when they added a little wine or milk if it was given them in alms. The superior worked with them in the fields and sometimes spent his time in copying books. When the number of his disciples increased, Benedict left to build a monastery in a more spacious place.

In a short time he had many religious under his direction, and at the same time exercised a general inspection over all the monasteries of Provence, Languedoc and Gascony, becoming eventually the director and overseer of all the monasteries in the empire; he reformed many with little or no opposition.

In order to have him close at hand, the Emperor Louis the Pious obliged Benedict to dwell first at the abbey of Maurmünster in Alsace and then, as he wanted him yet nearer, he built a monastery upon the Inde, later known as Cornelimünster, near Aachen, the residence of the emperor and court. Benedict lived in the monastery yet continued to help in the restoration of monastic observance throughout France and Germany. He was the chief instrument in drawing up the canons for the reformation of monks at the council of Aachen in 817, and presided in the same year over the assembly of abbots to enforce the restoration of discipline. His statutes, the *Capitula* of Aachen, were annexed to the Rule of St Benedict and imposed on all monks throughout the empire. Benedict also wrote the *Codex Regularum* (Code of Rules), a collection of all the monastic regulations which he found extant; he likewise compiled a book of homilies for the use of monks, collected from the works of the fathers; but his most important work was the *Concordia Regularum*, the Concord of Rules, in which he gives those of St Benedict of Nursia in combination with those of other patriarchs of monastic observance to show their similarity.

This great restorer of monasticism in the West, worn out by mortifications and fatigues, suffered much from continual sickness in the latter part of his days. He died at Inde with great tranquillity in 821, being then seventy-one years of age.

12 : ST MELETIUS, ARCHBISHOP OF ANTIOCH (A.D. 381)

MELETIUS belonged to one of the most distinguished families of Lesser Armenia, and was born at Melitene. His sincerity and kindly disposition gained for him the esteem of both Catholics and Arians, and he was promoted to the bishopric of Sebastea. However, he met with such violent opposition that he left it and retired, first into the desert and afterwards to Beroea in Syria, a town of which Socrates supposes him to have been bishop.

The church of Antioch had been oppressed by the Arians ever since the banishment of Eustathius in 331, several succeeding bishops having fostered the heresy. Eudoxus, the last of these, though an Arian, was expelled by a party of Arians in a sedition and shortly afterwards usurped the see of Constantinople. The Arians and some Catholics then agreed to raise Meletius to the chair of Antioch, and the emperor confirmed their choice in 361, although other Catholics refused to recognize him, as they regarded his election as irregular on account of the share which the Arians had taken in it. The Arians hoped that he would declare himself of their party, but they were undeceived when, on the arrival in Antioch of the

Emperor Constantius, he was ordered with several other prelates to expound the text in the Book of Proverbs concerning the wisdom of God: 'The Lord hath created me in the beginning of His ways'. First George of Laodicea explained it in an Arian sense, then Acacius of Caesarea gave it a meaning bordering on the heretical, but Meletius expounded it in the Catholic sense and connected it with the Incarnation. This public testimony angered the Arians, and Eudoxus at Constantinople persuaded the emperor to banish Meletius to Lesser Armenia. The Arians gave the see to Euzoius, who had previously been expelled from the Church by St Alexander, Archbishop of Alexandria. From this time dates the famous schism of Antioch, although it really originated with the banishment of St Eustathius about thirty years before. The death of the Emperor Valens in 378 put an end to the Arian persecution, and St Meletius was reinstated; but his difficulties were not at an end, for there was another orthodox hierarch, Paulinus, recognized by many as bishop of Antioch.

In 381 the second ecumenical council assembled at Constantinople, and St Meletius presided; but while the council was yet sitting death took this long-suffering bishop, to the great grief of the fathers and the Emperor Theodosius who had welcomed him to the imperial city with a great demonstration of affection. His funeral in Constantinople was attended by all the fathers of the council and the faithful of the city. One of the most eminent of the prelates, St Gregory of Nyssa, delivered his funeral oration.

13 : ST CATHERINE DEI RICCI, VIRGIN (A.D. 1590)

THIS saint was born in 1522 into a well-known Florentine family, and at her baptism was called Alexandrina. She took the name of Catherine at her religious clothing, when she was thirteen, in the Dominican convent of St Vincent at Prato, of which her uncle, Father Timothy dei Ricci, was director. Here for two years she suffered agonizing pain from a complication of diseases which remedies seemed only to aggravate; but she sanctified her sufferings by her exemplary patience, which she derived in great part from constant meditation on the passion of Christ. Catherine while still very young was chosen novice-mistress, then sub-prioress, and in her thirtieth year was appointed prioress in perpetuity. The reputation of her holiness and wisdom brought her visits from many lay people and clergy, including three cardinals, each of whom afterwards became pope.

St Philip Neri and St Catherine dei Ricci exchanged a number of letters, and although they never met in the body she appeared to him and talked with him in Rome—without ever having left her convent at Prato. This was expressly stated by St Philip Neri, who was always most cautious in giving credence to or publishing visions, and it was confirmed by the oaths of five witnesses. Catherine is famous for her extraordinary series of ecstasies in which she beheld and *enacted* in their order the scenes which preceded our Saviour's crucifixion. They began when she was twenty years old in February 1542, and they were renewed every week for twelve years continuously. Naturally they occasioned much talk, crowds of devout or curious people sought to visit the convent. The recollection of the community was interfered with, and the inconveniences resulting were only the more acutely felt when in 1552 she was herself elected prioress. Earnest supplication was made by all the nuns at her request that these manifestations might cease, and in 1554 they came to an end.

St Catherine dei Ricci died after a long illness at the age of sixty-eight on February 2, 1590.

14 : ST CYRIL AND ST METHODIUS, ARCHBISHOP OF SIRMIUM (A.D. 869 AND 884)

THESE brothers, natives of Thessalonika, are venerated as the apostles of the Southern Slavs and the fathers of Slavonic literary culture. Cyril, the younger of them, was baptized Constantine and assumed the name by which he is usually known only shortly before his death, when he received the habit of a monk. At an early age he was sent to Constantinople, where he studied at the imperial university under Leo the Grammarian and Photius. Here he learned all the profane sciences but no theology; however, he was ordained deacon (priest probably not till later) and in due course took over the chair of Photius, gaining for himself a great reputation, evidenced by the epithet 'the Philosopher'. For a time he retired to a religious house, but in 861 he was sent by the emperor, Michael III, on a religio-political mission to the ruler of the judaized Khazars between the Dnieper and the Volga. His elder brother, Methodius, who, after being governor of one of the Slav colonies in the Opsikion province, had become a monk, also took part in the mission to the Khazars, and on his return to Greece was elected abbot of an important monastery.

In 862 there arrived in Constantinople an ambassador charged by Rostislav, prince of Moravia, to ask that the emperor would send him missionaries capable of teaching his people in their own language. Photius, now patriarch of Constantinople, decided that Cyril and Methodius were most suitable for the work: they were learned men, who knew Slavonic, and the first requirement was the provision of characters in which the Slav tongue might be written. The characters now called 'cyrillic', from which are derived the present Russian, Serbian and Bulgarian letters, were invented from the Greek capitals, perhaps by the followers of St Cyril; the 'glagolithic' alphabet, in which the Slav-Roman liturgical books of certain Yugoslav Catholics are printed, may be that prepared for this occasion by Cyril himself.

In 863 the two brothers set out with a number of assistants and came to the court of Rostislav. The new missionaries made free use of the vernacular in their preaching and ministrations, and this made immediate appeal to the local people. To the German clergy this was objectionable, and their opposition was strengthened when the Emperor Louis the German forced Rostislav to take an oath of fealty to him. The Byzantine missionaries, armed with their pericopes from the Scriptures and liturgical hymns in Slavonic, pursued their way with much success, but were soon handicapped by their lack of a bishop to ordain more priests. The German prelate, the bishop of Passau, would not do it, and Cyril therefore determined to seek help elsewhere, presumably from Constantinople whence he came.

On their way the brothers arrived in Venice. It was at a bad moment.

Photius at Constantinople had incurred excommunication; the *protégés* of the Eastern emperor and their liturgical use of a new tongue were vehemently criticized. They came to Rome bringing with them alleged relics of Pope St Clement, which St Cyril had recovered when in the Crimea on his way back from the Khazars. Adrian II warmly welcomed the bearers of so great a gift. He examined their cause, and he gave judgement: Cyril and Methodius were to receive episcopal consecration, their neophytes were to be ordained, the use of the liturgy in Slavonic was approved.

While still in Rome Cyril died, on February 14, 869. He was buried with great pomp in the church of San Clemente on the Coelian, where the relics of St Clement had been enshrined. St Methodius now took up his brother's leadership. Having been consecrated bishop he returned, bearing a letter from the Holy See recommending him as a man of 'exact understanding and orthodoxy'. Kosel, prince of Pannonia, asked that the ancient archdiocese of Sirmium (now Mitrovitsa) be revived. Methodius was made metropolitan and the boundaries of his charge extended to the borders of Bulgaria. But the papal approval did not intimidate the Western clergy there, and the situation in Moravia had now changed. Rostislav's nephew, Svatopluk, had allied himself with Carloman of Bavaria and driven his uncle out. In 870 Methodius found himself haled before a synod of German bishops and interned in a leaking cell. Only after two years could the pope, now John VIII, get him released. John judged it prudent to withdraw the permission to use Slavonic ('a barbarous language', he called it), except for the purpose of preaching. At the same time he reminded the Germans that Pannonia and the disposition of sees throughout Illyricum belonged of old to the Holy See.

During the following years St Methodius continued his work of evangelization in Moravia, but he made an enemy of Svatopluk, whom he rebuked for the wickedness of his life. Accordingly in 878 the archbishop was delated to the Holy See both for continuing to conduct divine worship in Slavonic and for heresy, in that he omitted the words 'and the Son' from the creed (at that time these words had not been introduced everywhere in the West, and not in Rome). John VIII summoned him to Rome. Methodius was able to convince the pope both of his orthodoxy and of the desirability of the Slavonic liturgy, and John again conceded it, though with certain reservations. Unfortunately, in accordance with the wishes of Svatopluk, the pope also nominated to the see of Nitra, which was suffragan to Sirmium, a German priest called Wiching, an implacable opponent of Methodius. This unscrupulous prelate continued to persecute his metropolitan, even to the extent of forging pontifical documents. After his death, Wiching obtained the archiepiscopal see, banished the chief disciples of his predecessor, and undid much of his work in Moravia.

During the last four years of his life, according to the 'Pannonian legend', St Methodius completed the Slavonic translation of the Bible (except the books of Machabees) and also of the *Nomokanon*, a compilation of Byzantine ecclesiastical and civil law. This suggests that circumstances were preventing him from devoting all his time to missionary and episcopal concerns; in other words, he was fighting a losing battle with the German influence. He died, probably at Stare Mesto (Velehrad), worn out by his apostolic labours and the opposition of those who thought them misdirected, on April 6, 884.

15 : ST SIGFRID, BISHOP OF VÄXJÖ (c. A.D. 1045)

AFTER King Olaf Tryggvason of Norway had been converted to Christianity he asked the English king, Ethelred, to send him missionaries. Sigfrid, said to have been a priest of York (or possibly Glastonbury), went out from England as a missionary bishop, and with him also went two other bishops, John and Grimkel. They did not confine themselves to Norway, but passed on to Sweden which, after having been in part evangelized by St Anskar, had relapsed into idolatry. There they laboured under the protection of the archbishop of Bremen, and Sigfrid made his headquarters at Växjö. The king of Sweden, whose name also was Olaf, was himself converted by St Sigfrid, who baptized him at Husaby in a spring which afterwards bore Sigfrid's name and was the channel of many miracles. St. Sigfrid continued his labours successfully for many years, and at his death was buried in the church of Växjö. It is said that he ordained two bishops, for East and West Gothland. His three nephews, Unaman a priest, Sunaman a deacon, and Vinaman a subdeacon, were his chief assistants.

After a time, St Sigfrid entrusted the care of his diocese to these three and set off to carry the light of the gospel into more distant provinces. During his absence, a troop, partly out of hatred for Christianity and partly for booty, plundered the church of Växjö and murdered Unaman and his brothers, burying their bodies in a forest and placing their heads in a box which they sank in a pond. The heads were duly recovered and placed in a shrine, on which occasion, we are told, the three heads spoke. The king resolved to put the murderers to death, but St Sigfrid induced him to spare their lives. Olaf compelled them, however, to pay a heavy fine which he wished to bestow on the saint, who refused to accept any part of it, notwithstanding his extreme poverty and the difficulties with which he had to contend in rebuilding his church. He had inherited in an heroic degree the spirit of the apostles, and preached the gospel also in Denmark. Sigfrid is said, but doubtfully, to have been canonized by Pope Adrian IV, the Englishman who had himself laboured zealously for the propagation of the faith in the North over one hundred years after St Sigfrid. The Swedes honour St Sigfrid as their apostle.

16 : ST GILBERT OF SEMPRINGHAM, FOUNDER OF THE GILBERTINE ORDER (A.D. 1189)

ST GILBERT was born at Sempringham in Lincolnshire, and in due course was ordained priest. For some time he taught in a free school, but the advowson of the parsonages of Sempringham and Terrington being in the gift of his father, he was presented by him to the united livings in 1123. He gave the revenues of them to the poor, reserving only a small sum for bare necessities. By his care, his parishioners were led to sanctity of life, and he drew up a rule for seven young women who lived in strict enclosure in a house adjoining the parish church of St Andrew at Sempringham. This foundation grew, and Gilbert found it necessary to add first lay-sisters and then lay-brothers to work the nuns' land. In 1147 he went to Cîteaux to ask the abbot to take over the foundation. This the Cistercians were unable to do, and Gilbert was encouraged by Pope Eugenius III to carry on the work himself. Finally Gilbert added a fourth element, of canons regular, as chaplains to the nuns.

Thus the Gilbertines came into being, the only medieval religious order of English origin. Except for one house in Scotland, it never spread outside England and became extinct at the dissolution, when there were twenty-six monasteries. The nuns had the Rule of St Benedict and the canons St Augustine's. The houses were double, but it was mainly a women's order, though at its head was a canon, the master general. The discipline of the order was severe and strongly influenced by Cîteaux; and the insistence on simplicity in church-furnishing and worship went to the extent of celebrating the choir office 'in monotone in a spirit of humility, rather than to pervert the minds of the weak like the daughter of Herodias'.

Eventually St Gilbert himself assumed the office of master general of the order, but resigned the direction of it some time before his death, when the loss of his sight rendered adequate supervision impossible. So abstemious was he that others wondered how life could be supported on such slender fare. He always had at his table a dish which he called 'the plate of the Lord Jesus', into which he put all that was best of what was served up, and this was for the poor. He wore a hair-shirt, took his short rest sitting, and spent a great part of the night in prayer. During the exile of St Thomas of Canterbury, he and other superiors of his order were accused of having sent him assistance.

St Gilbert died in 1189 at the age of 106, and was canonized in 1202. His relics are said to have been taken by King Louis VIII to Toulouse, where what purports to be them are still kept in the church of St Sernin.

17 : THE SEVEN HOLY FOUNDERS OF THE SERVITE ORDER, (THIRTEENTH CENTURY)

BETWEEN the years 1225 and 1227 seven young Florentines joined the Confraternity of the Blessed Virgin—popularly known as the 'Laudesi' or Praisers. It was a period when the prosperous city of Florence was being rent by political factions and distracted by the heresy of the Cathari: it was also a time of general relaxation of morals even where devotional practices were retained. These young men were members of the most prominent families of the city. Whether they were all friends before they joined the Laudesi is not clear, but in that confraternity they became closely allied.

The eldest was Buonfiglio Monaldo, who became their leader. The others were Alexis Falconieri, Benedict dell' Antella, Bartholomew Amidei, Ricovero Uguccione, Gerardino Sostegni, and John Buonagiunta. They had as their spiritual director James of Poggibonsi, who was chaplain of the Laudesi, a man of great holiness and spiritual insight. All of them came to realize the call to a life of renunciation, and they determined to have recourse to our Lady in their perplexity. On the feast of the Assumption, as they were absorbed in prayer, they saw her in a vision, and were inspired by her to withdraw from the world into a solitary place and to live for God alone. There were difficulties, because, though three of them were celibates, four had been married and had ties, although two had become widowers. Suitable provision for their dependants was arranged, and with the approval of the bishop they withdrew from the world and betook themselves to a house called La Carmarzia, outside the gates of Florence, twenty-three days after they had received their call. Before long they found themselves so much disturbed by constant visitors from Florence that they decided to withdraw to the wild and deserted slopes of Monte Senario, where they built a simple church and hermitage and lived a life of almost incredible austerity.

In spite of difficulties, visitors sometimes found their way to the hermits and many wished to join them, but they refused to accept recruits. So they continued to live for several years, until they were visited by their bishop, Ardingo, and Cardinal Castiglione, who had heard about their sanctity. He was greatly edified, but made one adverse criticism: 'You treat yourselves in a manner bordering on barbarity: and you seem more desirous of dying to time than of living for eternity. Take heed: the enemy of souls often hides himself under the appearance of an angel of light . . . . Hearken to the counsels of your superiors.'

Again the solitaries gave themselves up to prayer for light, and again they had a vision of our Lady, who bore in her hand a black habit while an angel held a scroll inscribed with the title of Servants of Mary. She told them she had chosen them to be her servants, that she wished them to wear the black habit, and to follow the Rule of St Augustine. From that date, April 13, 1240, they were known as the Servants of Mary, or Servites.

They were clothed by the bishop himself, Buonfiglio being elected their superior. According to custom they selected names by which they should thenceforth be known, and became Brothers Bonfilius, Alexis, Amadeus, Hugh, Sostenes, Manettus and Buonagiunta. By the wish of the bishop, all except St Alexis, who in his humility begged to be excused, prepared to receive holy orders, and in due time they were fully professed and ordained priests. The new order, which took a form more like that of the mendicant friars than that of the monastic orders, increased amazingly, and it soon became necessary to form fresh houses. Siena, Pistoia and Arezzo were the first places chosen, and afterwards the houses at Carfaggio, the convent and church of the Santissima Annunziata in Florence, and the convent at Lucca were established. Meanwhile, although the Servites had the approval of their immediate superiors, they had not been recognized by the Holy See. It was only in 1259 that the order was practically recognized by Alexander IV, and not until 1304—over sixty years after its foundation—that it received the explicit and formal approbation of Bd Benedict XI. St Bonfilius had remained as prior general until 1256, when he begged to be relieved owing to old age. He died on new year's night, 1261.

St Buonagiunta, the youngest of the seven, was the second prior general, but not long after his election he breathed his last in chapel while the gospel of the Passion was being read. St Amadeus ruled over the important convent of Carfaggio, but returned to Monte Senario to end his days. St Manettus became fourth prior general and sent missionaries to Asia, but he retired to make way for St Philip Benizi, upon whose breast he died. St Hugh and St Sostenes went abroad—Sostenes to Paris and Hugh to found convents in

Germany. They were recalled in 1276, and, being attacked by illness, they passed away side by side the same night. St Alexis, the humble lay-brother, outlived them all, and he was the only one who survived to see the order fully and finally recognized. He is reported to have died at the age of one hundred and ten.

18 : ST THEOTONIUS, (A.D. 1166)

ST THEOTONIUS is held in great honour in Portugal. A nephew of Cresconius, Bishop of Coimbra, he had been destined for the priesthood from his earliest years; after his ordination he was appointed to Viseu, and in a short time the spiritual charge of all in that township was entrusted to him. A man of true holiness and austerity of life, he was also a great preacher whose fame spread far and wide. He resigned his office of archpriest to visit the Holy Land, but on his return continued to work at Viseu. The queen and her husband, Henry, Count of Portugal, repeatedly urged him to accept a bishopric, but he always refused. He had a great love for the poor and for the souls in Purgatory, for whom he used to sing solemn Mass every Friday. This was followed by a procession to the cemetery in which the whole population joined and in the course of which large sums of money were given in alms: these he invariably distributed amongst the poor. He was outspoken in rebuking vice, and the greatest in the land feared and respected him. When the widowed queen and Count Ferdinand (whose association with her was causing scandal) were present at one of his sermons, St Theotonius uttered from the pulpit stern words so obviously aimed at them that they were filled with confusion and beat a hasty retreat. On another occasion he was vested and about to celebrate a Mass of our Lady when he received a message from the queen, who was at the church, asking him to shorten the time he usually took. He sent back word that he was offering Mass in honour of a sovereign who was greater than any royal personage on earth, and that the queen was quite at liberty to stay or to go.

After a second pilgrimage to the Holy Land, St Theotonius found that his former preceptor, Tellus, was busied with a scheme of a new monastery at Coimbra to be composed of Canons Regular of St Augustine; and Theotonius decided to join them, being the twelfth on the original foundation, of which he soon became prior. King Alphonsus, who greatly venerated him, heaped gifts on this monastery of the Holy Cross, as did also Queen Mafalda, although she sought in vain to be permitted to cross the threshold. St Theotonius was remarkable for his insistence on the exact and reverent recitation of the daily offices: he would never allow them to be gabbled or hurried. The king attributed to the holy man's prayers his victories over his enemies and recovery from illness, and in his gratitude granted the saint's request that he should liberate all his Mozarabic Christian captives. Theotonius rose to be abbot of the monastery, where he spent the last thirty years of his life, dying at the age of eighty.

When Alphonsus heard of his death, he exclaimed, 'His soul will have gone up to Heaven before his body is lowered into the tomb'.

19 : ST BONIFACE, BISHOP OF LAUSANNE (A.D. 1260)

ST BONIFACE was born in Brussels and was sent at the age of seventeen to study at Paris, where he in due course became one of the best-known lecturers in the university. He remained in Paris for seven more years, but disputes arose between the masters and the students, and his pupils struck and would not attend his lectures any longer. This decided him to leave Paris and he betook himself to Cologne, where a post was assigned to him in the cathedral school. He had been there only two years when he was elected bishop of Lausanne. He went to his diocese full of zeal and laboured indefatigably, but he found himself continually opposed and misunderstood throughout the eight years of his episcopate. Perhaps his long connection with the University of Paris unfitted him for dealing tactfully with his difficult people; he appears to have publicly denounced from the pulpit the weaknesses of the clergy.

Having incurred the enmity of the Emperor Frederick II, Boniface was set upon and badly wounded in 1239. Convinced that he was unfit for his office, he went to the pope and begged to be released, and his request was granted. The saint went back to Brussels, to the Cistercian nunnery at La Cambre, where the abbess invited him to stay amongst them. This he seems to have done, donning the Cistercian habit if he did not actually take the vows, and living the rest of his life within the precincts of the abbey. His cult was approved in 1702.

20 : ST WULFRIC, (A.D. 1154)

BORN at Compton Martin, eight miles from Bristol, and trained for the priesthood, Wulfric lived a careless life even after his ordination, being engrossed with hawking and hunting. But while priest at Deverill, near Warminster, he was suddenly touched by divine grace, and his conversion was popularly attributed to a chance interview he had with a beggar.

St Wulfric was casting about for a solitary spot in which he might devote himself entirely to the service of God when a knight offered him a cell adjoining the church at Haselbury in Somerset. Here he gave himself up to great austerities, and by fasting and scourging reduced himself to skin and bone. He wore chain-mail next to his skin, and a curious miracle is recounted in detail of the cutting of the iron links with an ordinary pair of scissors or shears as if they were so much linen. The reason why Wulfric wanted his cuirass shortened was that it prevented him from making the innumerable prostrations which formed, perhaps as a survival of Celtic influences, so favourite a type of penitential exercise at that period. We are told that sometimes Wulfric would at night, summer or winter, strip and get into a tub of cold water, remaining there till he had recited the whole psalter; at other times he would spend the night in prayer in the church, where he offered Mass daily and was served by a boy named Osbern, afterwards parson of Haselbury, to whom we owe valuable information about the anchoret.

Wulfric employed himself in the copying of books (he sometimes had a secretary to help him), which he bound himself, and it looks as if he also made things for the church. The many wonders attributed to Wulfric show the veneration in which he was held, but it seems that it was for prophecy more than anything else that he was famous, even to far parts of the land: among his visitors were King Henry I and King Stephen.

St Wulfric (there is no reason to suppose that he was ever canonized) died on February 20, 1154, and was buried in the cell in which he had lived: the vestry of the present church at Haselbury stands on its site.

21 : ST PETER DAMIAN, CARDINAL-BISHOP OF OSTIA, DOCTOR OF THE CHURCH (A.D. 1072)

ST PETER DAMIAN was born at Ravenna and, having lost his parents when very young, he was left in the charge of a brother in whose house he was treated more like a slave than a kinsman. As soon as he was old enough he was sent to tend swine. Another brother, who was archpriest of Ravenna, took pity on the neglected lad and undertook to have him educated. Having found a father in this brother, Peter appears to have adopted from him the surname of Damian. Damian sent the boy to school, first at Faenza and then at Parma. He proved an apt pupil and became in time a master and a professor of great ability. He had early begun to inure himself to fasting, watching and prayer, and wore a hair shirt under his clothes to arm himself against the allurements of pleasure and the wiles of the Devil. Not only did he give away much in alms, but he was seldom without some poor persons at his table, and took pleasure in serving them with his own hands.

After a time Peter resolved to leave the world entirely and embrace a monastic life away from his own country. Whilst his mind was full of these thoughts, two religious of St Benedict, belonging to Fonte Avellana of the reform of St Romuald, happened to call at the house where he lived, and he was able to learn much from them about their rule and mode of life. This decided him, and he joined their hermitage, which was then in the greatest repute. The hermits, who dwelt in pairs in separate cells, occupied themselves chiefly in prayer and reading, and lived a life of great austerity.

He now devoted considerable time to sacred studies, and became as well versed in the Holy Scriptures as he formerly had been in profane literature. By the unanimous consent of the hermits he was ordered to take upon himself the government of the community in the event of the superior's death. Peter's extreme reluctance obliged the abbot to make it a matter of obedience. Accordingly after the abbot's decease about the year 1043, Peter assumed the direction of that holy family, which he governed with great wisdom and piety. He also founded five other hermitages in which he placed priors under his own general direction. His chief care was to foster in his disciples the spirit of solitude, charity and humility.

For years Peter Damian was much employed in the service of the Church by successive popes, and in 1057 Stephen IX prevailed upon him to quit his desert and made him cardinal-bishop of Ostia. Peter constantly solicited Nicholas II to grant him leave to resign his bishopric and return to his solitude, but the pope had always refused. His successor, Alexander II, out of affection for the holy man, was prevailed upon with difficulty to consent, but reserved the power to employ him in church matters of importance, as he might hereafter have need of his help. The saint from that time considered himself dispensed not only from the responsibility of governing his see, but from the supervision of the various religious settlements he had controlled, and reduced himself to the condition of a simple monk.

Whatever austerities he prescribed for others, he practised himself, remitting none of them even in his old age. He used to make wooden spoons and other little useful things that his hands might not be idle during the time he was not at work or at prayer. When Henry, Archbishop of Ravenna, had been excommunicated for grievous enormities, Peter was sent by Alexander II as legate to settle the troubles. Upon his arrival at Ravenna he found that the prelate had just died, but he brought the accomplices of his crimes to a sense of their guilt and imposed on them suitable penance. This was Damian's last undertaking for the Church. As he was returning towards Rome he was arrested by an acute attack of fever in a monastery outside Faenza, and died on the eighth day of this illness, whilst the monks were reciting Matins round about him, on February 22, 1072.

St Peter Damian was one of the chief forerunners of the Hildebrandine reform in the Church. His preaching was most eloquent and his writing voluminous, and he was declared a doctor of the Church in 1828.

22 : ST MARGARET OF CORTONA, (A.D. 1297)

MARGARET was the daughter of a small farmer of Laviano in Tuscany. She had the misfortune to lose a good mother when she was only seven years old, and the stepmother whom her father brought home two years later was a hard and masterful woman who had little sympathy with the high-spirited, pleasure-loving child.

Margaret fell an easy prey to a young cavalier from Montepulciano, who induced her to elope with him one night to his castle among the hills. For nine years she lived openly as his mistress and caused much scandal, especially when she rode through the streets of Montepulciano on a superb horse and splendidly attired. She was however, faithful to her lover whom she often entreated to marry her and to whom she bore one son. One day the young man went out to visit one of his estates and failed to return. All one night and the next day Margaret watched with growing anxiety, until at length she saw the dog that had accompanied him running back alone. He plucked at her dress and she followed him through a wood to the foot of an oak tree, where he began to scratch, and soon she perceived with horror the mangled body of her lover, who had been assassinated and then thrown into a pit and covered with leaves.

She recognized in this the judgement of God. As soon as she could she left Montepulciano, after having given the relations of the dead man all that was at her disposal except a few ornaments which she sold for the benefit of the poor. Clad in a robe of penitence and holding her little son by the hand, she returned to her father's house to ask forgiveness and admittance. Her father refused to receive her, and Margaret was almost reduced to despair when she was suddenly inspired to go to Cortona to seek the aid of the Friars Minor, of whose gentleness with sinners she seems to have heard. When she reached the town she did not know where to go and her evident misery attracted the attention of two ladies, Marinana and Raneria by name, who spoke to her and asked if they could help her. She told them her story and why she had come to Cortona, and they at once took her and her boy to their own home. Afterwards they introduced her to the Franciscans, who soon became her fathers in Christ. For three years Margaret had a hard struggle against temptation, for the flesh was not yet subdued to the spirit. She found her chief earthly support in the counsel of two friars, John da Castiglione and Giunta Bevegnati, who was her ordinary confessor and who afterwards wrote her 'legend'.

Margaret started to earn her living by nursing the ladies of the city, but she gave this up in order to devote herself to prayer and to looking after the sick poor. She left the home of the ladies who had befriended her, and took up her quarters in a small cottage in a more secluded part, where she began to subsist upon alms. Any unbroken food that was bestowed upon her she gave to the poor, and only what was left of the broken food did she use for herself and her child. At the end of three years her earlier struggles were over, and she reached a higher plane of spirituality when she began to realize by experience the love of Christ for her soul. She had long desired to become a member of the third order of St Francis, and the friars, who had waited until they were satisfied of her sincerity, at length consented to give her the habit. Soon afterwards her son was sent to school at Arezzo, where he remained until he entered the Franciscan Order. From the time she became a tertiary, St Margaret advanced rapidly in prayer and was drawn into very direct communion with her Saviour.

The communications she received did not all relate to herself. In one case she was told to send a message to Bishop William of Arezzo, warning him to amend his ways and to desist from fighting with the people of his diocese and Cortona in particular. In 1289 she strove to avert war when Bishop William was again at strife with the Guelfs. Margaret went to him in person but he would not listen, and ten days later he was slain in battle. The bishop had, however, done one good turn to Margaret and to Cortona, for in 1286 he had granted a charter which enabled her to start putting her work for the sick poor on a permanent basis. At first she seems to have nursed them by herself in her own cottage, but after a time she was joined by several women, one of whom, Diabella, gave her a house for the purpose. She enlisted the sympathy of Uguccio Casali, the leading citizen of Cortona, and he induced the city council to assist her in starting a hospital called the Spedale di Santa Maria della Misericordia, the nursing sisters of which were Franciscan tertiaries whom Margaret formed into a congregation with special statutes; they were called the Poverelle. She also founded the Confraternity of Our Lady of Mercy, pledged to support the hospital and to search out and assist the poor.

As Margaret advanced in life, so did she advance in the way of expiation. Her nights she spent, almost without sleep, in prayer and contemplation, and when she did lie down to rest, her bed was the bare ground. For food she took only a little bread and raw vegetables, with water to drink; she wore rough hair-cloth next her skin and disciplined her body to blood for her own sins and those of mankind.

She received the last rites from Fra Giunta and passed away at the age of fifty, after having spent twenty-nine years in penance. On the day of her death she was publicly acclaimed as a saint, and the citizens of Cortona in the same year began to build a church in her honour, although she was not formally canonized until 1728. Of the original church built by Nicholas and John Pisano nothing remains but a window; the present tasteless building, however, contains St Margaret's body under the high altar and a statue of the saint and her dog by John Pisano.

23 : ST POLYCARP, BISHOP OF SMYRNA, MARTYR (A.D. 155?)

ST POLYCARP was one of the most famous of the little group of early bishops known as 'the Apostolic Fathers', who, being the immediate disciples of the apostles, received instruction directly from them, as it were from the fountain head. Polycarp was a disciple of St John the Evangelist, and was respected by the faithful to the point of profound veneration. He trained many holy disciples, among whom were St Irenaeus and Papias.

St Polycarp kissed the chains of St Igantius when he passed by Smyrna on the road to his martyrdom, and Ignatius in turn recommended to him the care of his distant church of Antioch, supplementing this charge later on by a request that he would write in his name to those churches of Asia to which he had not leisure to write himself. Polycarp addressed a letter to the Philippians shortly after, which is still extant.

Polycarp undertook a journey to Rome to confer with Pope St Anicetus about certain points, especially about the time of keeping Easter, for the Asiatic churches differed from others in this matter. Anicetus could not persuade Polycarp, nor Polycarp Anicetus, and so it was agreed that both might follow their custom without breaking the bonds of charity. St Anicetus, to testify his respect, asked him to celebrate the Eucharist in his own papal church. We find no further particulars concerning Polycarp recorded before his martyrdom.

In the sixth year of Marcus Aurelius (according to Eusebius) a violent persecution broke out in Asia in which the faithful gave heroic proof of their courage. The holy man, though fearless, had been prevailed upon by his friends to conceal himself during the storm. When the persecutors came in search of him he changed his retreat, but was betrayed by a slave, who was threatened with the rack unless he disclosed his whereabouts. When the chief of police, Herod, sent horsemen by night to surround his lodging, Polycarp was upstairs in bed, but refused to make his escape, saying, 'God's will be done'. He went down, met them at the door, ordered them supper, and desired only some time for prayer before he went with them.

The holy man went cheerfully to the place where the people were assembled. He was led to the tribunal of the proconsul, who exhorted him to have regard for his age, to swear by the genius of Caesar, and to say, 'Away with the atheists', meaning the Christians. The saint, turning towards the crowd of ungodly people in the stadium, said, with a stern countenance, 'Away with the atheists! ' The proconsul repeated, 'Swear by the genius of

Caesar, and I will discharge you; revile Christ'. Polycarp replied, 'Fourscore and six years have I served Him and He hath done me no wrong. How then can I blaspheme my King and my Saviour? If you require of me to swear by the genius of Caesar, as you call it, hear my free confession: I am a Christian; and if you desire to learn the doctrines of Christianity, appoint a time and hear me.' The proconsul said, 'Persuade the people'. The martyr replied, 'I address myself to you; for we are taught to give due honour to princes, so far as is consistent with religion. But before these people I cannot justify myself.'

Whilst he said this and many other things, he appeared in a transport of joy and confidence, and his countenance shone with a certain heavenly grace, insomuch that the proconsul himself was struck with admiration. However, he ordered a crier to announce three times in the middle of the stadium, 'Polycarp hath confessed himself a Christian'. At this the whole multitude appealed to Philip the governor to let a lion loose upon Polycarp. He told them that it was not in his power, because he had brought the sports to a close. Then they all clamoured that he should be burnt alive. Their demand was no sooner granted than everyone ran with all speed to fetch wood from the bath-furnaces and workshops. The executioners would have nailed him to the stake, but he said, 'Suffer me to be as I am. He who gives me grace to endure the fire will enable me to remain at the pile unmoved.' They therefore contented themselves with tying his hands behind his back.

The flames, forming themselves like the sails of a ship swelled with the wind, gently encircled the body of the martyr, which stood in the middle, resembling not burning flesh but bread that is being baked or precious metal refined: And there was a fragrance like the smell of incense. The order was given that Polycarp should be pierced with a spear, which was done: and a dove came forth, and such quantity of blood as to quench the fire.

Nicetas advised the proconsul not to give up the body to the Christians, lest, said he, abandoning the crucified man, they should worship Polycarp. The centurion placed the body in the middle and burnt it to ashes. It was at two o'clock in the afternoon of February 23 about the year 155.

24 : ST PRAETEXTATUS, OR PRIX, BISHOP OF ROUEN, MARTYR (A.D. 586)

ST PRAETEXTATUS became bishop of Rouen in 549 and occupied that see for thirty-five years. During this long episcopate he suffered grievous difficulties, exile and in the end martyrdom due to the rivalry between King Clotaire I's sons Chilperic and Sigebert, and the deadly feud of Chilperic's mistress, Fredegund, with Sigebert's wife, Brunhilda, sister to the poisoned second wife of Chilperic. Fredegund contrived the murder of Sigebert in 575, and Chilperic threw Brunhilda into prison at Rouen, from whence she appealed for help to Meroveus, Chilperic's son by his first wife. The young man dreaded the power of Fredegund, and was not unwilling to take up arms against his father. Furthermore, he fell in love with his step-aunt Brunhilda and married her, thus making common cause with her. Praetextatus found himself placed in a very awkward position. Meroveus had made

Rouen his headquarters and expected or exacted contributions from the Church which it was difficult to refuse. The young man had been baptized by the bishop and the tie was then considered a very close one. Chilperic was ready to believe accusations against Praetextatus and summoned him to appear before a council of bishops in Paris on the charges of having broken the canons by marrying Meroveus to his aunt and also for fomenting the rebellion by giving aid to the prince.

At first the bishop would plead guilty to neither charge, but he was afterwards prevailed upon by false friends to acknowledge that he had favoured and helped Meroveus. He was condemned and banished to a little island off Coutances. His powerful enemies spared no trouble to blast his reputation, but St Gre'gory of Tours never wavered in his support. Meroveus and his brothers were put to death by order of the savage Fredegund, who was also suspected of causing the death of her husband to clear the way to the throne for her own son, Clotaire II. On the death of Chilperic, Praetextatus returned to his see by order of King Gontran of Burgundy, but sorely against the wishes of Fredegund. At the Council of Mâcon he was formally reinstated, and he took a prominent part in the deliberations of that body. He frequently remonstrated with the wicked queen, who often resided at Rouen, and her hatred for him became greater than ever. In 586 she said to him, 'The time is coming when you shall revisit the place of your exile.'—'I was bishop always, whether in exile or out of exile', replied the saint, 'and a bishop I shall remain; but you will not always enjoy your crown,' and he exhorted her to abandon her evil ways. On the following Sunday, soon after midnight, as he was saying Matins in church, an assassin sent by Fredegund stabbed him under the armpit. He was carried to his bed, where he died.

25 : ST TARASIUS, PATRIARCH OF CONSTANTINOPLE (A.D. 806)

ST TARASIUS, although a layman and chief secretary to the young Emperor Constantine VI and his mother Irene, was chosen patriarch of Constantinople by the court, clergy and people after having been nominated by his predecessor Paul IV, who had retired into a monastery. Tarasius came of a patrician family, had had a good upbringing and though surrounded by all that could flatter pride or gratify the senses, he had led a life of almost monastic severity. He was most loath to accept the dignity which had been conferred upon him, partly because he felt that a priest should have been chosen, but also on account of the position created by the succession of emperors, beginning with Leo III in 726, whose policy it was for various reasons to abolish the veneration of sacred images and banish ikons from the churches.

Tarasius was called to be patriarch at a time when the Empress Irene had the imperial power in her hands as regent for her son, Constantine VI, then only ten years old. She was an ambitious, artful and heartlessly cruel woman, but she was opposed to Iconoclasm. When therefore Tarasius had been consecrated on Christmas day 784, on the understanding that a council should be held to restore the unity of the churches disrupted by the campaign against images, the way was clear for such a gathering. This, the seventh ecumenical council, eventually assembled at Nicaea in 787, under the presidency of the legates of Pope Adrian I. After due discussion it was declared to be the sense of the Church to allow to holy pictures and other images a relative honour, but not of course that worship which is due to God alone. He who reveres the image, it was emphasized, reveres the person it represents. Tarasius, in obedience to the decision of the synod, restored holy images throughout his patriarchate.

Some years later the emperor became enamoured of Theodota, a maid of honour to his wife, the Empress Mary, whom he had been forced to marry by his mother and whom he now resolved to divorce. To further his purpose he tried to gain over the patriarch, and sent an officer to inform him that the empress was plotting to poison him. Tarasius answered the messenger sternly, 'Tell him I will suffer death rather than consent to his design'. The emperor, hoping to win him by flattery, sent for the patriarch and said to him, 'I can conceal nothing from you whom I regard as my father. No one can deny that I may divorce one who has attempted my life. The Empress Mary deserves death or perpetual penance.' He then produced a vessel full of poison which he pretended she had prepared for him. The patriarch, perceiving this to be an attempt to hoodwink him, replied that he was only too sure that Constantine's passion for Theodota was at the bottom of all his complaints against the empress; he also warned him that even if she were really guilty of the crime, a second marriage during her lifetime would be adulterous.

The emperor turned Mary out of the palace and forced her to take the veil. As Tarasius persisted in his refusal to marry him to Theodota, it was done by Abbot Joseph, an official of the church of Constantinople. Tarasius had to face the resentment of Constantine, who persecuted him during the remainder of his reign. We are told that spies were set to watch the patriarch's coming and goings, that none was suffered to associate with him without leave, and many of his relations and servants were banished. In the meantime, however, the Dowager Empress Irene, dissatisfied at being no longer at the head of the government, gained over the principal officers of the court and army, and having made her son prisoner caused his eyes to be put out. Irene reigned for five years, but was deposed by Nicephorus, who usurped the empire and banished her to the isle of Lesbos.

Under the reign of Nicephorus, Tarasius persevered peaceably in the functions of his pastoral office. Shortly before his death he fell into a trance, as his biographer, who was present, relates, and he seemed to be disputing with a number of accusers who were busily scrutinizing all the actions of his life and making accusations. He appeared to be in great agitation as he defended himself against their charges. But a wonderful serenity succeeded, and the holy man gave up his soul to God in great peace after he had ruled his patriarchal see for twenty-one years.

26 : ST ALEXANDER, BISHOP OF ALEXANDRIA (A.D. 328)

ST ALEXANDER, the successor of St Achillas in the see of Alexandria, is chiefly celebrated for the determined resistance he offered to the heresy which Arius, an Alexandrian priest, first began openly to propagate during his episcopate.

Alexander was a man of apostolic doctrine and life, charitable to the poor, and full of faith, zeal and fervour. He admitted to the ministry by preference those who had sanctified themselves in solitude, and was happy in his choice of bishops throughout Egypt. It seemed as though the Devil, enraged at the disrepute into which idolatry was falling, had endeavoured to repair his losses by fomenting this new and imperious heresy of Arius, who taught not only that Christ was not truly God, but also that the Son was a creature, that there was a time when He did not exist, and that He was capable of sinning. Some of the orthodox were disposed to be scandalized by the forbearance of St Alexander who, being one of the mildest of men, at first made use of gentle methods and by kindly expostulations and sound argument sought to bring Arius back to the true faith. As his efforts proved ineffectual and the Arian faction grew in strength, the bishop summoned Arius to appear in an assembly of the clergy, where being found to be obstinate and incorrigible he was excommunicated. At a council held in Alexandria, Arius was again tried, his sentence of excommunication being confirmed by the bishops who were present. St Alexander wrote a letter to Bishop Alexander of Constantinople and a circular epistle to the other bishops of the Church, giving them an account of the heresy and of the condemnation of the heretic, the only two communications that have survived from his large correspondence on the subject.

In due course, in the year 325, the first ecumenical council assembled at Nicaea to deal with the matter, Pope St Silvester being represented by legates. Arius was himself present, and both Marcellus of Ancyra and the deacon St Athanasius, whom St Alexander had brought with him, exposed the falsity of the new doctrines and completely confuted the Arians. The heresy was emphatically and finally condemned, and Arius and a few others banished by the Emperor Constantine to Illyricum. St Alexander, after this triumph of the faith, returned to Alexandria, where he died two years later, having named St Athanasius as his successor.

27 : ST GABRIEL POSSENTI, (A.D. 1862)

THIS young saint was the son of a distinguished advocate who held a succession of official appointments under the government of the States of the Church. There were thirteen children in the family of Sante Possenti, of whom the future saint, born in 1838 and christened Francis, was the eleventh. Several died in infancy and their mother died in 1842, when Francis was only four years old. Signor Possenti had just then become 'grand assessor' (or registrar) of Spoleto, and in the Jesuit college there Francis received most of his education.

As a youth he read novels, he was fond of gaiety and of the theatre, though seemingly the plays he frequented were innocent enough, and on account of his cheerfulness and good looks he was a universal favourite. There must have been a certain relative frivolity in these years, and his friends, we are told, used in playful exaggeration to call him *il damerino*, 'the ladies' man'. As a consequence the call of God does not seem to have been at once attended to even when it was clearly heard. Before his very promising career as a student was completed he fell dangerously ill, and he promised if he recovered to enter religion; but when he was restored to health he took no immediate step to carry his purpose into effect. After the lapse of a year or two he was again brought to death's door by an attack of laryngitis, or possibly quinsy, and he renewed his promise, having recourse in this extremity to a relic of the Jesuit martyr St Andrew Bobola, just then beatified. Once more he was cured, miraculously as he believed, and he made application to enter the Society of Jesus. But though he was accepted, he still delayed—after all, he was not yet even seventeen—possibly because he doubted whether God was not calling him to a more penitential life than that of the Society. Then his favourite sister died during an outbreak of cholera, and so, stricken with a sense of the precarious nature of all earthly ties, he at last, with the full approval of his Jesuit confessor, made choice of the Passionists. Thus in September 1856 he entered their noviceship at Morrovalle, where he was given the name in religion of Brother Gabriel-of-our-Lady-of-Sorrows.

After only four years spent in religion, in the course of which Brother Gabriel had given rise to the expectation of great and fruitful work for souls once the priesthood had been attained, symptoms of tuberculous disease manifested themselves so unmistakably that from henceforth he had to be exempted, very much against his will, from all the more arduous duties of community observance. Everyone was indescribably impressed by the example which he gave, but he himself shrank from any sort of favourable notice, and not long before his death, he succeeded in securing the destruction of all his private notes of the spiritual favours which God had bestowed upon him. He passed away in great peace in the early morning of February 27, 1862, at Isola di Gran Sasso in the Abruzzi. St Gabriel-of-our-Lady-of-Sorrows was canonized in 1920.

28 : ST ROMANUS, ABBOT (c. A.D. 460)

ST ROMANUS had reached the age of thirty-five when he withdrew into the forests of the Jura Mountains between Switzerland and France to live there as a hermit. He took with him Cassian's *Lives of the Fathers of the Desert*, a few tools and some seeds, and found his way to an uninhabited spot at the confluence of the Bienne and the Alière, enclosed between steep heights and difficult of access. Here under the shelter of an enormous fir tree he spent his time praying, reading and cultivating the soil. At first his solitude was disturbed only by the beasts and an occasional huntsman, but before long he was joined by his brother Lupicinus and by one or two more. Other recruits soon flocked to them, including their sister and a number of women.

The two brothers soon built the monastery of Condat and then that of Leuconne, two miles to the north, whilst for the women they established the nunnery of La Beaume (the site of the present village of Saint-Romain-de-la-Roche). The brothers ruled as joint abbots in perfect harmony, although Lupicinus was inclined to be the stricter; he generally lived at Leuconne, and when at one time the brethren at Condat were making their food more palatable, he came over and forbade the innovation. Although they strove to imitate the anchorites of the East, they were obliged to modify some of their austerities owing to climatic and other differences. These monks spent much of their time in very hard manual labour, but they never touched flesh-meat and were only allowed milk and eggs when they were ill. They wore wooden sabots and the skins of animals sewn together, which protected them from the rain, but not from the bitter cold in winter or from the summer rays of the sun reflected from the perpendicular rocks.

St Romanus made a pilgrimage to what is now Saint-Maurice in the Valais, to visit the place of martyrdom of the Theban Legion. He cured two lepers on the way, and, the fame of this miracle reaching Geneva, the bishop, the clergy and the whole town turned out to greet him as he was passing through. He died about the year 460, and was buried, as he had desired, in the church of the nunnery where his sister ruled.

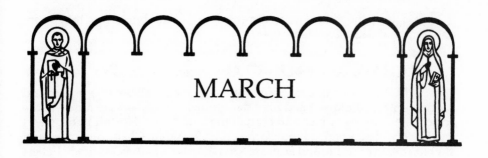

MARCH

1 : ST DAVID, OR **DEWI,** BISHOP IN MYNYW, PATRON OF WALES (A.D. 589 ?)

ACCORDING to legend David was the son of Sant, of princely family in Ceredigion, and of St Non (March 3), grand-daughter of Brychan of Brecknock; and he was born perhaps about the year 520. Ordained priest in due course, he afterwards retired to study for several years under the Welsh St Paulinus, who lived on an island which has not been identified. He is said to have restored sight to his master, who had become blind through much weeping. Upon emerging from the monastery, David seems to have embarked upon a period of great activity, the details of which, however, are at least for the most part pure invention. Finally, and here we are on surer ground, he settled in the extreme south-west corner of Wales, at Mynyw (Menevia), with a number of disciples and founded the principal of his many abbeys.

The community lived a life of extreme austerity. Hard manual labour was obligatory for all, and they were allowed no cattle to relieve them in tilling the ground. They might never speak without necessity, and they never ceased praying mentally, even when at work. Their food was bread, with vegetables and salt, and they drank only water, sometimes mingled with a little milk. For this reason St David was surnamed 'The Waterman'.

We are told that a synod was held at Brefi in Cardigan to suppress the Pelagian heresy, which was springing up in Britain for the second time. There is, however, no trace of any preoccupation about Pelagianism in the decrees which were said to have been passed by the assembly. St David was invited to attend, but was unwilling to go until St Deiniol and St Dubricius came in person to fetch him. At the synod David is said to have spoken with such grace and eloquence as to silence his opponents completely, and he was thereupon unanimously elected primate of the Cambrian church, Dubricius having resigned in his favour. St David was obliged to accept, but he did so on condition that the episcopal seat should be transferred from Caerleon to Mynyw—now Saint Davids—a quiet and solitary place.

At his death, which, according to Geoffrey of Monmouth, took place in his monastery at Mynyw, St Kentigern at Llanelwy saw his soul borne to Heaven by angels. His body was subsequently translated from the monastery church to Saint Davids cathedral, where the empty tomb is still shown.

It is said that the relics were removed to Glastonbury, but they were apparently at Saint Davids in 1346.

2 : ST CHAD, OR CEADDA, BISHOP OF LICHFIELD (A.D. 672)

S T CHAD was one of four holy brothers of whom all became priests and two—St Chad himself and his elder brother St Cedd—were raised to the episcopate. Angles by race and born in the kingdom of Northumbria, Cedd and Chad were trained at Lindisfarne under St Aidan. Chad went to Ireland after the death of Aidan and appears to have spent some years with St Egbert at Rathmelsigi. He was recalled to England, however, by St Cedd to take charge of the abbey at Lastingham which he had founded in a wild and solitary spot on the Yorkshire moors south-west of Whitby. The new abbot was not left long in his retirement. Within a year he was summoned by King Oswin to become bishop of York, although St Wilfrid had already been designated by Oswin's son Alcfrith (to whom he had given over part of the kingdom) and had actually gone to France to be consecrated by St Agilbert because he objected to being consecrated by those who held the Celtic view about the keeping of Easter.

'King Alcfrith', Bede writes, 'sent the priest Wilfrid to the king of the Gauls to have him consecrated for himself and his subjects. Now he sent him for ordination to Agilbert, who, as we stated above, had left Britain and had been made bishop of Paris. By him Wilfrid was consecrated with great pomp, several bishops having assembled for that purpose in a town called Compiègne belonging to the king. While he was still abroad, King Oswin, following his son's example, sent to Kent a holy man of modest character, well versed in the Scriptures and practising with diligence what he had learnt from them, to be ordained bishop of the church of York. This was a priest named Ceadda (or Chad) . . . . But when they reached Kent, they found that Archbishop Deusdedit had departed this life and that as yet no other had been appointed in his place. Thereupon they turned aside to the province of the West Saxons, where Wine was bishop, and by him the above-mentioned Chad was consecrated bishop, two bishops of the British nation, who kept Easter in contravention of canonical custom from the 14th to the 20th of the moon, being associated with him, for at that time there was no other bishop in all Britain canonically ordained besides Wine. As soon as Chad had been bishop, he began most strenuously to devote himself to ecclesiastical truth and purity of doctrine and to give attention to the practice of humility, self-denial and study: to travel about, not on horseback, but on foot, after the manner of the apostles, preaching the gospel in the towns and the open country, in cottages, villages and castles, for he was one of Aidan's disciples and tried to instruct his hearers by acting and behaving after the example of his master and of his brother Cedd.'

When St Theodore, the new archbishop of Canterbury, arrived in England in 669 and came on his first visitation to Northumbria, he adjudged the see of York to Wilfrid and charged Chad with being improperly ordained. The saint humbly replied, 'If you consider that I have not been properly consecrated, I willingly resign this charge of which I never thought myself worthy. I undertook it, though unworthy, under obedience.' St

Theodore was so deeply impressed by the respondent's humility and holiness that, before allowing him to retire to Lastingham, he supplied whatever was defective in his episcopal consecration, and soon after, at the death of Jaruman, Bishop of Mercia, he asked King Oswin to let St Chad have that see. In consideration of his age the archbishop forbade him to continue to make his visitations on foot, and to enforce his command lifted him on a horse with his own hands. St Chad moved the seat of the diocese from Repton to Lichfield. King Wulfhere gave him land on which to build a monastery at 'Ad Barvae' in the province of Lindsey, and the abbey of Bardney in the same district is believed to have owed its foundation to him. Hard by the church in Lichfield he built a house of retreat, and thither in his leisure time he was wont to betake himself, to pray and read with the seven or eight monks he had settled there, including his friend Owen.

Though St Chad only ruled over the Mercians for two and a half years, his virtues left a deep impression upon all that country. Thirty-one churches were dedicated in his honour in the Midlands and several wells bear his name.

3 : ST CUNEGUND, EMPRESS AND WIDOW (A.D. 1033)

ST CUNEGUND was piously trained from her earliest years by her parents. Siegfried of Luxemburg and his saintly wife Hedwig. She married St Henry, Duke of Bavaria, who gave her as a wedding present a crucifix of eastern workmanship which is said to be identical with one now existing in Munich. Later writers have asserted that they both took a vow of virginity on their wedding-day, but historians now seem to agree that there is no reliable evidence to corroborate the statement. Upon the death of the Emperor Otto III, Henry was elected king of the Romans, and his coronation by St Willigis at Mainz was followed, two months later, by that of his wife at Paderborn. In 1013 they went together to Rome to receive the imperial crown from Pope Benedict VIII.

It was partly at the instigation of St Cunegund that the emperor founded the monastery and cathedral of Bamberg, to the consecration of which Pope Benedict came in person, and she obtained for the city such privileges that by common report her silken threads were a better defence than walls. During a dangerous illness she had made a vow that if she recovered she would found a convent at Kaufungen, near Cassel, in Hesse. This she proceeded to do, and had nearly finished building a house for nuns of the Benedictine Order when St Henry died.

Her later biographers relate a quaint story about the first abbess. It appears that the empress had a young niece, called Judith or Jutta, to whom she was much attached, and whom she had educated with great care. When a superior had to be found for the new convent, St Cunegund appointed Judith and gave her many admonitions and much good advice. No sooner, however, did the young abbess find herself free, than she began to show symptoms of frivolity and lax observance: it was soon noticed that she was the first in the refectory and the last to come to chapel. The climax came when she failed to appear in the Sunday procession and was found feasting with some of the younger sisters. Filled with indignation St Cunegund sternly upbraided the culprit, and even struck her. The marks of her fingers remained impressed upon the abbess's cheek until her dying day, and the marvel not only converted her, but had a salutary effect upon the whole community.

On the anniversary of her husband's death in 1024 Cunegund invited a number of prelates to the dedication of her church at Kaufungen. When the gospel had been sung at Mass, she offered at the altar a piece of the true cross, and then, putting off her imperial robes, she was clothed in a nun's habit, and the bishop gave her the veil. Once she had been consecrated to God in religion, she seemed entirely to forget that she had ever been an empress and behaved as the lowest in the house, being convinced that she was so before God. She feared nothing more than anything that could recall her former dignity. She prayed and read much and especially made it her business to visit and comfort the sick. Thus she passed the last years of her life, dying on March 3, 1033 (or 1039). Her body was taken to Bamberg to be buried with her husband's.

4 : ST CASIMIR OF POLAND, (A.D. 1484)

ST CASIMIR, to whom the Poles gave the title of 'The Peace-maker', was born in 1458, the third of the thirteen children of Casimir IV, King of Poland, and of Elizabeth of Austria, daughter of the Emperor Albert II. Casimir was the second son; he and his two brothers, Ladislaus and John, had as their tutor John Dlugosz, the historian, a canon of Cracow and a man of extraordinary learning and piety. All the princes were warmly attached to the holy man, but Casimir profited the most by his teaching and example. Devout from his infancy, the boy gave himself up to devotion and penance. His bed was often the ground, and he was wont to spend a great part of the night in prayer and meditation, chiefly on the passion of our Saviour. His clothes were plain, and under them he wore a hair-shirt. Living always in the presence of God he was invariably serene and cheerful, and pleasant to all.

The saint's love of God showed itself in his love of the poor, and for the relief of these the young prince gave all he possessed, using in their behalf the influence he had with his father and with his brother Ladislaus when he became king of Bohemia. In honour of the Blessed Virgin Mary Casimir frequently recited the long Latin hymn '*Omni die dic Mariae*', a copy of which was by his desire buried with him. Though this hymn, part of which is familiar to us through Bittleston's version, 'Daily, daily sing to Mary', is not uncommonly called the Hymn of St Casimir, it was certainly not composed by him, but by Bernard of Cluny in the twelfth century.

The nobles of Hungary, dissatisfied with their king, Matthias Corvinus, in 1471 begged the King of Poland to allow them to place his son Casimir on the throne. The saint, at that time not fifteen years old, was very unwilling to consent, but in obedience to his father he went to the frontier at the head of an army. There, hearing that Matthias had himself assembled a large body of troops, and finding that his own soldiers were deserting in large numbers because they could not get their pay, he decided on the advice of his officers to return home. The knowledge that Pope Sixtus IV had sent an embassy to his father to deter him from the expedition made the young prince carry out his resolution with the firmer conviction that he was acting rightly. King Casimir, however, was greatly incensed at the failure of his ambitious projects and would not permit his son to return to Cracow, but relegated him to the castle of Dobzki. The young man obeyed and remained in confinement there for three months. Convinced of the injustice of the war upon which he had so nearly embarked, and determined to have no further part in these internecine conflicts which only facilitated the progress into Europe of the Turks, St Casimir could never again be persuaded to take up arms, though urged to do so by his father and invited once more by the disaffected Hungarian magnates. He returned to his studies and his prayers, though for a time he was viceroy in Poland during an absence of his father. An attempt was made to induce him to marry a daughter of the Emperor Frederick III, but he refused to relax the celibacy he had imposed on himself.

St Casimir's austerities did nothing to help the lung trouble from which he suffered, and he died at the age of twenty-three in 1484. He was buried at Vilna, where his relics still rest in the church of St Stanislaus. Miracles were reported at his tomb, and he was canonized in 1521.

5 : ST JOHN JOSEPH-OF-THE-CROSS, (A.D. 1734)

ON the feast of the Assumption 1654, in the island of Ischia, off Naples, a boy was born, who, being baptized the same day, received the names of Carlo Caetano. His parents, Joseph Calosirto and Laura Garguilo, were a well-to-do and most exemplary couple. Of their seven sons, five entered religion, but little Carlo was pre-eminent amongst them. Generally the boy's sanctity was recognised and approved by his relations, who left him free to follow his own devices.

Two Spanish Franciscan friars of the 'Alcantarine' reform in the course of a begging tour came to the house. Carlo was greatly impressed by their poverty and conversation and went to their convent in Naples, Santa Lucia del Monte, to consult with the superiors. Here he met Father Carlo-of-the-Wounds-of-Jesus, and this experienced director discerned in the youth the germs of a great vocation. For nine months he put him through a strenuous course of self-abnegation and trained him in the method of mental prayer bequeathed by St Peter of Alcantara. Then the aspirant, only sixteen years old, was clothed with the religious habit, and took the name of John Joseph-of-the-Cross. The new novice did not disappoint the expectation of his superiors: it is a proof of the high esteem in which he was held that when the Neapolitan Alcantarines were about to build a monastery at Piedimonte di Alife, they chose John Joseph to start a tradition of regular observance, although he was not yet twenty-one and was not a priest.

It had been his wish to remain a deacon in imitation of the Seraphic Father St Francis, but his superiors decided that he should be raised to the priesthood, and on Michaelmas day 1677 he celebrated his first Mass. A month later, when at an unusually early age he was entrusted to hear confessions, it was found that the young priest, who from his purity of heart had grown up ignorant of evil, was endowed with an extraordinary insight and wisdom in the tribunal of penance. About this time he formed the plan of building in the wood near the convent some little hermitages, like those of the early Franciscans, where he and his brethren could spend periods of retirement in even stricter austerity than was possible in the house.

From the congenial life the saint was recalled to the mother-house to be charged with the task of novice-master. Here again he acquitted himself successfully, inculcating upon his novices strict observance of the rule, but not exacting from them the austerities he practised himself. Indeed, he was most particular that they should have regular times of recreation. He was again transferred to Piedimonte to be superior, and though he obtained leave to lay down the office for a short period, which he devoted to the direction of souls, he was soon recalled to take up the charge of governing his brethren a second time. He was then passing through a season of great aridity and desolation, but he was consoled by a vision of a departed lay-brother who reassured him as to his condition. It was after this vision that St John Joseph began to show powers as a wonder-worker, not only by miracles of healing, but also by supplying and multiplying food for the house; his fame spread so rapidly that when he went back to Ischia, to visit his mother in her last illness, he had the unusual experience of being acclaimed as a saint in his native town. A second period as novice-master was succeeded by a third term as superior at Piedimonte, at the close of which an illness brought him to death's door—the malady had been brought on by hardships and austerities—and hardly had he recovered when he was called upon to take the lead in a crisis which threatened the very existence of the Italian Alcantarines.

It had been laid down by a papal brief that the office of minister provincial and other important charges among the Italian branch of Alcantarines should always be confided to Spaniards. This led to great friction, partly no doubt on account of racial differences, but also because of the fact that, as the Spanish friars in Italy were comparatively few, suitable superiors were often not forthcoming. The troubles increased until the Spaniards obtained entire separation from the Italians, with possession of the two Neapolitan houses, one of which was Santa Lucia del Monte. Disorganized and threatened with total suppression, the Italian friars turned to St John Joseph to help and direct them, and it was mainly through his wisdom, personality and reputation that they held together, lived down slander and opposition, and gained permission to turn themselves into a province. At one period in Naples it was as much as they could do to keep a roof over their heads, and they were without many of the ordinary necessaries of life—but Father John Joseph took all these hardships cheerfully, as being in keeping with the teaching of the founder.

In 1722 the two Neapolitan houses were restored to them, and St John Joseph returned to Santa Lucia where, as he had prophesied when he had left it, he was ultimately to lay his bones. As the day of his death approached, St John Joseph was divinely warned and spoke of it freely to those around him, but he continued to carry on his usual avocations. At two o'clock in the morning of March 1, 1734, he had a violent apoplectic seizure from which he never recovered, although he lingered on for five days, passing away at the age of eighty. He was buried at Santa Lucia del Monte and his tomb almost immediately became a very popular place of pilgrimage. He was canonized in 1839.

6 : ST COLETTE, VIRGIN (A.D. 1447)

THE circumstances of the Saint's birth were humble, her father being a carpenter at the abbey of Corbie in Picardy; her parents were devout people who gave to their little girl the name of Nicolette, in honour of St Nicholas of Myra. Both her parents died when Colette was seventeen, leaving her under the care of the abbot of Corbie; after a time in a convent, she distributed to the poor the little she had inherited and entered the third order of St Francis. The abbot gave her a small hermitage beside the church of Corbie, where she lived a life of such austerity that her fame spread far and wide and many sought her prayers and advice.

Colette had visions, in one of which the Seraphic Father St Francis appeared and charged her to restore the first rule of St Clare in all its original severity. Not unnaturally, she hesitated, but she received what she recognized as a sign from Heaven when she was struck blind for three days and dumb for three days more. Encouraged by Father Henry de Baume, her director, she left her cell in 1406, and straightway made an attempt to explain her mission in one or two convents, but soon discovered that, if she was to succeed, she must be invested with the proper authority. Barefoot, dressed in a habit made up of patches, Colette set out for Nice to seek Peter de Luna, who at that epoch of the great schism was acknowledged by the French as pope, under the name of Benedict XIII. He received her with great consideration, and not only professed her under the rule of St Clare, but was so much impressed that he constituted her superioress of all convents of Minoresses that she might reform or found, with a mission to the friars and tertiaries of St Francis as well. At the same time he appointed Father Henry de Baume to act as her assistant.

Armed with these powers, St Colette went from convent to convent, travelling through France, Savoy and Flanders, and at first she met with violent opposition, being treated as a fanatic and even accused of sorcery. But rebuffs, ill-will, and calumnies were all alike received with joy, and after a while she began to meet with a more favourable reception, especially in Savoy, where her reform gained both sympathizers and recruits, and from thence it passed to Burgundy, France, Flanders and Spain. Besançon was the first house of Poor Clares to receive her revised rule, in 1410. Altogether she founded seventeen new convents, besides reforming numerous old ones, and several houses of Franciscan friars accepted her reform.

It was in Flanders, where she had established several houses, that St Colette was seized with her last illness. She foretold her own death, received the last sacraments and died in her convent at Ghent in her sixty-seventh year. Her body was removed from Ghent by the Poor Clares when the Emperor Joseph II was suppressing a number of religious houses in Flanders, and borne to her convent at Poligny, thirty-two miles from Besançon. She was canonized in 1807.

7 : ST DRAUSIUS, OR DRAUSIN, BISHOP OF SOISSONS
(c. A.D. 674)

D RAUSIUS was educated by St Anseric, Bishop of Soissons, and was appointed archdeacon by Anseric's successor. So highly did Bishop Bettolin esteem his young subordinate that when he himself was about to retire, on the plea that his election had not been valid, he urged that Drausius should be chosen in his place. The new bishop soon proved himself a most zealous administrator, whilst by his sermons and instructions he gained many to Christ. His life was one constant fast, and although he suffered nearly all his life from most painful maladies, he added to his sufferings by voluntary mortifications.

He founded two religious houses, one for men and the other for women, that through the prayers of the communities the blessing of God might descend upon the city. From Bettolin he bought land beside the Aisne, and there he built his monastery for men at Rethondes. The nunnery was at Soissons itself, and in establishing it St Drausius was greatly assisted by Leutrude, the wife of Ebroin, mayor of the palace. In 664 the church of Notre-Dame de Soissons was completed and dedicated. Already at this date a single church was not considered sufficient for the needs of a great community, and St Drausius therefore built two other chapels, one for the abbess and obedientiaries, and another for sick nuns, guests and the poor whom they received. The holy bishop only lived long enough to complete his work, and died on March 5 about the year 674.

8 : ST JOHN OF GOD, FOUNDER OF THE BROTHERS HOSPITALLERS
(A.D. 1550)

T HIS St John was born at Monte Mor il Nuovo in Portugal and spent part of his youth in the service of the bailiff of the count of Oroprusa in Castile. In 1522 he enlisted in a company of soldiers raised by the count, and served in the wars between the French and the Spaniards and afterwards in Hungary against the Turks. The troop having been disbanded, he went to Andalusia, where he entered the service of a woman near Seville as a shepherd. At the age of about forty, stung with remorse for his past misconduct, he resolved to amend his life, and began to consider how he could best dedicate the rest of his life to God's service.

In Gibraltar the idea suggested itself that by turning pedlar and selling sacred pictures and books he might find opportunities of doing good to his customers. He succeeded well in this business, and in 1538, when he was forty-three, he was able to open a shop in Granada. On St Sebastian's day, which is kept as a great festival in that city, it happened that they had invited as special preacher the famous John of Avila. Amongst those who flocked to hear him was this other John, who was so affected by his sermon that he filled the church with his cries, beating his breast and imploring mercy. Then, as though demented, he ran about the streets, tearing his hair and behaving so wildly that he was pelted with sticks and stones and returned home a pitiable object. There he gave away his stock and began roaming the streets distractedly as before, until some kindly persons took him to Bd John of Avila. The holy man spoke to him in private, gave him advice and promised him help. John was quieted for a time, but soon returned to his extravagances and was carried off to a lunatic asylum, where, according to the practice of the times, the most brutal methods were employed to bring him to his senses. When John of Avila was informed of what had befallen, he came to visit his penitent and told him that he had practised his singular method of penance long enough, and advised him to occupy himself for the future in something more conducive to his own spiritual profit and that of his neighbour. This exhortation had the effect of instantly calming John—much to the astonishment of his keepers—but he remained in the hospital, waiting upon the sick, until St Ursula's day 1539, when he finally left it.

His mind was now set upon doing something to relieve the poor, and he began selling wood in the market-place to earn money for feeding the destitute. Soon afterwards he hired a house in which to harbour the sick poor, whom he served and catered for with such wisdom, zeal and economy as to astonish the whole city: this was the foundation of the order of Brothers of St John of God. John never thought of founding a religious order. The rules which bear his name were only drawn up six years after his death, and religious vows were not introduced among his brethren before 1570.

Worn out at last by ten years' hard service, St John fell ill. The immediate cause was over-fatigue through his efforts to save his wood and other things for the poor in a flood, and to rescue a drowning man. At first he concealed his symptoms that he might not be compelled to diminish his work, but he carefully went over the inventories of the hospital and inspected the accounts. He also revised the rules of administration, the time-tables, and the devotional exercises to be observed. As his disease gained greater hold it became impossible to conceal it, and the news quickly spread.

He named Antony Martin superior over his helpers, and before leaving he visited the Blessed Sacrament, remaining there so long that the masterful Lady Anne Ossorio caused him to be lifted forcibly into her coach, in which she conveyed him to her own home. He complained that whilst our Saviour in His agony drank gall, he, a miserable sinner, was served with good food. The magistrates begged him to give his benediction to his fellow townsfolk. This he was loath to do, saying that his sins made him the scandal and reproach of the place, but that he recommended to them his brethren, the poor and those who had served him. At last, at the wish of the archbishop, he gave the city his dying blessing. St John passed away, on his knees before the altar, on March 8, 1550, being exactly fifty-five years old. He was buried by the archbishop, and the whole of Granada followed in procession. He was canonized in 1690.

9 : ST FRANCES OF ROME, WIDOW (A.D. 1440)

FRANCES was born in the Trastevere district of Rome in 1384. Her parents, Paul Busso and Jacobella dei Roffredeschi, were of noble birth and ample means, and the child was brought up in the midst of luxury but in a pious household.

Frances was a precocious little girl, and when she was eleven she asked her parents to allow her to become a nun, only to be met by a point-blank refusal. Her parents had quite different plans for their attractive little daughter. Within a year they announced to her that they had arranged to betroth her to young Lorenzo Ponziano, whose position, character and wealth made him a suitable match. After a time Frances withdrew her objections, and the marriage was solemnized when she was barely thirteen. At first she found the new life very trying, although she did her best to please her husband as well as her parents-in-law, and Cannozza, the young wife of Lorenzo's brother Paluzzo, discovered her one day weeping bitterly. Frances told her of her frustrated hopes, and learnt to her surprise that this new sister of hers would also have preferred a life of retirement and prayer. This was the beginning of a close friendship which lasted till death, and the two young wives strove together henceforth to live a perfect life under a common rule. Plainly dressed they sallied out to visit the poor of Rome, ministering to their wants and relieving their distress, and their husbands, who were devoted to them, raised no object to their charities and austerities. They went daily to the hospital of Santo Spirito in Sassia to nurse the patients, singling out more particularly those suffering from the most repellent diseases.

In 1400 a son was born to Frances, and for a time she modified her way of life to devote herself to the care of little John Baptist (Battista). The following year Donna Cecilia died, and Frances was bidden by her father-in-law take her place at the head of the household. In vain she pleaded that Vannozza was the wife of the elder brother: Don Andrew and Vannozza insisted that she was the more suitable, and she was obliged to consent. She proved herself worthy of this position, discharging her duties efficiently whilst treating her household not as servants but as younger brothers and sisters, and trying to induce them to labour for their own salvation. In all the forty years that she lived with her husband there was never the slightest dispute or misunderstanding between them. In addition to the eldest, two other children of Frances are known, a younger boy, Evangelist, and a girl, Agnes; and she allowed no one but herself to look after them during childhood.

In 1408 the troops of Ladislaus of Naples, the ally of the antipope, had entered Rome and a soldier of fortune, Count Troja, had been appointed governor. The Ponziani had always supported the legitimate pope, and in one of the frequent conflicts Lorenzo was stabbed and carried home to Frances, to whose devoted nursing he owed his restoration to health. Troja resolved to leave the city after having wreaked his vengeance on the principal papal supporters. Amongst these were the Ponziani, and he not only arrested Vannozza's husband Paluzzo, but also demanded as a hostage little Battista; but while his mother Frances was praying in the church of Ara Coeli the boy was released in circumstances that seemed to be miraculous. Then, in 1410 when the cardinals were assembled at Bologna for the election of a new pope, Ladislaus again seized Rome. Lorenzo Ponziano, who as one of the heads of the papal party went in danger of his life, managed to escape, but it was impossible for his wife and family to follow him. His palace was plundered and Battista was taken captive by the soldiers of Ladislaus, though he afterwards got away and was able to join his father. The family possessions in the Campagna were destroyed, farms being burnt or pillaged and flocks slaughtered, whilst many of the peasants were murdered.

Frances lived in a corner of her ruined home with Evangelist, Agnes and Vannozza, whose husband was still a prisoner, and the two women devoted themselves to the care of the children and to relieving as far as their means would allow the sufferings of their still poorer neighbours. During another pestilence three years later, Evangelist died. Frances then turned part of the house into a hospital, and God rewarded her labours and prayers by bestowing on her the gift of healing.

Twelve months after the death of Evangelist, as his mother was praying one day, a bright light suddenly shone into the room and Evangelist appeared accompanied by an archangel. After telling her of his happiness in Heaven he said that he had come to warn her of the impending death of Agnes. A consolation was, however, to be vouchsafed to the bereaved mother. The archangel who accompanied Evangelist was henceforth to be her guide for twenty-three years. He was to be succeeded in the last epoch of her life by an angel of still higher dignity. Very soon Agnes began to fail, and a year later she passed away at the age of sixteen.

After many delays Pope John XXIII summoned the Council of Constance which was to prepare the healing of the Great Schism, and in that same year 1414 the Ponziani regained their property after being recalled from banishment. Lorenzo was now a broken man and lived in retirement, being tended with the utmost devotion by his faithful wife. It was his great wish to see his son Battista married and settled before his death, and he chose for him a beautiful girl called Mobilia, who proved to have a violent and overbearing temper. She conceived a great contempt for Frances, of whom she complained to her husband and his father, and whom she ridiculed in public. In the midst of a bitter speech she was struck down by a sudden illness, through which she was nursed by the saint. Won by her kindness Mobilia found her contempt turned to love, and thenceforward she sought to imitate her saintly mother-in-law. By this time the fame of the virtues and miracles of St Frances had spread over Rome, and she was appealed to from all quarters, not only to cure the sick but also to settle disputes and heal feuds. Lorenzo, whose love and reverence for her only increased with age, offered to release her from all the obligations of married life provided only that she would continue to live under his roof.

She was now able to carry out a project which had been taking shape in her mind of forming a society of women living in the world and bound by no vows, but pledged to make a simple offering of themselves to God and to serve the poor. The plan was approved by her confessor Dom Antonio, who obtained the affiliation of the congregation to the Benedictines of Monte Oliveto, to which he himself belonged. Known at first as the Oblates of Mary, they were afterwards called the Oblates of Tor de' Specchi. The society had lasted seven years when it was thought desirable to take a house adapted for a community, and the old building known as Tor de' Specchi was acquired. Whatever time she could spare from her home duties St Frances spent with the oblates, sharing in their daily life and duties. She never allowed them to refer to her as the foundress, but insisted that all should be subject to Agnes de Lellis who was chosen superioress. Three years later Lorenzo died and was laid beside Evangelist and Agnes; and St Frances announced her intention of retiring to Tor de' Specchi. On the feast of St Benedict she entered her foundation as a humble suppliant and was eagerly welcomed. Agnes de Lellis immediately insisted upon resigning office and Frances had to take her place in spite of her protestations.

One evening in the spring of 1440, though feeling very ill she tried to get back home after visiting Battista and Mobilia. On the way she met her director, Dom John Matteotti, who, shocked at her appearance, ordered her to return at once to her son's house. It was soon evident that she was dying, but she lingered on for seven days. On the evening of March 9 her face was seen to shine with a strange light: 'The angel has finished his task: he beckons me to follow him' were her last words. Hr body was removed to Santa Maria Nuova, and she was buried in the chapel of the church reserved for her oblates.

St Frances was canonized in 1608, and Santa Maria Nuova is now known as the church of Santa Francesca Romana.

10 : ST JOHN OGILVIE, MARTYR (A.D. 1615)

THE father of John Ogilvie was baron of Drum-na-Keith, lord of large territories in Banffshire and head of the younger branch of Ogilvies, whilst his mother, through whom he was connected with the Stewarts and the Douglases, was the daughter of Lady Douglas of Lockleven, Queen Mary's gaoler.

The family, like many Scottish families at that time, was partly Catholic and partly Presbyterian, but John's father, though not unfriendly to the old faith, brought his eldest son up as a Calvinist, and as such sent him at the age of thirteen to be educated on the continent. There the lad became interested in the religious controversies which then and until a much later date were popular in France and in lands under French influence. The best Catholic and Calvinistic protagonists took part in the disputations, which profoundly influenced the intellectual world. These and the testimony of the martyrs decided him, and it was in order to belong to the Church of the martyrs that he decided to become a Catholic and was received into the Church at the Scots College in Louvain in 1596, at the age of seventeen.

His next three years were spent in various continental educational centres. Lack of funds caused Father Crichton, the head of the Scots College, to dismiss many of his pupils, including John Ogilvie, who betook himself to the Scottish Benedictines at Ratisbon, with whom he remained six months. He next passed on to the Jesuit College at Olmütz, which he entered as a lay student, and henceforth we find him intimately connected with the Jesuits. Within a year John asked to be admitted to the Society, but at that very moment an outbreak of plague compelled the authorities to close the college. Not to be deterred, the young man followed the superior to Vienna, obtained his consent, and after probation was admitted a novice at Brünn. For the next ten years he worked and trained in Olmütz, Gratz and Vienna.

By the express command of Aquaviva, father-general of the Society, John Ogilvie came to the French province, and it was in Paris that he received priest's orders in 1610. In France the young man was brought into contact with two Jesuits who had undertaken missionary work in Scotland, and had made expeditions thither still hoping, through the nobles, to win over King James. Ogilvie formed the project to devoting his life to the work and he wrote to the father-general offering himself for the mission. After two and a half years of worrying and importunity he received orders to proceed to Scotland.

In consequence of the strict regulations against the entry of priests into Great Britain, he travelled under the name of John Watson, and figured henceforth sometimes as a horse-dealer and sometimes as a soldier returning from the European wars. He soon found out that the Catholic nobles on whom he had relied were only anxious to be left alone. Most of them had confirmed, at least outwardly, to the established religion, and none but a very few middle-class uninfluential families were prepared to receive a proscribed priest. Realizing this, he reverted to the methods attempted by the earlier Jesuits and went to London, where he got into touch with King James, or one of his ministers, to whom he proposed some semi-political project the details of which are lost. On the strength of this, he made a journey to Paris to consult his superior, Father Gordon, who rebuked him sharply for leaving his mission and sent him back to Scotland.

Upon his return to Edinburgh, John Ogilvie made his headquarters at the house of William Sinclair, a parliamentary advocate and a sincere Catholic. Here he met a Franciscan namesake, and the two ministered to the little congregations which met at the houses of Sinclair, John Philipps and Robert Wilkie. Ogilvie soon increased his flock and became famous for his insistence on greater devotion among Catholics. He also appears to have acted as tutor to Sinclair's elder boy Robert, who afterwards became a Jesuit. Warming to his work, he now began to extend it in other directions, and set about visiting Catholics in prison—a risky proceeding in a place where all visitors were watched—and he even climbed to the castle and obtained leave to see old Sir James MacDonald, who recalled his ministrations in after years. During the summer months of 1614 he made some converts, and Sinclair afterwards maintained that the number was great, considering the shortness of the time. Towards the end of August he went to Glasgow, where he was harboured by a widow called Marion Walker, who ended her days in prison for the faith.

In Glasgow he succeeded in entering into relations with Sir John Cleland and Lady Maxwell, who were both secret Catholics, and also in reconciling to the faith several members of the Renfrewshire gentry. At the same time he was building up a congregation among the bourgeoisie. Shortly after his return to Edinburgh, news came that five other persons in Glasgow wished to be reconciled and he hurried back to Glasgow. On May 4 he celebrated Mass, one of the five would-be converts, Adam Boyd by name, being present. After the service the man said he desired instruction, and requested the priest to come at four o'clock in the afternoon to the market-cross, where a messenger would meet him and conduct him to a safe place. Ogilvie agreed, and Boyd immediately went to Archbishop Spottiswoode, a former Presbyterian minister who was now one of the king's most capable lieutenants, and who from his residence in Glasgow kept watch upon Catholics and Presbyterians alike. It was agreed between them that one of the archbishop's most muscular servants, Andrew Hay, should meet Adam Boyd and Ogilvie in the market-place. At the same time Boyd denounced all those whom he suspected of having dealings with Ogilvie.

The appointment was kept, and the Jesuit arrived in the square accompanied by James Stewart, the son of the former provost, who, recognizing Hay, tried to induce Ogilvie to return home. Stewart and Hay fell into a dispute which ended in a free fight in which outsiders took part, but finally Ogilvie was borne along to the provost's house. The following morning he was brought before the archbishop and the burghal court of Glasgow, and was asked, 'Have you said Mass in the king's dominions?' Knowing that this came under the criminal law the prisoner replied, 'If this is a crime, it should be proved, not by my word, but by witnesses'. All question which would incriminate himself or endanger the life of others he refused to answer, and the trial dragged on until he had been without food for twenty-six hours and was trembling with fever.

When it was found that neither the threat of torture nor promises of the king's favour could obtain from the prisoner the betrayal of the unknown Catholics of Scotland, it was determined to deprive him of sleep and thus weaken his power of resistance. For eight days and nights he was kept from sleep by being prodded with sharp-pointed stakes, by being dragged from his couch, by shouts in his ears, by having his hair torn and by being flung upon the floor. Only because the doctors declared that another three hours would prove fatal was he allowed a day and night's rest before being brought up for his second examination, which took place in Edinburgh before the lords commissioners appointed by the king's missives for his examination and trial. The charge against him was now completely changed. Ogilvie, the authorities declared, had been guilty of high treason in refusing to acknowledge the king's jurisdiction in spiritual matters; but actually the whole object of the privy council was, not to convict him of saying Mass, or even condemn him for asserting the papal jurisdiction in Scotland, but to discover, through him, what Scotsmen would be prepared to welcome to return to the Catholic faith.

After the second trial, Ogilvie was taken back to Glasgow, where he seems to have been, at first, kindly treated. The report of his heroism in prison had gone through the length and breadth of Scotland, and even his keepers, including the archbishop, desired nothing so much as that he should recant and accept the royal supremacy. Soon, however, there came for the prisoner a questionnaire drawn up by King James himself. To these five questions, which dealt entirely with the relations between church and state, he could only return answers which practically sealed his fate. His treatment in prison grew more rigorous. Nevertheless he still continued to write, in Latin, an account of his arrest and subsequent treatment and managed to transmit the pages through the crack between the door and the floor to persons who were passing outside—ostensibly on their way to visit other prisoners.

Though the gallows had been erected in readiness, there was still the show of a trial to be gone through. For the last time Father Ogilvie appeared before his judges. He was told that he was being tried, not for saying Mass, but for the answers he had given to the king's questions.

He was accordingly condemned for high treason and sentenced to a traitor's death. His friend John Browne, who attended him to the end and heard his last words, asserted that even on the scaffold he was offered his freedom and a fat living if he would abjure his religion—a sure proof, if further proof were needed, that his offence was his faith and not his politics. He was canonized in 1976, the first Scottish saint for five hundred years.

11 : ST OENGUS, ABBOT-BISHOP (c. A.D. 824)

ST OENGUS sometimes called 'the Hagiographer', is better known as 'the Culdee' or 'God's Vassal'. He came of royal race in Ulster, and was born about the middle of the eighth century. In early youth he entered the famous monastery of Clonenagh in Leix, which, under its saintly abbot Maelaithgen, then enjoyed a great reputation for learning, for sanctity and for its numbers. Here he made rapid advance until he had reached a point at which it could be said of him that no one in his time could be found in Ireland to equal him in virtue and in sacred knowledge. To shun the world more entirely he retired to a cell at Dysartenos some seven miles from the monastery, where he hoped to continue unnoticed the austerities he practised. Besides making three hundred genuflexions, it was his custom to recite the whole Psalter daily, dividing it into three parts, one of which he recited in his cell, another under a spreading tree, and the third whilst he stood tied by the neck to a stake, with his body partially immersed in a tub of cold water. His fame soon attracted too many visitors, and he departed secretly from his hermitage.

He finally reached the great monastery of Tallaght near Dublin, and asked to be received as a serving-man—concealing his name and scholarship. He was accepted by the abbot, St Maelruain, and for seven years he was given the meanest and most laborious offices. His identity, however, was discovered in a singular way. One day as he was working in the monastery barn a school boy, who did not know his lesson and was therefore playing truant, took shelter in the granary and asked to be allowed to stay. Oengus took the little fellow in his arms and lulled him to sleep. When he awoke he had learnt his lesson perfectly. Whether Maelruain thought that a miracle had been performed, or whether he realized that the humble serving-man was a teacher of exceptional ability, he ran out to the barn and embraced St Oengus with tender affection, divining or eliciting that he was the missing Oengus of Dysartenos. From that moment the two saints became the closest of friends, and St Oengus, freed from menial work, set about composing the metrical hymn known in the Irish language as the *Félire*.

He remained on the some years at Tallaght, but after the death of St Maelruain in 792 he turned his steps back to Clonenagh, where he had spent his youth. Here he appears to have been made abbot in succession to Maelaithgen, and to have been raised to episcopal dignity.

As he felt his end approaching, he withdrew to Dysartbeagh and there finished his Félire and perhaps composed some of his other works now lost, but whether he built a monastery in that place or whether he had a hermitage whilst continuing to guide a religious community elsewhere is uncertain. The exact date of his death is contested, but it is not thought that he lived to a great age.

12 : ST THEOPHANES THE CHRONICLER, ABBOT (A.D. 817)

ST THEOPHANES grew up at the court of the Emperor Constantine V. His father had died early, leaving him heir to a large estate and entrusting him to the guardianship of the emperor. He was induced to marry, but by mutual agreement his wife became a nun; Theophaneş also retired from the world and seemingly built two monasteries, the first of which was situated on Mount Sigriana, near Cyzicus. When he established the second, on the island of Kalonymos, which was part of his heritage, he made this his home, and spent six years there. Eventually he returned to Mount Sigriana as abbot. In 787 Theophanes was invited to take part in the Second Council of Nicaea, which sanctioned the use and veneration of sacred images. But Leo the Armenian in 814 reversed the policy of his predecessors, and strove to suppress the cult of images. Recognizing how widespread was the authority and reputation of St Theophanes, he attempted to win him over to his side, but the holy man was well armed against all the devices which could be used to ensnare him. At the age of fifty he had begun to be grievously afflicted with the stone and with another painful internal disease; but, called to Constantinople by the emperor, he obeyed, although tortured by these agonizing infirmities.

Leo sent him a message that flattered and then threatened. To this Theophanes replied: 'Being now far advanced in years and much broken with pain and the weakness of my body, I have neither relish nor inclination for any of those things which I despised, for Christ's sake, in my youth. As to my monastery and my friends, I commend them to God. If you think to frighten me into compliance by your threats, as a child is awed by the rod, you are only losing your pains.' The emperor sent several emissaries to argue with him, but he remained inflexible. He was condemned to be scourged and imprisoned, and, after receiving 300 strokes was confined for two years in a stinking dungeon, where he was left almost without the necessaries of life, although his malady was increasing. At last he was banished to the island of Samothrace, where he died March 12, 817, seventeen days after his arrival, as the result of the treatment he had endured. He left a Chronography or short history of the world to the year 813, starting from A.D. 284; the date which terminated an earlier history written by his friend George Syncellus, secretary of the patriarch St Tarasius.

13 : ST EUPHRASIA, OR EUPRAXIA, VIRGIN (c. AD 420)

THE Emperor Theodosius I had a kinsman Antigonus, who died within a year of the birth of his daughter Euphrasia, and the emperor took the widow and her child under his protection. When the little girl was five years old he arranged to betroth her to the son of a wealthy senator—in accordance with the custom of the time—the marriage being deferred until the maiden should have reached a suitable age. The widow herself began to be sought in marriage, and she withdrew from the court and went with Euphrasia to Egypt, where she settled down near a convent of nuns. Euphrasia, then seven years of age, was greatly drawn to the nuns and begged to be allowed to stay with them. Her mother left her there for a little, expecting her soon to weary of the life, but the child was persistent and was clothed in the nun's habit. Soon afterwards the mother went to rejoin her husband in a better world, and Euphrasia grew up in the seclusion of the convent.

In due time the emperor, presumably Arcadius, sent for her to come to Constantinople to marry the senator to whom he had betrothed her. She was now twelve years old and an heiress, but she wrote him a letter begging him to allow her to follow her vocation and requesting him to distribute her parents' property to the poor as well as to enfranchise all her slaves. The emperor carried out her requests; but Euphrasia was sorely tried by vain imaginations and temptations to know more of the world she had forsaken. The abbess, to whom she opened her heart, set her some hard and humbling tasks to divert her attention. Once the abbess ordered her to remove a pile of stones from one place to another, and when the task was completed she continued to make her carry them backwards and forwards thirty times. In this and in whatever else she was bidden to do, Euphrasia complied cheerfully and promptly. Her meekness and humility were extraordinary.

As the saint lay on her death-bed, Julia, a beloved sister who shared her cell, besought Euphrasia to obtain for her the grace of being with her in Heaven as she had been her companion on earth, and three days after her friend's demise, Julia was taken also. The aged abbess who had originally received Euphrasia remained for a month together very sad at the loss of her dear ones. She prayed earnestly that she might not have to linger on now that the others had gone to their reward. The following morning when the nuns entered her cell they found only her lifeless body.

14 : ST LEOBINUS, or LUBIN, BISHOP OF CHARTRES (*C.* AD 558)

THE parents of St Lubin were peasants in the country near Poitiers, and from childhood he was set to work in the fields. As a boy he was keen to learn, and he went to a monastery—probably Noailles—where he was employed in menial tasks. As work occupied him all day, he was obliged to do most of his studying at night, screening his lamp because the monks complained that the light disturbed their slumbers. By humility and perseverance he advanced in religious knowledge until he had reached an honourable place in the house. In some way, however, he came into contact with St Carilef, and it was probably at his suggestion that Lubin sought out the hermit St Avitus, who recommended him to spend some time longer in a monastery and then to return to him in Le Perche.

After sundry misadventures Lubin settled down for five years in an abbey near Lyons, until in a war between the Franks and the Burgundians the monastery was raided and the monks took to flight, only Lubin and an old man remaining behind. The raiders, who were intent on plunder, tried to discover from the old man where the treasures were concealed, and he referred them to St Lubin. As they could obtain no information from him they had recourse to torture—fastening a cord round his head and tightening it. After this they tied his feet and dipped him, head first, into the river, but failing to make him divulge anything they eventually left him for dead. He recovered, however, and with two companions returned to Le Perche where St Avitus received him into his monastery. After the death of St Avitus, Lubin again lived the life of a hermit. Bishop Aetherius of Chartres nominated him abbot of Brou and raised him to the priesthood. He seems to have found his responsibilities too onerous and longed to become a simple monk at Lérins, but St Caesarius, to whom his own bishop sent him for advice, told him to go back to Brou and not to leave his people like sheep without a shepherd. He obeyed, but soon after his return was promoted to succeed Aetherius as bishop of Chartres. He brought about various reforms and continued to be very famous for his miracles. He took part in the Fifth Council of Orleans and in the Second Council of Paris, dying on March 14, about 558, after a long illness.

15 : ST LOUISE DE MARILLAC, WIDOW, CO-FOUNDRESS OF THE VINCENTIAN SISTERS OF CHARITY (A.D. 1660)

LOUISE, born in 1591, lost her mother when still a child, but had a good upbringing and education, thanks partly to the nuns of Poissy, and partly to the personal instruction of her own father, who, however, died when she was little more than fifteen.

She married Antony Le Gras, a man who seemed destined for a distinguished career. A son was born to them, and her twelve years of married life were happy except that before very long her husband fell ill of a lingering sickness in which she nursed him most devotedly.

Not long before the death of her husband, Louise made a vow not to marry again but to devote herself wholly to the service of God. He died in 1625, but before this she had already made the acquaintance of 'M. Vincent', as the holy priest known to us now as St Vincent de Paul was then called, and he, though showing reluctance at first, consented eventually to act as her confessor. Only after some five years personal association with Mlle Le Gras did M. Vincent, who was ever patient to abide God's own good time, send this devoted soul in May 1629 to make what we might call a visitation of the 'Charity' of Montmirail he had founded. This was the precursor of many similar missions, and in spite of much bad health, of which St Vincent himself was by no means inconsiderate, his deputy, with all her reckless self-sacrifice did not succumb. Quietly, however, and very gradually, as activities multiplied, in the by-ways of Paris as well as in the country, the need of robust helpers made itself felt.

Hence it came about that in 1633 a sort of training centre or noviceship was established in what was then known as the Rue des Fossé-Saint-Victor. This was the unfashionable dwelling Mlle Le Gras had rented for herself after her husband's death, and she now gave hospitality to the first candidates who were accepted for the service of the sick and poor.

These with Louise as their directress formed the grain of mustard seed which has grown into the world-wide organization known as the Sisters of

Charity of St Vincent de Paul. Soon it became evident that some rule of life and some guarantee of stability was desirable. Louise had long wanted to bind herself to this service by vow, but St Vincent, always prudent and content to wait for a clear manifestation of the will of God, had restrained her ardour. But in 1634 her desire was gratified; St Vincent had now complete confidence in his spiritual daughter, and it was she who drafted something in the nature of a rule of life to be followed by the members of their association. The substance of this document forms the kernel of the religious observance of the Sisters of Charity down to the present day. But although this was a great step forward, the recognition of the Sister of Charity as an institute of nuns was still far distant. St Vincent himself insisted that he had never dreamed of founding a religious order. It was not until 1642 that he allowed four of the company to take annual vows of poverty, chastity and obedience, and it was not until 1655 that Cardinal de Retz, Archbishop of Paris, despatched from Rome the formal approbation of the company and placed them definitely under the direction of St Vincent's own congregation of priests.

Meanwhile the good works of the Daughters of Charity had multiplied apace. The patients of the great Paris hospital of the Hôtel-Dieu had passed in large measure under their care, the brutal treatment of an abandoned child had led St Vincent to organize a home for foundlings, and despite the illiteracy of many of their own recruits the associates had found themselves compelled to undertake the teaching of children. In all these developments Mlle Le Gras had borne the heaviest part of the burden.

As we may learn from her letters to St Vincent and others, two things only troubled her; the one was the respect and veneration with which she found her visits welcomed, the other was her anxiety for the spiritual welfare of her son Michael. With all her occupations she never forgot him. He came with his wife and child to visit his mother on her deathbed and she blessed them tenderly.

St Louise de Marillac died on March 15, 1660, and St Vincent followed her only six months later. She was canonized in 1934.

16 : ST ABRAHAM KIDUNAIA, (SIXTH CENTURY)

THE birthplace of St Abraham was near Edessa in Mesopotamia, where his parents occupied an important position, being possessed of great riches. They chose for him a bride, and although he felt called to a celibate life he did not dare to oppose their wishes. In accordance with the custom of the time and country, a seven days' festivity preceded the actual marriage, and on the last day Abraham ran away to conceal himself in the desert. A search was made for the fugitive, who at length was discovered absorbed in prayer. All appeals and entreaties having failed to shake his resolution, his friends finally withdrew, and he walled up the door of his cell, leaving only a little window through which food could be passed. When his parents died, he inherited their riches, but he commissioned a friend to distribute all his goods to the poor. His only remaining possessions were a cloak, a goatskin garment, a bowl for food and drink, and a rush mat on which he slept. 'He was never seen to smile', says his biographer, 'and he regarded each day as his last . . . . And, what is even more surprising, never once, in fifty years, did he change his coat of goatskin, which was actually worn by others after his death.'

Not far from Abraham's cell there was a colony of idolaters who had resisted all attempts to evangelize them. The bishop of Edessa appealed to him to leave his hermitage and preach to the people. Reluctantly St Abraham allowed himself to be ordained priest and did as he was bidden. Coming to the town of Beth-Kiduna he found on all sides signs of idolatry and appalling abominations. He asked the bishop to build a Christian church and when it was completed, the saint felt that his time had come. After praying earnestly, he cast down the altars and destroyed every idol he could see. The infuriated villagers beat him and drove him from the village. During the night he returned, and was found in the morning praying in the church. Going out into the streets he began to harangue the people and to urge them to give up their superstitions, but they again turned on him, and seizing him dragged him away, stoned him and left him for dead. Upon recovering consciousness he again returned, and though constantly insulted, ill-treated and sometimes attacked with sticks and stones, he continued for three years to preach, without any apparent result. Suddenly the tide turned: the saint's meekness and patience convinced the people that he was indeed a holy man, and they began to listen.

For a year, he continued to build up his converts, and then, fearing that he himself was becoming too much absorbed in the things of this world, he determined to leave his flock to the care of others and stole away at night to hide himself once more in the desert. St Abraham lived to the age of seventy. At the news of his last illness, the whole countryside flocked to receive his benediction, and after his death each one sought to procure some fragment of his clothing.

17 : ST PATRICK, ARCHBISHOP OF ARMAGH, APOSTLE OF IRELAND
(A.D. 461)

WHETHER Patrick's birthplace was near Dumbarton on the Clyde, or in Cumberland to the south of Hadrian's Wall, or at the mouth of the Severn or elsewhere is of no great moment. We may infer from what he says of himself that he was of Romano-British origin. His father Calpurnius was a deacon and a municipal official, his grandfather a priest, for in those days no strict law of celibacy had yet been imposed on the Western clergy. We cannot be far wrong in supposing that he was born about 389, and that about 406 he with many others was carried off by raiders to become a slave among the still pagan inhabitants of Ireland. There amid the bodily hardships of this bondage his soul grew marvellously in holiness.

After six years he heard a voice in his sleep warning him to be ready for a brave effort which would bring him back to freedom in the land of his birth. Accordingly he ran away from his master and travelled 200 miles to the ship of whose approaching departure he had had some strange intimation. His request for free passage was refused at first, but, in answer to his silent prayer to God, the sailors called him back, and with them he made an adventurous journey. They were three days at sea, and when they reached land it was only to travel in company for a month through some uninhabited tract of country.

At length they reached human habitations—probably in Gaul—but the fugitive was safe, and thus eventually Patrick, at the age of twenty-two or twenty-three, was restored to his kinsfolk. They welcomed him warmly and besought him not to depart from them again, but after a while, in the watches of the night, fresh visions came to him, and he heard 'the voices of those who dwelt beside the wood of Foclut which is nigh to the western sea, and thus they cried, as if with one mouth, "We beseech thee, holy youth, to come and walk among us once more".' 'Thanks be to God', he adds 'that after many years the Lord granted to them according to their cry.'

With regard to the order of events which followed there is no certainty, and to trace in detail the course of the saint's heroic labours in the land of his former captivity is impossible, left as we are to the confused, legendary and sometimes contradictory data supplied by his later biographers.

When Patrick had gathered many disciples round him, such, for example, as Benignus, who was destined to be his successor, the work of evangeliza-tion was well under way. He maintained his contacts abroad, and it has been suggested that the 'approval' of which we read was a formal communication from Pope St Leo the Great. In 444, according to the Annals of Ulster, the cathedral church of Armagh, the primatial see of Ireland, was founded, and no long time probably elapsed before it became a centre of education as well as administration.

It seems possible that Patrick died and was buried, in or about the year 461, at Saul on Strangford Lough, where he had built his first church.

18 : ST CYRIL, ARCHBISHOP OF JERUSALEM, DOCTOR OF THE CHURCH (A.D. 386)

IF Cyril was not born in Jerusalem (about 315), he was certainly brought up there, and his parents, who were probably Christians, gave him an excellent education. He seems to have been ordained priest by the bishop of Jerusalem, St Maximus, who thought so highly of his abilities that he charged him with the important duty of instructing the catechumens. His catechetical lectures were delivered without a book, and the nineteen catechetical discourses which have come down to us are perhaps the only ones ever committed to writing. They are most valuable as containing an exposition of the teaching and ritual of the Church in the middle of the fourth century.

Not very long after Cyril's accession to the see of Jerusalem, misunder-standings began to arise between him and Bishop Acacius, primarily about the precedence and jurisdiction of their respective sees, but also over matters of faith, for Acacius had become imbued with the full Arian heresy. Disagreement increased to open strife, and finally Acacius called a small council of bishops of his own party, to which Cyril was summoned, but before which he refused to appear. To the charge of contumacy was added that of having sold church property during a famine to relieve the poor. This he had certainly done, as it was also done by St Ambrose, St Augustine and many other great prelates, who have been held fully justified. However, the packed meeting condemned him and he was driven out of Jerusalem. He made his way to Tarsus, where he was hospitably received by Silvanus, the semi-Arian biship, and where he remained pending the hearing of an appeal which he had sent to a higher court. Two years after his deposition, the appeal came before the Council of Seleucia, which consisted of semi-Arians, Arians and a very few members of the strictly orthodox party—all from Egypt. Cyril himself sat among the semi-Arians, the best of whom had befriended and supported him during his exile. Acacius took violent exception to his presence and departed in anger, though he soon returned and took a prominent part in the subsequent debates. His party, however, was in the minority, and he himself was deposed, whilst Cyril was vindicated and reinstated.

Acacius thereupon persuaded the Emperor Constantius to summon another council. Acacius triumphed and obtained a second decree of exile against Cyril within a year of his vindication. But upon the death of Constantius in 361, his successor Julian recalled all the bishops whom his predecessor had expelled, and Cyril returned to his see with the rest.

In 367 St Cyril was banished for the third time, Valens having decreed the expulsion of all prelates recalled by Julian, but about the date of the accession of Theodosius he was finally reinstated and enjoyed undisturbed possession of his see for the last eight years of his life. He was distressed on his return to find Jerusalem torn with schisms and party strife, overrun with heresy and stained by appalling crimes. The Council of Antioch sent St Gregory of Nyssa, who, however, soon departed, leaving to posterity a highly-coloured description of the morals of the holy city at this period.

In 381 both Cyril and Gregory were present at the great Council of Constantinople—the second ecumenical council—and the bishop of Jerusalem on this occasion took his place as a metropolitan with the patriarchs of Alexandria and Antioch. At this gathering the Nicene Creed was promulgated in its amended form, and Cyril, who subscribed to it with the rest, accepted the term 'Homoousios', which had come to be regarded as the test word of orthodoxy.

He is thought to have died in 386 at the age of nearly seventy, after an episcopate of thirty-five years, sixteen of which were spent in exile. He was declared a doctor of the Church in 1882.

19 : ST JOSEPH, HUSBAND OF OUR LADY ST MARY (FIRST CENTURY)

ACCORDING to the Roman Martyrology March 19 is 'the [heavenly] birthday of St Joseph, husband of the most Blessed Virgin Mary and confessor, whom the Supreme Pontiff Pius IX, assenting the desires and prayers of the whole Catholic world, had proclaimed patron of the Universal Church'.

What is told in the gospels is familiar: he was of royal descent and his genealogy has been set out for us both by St Matthew and by St Luke. He was the protector of our Lady's good name, and in that character of necessity the confidant of Heaven's secrets, and he was the foster-father of Jesus, charged with the guidance and support of the holy family, and responsible for the education of Him who, though divine, loved to call Himself 'the son of man'. It was Joseph's trade that Jesus learnt, it was his manner of speech that the boy will have imitated, it was he whom our Lady herself seemed to invest with full parental rights when she said without qualification, 'Thy father and I have sought thee sorrowing'.

None the less our positive knowledge concerning St Joseph's life is very restricted, and the 'tradition' enshrined in the apocryphal gospels must be pronounced to be quite worthless. We may assume that he was betrothed to Mary his bride with the formalities prescribed by Jewish ritual, but the nature of this ceremonial is not clearly known, especially in the case of the poor; and that Joseph and Mary were poor is proved by the offering of only a pair of turtle-doves at Mary's purification in the Temple. By this same poverty the story of the competition of twelve suitors for Mary's hand, of the rods deposited by them in the care of the High Priest and of the portents which distinguished the rod of Joseph from the rest, is shown to be quite improbable.

We must be content to know the simple facts that when Mary's pregnancy had saddened her husband his fears were set at rest by an angelic vision, that he was again warned by angels—first to seek refuge in Egypt, and afterwards to return to Palestine—that he was present at Bethlehem when our Lord was laid in the manger and the shepherds came to worship Him, that he was present also when the Infant was placed in the arms of Holy Simeon, and finally that he shared his wife's sorrow at the loss of her Son and her joy when they found Him debating with the doctors in the Temple. St Joseph's merit is summed up in the phrase that 'he was a just man', that is to say, a godly man. This was the eulogy of Holy Writ itself.

20 : ST CUTHBERT, BISHOP OF LINDISFARNE (A.D. 687)

THE name Cuthbert is undoubtedly Saxon and not Celtic. We-first make his acquaintance when he was about eight and under the charge of a widow named Kenswith, whom he regarded as a mother and who treated him as her son. The occupation to which he was bred—that of a shepherd—gave him ample opportunities of quiet communing with God on the great pasturages or folklands of Northumbria. At the end of August 651 Cuthbert, then about fifteen years of age, had a vision which decided him to consecrate his life to God.

Cuthbert was alone in prayer. Suddenly a beam of dazzling light shone across the black sky, and in it appeared a host of angels carrying, as though in a globe of fire, a soul to heaven. Later he learnt that the holy bishop St Aidan had died that night at Bamborough. Although this was the turning-point in his life, he does not appear at once to have given up the world. It has been suggested that he may have been called upon to fight against the Mercians, for it was on horseback and armed with a spear that he eventually appeared at the gate of Melrose Abbey and asked to be admitted amongst the brethren.

In the year 660 the abbot of Melrose received land for another monastery, and upon an elevation at the confluence of the rivers Ure and Skell was built the abbey of Ripon, to which St Eata came in 661, bringing Cuthbert with him. But their stay was short. A year later King Alcfrith transferred the abbey to St Wilfrid, and Cuthbert returned to Melrose. The whole country was being ravaged by a disease known as 'the yellow plague', and under the infliction men and women were again, as Bede tells us, putting faith in charms and amulets. To assist the stricken people and to revive Christianity St Cuthbert now entered upon a strenuous missionary effort which extended over the years that he was prior, first at Melrose, and afterwards at Lindisfarne.

Great changes were taking place at Lindisfarne, and it seemed at one moment as though Holy Island might lose the famous community which had made it the most venerable sanctuary in the north. The disputes over the date of Easter had culminated in the Council of Whitby, at which King Oswiu decided for the Roman use. St Colman returned to Lindisfarne, but soon decided that he could not conform and preferred to resign. Followed by all the Irish monks and thirty of the English, and bearing the body of St Aidan, he left England and made new homes in Ireland. To fill his place St Eata was recalled from Melrose and given the rank of Bishop, and Cuthbert accompanied him again to act as his prior.

After some years at Lindisfarne, the longing to lead a life of still closer union with God led him with his abbot's consent to seek solitude. His first hermitage was at no great distance from the abbey—probably in the islet off Holy Island which local tradition associates with him and calls St Cuthbert's Isle. The place, wherever it may have been, appears not to have been sufficiently secluded, for in 676 he moved to a bleak and desolate island of the Farne group, two miles from Bamborough. The spot was then uninhabited, and afforded him at first neither water nor corn, but he found a spring and though the first crop which he planted failed entirely the second crop—which was barley—yielded sufficient to sustain him. In spite of the storms which then, as now, rage round the islands, visitors persisted in coming, and St Cuthbert built a guest-house near the landing-stage to lodge them. Only once did he leave his retreat, and that was at the request of the abbess St Elfleda, King Oswiu's daughter. This meeting took place on Coquet Island, and Elfleda uged him on that occasion to accept a bishopric which King Egfrith was anxious to bestow upon him. Shortly afterwards he was elected bishop of Hexham. He refused to leave his island cell, and was only induced to consent when King Egfrith came in person to Farne, accompanied by Bishop Trumwin. Very reluctantly Cuthbert gave way, but stipulated to be allowed to remain in his hermitage for the six months that would elapse before his consecration. During that period he visited St Eata and arranged for an exchange of dioceses, whereby Eata would take Hexham and Cuthbert would have the see of Lindisfarne with charge of the monastery.

On Easter day 685, he was consecrated in York Minster by St Theodore, Archbishop of Canterbury. The two years of his episcopate were mainly spent in visiting his diocese, which extended far to the west and included Cumberland. He preached, taught, distributed alms, and wrought so many miracles of healing that he won during his lifetime the name of 'the Wonderworker of Britain', which the remarkable cures effected at his tomb caused him to retain after his death. He was making his first visitation of Carlisle, a few weeks after his consecration, when, by some strange telepathic gift or by divine revelation, he was apprised of the overthrow of the Northumbrian army and of the death in battle of King Egfrith.

Labours and austerities had sapped St Cuthbert's constitution, and he realized that he had not long to live. After a farewell visitation through the diocese, he laid down the pastoral staff, and after celebrating the Christmas of 686 with the monks in Holy Island, he withdrew to his beloved Farne to prepare for his end. His brethren often visited him during the last three months, although he would not allow anyone to stay and minister to him in his growing weakness. Fever set in and he endured terrible trials during a stormy period of five days, when no one could approach the island. He wanted to be buried in his retreat, but yielded to the entreaties of his monks who wished that his bones should rest amongst them at the abbey. 'You will bury me', he said, 'wrapped in the linen which I have kept for my shroud, out of love for the Abbess Werca, the friend of God, who gave it to me.'

He received the last sacraments and died peacefully, seated, with his hands uplifted and his eyes gazing heavenwards. A monk immediately climbed the rock on which the lighthouse now stands and waved two lighted torches—for it was night—to announce to the brethren at Lindisfarne that the great saint had passed to his rest. His body, which at first was laid in the abbey and remained at Lindisfarne for 188 years, was removed when the Danes began to descend upon the coast, and after many translations was deposited in a magnificent shrine in Durham Cathedral, which continued to be a favourite place of pilgrimage for the north of England until the Reformation. In the reign of Henry VIII the shrine was desecrated and plundered, but the monks secretly buried the relics. In 1827 St Cuthbert's body was again discovered, and the various articles through which it was identified were removed to the cathedral library. Although the genuineness of the relics is generally admitted, yet there is another tradition, according to which St Cuthbert's remains still lie interred in another part of the cathedral, known only to three members of the English Benedictine Congregation, who hand on the secret before they die.

St Cuthbert is usually represented as carrying in his hands the head of King Oswald. This was buried with him for safety, and was found when the bishop's coffin was opened and examined at Durham in 1104.

21 : ST ENDA, ABBOT, (c A.D. 530)

MUCH that we are told of St Enda's hidtory previous to his settlement at Aranmore is quite legendary, except perhaps for an important stay at Whithorn, the monastery founded by St Ninian in Galloway. Afterwards Enda went to Drogheda and built churches on both sides of the river Boyne. He crossed Ireland and went to see Oengus, King of Munster, who was married to one of his sisters, and lived at Cashel. From his brother-in-law he asked for the isle of Aran that he might found a religious establishment there. Oengus urged him to choose a more fertile place nearer at hand, but when St Enda persisted that Aran was to be the place of his resurrection and that it was good enough for him, Oengus yielded.

To this island St Enda brought his disciples, and the fame of his austerity and sanctity led many others to join them. The saint built, on the eastern side of Aranmore, a great monastery at Kelleany, over which he presided, and half the land was apportioned to it, whilst the rest of the island was divided between ten other smaller houses which he founded and over which he set superiors. We are told that not only did he live a most penitential life himself, but that he exacted a very strict discipline from all under his charge. A legend relates that every night he tested his brethren by putting them in turn into a curragh, or wicker-work canoe, and setting it afloat without the hide covering which rendered it watertight. If a man was free from sin, the water could not get in. All the monks—including the abbot himself—escaped a wetting, except Gigniat the cook, who when questioned admitted that he had added a little to his own portion of food from that of Kieran, son of the artificer. St Enda ordered him to leave the island, saying, 'There is no room here for a thief; I will not permit this at all'.

With St Finnian of Clonard, St Enda was a father of monachism in Ireland: with him organized monasticism, properly speaking, seems to have begun. One of his best-known desciples was St Kieran of Clonmacnois, just referred to.

22 : ST NICHOLAS OWEN, MARTYR (A.D. 1606)

PERHAPS no single person contributed more to the preservation of the Catholic religion in England during the penal times than Nicholas Owen, who in the reign of James I saved the lives of many priests by his extraordinary skill in devising hiding-places for them. Nothing is known of his antecedents or early life, but it is thought that he may have been a builder by trade. Familiarly known as 'Little John' and 'Little Michael', he also passed under the names of Andrewes and Draper.

Summarizing contemporary records Father Tanner says of him: 'A great servant of God in a diminutive body, Nicholas Odoenus, otherwise Owen, spent eighteen years with Fathers Henry Garnet and John Gerard in the capacity of a faithful and most useful servant. Born in England in an age of licence, he lived a singularly innocent life, untainted by the allurements of the world; his confessor, who had known his conscience from his earliest childhood, solemnly asserts that he preserved his baptismal innocence unsullied until death. With imcomparable skill he knew how to devise a place of safety for priests in subterranean passages, to hide them between walls, and to bury them in impenetrable recesses. But what was much more dificult of accomplishment, he so disguised the entrances to these as to make them most unlike what they really were. Moreover he kept these places so close a secret with himself, that he would never disclose their existence to anyone else. He alone was both their architect and their builder, working at them with inexhaustible industry and labour, for generally the thickest walls had to be broken into and large stones excavated, requiring stronger arms than were attached to a body so diminutive as to give him the nickname of 'Little John'. And by his skill many priests were preserved from the fury of the persecutors, nor is it easy to find anyone who had not often been indebted for his life to Owen's hiding-places—a benefit resounding to all Catholics, whose progress in virtue and whose access to the sacraments were thus due to him. His unwonted success in constructing these hiding-places would seem to have been a reward from Heaven for his remarkable piety; for when he as about to design one, he commenced the work by receiving the most holy Eucharist, sought to aid its progress by continual prayer, and offered the completion of it to God alone, accepting of no other reward for his toil than the merit of charity and the consolation of labouring for the good of Catholics.'

When he had worked for some years in this way, Father Garnet admitted him to the Society of Jesus, before 1580, and he was amongst the first English lay-brothers—although, for good reasons, his connection with the order was kept secret. He was with Father John Gerard when they were betrayed on St George's day 1594. He was imprisoned in the Counter and subjected to terrible tortures to force him to disclose the names of other Catholics. He and Brother Richard Fulwood were hung up for three hours together, with their arms fixed into iron rings, and their bodies hanging in the air, and Owen's suffering was increased by heavy weights which were attached to his feet. No information could be obtained from either of the prisoners, and Nicholas was released for a sum of money which a Catholic gentleman paid, because, as Father Gerard testified, his services in contriving priests' hiding-places were indispensable to them and many others.

He soon proved that he could do more than conceal them. The wonderful escape of Father Gerard from the Tower was almost certainly planned by Owen, although it was carried out by Brothers Fulwood and Lilly, who were less well-known to the prison authorities. Owen himself was waiting with horses.

At length, after a faithful service of twenty years, Owen fell once more into the hands of his enemies together with Father Garnet and Father Oldcorne. He came voluntarily out of the hiding-place in which he had carefully concealed them, in order that he might be captured and, by passing for a priest, save the lives of the fathers. He was apprehended with Brother Ralph Ashley, the servant of Father Oldcorne. At first a 'free custody' was allowed in order that those who visited him might be watched, but Owen's prudence baulked the intentions of his captors. He was then removed from the Marshalsea to the Tower of London, the keeper of which, Wade, kept his victim suspended day after day, sometimes for six hours together, although he was ill and suffering from a hernia, which was girt with an iron band. Owen consistently refused to answer Wade's questions and in the end the prolonged strain so extended the martyr's body that his bowels broke in a terrible way, the iron band assisting to tear and enlarge the wound. In the midst of terrible anguish Brother Nicholas passed to his eternal reward on March 2, 1606.

23 : ST TURIBIUS, ARCHBISHOP OF LIMA (A.D. 1606)

TURIBIUS, Toribio Alfonso de Mogrovejo, was born in 1538 at Mayorga in Spain. His childhood and youth were notably religious, but he had no intention of becoming a priest and was, in fact, educated for the law. He was so brilliant a scholar that he became professor of law in the University of Salamanca, and while there he attracted the notice of King Philip II (widower of Mary I of England), who eventually made him chief judge of the ecclesiastical court of the Inquisition at Granada. After some years the archbishopric of Lima in the Spanish colony of Peru became vacant. Turibius had carried out his judge's duties so well, and displayed such a fine missionary spirit, that it was decided to send him to Peru as archbishop: he seemed to be the one person who had force of character sufficient to remedy the serious scandals which stood in the way of the conversion of the Peruvians.

Turibius himself was shocked by the decision, and he wrote forthwith to the royal council, pleading his incapacity and appealing to the canons which forbade the promotion of laymen to ecclesiastical dignities. His objections were overruled; he received all the orders and episcopal consecration, and immediately afterwards sailed for Peru. Arriving in Lima in 1581, it did not take him long to realize the arduous nature of the charge which had been laid upon him. His diocese stretched for some 400 miles along the coast, and inland amongst the spurs of the Andes, a most difficult country to traverse. Far more serious, however, than the physical difficulties were those created by the attitude of the Spanish conquerors towards the native population.

The clergy themselves were often among the most notorious offenders, and it was the first care of Turibius to restore ecclesiastical discipline. He at once undertook a visitation of his diocese, and was inflexible in regard to scandals amongst the clergy. Without respect of persons, he reproved injustice and vice, using his authority always to protect the poor from oppression. The archbishop succeeded in eradicating some of the worst abuses, and he founded numerous churches, religious houses and hospitals; in 1591 he established at Lima the first ecclesiastical seminary in the New World.

Right on into old age St Turibius continued to study the Indian dialects so that he could address the people in their own speech and not through an interpreter. Thus he succeeded in making many conversions. In order to teach his flock he would sometimes stay two or three days in a place where he had neither bed nor sufficient food. Every part of his vast diocese was visited, and when danger threatened from marauders or physical obstacles he would say that Christ came from Heaven to save man and that we ought not to fear danger for His glory. The archbishop offered Mass daily, even when on a journey, and always with intense fervour, and every morning he made his confession to his chaplain. Among those St Turibius confirmed, as well as St Rose, are said to have been St Martin Porres and St John Massias. From 1590 he had the help of another great missionary, the Franciscan St Francis Solano, whose denunciations of the wickedness of Lima so alarmed the people that the viceroy had to call on the archbishop to calm them.

St Turibius was in his sixty-eighth year when he fell ill at Pacasmayo, far to the north of Lima. Working to the last, he struggled as far as Santa, where he realized the end was at hand. He made his will, giving his personal belongings to his servants and all the rest of his property for the benefit of the poor. He asked to be carried into the church to receive viaticum, and was then brought back to bed and anointed. While those about him sang the psalm, 'I was glad when they said unto me, We will go into the house of the Lord', St Turibius died on March 23, 1606. In 1726 he was canonized.

24 : ST IRENAEUS, BISHOP OF SIRMIUM, MARTYR (A.D. 304)

SIRMIUM, then the capital of Pannonia, stood on the site of the present Mitrovica, forty miles or more to the west of Belgrade, and St Irenaeus, quite apart from his position as leader of the Christians, must have been a man of considerable local importance. During the persecution of Diocletian he was as a Christian arrested and brought before Probus, governor of Pannonia. When commanded to offer sacrifice to the gods he refused and was put to the rack, but his resolution remained unshaken. All the bishop's relations and friends were greatly distressed. His mother, his wife and his children surrounded him. His wife, in tears, threw her arms around his neck and begged him to preserve his life for her sake and for that of his innocent children. His sons and daughters cried, whilst his mother sobbed aloud, and servants, neighbours and friends filled the court-house with their lamentations.

The martyr steeled himself against their appeals and avoided making any direct answer to their entreaties. He was again committed to prison, where he was detained a long time, suffering still more hardships and bodily torments, by which it was hoped to shake his constancy. A second public examination produced no more effect than the first and in the end sentence was passed that for disobedience to the imperial edict he should be drowned in the river. Irenacus is said to have protested that such a death was unworthy of the cause for which he suffered. He begged to be given an opportunity to prove that a Christian, strong in his belief in the one true God, could face without flinching the persecutor's most cruel torments. It was conceded to him that he should first be beheaded and his body cast from the bridge into the river.

25 : ST LUCY FILIPPINI, VIRGIN (A.D. 1732)

BORN in 1672 at Tarquinia in Tuscany, about sixty miles from Rome, Lucy was left an orphan at an early age. When still quite young her seriousness of purpose, her great piety and remarkable gifts brought her to the notice of the bishop of the diocese, Cardinal Marcantonio Barbarigo, who persuaded her to come to Montefiascone to take part in an educational institute for training teachers he had established. Lucy threw herself heart and soul into the work and was there brought into contact with Bd Rose Venerini, whom as the successful and most devoted organizer of a similar work in Viterbo, the cardinal had summoned to Montefiascone, that she might give his own foundation the benefit of her experience.

No pupil could have shown more aptitude than St Lucy. Her modesty, her charity, her intense conviction of the value of the things of the spirit, together with her courage and her practical common sense, won all hearts. The work prospered amazingly. New schools for girls and educational centres multiplied and in 1707, at the express desire of Pope Clement XI, she came to Rome and founded the first school of the Maestre Pie in the Via delle Chiavi d'Oro. She was only able to remain in the city a little more than six months, her duties calling her elsewhere, but children came in crowds which far exceeded the accommodation which could be provided for them.

Lucy before she left was known to half the district as the *Maestra santa* (the holy schoolmistress). Like Rose Venerini, she had a great gift of easy and convincing speech. Unfortunately her strength was not equal to the strain that was put on it. She became seriously ill in 1726, and in spite of medical care in Rome itself was never able to regain her normal health, dying a most holy death on March 25, 1732, the day she had herself predicted. St Lucy Filippini was canonized in 1930.

26 : ST BRAULIO, BISHOP OF SARAGOSSA (A.D. 651)

AT the college founded in Seville by St Isidore, one of the more promising of the alumni was a boy of noble birth called Braulio, who grew up to be so eminent a scholar that Isidore regarded him as a friend and disciple rather than a pupil, and used to send him his own writings to correct and revise. Braulio prepared for the priesthood and was ordained, and when in 631 the see of Saragossa became vacant at the death of his brother Bishop John, the neighbouring prelates assembled to elect a successor and their choice fell upon Braulio. As a pastor, St Braulio laboured zealously to teach and encourage his people, and at the same time to extirpate the Arian heresy which continued to flourish even after the conversion of King Reccared. He kept in close touch with St Isidore, whom he assisted in his task of restoring church order and regularizing ecclesiastical discipline: a small portion of the correspondence between the two saints has survived.

He took part in the fourth Council of Toledo, which was presided over by his friend and master St Isidore, and also in the fifth and sixth. The last-named assembly charged him to write an answer to Pope Honorius I, who had accused the Spanish bishops of negligence in the fulfilment of their duties. His defence was dignified and convincing.

The good bishop's duties did not prevent his constant ministrations in his cathedral church and in that of our Lady 'del Pilar', where he spent many hours of the day and night in prayer. Luxury of all kinds he abhorred: his garments were rough and plain, his food simple and his life austere. An eloquent preacher and a keen controversialist, he could carry conviction by his telling arguments and absolute sincerity. His liberality to the poor was only matched by his tender care of all his flock. The close of his life was saddened by failing eyesight—a heavy trial to anyone, but especially to a scholar. As his end drew near, he realized that he was dying, and the last day of his life was spent in the recitation of psalms.

27 : ST JOHN OF EGYPT, (A.D.394)

JOHN was born in the Lower Thebaïd at Lycopolis, the site of the present city of Asyut, and was brought up to the trade of a carpenter. At the age of twenty-five, he abandoned the world and placed himself under the direction of an aged anchoret, who for ten or twelve years trained him in obedience and self-surrender. John obeyed unquestioningly, however unreasonable the task imposed: for a whole year, at the command of his spiritual father, he daily watered a dry stick as though it had been a live plant and carried out other equally ridiculous orders. He continued thus until the old man's death, and it is to his humility and ready obedience that Cassian attributes the extraordinary gifts which he afterwards received from God.

Another four or five years seem to have been spent in visiting various monasteries. Finally he retired to the top of a steep hill near Lycopolis and made in the rock a succession of three little cells—one as a bedroom, another as a workroom and living-room, and the third as an oratory. He then walled himself up, leaving only a little window through which he received the necessaries of life and spoke to those who visited him. During five days of the week he conversed only with God, but on Saturdays and Sundays men—but not women—had free access to him for his instructions and spiritual advice. He never ate until sunset, and his fare was dried fruit and vegetables. At first and until he became inured, he suffered severely because he would not eat bread or anything that had been cooked by fire, but he continued this diet from his fortieth year until he was ninety.

He founded no community, but was regarded as a father by all the ascetics of the neighbourhood, and when his visitors became so numerous that it seemed necessary to build a hospice for their reception, the establishment was managed by his disciples. St John was especially famous for his prophecies, his miracles and his power of reading the thoughts and of discovering the secret sins of those who visited him. Wonderful cures were effected by the application to the sick and blind of oil which the man of God had blessed.

Shortly before St John's death he was visited by Palladius, who gives a most interesting account of his journey and reception. The venerable hermit told him that he was destined one day to be consecrated bishop, and made other disclosures of things of which he could not normally have knowledge. Similarly, when some monks came from Jerusalem, John recognized at once that one of them was a deacon, though the fact had been suppressed. The recluse was then ninety years of age and died shortly afterwards. Divinely warned of his approaching end, he had shut his window and commanded that no one should come near him for three days. He died peacefully at the end of that period, when on his knees at prayer. In 1901 the cell he had occupied was discovered near Asyut.

28 : ST TUTILO, (c A.D. 915)

ST TUTILO was educated by Iso and Marcellus in the celebrated Benedictine monastery of Saint-Gall, where he had as schoolfellows Bd Notker Balbulus and Ratpert. They all three became monks in the abbey, Tutilo being appointed head of the cloister school and Notker librarian. Handsome, eloquent and quick-witted, St Tutilo appears to have been a universal genius, for he is described as a poet, an orator, an architect, a painter, a sculptor, a metal worker and a mechanic. Music, however, was his passion, and he could play all the various instruments taught to the monastery scholars. Although he did not invent liturgical tropes, he certainly cultivated them, and he was probably associated with his friend Notker in writing sequences and in fitting words to the final Alleluia in the gradual.

King Charles the Fat had a great admiration for St Tutilo, and remarked that it was a pity such a genius should be hidden away in a monastery. The saint himself shrank from publicity, and when obliged to go to large cities like Metz and Mainz, where his artistic talents were in great request, he strove to avoid notice and shrank from compliments. He was wont to adorn his pictures and sculptures with an epigram or motto, and there are still at Constance, Metz, Saint-Gall and Mainz paintings attributed to him, but of his poetical and musical works only three little elegies and one hymn have been printed. He died about the year 915 and was buried in the chapel of St Catherine, which was renamed St Tutilo's in his honour.

29 : ST RUPERT, BISHOP OF SALZBURG (c. A.D. 710)

THE early history of St Rupert was formerly very obscure, and there has been considerable difference of opinion as to the date at which he actually flourished. According to the most reliable sources he was a Frank, though Colgan claims him as an Irishman whose Gaelic name was Robertach. It may now be affirmed with certainty that before his missionary undertakings began he was already bishop at Worms, and in that case there is no great likelihood that he paid a visit to Rome, for, as bishop, he would not require any special authorization for such an enterprise.

It was probably about the year 697 that he arrived with several companions at Regensburg and presented himself before Duke Theodo, without whose permission nothing much could be done. He may have brought credentials from the French King Childebert III, who was always anxious for the conversion of recently subjugated provinces. The duke, it seems, was still a pagan, but his sister is said to have been a Christian, and there is no room for doubt that many in Bavaria had received the message of the gospel before this date. Theodo not only gave the newcomers a welcome, but consented to listen to their preaching and to receive instruction. His conversion and baptism were followed by that of many of the nobles, and no serious opposition was offered to the work of the missionaries. The people were well disposed, and St Rupert and his followers met with conspicuous success. One heathen temple at Regensburg and another at Altötting were almost immediately adapted for Christian worship. Other churches were built and nearly the whole population was re-established in the Christian faith. The missionaries pushed their way also along the Danube, and at Lorch St Rupert made many converts and performed several miracles of healing.

It was, however, neither Regensburg nor Lorch which the saint made his headquarters, but the old ruined town of Juvavum, which the duke gave him and which was rebuilt and called Salzburg. Theodo's generosity enabled Rupert to erect there a church and a monastery with a school which were dedicated to St Peter, besides other sacred edifices. The neighbouring valley with its salt springs formed part of the duke's donation. St Rupert had been ably seconded by his companions, three of whom, Vitalis, Chuniald and Gislar, were afterwards reckoned as saints, but before long it became imperative to obtain more help. He therefore returned to his native land to enlist recruits, and succeeded in obtaining twelve more workers. He also induced his sister or niece St Erentrudis to enter a nunnery which he built at Nonnberg and of which she became the first abbess. A considerable number of churches and places bear St Rupert's name and are traditionally connected with him, but many of them were no doubt dedicated to him in after times. Besides the great work of evangelization, the saint did much to civilize his converts and promoted the development of the salt mines. It was he who gave to Juvavum its modern name of Salzburg, and it was there that he died, probably about the year 710.

30 : ST ZOSIMUS, BISHOP OF SYRACUSE (c. A.D. 660)

THE parents of St Zosimus were Sicilian landowners, who dedicated their little boy to the service of St Lucy and placed him, when he was seven years old, in the monastery that bore her name near Syracuse, not far from their home. There his main occupation seems to have been to watch near the relics of the saint. The duty was not altogether congenial to the little lad, accustomed as he was to a free open-air life on a farm, and once, when the abbot Faustus had sent him a particularly distasteful task, he ran away and went home. He was brought back in disgrace, and the enormity of his offence impressed upon him. That night, in his dreams, he saw St Lucy rise from her shrine and stand over him with a menacing countenance. As he lay in terror, there appeared beside her the gracious figure of our Lady interceding for him, and promising in his name that he would never do such a thing again. As time went by, Zosimus became more reconciled to the life of the cloister, his visits home became fewer and shorter, and he settled down to the regular round of prayer, praise and contemplation with the other monks.

For thirty years he lived almost forgotten. then the abbot of Santa Lucia died, and there was great uncertainty and discussion over the choice of a successor. Finally the monks went in a body to the bishop of Syracuse and begged him to make the appointment for them. The prelate, after scrutinizing them all, asked if there was no other monk belonging to the convent. Thereupon they remembered Brother Zosimus, whom they had left to mind the shrine and to answer the door. He was sent for, and no sooner had the bishop set eyes upon him than he exclaimed, 'Behold him whom the Lord hath chosen'. So Zosimus was appointed abbot, and a few days later the bishop ordained him a priest. His biographer says that he ruled the monastery of Santa Lucia with such wisdom, love and prudence that he surpassed all his predeccessors and all his successors. When the see of Syracuse fell vacant in 649, the people elected Zosimus, who, however, did not wish to be raised to the dignity, whilst the clergy chose a priest called Vanerius, a vain and ambitious man. Appeal was made to Pope Theodore, who decided for Zosimus and consecrated him. In his episcopate the holy man was remarkable for his zeal in teaching the people and for his liberality to the poor.

At the age of nearly ninety St Zosimus died, about the year 660.

31 : ST GUY OF POMPOSA, ABBOT (A.D. 1046)

ST GUY, or Guido, who is also called Guion, Wido, Witen and Wit, was born near Ravenna, and his father and mother took great pride in him; and, mainly to please them, he was very careful of his appearance and dress. One day, however, he was smitten with compunction for this form of vanity. He went to Ravenna, where the patronal feast of St Apollinaris was being celebrated, and stripping off his fine clothes he gave them to the poor and donned the shabbiest garments he could find. To his parents' mortification, he started off in that garb for Rome, and whilst he was there he received the tonsure. A divine inspiration led him to place himself under the guidance of a hermit called Martin, who lived on a little island in the river Po. For three years they remained together, and then the recluse sent him to the abbey of Pomposa, near Ferrara, to learn monastic life in a large community. That monastery and that of St Severus at Ravenna were actually under the ultimate direction of the hermit, who decided the appointment of the superiors.

St Guy's outstanding merits were such that he rose to high office, becoming abbot first of St Severus and then of Pomposa upon the nomination of Martin, confirmed by the vote of the monks. His reputation drew so many (including his father and his brother) to join the community, that the number of monks was doubled, and it became necessary for St Guy to build another monastery to accommodate all. After a time he delegated to others the secular part of his office, and concentrated on the more purely spiritual side, especially on the direction of souls. At certain seasons of the year he was accustomed to withdraw to a cell about three miles from the abbey, where he lived in such unbroken abstinence and devotion that he seemed to be sustained by fasting and prayer. During Lent especially, he treated his body with a severity which tortures could hardly have surpassed, and yet he was extraordinarily tender to his monks and they were devoted to him. St Peter Damian, who at his request delivered lectures on the Sacred Scriptures in the abbey of Pomposa for two years, dedicated to St Guy his book *De perfectione monachorum*.

Towards the close of his life, St Guy retired into solitude, but he was summoned to Piacenza by the Emperor Henry III, who had come to Italy and wished to consult the abbot, of whose sanctity and wisdom he had heard much. The aged man obeyed very unwillingly, and took a tender farewell of his brethren, telling them that he would see their faces no more. He had arrived at Borgo San Donnino near Parma, when he was attacked by a sudden illness, from which he died on the third day. A contest took place for the custody of his body between Pomposa and Parma; the emperor settled the matter by having the relics taken to the church of St John the Evangelist at Speyer, which was afterwards renamed St Guido-Stift.

APRIL

1 : ST HUGH, BISHOP OF GRENOBLE (A.D. 1132)

ST HUGH was born at Châteauneuf, near Valence in the Dauphiné, in the year 1052. His father, Odilo, after being twice married, became a Carthusian, and died at the age of 100, receiving viaticum from his son in whose arms he passed away. After an education begun in Valence and completed with distinction in foreign centres of learning, Hugh was presented to a canonry in the cathedral of Valence though still a layman—such benefices at that period being often conferred on young students without orders. Very young, good-looking, and extremely bashful, he soon won all hearts by his courtesy and by the modesty which led him to conceal and underrate his talents and learning.

The bishop of Die, another Hugh, was so charmed by his namesake when he came to Valence that he insisted upon attaching him to his household. The prelate soon proved the young canon's worth by entrusting him with some difficult negotiations in the campaign then directed against simony; and in 1080 he took him to a synod at Avignon, called to consider, amongst other matters, the disorders which had crept into the vacant see of Grenoble. The council and the delegates from Grenoble severally and collectively appear to have looked on Canon Hugh as the one man who was capable of dealing with the disorders complained of; but though unanimously elected it was with the greatest reluctance that he consented to accept the office. The legate himself conferred on him holy orders up to the priesthood, and took him to Rome that he might receive consecration as bishop from the pope. Immediately after his consecration, St Hugh hurried off to his diocese, but he was appalled by the state of his flock.

For two years he laboured unremittingly. The excellent results he was obtaining were clear to all but to himself: he only saw his failures and blamed his own incompetence. Discouraged, he quietly withdrew to the Cluniac abbey of Chaise-Dieu, where he received the Benedictine habit. He did not remain there long, for Pope Gregory commanded him to resume his pastoral charge and return to Grenoble. It was to St Hugh of Grenoble that St Bruno and his companions addressed themselves when they decided to forsake the world, and it was he who granted to them the desert called the Chartreuse which gave its name to their order. The bishop became greatly attached to the monks: it was his delight to visit them in their solitude, joining in their exercises and performing the most menial offices. Sometimes he would linger so long in these congenial surroundings that St Bruno was constrained to remind him of his flock and of his episcopal duties.

A generous almsgiver, St Hugh in a time of famine sold a gold chalice as well as rings and precious stones from his church treasury; and rich men were stirred by his example to give liberally to feed the hungry and supply the needs of the diocese. Although at the end of life his soul was further purified by a lingering illness of a very painful character, Hugh never uttered a word of complaint, nor would he speak of what he endured. A short time before his death he lost his memory for everything but prayer, and would recite the psalter or the Lord's Prayer without intermission. St Hugh died on April 1, 1132, two months before attaining the age of eighty, having been a bishop for fifty-two years. Pope Innocent II canonized him two years later.

2 : ST FRANCIS OF PAOLA, FOUNDER OF THE MINIM FRIARS (A.D. 1507)

ST FRANCIS was born about the year 1416 at Paola, a small town in Calabria. His parents were humble, industrious people who made it their chief aim to love and to serve God. As they were still childless after several years of married life, they prayed earnestly for a son, and when at last a boy was born to them, they named him after St Francis of Assisi, whose intercession they had specially sought. In his thirteenth year he was placed in the Franciscan friary at San Marco, where he learnt to read and where he laid the foundation of the austere life which he ever afterwards led.

After spending a year there he accompanied his parents on a pilgrimage which included Assisi and Rome. Upon his return to Paola, with their consent, he retired first to a place about half a mile from the town, and afterwards to a more remote seclusion by the sea, where he occupied a cave. He was scarcely fifteen years old. Before he was twenty, he was joined by two other men. The neighbours built them three cells and a chapel in which they sang the divine praises and in which Mass was offered for them by a priest from the nearest church.

This date, 1452, is reckoned as that of the foundation of his order. Nearly seventeen years later a church and a monastery were built for them in the same place, with the sanction of the archbishop of Cosenza. So greatly were they beloved by the people that the whole countryside joined in the work of construction. When the house was finished, the saint set himself to establish regular discipline in the community, whilst never mitigating anything of the austerity he practised. Though his bed was no longer a rock, it was a plank or the bare ground, with a log or a stone by way of a pillow. Only in extreme old age would he allow himself a mat. Penance, charity and humility formed the basis of his rule: charity was the motto he chose; but humility was the virtue which he inculcated continually on his followers. In addition to the three usual monastic obligations he imposed upon them a fourth, which bound them to observe a perpetual Lent, with abstinence not only from flesh but also from eggs and anything made with milk.

The new order received the sanction of the Holy See in 1474. At that time the community was composed of uneducated men, with only one priest. They were then called Hermits of St Francis of Assisi, and it was not until 1492 that their name was changed to that of 'Minims', at the desire of the founder, who wished his followers to be reckoned as the least (*minimi*) in the household of God.

In 1481 Louis XI, King of France, was slowly dying. Realizing that he was steadily growing worse, he sent into Calabria to beg St Francis to come and heal him, making many promises to assist him and his order. Then, as his request was not acceded to, he appealed to Pope Sixtus IV, who told Francis to go. He at once set out; and King Louis sent the dauphin to escort him to Plessis-les-Tours. Louis, falling on his knees, besought Francis to heal him. The saint replied that the lives of kings are in the hands of God and have their appointed limits; prayer should be addressed to Him. Many interviews followed between the sovereign and his guest. Although Francis was an unlearned man, Philip de Commines, who often heard him, wrote that his words were so full of wisdom that all present were convinced that the Holy Spirit spoke through his lips. By his prayers and example he wrought a change of heart in the king, who died in resignation in his arms. Charles VIII honoured Francis as his father had done, and would do nothing in the affairs of his conscience or even in state matters without his advice. He built for his friars a monastery in the park of Plessias and another at Amboise, at the spot where they had first met. Moreover, in Rome, he built for the Minims the monastery of Santa Trinità del Monte on the Pincian Hill, to which none but Frenchmen might be admitted.

St Francis passed twenty-five years in France, and died there. On Palm Sunday 1507 he fell ill, and on Maundy Thursday assembled his brethren and exhorted them to the love of God, to charity and to a strict observance of all the duties of their rule. Then he received viaticum barefoot with a rope round his neck, according to the custom of his order. He died on the following day, Good Friday, being then ninety-one years of age. His canonization took place in 1519.

3 : ST RICHARD OF WYCHE, BISHOP OF CHICHESTER (A.D. 1253)

RICHARD DE WYCHE, or Richard of Burford, as he is sometimes called, was born *c.* 1197 at Wyche, the present Droitwich. His father was a landed proprietor or small squire, but both he and his wife died when their children were very young, leaving the estate in the charge of a negligent guardian who allowed it to go to rack and ruin. Richard, the younger son, although addicted to study from childhood, was of a much more virile temperament than his brother, and, as soon as he realized the state of affairs worked like a common labourer until he had retrieved the family fortunes. In a fit of gratitude, the elder, Robert, made over to him the title deeds, but when Richard discovered that a wealthy bride was being found for him and also that Robert was repenting of his generosity, he resigned to him both the land and the lady, departing almost penniless to take up a new life in the University of Oxford.

They had great masters at Oxford in those days. Grosseteste was lecturing in the Franciscan house of studies, and the Dominicans, who arrived in the city in 1221, at once gathered round them a host of brilliant men. From Oxford Richard went to Paris, but returned to his *alma mater* to take his M.A. degree, and then, some years later, proceeded to Bologna to study canon law in what was regarded as the chief law school of Europe. He stayed there seven years, receiving the degree of doctor and winning general esteem, but when one of his tutors offered to make him his heir and to give him his daughter in marriage, Richard, who felt himself called to a celibate life, made a courteous excuse and returned to Oxford. Almost immediately he was appointed chancellor of the university, and soon afterwards both St Edmund Rich, archbishop of Canterbury, and Grosseteste, bishop of Lincoln, invited him to become their chancellor. He accepted Edmund's offer and henceforth became his close companion and right-hand man, relieving him as much as he could of his heavy burdens.

St Edmund needed all his chancellor's help and sympathy in face of his well-nigh overwhelming difficulties, the greatest of which arose from Henry III's reprehensible and obstinate practice of either keeping benefices vacant that he might enjoy their revenues or else filling them with unworthy favourites of his own. When the archbishop, sick and despairing, retired to the Cistercian monastery of Pontigny, St Richard accompanied him and nursed him until his death. Unwilling to remain on without his master, the ex-chancellor then left Pontigny for the Dominican house of studies in Orleans, where he continued reading and lecturing for two years, and it was in the friars' church that he was ordained priest in 1243. Although he certainly contemplated eventually joining the Order of Preachers, he returned to England, for some reason unknown, to work as a parish priest at Deal, the prebendal stall of which had probably been conferred upon him by St Edmund, as it was in the gift of the archbishop. A man of his outstanding merits and qualifications could not long remain in obscurity, and he was shortly afterwards recalled to his former chancellorship by the new archbishop of Canterbury, Boniface of Savoy.

In 1244 Ralph Neville, bishop of Chichester, died, and Henry III, by putting pressure on the canons, obtained the election of Robert Passelewe. The archbishop refused to confirm the election and called a chapter of his suffragans who declared the election invalid, and chose Richard, the primate's nominee, to fill the vacant see. Upon hearing the news, King Henry was violently enraged: he kept in his own hands all the temporalities and forbade the admission of St Richard to any barony or secular possession attached to his see.

At last, however, both he and the king carried the case to Pope Innocent IV, who was presiding over the council of Lyons, and he decided in favour of St Richard, whom he consecrated himself on March 5, 1245. Landing once more in England the new bishop was met by the news that the king, far from giving up the temporalities, had forbidden anyone to lend St Richard money or even to give him houseroom. At Chichester he found the palace gates closed against him: it seemed as though he would have to wander about his diocese a homeless outcast. However, a good priest, Simon of Tarring, opened his house to him, and from this modest centre St Richard worked for two years like a missionary bishop, visiting fisherfolk and downsmen, travelling about mainly on foot, and succeeding under great difficulties in holding synods—as we learn from the Constitutions of St Richard, a body of statutes drawn up at this period and dealing with the various abuses which had come to his notice.

Only when the pope threatened to excommunicate him would Henry acknowledge the bishop and yield up the temporalities, but even then much of the money which should have been restored to him remained unpaid until after his death. Still, St Richard's position was now totally changed: he was enthroned and could henceforth dispense some of that general hospitality combined with liberal almsgiving which was expected of a medieval prelate.

In the course of his eight years' episcopate he won the affection of his people to a remarkable extent, but though fatherly and tender he could be very stern when he discovered avarice, heresy or immorality amongst his clergy. To the strenuous duties of his office, the pope added that of preaching a new crusade against the Saracens, and it was upon reaching Dover after conducting a strenuous campaign along the coast that St Richard was seized with a fever which he knew would prove fatal. He died at the house for poor priests and pilgrims called the Maison-Dieu, surrounded on his death-bed by devoted friends. He was then in his fifty-fifth year, and he was canonized only nine years later.

4 : ST ISIDORE, BISHOP OF SEVILLE, DOCTOR OF THE CHURCH (A.D. 636)

ISIDORE'S father, Severian, who came from Cartagena, was probably of Roman origin, but he was closely connected with the Visigothic kings. Two of St Isidore's brothers, Leander, who was greatly his senior, and Fulgentius, became, like himself, saints as well as bishops, and of his sisters one was St Florentina, abbess of many convents. Isidore's education was entrusted to his brother Leander, who seems to have been a somewhat severe master. Nonetheless, the system had good results, for Isidore became the most learned man of his age and, what is even more remarkable in the circumstances, an ardent educationist. Although it is almost certain that he never was a monk, he had a great love for the religious orders, and at their request drew up a code of rules for them which bore his name and was generally followed throughout Spain.

It seems probable that Isidore assisted St Leander in ruling the diocese of Seville, and then succeeded to it after his brother's death. During the thirty-seven years of his episcopate, which extended through the reigns of six kings, he completed the work begun by St Leander of converting the Visigoths from Arianism to Catholicism. He also continued his brother's practice of settling the discipline of the Spanish church in councils, the arrangement and organization of which were largely due to Leander and Isidore.

St Isidore presided over the second Council of Seville in 619 and again over the fourth Council of Toledo in 633, where he was given precedence over the archbishop of Toledo on the ground of his exceptional merit as the greatest teacher in Spain. Many of the enactments of the council emanated from St Isidore himself, notably the decree that a seminary or cathedral school should be established in every diocese. The aged prelate's educational scheme was extraordinarily wide and progressive: far from desiring a mere counterpart of the conventional classical curriculum, his system embraced every known branch of knowledge. The liberal arts, medicine, and law were to be taught as well as Hebrew and Greek; and Aristotle was studied in the Spanish schools long before he was reintroduced by the Arabs. His crowning contribution to education was the compilation of a sort of encyclopedia, called the Etymologies or Origins, which gathered into compact form all the knowledge of his age.

St Isidore was a voluminous writer, his earlier works including a dictionary of synonyms, a treatise on astronomy and physical geography, a summary of the principal events of the world from the creation, a biography of illustrious men, a book of Old and New Testament worthies, his rules for monks, extensive theological and ecclesiastical works, and the history of the Goths, Vandals and Suevi. Another service which St Isidore rendered to the church in Spain was the completion of the Mozarabic missal and breviary which St Leander had begun to adapt for the use of the Goths from the earlier Spanish liturgy.

When he felt that his end was drawing near, he invited two bishops to come to see him. In their company he went to the church where one of them covered him with sackcloth, while the other put ashes upon his head. Thus clad in the habit of penance, he raised his hands towards Heaven, praying earnestly and aloud for the forgiveness of his sins. Afterwards he received viaticum, commended himself to the prayers of those present, forgave his debtors, exhorted the people to charity, and distributed to the poor the rest of his possessions. He then returned to his house where shortly afterwards he peacefully departed this life.

St Isidore was declared a doctor of the Church in 1722.

5 : ST VINCENT FERRER, (A.D. 1419)

THE descendant of an Englishman or a Scotsman settled in Spain, St Vincent Ferrer was born at Valencia, probably in the year 1350. His parents instilled into him an intense devotion to our Lord and His blessed Mother and a great love for the poor.

He entered the Dominican priory of Valencia, where he received the habit in 1367, and before he was twenty-one he was appointed reader in philosophy at Lerida, the most famous university in Catalonia. Whilst still occupying that chair he published two treatises, both of which were considered of great merit. At Barcelona, whither he was afterwards transferred, he was set to preach, although he was still only a deacon. The city was suffering from famine; corn which had been despatched by sea had not arrived and the people were nearly desperate. St Vincent, in the course of a sermon in the open air, foretold that the ships would come in that day before nightfall. His prior censured him severely for making predictions, but the ships duly appeared—to the joy of the people who rushed to the priory to acclaim the prophet. His superiors, however, deemed it wise to transfer him to Toulouse, where he remained for a year. He was then recalled to his own country, and his lectures and sermons met with extraordinary success.

He soon became famous as a preacher, whose eloquence roused to penitence and fervour multitudes of careless Catholics, besides converting to the Christian faith a number of Jews, notably the Rabbi Paul of Burgos, who died bishop of Cartagena in 1435.

This was the time of the 'great schism', when rival popes were reigning at Rome and Avignon and when even great saints were divided in their allegiance. That terrible scandal had begun in 1378 when, upon the death of Gregory XI, sixteen of the twenty-three cardinals had hastily elected Urban VI in deference to the popular cry for an Italian pope. Under the plea that they had been terrorized, they then, with the other cardinals, held a conclave at which they elected Cardinal Robert of Geneva, a Frenchman. He took the name of Clement VII and ruled at Avignon, whilst Urban reigned in Rome. St Vincent Ferrer, who had been amongst those who recognized Clement, naturally upon his death accepted as pope his successor, Peter de Luna or Benedict XIII as he was called, who summoned the Dominican to his side.

St Vincent duly arrived in Avignon where he had great favour shown him, including the offer of a bishopric, which he refused; but he found his position very difficult. He soon realized that Benedict by his obstinacy was hindering all efforts that were being made towards unity. In vain did Vincent urge him to come to some sort of understanding with his rival in Rome. Even when a council of theologians in Paris declared against his claim, the Avignon pontiff would not stir an inch. The strain upon the saint as his confessor and adviser was so great that he fell ill. Upon his recovery he with great difficulty obtained permission to leave the court and devote himself to missionary work. He set forth from Avignon in 1399 and preached to enormous congregations in Carpetras, Arles, Aix, Marseilles.

Between 1401 and 1403 the saint was preaching in the Dauphiné, in Savoy and in the Alpine valleys: he then went on to Lucerne, Lausanne, Tarentaise, Grenoble and Turin. Everywhere crowds flocked to hear him; everywhere innumerable conversions and remarkable miracles were reported. In 1405 St Vincent was in Genoa, from whence he reached a port from which he could sail for Flanders. Amongst other reforms he induced the Ligurian ladies to modify their fantastic head-dress—'the greatest of all his marvellous deeds', as one of his biographers avers. In the Netherlands he wrought so many miracles that an hour was set apart every day for the healing of the sick. In 1407 he returned to Spain.

Grenada was then under Moorish rule, but Vincent preached there, with the result that 8000 Moors are said to have asked to be baptized. In Seville and Cordova the missions had to be conducted in the open air, because no church could accommodate the congregations. At Valencia, which he revisited after fifteen years, he preached, worked many miracles, and healed the dissensions which were rending the town.

St Vincent had never ceased being deeply concerned at the disunity within the Church, especially since after 1409 there had been no less than three claimants to the papacy, to the great scandal of Christendom. The Council of Constance in 1414 proceeded to depose one of them, John XXIII, and to demand the resignation of the other two with a view to a new election. Gregory XII expressed his willingness, but Benedict XIII still held out. St Vincent went to Perpignan to entreat him to abdicate, but in vain. Thereupon, being asked by King Ferdinand of Castile and Aragon to give his own judgement in the matter, the saint declared that because Benedict was hindering the union which was vital to the Church, the faithful were justified in withdrawing their allegiance. Ferdinand acted accordingly, and at length Benedict, Peter de Luna, found himself deposed. 'But for you', wrote Gerson to St Vincent, 'this union could never have been achieved.'

The last three years of the saint's life were spent in France. Brittany and Normandy were the scene of the last labours of this 'legate from the side of Christ'. When, early in 1419, he returned to Vannes after a course of sermons in Nantes, it was clear that he was dying, and on the Wednesday in Passion Week 1419 he passed away, being then in his seventieth year. His death was greeted by an outburst of popular veneration, and in 1455 St Vincent Ferrer was canonized.

6 : ST WILLIAM OF ESKILSOË, ABBOT (A.D. 1203)

ON this day the Roman martyrology mentions the death in Denmark of St William, 'famous for his life and miracles'. He was born about 1125, at Saint-Germain, Crépy-en-Valois, and became a canon of the collegiate church of St Genevieve in Paris. In 1148 Suger, abbot of Saint-Denis, carrying out the wishes of the pope, Bd Eugenius III, established canons regular in this church, and William was one of those who accepted a more austere and regular life with enthusiasm. In time his reputation for canonical discipline and holiness of life reached so far as Denmark, for, about 1170, he received a visit from a young Dane, Saxo Grammaticus, who was to become famous as an historian. Saxo had been sent by the bishop of Roskilde, Absalom or Axel, to invite William to undertake the restoration of discipline in the monastic houses of his diocese. William agreed, and began his labours with the canons regular at Eskilsoë on the Ise Fiord, where his delicate task was successfully carried out, but only after a hard struggle.

Having established the monastery of St Thomas on Seeland, William undertook to reform other religious houses, and in all his very considerable difficulties he had the support of Axel, who had become archbishop of Lund. During his later years he left Denmark for a time, having embroiled himself in some semi- political affairs; but he returned to his abbey, where he died peacefully on April 6, 1203.

St William of Eskilsoë was canonized in 1224.

7 : ST JOHN BAPTIST DE LA SALLE, FOUNDER OF THE BROTHERS OF THE CHRISTIAN SCHOOLS (A.D. 1719)

THE founder of the Institute of the Brothers of the Christian Schools was born at Rheims on April 30, 1651. His parents were both of noble family. From the instructions of a devout mother, the boy, John Baptist, early gave evidence of such piety that he was designated for the priesthood. He received the tonsure when he was only eleven, and became a member of the cathedral chapter of Rheims at the age of sixteen; in 1670 he entered the seminary of St Sulpice in Paris, being ordained priest in 1678. A young man of striking appearance, well connected, refined and scholarly, he seemed assured of a life of dignified ease or of high preferment in the Church.

But in 1679 he met a layman, Adrian Nyel, who had come to Rheims with the idea of opening a school for poor boys. Canon de la Salle gave him every encouragement, and, somewhat prematurely, two schools were started. Gradually the young canon became more and more drawn into the work and grew interested in the seven masters who taught in these schools. He rented a house for them, fed them from his own table, and tried to instil into them the high educational ideals which were gradually taking shape in his own mind. In 1681 he decided to invite them to live in his own home that he might have them under his constant supervision. The result must have been a great disappointment. Not only did two of his brothers indignantly leave his house but five of the schoolmasters soon took their departure, unable or unwilling to submit to a discipline for which they had never bargained. The reformer waited, and his patience was rewarded. Other men presented themselves, and these formed the nucleus of what was to prove a new congregation. To house them the saint gave up his paternal home, and moved with them to more suitable premises in the Rue Neuve. As the movement became known, requests began to come in from outside for schoolmasters trained on the new method, and de la Salle found his time fully engrossed. Partly for that reason, and partly because he realized the contrast his disciples drew between his assured official income and their own uncertain position, he decided to give up his canonry.

Four schools were soon opened, but de la Salle's great problem at this stage was that of training teachers. Eventually he called a conference of twelve of his men, and it was decided to make provisional regulations, with a vow of obedience yearly renewable until vocations became certain. At the same time a name was decided upon for members of the community. They were to be called the Brothers of the Christian Schools.

Hitherto recruits had been full-grown men, but now applications began to be received from boys between the ages of fifteen and twenty. De la Salle, in 1685, accordingly decided to set up a junior novitiate. He lodged the youths in an adjoining house, gave them a simple rule of life, and entrusted their training to a wise brother, whilst retaining supervision of them himself. But soon there appeared another class of candidate who also, like the boys, could not well be refused and who likewise required to be dealt with apart. These were young men who were sent by their parish priests to the saint with a request that he would train them as schoolmasters, and send them back to teach in their own villages. He accepted them, found them a domicile, undertook their training, and thus founded the first training-college for teachers, at Rheims in 1687; others followed, at Paris (1699) and at Saint-Denis (1709).

All this time the work of teaching poor boys had been steadily going on, although hitherto it had been restricted to Rheims. In 1688 the saint, at the request of the curé of St Sulpice in Paris, took over a school in that parish. The brothers were so successful that a second school was opened in the same district. The control of these Paris foundations was entrusted to

Brother L'Heureux, a gifted and capable man whom de la Salle designed to be his successor, and whom he was about to present for ordination. It had been his intention to have priests in his institution to take charge of each house, but Brother L'Heureux's unexpected death made him doubt whether his design had been according to God's will. After much prayer it was borne in upon him that if his order was to confine itself strictly to the work of teaching, for which it had been founded, and to remain free from 'caste' distinctions the brothers must continue to be laymen. He therefore laid down the statute that no Brother of the Christian Schools should ever be a priest, and that no priest should ever become a member of the order.

About 1695, de la Salle drew up the first draft of the matured rule, with provision for the taking of life vows. He also wrote his manual of the *Conduct of Schools* which sets forth the system of education to be carried out—a system which revolutionized elementary education and is successfully pursued at the present day. It replaced the old method of individual instruction by class teaching and the 'simultaneous method', it insisted on silence while the lessons were being given, and it taught in French and through French—not through Latin.

As early as 1700 Brother Drolin had been sent to found a school in Rome, and in France schools were started at Avignon, at Calais, in Languedoc, in Provence, at Rouen, and at Dijon. In 1705 the novitiate was transferred to St Yon in Rouen. There a boarding- school was opened, and an establishment for troublesome boys, which afterwards developed into a reformatory-school. In 1717 the founder decided finally to resign; from that moment he would give no orders, and lived like the humblest of the brothers. He taught novices and boarders, for whom he wrote several books, including a method of mental prayer.

In Lent, 1719, St John Baptist suffered a good deal from asthma and rheumatism, but would give up none of his habitual austerities. Then he met with an accident, and gradually grew weaker. He passed away on Good Friday, April 7, 1719, in the sixty-eighth year of his age. The Church has shown her appreciation of the character of this man, a thinker and initiator of the first importance in the history of education, by canonizing him in 1900, and in 1950 Pope Pius XII declared him the heavenly patron of all school-teachers.

8 : ST JULIA BILLIART, VIRGIN, CO-FOUNDRESS OF THE INSTITUTE OF NOTRE DAME OF NAMUR (A.D. 1816)

MARY ROSE JULIA BILLIART came of a family of fairly well-to-do peasant farmers, who also owned a little shop at Cuvilly in Picardy, where she was born in 1751. As the result of shock caused by the firing of a gun through a window at her father beside whom she was sitting, there came upon her a mysterious illness, attended with great pain, which gradually deprived her of the use of her limbs. Thus reduced to the condition of an invalid, she lived a life of even closer union with God.

In 1790, when the curé of Cuvilly was superseded by a constitutional priest who had taken the oath prescribed by the revolutionary authorities, it was mainly Julia's influence which induced the people to boycott the intruder. For that reason and because she was known to have helped to find hiding-places for fugitive priests, she was taken to Compiègne, where she was hunted from one lodging to another.

In the first lull which followed the end of the Reign of Terror, an old friend rescued Julia and brought her to Amiens to the house of Viscount Blin de Bourdon. In that hospitable home the invalid recovered and there, met Frances Blin de Bourdon, Viscountess de Gézaincourt, who was henceforth to be her close friend and her associate in all her work. In the sickroom, where the Holy Sacrifice was daily offered, gathered a little party of women who were inspired by the invalid and spent their time and money in good works; but a recrudescence of persecution scattered them, and forced Julia and her new friend to retire to a house belonging to the Doria family at Bettencourt.

During their stay at Bettencourt, they were several times visited by Father Joseph Varin, who was immensely struck by the personality and capabilities of Julia. He was convinced that God intended her to do great things. Under his direction, as soon as they could return to Amiens, were laid the foundations of the Institute of Notre Dame which was to devote itself primarily to the spiritual care of poor children, but also to the Christian education of girls of all classes and to the training of religious teachers. The rules were in some respects a great departure from those of existing orders, notably in the abolition of the distinction between choir and lay sisters.

In 1804, when the Fathers of the Faith held a great mission in Amiens, they entrusted the teaching of the women to the Sisters of Notre Dame. The close of that mission was followed by an event that made a great sensation. Father Enfantin asked Julia to join him in a novena for an unknown intention. On the fifth day—the feast of the Sacred Heart—he approached the invalid of twenty-two years' standing and said to her, 'Mother, if you have any faith, take one step in honour of the Sacred Heart of Jesus'. She at once got up, and realized that she was completely cured.

Her activity now fully restored, Mother Julia was able not only to consolidate and extend the new institute, but also to give her personal assistance to the missions which were conducted by the Fathers of the Faith in other towns, until their activities in that direction were checked by the action of the government. The educational work of the sisters continued to increase rapidly; convents were opened by them at Namur, Ghent and Tournai, and everything seemed to augur well for their future when a disastrous set-back was experienced which threatened the very existence of the new community. Father Varin had been obliged to leave Amiens, and the post of confessor to the Sisters of Notre Dame fell to a capable but most injudicious, self-opinionated young priest who managed for a time to estrange her from the Bishop of Amiens, who virtually demanded her withdrawal from his diocese. Accompanied by nearly all the sisters she retired to the house at Namur, where the bishop of that city received her warmly. Before long St Julia was fully vindicated and she was invited to return to Amiens; but it was found impracticable to restart the work there, so Namur became permanently the mother-house.

In 1816 it became evident to herself and to her community that she was failing fast. On April 8, while she was gently repeating the *Magnificat*, the foundress of the Institute of Notre Dame of Namur passed to her reward. She was canonized in 1969.

9 : ST WALDETRUDIS, OR WAUDRU, WIDOW (c. A.D. 688)

ST WALDETRUDIS, called in French Waltrude or Waudru, belonged to a family of remarkable holiness. Her parents were St Walbert and St Bertilia, her sister St Aldegundis of Maubeuge, her husband St Vincent Madelgar, and their four children St Landericus, St Dentelinus, St Aldetrudis and St Madelberta, the last two named both both being abbess of Maubeuge. She married a young nobleman called Madelgar, with whom she led a happy life of devotion and good works. Some time after the birth of the last of their children, Madelgar withdrew into the abbey of Haumont which he had founded, taking the name of Vincent.

Waldetrudis remained in the world two years longer than her husband and then she also withdrew, retiring into a very humble little house, built in accordance with her instructions, where she lived in poverty and simplicity. Her sister repeatedly invited her to join her at Maubeuge, but she wished for greater austerity than she could have at the abbey. Her solitude was so often broken in upon by those who sought her advice and direction that she eventually founded a convent. This place, which afterwards became known as Chateaulieu (Castri locus in Monte), was in the centre of what is now the town of Mons. Throughout her life St Waldetrudis was greatly given to works of mercy, and she became celebrated for the miracles of healing which were wrought through her both before and after her death.

10 : ST FULBERT, BISHOP OF CHARTRES (A.D. 1029)

ST FULBERT was of humble extraction, but we know little of his early years beyond the fact that he was born in Italy and spent his boyhood there. He was later a student in Rheims and must have been one of its most distinguished scholars, for when the celebrated Gerbert, who taught him mathematics and philosophy, was raised to the papacy under the title of Silvester II, he summoned Fulbert to his side. When another pope succeeded, Fulbert returned to France, where Bishop Odo of Chartres bestowed upon him a canonry and appointed him chancellor. Moreover, the cathedral schools of Chartres were placed under his care, and he soon made them the greatest educational centre in France, attracting pupils from Germany, Italy and England. Upon the death of Bishop Roger, Fulbert was chosen to succeed him in the see of Chartres.

Fulbert's influence was now immense, for besides retaining direction of the school he became the recognized counsellor of the spiritual and temporal leaders of France. Yet external affairs were never allowed to interfere with the duty he owed to his diocese: he preached regularly from his cathedral pulpit and exerted himself to spread instruction in the territories under his jurisdiction. When, soon after his elevation, the cathedral of Chartres was burnt down, he at once set about rebuilding it with great magnificence, though this is not the cathedral which is now one of the glories of Christendom; people of all classes came to his assistance, including Canute,

King of England, who contributed a large sum. St Fulbert had a great devotion to our Lady, in whose honour he composed several hymns, and when the beautiful new cathedral was opened he caused the recently introduced feast of her birthday to be celebrated there with great solemnity, as well as to be observed throughout the diocese.

Like most of the more eminent churchmen of his century he was an outspoken opponent of simony and of bestowing ecclesiastical endowments upon laymen. After an episcopate of nearly twenty-two years, he died on April 10, 1029.

11 : ST STANISLAUS, BISHOP OF CRACOW, MARTYR (A.D. 1079)

STANISLAUS SZCZEPANOWSKI was born on July 26, 1030, at Szczepanow. He came of noble parents, who had been childless for many years until this son was vouchsafed to them in answer to prayer. They devoted him from his birth to the service of God, and encouraged in every way the piety which he evinced from early childhood. He was educated at Gnesen and afterwards he was ordained priest by Lampert Zula, bishop of Cracow, who gave him a canonry in the cathedral and subsequently appointed him his preacher and archdeacon. The eloquence of the young priest and his saintly example brought about a great reformation of morals amongst his penitents—clergy as well as laity flocking to him from all quarters for spiritual advice. Bishop Lampert wished to resign the episcopal office in his favour, but Stanislaus refused to consider the suggestion. However, upon Lampert's death, he could not resist the will of the people seconded by an order from Pope Alexander II, and he was consecrated bishop in 1072.

Poland at that epoch was ruled by Boleslaus II, a prince whose finer qualities were completely eclipsed by his unbridled lust and savage cruelty. Stanislaus alone ventured to beard the tyrant and to remonstrate with him at the scandal his conduct was causing. At first the king endeavoured to vindicate his behaviour, but when pressed more closely he made some show of repentance. The good effects of the admonition, however, soon wore off: Boleslaus relapsed into his evil ways. There were acts of rapacity and political injustice which brought him into conflict with the bishop and at length he perpetrated an outrage which caused general indignation. A certain nobleman had a wife who was very beautiful. Upon this lady Boleslaus cast lustful eyes, and when she repelled his advances he caused her to be carried off by force and lodged in his palace. The Polish nobles called upon the archbishop of Gnesen and the court prelates to expostulate with the monarch. Fear of offending the king closed their lips, and the people openly accused them of conniving at the crime. St Stanislaus, when appealed to, had no such hesitation, he went again to Boleslaus and rebuked him for his sin. He closed his exhortation by reminding the prince that if he persisted in his evil courses he would bring upon himself the censure of the Church.

Finding all remonstrance useless, Stanislaus launched against him a formal sentence of excommunication. The tyrant professed to disregard the ban, but when he entered the cathedral of Cracow he found that the services were at once suspended by order of the bishop. Furious with rage, he pursued the saint to the little chapel of St Michael outside the city, where he was celebrating Mass, and ordered some of his guards to enter and slay him. The men, however, returned, saying that they could not kill the saint as he was surrounded by a heavenly light. Upbraiding them for cowardice, the king himself entered the building and dispatched the bishop with his own hand. The guards then cut the body into pieces and scattered them abroad to be devoured by beasts of prey: the sacred relics were rescued three days later by the cathedral canons and privately buried at the door of the chapel in which Stanislaus had been slain.

There seems no doubt that there were some political considerations behind the murder of St Stanislaus, though the whole business is very uncertain and obscure. It is not true that the action of Boleslaus led to an immediate rising of the people which drove him from Poland; but it certainly hastened his fall from power. Pope St Gregory VII laid the country under an interdict, and nearly two centuries later, in 1253, St Stanislaus was canonized by Pope Innocent IV.

12 : ST ALFERIUS, ABBOT (A.D. 1050)

ALFERIUS belonged to the Pappacarboni family which was descended from the ancient Lombard princes. Sent by Gisulf, duke of Salerno, as ambassador to the French court, he fell dangerously ill, and vowed that if he should regain his health he would embrace the religious life. Upon his recovery he entered the abbey of Cluny, then under the rule of St Odilo, but was recalled by the duke of Salerno, who wished him to reform the monasteries in the principality.

The task appeared beyond his power, and he retired about the year 1011 to a lonely spot, picturesquely situated in the mountainous region about three miles north-west of Salerno, where he was soon joined by disciples. Of these he would only accept twelve—at any rate at first—but they formed the nucleus around which gradually grew the abbey of La Cava which afterwards attained to great celebrity. Alferius is said to have lived to the age of 120 and to have died on Maundy Thursday, alone in his cell, after he had celebrated Mass and washed the feet of his brethren. Only a very few years after his death there were, in south Italy and Sicily, over 30 abbeys and churches dependent upon La Cava and 3000 monks. Amongst his disciples had been Desiderius, who subsequently became Pope Victor III and a *beatus*.

13 : ST HERMENEGILD, MARTYR (A.D. 585)

HERMENEGILD and his brother Reccared were the two sons of the Visigothic king of Spain, Leovigild, by his first wife Theodosia. They were educated by their father in the Arian heresy, but Hermenegild married a zealous Catholic, Indegundis or Ingunda, daughter of Sigebert, king of Austrasia; his conversion to the true faith was due as much to her example and prayers as to the teaching of St Leander, archbishop of Seville. Leovigild was furious when he heard of his son's open profession of the faith, and called upon him to resign all his dignities and possessions. This Hermenegild refused to do.

He raised the standard of revolt and, as the Arians were all-powerful in Visigothic Spain, he sent St Leander to Constantinople to obtain support and assistance. Disappointed in that quarter, Hermenegild implored the help of the Roman generals who, with a small army, still ruled the strip of Spanish land along the Mediterranean coast which remained in the possession of the Empire. They took his wife and infant son as hostages and made promises which they failed to fulfil. For over a year Hermenegild was besieged in Seville by his father's troops, and when he could hold out no longer he fled to the Roman camp—only to be warned that those he had reckoned upon as his friends had been bribed by Leovigild to betray him. Despairing of all human aid, he entered a church and sought refuge at the altar. Leovigild did not venture to violate the sanctuary, but permitted his younger son Reccared, who was still an Arian, to go to his brother with an offer of forgiveness if he would submit and ask for pardon. Hermenegild took his father at his word and a reconciliation took place, the genuineness of which there seems no reason to doubt. Leovigild appears to have restored his elder son to some measure of his former dignities; but the king's second wife, Gosvinda, soon succeeded in estranging him once more from the unfortunate prince, and Hermenegild was imprisoned at Tarragona. He was no longer accused of treason but of heresy, his liberty being offered to him at the price of recantation. With fervent prayer he asked God to give him fortitude in his combat for the truth, adding voluntary mortifications to his enforced sufferings and clothing himself in sackcloth.

At Easter his father sent him an Arian bishop, offering to restore him to favour if he would receive communion from the prelate. Upon learning that Hermenegild had absolutely refused, Leovigild fell into one of the paroxysms of rage to which he was subject, and despatched soldiers to the prison with orders to put the young prince to death. They found him fully prepared and quite resigned to his fate. He was killed instantaneously by one blow from an axe. St Gregory the Great attributes to the merits of St Hermenegild the conversion of his brother Reccared and of the whole of Visigothic Spain.

14 : ST BÉNEZET, (A.D. 1184)

THE boyhood of Bénezet, or Little Benedict the Bridge Builder, was spent in minding his mother's sheep either in Savoy or in the Ardenne. He was a pious lad, thoughtful beyond his years, and seems to have reflected much on the perils encountered by people who sought to cross the Rhône.

One day, during an eclipse of the sun, he heard a voice which addressed him three times out of the darkness, bidding him go to Avignon and build a bridge over the river which was extremely rapid there. The construction and the repair of bridges was regarded in the middle ages as a work of mercy, for which rich men were often urged to make provision in their wills; but Bénezet was only an ignorant, undersized youth, without experience, influence or money. Nevertheless he did not hesitate to obey the call. As may be imagined, the Bishop of Avignon, to whom he addressed himself upon his arrival in the city, was not disposed at first to take him seriously, but the lad was able by miracles to prove his mission to the good bishop's satisfaction; and with his approval the work of building a stone bridge over the Rhône was begun in A.D. 1177. For seven years little Benedict directed the operations, and when he died in 1184 the main difficulties of the enterprise had been overcome.

15 : ST HUNNA, MATRON (*C*. A.D. 679)

ST HUNNA, or Huva, came of the reigning ducal family of Alsace and was married to a nobleman, Huno of Hunnaweyer, a village in the diocese of Strasbourg. Because she undertook to do the washing for her needy neighbours, she was nicknamed by her contemporaries 'The Holy Washerwoman'. Her family seems to have been influenced by St Deodatus (Dié), Bishop of Nevers, for St Hunna's son, who was his namesake, was baptized by him and subsequently entered the monastery which he founded at Ebersheim. St Hunna died in 679 and was canonized in 1520 by Leo X at the instance of Duke Ulric of Würtemberg.

16 : ST BERNADETTE, VIRGIN (A.D. 1879)

SHE was born on January 7, 1844, the oldest of a family of six, and though christened Marie Bernarde, was known to the family and neighbours by the pet name of Bernadette. The father was by trade a miller, and in 1844 he rented a mill of his own, but thrift and efficiency were not the distinguishing virtues of either Francis Soubirous or his wife, Louise Casterot, then still in her teens and eighteen years younger than her husband. Bernadette was always a most delicate girl, afflicted with asthma and other ailments, and the fact that she was one of the sufferers in the cholera epidemic of 1854 cannot have helped to make her more robust. Meanwhile the family was gradually sinking into dire poverty.

Beginning on 11 February 1858 Bernadette had eighteen visions at the grotto of Massabielle, beside the River Gave. By 4 March the crowds accompanying her to the sight of the apparitions had grown to 200,000 people. The Lady of the visions instructed Bernadette to have a chapel built on the spot, to which pilgrims might come in procession, and to wash in, and drink from, the spring which had gushed out at the foot of the rock when the young saint dug. On 25 March the vision proclaimed, using the local patois, 'I am the Immaculate Conception'. The last time she appeared was on 16 July, the Feast of Our Lady of Mount Carmel.

At the date of the first apparition (February 11, 1858) the family were living in the dark airless basement of a dilapidated building in the rue des Petits Fossés. The child herself, though fourteen years of age, had not yet made her first communion and was regarded as a very dull pupil, but she was notably good, obedient and kind to her younger brothers and sisters, in spite of the fact that she was continually ailing.

The apparitions and the popular excitement which accompanied them did eventually have some effect in relieving the destitution of the Soubirous family, for people interested themselves to find work for the father; but for Bernadette, apart from the spiritual consolation of these visions, which had come to an end in less than a couple of months, they left a heavy load of embarrassment from the ceaseless and indiscreet questionings which allowed her no peace. As a measure of protection, she was after a while taken to reside with the nuns at the hospice (1861–6), but even there there were often visitors who could not be denied.

In 1864 she offered herself, under advice, to the sisters of Notre-Dame de Nevers. Attacks of illness postponed her departure from Lourdes, but in 1866 she was allowed to join the novitiate in the mother-house of the order. Separation from her family and from the grotto cost her much, but with her fellow-novices at Nevers she was gay, while remaining still the humble and patient child she had always been. Her ill-health continued, so that within four months of her arrival she received the last sacraments and by dispensation was permitted to take her first vows. She recovered, however, and had strength enough to act as infirmarian and afterwards as sacristan, but the asthma from which she suffered never lost its hold, and before the end came she suffered grievously from further complications.

Bernadette Soubirous died on April 16, 1879; she was thirty-five years old. In 1933 she was canonized, and she now appears in the Church's official records as St Mary Bernarda.

17 : ST STEPHEN HARDING, ABBOT OF CÎTEAUX, CO-FOUNDER OF THE CISTERCIAN ORDER (A.D. 1134)

ST STEPHEN HARDING, the Englishman who helped to found the monastery of Cîteaux, and who actually framed the Cistercian constitution, was educated at the abbey of Sherborne in Dorsetshire. Nothing is known of his parentage or family. He seems to have left the abbey without any very definite idea of becoming a monk, and went first to Scotland and then to Paris, probably to study and to see something of the world.

With a friend, he made a journey to Rome. On the way back, as they passed through a forest in Burgundy, they came upon a collection of rough huts, inhabited by monks who were living a life of poverty, their time being divided between prayer and the hard manual work which provided them with vegetables. Their self-abnegation and austerity made an immediate appeal to Stephen, and, leaving his friend to continue his journey alone, he remained at Molesmes and threw in his lot with the monks. In St Robert the abbot and St Alberic the prior he found kindred spirits, and all rejoiced in their holy fellowship of prayer and mortification as well as in a poverty which sometimes amounted to absolute want. After some years, however it seemed to Stephen and to some of the others that the spirit of the place had departed; and in 1098 Abbot Robert accompanied by Alberic, Stephen and four others, went to Lyons and, in an interview with Archbishop Hugh, who was also the papal legate in France, they applied for permission to leave Molesmes. He at once appreciated their aims and gave them the authorization in a document the terms of which have been preserved. St Robert released the brethren from their vows of obedience to him, and he and twenty of the monks left Molesmes.

They found their way to Cîteaux, then a gloomy place in the heart of the forest, far removed from any human habitation. Rainald, the lord of Beune, willingly gave them the site, and Odo, Duke of Burgundy, who had heard of them from Archbishop Hugh, sent some workmen to assist them in building their monastery.

On March 21, 1098, the new abbey was inaugurated, with Robert as abbot, Alberic as prior, and Stephen as sub-prior, but the following year the monks of Molesmes, finding that they fared very badly without their former abbot, petitioned Rome that Robert should be sent back to them. He had never really been a leader in the migration to Cîteaux and he seems to have been glad to return to Molesmes.

Alberic now became abbot of Cîteaux with Stephen as prior, but in 1109 Bd Alberic died and Stephen was elected abbot in his place. His first act was to decree that magnates should no longer be permitted to hold their courts at Cîteaux—thus apparently cutting off the abbey's greatest earthly support and alienating for a time Odo's successor, Duke Hugh. His second measure was even more severe. He forbade the use of anything costly in the service of God: there must be nothing which tended to pomp. Chalices were to be silver gilt, chasubles of good common stuff, and so forth. But the immediate result of these regulations was to discourage visitors and to dry up still further the supply of novices—already a source of anxiety.

Their numbers diminished. A mysterious disease appeared amongst them which carried off one monk after another, until even Stephen's stout heart quailed before the prospect of the future, and he began to wonder if he were really doing the will of God. Certainly no one could have foreseen how dramatically that answer would come.

At the monastery gates appeared one day a troop of thirty men, who announced to the astonished porter that they had come to crave admittance and to offer themselves to the religious life. They were all of noble lineage, and they had as their leader and spokesman a young man whose name was Bernard. He had been moved to give up the world, but being of keen affections he had no mind to enter the way of perfection himself and leave his friends outside. He had gained over his brothers, his uncle, and a number of his acquaintances. From henceforth there was no lack of novices and no fear of starvation, for the new foundation was drawing upon itself the attention and admiration of France.

Increasing numbers soon necessitated a daughter house, and a foundation was made at Pontigny. Two other houses, Morimond and then Clairvaux, followed, and to the general surprise Stephen appointed Bernard abbot of Clairvaux, although he was only twenty-four years of age. To bind these monasteries to Cîteaux, Stephen instituted an annual general chapter which the heads of the affiliated abbeys were bound to attend. In 1119, when nine abbeys had sprung from Cîteaux and Clairvaux, St Stephen drew up a body of statutes, the Charter of Charity, which both organized the Cistercians as an order and regulated their mode of life.

It was only when he was old and very nearly blind that St Stephen laid down his pastoral staff to prepare for the end.

18 : ST GALDINUS, ARCHBISHOP OF MILAN AND CARDINAL (A.D. 1176)

A MEMBER of the famous Della Scala family, Galdinus occupied the posts of chancellor and archdeacon under two archbishops of Milan, winning the confidence of clergy and people by the manner in which he shouldered his responsibilities at a very difficult epoch. When Pope Alexander III was elected in 1159, a few dissentient cardinals promptly elected a rival pope more favourable to the pretensions of the Emperor Frederick Barbarossa. Milan had already offended the emperor by claiming the right to select its own magistrates, but when the citizens acknowledged Alexander III he became further incensed against them. Archbishop Hubert and his archdeacon Galdinus were obliged to withdraw into exile, and the following year Frederick, with a great army, invested the city, which surrendered after a siege. It was by his orders that the reputed bodies of the Three Magi were then removed from the church of St Eustorgius to Cologne, where the greater part of these 'relics' still remain.

In 1165 Galdinus was created cardinal, and the following year, upon the death of Archbishop Hubert, he was appointed his successor. The new prelate made it his first care to comfort and encourage his distressed flock; the Lombard states had entered into a league to rebuild Milan, and St Galdinus threw himself heart and soul into the new undertaking. He preached constantly, and assisted the poor whom he sought out in their homes. Amongst his clergy he enforced discipline, which had inevitably become relaxed during the troublous times through which they had been passing. His wisdom and eloquence, which had at first been mainly directed towards healing the chism, were afterwards exerted to confute the doctrines of the Cathari, then widely prevalent in Lombardy. On the last day of his life, although too weak to celebrate Mass, he succeeded in delivering an impassioned sermon against false doctrine. The effort was too much for him: he lost consciousness before he could leave the pulpit, and died as the Mass was ending.

19 : ST ALPHEGE, ARCHBISHOP OF CANTERBURY, MARTYR (A.D. 1012)

ST ALPHEGE (Aelfheah; Elphege) when a young man entered the monastery of Deerhurst in Gloucestershire. Afterwards he withdrew to a deserted place near Bath as a solitary, and eventually became abbot of the monastery at Bath. Upon the death of St Ethelwold in 984, St Dunstan obliged Alphege to accept the bishopric of Winchester, although he was only thirty years of age and shrank from the responsibility. In this position his high qualities and exceptional abilities found a wider scope. His liberality to the poor was so great that during the period of his episcopate there were no beggars in the diocese of Winchester. Adhering to the austerity of his monastic days, he became so thin through prolonged fasts that men declared they could see through his hands when he uplifted them at Mass. The holy prelate had ruled his see wisely for twenty-two years when he was translated to Canterbury in succession to Archbishop Aelfric. In order to be invested with the pallium, he paid a visit to Rome, where he was received by Pope John XVIII.

At this period England was suffering severely from the ravages of the Danes. Joining forces in 1011 with the rebel earl Edric, they marched into Kent and laid siege to Canterbury; the leading citizens urged St Alphege to seek safety in flight. This he absolutely refused to do. The city was betrayed, when a terrible massacre ensued, men and women, old and young, being put to the sword. St Alphege hastened to the place where the worst deeds of cruelty were being perpetrated. Pressing through the crowd, he appealed to the Danes to cease their carnage. He was immediately seized, roughly handled, and then confined in a dungeon. Several months later he was released from prison because a mysterious epidemic had broken out amongst the Danes, but although he cured many of the sick by prayer and by giving them blessed bread, the barbarians demanded three thousand gold crowns for his ransom. The archbishop declared that the country was too poor to pay such a sum. He was therefore taken to Greenwich and upon a second refusal to pay the money demanded he was barbarously put to death.

His body was recovered and buried at St Paul's in London, but was translated to Canterbury with great honour by the Danish King Canute in 1023. That St Alphege did not actually die for the faith was pointed out by one of his successors, Lanfranc, to St Anselm, but the latter replied that in his opinion to die for justice was tantamount to martyrdom.

20 : ST AGNES OF MONTEPULCIANO, VIRGIN (A.D. 1317)

IN the little Tuscan village of Gracchiano-Vecchio, some three miles from Montepulciano, there was born about the year 1268 to a well-to-do couple a little girl who was destined to become one of the great women saints of the Order of Preachers. When she was nine years old she induced her parents to place her in a convent at Montepulciano, occupied by a community of austere nuns who were popularly nicknamed *Sacchine*, from the coarse material of their habits. Her religious formation was entrusted to an experienced old sister called Margaret, and she soon edified the whole house by her exceptional progress. Moreover she was wise beyond her years and was made housekeeper when she was only fourteen. One day there arrived at the convent a request from Procena that a nun might be sent to take charge of a new convent in their town. Sister Margaret, who was selected for the purpose, stipulated that she should have Agnes as her assistant. As soon as it became known that Agnes was at Procena, a number of girls offered themselves to the new foundation, and before long she was elected abbess. A special dispensation had to be obtained from Pope Nicholas IV to authorize the appointment of a girl of fifteen to such a post. From that moment Agnes redoubled her austerities. For fifteen years she lived on bread and water, sleeping on the ground with a stone for a pillow.

The inhabitants of Montepulciano were becoming anxious to bring back to their town a fellow citizen whose fame had become widespread. It was ascertained that Agnes was favourably disposed towards a proposal to build a convent for her; and it was decided at her suggestion that the new convent should be placed under Dominican patronage. The building was erected on the site previously occupied by several houses of ill fame which had been a disgrace to the town. Upon her arrival at Montepulciano Agnes was installed as prioress, a post she continued to fill until her death, and the priory at Montepulciano flourished greatly under her rule. A painful illness afflicted her later days, but she never allowed it to interfere with her usual occupations.

In compliance with the entreaties of her anxious daughters she resorted to some medicinal springs in the neighbourhood—the convent was not enclosed—but she derived no benefit from them and returned to Montepulciano to die. She had reached the age of forty-nine.

21 : ST ANSELM, ARCHBISHOP OF CANTERBURY AND DOCTOR OF THE CHURCH (A.D. 1109)

ST ANSELM was born at Aosta in Piedmont about the year 1033. He wished to enter a monastery when he was fifteen years old, but the abbot to whom he applied refused to accept him, apprehending his father's displeasure.

There was no sympathy between him and his father, who by his harshness practically drove Anselm from home, after his mother's death, to prosecute his studies in Burgundy. Three years later he went to Bec in Normandy attracted by the fame of its great abbot Lanfranc, whose pupil, disciple and friend he became, and also a monk at Bec at the age of twenty-seven in 1060. He had only been a religious for three years when Lanfranc was appointed abbot of St Stephen's at Caen, and he himself was elected prior of Bec.

An original and independent thinker, endowed with profound learning, St Anselm was the greatest theologian of his age and the '"father of Scholasticism'; as a metaphysician he surpassed all Christian doctors since the days of St Augustine. Whilst still prior of Bec, he wrote his *Monologion*, in which he gave metaphysical proofs of the existence and nature of God, his *Proslogion*, or contemplation of God's attributes, as well as treatises on truth, on freewill, on the origin of evil, and a work on the art of reasoning.

In 1078, after he had been prior for fifteen years, Anselm was chosen abbot of Bec. This entailed occasional visits to England, where the abbey possessed property and where his friend Lanfranc was now archbishop of Canterbury. Anselm was in England in 1092, three years after Lanfranc's death, when the see of Canterbury was being kept vacant for the sake of its revenues by King William Rufus. The king was, however, induced to change his mind by a sudden illness. Stricken with fear, he promised that in future he would govern according to law and nominated Anselm to the archbishopric. The good abbot pleaded his age, ill-health and unfitness for the management of public affairs; but the bishops and others present forced the pastoral staff into his hand and bore him away to the church where they sang a *Te Deum*.

But the heart of Rufus, though temporarily softened by the fear of death, had not really changed. The new archbishop had not long been installed when the king, with a view to wresting the duchy of Normandy out of his brother Robert's hands, began to make large demands for supplies. Not content with Anselm's offer of five hundred marks the monarch required him to pay a thousand, as the price of his nomination to the see. St Anselm absolutely refused to comply. Moreover, he did not hesitate to urge the king to fill the vacant abbeys and to sanction the convening of those synods whose office it was to repress abuses among clergy and laity. The king angrily replied that his abbeys were no more to be extorted from him than his crown, and from that moment he sought to deprive Anselm of his see. He succeeded in detaching from their obedience a number of bishops, but when he bade the barons disavow the action of the primate he was met with a blank refusal. An attempt to persuade Pope Urban II to depose the saint was equally futile. The very legate who was charged to tell William that his desire could not be granted brought the pallium which rendered Anselm's position unassailable.

Finding that King William was determined on every possible occasion to oppress the Church unless the clergy would yield to his will, St Anselm sought permission to leave the country that he might consult the Holy See. Twice he was met with refusal, but eventually he was told by the monarch that he might depart if he liked, but that if he did so his revenues would be confiscated and he would never be allowed to return. Nevertheless he set out from Canterbury in October 1097.

Upon his arrival in Rome, he laid his case before the pope, who not only assured him of his protection, but wrote to the English king to demand Anselm's re-establishment in his rights and possessions. It was while the archbishop was staying in a Campanian monastery, whither he had betaken himself from Rome for the benefit of his health, that he completed his famous book, *Cur Deus Homo*, the most famous treatise on the Incarnation ever written. Despairing of doing any good at Canterbury, and convinced that he could serve God better in a private capacity, he asked the pope to relieve him of his office, but his request was refused, although, as it was obviously impossible for him to return to England at the moment, he was allowed to remain in his Campanian retreat. While there Anselm attended the Council of Bari in 1098, and distinguished himself by his dealing with the difficulties of the Italo-Greek bishops on the matter of the *Filioque*. The council proceeded to denounce the king of England for his simony, his oppression of the Church, his persecution of Anselm and his personal depravity. A solemn anathema was only prevented by the entreaties of the archbishop, who persuaded Pope Urban to confine himself to a threat of excommunication.

The death of William Rufus put an end to St Anselm's exile, and he came back to England amid the rejoicings of king and people. The harmony did not last long. Difficulties arose as soon as Henry I wanted Anselm to be reinvested by him and to make the customary homage for his see. This was contrary to the enactments of a Roman synod in 1099 which had forbidden lay investiture in respect of cathedrals and abbeys, and the archbishop refused. But at this time great apprehension was being felt at the threatened invasion of England by Robert of Normandy, whom many of the barons were not indisposed to support. Eager to have the Church on his side, Henry made lavish promises of future obedience to the Holy See, whilst

Anselm did his utmost to prevent a rebellion. Henry owed the retention of his crown in no small measure to St Anselm, yet, as soon as all danger of invasion was passed, he renewed his claim to the right of investiture. The archbishop, on the other hand, absolutely declined to consecrate bishops nominated by the king unless they were canonically elected; and the divergence grew daily more acute. At last Anselm was persuaded to go in person to lay the questions before the pope, Henry at the same time sending a deputy to state his own case. After due consideration Paschal II confirmed his predecessor's decisions, and Henry thereupon sent word to St Anselm forbidding his return if he continued recalcitrant, and pronouncing the confiscation of his revenues. Eventually the rumour that St Anselm was about to excommunicate him seems thoroughly to have alarmed the English monarch, and at a meeting in Normandy some sort of reconciliation took place. Afterwards in England at a royal council the king renounced the right of investiture to bishoprics or abbeys, whilst Anselm, with the pope's consent, agreed that English bishops should be free to do homage for their temporal possessions. The pact thus made was loyally kept by King Henry, who came to regard the saint with such confidence that he made him regent during an absence in Normandy in 1108. Anselm's health, however, had long been failing—he was by this time an old man—and he died the following year, 1109, amongst the monks of Canterbury.

His was a character of singular charm. It was conspicuous for a sympathy and sincerity which won him the affection of men of all classes and nationalities. His care extended to the very poorest of his people. He was one of the first to stand forward as an opponent of the slave trade. When in 1102 he held a national council at Westminster, primarily for settling ecclesiastical affairs, the archbishop obtained the passing of a resolution to prohibit the practice of selling men like cattle. St Anselm was in 1720 declared a doctor of the Church, though never formally canonized. In Dante's *Paradiso* we find him among the spirits of light and power in the sphere of the sun, next to St John Chrysostom.

22 : ST THEODORE OF SYKEON, BISHOP OF ANASTASIOPOLIS
(A.D. 613)

ST THEODORE was born in the Galatian town of Sykeon in Asia Minor, the son of a harlot who kept an inn. From infancy he was so given to prayer that as a schoolboy he often deprived himself of his meal to spend the dinner hour in church. At an early age he shut himself up, first in a cellar of his mother's house and then in a cave under a disused chapel. The desire to escape still more completely from the world led him subsequently to take up his abode for a time on a mountain. He assumed the monastic habit when on a pilgrimage to Jerusalem, and received ordination to the priesthood from his own bishop. His life was extremely austere. Vegetables were his only food, but of these he partook most sparingly, and he wore an iron girdle about his body. Endowed with the gifts of phrophecy and of miracles, he obtained by his prayers, when on a second visit to the Holy Land, an abundant fall of rain after a severe drought.

Several monasteries were founded by St Theodore, notably one near an ancient chapel dedicated in honour of St George, to whom he had a great devotion, and another at his native town of Sykeon. Over the latter he ruled as abbot, although he continued to reside mainly in a remote and secluded cell. Theodore was consecrated bishop of Anastasiopolis—a post for which he felt himself totally unfitted—but after ten years he succeeded in obtaining leave to resign. From Sykeon whither he joyfully retired he was recalled to Constantinople to bless the emperor and senate, and he then cured one of the emperor's sons of a skin disease, supposed to be leprosy. St Theodore died at Sykeon on April 22, 613. He had done much to propagate and popularize the cult of St George.

23 : ST GEORGE, MARTYR, PROTECTOR OF THE KINGDOM OF ENG- LAND (A.D. 303?)

WE are told that St George was a Christian knight and that he was born in Cappadocia. It chanced, however, that he was riding one day in the province of Lybia, and there he came upon a city called Sylene, near which was a marshy swamp. In this lived a dragon. The people had mustered together to attack and kill it, but its breath was so terrible that all had fled. To prevent its coming nearer they supplied it every day with two sheep, but when the sheep grew scarce, a human victim had to be substituted. This victim was selected by lot, and the lot just then had fallen on the king's own daughter. No one was willing to take her place, and the maiden had gone forth dressed as a bride to meet her doom. Then St George, coming upon the scene, attacked the dragon and transfixed it with his lance. Further; he borrowed the maiden's girdle, fastened it round the dragon's neck, and with this aid she led the monster captive into the city. The people in mortal terror were about to take to flight, but St George told them to have no fear. If only they would believe in Jesus Christ and be baptized, he would slay the dragon. The king and all his subjects gladly assented. The dragon was killed and four ox-carts were needed to carry the carcass to a safe distance.

It should be noted, however, that the story of the dragon, though given so much prominence, was a later accretion, of which we have no sure traces before the twelfth century.

There is every reason to believe that St George was a real martyr who suffered at Diospolis (*i.e.* Lydda) in Palestine, probably before the time of Constantine. Beyond this there seems to be nothing which can be affirmed with any confidence. The cult is certainly early.

It is not quite clear how St George came to be specially chosen as the patron saint of England. His fame had certainly travelled to the British Isles long before the Norman Conquest. The *Félire* of Oengus, under April 23, speaks of 'George, a sun of victories with thirty great thousands', while Abbot Aelfric tells the whole extravagant story in a metrical homily. William of Malmesbury states that Saints George and Demetrius, 'the martyr knights', were seen assisting the Franks at the battle of Antioch in 1098, and it seems likely that the crusaders, notably King Richard I, came back from the east with a great idea of the power of St George's intercession. At the national synod of Oxford in 1222 St George's day was included among the lesser holidays, and in 1415 the constitution of Archbishop Chichele made it one of the chief feasts of the year. In the interval King Edward III had founded the Order of the Garter, of which St George has always been the patron. During the seventeenth and eighteenth centuries (till 1778) his feast was a holiday of obligation for English Catholics, and Pope Benedict XIV recognized him as the Protector of the Kingdom.

24 : ST FIDELIS OF SIGMARINGEN, MARTYR (A.D. 1622)

THE Congregation *de Propaganda Fide* honours as its protomartyr the Capuchin priest St Fidelis, otherwise known as Mark Rey. A native of Sigmaringen in Hohenzollern, he was sent to the university of Freiburg in Breisgau, where he taught philosophy whilst he was working for a legal degree. In 1604 he was appointed tutor to a small party of aristocratic Swabian youths who wished to complete their education by supplementary studies in the chief cities of western Europe. During this tour, which seems to have lasted for six years, he won the affection and esteem of his companions, to whom he set the example of religious devotion and of liberality towards the poor, to whom he sometimes gave the clothes off his back. Upon his return to Germany, he took his degree as doctor of laws, and began to practise as an advocate at Ensisheim in Upper Alsace. He soon became known for his integrity and for his studied avoidance of the invective and personalities then too often employed to damage an opponent's case. His espousal of the cause of the oppressed earned him the nickname of The Poor Man's Lawyer; but the unscrupulous and crooked expedients adopted by his colleagues gave him a disgust for the law, and he decided to enter the Capuchin branch of the Franciscan Order, of which his brother George was already a member. After having received holy orders Mark took the habit, together with the name of Fidelis.

As soon as his theological course was completed, the young Capuchin was employed in preaching and in hearing confessions. He was appointed guardian successively at Rheinfelden, Freiburg and Feldkirch, and whilst he held this last office he not only brought about a reform in the town and in several outlying districts, but also converted numerous Protestants. His great devotion to the sick, many of whom he cured during a severe epidemic, still further enhanced his reputation, and at the request of the bishop of Chur his superiors sent him to preach among the Zwinglians of the Grisons, with eight other Capuchins. This first attempt since the Reformation to reclaim that land from heresy was received by the leading Protestants with threats of violence which Fidelis affected to disregard, although fully aware of the fate that probably awaited him.

From the outset the mission was abundantly blessed, and the newly established Congregation for the Spreading of the Faith formally appointed Father Fidelis leader of the Grisons enterprise. The wonderful effects of his zeal inflamed the rage of his adversaries. They roused the peasants against him by representing him as the opponent of their national aspirations for independence and the agent of the Austrian emperor, to whose rule he was said to have counselled submission. St Fidelis, who had been warned, spent several nights in prayer before the Blessed Sacrament or before his crucifix. On April 24, 1622, he preached at Grüsch. He then proceeded to Sewis, and was in the midst of a sermon on 'One Lord, one faith, one baptism', when a gun was fired at him; but the bullet missed, lodging in the wall.

There was a great tumult, the Austrian soldiers who were about the place were set upon, and a Protestant offered to shelter Fidelis, who thanked him but declined, saying his life was in God's hands. He tried to retake the road back to Grüsch, but was attacked by a score of armed men, clamouring that he should repudiate his faith. He refused and was struck down, calling on God to forgive his murderers as they mangled his body with their weapons. He was forty-five years old.

The conversion of a Zwinglian minister who was present was one of the first fruits of the martyrdom of St Fidelis of Sigmaringen, who was canonized by Pope Benedict XIV.

25 : ST MARK, EVANGELIST (c. A.D. 74)

IT is generally believed that he must be identical with the 'John surnamed Mark' of Acts xii 12 and 25, and that the Mary whose house in Jerusalem was a kind of rendezvous for the apostles was consequently his mother. From Col. iv 10 we learn that Mark was a kinsman of St Barnabas who, as stated in Acts iv 36, was a Levite and a Cypriot, and from this it is not unlikely that St Mark was of a levitical family himself. When Paul and Barnabas returned to Antioch, after leaving in Jerusalem the alms they had brought, they took John surnamed Mark with them, and in their apostolic mission at Salamis in Cyprus, Mark helped them in their ministry (Acts xiii 5), but when they were at Perga in Pamphylia he left and returned to Jerusalem (Acts xiii 13). St Paul seems consequently to have suspected Mark of a certain instability, and later, when preparing for a visitation of the churches in Cilicia and the rest of Asia Minor, he refused to include John Mark, though Barnabas desired his company. The difference of opinion ended in Barnabas separating from St Paul and going with Mark again to Cyprus. None the less when Paul was undergoing his first captivity in Rome, Mark was with him and a help to him (Col. iv 10). Also in his second Roman captivity, shortly before his martyrdom, St Paul writes to Timothy, then at Ephesus, enjoining him to 'take Mark and bring him with thee, for he is profitable to me for the ministry'.

On the other hand tradition testifies strongly in the sense that the author of the second gospel was intimately associated with St Peter. Clement of Alexandria (as reported by Eusebius), Irenaeus and Papias speak of St Mark as the interpreter or mouthpiece of St Peter, though Papias declares that Mark had not heard the Lord and had not been His disciple. In spite of this last utterance, many commentators incline to the view that the young man (Mark xiv 51) who followed our Lord after His arrest was Mark himself. What is certain is that St Peter, writing from Rome (1 Peter v 13), speaks of 'my son Mark' who apparently was there with him. We can hardly doubt that this was the evangelist, and there is at any rate nothing which conclusively shows that this young man is a different person from the 'John surnamed Mark' of the Acts.

That St Mark lived for some years in Alexandria and became bishop of that see is an ancient tradition, though his connection with their native city is not mentioned either by Clement of Alexandria or by Origen.

The city of Venice claims to possess the body of St Mark which is supposed to have been brought there from Alexandria early in the ninth century. The authenticity of the remains preserved for so many hundred years has not passed unquestioned. It is certain, however, that St Mark has been honoured from time immemorial as principal patron of the city.

26 : ST STEPHEN, BISHOP OF PERM (A.D. 1396)

FROM their early Christian days the Russians had sent out missions to the heathen, such as the Mongols and Finns, and in the revival of this zeal during the fourteenth century the outstanding figure was Bishop St Stephen. He was a monk of Rostov, who sometime after 1370 went to preach the gospel to the Zyriane or Permiaks, a people who lived far to the east of the Volga river but south-west of the Ural mountains, among whom he had been born though himself a Russian.

St Stephen was a very worthy successor of St Cyril and St Methodius and his missionary methods are reminiscent of theirs. He believed, as his biographer tells us, that every people should worship God in its own tongue, since languages also are from God, and so one of his first undertakings was to translate the necessary parts of the liturgical services into the language of the Zyriane, and portions of the Holy Scriptures likewise. So convinced was Stephen that every people has its own peculiar contribution to make to God's service that he would not give his converts even the Russian characters: instead he invented an alphabet of letters based on details in the patterns of their embroideries and carvings. And he established schools wherein the use of this alphabet could be learned. Like other Russian missionaries St Stephen used the celebration of public worship as an initial means of attracting the heathen by its beauty and impressive solemnity. He distinguished himself not only as a missionary, but also as a champion of the downtrodden and oppressed so far away as Novgorod and Moscow.

In 1383 his work was recognized by the conferring of episcopal orders, and he became the first bishop of Perm, where he had to oppose by writing and preaching the people called Strigolniks, the first Russian dissenters, who had much in common with the Lollards and Hussites. St Stephen died at Moscow in 1396.

27 : ST ZITA, VIRGIN (A.D. 1278)

ZITA'S parents were devout Christians, her elder sister afterwards became a Cistercian nun, and her uncle Graziano was a hermit who was locally regarded as a saint. At the age of twelve, she went to be a servant at Lucca, eight miles from her native village of Monte Sagrati, in the house of Pagano di Fatinelli, who carried on a wool and silk-weaving business. From the outset she formed the habit of rising during the night for prayer and of attending daily the first Mass at the church of San Frediano. The good food with which she was provided she would distribute to the poor, and more often than not she slept on the bare ground, her bed having been given up to a beggar. Her work indeed was part of her religion.

The children of the family were committed to her care, and she was made housekeeper. In time Zita became the friend and adviser of the whole house, and the only person who could cope with the master in his rages; but the general veneration with which she was regarded embarrassed her far more than the slights she had had to bear in her earlier years. On the other hand, she found herself relieved of much of her domestic work and free to visit to her heart's content the sick, the poor and the prisoners. She had a special devotion to criminals under sentence of death, on whose behalf she would spend hours of prayer. In such works of mercy and in divine contemplation she spent the evening of her life. She died very peacefully, on April 27, 1278. She was sixty years of age and had served the same family for forty-eight years.

28 : ST PETER MARY CHANEL, MARTYR (A.D. 1841)

THE first martyr of Oceania and of the Society of Mary, Peter Louis Mary Chanel, was born in 1803 in the diocese of Belley. Set to mind his father's sheep from the age of seven, he was one day noticed by the Abbé Trompier, parish priest of Cras, who was struck by his intelligence and piety, and obtained leave from the boy's parents to educate him in the little Latin school which he had started. Both as a student at Cras and in the seminary Peter won the affectionate esteem of masters and pupils alike.

A year after his ordination he was appointed to the parish of Crozet—a district which bore a bad reputation. In the three years he remained there he brought about a great revival of religion, his devotion to the sick opening to him many doors which would otherwise have remained closed. But his heart had long been set on missionary work, and in 1831 he joined the Marists, who had recently formed themselves into a society for evangelistic work at home and abroad. His aspirations were not at once realized, for he was given professorial work for five years in the seminary of Belley.

However, in 1836, Pope Gregory XVI gave canonical approval to the new congregation, and St Peter was one of a small band of missionaries commissioned to carry the faith to the islands of the Pacific. Peter with one companion went to the island of Futuna in the New Hebrides. They were well received by the people, whose confidence they gained by healing the sick. But after the missionaries had acquired the language and had begun to teach, the chieftain's jealousy was aroused. Suspicion turned to hatred when his own son expressed a desire for baptism, and on April 28, 1841, he sent a band of warriors, one of whom felled St Peter with his club and the rest cut up the martyr's body with their hatchets. The missionary's death swiftly completed the work he had begun, and within a few months the whole island was Christian. Peter was canonized in 1954.

29 : ST CATHERINE OF SIENA, VIRGIN (A.D. 1380)

ST CATHERINE was born in Siena on the feast of the Annunciation 1347, she and a twin sister who did not long survive her birth being the youngest of twenty-five children. Their father, Giacomo Benincasa, a well-to-do dyer, lived with his wife Lapa, daughter of a now forgotten poet, in the spacious house which the piety of the Sienese has preserved almost intact to the present day. Catherine as a little girl is described as having been very merry, and sometimes on her way up or downstairs she used to kneel on every step to repeat a Hail Mary. She was only six years old when she had the remarkable mystical experience which may be said to have sealed her vocation.

When she had reached the age of twelve, her parents urged her to devote more care to her personal appearance. In order to please her mother and her sister Bonaventura she submitted for a time to have her hair dressed and to be decked out in the fashion, but she soon repented of her concession. Uncompromisingly she now declared that she would never marry, and as her parents still persisted in trying to find her a husband she cut off her golden-brown hair—her chief beauty. The family, roused to indignation, tried to overcome her resolution. She was harried and scolded from morning to night, set to do all the menial work of the house, and because she was known to love privacy she was never allowed to be alone, even her little bedroom being taken from her. All these trials she bore with patience which nothing could ever ruffle. At last her father realized that further opposition was useless, and Catherine was allowed to lead the life to which she felt called. She obtained what she had ardently desired—permission to receive the habit of a Dominican tertiary.

On Shrove Tuesday, 1366, while Siena was keeping carnival, she was praying in her room when the Saviour appeared to her, accompanied by His blessed Mother and a crowd of the heavenly host. Taking the girl's hand, our Lady held it up to her Son who placed a ring upon it and espoused Catherine to Himself, bidding her to be of good courage, for she was now armed with faith to overcome the assaults of the enemy. The ring remained visible to her though invisible to others. This spiritual betrothal marked the end of the years of solitude and preparation. Very shortly afterwards, it was revealed to Catherine that she must now go forth into the world to promote the salvation of her neighbour, and she began gradually to mix again with her fellow creatures. Gradually there gathered round her a band of friends and disciples—her Fellowship or Family, all of whom called her 'Mamma'.

As may be readily supposed, public opinion in Siena was sharply divided about Catherine, especially at this period. It may have been in consequence of accusations made against her that she was summoned to Florence, to appear before the chapter general of the Dominicans. If any charges were made, they were certainly disproved, and shortly afterwards the new lector to Siena, Bd Raymund of Capua, was appointed her confessor. Their association was a happy one for both. The learned Dominican became not only her director but in a great measure her disciple, whilst she obtained through him the support of the order. In later life he was to be the master general of the Dominicans and the biographer of his spiritual daughter.

Her reputation for holiness and wonders had by this time won for her a unique place in the estimation of her fellow citizens, many of whom proudly called her 'La Beata Popolana' and resorted to her in their various difficulties: three Dominicans were specially charged to hear the confessions of those who were induced by her to amend their lives. Moreover, because of her success in healing feuds, she was constantly being called upon to arbitrate. It was partly no doubt with a view to turning the belligerent energies of Christendom from fratricidal struggles that Catherine was moved to throw herself energetically into Pope Gregory XI's appeal for another crusade to wrest the Holy Sepulchre from the Turks. Her efforts in this direction brought her into direct correspondence with the pontiff himself.

In February 1375 she accepted an invitation to visit Pisa. She had only been in the city a few days when she had another of those great spiritual experiences which appear to have preluded new developments in her career. After making her communion in the little church of St Christina, she had been looking at the crucifix, rapt in meditation, when suddenly there seemed to come from it five blood-red rays which pierced her hands, feet and heart, causing such acute pain that she swooned. The wounds remained as stigmata, apparent to herself alone during her life, but clearly visible after her death.

She was still at Pisa when she received word that the people of Florence and Perugia had entered into a league against the Holy See and its French legates; and Bologna, Viterbo, Ancona, together with other cities, not without provocation from the mismanagement of papal officials, promptly rallied to the insurgents. That Lucca as well as Pisa and Siena held back for a time was largely due to the untiring efforts of Catherine, who paid a special visit to Lucca besides writing numerous letters of exhortation to all three towns. From Avignon, after an unsuccessful appeal to the Florentines, Pope Gregory despatched his legate Cardinal Robert of Geneva with an army, and laid Florence under an interdict. This ban soon entailed such serious effects upon the city that its rulers in alarm sent to Siena, to accept Catherine's offer to become their mediatrix with the Holy See.

Catherine arrived at Avignon on June 18, 1376, and soon had a conference with Pope Gregory. But the Florentine ambassadors disclaimed Catherine, and the pope's peace terms were so severe that nothing could be done.

Although the immediate purpose of her visit to Avignon had thus failed, Catherine's efforts in another direction were crowned with success. For seventy-four years the popes had been absent from Rome, living in Avignon, where the curia had become almost entirely French. It was a state of things deplored by all earnest Christians outside France, and the greatest men of the age had remonstrated against it in vain. Gregory XI had indeed himself proposed to transfer his residence to the Holy City, but had been deterred by the opposition of his French cardinals. Since Catherine in her letters had urged his return to Rome, it was only natural that the pope should talk with her on the subject when they came face to face. 'Fulfil what you have promised', was her reply—recalling to him, it is said, a vow which he had never disclosed to any human being. Gregory decided to act without loss of time. On September 13, 1376, he started from Avignon to travel by water to Rome, Catherine and her friends leaving the city on the same day to return overland to Siena. The two parties met again, almost accidentally, in Genoa, where Catherine was detained by the illness of two of her secretaries.

It was a month before she was back in Siena, from whence she continued to write to Pope Gregory, exhorting him to contribute by all means possible to the peace of Italy. By his special desire she went again to Florence, still rent by factions and obstinate in its disobedience. There she remained for some time, amidst daily murders and confiscations, in danger of her life but ever undaunted, even when swords were drawn against her. Finally she did indeed establish peace with the Holy See, although not during Gregory's reign. After this memorable reconciliation the saint returned to Siena where, as Raymund of Capua tells us, 'she occupied herself actively in the composition of a book which she dictated under the inspiration of the Holy Ghost'. This was the celebrated mystical work, written in four treatises, known as the 'Dialogue of St Catherine'.

But within two years of the ending of the papal 'captivity' at Avignon began the scandal of the great schism which followed the death of Gregory XI in 1378, when Urban VI was chosen in Rome and a rival pope was set up in Avignon by certain cardinals who declared Urban's election illegal. Christendom was divided into two camps, and Catherine wore herself out in her efforts to obtain for Urban the recognition which was his due. Letter after letter she addressed to the princes and leaders of the various European countries. To Urban himself she continued to write, sometimes to urge him to bear up under his trials, sometimes admonishing him to abate a harshness which was alienating even his supporters. Far from resenting her reproof, the pope told her to come to Rome that he might profit by her advice and assistance. In obedience to the call she took up her residence in the City, labouring indefatigably by her prayers, exhortations and letters to gain fresh adherents to the true pontiff. Her life, however, was almost ended. Early in 1380 she had a strange seizure, when a visible presentment of the ship of the Church seemed to crush her to the earth and she offered herself a victim for it. After this she never really recovered. On April 21 there supervened a paralytic stroke which disabled her from the waist downwards, and eight days later, at the age of thirty-three, St Catherine of Siena passed away in the arms of Alessia Saracini. She was canonized in 1461, and declared a doctor of the church in 1970.

30 : ST PIUS V, POPE (A.D. 1572)

MICHAEL GHISLIERI was born in 1504 at Bosco, in the diocese of Tortona, and received the Dominican habit at the age of fourteen in the priory of Voghera. After his ordination to the priesthood he was lector in theology and philosophy for sixteen years, and for a considerable time was employed as novice master and in governing houses of the order—everywhere endeavouring to maintain the spirit of the founder. In 1556 he was chosen bishop of Nepi and Sutri, and the following year was appointed inquisitor general, and also cardinal—in order, as he ruefully remarked, that irons should be riveted to his feet to prevent him from creeping back into the peace of the cloister. Pope Pius IV transferred him to the Piedmontese bishopric of Mondovi—a church reduced almost to ruin by the ravages of war. Within a short time of his accession the newly-appointed prelate had done much to restore calm and prosperity in his diocese, but he was soon recalled to Rome in connection with other business. Here, though his opinions were often at variance with those of Pius IV, he never shrank from openly stating his convictions.

In December 1565 Pius IV died, and Michael Ghislieri was chosen pope, largely through the efforts of St Charles Borromeo, who saw in him the reformer of whom the Church stood in need. He took the name of Pius V, and from the outset made it abundantly clear that he was determined to enforce the letter as well as the spirit of the recommendations of the Council of Trent. On the occasion of his coronation, the largesses usually scattered indiscriminately amongst the crowd were bestowed upon hospitals and the really poor, whilst the money which was wont to be spent in providing a banquet for the cardinals, ambassadors and other great persons was sent to the poorer convents of the city. One of his first injunctions was that all bishops should reside in their dioceses, and parish priests in the cures to which they had been appointed—severe penalties being imposed for disobedience.

The new pope's activities extended from a drastic purge of the Roman *curia* to the clearing of the papal states of brigands, from legislation against prostitution to the prohibition of bull-fighting. In a time of famine, he imported from Sicily and France at his own expense large quantities of corn, a considerable proportion of which was freely distributed to the poor or was sold under cost price. A determined opponent of nepotism, he kept his relatives at a distance, and although he was persuaded to follow tradition by making one of his nephews a cardinal, he gave him little influence or power. In the new Breviary which was published in 1568, certain saints' days and some extravagant legends were omitted and lessons from the Holy Scriptures regained their proper place, whilst the Missal, issued two years later, was as much a restoration of ancient usage as a revision adapted to the needs of the time. To Pius the Church owed the best edition of St Thomas Aquinas which had yet appeared and the solemn recognition of St Thomas as a doctor of the Church. The catechism, too, which had been ordered by the Council of Trent was completed during his pontificate, and he at once ordered translations to be made into foreign tongues. Moreover, he made the catechetical instruction of the young a duty incumbent on all parish priests.

By the terms used when Pius V re-issued the bull 'In cena Domini' (1568), it was made clear that as pope he claimed a certain suzerainty over secular princes. For a long time he cherished hopes of winning to the faith Queen Elizabeth of England, but in 1570 he issued a bull of excommunication ('Regnans in excelsis') against her, absolving her subjects from their allegiance and forbidding them to recognize her as their sovereign. Its only result was to increase the difficulties of loyal English Catholics and to lend some appearance of justification to the accusation of treason so frequently brought against them; and to aggravate those controversies about oaths and tests which vexed and weakened their body from the Oath of Obedience in 1606 until Emancipation in 1829.

Pius V's disappointment in England was compensated for in the following year when, aided politically and materially by the Holy See, Don John of Austria and Marcantonio Colonna broke the Turkish power in the Mediterranean. Their force, which comprised 20,000 soldiers, sailed from Corfu and came upon the Turks in the Gulf of Lepanto. There, in one of the world's greatest maritime battles, the Ottoman fleet was completely defeated. From the moment the expedition started the pope had prayed for it almost unceasingly—often with uplifted hands like Moses on the mountain. He had also prescribed public devotions and private fasts and, at the very hour that the contest was raging, the procession of the rosary in the church of the Minerva was pouring forth petitions for victory. To commemorate the great deliverance he afterwards inserted the words 'Help of Christians' in the Litany of Our Lady and instituted the festival of the Holy Rosary. The victory was won on October 7, 1571. In the following year the pope was struck down by a painful disorder from which he had long suffered and which his austerities had aggravated: it carried him off on May 1, 1572, at the age of sixty-eight.

St Pius V was canonized in 1712, the last pope to be raised to the Church's altars till the beatification of Pius X.

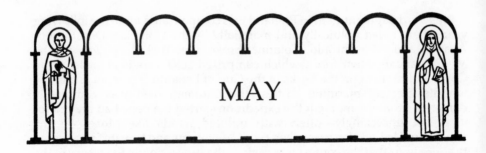

MAY

1 : ST MARCULF, OR MARCOUL, ABBOT (c. A.D. 558)

THE name of St Marcoul was formerly celebrated throughout the length and breadth of France because for centuries it was usual for the king, after his coronation at Rheims, to proceed to Corbeny to venerate the relics of St Marcoul, in whose honour a novena was observed by the sovereign in person or, vicariously, by his grand-almoner. It was through St Marcoul that the king was popularly believed to derive the gift of healing known as 'touching for the King's Evil,' or scrofula.

Marcoul was born at Bayeaux of noble parents. At the age of thirty he was ordained by Possessor, bishop of Coutances, who sent him forth to preach. Although successful in winning souls, Marcoul always longed for solitude and closer union with God, and would retire to a lonely island, where he would spend his days as a hermit. After some time he obtained from King Childebert a grant of land at Nanteuil, on which he built some huts for a few disciples who also wished to live a retired life. From this small nucleus there soon grew a great monastery. Many of the monks continued to live, like their founder, the eremitic life, and several of them, including St Helier, went to settle in the island of Jersey. We read that St Marcoul at one period stayed there with them, and by his intercession saved the inhabitants from a raid of marauding Saxons. So violent a storm arose when he prayed that the invaders were dashed to pieces on the rocks. Marcoul died about the year 558, on May 1, and tradition says that his two most faithful disciples, St Domardus and St Cariulfus (St Criou), passed away on the same day. St Marcoul was regarded as a patron who cured skin diseases, and as late as 1680 sufferers made pilgrimages to his shrine at Nanteuil and bathed in the springs connected with the church.

2 : ST ATHANASIUS, ARCHBISHOP OF ALEXANDRIA, DOCTOR OF THE CHURCH (A.D. 373)

ST ATHANASIUS, 'the Champion of Orthodoxy,' was probably born about the year 297 at Alexandria. Of his family nothing is known except that his parents were Christians, and that he had a brother called Peter. He received an excellent education, which embraced Greek literature and philosophy, rhetoric, jurisprudence and Christian doctrine. His familiarity with the text of the Bible was quite exceptional. We have it on his own authority that he learnt theology from teachers who had been confessors during the persecution under Maximian, which had raged in Alexandria when he was almost an infant. It is interesting to note that from his early youth Athanasius appears to have had close relations with the hermits of the desert—more especially with the great St Antony.

It is not until the year 318, when he was about 21, that Athanasius makes his first actual appearance upon the stage of history. He then received the diaconate, and he was appointed secretary to Bishop Alexander. It was probably at this period that he produced his first literary work, the famous treatise on the Incarnation, in which he expounded the redemptive work of Christ.

It was probably about the year 323 that scandal began to be aroused in Alexandria by the priest of the church of Baukalis, Arius by name, who was publicly teaching that the Word of God is not eternal, that He was created in time by the Eternal Father, and that therefore He could only figuratively be described as the Son of God. The bishop demanded a statement of these doctrines, which he laid first before the Alexandrian clergy and afterwards before a council of Egyptian bishops. With only two dissentients the assembly condemned the heresy, deposing Arius together with eleven priests and deacons who adhered to his tenets. The heresiarch retired to Caesarea, where he continued to propagate his teaching, having enlisted the support of Eusebius of Nicomedia and other Syrian prelates. In Egypt he had won over the Meletians, a disaffected body, and many of the 'intellectuals,' whilst his doctrines, embodied in hymns or songs set to popular tunes, were popularized in the market-place and carried by sailors and traders in an incredibly short time all along the Mediterranean shores.

Athanasius, as the bishop's archdeacon and secretary, was present at the great Council of Nicaea in which the true doctrine of the Church was set forth, the sentence of excommunication against Arius confirmed, and the confession of faith known as the Nicene Creed promulgated and subscribed.

Shortly after the close of the council Alexander died, and Athanasius, whom he had nominated as his successor, was chosen bishop of Alexandria, although he was not yet thirty years old. Almost immediately he undertook a visitation of his enormous diocese, including the Thebaid and other great monastic settlements, where he was warmly welcomed as being himself an ascetic. He also appointed a bishop for Ethiopia, a country in which the Christian faith had recently found a footing.

In 330 the Arian bishop of Nicomedia, Eusebius, returned from exile and succeeded in persuading the Emperor Constantine, whose favourite residence was in his diocese, to write to Athanasius, bidding him re-admit Arius into communion. The bishop replied that the Catholic Church could hold no communion with heretics who attacked the divinity of Christ. Eusebius then addressed an ingratiating letter to Athanasius, in which he sought to justify Arius.

The bishop of Nicomedia's next move was to write to the Egyptian Meletians urging them to impeach Athanasius. They responded by bringing against him charges of having exacted a tribute of linen for use in his church, of having sent gold to a certain Philomenus, suspected of treason against the emperor, and of having authorized one of his deputies to destroy a chalice which was being used at the altar by a Meletian priest called Iskhyras. In a trial before the emperor, Athanasius cleared himself of all these accusations and returned in triumph to Alexandria, bearing with him a commendatory letter from Constantinople. His enemies, however, were not discouraged. He was now charged with having murdered a Meletian bishop, Arsenius, and was cited to attend a council at Caesarea. Aware that his supposed victim was alive and in hiding, Athanasius ignored the summons. Nevertheless he found himself compelled by a command from the emperor to appear before another council summoned at Tyre in 335—an assembly which, as it turned out, was packed by his opponents and presided over by an Arian who had usurped the see of Antioch. Various offences were preferred against him, of which the first was that of the broken chalice. Several of the charges he disposed of at once: in regard to others he demanded time in which to obtain evidence. Realizing, however, that his condemnation had been decided beforehand, he abruptly left the assembly and embarked for Constantinople. Upon his arrival he accosted the emperor in the street in the attitude of a suppliant, and obtained an interview. So completely did he seem to have vindicated himself that Constantine, in reply to a letter from the Council of Tyre announcing that Athanasius had been condemned and deposed, wrote to the signatories a severe reply summoning them to Constantinople for a retrial of the case. But before the first letter could reach its destination, a second one was despatched which confirmed the sentences of the Council of Tyre and banished Athanasius to Trier in Belgian Gaul.

In 337 the Emperor Constantine died, and his empire was divided betweeen his threee sons, Constantine II, Constantius and Constans. The various exiled prelates were immediately recalled, and one of the first acts of Constantine II was to restore Athanasius to his see. The bishop re-entered his diocesan city in seeming triumph, but his enemies were as relentless as ever, and Eusebius of Nicomedia completely won over the Emperor Constantius, within whose jurisdiction Alexandria was situated. Athanasius was accused before the monarch of raising sedition, of promoting bloodshed and of detaining for his own use corn which was destined for widows and the poor. His old adversary Eusebius furthermore obtained from a council which met at Antioch a second sentence of deposition, and the ratification of the election of an Arian bishop of Alexandria. By this assembly a letter was written to Pope St Julius inviting his intervention and the condemnation of Athanasius. This was followed by an encyclical, drawn up by the orthodox Egyptian hierarchy and sent to the pope and the other Catholic bishops, in which the case for Athanasius was duly set forth. The Roman pontiff replied accepting the suggestion of the Eusebians that a synod should be held to settle the question.

In the meantime a Cappadocian named Gregory had been installed in the see of Alexandria; and in the face of the scenes of violence and sacrilege that ensued, Athanasius betook himself to Rome to await the hearing of his case. The synod was duly summoned, but as the Eusebians who had demanded it failed to appear, it was held without them. The result was the complete vindication of the saint—a declaration which was afterwards endorsed by the Council of Sardica. Nevertheless he was unable to return to Alexandria till after the death of the Cappadocian Gregory, and then only because the Emperor Constantius, on the eve of a war with Persia, thought it politic to propitiate his brother Constans by restoring Athanasius to his see. After an absence of eight years the bishop returned to Alexandria amidst scenes of unparalleled rejoicing, and for three or four years the wars and disturbances in which the rulers of the empire were involved left him in comparative peace. But the murder of Constans removed the most powerful support of orthodoxy, and Constantius, once he felt himself securely master of the west and of the east, set himself deliberately to crush the man whom he had come to regard as a personal enemy. At Arles in 353 he obtained the condemnation of the saint from a council of time-serving prelates, and again in 355 at Milan.

In Egypt Athanasius held on with the support of his clergy and people, but not for long. One night, when he was celebrating a vigil in church, soldiers forced open the doors, killing some of the congregation and wounding others. Athanasius escaped and disappeared into the desert, where the watchful care of the monks kept him safely hidden for six years.

The death of Constantius in 361 was followed soon afterwards by the murder, at the hands of the populace, of the Arian who had usurped the Alexandrian see. The new emperor, Julian, had revoked the sentences of banishment enacted by his predecessor, and Athanasius returned to his city. But it was only for a few months. The Apostate's plans for the paganizing of the Christian world could make little way as long as the champion of the Catholic faith ruled in Egypt. Julian therefore banished him as 'a disturber of the peace and an enemy of the gods,' and Athanasius once more sought refuge in the desert. During this fourth exile Athanasius seems to have explored the Thebaïr from end to end. He was at Antinopolis when he was informed by two solitaries of the death of Julian, who had at that moment expired, slain by an arrow in Persia.

At once he returned to Alexandria, and some months later he proceeded to Antioch at the invitation of the Emperor Jovian, who had revoked his sentence of banishment. Jovian's reign, however, was a short one; and the Emperor Valens in May 365 issued an order banishing all the orthodox bishops who had been exiled by Constantius and restored by his successors. Again Athanasius was forced to withdraw. Four months later Valens revoked his edict—possibly fearing a rising among the Egyptians, who had become devotedly attached to their much-persecuted bishop. With great demonstrations of joy the people escorted him back. Five times Athanasius had been banished; seventeen years he had spent in exile: but for the last seven years of his life he was left in the unchallenged occupation of his see. It was probably at this time that he wrote the Life of St Antony. He died in Alexandria on May 2, 373, and his body was translated later, first to Constantinople, and then to Venice.

3 : SS. PHILIP AND JAMES, APOSTLES

S T PHILIP the apostle came from Bethsaida in Galilee, and seems to have belonged to a little group of earnest men who had already fallen under the influence of St John the Baptist. In the synoptic gospels there is no mention of Philip except in the list of apostles which occurs in each. But St John's gospel introduces his name several times, recording in particular that the call of Philip came the day after that given to St Peter and St Andrew. Jesus, we are told, 'found Philip' and said to him, 'Follow me.'

From the account given by the evangelist, we should naturally infer that Philip responded without hesitation to the call he had received. He goes at once to find his friend Nathanael and tells him, 'We have found him of whom Moses, in the law and the prophets did write.' At the same time Philip gives proof of a sober discretion in his missionary zeal. He does not attempt to force his discovery upon unwilling ears. When Bathanael objects, 'Can anything good come from Nazareth?' his answer is not indignant declamation, but an appeal for personal inquiry—'Come and see.' In the description of the feeding of the five thousand Philip figures again. 'When Jesus,' we are told, 'had lifted up His eyes and seen that a very great multitude cometh to Him, He said to Philip, 'Whence shall we buy bread that these may eat?' And this He said to try him; for He Himself knew what He would do.' Once more we get an impression of the sober literalness of St Philip's mental outlook when he replies: 'Two hundred pennyworth of bread is not sufficient for them that every one may take a little.' It is in accord with the same amiable type of character which hesitates before responsibilities that, when certain Gentiles among the crowds who thronged to Jerusalem for the pasch came to Philip saying, 'Sir, we would see Jesus,' we find him reluctant to deal with the request without taking counsel. 'Philip cometh and telleth Andrew. Again Andrew and Philip told Jesus.' Finally another glimpse is afforded us of the apostle's earnestness and devotion conjoined with defective spiritual insight, when on the evening before the Passion our Lord announced, 'No man cometh to the Father but by me. If you had known me, you would without doubt have known my Father also: and from henceforth you shall know Him, and you have seen Him.' Philip saith to Him: 'Lord, show us the Father, and it is enough for us.' Jesus saith to him: 'Have I been so long a time with you; and have you not known me? Philip, he that seeth me seeth the Father also. How sayest thou: Show us the Father?' (John xiv6–9).

Apart from the fact that St Philip is named with the other apostles who spent ten days in the upper room awaiting the coming of the Holy Ghost at Pentecost, this is all we know about him with any degree of certainty.

The apostle St James—the Less, or the younger—here associated with St Philip, is most commonly held to be the same individual who is variously designated 'James, the son of Alpheus' (e.g. Matt. x 3, and Acts i 13), and 'James, the brother of the Lord' (Matt. xiii 55; Gal. i 19). He may also possibly be identical with James, son of Mary and brother of Joseph (Mark xv 40). This, however, is not the place to discuss the rather intricate problem of the 'Brethren of our Lord' and the question connected with it. It may be assumed then, as Alban Butler infers, that the apostle James who became bishop of Jerusalem (Acts xv and xxi 18) was the son of Alpheus and 'brother' (i.e. first cousin) of Jesus Christ. Although no prominence is given to this James in the gospel narrative, we learn from St Paul that he was favoured with a special appearing of our Lord before the Ascension. Further, when St Paul, three years after his conversion, went up to

Jerusalem and was still regarded with some suspicion by the apostles who remained there, James, with St. Peter, seems to have bid him a cordial welcome. Later we learn that Peter, after his escape from prison, sent a special intimation to James, apparently as to one whose pre-eminence was recognized among the Christians of the holy city. At what is called the Council of Jerusalem, where it was decided that the Gentiles who accepted Christian teaching need not be circumcised, it was St James who, after listening to St Peter's advice, voiced the conclusion of the assembly in the words, 'it hath seemed good to the Holy Ghost and to us' (Acts XV). He was, in fact, the bishop of Jerusalem, as Clement of Alexandria and Eusebius expressly state. Even Josephus, the Jewish historian, bears testimony to the repute in which James was held, and declares, so Eusebius asserts, that the terrible calamities which fell upon the people of that city were a retribution for their treatment of one'who was the most righteous of men.'

Josephus also informs us that James was stoned to death, and assigns this to the year 62. This St James is commonly held to be the author of the epistle in the New Testament which bears his name.

4 : ST GODEHARD, OR GOTHARD, BISHOP OF HILDESHEIM (A.D. 1038)

THE birthplace of St Godehard was the Bavarian village of Reichersdorf, where his father was an employee in the service of the canons, who at that period occupied what had formerly been the Benedictine abbey of Nieder-Altaich. The boy was educated by the canons and he attracted the notice of the bishops of Passau and Regensburg and the favour of Archbishop Frederick of Salzburg. The last named not only took him to Rome, but also made him provost of the canons at the age of nineteen. When, mainly through the efforts of the three prelates, the Benedictine rule was restored in Nieder-Altaich in 990, Godehard, by this time a priest, received the monastic habit together with several other canons. He rose to be abbot, his installation being honoured by the presence of St Henry, then duke of Bavaria—afterwards emperor—who always held him in the utmost esteem. A girdle worked for him by the Empress Cunegund was long venerated as a relic. The excellent order kept by Godehard at Nieder-Altaich prompted St Henry to send him to reform the monasteries of Tegernsee, in the diocese of Freising, Hersfeld, in Thuringia, and Kremsmünster in the diocese of Passau. This difficult task he accomplished satisfactorily whilst retaining the direction of Nieder-Altaich, which was ruled by a deputy during his long absences. In the course of twenty-five years he formed nine abbots for various houses.

St Bernwald, bishop of Hildesheim, died in 1022, and the Emperor Henry immediately decided to nominate Godehard to be his successor. He was obliged to comply with the wishes of the monarch, supported by the local clergy. Although he was sixty years of age he threw himself into the work of his diocese with the zest and energy of a young man. He built and restored churches: he did much to foster education, especially in the cathedral school; he established such strict order in his chapter that it resembled a monastery; and, on a swampy piece of land which he reclaimed on the outskirts of Hildesheim, he built a hospice where the sick and poor were tenderly cared for. He had a great love for the really necessitous, but he looked with less favour on able-bodied professional tramps; he called them 'peripatetics,' and would not allow them to stay for more than two or three days in the hospice. The holy bishop died in 1038 and was canonized in 1131.

5 : ST HILARY, BISHOP OF ARLES (A.D. 449)

THE birthplace of St Hilary of Arles is not known, but he came of a noble family and was nearly related to St Honoratus, the founder and first abbot of the monastery of Lérins. Having received an excellent education and being endowed with exceptional abilities, he had the prospect of a successful career in the world. But St Honoratus, who had always loved him, was convinced that he was called to the special service of God. The holy abbot actually abandoned for a short time his island retreat to seek out his young kinsman with the object of inducing him to embrace the religious life. Hilary, however, seemed proof against all his entreaties and fears.

He found himself a prey to a violent interior contest. 'On the one side I felt that the Lord was calling me, whilst on the other hand the seductions of the world held me back,' he afterwards wrote. 'My will swayed backwards and forwards, now consenting, now refusing. But at last Christ triumphed in me.' Once he had definitely made up his mind, he had never looked back: he distributed to the poor the proceeds of his patrimony, which he sold to his brother, and then went to join St Honoratus at Lérins.

In 426 St Honoratus was elected of Arles and being an old man, greatly desired the assistance and companionship of his favourite relation. Hilary was loth to leave Lérins, but Honoratus went in person to fetch him and they remained together until the bishop's death. Grieved though he was at the loss of his spiritual father, the young monk rejoiced at the prospect of returning to his abbey. He had started on his journey when he was overtaken by messengers, sent by the citizens of Arles, who desired to have him for their archbishop. He was obliged to consent and was duly consecrated, although only twenty-nine years of age.

In his new station Hilary observed the austerities of the cloister, while carrying out with immense energy all the duties of his office. He presided over several church councils; but his very zeal, and, perhaps, a somewhat autocratic temper, caused him on more than one occasion to act in a way which had serious consequences for himself. The limits of his province as metropolitan of Southern Gaul had never been satisfactorily settled, and once, when he was on a visitation in debatable territory, he deposed a certain bishop called Chelidonius on the plea that before he had received holy orders he had married a widow and, as a magistrate, had passed a death sentence. Either of these charges, if substantiated, would have disqualified him for the episcopate. Chelidonius forthwith set out for Rome, where he cleared himself of the imputations to the satisfaction of Pope St Leo the Great. As soon as St Hilary realized that the prelate he had deposed had gone to the Holy City, he followed him thither. To settle the matter a council was called, which Hilary attended—not, however, to defend his action, but to contend that the case ought to have been tried by the papal commissaries in Gaul. He did not even await the verdict. Realizing that he was being kept under supervision, and fearing lest he might be forced to communicate with Chelidonius, he left Rome secretly and returned to Arles. Judgement was given against him, and soon afterwards another complaint against him reached the Holy See. Whilst a Gaulish bishop called Projectus was still living—though apparently at the point of death—Hilary had appointed another bishop to the see. The sick man recovered, and there were two prelates claiming the same diocese. Hilary supported his own nominee, perhaps because the other claimant was too infirm to carry out his duties, but St Leo, to whom the matter was referred, rightly judged that Hilary's proceedings had been irregular and were likely to lead to schism. He therefore censured him, forbade him to appoint any more bishops and transferred the dignity of metropolitan to the bishop of Fréjus.

We know little about St Hilary's last years, except that he continued to labour in his own diocese with the same zeal as before, and that he died in his forty-ninth year.

6 : ST PETRONAX, ABBOT OF MONTE CASSINO (c. A.D. 747)

THE second founder of the abbey of Monte Cassino, St Petronax was a native of Brescia. He seems to have been induced by Pope St Gregory II to make a pilgrimage to the tomb of St Benedict in the year 717. There, among the ruins of the old monastery which had been destroyed by the Lombards in 581, he found a few solitaries, who elected him their superior. Other disciples soon gathered round them. Through the generosity of prominent nobles, chief amongst whom was the Lombard duke of Beneventum, and with the strong support of three popes, he succeeded in rebuilding Monte Cassino, which, under his long and vigorous rule, regained its old eminence. The English St Willibald, afterwards bishop of Eichstätt, received the habit at his hands. St Sturmius, founder of the abbey of Fulda, spent some time at Monte Cassino learning the primitive Benedictine rule, and great men of all kinds, princes as well as ecclesiastics, stayed within its hospitable walls. St Petronax ruled over the community until his death, the date of which was probably 747.

7 : ST JOHN OF BEVERLEY, BISHOP OF YORK (A.D. 721)

THE saint was born at Harpham, a village in Yorkshire. As a young man, he was attracted to Kent by the famous school of St Theodore in which he became a distinguished student under the holy abbot Adrian. Upon his return to his own county, he entered the double abbey of Whitby, then under the rule of the Abbess Hilda. His exceptional abilities marked him out for preferment, and after the death of St Eata he was appointed bishop of Hexham. Whatever time he could spare from the duties of his office he devoted to heavenly contemplation, retiring for that purpose at stated periods to a cell beside the church of St Michael beyond the Tyne, near Hexham.

After the death of St Bosa, John was appointed bishop of York. The Venerable Bede, who received holy orders from St John when bishop of

Hexham, refers to him at some length in his *Ecclesiastical History*, giving ample testimony to his sanctity, and recounting several miracles which had been described to him by such reliable eye-witnesses as the abbots of Beverley and of Tynemouth. After St John had been translated to York he continued his practice of a periodical retirement from the world for spiritual refreshment. He chose for his retreat an abbey which he had built at Beverley, then a forest. In 717, when he was much worn by age and fatigue, St John resigned his bishopric to his chaplain, St Wilfrid the Younger, and retired to Beverley, where he spent the four last years of his life in the faithful performance of monastic duties. St John died on May 7, 721.

8 : ST PETER, ARCHBISHOP OF TARENTAISE (A.D. 1175)

ST PETER of Tarentaise was born near Vienne in the French province of the Dauphiné. He early displayed a remarkable memory, coupled with a great inclination for religious studies, and at the age of twenty he entered the abbey of Bonnevaux. After a time, his father and the other two sons followed Peter to Bonnevaux, whilst his mother, with the only daughter, entered a neighbouring Cistercian nunnery.

He was not quite thirty when he was chosen superior of a new house built at Tamié, in the desert mountains of Tarentaise. It overlooked the pass which was then the chief route from Geneva to Savoy, and the monks were able to be of great use to travellers. There, with the help of Amadeus III, Count of Savoy, who held him in high esteem, he founded a hospice for the sick and for strangers, in which he was wont to wait upon his guests with his own hands.

In 1142 came his election to the archbishopric of Tarentaise, and Peter was compelled by St Bernard and the general chapter of his order, though much against the grain, to accept the office. He found the diocese in a deplorable state, due mainly to the mismanagement of his predecessor, an unworthy man who had eventually to be deposed. In place of the cathedral clergy whom he found lax and careless, St Peter substituted canons regular of St Augustine. He undertook the constant visitation of his diocese; recovered property which had been alienated; appointed good priests to various parishes; made excellent foundations for the education of the young and relief of the poor; and everywhere provided for the due celebration of the services of the Church. The author of his life, who was his constant companion at this period, testifies to numerous miracles which he wrought, mainly in curing the sick and multiplying provisions in time of famine.

In 1155, after he had administered the diocese for thirteen years, Peter suddenly disappeared. Actually he had made his way to a remote Cistercian abbey in Switzerland, where, he was accepted as a lay-brother. Not until a year later was he discovered. His identity having been revealed to his new superiors, Peter was obliged to leave and return to his see, where he was greeted with great joy. He took up his duties more zealously than ever. He rebuilt the hospice of the Little St Bernard and founded other similar refuges for travellers in the Alps.

His chief political efforts were directed to supporting the cause of the true pope, Alexander III, against the pretensions of the antipope, Victor, who had behind him the redoubtable Emperor Frederick Barbarossa. At one time, indeed, it seemed as though the archbishop of Tarentaise was the only subject of the empire who dared openly to oppose the pretender, but it soon became apparent that he carried with him the whole of the great Cistercian Order. To establish the claims of the true pontiff, St Peter preached in Alsace, Lorraine, Burgundy and many parts of Italy. He also spoke out fearlessly in various councils and even in the presence of the emperor himself, who was so far impressed by his sanctity and courage as to permit in him a freedom of speech he would endure from no one else.

It was not granted to the saint to die amongst his mountain flock. His reputation as a peacemaker led Alexander III to send him in 1174 to try effect a reconciliation between King Louis VII of France and Henry II of England. St Peter, though he was old, set out at once, preaching everywhere on his way. As he approached Chaumont in the Vexin, where the French court was being held, he was met by King Louis and by Prince Henry, the rebellious heir to the English throne. The latter, alighting from his horse to receive the archbishop's blessing, asked for the saint's old cloak, which he reverently kissed. Both at Chaumont and at Gisors where he interviewed the English king, St Peter was treated with utmost honour, but the reconciliation for which he laboured did not take place until after his death. As he was returning to his diocese he was taken ill on the road near Besançon, and died as he was being carried into the abbey of Bellevaux. This St Peter was canonized in 1191.

9 : ST PACHOMIUS, ABBOT (A.D. 348)

PACHOMIUS was born of heathen parents in the Upper Thebaîd about the year 292, and when twenty was conscripted for the emperor's army. As he and other recruits were being conveyed down the Nile under wretched conditions, they received great kindness from the Christians of Latopolis (Esneh), who were moved with compassion for them. This disinterested charity Pachomius never forgot; and as soon as the army was disbanded, he made his way back home to Khenoboskion (Kasr as-Syad), where there was a Christian church, and enrolled himself among the catechumens. After his baptism his one preoccupation was how best to correspond with the grace he had received. Having heard that an old hermit called Palaemon was serving God with great perfection in the desert, he sought him out and begged him to receive him as a disciple. The life they led together was one of extreme austerity: their diet was bread and salt; they drank no wine and used no oil; they always watched half the night and frequently passed the whole of it without sleep. Sometimes they would repeat the entire psalter together; at other times they would occupy themselves in manual labour accompanied by interior prayer.

One day when Pachomius was visiting, as he occasionally did, a vast uninhabited desert on the banks of the Nile called Tabennisi, he is said to have heard a voice bidding him begin a monastery there, and about the same time he had a vision of an angel who gave him certain instructions regarding the religious life. These revelations he imparted to Palaemon, who accompanied him to Tabennisi about the year 318, helped him to construct a cell and remained with him for some time before returning to his solitude.

The first disciple to receive the habit at Tabennisi from St Pachomius was his own eldest brother John: others followed, and within a comparatively short time the number of his monks exceeded one hundred. He established six other monasteries in the Thebaïd, and from the year 336 resided often at Pabau, near Thebes, which became a larger and even more famous community than Tabennisi. He built for the benefit of the poor shepherds a church in which for some time he acted as lector, but he could never be induced to offer himself for the priesthood, or to present any of his monks for ordination.

He zealously opposed the Arians, and in 333 had a visit from St Athanasius. For the benefit of his sister whom, however, he never would see, he built a nunnery on the opposite side of the Nile. Pachomius died on May 15, 348, of an epidemic disease which had already carried off many of his brethren. He had lived to see three thousand monks in the nine monasteries under his charge.

10 : ST ANTONINUS, ARCHBISHOP OF FLORENCE (A.D. 1459)

ANTONINUS' father, a citizen of good family, and notary to the republic, was called Nicholas Pierozzi, and he himself received in baptism the name of Antony. The diminutive, Antonino, which clung to him all his life, was given him in childhood because of his small stature and gentle disposition. A serious boy, much addicted to prayer, he loved to listen to the sermons of Bd John Dominici, then prior of Santa Maria Novella, and when he was fifteen he asked the friar to admit him to the Dominican Order. The saintly John, judging him too weakly for the life, tried to put him off by bidding him study for a time and learn the *Decretum Gratiani*; but when, within a year, the lad returned, having committed the whole of the treatise to memory, he was received without further hesitation.

Antoninus early gave evidence of exceptional gifts as a scholar and as a leader. He was chosen when very young to govern the great convent of the Minerva in Rome; and afterwards he was successively prior at Naples, Gaeta, Cortona, Siena, Fiesole and Florence. As superior of the reformed Tuscan and Neapolitan congregations, and also as prior provincial of the whole Roman province, he zealously enforced the measures initiated by Bd John Dominici with a view to restoring the primitive rule. At Florence in 1436 he founded the famous convent of San Marco in buildings taken over from the Silvestrines, but practically rebuilt by him after designs by Michelozzi and decorated with the frescoes of Fra Angelico who had been a novice with him.

The adjacent late thirteenth-century church was rebuilt with great magnificence by Cosimo de'Medici to serve the new Dominican house. In addition to his official duties, St Antoninus preached often and wrote works which made him famous among his contemporaries. He was consulted from Rome and from all quarters, especially in intricate cases of canon law. Pope Eugenius IV summoned him to attend the general Council of Florence, and he assisted at all its sessions. He was occupied with reforming houses in the province of Naples when he learnt to his dismay that the pope had nominated him to be archbishop of Florence. He was consecrated in March 1446 amid the rejoicings of the citizens.

In his new capacity St Antoninus continued to practise all the observances of his rule, as far as his duties would permit. He gave audience daily to all comers, whilst declaring himself especially the protector of the poor, at whose disposal he kept his purse and granaries. When these were exhausted he gave away his furniture and his clothes. He put down gambling in his diocese, was the determined foe of both usury and magic, and reformed abuses of all kinds. In addition to preaching nearly every Sunday and festival, he visited his whole diocese once a year, always on foot. His reputation for wisdom and integrity was such that he was unceasingly consulted by those in authority, laymen as well as ecclesiastics; and his decisions were so judicious that they won for him the title of 'the Counsellor.' When Pope Eugenius IV was dying he summoned Antoninus to Rome, received from him the last sacraments and died in his arms. Nicholas V sought his advice on matters of church and state, forbade any appeal to be made to Rome from the archbishop's judgements, and declared that Antonino in his lifetime was as worthy of canonization as the dead Bernardino (da Siena), whom he was about to raise to the altars. Pius II nominated him to a commission charged with reforming the Roman court. The Florentine government charged him with important embassies on behalf of the republic and would have sent him as their representative to the emperor if illness had not prevented him from leav! ng Florence.

Cosimo de'Medici publicly asserted that the preservation of the republic from the dangers which threatened it was largely due to the merits and prayers of the holy archbishop. St Antoninus was canonized in 1523.

11 : ST FRANCIS DI GIROLAMA, A.D. 1716)

FRANCIS an the eldest of a family of eleven, was born in 1642 at Grottaglie, near Taranto. After he had made his first communion, at the age of twelve, he was received into the house of some secular priests in the neighbourhood who lived a community life. The good fathers were not slow to perceive that their young charge was no ordinary boy; from leaving him in charge of their church they promoted him to teaching the catechism, and he received the tonsure when he was barely sixteen. With a view to learning canon and civil law, he went to Naples in the company of a brother who desired to study under an eminent painter. In 1666 Francis was ordained priest, for which a dispensation had to be obtained as he was not yet twenty-four. For the next five years he taught at Naples in the Jesuit Collegio dei Nobili. At the age of twenty-eight, having overcome the opposition of his parents, he entered the Society of Jesus.

During the first year of novitiate Francis was subjected to exceptionally severe tests by his superiors, who were so completely satisfied that at its close they sent him to help the celebrated preacher Father Agnello Bruno in his mission work. From 1671 till 1674, the two priests laboured untiringly and with great success, mainly amongst the peasants of the province of

Otranto. At the close of that mission Francis was recalled to Naples where he completed his theological studies and was professed. He was now appointed preacher at the Neapolitan church known as the Gesu Nuovo. From the outset his preaching attracted huge congregations and was rewarded by such excellent results that he was set to train other missionaries. In the provinces he conducted at least 100 missions. Wherever he went, men and women hung upon his lips and crowded to his confessional. He would visit the prisons, the hospitals and even the galleys, in one of which—a Spanish one—he brought to the faith twenty Turkish prisoners. Often he would preach in the streets—occasionally on the spur of the moment.

Amid his numerous penitents of all classes, perhaps the most remarkable was a woman, French by birth, called Mary Alvira Cassier. She had murdered her father and had afterwards served in the Spanish army, disguised as a man. Under the direction of St Francis she not only was brought to penitence, but attained to a high degree of holiness.

The effects of the preaching of the holy Jesuit were enhanced by his reputation as a wonder-worker, but he consistently disclaimed any extraordinary powers, attributing the numerous cures which attended his ministrations to the intercession of St Cyrus (January 31), for whom he had a special veneration. St Francis di Girolamo died at the age of seventy-four, after much suffering, and his remains were interred in the Jesuit church of Naples where they still lie. He was canonized in 1839.

12 : ST GERMANUS, PATRIARCH OF CONSTANTINOPLE (A.D. 732)

ST GERMANUS was the son of a senator of Constantinople, was educated for the priesthood, and was for some time attached to the metropolitan church; but after his father's death, at a date which is not recorded, he was appointed bishop of Cyzicus. Under Anastasius II Germanus was translated from Cyzicus to the see of Constantinople. Within a year of his accession he called a synod of 100 bishops at which the true doctrine of the Church was asserted against the monothelite heresy.

After Leo the Isaurian had ascended the imperial throne in 717, St Germanus crowned him in the church of the Holy Wisdom, and the emperor solemnly swore to preserve the Catholic faith. Ten years later, when Leo declared himself in sympathy with the iconoclasts and set himself against the veneration of images, St Germanus reminded him of the vow he had made. In spite of this remonstrance, the emperor issued an edict prohibiting the outward display of reverence to religious statues and pictures, all of which were to be raised to a height which precluded the public from kissing them. A later and still more drastic decree ordered the general destruction of sacred images and the whitewashing of church walls. The patriarch, though a very old man, spoke out fearlessly in defence of images and wrote letters upholding the Catholic tradition to bishops inclined to favour the iconoclasts.

Over and over again did Leo attempt to win over the aged prelate, but finally, in 730, realizing that his efforts remained fruitless, he practically compelled St Germanus to relinquish his office. The saint then retired to his paternal home, where he spent the remainder of his life in monastic seclusion, preparing for his death which took place when he was over ninety.

13 : ST JOHN THE SILENT, (A.D. 558)

HE was born in the year 454, at Nicopolis in Armenia, of a family which had supplied generals and governors for that part of the empire. After the death of his parents he built a monastery in which, at the age of eighteen, he shut himself up with ten companions. Here, under the direction of their youthful superior, the little community led a most edifying life of devotion and hard work. The great reputation St John acquired for sanctity and leadership led the archbishop of Sebaste to consecrate him bishop of Colonia in Armenia, much against his will, when he was only twenty-eight. For nine years he exercised his episcopal functions, zealously instructing his flock, depriving himself of even the necessaries of life that he might relieve the poor, and continuing to practise as far as possible the austerities of his former life. Then his inability to remedy certain evils, combined with a strong desire for a secluded life, decided him to lay down his charge. Instead of returning to Armenia he quietly went to Jerusalem—uncertain as to his future vocation.

His biographer assures us that whilst John was watching one night in prayer he saw before him a bright cross in the air and heard a voice which said, 'If thou desirest to be saved, follow this light.' The cross then moved before him, and at length directed him to the laura (monastery) of St Sabas. Convinced that he now knew God's will, St John immediately betook himself to the laura, which contained one hundred and fifty monks. He was then thirty-eight years old. St Sabas at first placed him under the steward to fetch water, carry stone, and serve the workmen in building a new hospital. After this test, the experienced superior made him guestmaster. By this time St Sabas recognized that his novice was on the road to perfection and, in order to give him opportunities for uninterrupted contemplation, he allowed him to occupy a separate hermitage. During five consecutive days of the week, which he passed fasting, John never left his cell; but on Saturdays and Sundays he attended public worship in church. After three years spent in this eremitic life, he was made steward of the laura.

Four years later St Sabas thought him worthy of the priesthood and decided to present him to the Patriarch Elias. Upon their arrival at the church of Mount Calvary, where the ordination was to take place, John said to the patriarch, 'Holy father, I have something to impart to you in private: afterwards, if you judge me suitable, I will receive holy orders.' The patriarch granted him a private interview, and St John, when he had bound him to secrecy, said, 'Father, I have been consecrated bishop: but on account of my many sins I have fled and have sought out this desert to await the coming of the Lord.' Elias was startled, and having summoned St Sabas, declared, 'I cannot ordain this man, because of certain particulars he has communicated to me.' St Sabas returned home deeply grieved because he feared that John must have committed some terrible crime, but in answer to his earnest prayer the truth was made known to him by revelation. He was, however, directed not to divulge the secret to others.

In the year 503 the factious spirit of certain turbulent monks obliged St Sabas to leave his laura; St John at the same time withdrew into a neighbouring desert, where he spent six years. When St Sabas was recalled to his community, St John returned to the laura and there lived in his cell for forty years. His love of obscurity and his humility made him desire more than ever to live unknown. Nevertheless the fame of his sanctity made it impossible for him to realize his ambition, and he now no longer refused to see those who resorted to him for advice. Both by example and precept St John led many souls to God, and continued in his hermitage to emulate, as far as this mortal state will allow, the glorious employment of the heavenly spirits in an uninterrupted exercise of love and praise. He passed to their blessed company in A.D. 558—having lived in solitude for seventy-six years, interrupted only by the nine years of his episcopate.

14 : ST MICHAEL GARICOÏTS, FOUNDER OF THE PRIESTS OF THE SACRED HEART OF BÉTHARRAM (A.D. 1863)

TOWARDS the close of the eighteenth century, and in the early part of the nineteenth, there was living in the Lower Pyrenees, at the hamlet of Ibarra, a family of poor peasants named Garicoïts. Their cottage was humble enough but its hospitable door was always open to proscribed priests who, from time to time during the French Revolution and the years immediately following, came to minister in secret to the faithful. Here on April 15, 1797, there was born to Arnold and Gratianne Garicoïts their eldest son Michael. Life is hard in those mountain regions, and the boy was a mere child when he was hired out to be shepherd-boy to a farmer. His own often expressed desire was to be a priest, but his parents always replied, 'No, we are too poor.' The old grandmother thought otherwise. One day she went to talk the matter over with the parish priest of Saint-Palais, who in times past had often found a hiding-place in the Garicoïts' cottage. Through his efforts the boy was received first into the College of S. Palais and afterwards at Bayonne, arrangements having been made that he should earn his expenses by working out of school hours for the clergy and in the bishop's kitchen. Philosophy he studied at Aire and theology in the *grand séminaire* at Dax; and in December 1823 he was ordained priest in Bayonne cathedral by Bishop d'Astros.

Michael's first parochial experience was gained at Cambo, whither he was sent to act as *vicaire* to the *curé*, who was in feeble health. In the two years he remained there he did much to revive religion, combating Jansenism by the custom of frequent communion as well as by introducing Sacred Heart devotions. Father Garicoïts' next call was to a professorship in the senior seminary for priests at Bétharram, and then to be superior—a congenial post which he filled with conspicuous ability and success. The bishop, however, suddenly decided to merge the seminary with that of Bayonne, and Michael Garicoïts found himself with two other priests left alone to carry on the services.

During this period, there began to take shape in his mind a scheme for training priests to do mission work among the people. With two or three companions he started to live a community life, and then, in order that he might better know God's will, he went to Toulouse to attend a retreat given by Father Le Blanc, a Jesuit. To this good priest he opened his heart, and was encouraged to persevere. 'You will be the father of a congregation that will be our sister,' said the Jesuit, and Father Garicoïts drew up in 1838 a constitution largely based on that of the sons of St Ignatius. Like them, his missionaries were to take life vows and to spread far and wide. Associates gathered round him at Bétharram, and all seemed promising, when a check came from an unexpected quarter. The bishop who had been his patron and had ordained him was replaced by another, who viewed with disapproval this idea of founding a new congregation. His constitutions were subjected to a fundamental revision, he was told to confine himself to the diocese, and to work only under the direction of the bishop. Not till 1852 was the community allowed to choose its own superior, and even then it was tied down by regulations which hampered its activity. Father Garicoïts submitted, but with a heavy heart. 'What pangs accompany the birth of a congregation!' he once said to one of his sons; but generally he bore his trials in silence. He died on Ascension-day, May 14, 1863.

Fourteen years later the Society of Priests of the Sacred Heart of Bétharram was approved by the Holy See on the lines the founder had laid down.

15 : ST ISIDORE THE FARMER, (A.D. 1130)

THE patron of Madrid was born in the Spanish capital of poor parents, and was christened Isidore after the celebrated archbishop of Seville. As soon as he was old enough to work, Isidore entered the service of John de Vergas, a wealthy resident of Madrid, as a farm labourer on his estate outside the city, and with that one employer he remained all his life. He married a girl as poor and as good as himself, but after the birth of one son, who died young, they agreed to serve God in perfect continence. Isidore's whole life was a model of Christian perfection lived in the world. He would rise early to go to church, and all day long, whilst his hand guided the plough, he would be communing with God, with his guardian angel or with the holy saints. Public holidays he would spend in visiting the churches of Madrid and the neighbouring districts. The saint's liberality to the poor was so great that he was wont to share his meals with them, often reserving for himself only the scraps they left over.

Amongst the numerous stories told of the holy man is one which illustrates his love for animals. On a snowy winter's day, as he was carrying a sack of corn to be ground, he saw a number of birds perched disconsolately on the bare branches, obviously unable to find anything to eat. Isadore opened the sack and, in spite of the jeers of a companion, poured out half its contents upon the ground. When, however, they reached their destination the sack proved to be still full and the corn, when ground, produced double the usual amount of flour.

St Isidore died on May 15, 1130. His wife survived him for several years and, like him, is honoured as a saint. Forty years after the death of St Isidore his body was transferred to a more honourable shrine, and a great impetus was given to his cult by the report of many miracles worked through his intercession. In 1211 he is said to have appeared in a vision to King Alphonsus of Castile, then fighting the Moors in the pass of Navas de Tolosa, and to have shown him an unknown path by means of which he was able to surprise and defeat the enemy.

The Spanish royal family had long desired to have St Isidore formally enrolled amongst the saints, and in March 1622 he was duly canonized.

16 : ST BRENDAN, ABBOT OF CLONFERT (A.D. 577 OR 583)

BRENDAN was a real personage, and exercised great influence amongst his contemporaries in the sixth century. He was probably born near Tralee on the west coast of Ireland, and Findlugh is given as his father's name. For five years as a tiny child he was committed to the care of St Ita, and after that he was watched over by Bishop Erc who had already baptized him as an infant and who was in due time to ordain him priest. St Jarlath of Tuam is also named as one of the holy men whom he visited with the view of obtaining edification and counsel.

To determine the chronological sequence of events is quite impossible, but we should be led to infer that shortly after being raised to the priesthood, St Brendan assumed the habit of a monk and gathered followers around him in a settled community. How he could have left these behind to start off with sixty chosen companions in skin-covered coracles to discover the Isles of the Blessed is a difficulty which does not seem to have troubled his biographers.

The most reliable fact which we can connect with the life of St Brendan is his foundation of a monastic community at Clonfert in 559(?). His biographers speak of his governing a community of three thousand monks. He is also said to have had a rule of life dictated to him by an angel. We know nothing of its nature, but we are told that the rule was followed 'down to the present day' by those who succeeded him in the office of abbot. There seems, again, no sufficient reason for questioning the statement that he did not die at Clonfert, but that God called him to his reward when he was paying a visit to his sister, Brig, who governed a community at Enach Duin. Foreseeing that attempts would be made to detain his body, he directed that his death should be kept secret for a time, while his remains were taken back to Clonfert in a cart, disguised as luggage he was sending on in advance of his own return.

17 : ST PASCHAL BAYLON, (A.D. 1592)

THANKS mainly to his fellow religious, superior and biographer, Father Ximenes, we are well informed regarding Paschal's early days. He first saw the light at Torre Hermosa, on the borders of Castile and Aragon, on a Whitsunday, and to that accident he seems to have owed his Christian name, for in Spain, as well as in Italy, the term *Pascua* is given to other great feasts of the year besides Easter. So the little son born to Martin Baylon and his wife Elizabeth Jubera was called Pascual.

From his seventh to his twenty-fourth year Paschal, first as the deputy of his own father, and then serving other employers, led the life of a shepherd. When Paschal, seemingly about the age of eighteen or nineteen, first sought admission among the barefooted Friars Minor, St Peter of Alacantara, the author of the reform, was still living. Probably the friars of the Loreto convent, knowing nothing of the young shepherd who came from a district two hundred miles away, doubted his fortitude. At any rate, they put him off, but when they admitted him some few years later, they soon realized that God had committed a treasure to their keeping. The community lived at the level of the first fervour of the reform, but Brother Paschal even in this ascetical atmosphere was recognized as being eminent in every religious virtue.

It is, however, as the Saint of the Eucharist that St Paschal is best remembered outside his own country. The long hours which he spent before the tabernacle, kneeling without support, his clasped hands held up in front of, or higher than, his face, had left a deep impression upon his brethren. He was on one occasion sent into France as the bearer of an important communication to Father Christopher de Cheffontaines, the very learned Breton scholar who at that time was minister general of the Observants. For a friar wearing the habit of his order the journey across France at that time, when the wars of religion had reached their most acute phase, was extremely dangerous. He succeeded in his mission, but was very roughly handled; on several occasions barely escaping with his life. At one town in particular, where he was stoned by a party of Huguenots, he seems to have sustained an injury to his shoulder which was a cause of suffering for the rest of his days.

St Paschal died, as he was born, on a Whitsunday, in the friary at Villareal. He was fifty-two years old. It was held to be significant of his life-long devotion to the Blessed Sacrament that, with the holy name of Jesus on his lips, he passed away just as the bell was tolling to announce the consecration at the high Mass. St Paschal's canonization took place in 1690.

18 : ST ERIC OF SWEDEN, MARTYR (A.D. 1161)

ST ERIC was acknowledged king in most parts of Sweden in 1150, and his line subsisted for a hundred years. He did much to establish Christianity in Upper Sweden and built or completed at Old Uppsala the first large church to be erected in his country. It is said that the ancient laws and constitutions of the kingdom were by his orders collected into one volume, which became known as King Eric's Law or the Code of Uppland. The king soon had to take up arms against the heathen Finns.

He vanquished them in battle, and at his desire, St Henry, Bishop of Uppsala, an Englishman, who had accompanied him on the expedition, remained in Finland to evangelize the people.

The king's zeal for the faith was far from pleasing to some of his nobles, and we are told that they entered into a conspiracy with Magnus, the son of the king of Denmark. St Eric was hearing Mass on the day after the feast of the Ascension when news was brought that a Danish army, swollen with Swedish rebels, was marching against him and was close at hand. He answered calmly, 'Let us at least finish the sacrifice; the rest of the feast I shall keep elsewhere'. After Mass was over, he recommended his soul to God, and marched forth in advance of his guards. The conspirators rushed upon him, beat him down from his horse, and cut off his head. His death occurred on May 18, 1161.

The king's relics are preserved in the cathedral of Uppsala, and his effigy appears in the arms of Stockholm.

19 : ST DUNSTAN, ARCHBISHOP OF CANTERBURY (A.D. 988)

ST DUNSTAN, the most famous of all the Anglo-Saxon saints, was born (*c*. A.D. 910) near Glastonbury of a noble family closely allied to the ruling house. He received his early education from some Irish scholars and others at Glastonbury, and then, while still a lad, he was sent to the court of King Athelstan. He had already received the tonsure, and his uncle, St Alphege the Bald, Bishop of Winchester, urged him to embrace the religious life. Dunstan demurred for a time, but after his recovery from a skin trouble which he took to be leprosy he hesitated no longer, receiving the habit and subsequently holy orders at the hands of his saintly kinsman. Returning to Glastonbury, he is said to have built himself a small cell adjoining the old church. There he divided his time between prayer, study, and manual labour which took the form of making bells and sacred vessels for the church and of copying or illuminating books. He also played the harp, for he was very musical.

Athelstan's successor, Edmund, recalled St Dunstan to court and in 943 appointed him abbott of Glastonbury. At once the new abbot set about reconstructing the monastic buildings and restoring the church of St Peter. By introducing monks amongst the clerks already in residence, he was able without too much friction to enforce regular discipline. Moreover, he made of the abbey a great school of learning. Other monasteries were revived from Glastonbury, and the work was carried on as well by St Ethelwold from Abingdon and St Oswald from Westbury.

The murder of King Edmund after a reign of six and a half years was followed by the accession of his brother Edred. The new monarch made Dunstan practically his chief adviser. The policy which the saint then initiated and which continued to be his throughout his career was vigorous and far-seeing; he stood out for reform—especially in morals—for the spread of regular observance to counteract the laxity of the secular clergy, and for the unification of the country by conciliating the Danish element. He became the acknowledged leader of a party which found its chief support in East Anglia and in the north, but he made made bitter enemies amongst those whose vices he opposed and amongst the mass of West Saxon nobles who were reactionary in their views. Edred died in 955 and was succeeded by his nephew Edwy, a boy of sixteen, who on the very day of his coronation left the royal banquet to seek the society of a girl called Elgiva and her mother, and was sternly rebuked by St Dunstan for his unseemly conduct. This reproof the young prince bitterly resented. With the support of the opposition party St Dunstan was disgraced, his property confiscated, and he was driven into exile. He found a refuge in Flanders, where he came into contact for the first time with continental monasticism, then in the fulness of its renewed vigour; it gave him a vision of Benedictine perfection which was to be an inspiration to him in all his after labours. His banishment, however, did not last long. A rebellion broke out in England, and the north and east, throwing off Edwy's yoke, chose for their ruler his brother Edgar. The new monarch immediately recalled St Dunstan, upon whom he bestowed first the see of Worcester and afterwards that of London. Upon Edwy's death in 959 the kingdom was reunited under Edgar, and St Dunstan became archbishop of Canterbury. Upon going to Rome to receive the pallium he was appointed by Pope John XII a legate of the Holy See. Armed with this authority the saint set himself energetically to re-establish ecclesiastical discipline, being powerfully protected by King Edgar and ably assisted by St Ethelwold, Bishop of Winchester, and St Oswald, Bishop of Worcester and Archbishop of York. These three prelates restored most of the great monasteries which had been destroyed during the Danish incursions and founded new ones. They were no less zealous in reforming the clergy, many of whom were leading worldly or scandalous lives, openly disregarding the canonical law binding them to celibacy. Where the seculars proved recalcitrant they were ejected, their places being supplied by monks.

Throughout the sixteen years' reign of Edgar, St Dunstan remained his chief adviser and he continued to direct the state during the short reign of the next king, Edward the Martyr. The death of the young prince was a grievous blow to his ecclesiastical prime minister, who when he crowned Edward's half-brother Ethelred in 970 foretold the calamities which were to mark his reign.

The archbishop's political career was now over. He took no further part in state matters, but retired to Canterbury. On the feast of the Ascension, 988, the archbishop, though ill, celebrated Mass and preached thrice to his people, to whom he announced his impending death. In the afternoon he went again to the cathedral and chose a place for his burial. Two days later he died peacefully.

20 : ST BERNARDINO OF SIENA, (A.D. 1444)

S T BERNARDINO was born in the Tuscan town of Massa Marittima, in which his father, a member of the noble Sienese family of the Albizeschi, occupied the post of governor. The little boy lost both his parents before he was seven and was entrusted to the care of a maternal aunt and her daughter who gave him a religious training and loved him as though he had been their own child. Upon reaching the age of eleven or twelve he was placed by his uncles at school in Siena, where he passed with great credit through the course of studies.

In 1400 Siena was visited by the plague. Twelve to twenty persons died daily in the famous hospital of Santa Maria della Scala, which found itself bereft of almost all who tended the sick. Bernardino offered to take charge of the establishment, with the help of some other young men whom he had fired with the determination to sacrifice their lives if necessary to aid the sufferers. For four months they worked tirelessly, day and night, under the direction of Bernardino, who, besides nursing the patients and preparing them for death, saw to everything and brought order as well as cleanliness into the hospital. Though several of his companions died, Berbardino escaped the contagion and returned home after the epidemic was over. He was, however, so exhausted by his labours that he fell an easy prey to a fever which laid him low for several months.

Upon his recovery he found that his immediate duty lay close at hand. An aunt named Bartolomea, to whom he was much attached, had become blind as well as bedridden, and to her he devoted himself as he had done to the plague-stricken in the hospital. When, fourteen months later, God called the invalid to Himself, it was in the arms of her nephew that she breathed her last. Free now from all earthly ties, Bernardino set himself by prayer and fasting to learn God's will as to his future. He was led to enter the Franciscan Order, the habit of which he received shortly afterwards in Siena. The house, however, proved too accessible to the novice's many friends and relations, and with the consent of his superiors he retired to the convent of Colombaio outside the city, where the rule of St Francis was strictly observed. Here in 1403 he was professed and here he was ordained priest—exactly a year later, on the feast of the Birthday of our Lady which was his birthday.

During the next twelve years he preached occasionally, but his life was mainly spent in retirement. Gradually he was being prepared by God for the twofold mission of apostle and reformer. He opened his apostolic career at Milan to which he went as a complete stranger towards the end of 1417, but soon his eloquence and zeal began to attract enormous congregations. Before he was allowed to leave the city to preach elsewhere in Lombardy he was obliged to promise that he would return the following year.

It is impossible to follow him on his missionary journeys, for in them he covered nearly the whole of Italy with the exception of the kingdom of Naples. He travelled always on foot, preached sometimes for three or four consecutive hours and often delivered several sermons on the same day. All over Italy people spoke of the wonderful fruit of St Bernardino's missions. Nevertheless there were some who took exception to his teaching and accused him of encouraging superstitious practices. They went so far as to denounce him to Pope Martin V, who for a time commanded him to keep silence. However, an examination of his doctrine and conduct led to a complete vindication and he received permission to preach wherever he liked. The same pope, in 1427, urged him to accept the bishopric of Siena but he refused it, as he afterwards declined the sees of Ferrara and of Urbino.

In 1430, however, he was obliged to give up missionary work to become vicar general of the friars of the Strict Observance. He accomplished this task with so much wisdom and tact that many convents passed voluntarily and without friction from the Conventual to the Observant rule. The original Observants had shunned scholarship as they had shunned riches, but St Bernardino insisted upon instruction in theology and canon law as part of the regular curriculum.

The saint longed to return to his apostolic labours which he regarded as his only vocation, and in 1442 he obtained permission from the pope to resign his office as vicar general. He then resumed his missionary journeys, which led him through the Romagna, Ferrara and Lombardy. He was by this time in failing health, yet at Massa Marittima in 1444 he preached on fifty consecutive days. Though obviously dying, he still continued his apostolic work and set out for Naples, preaching as he went. He succeeded in reaching Aquila, but there his strength gave out and he died on the eve of the Ascension, May 20, 1444, in the monastery of the Conventuals. He had almost reached the age of sixty-four years, forty-two of which he had spent as a religious. His tomb at Aquila was honoured by many miracles and he was canonized within six years of his death.

21 : ST ANDREW BOBOLA, MARTYR (A.D. 1657)

ST ANDREW BOBOLA came of an aristocratic Polish family and was born in the palatinate of Sandomir in 1591. He entered in 1609 the Jesuit noviciate at Vilna in Lithuania, which had become united with Poland in 1391 through the marriage of queen Hedwig with Duke Jagiello. After he had been raised to the priesthood, Andrew was appointed preacher in the church of St Casimir at Vilna, where his apostolic zeal made a great impression upon the people. At a later date he was chosen superior of the Jesuit house at Bobrinsk and, during his term of office, distinguished himself by his devotion to the sick and dying when a terrible epidemic was raging.

As soon as he was relieved of his charge, he resumed the missionary career which he had pursued for more than twenty years. His success brought upon him hatred and opposition. Poland at this time had become the scene of a sanguinary conflict in which the Cossacks took a prominent part. The Jesuit missionaries were driven from their churches and colleges, and they took refuge in a district of swamps, lakes and marshland formed by branches of the Pripet and Berezina and known as Podlesia. Thither Prince Radziwell invited the Jesuits, to whom he offered one of his residences at Pinsk in 1652. St Andrew accepted the invitation although he fully anticipated the fate that was in store for him.

In May 1657 some Cossacks made a sudden attack on Pinsk. Father Bobola was seized near Janow, and made to run back there at the heels of a Cossack's horse. He was invited to abjure Catholicism, and on his refusal was mercilessly beaten. He was then interrogated, and his firm answers so infuriated the officer that he slashed at him with his sword and nearly severed one of the priest's hands. He was then put to a slow death with the most revolting barbarity. In the public slaughterhouse he was stripped of his clothes, scorched all over like a dead pig, half flayed, his nose and lips cut off, and his tongue torn out through his neck with pincers. His prayers to Christ and His mother seemed only to increase his tormentors' savagery. At last his head was struck off, and the mutilated body cast on a dungheap.

22 : ST RITA OF CASCIA, WIDOW (A.D. 1457)

RITA was born in 1381 in Roccaborena in the central Apennines. She showed from her earliest years extraordinary piety and love of prayer. She had set her heart upon dedicating herself to God in the Augustinian convent at Cascia, but when her father and mother decreed that she should marry, she sorrowfully submitted, deeming that in obeying them she was fulfilling God's will. Her parents' choice was an unfortunate one. Her husband proved to be brutal, dissolute and so violent that his temper was the terror of the neighbourhood. For eighteen years with unflinching patience and gentleness Rita bore with his insults and infidelities. As with a breaking heart she watched her two sons fall more and more under their father's evil influence, she shed many tears in secret and prayed for them without ceasing. Eventually there came a day when her husband's conscience was touched, so that he begged her forgiveness for all the suffering he had caused her: but shortly afterwards he was carried home dead covered with wounds.

Her sons vowed to avenge their father's death, and in an agony of sorrow she prayed that they might die rather than commit murder. Her prayer was answered. Before they had carried out their purpose they contracted an illness which proved fatal. Their mother nursed them tenderly and succeeded in bringing them to a better mind, so that they died forgiving and forgiven. Left alone in the world, Rita's longing for the religious life returned, and she tried to enter the convent at Cascia. She was informed, however, to her dismay that the constitutions forbade the reception of any but virgins. Three times she made application, and three times the prioress reluctantly refused her. But her persistence triumphed: the rules were relaxed in her favour and she received the habit in 1413.

In the convent St Rita displayed the same submission to authority which she had shown as a daughter and wife. No fault could be found with her observance of the rule. On the other hand, where latitude was allowed by the rule—as in the matter of extra austerities—she was pitiless to herself. Her charity to her neighbour expressed itself in her care for her fellow religious during illness and for the conversion of negligent Christians. From childhood she had had a special devotion to the sufferings of our Lord, and when in 1441 she heard an eloquent sermon on the crown of thorns from St James della Marca, a strange physical reaction seems to have followed. While she knelt, absorbed in prayer, she became acutely conscious of pain—as of a thorn which had detached itself from the crucifix and embedded itself in her forehead. It developed into an open wound which suppurated and became so offensive that she had to be secluded from the rest. The wound was healed for a season to enable her to accompany her sisters on a pilgrimage to Rome during the year of the jubilee, 1450, but it was renewed after her return and remained with her until her death, obliging her to live practically as a recluse.

She died on May 22, 1457, and her body has remained incorrupt until modern times.

23 : ST JOHN BAPTIST ROSSI, (A.D. 1764)

THIS holy priest was born in 1698 at the village of Voltaggio in the diocese of Genoa, one of four children. When he was ten, a nobleman and his wife who were spending the summer at Voltaggio obtained permission from his parents to take him back with them to Genoa to be trained in their house. He remained with them three years, winning golden opinions from all, notably from two Capuchin friars who came to his patron's home. They carried such a favourable report of the boy to his uncle, who was then minister provincial of the Capuchins, that a cousin, Lorenzo Rossi, a canon of Santa Maria in Cosmedin, invited him to come to Rome. The offer was accepted, and John Baptist entered the Roman College at the age of thirteen. He had completed the classical course with distinction when the reading of an ascetical book led him to embark on excessive mortifications. The strain on his strength at a time when he was working hard led to a complete breakdown, which obliged him to leave the Roman College. He recovered sufficiently to complete his training at the Minerva, but he never was again really robust.

On March 8, 1721, at the age of twenty-three, John Baptist was ordained, and his first Mass was celebrated in the Roman College. Even in his student days he had been in the habit of visiting the hospitals. Now, as a priest, he could do far more for the patients. Very particularly did he love the hospice of St Galla, a night refuge for paupers which had been founded by Pope Celestine III. For forty years he laboured amongst the inmates, consoling and instructing them. The hospital of the Trinità dei Pellegrini was also a field of his labours. But there were other poor people for whom, as he discovered, no provision had hitherto been made; there were the cattle-drovers who came from the country to sell their beasts at the market then held in the Roman Forum. In the early morning and late evening he would go amongst them, winning their confidence, instructing them and preparing them for the sacraments. Another class to whom his pity was extended comprised the homeless women and girls who wandered about begging, or who haunted the streets by night. He had absolutely no money except the little that came as Mass stipends, but with the help of 500 scudi from a charitable person and of 400 scudi from the pope, he hired a house behind the hospice of St Galla and made of it a refuge which he placed under the protection of St Aloysius Gonzaga.

In the year 1731, Canon Rossi obtained for his kinsman the post of assistant priest at Sta Maria in Cosmedin. The church, partly owing to its position, had been poorly attended, but it soon began to fill with penitents of all classes who flocked to St John Baptist's confessional. Upon the death of Canon Lorenzo Rossi in 1736 his canonry was conferred upon his cousin, who accepted it but gave up its emoluments to provide the church with an organ and the stipend of an organist. Even the house which he inherited from Canon Lorenzo he presented to the chapter, whilst he himself went to live in an attic

One very congenial task was undertaken at the request of Pope Benedict XIV, who inaugurated courses of instruction for prison officials and other state servants and selected this young priest to deliver them. Amongst his penitents was the public hangman. As a preacher the saint was in great demand also for missions and for giving addresses in religious houses of both men and women. But failing health obliged him, in 1763, to take up his residence in the Trinità dei Pellegrini, and in the December of that year he had a stroke and received the last sacraments. He rallied sufficiently to resume celebrating Mass, but he suffered greatly and on May 23, 1764, he succumbed to another apoplectic seizure. He was sixty-six years of age. He left so little money that the hospital of the Trinità had to undertake to pay for his burial. As it turned out, however, he was accorded a magnificent funeral: two hundred and sixty priests, many religious, and innumerable lay persons took part in the procession; Archbishop Lercari of Adrianople pontificated at the requiem in the church of the Trinità, whilst the papal choir provided the music.

The process of his beatification, begun in 1781, was completed by the bull of canonization in 1881.

24 : ST VINCENT OF LÉRINS, (c. A.D. 445)

ST VINCENT of Lérins is described by St Eucherius in his *Instructiones* and in his letter *De Laude Eremi* as a man 'pre-eminent in eloquence and learning'. He is supposed to have been the brother of St Lupus of Troyes, and he would seem to have been a soldier before he took the religious habit at the abbey of Lérins on the island off the coast of Cannes now called Saint-Honorat, after the founder of the monastery. St Vincent was living there as a monk and a priest when, in the year 434—nearly three years after the close of the Council of Ephesus—he composed the book upon which his fame rests, his so-called *Commonitorium* against heresies. In this book he explains that, in the course of his reading, he had gathered from the fathers certain principles or rules for distinguishing Christian truth from falsehood, and that he had jotted them down primarily for his own use, to aid his poor memory. These notes he expanded into a treatise in two parts, the second of which dealt with the recent Council of Ephesus. This latter portion, however, was lost or stolen, and St Vincent contented himself with adding to the first part a general summary or recapitulation of the whole. In this book of forty-two short chapters, we find enunciated for the first time the axiom that for a dogma to be regarded as Catholic truth it must have been held always, everywhere, and by all the faithful. ·

An immense body of literature has been provoked by his treatise and it has been very variously judged. It appeared at a time when the controversy over grace and free-will was raging, especially in the south of France, and many authorities regard the book as a thinly-veiled attack upon the extreme Augustinian doctrine of predestination. In support of this view they point to the fact that at the time when the *Commonitorium* was written, the abbot of Lérins and many of the monks were semi-Pelagians. If St Vincent erred in that direction he erred in company with many other holy men. The exact date of his death is not certain, but it seems to have been about the year 445.

25 : ST MADELEINE SOPHIE BARAT, VIRGIN, FOUNDRESS OF THE SOCIETY OF THE SACRED HEART (A.D. 1865)

MADELEINE SOPHIE BARAT was born on December 12, 1779, in the Burgundian town of Joigny, where her father was a cooper and the owner of a small vineyard. At her baptism, a brother eleven years her senior stood godfather. Louis was intended for the priesthood, and when, after completing his course at Sens, he returned as a deacon to take up a post as master in the college of his native city, he found his godchild a sprightly intelligent little girl of ten. Almost immediately the conviction forced itself upon him that she was destined by God to accomplish some great work for which it was his duty to fit her. This he proceeded to do by imparting to her an education similar to that which his boy pupils received, coupled with a discipline calculated to teach her to restrain her emotions and control her will.

In the year 1793, which saw the execution of Louis XVI and the inauguration of the Reign of Terror, Louis Barat, who had openly withdrawn his adherence to the civil constitution of the clergy as soon as it had been condemned by the pope, fled Joigny to escape prosecution, only to be arrested in Paris and to remain for two years a prisoner in constant expectation of death. Sophie in the meantime had grown up a charming and vivacious girl, the idol of her parents and the centre of an admiring circle of friends. To Louis, when he revisited Joigny as a priest after his liberation, there seemed real danger that she might lose that sense of vocation to the religious life which she had formerly evinced, and he transplanted her to Paris, where he was living and where he could resume his course of training.

As soon as the first fury of the French Revolution had spent itself, thoughtful people were confronted with the problem of providing education for the younger generation, seeing that all Christian schools had been swept away. Amongst those who took a deep interest in this was a group of young priests who had formed an association pledged to work for the restoration of the Society of Jesus, suppressed by Pope Clement XIV thirty years earlier. Their superior, Father Varin, had for some time been desirous of forming an institute of consecrated women for the training of girls, and when he heard from the Abbé Barat of his sister's abilities and training, he sent for her and questioned her. He then expounded to her his ideal of a great educational work for girls, a work deriving its inspiration from devotion to the Sacred Heart of Jesus. Humbly and diffidently she responded to the call.

On November 21, 1800, Madeleine Sophie and three other postulants began their religious life, and the following year she was sent to Amiens to teach in a school which had been taken over and which was the first convent of the new order. Soon a second school—a free one for poor children—was opened. More postulants came to the little community, but their first superior left them after two years, having proved herself devoid of ability to govern and lacking a true vocation. To her dismay Madeleine Sophie was appointed superior by Father Varin although she was only twenty-three and the youngest of all. She was to retain that office for sixty-three years.

The success of their educational ventures in Amiens led to requests for other foundations, and in 1804 Mother Barat travelled to Grenoble to take over the derelict convent of Sainte Marie-d'en-Haut as well as to receive into her institute the remnant of a community of Visitation nuns which it had sheltered.

The next settlement was at Poitiers, where an ancient Cistercian house, the abbey of the Feuillants, had been offered as a gift. St Madeleine Sophie made it the novitiate, and it became her headquarters for two years, which were perhaps the happiest of her life. There she trained her novices and from there she made occasional journeys across France and into Flanders to open fresh houses at Belley, Niort, Ghent and Cugnières.

In 1818 Mother Philippine Duchesne was sent with four companions to North America. Two years later Mother Barat summoned all the available local superiors to Paris—now the headquarters of the order—to draw up a general plan of study for the schools. Certain definite principles were laid down, but with characteristic clear-sightedness she insisted from the first that there should be facilities for development and adaptation.

In the December of 1826, in response to a memorandum drawn up by St Madeleine Sophie and presented by her to Pope Leo XII, the Society of the Sacred Heart received formal approbation. She lived to see her daughters firmly established in twelve countries of two continents. In 1864, when eighty-five years of age, she begged the general congregation to allow her to lay down her office, but all she could obtain was permission to choose a vicaress to assist her. The following year on May 21 she was stricken with paralysis and four days later, on the feast of the Ascension, her soul went to God. She was canonized in 1925.

26 : ST PHILIP NERI, (A.D. 1595)

ST PHILIP NERI was born in Florence in the year 1515, one of the four children of a notary called Francis Neri. Their mother died while they were very young, but her place was well supplied by an excellent stepmother. When Philip was eighteen he was sent to San Germano, to a childless kinsman who was supposed to have a flourishing business and who was likely to make him his heir. However, he did not stay there long. Soon after his arrival he passed through a mystical experience which in after years he spoke of as 'conversion', and from thenceforth worldly affairs had no more attraction for him. The atmosphere in which he was living became uncongenial, and he set out for Rome, without money and without plans, trusting entirely to the guidance of divine providence. In Rome he found shelter under the roof of Galeotto Caccia, a Florentine customs-official, who provided him with an attic and the bare necessaries of life. In return for his hospitality Philip gave lessons to his host's two small sons.

Except for the hours he devoted to his charges, St Philip seems to have spent the first two years of his residence in Rome almost like a recluse, giving up whole days and nights to prayer in his garret. It proved to be a period of inward preparation, at the close of which he emerged from his retreat, with his spiritual life strengthened and his determination fo live for God confirmed, while he proceeded to take up courses of philosophy and theology at the Sapienza and at Sant' Agostino. For three years he worked with diligence. Then, quite suddenly, he threw up his studies, sold most of his books and embarked upon an apostolate amongst the people. Religion at that time was at a low ebb in Rome, which was very slowly recovering from the effects of the sacking of 1527.

He began in a small way. He would stand about the street-corners and market place, entering into conversation with all sorts of people—especially with the young Florentines employed in the banks and shops of the Sant' Angelo quarter. He found them willing enough to respond provided he would show them the way. So he took them with him to wait upon the sick in the hospitals and to visit the Seven Churches—a favourite devotion of his own.

In the year 1548, with the help of his confessor, Father Persiano Rossa, who lived at San Girolamo della Carità, St Philip founded a confraternity of poor laymen who met for spiritual exercises in the church of San Salvatore in Campo. With their aid he popularized in Rome the devotion of the forty hours and undertook the care of needy pilgrims. This work was greatly blessed and developed into the celebrated hospital of Santa Trinità dei Pellegrini, which in the year of jubilee 1575 assisted no less than 145,000 pilgrims, and afterwards undertook the charge of poor convalescents. By the time he was thirty-four, St Philip Neri had accomplished much; but his confessor was convinced that he could do still more as a priest.

He was ordained on May 23, 1551, and went to live with Father Rossa and other priests at San Girolamo della Carità. His apostolate was now exercised mainly through the confessional. He had a wonderful power of reading the thoughts of those who resorted to him and effected an enormous number of conversions. For the benefit of these penitents he would hold informal spiritual conferences and discussions, followed by visits to churches or attendance at Vespers and Complin.

A large room was built over the nave of San Girolamo to accommodate the increasing numbers of those who attended the conferences, in the direction of which St Philip was aided by several other priests. The people called them Oratorians, because they rang a little bell to summon the faithful to prayers in their oratory, but the real foundation of the congregation so-named was laid a few years later, when St Philip presented five of his young disciples for ordination and sent them to serve the church of San Giovanni, the charge of which had been entrusted to him by his fellow Florentines in Rome. For these young priests, amongst whom was Cesare Baronius, the future historian, he drew up some simple rules of life. They shared a common table and spiritual exercises under his obedience, but he forbade them to bind themselves to this state by vows or to renounce their property if they had any. Others joined them and their organization and work developed rapidly, and in 1575 the new society received the formal approbation of Pope Gregory XIII, who gave it the ancient church of Sta Maria in Vallicella. St Philip decided to demolish it and rebuild it on a large scale. He had no money, but contributions came in from rich and poor. The pope and St Charles Borromeo were generous in their donations, as were many of the most prominent men in Rome.

By April 1577, work on the Chiesa Nuova, as it was called, had advanced sufficiently for the Congregation of the Oratory to be transferred to the Vallicella, but their superior went on living at San Girolamo as before. He had become attached to the room he had occupied for thirty-three years, and it was not until 1584 that he took up residence at the Chiesa Nuova, in compliance with the pope's expressed wish. Even then he continued to live and have his meals apart from the community, although his spiritual sons had free access to him.

On the feast of Corpus Christi, May 25, 1595, the saint appeared to be in a radiantly happy mood, bordering on exultation, and his physician told him he had not looked so well for ten years. St Philip alone realized that his hour had come. All day long he heard confessions and saw visitors as usual, but before retiring he said, 'Last of all, we must die'. About midnight he was seized with an attack of haemorrhage so severe that the fathers were called. He was obviously dying, and Baronius, who read the commendatory prayers, besought him to say a parting word, or at least to bless his sons. Though St Philip was past speaking, he raised his hand, and in bestowing his blessing passed to his eternal reward. He was eighty years of age. His body rests in the Chiesa Nuova, which the Oratorians serve to this day. St Philip Neri was canonized in 1622.

27 : ST AUGUSTINE, ARCHBISHOP OF CANTERBURY (c. A.D. 605)

WHEN Pope St Gregory the Great decided that the time had come for the evangelization of Anglo-Saxon England, he chose as missionaries some thirty or more monks from his monastery of St Andrew on the Coelian Hill. As their leader he gave them their own prior, Augustine. The party set out from Rome in the year 596; but no sooner had they arrived in Provence than they were assailed with warnings about the ferocity of the Anglo-Saxons and the dangers of the Channel. Greatly discouraged, they persuaded Augustine to return to Rome and obtain leave to abandon the enterprise. St Gregory, however, had received definite assurance that the English were well disposed towards the Christian faith; he therefore sent Augustine back to his brethren with words of encouragement which gave them heart to proceed on their way. They landed in the Isle of Thanet in the territory of Ethelbert, king of Kent, who was baptized at Pentecost 597. Almost immediately afterwards St Augustine paid a visit to France, where he was consecrated bishop of the English by St Virgilius, metropolitan of Arles. At Christmas of that same year, many of Ethelbert's subjects were baptized, as St Gregory joyfully related in a letter to Eulogius, the patriarch of Alexandria. Augustine sent two of his monks, Laurence and Peter, to Rome to give a full report of his mission, to ask for more helpers and obtain advice on various points. They came back bringing the pallium for Augustine and accompanied by a fresh band of missionaries, amongst whom were St Mellitus, St Justus and St Paulinus.

Gregory outlined for Augustine the course he should take to develop a hierarchy for the whole country, and both to him and to Mellitus gave very practical instructions on other points. Pagan temples were not to be destroyed, but were to be purified and consecrated for Christian worship. Local customs were as far as possible to be retained, days of dedication and feasts of martyrs being substituted for heathen festivals.

In Canterbury itself St Augustine rebuilt an ancient church which, with an old wooden house, formed the nucleus for his metropolitan basilica and for the later monastery of Christ Church. These buildings stood on the site of the present cathedral begun by Lanfranc in 1070. Outside the walls of Canterbury he made a monastic foundation, which he dedicated in honour of St Peter and St Paul. After his death this abbey became known as St Augustine's, and was the burial place of the early archbishops.

Cut off from much communication with the outside world, the British church clung to certain usages at variance with those of the Roman tradition. St Augustine invited the leading ecclesiastics to meet him at some place just on the confines of Wessex, still known in Bede's day as Augustine's Oak. There he urged them to comply with the practices of the rest of Western Christendom, and more especially to co-operate with him in evangelizing the Anglo-Saxons. Fidelity to their local traditions, however, made them unwilling. A second conference proved a sad failure. Because St Augustine failed to rise when they arrived, the British bishops decided that he was lacking in humility and would neither listen to him nor acknowledge him as their metropolitan.

The saint's last years were spent in spreading and consolidating the faith throughout Ethelbert's realm, and episcopal sees were established at London and Rochester. About seven years after his arrival in England, St Augustine passed to his reward, on May 26, c. 605.

28 : ST GERMANUS, BISHOP OF PARIS (A.D. 576)

ST GERMANUS (Germain), was born near Autun about the year 496. After a careful training he was ordained priest by St Agrippinus, and was subsequently chosen abbot of St Symphorian in one of the suburbs of Autun. Happening to be in Paris when that see became vacant, he was nominated by King Childebert I to fill the chair. His promotion made no change in the austerity of his life: he retained his simplicity of dress and food, but his house was always crowded by a throng of beggars whom he entertained at his own table. Through his eloquence and example he brought many sinners and careless Christians to repentance, including the king himself who, from being entirely absorbed in worldly interests, became a generous benefactor to the poor and the founder of religious establishments.

Among Childebert's foundations was a church in Paris which, with the adjoining monastery, was dedicated to God in honour of the Holy Cross and St Vincent; it was consecrated by St Germanus, who added to it the chapel of St Symphorian, which eventually contained his tomb. After his death the church was renamed Saint-Germain-des-Prés and became for several generations the burial place of the royal family. Throughout his episcopate St Germanus strove to check the licentiousness of the nobles. He did not scruple to reprove and even to excommunicate King Charibert for his shameless wickedness. During the fratricidal wars in which the nephews of Childebert became involved, he made every effort to induce them to suspend their hostilities, even writing to Queen Brunhildis in the hope of enlisting her influence with her husband to that end. All his remonstrances and appeals, however, were ineffectual. The saint died on May 28, 576, at the age of eighty, mourned by all the people.

29 : WILLIAM OF TOULOUSE, STEPHEN, RAYMUND
AND THEIR COMPANIONS, MARTYRS·(A.D. 1242)

THE twelve martyrs who are commemorated together on this day were all directly or indirectly connected with the branch of the Inquisition which had been set up at Toulouse in 1228 to combat the errors of the Albigensians and other false teachers in Languedoc. Pope Gregory IX specially commissioned the Order of Preachers to expound the faith in Toulouse and the neighbouring districts, and to deliver heretics over to the secular arm. The Dominicans encountered great hostility and drew upon themselves the bitter hatred of the Albigensians; they were driven out of Toulouse, Narbonne and other places by the mob. As they went, the friars, undaunted by the treatment they were receiving, chanted aloud the 'Salve Regina' and the Apostles' Creed. At Avignonet, to the south-west of Toulouse, they conducted a preaching mission with the assistance of other priests, and were offered hospitality in the local castle, which belonged to Count Raymond VII of Toulouse but which was then in charge of his bailiff. All unsuspecting, they accepted the invitation. As they were retiring for the night, they were set upon and butchered by a band of soldiers who had been secretly introduced into the building. They uttered no cry, but with their dying breath praised God in the words of the Te Deum. The little company included three Dominicans—William Arnaud and two others—two Friars Minor, Stephen and Raymund, two Benedictines, four other clerics and a layman. Many cures reported at their grave led to a cult that was confirmed more than six hundred years later, in 1856.

30 : ST JOAN OF ARC, VIRGIN (A.D. 1431)

ST JEANNE LA PUCELLE, or Joan of Arc as she has always been called in England, was born on the feast of the Epiphany 1412, at Domrémy, a little village of Champagne on the bank of the Meuse. Her father, Jacques d'Arc, was a peasant farmer of some local standing, a worthy man, frugal and rather morose; but his wife was a gentle affectionate mother to their five children.

Joan was very young when Henry V of England invaded France, overran Normandy and claimed the crown of the insane king, Charles VI. France, in the throes of civil war between the contending parties of the Duke of Burgundy and Orleans, was in no condition to put up an adequate resistance, and after the Duke of Burgundy had been treacherously murdered by the Dauphin's servants the Burgundians threw in their lot with the English, who supported their claims. The death of the rival kings in 1422 brought no relief to France.

St Joan was in her fourteenth year when she experienced the earliest of those supernatural manifestations which were to lead her through the path of patriotism to death at the stake. At first it was a single voice addressing her apparently from near by, and accompanied by a blaze of light: afterwards, as the voices increased in number, she was able to see her interlocutors whom she identified as St Michael, St Catherine, St Margaret and others. Only very gradually did they unfold her mission: but by May

1428 they had become insistent and explicit: she must present herself at once to Robert Baudricourt, who commanded the king's forces in the neighbouring town of Vaucouleurs. Joan succeeded in persuading an uncle who lived near Vaucouleurs to take her to him, but Baudricourt only laughed and dismissed her, saying that her father ought to give her a good hiding.

After Joan's return to Domrémy her Voices gave her no rest. When she protested that she was a poor girl who could neither ride nor fight, they replied: 'It is God who commands it'. Unable to resist such a call she secretly left home and went back to Vaucouleurs. Baudricourt's scepticism as to her mission was somewhat shaken when official confirmation reached him of a serious defeat of the French which Joan had previously announced to him. He now not only consented to send her to the king but gave her an escort of three men-at-arms. At her own request she travelled in male dress to protect herself. Although the little party reached Chinon, where the king was residing, on March 6, 1429, it was not till two days later that Joan was admitted to his presence. Charles had purposely disguised himself, but she identified him at once and, by a secret sign communicated to her by her Voices and imparted by her to him alone, she obliged him to believe in the supernatural nature of her mission. She then asked him for soldiers whom she might lead to the relief of Orleans. This request was opposed by La Trémouille, the king's favourite, and by a large section of the court, who regarded the girl as a crazy visionary or a scheming impostor. To settle the matter it was decided to send her to be examined by a learned body of theologians at Poitiers.

After a searching interrogatory extending over three weeks this council decided that they found nothing to disapprove of, and advised Charles to make prudent use of her services. Accordingly after her return to Chinon arrangements were pushed forward to equip her to lead an expeditionary force. A special standard was made for her bearing the words 'Jesus: Maria', together with a representation of the Eternal Father to whom two kneeling angels were presenting a fleur-de-lis. On April 27 the army left Blois with Joan at its head clad in white armour, and she entered Orleans on April 29. Her presence in the city wrought marvels. By May 8, the English forts which surrounded Orleans had been captured and the siege raised, after she herself had been wounded in the breast by an arrow.

The Maid was allowed to undertake a short campaign on the Loire with the Duc d'Alençon, one of her best friends. It was completely successful and ended with a victory at Patay in which the English forces under Sir John Fastolf suffered a crushing defeat. Joan now pressed for the immediate coronation of the Dauphin. The road to Rheims had practically been cleared and the last obstacle was removed by the unexpected surrender of Troyes.

But the French leaders dallied, and only very reluctantly did they consent to follow her to Rheims where, on July 17, 1429, Charles VII was solemnly crowned, Joan standing at his side with her standard. That event, which completed the mission originally entrusted to her by her Voices, marked also the close of her military successes. A boldly planned attack on Paris failed, mainly for lack of Charles's promised support and presence. During the action Joan was wounded in the thigh by an arrow and had to be almost dragged into safety by Alençon. Then followed a truce which entailed a winter of inaction spent for the most part in the entourage of a worldly court, where Joan was regarded with thinly veiled suspicion. Upon the resumption of hostilities she hurried to the relief of Compiègne which was holding out against the Burgundians. She entered the city at sunrise on May 23, 1430, and that same day led an unsuccessful sortie. The drawbridge over which her company was retiring was raised too soon, leaving Joan and some of her men outside at the mercy of the enemy. She was dragged from her horse and led to the quarters of John of Luxembourg, one of whose soldiers had been her captor. From that time until the late autumn she remained the prisoner of the Duke of Burgundy. Never during that period or afterwards was the slightest effort made on her behalf by King Charles or any of his subjects.

But the English leaders desired to have her if the French did not: and on November 21 she was sold to them. Once in their hands her execution was a foregone conclusion. Though they could not condemn her to death for defeating them on open warfare, they could have her sentenced as a sorceress and a heretic. On February 21, 1431, she appeared for the first time before a tribunal presided over by Peter Cauchon, bishop of Beauvais, an unscrupulous man who hoped through English influence to become archbishop of Rouen. The judges were composed of dignitaries and doctors carefully selected by Cauchon, as well as of the ordinary officials of an ecclesiastical court. During the course of six public and nine private sessions the prisoner was examined and cross-examined as to her visions and 'voices', her assumption of male attire, her faith and her willingness to submit to the Church. At the conclusion of the sittings a grossly unfair summing-up of her statements was drawn up and submitted first to the judges, who on the strength of it declared her revelations to have been diabolical, and then to the University of Paris, which denounced her in violent terms.

In a final deliberation the tribunal decided that she must be handed over to the secular arm as a heretic if she refused to retract. This she declined to do, though threatened with torture. Only when she was brought into the cemetery of St Ouen before a huge crowd, to be finally admonished and sentenced, was she intimidated into making some sort of retractation. The actual terms of this retractation are uncertain and have been the occasion of much controversy. She was led back to prison but her respite was a short one. Either as the result of a trick played by those who thirsted for her blood or else deliberately of her own free-will, she resumed the male dress which she had consented to discard; and when Cauchon with some of his hench-men visited her in her cell to question her concerning what they chose to regard as a relapse, they found that she had recovered from her weakness. Once again she declared that God had truly sent her and that her voices came from God. On Tuesday, May 29, 1431, the judges after hearing Cauchon's report condemned her as a relapsed heretic to be delivered over to the secular arm, and the following morning at eight o'clock Joan was led out into the market-place of Rouen to be burned at the stake.

She was not yet twenty years old. After her death her ashes were contemptuously cast into the Seine, but twenty-three years later Joan's mother and her two brothers appealed for a reopening of the case, and Pope Callistus III appointed a commission for the purpose. Its labours resulted, on July 7, 1456, in the quashing of the trial and verdict and the complete rehabilitation of the Maid. Over four hundred and fifty years later, on May 16, 1920, she was canonized.

31 : ST MECHTILDIS OF EDELSTETTEN, VIRGIN (A.D. 1160)

THIS Mechtildis was only five years old when she was placed by her parents, Count Berthold of Andechs and his wife Sophia, in the double monastery they had founded on their own estate at Diessen, on the Ammersee in Bavaria. Trained by the nuns, Mechtildis grew up a devout and exemplary maiden, much given to prayer and austerities. In later life she was remarkable for her silence, and it was said of her by the Cistercian monk Engelhard that on the rare occasions when she opened her lips to speak her words were as those of an angel. After she had received the habit, she made still further advance along the path of perfection. Upon the death of the superior, she was elected abbess.

She was so highly esteemed by the Bishop of Augsburg that he requested her to take charge of the convent of Edelstetten which stood in great need of reform. Mechtildis shrank from the task: she was only twenty-eight, and felt incapable of coping with the difficulties of the situation. Nevertheless, in compliance with an injunction from Pope Anastasius IV she allowed herself to be installed abbess of Edelstetten. At first she was well received, for her youth and noble rank commended her to her new daughters. But when she proceeded to enforce the rule, to insist upon enclosure and generally to tighten the reins of discipline she met opposition. Finally it became necessary for the bishop to order the expulsion of the chief malcontents. The rest of the nuns were won over by the holy life of their superior, enhanced as it was by the extraordinary gifts and graces which, from this period onwards, became manifest to all. She healed the sick, restored speech to the dumb, and the sight of an eye to one of the nuns. Very often she was rapt in ecstasies which lasted for a long period. Her fame spread far and wide, and the Emperor Frederick I was proud to claim her as a kinswoman. Shortly before her death she had a premonition that her end was near; she thereupon laid down her office and returned to Diessen, where she died on May 31, 1160.

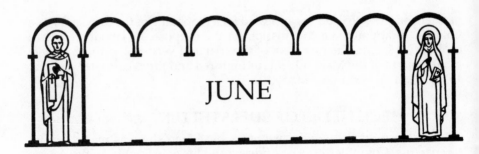

JUNE

1 : ST ENECO, OR IÑIGO, (A.D. 1057)

ABOUT the year 1010 Sancho, Count of Castile, founded a religious house at Oña, which he placed under the rule of his daughter Tigrida, who is venerated as a saint. It was probably a double monastery, but we only hear about the nuns. It seems that after a time they fell into lax observance and King Sancho the Great determined to restore discipline in his father-in-law's foundation. He was an ardent supporter of the Cluniac reform, which he had introduced into his dominions. From the abbey of San Juan de Peña, the first monastery to accept the revised rule, he drafted monks to Oña to replace the nuns, about the year 1029. Over them he appointed a disciple of St Odilo's called Garcia who, however, died before he had consolidated his work. It was therefore essential that a suitable successor should be found. At the time there was living in the mountains of Aragon a saintly hermit named Eneco, or Iñigo. Said to have been a native of Calatayud in the province of Bilbao, he had taken the habit at San Juan de Peña. According to one account he had risen to be prior, when the call came to him to resume the solitary life which he had practised in his pre-monastic days. King Sancho decided that he had all the necessary qualifications, but the efforts he made through envoys to induce Eneco to leave his retreat were unavailing. Only when he himself visited the saint did he succeed in persuading him to take up the charge.

The choice proved an excellent one. The abbey under his government increased rapidly in sanctity as well as in numbers. St Eneco's influence extended far beyond the walls of the monastery. He made peace between communities and individuals who had long been at bitter variance and he tamed men of violent passions. When a severe drought threatened a total failure of the crops, St Eneco prayed, and rain fell in abundance. On another occasion he is said to have fed a great multitude with three loaves. He was two leagues from the abbey when he was seized with the malady which was to prove fatal. He was carried home, and upon his arrival he asked that refreshment should be given to the boys who had escorted the party with torches. As no one else had seen the boys, it was concluded that they must have been angels. He passed away on June 1, 1057, and seems to have been canonized by Pope Alexander III about a century later.

2 : ST ERASMUS, OR ELMO, BISHOP AND MARTYR (A.D. 303 ?)

ST ERASMUS, or St Elmo, formerly widely venerated as the patron of
sailors and as one of the Fourteen Holy Helpers, is described as bishop of
Formiae, in the Campagna, and we know from St Gregory the Great that his
relics were preserved in the cathedral of that town in the sixth century.
When Formiae was destroyed by the Saracens in 842, the body of St Erasmus
was translated to Gaëta, of which city he still remains a principal patron.
Nothing is actually known of his history, his so-called 'acts' being late
compilations based on legends which confuse him with a namesake, a
martyr bishop of Antioch.

In Belgium, France and elsewhere St Erasmus is popularly represented
with a large aperture in his body through which his intestines have been
wound, or are being wound, round a windlass which stands beside him. He
is accordingly invoked against cramp and colic, especially in children. The
blue lights sometimes seen at mastheads before and after storms were
reckoned by Neapolitan seamen as signs of their patron's protection and
were called by them 'St Elmo's Fire'.

3 : SS. CHARLES LWANGA, JOSEPH MKASA, AND THEIR
COMPANIONS, THE MARTYRS OF UGANDA (A.D. 1886)

IN the interior of central Africa the first Catholic missions were established
by Cardinal Lavigerie's White Fathers in 1879. In Uganda some progress
was made under the not unfriendly local ruler, Mtesa; but his successor,
Mwanga, determined to root out Christianity among his people, especially
after a Catholic subject, St Joseph Mkasa, reproached him for his de-
bauchery and for his massacre of the Protestant missionary James Hanning-
ton and his caravan. Mwanga was addicted to unnatural vice and his anger
against Christianity, already kindled by ambitious officers who played on
his fears, was kept alight by the refusal of Christian boys in his service to
minister to his wickedness.

Joseph Mkasa himself was the first victim: Mwanga seized on a trifling
pretext and on November 15, 1885, had him beheaded. To the chieftain's
astonishment the Christians were not cowed by this sudden outrage, and in
May of the following year the storm burst. When he called for a young 'page'
called Mwafu, Mwanga learned that he had been receiving religious
instruction from another page, St Denis Sebuggwawo; Denis was sent for,
and the king thrust a spear through his throat. That night guards were
posted round the royal residence to prevent anyone from escaping.

St Charles Lwanga, who had succeeded Joseph Mkasa in charge of the
'pages', secretly baptized four of them who were catechumens; among them
St Kizito, a boy of thirteen whom Lwanga had repeatedly saved from the
designs of the king. Next morning the pages were all drawn up before
Mwanga, and Christians were ordered to separate themselves from the rest:
led by Lwanga and Kizito, the oldest and youngest, they did so—fifteen
young men, all under twenty-five years of age. They were joined by two
others already under arrest and by two soldiers. Mwanga asked them if they

intended to remain Christians. 'Till death! ' came the reponse. 'Then put them to death! '

The appointed place of execution, Namugongo, was thirty-seven miles away, and the convoy set out at once. Three of the youths were killed on the road; the others underwent a cruel imprisonment of seven days at Namugongo while a huge pyre was prepared. Then on Ascension day, June 3, 1886, they were brought out, stripped of their clothing, bound, and each wrapped in a mat of reed: the living faggots were laid on the pyre (one boy, St Mbaga, was first killed by a blow on the neck by order of his father who was the chief executioner), and it was set alight.

The persecution spread and Protestants as well as Catholics gave their lives rather than deny Christ. A leader among the confessors was St Matthias Murumba, who was put to death with revolting cruelty; he was a middle-aged man, assistant judge to the provincial chief, who first heard of Jesus Christ from Protestant missionaries and later was baptized by Father Livinhac, w.f. Another older victim, who was beheaded, was St Andrew Kagwa, chief of Kigowa, who had been the instrument of his wife's conversion and had gathered a large body of catechumens round him. This Andrew together with Charles Lwanga and Matthias Murumba and nineteen others (seventeen of the total being young royal servants) were solemnly beatified in 1920. They were canonized in 1964.

4 : ST FRANCIS CARACCIOLO, FOUNDER OF THE MINOR CLERKS REGULAR (A.D. 1608)

THE saint whom the Church specially honours on this day was born on October 13, 1563, at Villa Santa Maria, in the Abruzzi. His father belonged to the Pisquizio branch of the Neapolitan princes of Caraccioli, and his mother's family could claim relationship with St Thomas Aquinas. He received the name of Ascanio.

When he was twenty-two he developed a skin disease which seemed akin to leprosy and it soon assumed so virulent a form that his case was considered hopeless. He vowed that if he regained his health he would devote the rest of his life to God and to the service of others. He recovered so speedily that the cure was held to be miraculous. Eager to carry out his promise, he went to Naples to study for the priesthood. After his ordination he joined a confraternity called the *Bianchi della Giustizia*, the members of which were specially concerned with caring for prisoners and with preparing condemned criminals to die a holy death.

In the year 1588, John Augustine Adorno, a Genoese was inspired with the idea of founding an association of priests pledged to combine the active with the contemplative life. He consulted Fabriccio Caracciolo, the dean of the collegiate church of Santa Maria Maggiore in Naples, and a letter inviting the co-operation of another Ascanio Caracciolo-a distant kinsman-was by mistake delivered to our saint. So entirely, however, did Adorno's aspirations coincide with his own, that the recipient hastened to associate himself with Adorno. By way of preparation they made a forty-days' retreat in the Carmaldolese settlement near Naples where, after a strict fast and earnest prayer, they drew up rules for the proposed order. Then, as soon as their company numbered twelve, Caracciolo and Adorno went to Rome to obtain the approval of the sovereign pontiff. On June 1, 1588, Sixtus V solemnly ratified their new society, under the title of the Minor Clerks Regular, and on April 9 of the following year, the two founders made their solemn profession, Caracciolo taking the name of Francis, out of devotion to the great saint of Assisi. In addition to the usual three vows, the members of the new association took a fourth, never to seek any office or dignity either within the order or outside it.

Francis and Adorno settled their companions in a house in a suburb of Naples and set off for Spain in compliance with the pope's desire that they should establish themselves there, seeing that it was a country with which Adorno was well acquainted. However, the time was not yet ripe: the court of Madrid would not allow them to found a house, and they had to return. On the way home they were shipwrecked, but when they reached Naples they discovered that their new foundation could not contain all who wished to enter. Soon afterwards they were invited to take over Santa Maria Maggiore, the former superior of which, Fabriccio Caracciolo, had become one of their number. The Minor Clerks Regular worked mainly as missioners, but some of them devoted themselves to priestly work in hospitals and prisons. They also had places which they called hermitages for those who felt called to a life of contemplation.

St Francis contracted a serious illness, from which he had scarcely recovered when he had the great grief of losing his friend Adorno, who died at the age of forty, shortly after his return from a visit to Rome in connection with the affairs of the institute of which he was superior. Very much against his wishes, Francis was chosen to take his place. He insisted on taking his turn with the others in sweeping rooms, making beds and washing up in the kitchen.

In the interest of his society Francis paid a second and a third visit to Spain in the years 1595 and 1598, and succeeded in founding houses in Madrid, Valladolid and Alcalá; but for seven years he was obliged to retain the position of general superior. At last he obtained permission from Pope Clement VIII to resign, and then he became prior of Santa Maria Maggiore and novice-master. In 1607 he was relieved of all administrative duties and was allowed to give himself to contemplation and to preparing for death. He chose as his cell a recess under the staircase of the Neapolitan house and was often found lying there in ecstasy with outstretched arms.

He was not destined to die in Naples. St Philip Neri had offered the Minor Clerks Regular a house at Agnone, in the Abruzzi, as a novitiate, and it was thought desirable that St Francis should go to help with the new foundation. He arrived at Agnone apparently in his usual health, but he himself was under no illusion. On the first day of June he was seized with a fever which rapidly increased, and he dictated a fervent letter in which he urged the members of the society to remain faithful to the rule. He then seemed absorbed in meditation until an hour before sunset when he suddenly cried out, 'Let us go! Let us go! ' And where do you want to go, Brother Francis?' inquired one of the watchers. 'To Heaven! To Heaven! ' came the answer in clear and triumphant accents. Scarcely had the words been uttered when the wish was realized, and the speaker passed to his reward. He was forty-four years of age; and was canonized in 1807.

5 : ST BONIFACE, ARCHBISHOP OF MAINZ, MARTYR (A.D. 754)

BONIFACE, or Winfrid—to give him his baptismal name—was born about the year 680, probably at Crediton in Devonshire. At the age of five, after listening to the conversation of some monastic visitors to his home, he determined to be a monk, and when he was seven he was sent to school to a monastery near Exeter. Some seven years later he went to the abbey of Nursling, in the diocese of Winchester. There he became the apt pupil of its learned abbot, Winbert, and after completing his own studies, he was made director of the school. His skill in teaching and his personal popularity attracted many scholars, for whose benefit he wrote the first Latin grammar known to have been compiled in England. At the age of thirty he was ordained to the priesthood, and found further scope for his talents in sermons and instructions.

In Friesland St Willibrord had long been striving against great odds to bring the truths of the Gospel home to the people. Here seemed to Winfrid the place to which he was specially called. Having wrung a reluctant consent from his abbot, he set forth and landed with two companions at Duurstede in the spring of 716. The time was, however, inauspicious, and Winfrid, realizing that it was useless to stay, returned to England in the autumn. His brethren at Nursling, delighted to welcome him back, tried to retain him by electing him abbot upon the death of Winbert, but he was not to be deflected. His first attempt had convinced him that if he was to succeed he must have a direct commission from the pope; and in 718 he presented himself before St Gregory II in Rome. The pontiff in due course despatched him with a general commission to preach the word of God to the heathen. He also changed his name Winfrid to that of Boniface. The saint took the road to Germany, crossed the lower Alps, and travelled through Bavaria into Hesse.

Scarcely had he embarked upon his new work when he was informed of the death of the pagan ruler Radbod, and of the hopeful prospect opened up through the accession of a friendly successor. In obedience to what appeared like a recall to his original mission, St Boniface returned to Friesland, where for three years he laboured energetically under St Willibrord. But when St Willibrord, now a very old man, would have made him his coadjutor and successor, St Boniface declined, alleging that his commission had been a general one, not confined to any one diocese. Then, fearing he might be forced to consent he returned to Hesse.

Boniface was able to make such a satisfactory report to the Holy See that the pope summoned him to Rome. On St Andrew's day, 722, he was consecrated a regionary bishop with a general jurisdiction over Germany; and Gregory gave him a special letter to the powerful Charles Martel. This letter, which the newly ordained bishop presented in person on his way back to Germany, obtained for him the valuable concession of a sealed pledge of protection. Boniface, on his return to Hesse, made a bold attempt to strike at the root of the pagan superstitions. On a day which had been publicly announced, and in the midst of an awestruck crowd, he attacked with an axe one of the chief objects of popular veneration, Donar's sacred oak, which stood on the summit of Mount Gudenberg at Geismar, near Fritzlar. Almost as the first blows fell upon it, the huge tree crashed, splitting into four parts, and the poeple who had expected a judgement to descend upon the perpetrators of such an outrage acknowledged that their gods were powerless to protect their own sanctuaries. From that time the work of evangelization advanced steadily, but success in one field only spurred St Boniface to further efforts, and as soon as he felt that he could safely leave his Hessian converts for a time, he passed on into Thuringia.

Here he found a sprinkling of Christians, including a few Celtic and Frankish priests, but they tended to be more of a hindrance than a help. At Ohrdruf, near Gotha, he established his second monastery, to serve as a missionary centre for Thuringia. Everywhere he found the people ready to listen; it was the teachers who were lacking. To obtain them he applied to the English monasteries; and for several years in succession parties of monks and nuns crossed the sea to place themselves at his disposal and to assist in preaching the Gospel. The two existing monasteries were enlarged, and many new ones founded. Foremost among the English missionaries were St Lull, who was to succeed St Boniface at Mainz, St Eoban, who was to share his martyrdom, St Burchard and St Wigbert; whilst the women included St Thecla, St Walburga, and Boniface's beautiful and learned young cousin, St Lioba.

In 731 Pope Gregory II died, and his successor, Gregory III, to whom St Boniface had written, sent him the pallium and constituted him metropolitan of Germany beyond the Rhine, with authority to found bishoprics wherever he thought fit. Several years later the saint went to Rome for the third time, in order to confer about the churches he had founded. He was then appointed legate of the Apostolic See; and at Monte Cassino he obtained another missionary for Germany in the person of St Walburga's brother, St Willibald. In his capacity of legate he then went to Bavaria; where he organized its hierarchy, besides deposing unworthy priests and remedying abuses. From Bavaria he returned to his mission-fields. There he proceeded to found other bishoprics—Erfurt for Thuringia, Buraburg for Hesse, and Würzburg for Franconia. At a later date he established an episcopal seat also in the Nordgau—at Eichstätt. In charge of each diocese he placed one of his English disciples. To the year 741 belongs the commencement of the abbey of Fulda, of which he and his young disciple, St Sturmi, are reckoned as the joint founders.

The death of Charles Martel in 741, and the accession of his sons, Pepin and Carloman, provided an opportunity which St Boniface was not slow to seize. Carloman was earnestly devout; it was, therefore, a comparatively easy matter for St Boniface, whom he greatly venerated, to persuade him to call a synod to deal with abuses. The first assembly was followed by a second in 743. Pepin summoned a synod for Gaul, which was succeeded in 745 by a general council for the two provinces. St Boniface presided over them all, and succeeded in carrying all the reforms he had most at heart. Fresh vigour was infused into the Church, and as the result of five years' work Boniface had restored the Church of Gaul to her former greatness. The date of the fifth Frankish council, 747, was in other respects a memorable one for Boniface. Until then he had held a general commission; the time had come for him to have a fixed metropolitan see. Mainz was chosen, and Pope St Zachary created him primate of Germany as well as apostolic legate for Germany and Gaul.

No sooner had this matter been arranged than Boniface lost his ally Carloman, who decided to retire into a monastery. However, Pepin, who then united France under one rule, continued to give him the general support he still needed. And as papal legate it was Boniface who crowned Pepin at Soissons.

Boniface was now growing old, and he realized that the administration of his vast fold required the vigour of a younger man. He obtained the appointment of his disciple Lull to be his successor; but the missionary zeal burned within him as ardently as ever, and he was resolved to spend his last years amongst his first converts, the Frieslanders, who since the death of St Willibrord were relapsing once more into paganism. Now a man of about seventy-three, he embarked with some companions to sail down the Rhine. At Utrecht they were joined by Bishop Eoban. At first they worked to reclaim the lapsed in that part of the country which had been previously evangelized, but in early spring of the following year they crossed the lake which then divided Friesland into two parts, and bore their message to the wholly unevangelized tribes of north-east Friesland. Their efforts seemed crowned with success and large numbers were baptized. St Boniface arranged to hold a confirmation on Whitsun eve in the open fields on the plain of Dokkum, near the banks of the little river Borne.

He was quietly reading in his tent while awaiting the arrival of the new converts, when a hostile band suddenly descended upon the encampment. The attendants would have defended the saint, but he would not allow them. As he was exhorting them to trust in God and to welcome the prospect of dying for the faith, they were attacked—St Boniface being one of the first to fall. His companions shared his fate. The body of Boniface was taken finally to Fulda, where it still rests.

6 : ST NORBERT, ARCHBISHOP OF MAGDEBURG, FOUNDER OF THE CANONS REGULAR OF PRÉMONTRÉ (A.D. 1134)

XANTEN, in the duchy of Cleves, was the birthplace of St Norbert. His father, Heribert, Count of Gennep, was related to the emperor, and his mother, Hedwig of Guise, derived her pedigree from the house of Lorraine. Although he appeared to cherish no higher ambition than to lead a life of pleasure, he received minor orders, including the subdiaconate, and was presented to a canonry in the church of St Victor at Xanten, as well as to other benefices. At the court of the Emperor Henry V, who appointed him his almoner, Norbert joined in all the diversions. One day, when he was riding near the Westphalian village of Wreden, he was overtaken in open country by a violent thunderstorm. His horse threw its rider, who lay on the ground as though dead for nearly an hour. His first words on regaining consciousness were those of Saul on the road to Damascus: 'Lord, what wilt thou have me to do?' To which an inner voice replied: 'Turn from evil and do good: seek after peace and pursue it.'

This conversion was as sudden and complete as that of the great Apostle of the Gentiles. Norbert retired to Xanten, where he gave himself up to prayer, fasting, meditation and a review of his past life. He then made a retreat at the abbey of Siegburg, near Cologne, where he came under the influence of its Abbot Conon. Frederick, archbishop of Cologne, conferred on him the diaconate and the priesthood in 1115.

After another forty days' retreat he returned to Xanten determined to lead 'an evangelical and apostolic life'; but the vigour of his exhortations, joined apparently with a certain eccentricity of behaviour, made enemies for him, and at the Council of Fritzlar in 1118 he found himself denounced to the papal legate as a hypocrite and an innovator, and charged with preaching without a licence or commission. Any doubt as to his sincerity must have been dispelled by his next step. He sold all his estates and gave all he possessed to the poor, reserving only forty silver marks, a mule (which soon died), a missal, a few vestments, a chalice, and a paten. Then, accompanied by two attendants who refused to leave him, he travelled barefoot to Saint-Gilles in Languedoc, where Pope Gelasius II was residing in exile. At the feet of the vicar of Christ he made a general confession of his misdeeds and irregularities, and offered himself for any penance that might be laid upon him. In response to his petition the pope granted him leave to preach the Gospel wherever he chose.

Armed with this permission St Norbert started forth again, barefoot in the snow—for it was mid-winter—and seemingly insensible to the inclemency of the weather. At Valenciennes his companions fell ill and died. He was still at Valenciennes, however, when he received a visit from Burchard, archbishop of Cambrai, and his young chaplain Bd Hugh of Fosses. The bishop was amazed at the change in one whom he had formerly known as a frivolous courtier, whilst Hugh was so impressed that he elected to follow him. He became St Norbert's most trusted follower, and eventually succeeded him as head of his order. Pope Callistus II having succeeded Gelasius II in 1119, St Norbert, with a view to obtaining a renewal of the sanction he had received from Gelasius, went to Rheims, where the pontiff was holding a council. Although the saint does not seem to have achieved his main purpose, Bartholomew, bishop of Laon, received permission to retain the missioner in his diocese to assist him in reforming the canons regular of St Martin's at Laon. But as the canons could not be induced to accept St Norbert's strict regulations, the bishop offered the holy man his choice of several places in which to found a community of his own. Norbert chose a lonely valley called Prémontré in the forest of Coucy, which had been abandoned by the monks of St Vincent at Laon because of the poverty of the soil. There a beginning was made with thirteen disciples. Their number soon increased to forty, who made their profession on Christmas day, 1121. They wore a white habit and kept the rule of St Augustine with certain additional regulations.

When the new organization could number eight abbeys as well as one or two nunneries, St Norbert wanted a more formal approbation for its constitutions. With that object in view he in 1125 undertook a journey to

Rome, where he obtained from Pope Honorius II all that he asked for.

Theobald, Count of Champagne, aspired to enter the order, but St Norbert dissuaded him, urging him rather to carry out the duties of his station and to marry. When the count went to Germany to conclude a marriage treaty in 1126, he took the saint with him. On their way they visited Speyer, where the Emperor Lothair was holding a diet. At the same time deputies arrived from Magdeburg to ask the monarch to nominate a bishop to their vacant see. Lothair chose St Norbert. The deputies led him back to Magdeburg, where he entered the city barefoot, and so meanly clad that the porter at his episcopal residence is said to have denied him admission.

He still practised the austerity of a monk, whilst his residence came to resemble a cloister. But though personally humble, he was unflinching in his determination to resist all attempts to deprive the Church of her rights. Under the weak rule of his predecessors, laymen, sometimes local magnates, had alienated much ecclesiastical property. St Norbert did not hesitate to take action against them, for he regarded them as little better than robbers. Many of the clergy were leading careless—sometimes scandalous—lives, neglecting their parishes and disregarding the obligations of celibacy. Where they would not listen to reason the bishop resorted to compulsion, punishing some, dispossessing others, and occasionally replacing them by his own Premonstratensian canons.

His reforms met with much opposition. On two or three occasions he narrowly escaped assassination, so Norbert at last decided to retire from the city for a time and leave the people to their own devices. The citizens, finding themselves under ecclesiastical censure and fearing the emperor's displeasure, soon sent to beg him to return, promising to be more submissive for the future. Before the end of St Norbert's life he had successfully carried through the greater part of his projected reforms. All this time he was also directing his Premonstratensian houses through his lieutenant Bd Hugh, and for several years before his death he was taking an important part in the politics of the papacy and the empire.

After the death of Pope Honorius II, an unhappy schism divided the Church. One section of cardinals had elected Cardinal Gregory Papareschi, who adopted the name of Innocent II, whilst the rest chose Cardinal Pierleone. The latter, who called himself 'Anacletus II', was the favourite in Rome, and Innocent found himself obliged to escape to France. There he was accepted as the lawful pontiff, largely through the efforts of St Bernard and of St Hugh of Grenoble. A council which he held at Rheims was attended by St Norbert, who embraced his cause and won favour for it in Germany as St Bernard had done in France. He it was who persuaded the emperor to declare himself for Innocent. Furthermore, when it became evident that although France, Germany, England and Spain had acknowledged Innocent, he could only enter Rome with the help of armed forces, it was mainly through the influence of St Norbert that Lothair consented to lead an army into Italy. In March 1133, the emperor and the pope entered the Holy City accompanied by St Norbert and St Bernard.

In recognition of his outstanding services St Norbert was invested with the pallium, but his activities were nearly at an end. Although after their return from Italy the emperor insisted upon making him his chancellor, it was evident that his health was failing fast. He expired at Magdeburg on June 6, 1134, in the fifty-third year of his life. His relics were translated in 1627 by the Emperor Ferdinand II to the Premonstratensian abbey of Strahov in Bohemia; he was formally recognized as a saint by Pope Gregory XIII in 1582.

7 : ST ANTONY GIANELLI, BISHOP OF BOBBIO, FOUNDER OF THE MISSIONERS OF ST ALPHONSUS AND THE SISTERS OF ST MARY DELL' ORTO (A.D. 1846)

ANTONY Gianelli was born in the diocese of Genoa in 1789 of a middle-class family. As a youth he was conspicuous for his gentle docility and industry and for the promise of more than ordinary intellectual gifts. A generous benefactress made it possible for him to pursue his studies at Genoa, and there, entering the ecclesiastical seminary, he so distinguished himself that when still only a subdeacon he was allowed to preach and attracted great crowds by his eloquence. By special dispensation he was ordained priest in 1812 before he had reached the canonical age.

Though employed in important educational work he stil found time to deliver sermons and give missions resulting in a great harvest of souls, as well as to discharge the functions of an ordinary parish priest, his confessional being at all times besieged by penitents. Before he was forty he had organized two religious congregations, the one of priests who were known as the Missioners of St Alphonsus Liguori, the other of women living under rule whose activities in teaching poor children and nursing the sick were dedicated in honour of Santa Maria dell' Orto ('of the Garden'.) These sisters are now well known in Italy and they have houses in other parts of Europe as well as in America and Asia. Meanwhile, in the year 1838, St Antony was appointed bishop of Bobbio, and in that office he gave an extraordinary example of virtue, prudence and firm government. He died, all too soon, in 1846, and he was canonized in 1951.

8 : ST WILLIAM, ARCHBISHOP OF YORK (A.D. 1154)

ST WILLIAM Fitzherbert, also known as William of Thwayt, is stated to have been the son of King Stephen's half-sister Emma and of Count Herbert, treasurer to Henry I, and while yet young William himself was appointed treasurer of the church of York. He appears to have been somewhat indolent, but he was personally popular and, on the death of Archbishop Thurstan of York in 1140, he was chosen to fill the vacancy. The validity of the election, however, was contested by Archdeacon Walter of York, together with a number of Cistercian abbots and Augustinian priors, who alleged unchastity and simony on the part of William and undue influence on the part of the king. Stephen invested him with the temporalities of the see, but the archbishop of Canterbury, Theobald, hesitated to consecrate him, and the parties carried their case to Rome, where the objectors relied chiefly on the charge of intrusion into the see. Pope Innocent decided that the election might be regarded as valid provided the dean of York, also called William, should appear before a court to be held by Henry of Blois, who was bishop of Winchester and papal legate, and there swear that the chapter had received no mandate from the king.

Dean William, who just at this time was made bishop of Durham, did not take that oath—it is possible that he could not without committing perjury. But in consequence of another papal letter, whose origins are uncertain and not altogether above suspicion, William Fitzherbert was able to satisfy Henry of Winchester, who duly consecrated him, and he was warmly welcomed by the clergy and people of York. He governed his diocese well, promoting peace so far as in him lay. But his opponents had abated none of their energy; and William, through, says a chronicler, his easy-goingness and tendency to procrastination, made a mistake that played into their hands. He failed to make arrangements for receiving the pallium which Pope Lucius II had sent by the hands of his legate, Cardinal Imar of Tusculum. Lucius died while the pallium was yet unconferred, and Imar took it back to Rome. To sue for it William was obliged to go again to Rome, selling or pledging some of the treasures of York to pay his expenses. But the new pope, Eugenius III, was a Cistercian and completely under the influence of St Bernard of Clairvaux, who had all along vigorously supported the cause of William's opponents. Though the majority of the cardinals were in his favour, William was suspended on the ground that the bishop of Durham had not taken the oath prescribed by Innocent II. Thereupon the archbishop retired to the hospitality of his relative King Roger of Sicily. But his supporters in England, directly the news of the papal decision reached York, made an attack on Fountains Abbey, of which Henry Murdac, formerly a monk with Pope Eugenius, was abbot, and burnt its farms; they also seized and mutilated Archdeacon Walter. This criminality still further prejudiced William's cause, and in 1147 the pope deposed him. Soon after Henry Murdac was nominated to be archbishop of York in his stead.

Upon his return to England William took refuge with his uncle, Henry of Winchester, who treated him with honour; but the deposed prelate was chastened by his misfortunes; he now shunned the luxury to which he had been accustomed, and elected to lead a penitential and austere life in the cathedral monastery. He remained thus in Winchester for six years, when in 1153 Pope Eugenius, St Bernard and Murdac all died within three months of one another: whereupon William went to Rome to plead for the restoration of his see with Pope Anastasius IV. The new pontiff granted his petition, and conferred the pallium on him before he returned home.

St William re-entered York in May 1154 amid popular demonstrations of joy. Under the weight of the crowds gathered to welcome him, the wooden bridge over the Ouse broke down, throwing many into the river. The rescue of these unfortunates, not one of whom sustained injury, was attributed by the citizens to the prayers of their restored archbishop. William showed no resentment towards his adversaries and almost at once visited Fountains Abbey, to which he promised restitution for the damage it had received from his violent relatives. But he did not live to carry out his projects for the benefit of his province. A month after his return to York he was taken with violent pain after celebrating a solemn Mass, and within a few days, on June 8, he was dead. Pope Honorius III canonized St William in 1227, after inquiry into the many wonders reported at his tomb.

9 : ST EPHRAEM, DOCTOR OF THE CHURCH (A.D. 373?)

FAMOUS in his lifetime as a great teacher, orator, poet, commentator and defender of the faith, St Ephraem is the only Syrian father who is honoured as a doctor of the Universal Church (since 1920); the Syrians, both Catholic and separated, style him 'the Harp of the Holy Ghost', and enrich their liturgies with his homilies and hymns.

St Ephraem was born about the year 306 at Nisibis in Mesopotamia, then still under Roman rule. That his parents were Christians is asserted in what purport to be his own words. 'I was born in the way of truth', he tells us. 'Although my boyhood did not understand the greatness of it, I knew it when trial came.' Elsewhere, in the same doubtful source, he is made to say: 'I had been early taught about Christ by my parents: they who begat me after the flesh had trained me in the fear of the Lord . . . My parents were confessors before the judge: yea, I am of the kindred of the martyrs'. He was baptized at the age of eighteen, and attached himself to the famous bishop of Nisibis, St Jacob (or James), whom he is said to have accompanied to the Council of Nicaea in 325. After St Jacob's death, Ephraem remained in close relation with the three succeeding hierarchs, probably as head of their school. He was living at Nisibis through the three sieges laid to it by the Persians, and in some of his Nisibeian hymns are to be found descriptions of the city's perils, of its defences, and of the final repulse of the enemy in 350. But although the Persians failed to capture Nisibis by direct attack, they obtained it thirteen years later as part of the price of the peace the Emperor Jovian was forced to negotiate after the defeat and death of Julian. The Christians abandoned the city, and Ephraem retired finally to a cave in a rocky height overlooking Edessa. Here he led a most austere life, sustained only by a little barley bread and a few vegetables, and here he wrote the greater part of his spiritual works.

His appearance was indeed that of an ascetic: he was of small stature, we are told, bald, beardless, and with skin shrivelled and dried up like a potsherd; his gown was all patches, the colour of dirt, he wept much and never laughed.

St Ephraem recognized the potentialities of sacred song as an adjunct to public worship. Partly no doubt through his personal prestige but largely through the superior merit of his own compositions, which he caused to be sung in church by a women's choir, he succeeded in completely supplanting gnostic hymns by his own. It was not until late in his life that he was raised to the diaconate. Humility had made him shrink from ordination and the fact that he is often designated as St Ephraem the Deacon supports the assertion made by some of his biographers that he never attained to higher rank. On the other hand, there are passages in his own writings which seem to indicate that he held the priestly office.

About the year 370 he undertook a journey from Edessa to Caesarea in Cappadocia in order to visit St Basil, of whom he had heard much. The last time that he took part in public affairs was in the winter of 372, shortly before his death. There was famine in the land and his heart was wrung by the sufferings of the poor. He administered large sums of money and stores entrusted to him to the satisfaction of all, besides organizing a relief service which included the provision of 300 litters for carrying the sick. Perhaps he

THE LIVES OF THE SAINTS

overtaxed his strength, for he only survived his return to the cave for one month. The date of his death is given by the Chronicle of Edessa and the best authorities as 373, but some writers have asserted that he lived until 378 or 379.

10 : ST ITHAMAR, BISHOP OF ROCHESTER (c. A.D. 656)

ST ITHAMAR has a special claim upon our interest, because he was the first Englishman to occupy an English bishopric. Unfortunately, we know very little about him. St Honorius, archbishop of Canterbury, consecrated him to the see of Rochester after the death of St Paulinus, and Bede tells us that 'though he was a man of Kent', yet in piety as well as in learning he was the equal of his predecessors, St Justus and St Paulinus, both of whom had been Italian missionaries under St Augustine. In 655 St Ithamar consecrated a fellow-countryman—Frithona or Deusdedit—to be archbishop of Canterbury. His death appears to have taken place the following year. On account of his reputation for miracles, several churches were dedicated in his honour, and his relics were enshrined in 1100.

11 : ST BARNABAS, APOSTLE (FIRST CENTURY)

ALTHOUGH St Barnabas was not one of the twelve chosen by our Lord, yet he is styled an apostle by the early fathers and by St Luke himself on account of the special commission he received from the Holy Ghost and the great part he took in apostolic work. He was a Jew of the tribe of Levi, but was born in Cyprus; his name was originally Joseph, but the apostles changed it to Barnabas—which word St Luke interprets as meaning 'man of encouragement'. The first mention we find of him in the Holy Scriptures is in the fourth chapter of the Acts of the Apostles, where it is stated that the first converts at Jerusalem lived in common and that as many as were owners of lands or houses sold them and laid the proceeds at the feet of the apostles for distribution. St Barnabas's sale of his estate is singled out for mention on this occasion. When St Paul came to Jerusalem three years after his conversion the faithful were suspicious of the genuineness of this conversion, and avoided him. Barnabas it was who then 'took him by the hand' and vouched for him among the other apostles.

Some time later, certain disciples having preached the Gospel with success at Antioch, it was thought desirable that someone should be sent by the Church in Jerusalem to guide and confirm the neophytes. The man selected was St Barnabas—'a good man, full of the Holy Ghost and of faith,' as we read in the Acts of the Apostles. Upon his arrival he rejoiced exceedingly at the progress the Gospel had made and by his preaching added greatly to the number of converts. Finding himself in need of an able assistant he went to Tarsus to enlist the co-operation of St Paul, who accompanied him back and spent a whole year at Antioch. Their labours were crowned with success, and it was in that same city and at this period that the name 'Christians' was first given to the followers of our Lord.

A little later the flourishing church of Antioch raised money for the relief of the poor brethren in Judaea during a famine. This they sent to the heads of the church of Jerusalem by the hands of Paul and Barnabas, who returned accompanied by John Mark. Antioch was by this time well supplied with teachers and prophets, amongst whom were Simeon called Niger, Lucius of Cyrene, and Herod's foster-brother Manahen. As they were worshipping God, the Holy Ghost said to them by some of these prophets, 'Separate me Paul and Barnabas for the work whereunto I have taken them'. Accordingly, after all had fasted and prayed, Paul and Barnabas received their commission by the laying on of hands and set forth on their first missionary journey. Taking with them John Mark, they went first to Seleucia and then to Salamis in Cyprus. After they had preached Christ there in the synagogues they proceeded to Paphos, where they converted Sergius Paulus, the Roman proconsul. Embarking again at Paphos, they sailed to Perga in Pamphylia. At this stage John Mark left them to return by himself to Jerusalem. Paul and Barnabas then travelled north of Antioch in Pisidia; they addressed themselves first to the jews, but finding them bitterly hostile they now openly declared that henceforth they would preach the Gospel to the Gentiles.

At Iconium, the capital of Lycaonia, they narrowly escaped stoning at the hands of the mob whom the rulers had stirred up against them. A miraculous cure wrought by St Paul upon a cripple at Lystra led the pagan inhabitants to conclude that the gods were come amongst them. They hailed St Paul as Hermes or Mercury because he was the chief speaker, and St Barnabas as Zeus or Jupiter and were with difficulty restrained from offering sacrifices to them. But, with the proverbial fickleness of the mob, they soon rushed to the other extreme and stoned St Paul, severely wounding him. After a stay at Derbe, where they made many converts, the two apostles retraced their steps, passing through the cities they had previously visited in order to confirm the converts and to ordain presbyters. Their first missionary journey thus completed, they returned to Antioch in Syria.

Shortly afterwards a dispute arose in the church of Antioch with regard to the observance of Jewish rites, some maintaining in opposition to the opinion of St Paul and St Barnabas that pagans entering the Church must be circumcised as well as baptized. This led to the calling of a council at Jerusalem. and in the presence of this assembly St Paul and St Barnabas gave a full account of their labours among the Gentiles and received approbation of their mission. The council, moreover, emphatically declared that Gentile converts were exempt from the obligation to be circumcised. Nevertheless, there continued to be such a marked division between Jewish and Gentile converts that St Peter, when on a visit to Antioch, refrained from eating with the Gentiles out of deference for the susceptibilities of the Jews—an example which St Barnabas followed. St Paul upbraided them both, and his expostulations carried the day. Another difference, however, arose between him and St Barnabas on the eve of their departure on a visitation to the churches they had founded, for St Barnabas wished to take John Mark, and St Paul demurred in view of the young man's previous defection. The contention between them became so sharp that they separated, St Paul proceeding on his projected tour with Silas, whilst St Barnabas sailed to Cyprus with John Mark. Here the Acts leave him without further mention. It seems clear, from the allusion to Barnabas in I Corinthians ix, 5 and 6 that he was living and working in A.D. 56 or 57, but St Paul's subsequent invitation to John Mark to join him when he was a prisoner in Rome leads us to infer that by A.D. 60 or 61 St Barnabas must have been dead: he is said to have been stoned to death at Salamis.

12 : ST JOHN OF SAHAGUN, (A.D. 1479)

THERE was an early Spanish martyr named Facundus, and he seems to have been adopted as patron by the abbey of Sahagun or San Fagondez in the kingdom of Leon. This locality was the birthplace of this John, and from it he derives his distinctive surname. His early education he received from the monks in the Benedictine monastery just mentioned. While he was yet a boy, his father, Don Juan Gonzalez de Castrillo, procured for him a small benefice, and when he was twenty the bishop of Burgos gave him a canonry in his cathedral, although the abbot of San Fagondez had already presented him with three other livings. He received the priesthood in 1445, and his conscience reproached him for disobeying the Church's ordinances against pluralities. He accordingly resigned all his benefices except the chapel of St Agatha in Burgos. There he daily celebrated Mass, frequently catechized the ignorant, and preached, leading the while a very mortified life in evangelical poverty. Realizing the necessity for a sounder knowledge of theology, he then obtained the bishop's permission to go to Salamanca University, where he studied for four years.

His course completed, he soon won a great reputation as a preacher and director of souls in the parish of St Sebastian, Salamanca, which he seems to have worked while holding one of the chaplaincies in the College of St Bartholomew. Nine years were thus spent, and then St John, faced with the ordeal of a severe operation, vowed that if his life were spared he would receive the religious habit. The operation having proved successful, he made his application to the superior of the local community of Augustinian friars, who admitted him with alacrity, for his merits were known to all. A year later, on August 28, 1464, he was professed.

Soon after his profession St John was appointed novice-master, an office he discharged with great wisdom. Seven times in succession he was definitor and he also became prior of Salamanca. He was endowed with a judicious discernment and with a remarkable gift for reading the thoughts of his penitents. He heard the confessions of all who presented themselves, but was rigid in refusing, or at least deferring, absolution in the case of habitual sinners, or of ecclesiastics who did not live in accordance with the spirit of their profession. His fervour in offering the divine sacrifice edified all present. We are also told that he was one of those to whom it has been granted to behold with bodily eyes the human form of our Lord at the moment of consecration. The graces he received in his prayers and communions also gave him courage and eloquence in the pulpit. Without respect of persons he reproved vice in high places with a vigour which sometimes drew upon him persecution and even physical violence.

A sermon at Alba, in the course of which he sternly denounced rich landlords who oppressed their poor tenants, so enraged the Duke of Alba that he sent two assassins to kill the bold preacher. In the presence of their intended victim, however, the men were struck with remorse, confessed their errand and humbly implored his forgiveness. Then a prominent personage whose unblushing association with a woman not his wife was causing grave scandal in Salamanca was induced by St John to sever the connection entirely. The woman vowed vengeance on the holy man and it was generally believed that the disorder of which he died was occasioned by poison administered at her instigation. He passed away on June 11, 1479. He was glorified by many miracles, both before and after his death, and was canonized in 1690.

13 : ST ANTONY OF PADUA, DOCTOR OF THE CHURCH (A.D. 1231)

A PORTUGUESE by nationality and a native of Lisbon, St Antony nevertheless derives his surname from the Italian city of Padua where he made his last home and where his relics are still venerated. He was born in 1195 and was baptized Ferdinand, a name which he was to change to that of Antony when he entered the Order of Friars Minor, out of devotion to the great patriarch of monks who was titular saint of the chapel in which he received the Franciscan habit.

His parents, young members of the Portuguese nobility, confided his early education to the clergy of the cathedral of Lisbon, but at the age of fifteen he joined the regular canons of St Augustine who were settled near the city. Two years later he obtained leave to be transferred to the priory at Coîmbra—then the capital of Portugal—in order to avoid the distractions caused by the numerous visits of friends. There he devoted himself to prayer and study, acquiring, with the help of an unusually retentive memory, an extraordinary knowledge of the Bible. He had been living at Coîmbra for eight years when Don Pedro of Portugal brought from Morocco in 1220 the relics of the Franciscans who had there lately suffered a glorious martyrdom. Ferdinand was profoundly moved, and conceived an ardent desire to lay down his life for Christ—an aspiration he had little prospect of realizing as a canon regular. To some Franciscans who came to his monastery of Holy Cross to beg, he laid open his heart, and eventually he was admitted to their order in 1221.

Within a very short time he was permitted to embark for Morocco with the intention of preaching the Gospel there. But he was prostrated by a severe illness which eventually necessitated his return to Europe. The vessel in which he sailed was driven off its course and he found himself at Messina in Sicily. He made his way to Assisi where, as he had learnt from his Sicilian brethren, a general chapter was about to be held. It was the great gathering of 1221—the last chapter open to all members of the order—and was presided over by Brother Elias as vicar general, with St Francis seated at his feet. It cannot fail to have deeply impressed the young Portuguese friar. At the close the brethren returned to the posts allocated to them, and Antony was appointed to the lonely hermitage of San Paolo near Forli. It happened that an ordination was held at Forli, on which occasion the Dominican and Franciscan candidates were entertained at the Minorite convent there. Through some misunderstanding none of the Dominicans had come prepared to deliver the customary address at the ceremony, and as no one among the Franciscans seemed capable of filling the breach St Antony, who was present, was told to come forward and speak whatever the Holy Spirit should put into his mouth. Very diffidently he obeyed; but once he had begun he delivered an address which amazed all who heard it by its eloquence, its fervour, and the learning it displayed. The minister provincial, informed of the talent possessed by the young friar he had brought from Assisi, promptly recalled him from his retreat and sent him to preach in various parts of Romagna, which then comprised the whole of Lombardy.

In addition to his commission as a preacher, he was appointed lector in theology to his brethren—the first member of his order to fill such a post. But it became more and more evident that his true mission lay in the pulpit. He had indeed all the qualifications—learning, eloquence, great power of persuasion, a burning zeal for souls and a sonorous voice which carried far. Though undersized and inclined to corpulence, he had an attractive, almost magnetic, personality. Sometimes the mere sight of him brought sinners to their knees: he appeared to radiate holiness. Wherever he went crowds flocked to hear him and hardened criminals, careless folk, and heretics alike were converted and brought to confession.

Shortly after the death of St Francis he was recalled to Italy, apparently to be minister provincial of Emilia or Romagna. He seems to have acted as envoy from the chapter general in 1226 to Pope Gregory IX, charged to lay before him for his decision the questions that had arisen. Antony on that occasion obtained from the pope his release from office that he might devote himself to preaching.

From that time St Antony resided at Padua—a city where he had previously laboured, where he was greatly beloved, and where, more than anywhere else, he was privileged to see the great fruit which resulted from his ministry.

After preaching a course of sermons in the spring of 1231, St Antony's strength gave out and he retired with two other friars to a woodland retreat at Camposanpiero. It was soon clear that his days were numbered, and he asked to be taken back to Padua. He never reached the city, but only its outskirts. On June 13, 1231, in the apartment reserved for the chaplain of the Poor Clares of Arcella, he received the last rites and passed to his eternal reward. He was only thirty-six.

Within a year of his death Antony was canonized; on that occasion Pope Gregory IX intoned the anthem 'O doctor optime' in his honour, thus anticipating the year 1946 when Pope Pius XII declared him a doctor of the Church.

14 : ST METHODIUS I, PATRIARCH OF CONSTANTINOPLE (A.D. 847)

METHODIUS was a Sicilian by birth, and received an excellent education in his native town of Syracuse. He went to Constantinople with the object of obtaining a post at court, but through the influence of a monk he decided to abandon the world for the religious life. He built a monastery in the island of Chios, from whence he was called to Constantinople by the Patriarch Nicephorus. At the second outbreak of the iconoclastic persecution, under Leo the Armenian in 815, he stood out boldly in favour of the veneration of sacred images. After the deposition and exile of St Nicephor-us, however, he went to Rome, apparently charged to inform Pope St Paschal I of the condition of affairs; and he remained there until the death of Leo V. Great hopes were entertained of the next emperor, Michael the Stammerer, and St Methodius in 821 returned to Constantinople, following upon a letter from Pope Paschal which requested the reinstatement of St Nicephorus. But the emperor after reading the letter denounced Methodius as a stirrer-up of sedition and ordered that he should be scourged and deported.

He was confined for seven years in a tomb or mausoleum with two thieves one of whom died, and was left, we are told, to rot in the prison. He was released looking like a skeleton, but his spirit was unbroken. Fresh persecution then broke out under the new emperor, Theophilus, and Methodius was summoned before him. Blamed for his past activities and for the letter which he was supposed to have incited the pope to write, he replied boldly, 'If an image is so worthless in your eyes, how is it that when you condemn the images of Christ you do not also condemn the veneration paid to representations of yourself? Far from doing so, you are continually causing them to be multiplied.' The death of the emperor in 842 was followed by the proclamation of his widow, Theodora, as regent for her infant son, Michael III, and she now came forward as the champion of images. Exiled clergy were recalled, and within thirty days sacred images had been replaced in the churches of Constantinople amid great rejoicings. John the Grammarian, an iconoclast, was deposed from the patriarchate, St Methodius being installed in his place.

The chief events that marked the patriarchate of St Methodius were the holding in Constantinople of a synod which endorsed the decrees about eikons of the second Council of Nicaea, the institution of a festival called the feast of Orthodoxy and the translation to Constantinople of the body of his predecessor, St Nicephorus. On the other hand, this period of reconciliation was marred by a very unfortunate quarrel with the Studite monks, who had formerly been Methodius's most ardent supporters; one cause of this difference was apparently the patriarch's condemnation of some of the writings of St Theodore Studites. After ruling for four years, St Methodius died of dropsy on June 14, 847.

15 : ST GERMAINE OF PIBRAC, VIRGIN (A.D. 1601)

GERMAINE was the daughter of Laurent Cousin, an agricultural labourer, and was born about the year 1579 at Pibrac, a village near Toulouse. Her mother, Marie Laroche, died when her little girl was scarcely out of the cradle. From her birth Germaine suffered from ill-health; she was scrofulous, and her right hand was powerless and deformed. Her father had no affection for her, whilst his second wife actively disliked her. She treated her stepdaughter most harshly, and after the birth of her own children she kept Germaine away from her healthier stepbrothers and sisters. The poor girl was made to sleep in the stable, or under the stairs, was fed on scraps, and as soon as she was old enough was sent out to mind sheep in the pastures.

Out in the fields however, alone with nature, she learned to commune with her Creator. Nothing could keep her from Mass. If she heard the bell when she was in the fields, she would plant her crook and her distaff in the ground, commend her flock to her angel guardian, and hurry off to church. Never once on her return did she find that a sheep had strayed, or had fallen a prey to the wolves that lurked in the neighbouring forest of Boucône, ever-ready to pounce upon unattended sheep. As often as she could she made her communion, and her fervour was long remembered in the village.

It might have been thought that anyone so poor as Germaine would be unable to exercise the corporal works of mercy. Love, however, can always find a way, and the scanty food that was grudgingly doled out to her was shared with beggars. Even this was made a cause for complaint. One cold winter's day her stepmother pursued her with a stick, declaring that she was concealing stolen bread in her apron. To the amazement of the pitying neighbours, who would have protected her, that which fell from the apron was not bread, but summer flowers. Contempt now gave way to veneration, and the inhabitants of Pibrac began to realize that they had a saint in their midst. Even her father and stepmother relented towards her; they would now have allowed her to take her proper place in their home, but Germaine chose to continue to live as before. It was not for long. One morning she was found lying dead on her straw pallet under the stairs. She was twenty-two years old.

Her body, which was buried in the church of Pibrac, was accidentally exhumed in 1644, forty-three years after her death, and was found in perfect preservation. It was afterwards enclosed in a leaden coffin, which was placed in the sacristy. Sixteen years later it was still flexible and well preserved. This circumstance, and the numerous miracles which were ascribed to her, encouraged a desire for official sanction of her cult. Owing to the French Revolution, however, and other hindrances, her beatification and canonization were deferred until the pontificate of Pius IX. An annual pilgrimage takes place on June 15 to Pibrac church, where her relics still rest.

16 : ST LUTGARDIS, VIRGIN (A.D. 1246)

AMONGST the notable women mystics of the twelfth and thirteenth centuries there is no more sympathetic or lovable figure than that of St Lutgardis. Born in 1182, the daughter of a citizen of Tongres in the Netherlands, she was placed at the age of twelve in the Benedictine convent of St Catherine near Saint-Trond, for no better reason than that the money intended for her marriage-portion had been lost in a business speculation, and that without it she was unlikely to find a suitable husband. She was an attractive girl, fond of pretty clothes and of innocent amusement, without any apparent religious vocation, and she seems to have lived at first as a kind of boarder, free to come and go, as well as to receive visitors of both sexes.

One day, however, while she was entertaining a friend, our Lord appeared to her, and, showing her His sacred wounds, bade her love Him and Him only. Accepting Him instantly as her heavenly Bridegroom, she renounced from that moment all earthly concerns. Some of the nuns who observed her sudden fervour prophesied that it would not last; but it only increased. So vividly did she come to realize God's presence that, when engaged in prayer, she beheld our Lord as with her bodily eyes. She would speak with Him familiarly, and if summoned away to perform some duty she would say, quite simply, 'Wait here, Lord Jesus, and I will come back directly I have finished this task.' In her meditations on our Lord's passion she was permitted to have a mystical share in her Saviour's sufferings, and her forehead and hair appeared at such seasons to be bedewed with drops of blood.

Lutgardis had been at St Catherine's twelve years when she was inspired or counselled to place herself under the stricter rule of the Cistercians. Although she would have preferred a German-speaking house, she selected the convent of Aywières, upon the advice of her confessor and of her friend, St Christine the Astonishing, who was then living at St Catherine's. Only French was spoken at Aywières, and St Lutgardis never mastered French. In after years, her ignorance of the language served her as a valid excuse for refusing to hold office at Aywières or elsewhere.

God endowed her with the gifts of healing and prophecy as well as an infused knowledge of the meaning of the Holy Scriptures. In spite of her imperfect French, she had great success in imparting spiritual consolation. When, eleven years before her death, she lost her sight, this affliction she accepted with joy, as a God-sent means of detaching her from the visible world. It was after she had become blind that she undertook the last of several prolonged fasts. Our Lord appeared to her to warn her o& her approaching death, and to bid her prepare for it in three ways. She was to give praise to God for what she had received; she was to pray unremittingly for the conversion of sinners; and she was to rely in all things on God alone, awaiting the time when she would possess Him for ever. St Lutgardis died, as she had predicted, on the Saturday night after the feast of the Holy Trinity, just as the night office for Sunday was beginning. It was June 16, 1246.

17 : SS. TERESA AND SANCHIA OF PORTUGAL, (A.D. 1250 AND 1229)

SANCHO I, King of Portugal, had three daughters, Teresa Sanchia and Mafalda, all of whom are honoured by the Church. Teresa, the eldest, became the wife of her cousin, Alfonso IX, King of León, by whom she had several children. The marriage, however, was after some years pronounced invalid, because it had been contracted within prohibited degrees without dispensation. Teresa was attached to her husband and loth to leave him, but eventually they agreed to part. Teresa returned to Portugal, and at Lorvão she found on her estate an abbey of Benedictine monks now fallen low in numbers and observance. These she ejected and replaced by a community of women pledged to the Cistercian rule. She rebuilt the church, besides restoring and extending the buildings to accommodate 300 nuns. Although she made her home with them, taking full part in their life, yet she retained the direction of her affairs, the disposal of her property, and the right to come and go as she pleased.

Teresa's sister, Sanchia, who never married, had lived since their father's death on her estates at Alenquer, where she devoted herself to good works. She welcomed the Franciscan and Dominican friars into Portugal, and founded the convent of Cellas, for women under the Augustinian rule. But during a visit to her sister she was so impressed by the life led by the community at Lorvao that she afterwards converted Cellas into a Cistercian abbey, and herself took the veil there. Sanchia died in 1229, at the age of forty-seven; Teresa surreptitiously smuggled her sister's body out of the choir at Cellas, where it lay on a bier, and conveyed it to Lorväo, where it was buried. The last public appearance of Teresa occurred two or three years later. It was made in response to an earnest entreaty from Berengaria, the widow of her former husband, that she would intervene to settle the quarrels between their respective children over the succession to the kingdom of León. Teresa went, and through her mediation an equitable arrangement was arrived at and peace was restored. Her work in the world, she felt, was now done and she determined never again to leave the convent. It was probably at this time that she actually received the veil. She survived until 1250, and at her death was buried beside St Sanchia. Their *cult* was approved in 1705.

18 : ST ELIZABETH OF SCHÖNAU, VIRGIN (A.D. 1164)

THREE German monasteries have borne the name of Schönau: one, a community of Cistercian monks near Heidelberg; another, a nunnery in Franconia; and the third, a double house of Benedictines not far from Bonn, built by Hildelin, who became its first abbot in 1125. Into the great nunnery of Hildelin's foundation, Elizabeth, a girl of humble extraction, entered at the age of twelve. Some six years later, in 1147, she was professed.

From her twenty-third year onwards she was subject to extraordinary supernatural manifestations, celestial visions, and diabolic persecutions. In a letter addressed to her friend St Hildegard, Elizabeth describes how an angel had told her to proclaim a series of judgements that would fall on the people unless they did penance, and how, because she had delayed obeying him, he had beaten her so severely with a whip that she had been ill for three days! At a later date, when some of her prophecies had failed in their fulfilment, the angel informed her that penance had actually averted the impending doom. For a time she was assailed by terrible temptations, but this period of trial was the prelude to great consolations and heavenly visitations. On Sundays and festivals in particular she would fall into ecstasies during the saying of the Office or at Mass. She recorded some of her visions on wax tablets which, at the bidding of Abbot Hildelin, she sent to her brother Egbert, a canon of Bonn, who subsequently took the habit at Schönau and succeeded Hildelin as abbot. These notes, supplemented by her oral explanations, Egbert embodied in three books of her visions, which he published with a preface of his own and a chronological list of her chief religious experiences.

The first book is written in simple language, such as Elizabeth herself might have used; but the others are more sophisticated in terminology and in thought, evincing at times a theological training more suggestive of Egbert than of his sister. The last of Elizabeth's books, as well as the most famous, was her contribution to the Ursuline Legend. It has a curious history. Excavations, which had been made on several occasions since the beginning of the twelfth century in a certain district of Cologne, had resulted in the discovery of a great number of human bones, thought to be those of St Ursula's eleven thousand virgins. Mingled with the rest, however, were the skeletons of men, and a number of tablets—now known to have been forgeries—ostensibly bearing names of the supposed martyrs. Gerlac, abbot of Deutz, who had assisted in translating the alleged relics of St Ursula in 1142, and who had spent nine years searching for the remains of her companions, addressed himself to Egbert in the hope that Elizabeth, through her visions, might be able to throw light on the problem thus presented.

Under strong pressure from her brother, as it would appear, she evolved an elaboration of the already fantastic story of St Ursula, into which she introduced a Pope Cyriacus, who never existed, and all the newly discovered 'martyrs'.

She must however, have been a woman of judgement or she could scarcely have held, as she did, the post of superioress during the last seven years of her life. Her office was second only to that of the abbot, who ruled the double community. She died on June 18, 1164, in her thirty-eighth year.

19 : ST JULIANA FALCONIERI, VIRGIN, FOUNDRESS OF THE
SERVITE NUNS (A.D. 1341)

ST JULIANA was one of the two glories of the noble family of the Falconieri, the other being her uncle, St Alexis, one of the Seven Holy Founders of the Servite Order. Her father, Chiarissimo, and her mother, Riguardata, were a devout couple of great wealth who had built at their own cost the magnificent church of the Annunziata in Florence. They were childless and already well advanced in age when, in 1270, Juliana was born—the answer to prayer. After the death of her father, which occurred while she was still quite young, her uncle Alexis shared with Riguardata the direction of her upbringing. She never cared for the amusements and occupations which interested other girls, and when she found that her relations were trying to arrange a suitable match for her she expressed her determination to consecrate herself to God and to renounce the world. She was then fifteen. After being carefully instructed by her uncle Alexis, she was invested with the Servite habit by St Philip Benizi in the church of the Annunziata, and a year later she was professed a tertiary of the order.

Juliana continued to live at home, and Riguardata, who had originally opposed her profession, ended by placing herself under her daughter's direction. Bereft of her mother in 1304, when she was thirty-four, Juliana moved to another house, where she led a community life with a number of women who devoted themselves to prayer and works of mercy. Their habit resembled that of the men of the Servite Order, but to facilitate their work they wore short sleeves, which caused them to be nicknamed 'Mantellate', a term subsequently applied to women tertiaries in general. With great reluctance Juliana accepted the post of superior at the urgent desire of her companions. For them she drew up a code of regulations which was formally confirmed 120 years later for their successors by Pope Martin V. Just as the Order of the Servants of Mary is commonly ascribed to St Philip Benizi because he framed their constitutions, so also for the same reason St Juliana is honoured as a foundress by all the women religious of the Servite Order, although she was not the first to be admitted into its ranks.

Her mortifications seriously impaired her health, and towards the close of her life she suffered much from gastric derangement. She had been in the habit of making her communion three times a week, and it was a source of deep sorrow to her in her last illness that her frequent attacks of sickness precluded her from receiving the sacrament of the altar. Juliana died in 1341, in her seventy-first year, and she was canonized in 1737.

20 : ST SILVERIUS, POPE AND MARTYR (c. A.D. 537)

SILVERIUS, the son of Pope St Hormisdas, was only a subdeacon when, on the death of Pope St Agapitus I at Constantinople on April 22, 536, he was forced as bishop on the Roman church by the Ostrogothic king of Italy, Theoldehad, who foresaw the appearance of a Byzantine candidate; however, after Silverius had been consecrated the clergy of Rome agreed to accept him. The Empress Theodora wrote asking him to recognize as patriarchs the monophysites Anthimus at Constantinople and Severus at Antioch; Silverius replied politely with what was in effect a refusal, and he is said to have remarked as he did so that he was signing his own death warrant. He was right; Theodora was a woman who would tolerate no opposition: but she could afford to wait.

After the devastation of suburban Rome by the Ostrogothic general Vitiges, the pope and the senate willingly opened the gates of the City to his Byzantine opponent Belisarius—and Theodora had her chance. An attempt to entrap Silverius by means of a forged letter in a charge of treasonable conspiracy with the Goths having apparently failed, he was kidnapped and carried away to Patara in Lycia in Asia Minor; and the next day Belisarius— who was acting under pressure from his wife Antonina—proclaimed as pope in his stead the Empress Theodora's nominee, the deacon Vigilius.

Apparently the Emperor Justinian had been kept in ignorance of what was going on; and when he was told by the bishop of Patara of what had happened, he ordered that Silverius be sent back to Rome and an inquiry instituted. But when the pope landed in Italy the supporters of Vigilius intercepted and captured him; and Antonina, eager to gratify Theodora, prevailed on her husband to let them deal with him as they chose. Accordingly Silverius was taken under escort to the island of Palmarola in the Tyrrhenian Sea, off Naples.

There, or perhaps in the neighbouring island of Ponza, he ended his days soon afterwards, as the result of the ill-treatment he received: the feast of St Silverius is kept as that of a martyr.

It is not at all clear how the appointment of Vigilius to the papal see came to be regularized; but once he was recognized as pope his patroness Theodora experienced disappointment, for he ceased to support her intrigues on behalf of Monophysism and stood forward as the upholder of orthodoxy—which after all is what is expected of a pope.

21 : ST ALOYSIUS, (A.D. 1591)

THE patron of Catholic youth, St Aloysius, or Luigi Gonzaga, was born on March 9, 1568, in the castle of Castiglione delle Stivieri in Lombardy. He was the eldest son of Ferrante, Marquis of Castiglione, and of Marta Tana Santena, lady of honour to the wife of Philip II of Spain, in whose court the marquis also held a high position. His father's one ambition was that his first-born son should become a great soldier. He was about seven when he experienced what may perhaps best be described as a spiritual quickening or sudden development of his religious faculties. He had said his morning and evening prayers from babyhood; now he began every day to recite the Office of our Lady, the seven penitential psalms, and other devotions.

In 1577 his father took him and his brother, Ridolfo, to Florence, and left them there under the charge of tutors to improve their Latin and to learn to speak the pure Italian of Tuscany. Whatever may have been his progress in those secular subjects, Aloysius made such rapid strides in the science of the saints that he used to call Florence the mother of piety. The boys had been living in Florence a little more than two years when their father removed them and placed them at the court of the Duke of Mantua, who had lately made him governor of Montserrat. This was in November 1579, when Aloysius was eleven and eight months. Even then he had it in his mind to resign to his brother his right of succession to the marquisate of Castiglione, although he had already received investiture from the emperor. A painful kidney disease furnished him with an adequate excuse for appearing little in public, and he spent most of his time in prayer and in reading the collection of the Lives of the Saints made by Surius.

Another book he read about this time, describing the experiences of the Jesuit missionaries in India, seems to have suggested the idea of entering the Society of Jesus in order to labour for the conversion of the heathen. As a first step to a future missionary career he set about instructing the poor boys of Castiglione in the catechism, during the summer holidays. At Casale-Monferrato, where the winter was spent, he haunted the churches of the Capuchins and the Barnabites: he also began to practise the austerities of a monk, fasting three days a week on bread and water, scourging himself with his dog-whip and rising at midnight to pray on the stone floor of a room in which he would suffer no fire to be lighted however bitter the weather.

In 1581 Don Ferrante was summoned to attend the Empress Mary of Austria on her journey from Bohemia to Spain. His family accompanied him, and on their arrival in Spain, Aloysius and Ridolfo were appointed pages to Don Diego, Prince of the Asturias. Although, as in duty bound, Aloysius waited on the young *infante* and shared his studies, yet he never omitted or curtailed his devotions.

He was now quite resolved to become a Jesuit. His mother, whom he first approached, approved, but when she communicated their son's decision to his father, Don Ferrante was furious. However, through the mediation of friends, he so far relented as to give a grudging and provisional consent. The death of the *infante* released the young Gonzagas from their court duties, and after a two-years' stay in Spain they returned to Italy in July, 1584. Upon their arrival at Castiglione the contest broke out again, and Aloysius found his vocation opposed not only by his father but by most of his relations, including the Duke of Mantua. Eminent churchmen and laymen were sent to argue with him, and promises and threats employed by turns as dissuasives. Don Ferrante insisted on sending him to visit all the rulers of Northern Italy and then engaged him in a number of secular commissions in the hope of awakening some new interest, or at least of putting off the evil hour. But nothing could move Aloysius. After giving his consent and retracting it several times, Don Ferrante finally capitulated when the imperial commission arrived transferring the succession to Ridolfo. Shortly afterwards Aloysius set out for Rome, and, on November 25, 1585, he entered the Jesuit novitiate house of Sant' Andrea.

There is little to be said about St Aloysius during the next two years except that he proved in all respects an ideal novice. Being under regular discipline he was obliged to take recreation, to eat more, and to distract his mind. Moreover, because of his weak health, he was forbidden to pray or meditate except at stated times. He was at Milan when one day, during his morning prayers, he had a revelation that he had not long to live. This filled him with joy and weaned his heart still more from the things of the world. Out of consideration for his precarious health he was recalled from Milan to Rome to complete his theological course in the City.

In 1591 an epidemic of plague caused great ravages in Rome. The Jesuits opened a hospital of their own, in which the father general himself and many members of the order rendered personal service. Aloysius, at his own entreaty, was one of the number. He instructed and exhorted the patients, washed them, made their beds, and performed with zeal the lowliest offices of the hospital. Several of the fathers fell victims to the disease and Aloysius caught it. He believed that he was dying, and, with a joy which he afterwards feared might have been impatience, he received viaticum and was anointed. Contrary to all expectation he recovered from the plague, but only to fall into a low fever which in three months reduced him to great weakness. As long as he possibly could, he would rise from his bed at night to worship before his crucifix and would kiss his sacred pictures, going from one to another; then he would kneel in prayer, propped up between the bed and the wall. Very humbly and anxiously he asked his confessor, St Robert Bellarmine, if he thought that anyone could go straight into the presence of God without passing through Purgatory. St Robert replied in the affirmative and, from his knowledge of Aloysius, encouraged him to hope that this grace might be his. Aloysius immediately fell into an ecstasy which lasted throughout the night, and during which he learnt that he would die on the octave of Corpus Christi.

On the octave-day he seemed so much better that the rector spoke of sending him to Frascati. Aloysius, however, maintained that he would die before the morrow and again received viaticum. In the evening, as he was thought to be in no immediate danger, all but two or three watchers were told to retire to rest. Nevertheless, at the request of Aloysius, Father Bellarmine recited the prayers for the departing. Afterwards the patient lay very still, occasionally murmuring, 'Into they hands'. Between ten and eleven a change came over him and it was evident that he was sinking. With his eyes fixed on the crucifix and with the name of Jesus upon his lips he died about midnight between June 20 and 21, 1591. He had attained the age of twenty-three years and eight months. The relics of St Aloysius now lie under the altar in the Lancellotti chapel of the church of St Ignatius in Rome; he was canonized in 1726.

22 : ST JOHN FISHER, BISHOP OF ROCHESTER AND CARDINAL, MARTYR (A.D. 1535)

BORN in Beverley, Yorkshire in 1469, the son of a small mercer who died when his children were very young, John Fisher was sent to Cambridge University at the age of fourteen. There he distingusihed himself greatly in his studies, was elected a fellow of Michaelhouse (since merged into Trinity), and was ordained priest by special permission when he was only twenty-two. He became successively senior proctor, doctor of divinity, master of Michaelhouse, and vice-chancellor of the university. In 1502 he resigned his mastership to become the chaplain of the king's mother, Lady Margaret Beaufort, Countess of Richmond and Derby.

Under his guidance she made a noble use of her fortune. By founding Christ's College and St John's College, Cambridge, and by establishing there, as well as at Oxford, a Lady Margaret divinity chair, and by other princely gifts, she has come to be regarded—and justly so—as the greatest benefactress Cambridge has ever known. The university's debt to St John Fisher is not so universally recognized. When he went to Cambridge its scholarship had sunk to a low ebb: no Greek or Hebrew was taught, and the library had been reduced to 300 volumes. Not only did all the administrative work in connection with Lady Margaret's benefactions fall upon him but he did much, entirely on his own initiative, to foster learning in the university. He endowed scholarships, he re-introduced Greek and Hebrew into the curriculum, and he brought Erasmus over to teach and to lecture.

In 1504 he was elected chancellor of the University of Cambridge—a post which he continued to hold until his death. Later in that same year King Henry VII nominated him to the bishopric of Rochester, although he was only thirty-five years of age. He accepted with reluctance an office which added the cares of a diocese to his work for Cambridge. Nevertheless, he carried out his pastoral duties with zeal and thoroughness. He held visitations, administered confirmation, disciplined his clergy, visited the sick poor, distributed alms with his own hands, and exercised generous hospitality. Moreover, he found time to write books and to continue his studies. He was forty-eight when he began to learn Greek, and fifty-one when he started upon Hebrew.

John Fisher's private life was most austere: he limited his sleep to four hours, used the discipline freely and, though his fare was of the scantiest, he kept a skull before him at meal-times to remind himself of death. Books were his one earthly pleasure: and, with a view to bequeathing his books to Cambridge, he formed a library which was among the finest in Europe. Because of his learning and eloquence, he was specially selected to preach against Lutheranism when it was found to be making headway— particularly in London and in the universities. He also wrote four weighty volumes against Luther which can claim the distinction of being the first books to be published in refutation of the new doctrines.

He was himself a reformer. At a synod called by Cardinal Wolsey in 1518 he boldly protested against the worldliness, the laxity and the vanity of the higher clergy, the greater part of whom had won their preferments through secular service to the state or by private interest. Because, unlike them, he was not trying to serve two masters, he had no hesitation, some nine years later, in upholding the validity of King Henry's marriage to Catherine of Aragon when other men in high office were temporizing or yielding. He was chosen to be one of the queen's counsellors in the nullity suit begun before Cardinal Campeggio at Blackfriars in 1529, and he proved to be her ablest champion.

As a member of the House of Lords he denounced the measures against the clergy which were being forced through the Commons. He uttered another great protest in Convocation when that assembly was called upon to agree that Henry VIII was head of the Church in England. To him it was due that the words 'So far as the law of Christ allows' were added to the form of assent that was eventually signed, but he regarded even that as too much in the nature of a compromise.

The warnings of friends and the threats of his enemies were not necessary to bring home to Bishop Fisher the danger he now ran by his opposition to the ruling powers. Twice already he had suffered short terms of imprisonment, at least one attempt was made to poison him, and on another occasion a shot fired from across the river penetrated his library window. Then came an unsuccessful effort on the part of Thomas Cromwell to connect him with the affair of Elizabeth Barton, the 'Holy Maid of Kent'. Eventually the passage into law of the bill of succession provided his enemies with the means of securing his downfall. He was summoned to Lambeth to subscribe to it, although he was so ill that he fainted on the road between Rochester and London. To the actual succession he would have been willing to agree, but he absolutely refused to take the oath in the form presented because it was so worded as to make it practically an oath of supremacy.

John of Rochester was arrested and conveyed to the Tower. An act of attainder of misprision of treason was then passed against the prisoner: he was declared to be degraded from his office and his see was pronounced vacant. He was sixty-six years of age, but looked more like a man of eighty-six. His wasted body, we are told, could scarcely bear the weight of his clothes. In November 1534, a second act of attainder was passed upon him, but he still lingered on in prison. By sending him the cardinal's hat, six months later, Pope Paul III infuriated Henry VIII and hastened the end.

The result of his trial was a foregone conclusion, for the king's will was law. Though some of the judges wept when the sentence was declared, John Fisher was condemned to death on June 17, 1535. Five days later, at five in the morning, he was roused with the news, that he was to be executed that day. He asked to be allowed to rest a little longer and he slept soundly for two hours. He then dressed, putting on a fur tippet 'to keep me warm for the while until the very time of execution'; then he took his little New Testament, and, with great difficulty owing to his excessive weakness, went down the steps to the entrance from whence he was conveyed in a chair to the Tower gate. He walked up Tower Hill, mounted the scaffold unassisted, and in the customary terms pardoned his executioner. As he stood up to address the crowd his tall emaciated figure made him appear like a living skeleton. With a clear voice he said that he was dying for the faith of Christ's holy Catholic Church, and he asked the people to pray that he might be steadfast to the end. After he had recited the *Te Deum* and the psalm *In te Domine speravi*, he was blindfolded, and with one blow from the axe his head was severed from his body.

In May 1935, almost exactly four hundred years after his death, John Fisher was solemnly numbered among the saints, together with his friend and fellow martyr, Sir Thomas More.

23 : ST THOMAS GARNET, MARTYR (A.D. 1608)

THOMAS GARNET was the nephew of the famous Jesuit, Father Henry Garnet, and the son of Mr Richard Garnet, a faithful Catholic who had been a distinguished fellow of Balliol College, Oxford. His early education Thomas received at Horsham Grammar School, but at the age of sixteen or seventeen he was sent across the Channel to the newly opened College of St Omer. In January 1595 he and several of the other students set sail for Spain, but not till fourteen months later, after many adventures which included a term of imprisonment in England, did he succeed in reaching his destination—the English Jesuit college at Valladolid. There, at the close of his theological course, he was ordained priest. He was then sent on the English Mission with Bd Mark Barkworth. His manner of life for the next six years he described in a few words in his evidence when on trial: 'I wandered from place to place to recover souls which had gone astray and were in error as to the knowledge of the true Catholic Church'.

He was arrested near Warwick shortly after the discovery of the Gunpowder Plot, and was imprisoned first in the Gatehouse and then at Newgate. Because he had been staying in the house of Mr Ambrose Rookwood, who was implicated in the conspiracy, and because he was so closely related to Father Henry Garnet, it was hoped that important information could be extracted from him, but neither threats of the rack nor the strictest cross-examination could elicit any incriminating admission. After eight or nine months spent in a damp cell with no better bed that the bare ground, he was deported to Flanders with some forty-six other priests. While still in England St Thomas had been admitted to the Society of Jesus by his uncle, and he now proceeded to Louvain for his novitiate. The following year, in September, he returned to England. Six weeks later he was betrayed by an apostate priest and rearrested.

At the Old Bailey he was charged with high treason on the ground that he had been made a priest by authority derived from Rome and that he had returned to England in defiance of the law. His priesthood he neither admitted nor denied, but he firmly refused to take the new oath of supremacy. On the evidence of three witnesses who declared that when he was in the Tower he had signed himself Thomas Garnet, Priest, he was declared guilty and was condemned to death. On the scaffold he proclaimed himself a priest and a Jesuit, explaining that he had not acknowledged this at his trial lest he should be his own accuser or oblige his judges to condemn him against their consciences. The Earl of Essex and others tried up to the last to persuade him to save his life by taking the oath, and when the end came and the cart was drawn away they would not allow him to be cut down until it was certain that he was quite dead.

24 : ST BARTHOLOMEW OF FARNE, (A.D. 1193)

OF the many pious men who were led by the example of St Cuthbert to become solitaries on the island of Farne, off the Northumbrian coast, not the least remarkable was this Bartholomew, for he spent no less than forty-two years upon that desolate haunt of birds. He was a north-countryman, a native of Whitby. His parents, who may have been of Scandinavian origin, called him Tostig, but because the name made him a laughing-stock it was changed to William. He determined to go abroad, and his wanderings led him to Norway, where he remained long enough to receive ordination as a priest. He returned home, and went to Durham, where he took the monastic habit, assuming the name of Bartholomew. A vision he had of St Cuthbert inspired him to dedicate the rest of his life to God in the cell which Cuthbert had once occupied at Farne.

Upon his arrival he found another hermit already installed—a certain Brother Ebwin, who strongly resented his intrusion and who strove by petty persecution to drive him away. Bartholomew attempted no reprisals, but made it quite evident that he had come to stay, and Ebwin eventually retired, leaving him in solitary possession. The mode of life he embraced was one of extreme austerity, modelled upon that of the fathers in the desert. Later he was joined by a former prior of Durham called Thomas; but they could not agree. Their chief cause of dissension—sad to relate—was the amount of the food ration. Thomas could not manage with as little as Bartholomew, and he went so far as to question the genuineness of what appeared to be his brother's extraordinary abstemiousness. Bartholomew, who seems to have been sensitive to criticism, was so offended at being charged with hypocrisy that he left the island and returned to Durham. There he remained in spite of the apologies of Thomas, until the bishop, a year later, ordered him back to Farne, when a reconciliation then took place. Forewarned of his approaching death, Bartholomew announced it to some monks, who were with him when he died, and buried him in the island. He left a reputation for holiness and miracles, but there is no evidence of liturgical cult.

25 : ST WILLIAM OF VERCELLI, ABBOT OF MONTE VERGINE (A.D. 1142)

THE founder of the religious congregation known as the Hermits of Monte Vergine came of a Piedmontese family and was born at Vercelli in 1085. After the death of his parents he was kindly cared for by relations, but at the age of fourteen he abandoned his home and set out as a poor pilgrim for Compostela in Spain. Not satisfied with the hardships such a journey entailed, he had two iron bands fastened round his body. How long William remained in Spain is not recorded. We hear of him next in 1106, when he was at Melfi in the Italian Basilicata, and then at Monte Solicoli, on the slopes of which he remained for two years, leading a penitential life with a hermit. To this period belongs St William's first miracle, the restoration of sight to a blind man. The cure made him famous, and to avoid being acclaimed as a wonder-worker he left the neighbourhood to stay with St John of Matera. They were kindred spirits and became close friends. It was St William's intention to proceed on a pilgrimage to Jerusalem, and he would not allow himself to be deterred by John's assurance that God had other work for him to do. He actually started, but he had not got far when he was attacked by robbers. He took this as a sign that John was right, and relinquished his journey.

He now betook himself to a height between Nola and Benevento, which was then called Monte Virgiliano—possibly after the great Virgil, who is said to have sojourned there. At first William attempted to live there as a hermit, but he was soon joined by would-be disciples, both priests and laymen. He formed them into a community and from the church which he built in 1124, under the name of our Lady, the mountain has derived its present name of Monte Vergine. The rule he instituted was most austere: no wine, meat or dairy produce was allowed, and on three days of the week only vegetables and dry bread. After the first fervour had cooled, murmurs arose and there was a general demand for relaxation. William had no desire to constrain the malcontents, though for himself any relaxation seemed unthinkable. He therefore chose a prior to rule the community, and then departed with five faithful followers. With St John of Matera, who now joined him, he made a second settlement at Monte Laceno, in Apulia. Here, however, the barrenness of the soil, the exposed position and the high altitude made life a misery to all but the most hardy, and even they could with difficulty hold out through the winter. St John had more than once urged removal, when a fire which destroyed their huts compelled them to descend into the valley. here the two holy men parted: John to go east and found one monastery at Pulsano on Monte Gargano, and William to found another on Monte Cognato in the Basilicata.

When that community was well established St William treated it as he had treated the monastery at Monte Vergine—he gave it a prior and left it to govern itself. At Conza, in Apulia, he founded a monastery for men, and at Guglietto, near Nusco, he established two communities, one of men and the other of women. King Roger II of Naples afterwards drew him to Salerno, in order that he might have the benefit of his counsel and help.

St William died at Guglietto on June 25, 1142. He left no written constitutions, but a code of regulations bringing the order into conformity with the Benedictine rule was drawn up by the third abbot general Robert. The only monastery of William's foundation which exists at the present day is that of Monte Vergine. It now belongs to the Benedictine congregation of Subiaco, and has a much venerated picture of our Lady of Constantinople, to which pilgrimages are frequently made.

26 : ST ANTHELM, BISHOP OF BELLEY (A.D. 1178)

ANTHELM was born in 1107 at the castle of Chignin, six miles from Chambéry. He was a high-principled young priest, hospitable and generous, but interested primarily in the things of this world. However, he had relatives among the Carthusians, and visits to the monastery of Portes completely changed his outlook. He accordingly abandoned the world to assume the habit of St Bruno about 1137. Before he had completed his noviciate he was sent to the Grande Chartreuse which had recently lost the greater part of its buildings through the fall of an avalanche; and Anthelm did much by his example and business-like qualities to revive the fervour and restore the prosperity of the monastery. After the resignation of Hugh I in 1139, he was elected seventh prior of the Grande Chartreuse.

He made it his first care to repair the ruined buildings, which he then encircled by a wall. He brought water through an aqueduct and renewed the farm premises and sheep-folds, and all the time he was enforcing the rule in its primitive simplicity, and had the satisfaction of seeing his efforts crowned with success. Until his time all the charterhouses had been independent of one another, each one being subject only to the bishop. He was responsible for summoning the first general chapter. By it the Grande Chartreuse was constituted the mother house, and he became, in fact if not in name, the first minister general of the order. It is not surprising that his reputation for sanctity and wisdom brought him many recruits; amongst those who received the habit at his hands were his own father, one of his brothers, and William, Count of Nivernais, who became a lay-brother.

After governing the Grande Chartreuse for twelve years he succeeded in 1152, to his great satisfaction, in resigning an office he had never desired. He was not allowed to remain long, however, in the seclusion of a solitary cell. Old age had compelled Bernard, the founder and first prior of Portes, to lay down his charge, and at his request Anthelm was appointed his successor. The toil of the monks had brought great prosperity to the monastery, whose treasury and barns were full to overflowing. Such superfluity the new prior regarded as incompatible with evangelical poverty, and in view of the scarcity that prevailed in the surrounding countryside he ordered free distribution to be made to all who were in need. He even sold some of the ornaments of the church to provide alms. Two years later he returned to the Grande Chartreuse to live for a while the contemplative life of a simple monk, but it was then that there came to him the first call to deal with ecclesiastical matters outside the order.

In 1159 western Christendom was split into two camps, the one favouring the claims of the true pope, Alexander III, the other supporting the antipope 'Victor IV', who was the nominee of the Emperor Frederick Barbarossa. Anthelm threw himself into the fray in conjunction with Geoffrey, the learned Cistercian abbot of Hautecombe. They succeeded in recruiting their own brethren and the religious of other communities, who declared for Alexander and organized his cause in France, in Spain and even in England. Partly no doubt in recognition of these services, Pope Alexander listened to an appeal made to him regarding the vacant see of Belley, to set aside the selected candidates and to nominate Anthelm. In vain did the Carthusian entreat—even with tears—to be excused. the pope was insistent, and Anthelm was obliged to consent. He was consecrated on September 8, 1163.

There was much in his diocese that called for reform, and he set to work with characteristic thoroughness. In his first synod he made an impassioned appeal to his clergy to live up to their high calling; the observance of clerical celibacy had largely fallen into abeyance and not a few priests openly lived as married men. At first the bishop used only persuasion and warnings, but after two years, finding that his injunctions were still being disregarded in certain quarters, he made an example of the worst offenders by depriving them of their benefices. He was equally firm in dealing with disorder and oppression among the laity: no previous bishop of Belley had ever been so fearless or so uncompromising.

Any leisure time he could secure was spent at the Grande Chartreuse and the houses of his order. Two other institutions were specially dear to him: the one was a community of women solitaries at a place called Bons, the other a leper house where he loved to tend the sufferers with his own hands. St Anthelm passed away on June 26, 1178, at the age of seventy-two.

27 : ST CYRIL, ARCHBISHOP OF ALEXANDRIA, DOCTOR OF THE CHURCH (A.D. 444)

ST CYRIL has been called the Doctor of the Incarnation, as St Augustine was styled the Doctor of Divine Grace: in the great intercession of the Syrian and Maronite Mass he is commemorated as 'a tower of truth and interpreter of the Word of God made flesh'. Throughout his life he made it a rule never to advance any doctrine which he had not learnt from the ancient fathers, but his books against Julian the Apostate show that he had also read the profane writers. H often said himself that he neglected human eloquence, and it is certainly to be regretted that he did not cultivate a clearer style and write purer Greek. Upon the death of his uncle Theophilus in 412, he was raised to the see of Alexandria. He began to exert his authority by causing the churches of the Novations to be closed and their sacred vessels to be seized.

He next drove out the Jews, which incensed Orestes the governor, although it was approved by the Emperor Theodosius. This disagreement with Orestes led to grievous results. Hypatia, a pagan woman of noble character, was the most influential teacher of philosophy at that time in Alexandria, and her reputation was so great that disciples flocked to her from all parts. Among these was the great Bishop Synesius, who submitted his works to her criticism. She was much respected by the governor, who used to consult her even on matters of civil administration. Acting upon a suspicion that Hypatia had incensed the governor against their bishop, the mob in 417 attacked her in the streets, pulled her out of her chariot, and tore her body in pieces.

In the year 428 Nestorius, a priest-monk of Antioch, was made archbishop of Constantinople; and he there taught with some of his clergy that there were two distinct persons in Christ, that of God and that of man, joined only by a moral union. Cyril sent him a mild expostulation, but was answered with haughtiness and contempt. Both parties appealed to Pope St Celestine I who, after examining the doctrine in a council at Rome, condemned it and pronounced a sentence of excommunication and deposition against Nestorius unless, within ten days of receiving notice of the sentence, he publicly retracted his errors. St Cyril, who was appointed to see the sentence carried out, sent Nestorius, with his third and last summons, twelve propositions with anathemas to be signed by him as a proof of his orthodoxy. Nestorius, however, showed himself more obstinate than ever.

This occasioned the summoning of the third general council which was held at Ephesus in 431, attended by two hundred bishops with St Cyril at their head as senior bishop and Pope Celestine's representative. Nestorius was present in the town, but refused to appear; so after his sermons had been read and other evidence received against him, his doctrines were condemned, and a sentence of excommunication and deposition was pronounced. Six days later there arrived at Ephesus Archbishop John of Antioch, with forty-one bishops who had not been able to reach Ephesus in time. They were in favour of Nestorius, although they did not share his errors, of which indeed they deemed him innocent. Instead of associating themselves with the council, they assembled by themselves and presumed to depose St Cyril, accusing him in turn of heresy. Both sides appealed to the emperor, by whose order St Cyril and Nestorius were both arrested and kept in confinement. When three legates arrived from Pope Celestine, the matter took another turn. After careful consideration of what had been done, the legates confirmed the condemnation of Nestorius, approved Cyril's con-duct, añd declared the sentence pronouced against him null and void. Thus he was vindicated with honour and, though the bishops of the Antiochene province continued their schism for a while, they made peace with St Cyril in 433, when they condemned Nestorius and gave a clear and orthodox declaration of their own faith. Nestorius retired to his old monastery at Antioch, but later was exiled to the Egyptian desert.

St Cyril, was declared a doctor of the Universal Church in 1882.

28 : ST IRENAEUS, BISHOP OF LYONS (c. A.D. 203)

IRENAEUS was born, probably about the year 125, in one of those maritime provinces of Asia Minor where the memory of the Apostles was still cherished and where Christians were numerous. He received what must have been an exceptionally liberal education, for it gave him a thorough knowledge of the text of Holy Scripture and a good general acquaintance with Greek philosophy and literature. Moreover, he had the inestimable privilege of sitting at the feet of men who had known the Apostles or their immediate disciples.

Commercial relations had existed from early times between the ports of Asia Minor and Marseilles, and in the second century of our era Levantine traders were regularly conveying their wares up the Rhone as far as Lyons, which became in consequence the chief mart of western Europe and the most populous city in Gaul. In the train of the traders many of whom settled in Lyons, came their priests and missionaries who brought the Gospel to the pagan Gauls and founded a vigorous local church. To this church of Lyons Irenaeus came to serve as a priest under its first bishop, St Pothinus, an oriental like himself; to it he was to remain permanently attached. The high opinion held of him by his brother clergy was evinced in the year 177, when he was dispatched on a somewhat delicate mission to Rome. It was after the outbreak of the terrible persecution, and some of the leaders of the church of

Lyons were already in prison. Their captivity, however, did not prevent them from continuing to take a deep interest in their fellow Christians in Asia Minor. Conscious of the sympathetic hearing to which they were entitled as confessors in imminent peril of death, they sent to Pope St Eleutherius, by the hands of Irenaeus, what is described by Eusebius as 'a most religious and most orthodox' letter, in which they appealed to him—in the interest of the peace and unity of the Church—to deal leniently with their Montanist brethren in Phrygia.

This mission, entailing as it did absence from Lyons, explains how it was that Irenaeus was not called upon to share the martyrdom of St Pothinus and his fellow-sufferers, and does not seem to have witnessed it. How long he remained in Rome we do not know, but when he returned to Lyons it was to occupy its vacant bishopric. By that time the persecution was over and the twenty or more years of his episcopate were years of relative peace. Information about his activities is scanty, but it is clear that in addition to his purely pastoral duties he did much to evangelize the neighbouring lands. It was the spread of Gnosticism in Gaul, and the ravages it was making amongst the Christians of his diocese, that inspired him to undertake the task of exposing its errors.

He produced a treatise in five books in which he sets forth fully the inner doctrines of the various sects and afterwards contrasts them with the teaching of the Apostles and the text of Holy Scripture.

Irenaeus was firmly convinced that a great part of the attractiveness of Gnosticism lay in the veil of secrecy with which it surrounded itself, and he was determined to 'strip the fox' as he expressed it. The event proved him to have been right. His work, written in Greek but quickly translated into Latin, was widely circulated and succeeded in dealing to second-century Gnosticism what appears to have been its death-blow. At any rate, from that time onwards, it ceased to offer a serious menace to the Catholic faith.

Thirteen or fourteen years after his mission to Pope Eleutherius, Irenaeus again acted as mediator between a pope and a body of Christians in Asia Minor. Because the Quartodecimans refused to keep Easter in accordance with the Western use they had been excommunicated by Victor III, and there was in consequence a real danger of schism. Irenaeus intervened on their behalf. The outcome of his representations was the restoration of good relations between the two parties and a peace which proved permanent. After the Council of Nicaea in 325, the Quartodecimans voluntarily conformed to the Roman usage without any pressure from the Holy See.

The date of the death of St Irenaeus is not known: it is usually assigned approximately to the year 202.

29 : ST PETER, PRINCE OF THE APOSTLES (A.D. 64?)

THE story of St Peter as recounted in the gospels is so familiar that there can be no need to retrace it here in detail. We know that he was a Galilean, that his original home was at Bethsaida, that he was married, a fisherman, and that he was brother to the apostle St Andrew. His name was Simon, but our Lord, on first meeting him told him that he should be called Kephas, the Aramaic equivalent of the Greek word whose English form is

Peter (*i.e.* rock). No one who reads the New Testament can be blind to the predominant role which is everywhere accorded to him among the immediate followers of Jesus. It was he who, as spokesman of the rest, made the sublime profession of faith: 'Thou art the Christ, the Son of the living God'.

Not less familiar is the story of Peter's triple denial of his Master in spite of the warning he had previously received. The very fact that his fall is recorded by all four evangelists with a fullness of detail which seems out of proportion to its relative insignificance amid the incidents of our Saviour's passion, is itself a tribute to the position which St Peter occupied among his fellows. After the Ascension we still find St Peter everywhere taking a leading part. Almost all that we know for certain about the later life of St Peter is derived from the Acts of the Apostles and from slight allusions in his own epistles and those of St Paul. Of special importance is the account of the conversion of the centurion Cornelius; for this raised the question of the continuance of the rite of circumcision and the maintenance of the prescriptions of the Jewish law in such matters as food and intercourse with the Gentiles.

The passion of St Peter took place in Rome during the reign of Nero (A.D. 54–68), but no written account of it (if there was such a thing) has survived. According to an old but unverifiable tradition he was confined in the Mamertine prison, where the church of San Pietro in Carcere now stands. Tertullian (d. *c.* 225) says that the apostle was crucified; and Eusebius adds, on the authority of Origen (d. 253), that by his own desire he suffered head downwards. The place has always been believed to be the gardens of Nero, which saw so many scenes of terror and glory at this time. The, at one time, generally accepted tradition that St Peter's pontificate lasted twenty-five years is probably no more than a deduction based upon inconsistent chronological data.

The joint feast of SS. Peter and Paul seems always to have been kept at Rome on June 29, and Duchesne considers that the practice goes back at least to the time of Constantine; but the celebration in the East was at first commonly assigned to December 28.

30 : THE FIRST MARTYRS OF THE CHURCH OF ROME,
(A.D. 64)

THESE confessors, whose number and names are known only to God, are described in the Roman Martyrology as 'the first fruits with which Rome, so fruitful in that seed, had peopled heaven'. It is interesting to note that the first of the Caesars to persecute Christians was Nero, perhaps the most unprincipled of them all.

In July 64, the tenth year of his reign, a terrible fire devastated Rome. It began near the Great Circus, in a district of shops and booths full of inflammable goods, and quickly spread in all directions. After it had raged for six days and seven nights and had been got under by the demolition of numerous buildings, it burst forth again in the garden of Tigellinus, the prefect of the praetorian guard, and continued for three days more. By the time it had finally died down, two-thirds of Rome was a mass of smouldering ruins. On the third day of the fire Nero came from Antium to survey the scene. It is said that, clad in theatrical costume, he went to the top of the Tower of Maecenas, and to the accompaniment of his lyre recited Priam's lament over the burning of Troy. His savage delight at watching the flames gave rise to the belief that he had ordered the conflagration, or at any rate had prevented it from being extinguished.

The belief rapidly gained ground. It was said that flaming torches were thrown into houses by mysterious individuals who declared themselves to be acting under orders. How far Nero was responsible remains a moot point to this day. In view of the numerous destructive fires which have afflicted Rome throughout the ages, it is more than likely that this, perhaps the worst of them all, was due to accident. At the time, however, suspicion was so widespread that Nero was alarmed, and sought to divert it from himself by accusing the Christians of setting fire to the city.

Although, as we know from the historian Tacitus, no one believed them to be guilty of the crime, they were seized, exposed to the scorn and derision of the people, and put to death with the utmost cruelty. Some were sewn up in the skins of wild beasts and delivered to hungry dogs who tore them to pieces; some were crucified; others again were smeared over with wax, pitch and other combustible material, and after being impaled with sharp stakes under their chins were ignited to serve as torches. All these barbarities took place at a public nocturnal fête which Nero gave in his own gardens. They served as side-shows whilst the emperor diverted his guests with chariot races, mixing with the crowd in plebeian attire or driving himself in a chariot. Hardened though the Romans were to gladiatorial shows, the savage cruelty of these tortures aroused horror and pity in many of those who witnessed them.

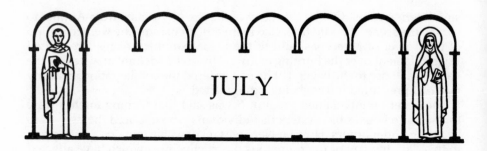

JULY

1 : ST OLIVER PLUNKET, ARCHBISHOP OF ARMAGH, MARTYR (A.D. 1681)

THE last Catholic to die for his faith at Tyburn and the first of the Irish martyrs to be beatified was born in 1629 at Loughcrew, in county Meath; through his father he was connected with the earl of Fingall and the barons of Dunsany and Locriff, and his mother was a Dillon and near kin to the earl of Roscommon. He was given his name after that young Oliver Plunket who had been done to death when the Spanish prisoners were massacred at Smerwick in Kerry in 1580. His youth was spent in the turmoil and confusion of parties consequent on the rebellion against King Charles I in England, the Plunkets naturally being among those Catholic nobles and gentry who were for the king's prerogative and freedom for the Irish; but Oliver himself was already destined for the priesthood and studied under his kinsman Patrick Plunket, Benedictine abbot of St Mary's, in Dublin.

In 1645, when he was sixteen, he went to Rome with four other young men who had been chosen to be educated at his own expense for the priesthood by Father Pierfrancesco Scarampi, the Oratorian who had been sent in 1643 by Pope Urban VIII to assist at the supreme council of the Irish Confederate party. He did brilliantly under the Jesuits at the then lately established Irish College, followed the course of civil and canon law at the *Sapienza*, and was ordained in 1654. The state of affairs in Ireland made it impossible for him at once to go on the mission there, so by the good offices of Father Scarampi he was appointed to the chair of theology in the College *de Propaganda Fide*. He lodged with the Oratorians, and was appointed a consultor of the Sacred Congregation of the Index and procurator for the Irish bishops to the Holy See. He thus lived a busy and devoted life in Rome for twelve years.

In March 1669 Edmund O'Reilly, Archbishop of Armagh and Primate of All Ireland died in exile in France. Pope Clement IX chose to succeed him Dr Oliver Plunket, and in November of that year he was consecrated at Ghent. He then went on to London, where he was weather-bound and was secretly lodged in his own apartments by Father Philip Howard, O.P. (afterwards cardinal), almoner of Charles II's queen, Catherine of Braganza. He reached Dublin in March 1670, where he was received by his noble relatives, including his former tutor, Dom Patrick Plunket, now bishop of Meath. He was one of the two bishops in Ireland, the aged and worn-out bishop of

Kilmore being the other; there were only three others, and they were in exile: Oliver's predecessor, O'Reilly, had been able to pass only two of his twelve years of episcopate in the country. The new archbishop within three months held a provincial synod, two ordinations, and confirmed ten thousand persons of all ages—and still there were fifty thousand unconfirmed in his province. The first two years of his rule were peaceful, owing to the fairness and moderation of the viceroy, Lord Berkeley of Stratton; he was tolerant to Catholics and personally friendly towards Oliver. Unhappily this peace was marred by a dispute among Catholics, in this case between the Archbishop of Armagh and his cousin the Archbishop of Dublin, Peter Talbot, as to the extent and implications of Armagh's primacy, a matter of considerable canonical importance to the Church of Ireland. Oliver interpreted his primacy as being not merely titular but carrying with it primatial jurisdiction over the other metropolitans; Dr Talbot saw in it only a precedence of rank.

These two years were not otherwise uneventful, but a period of tremendously hard and difficult work, of clearing the ground for an improvement of the spiritual state of the people which the new primate was not to see. The Synod of Clones legislated rigorously against abuses among both clergy and laity. He established the Jesuits in Drogheda, where they ran a school for boys and a college for ecclesiastical students; he even aspired to extend his ministry to the Gaelic-speaking Catholics of the highlands and isles of Scotland, but the difficulties were too great; he laboured to maintain discipline among his clergy, to put into force the decrees of the Council of Trent, and to forestall Jansenist infiltration through those who had been trained in France and Flanders, to enforce better observance among the friars, and to adjust the strained relationships both between seculars and regulars and between the orders themselves, whose differences were deliberately aggravated by the civil authorities for political ends. All this, the day-to-day care of his flock, and much more, had to be done with one eye all the time on the likelihood of incurring the penalties of *praemunire* for acknowledging the Pope's jurisdiction and resorting to the Holy See; moreover, it had to be done under conditions of 'astounding poverty', which Oliver shared with all his brother bishops and clergy. He was on friendly terms with the Protestant bishops and gentry of Ulster, who had great regard for him and for his sake were disposed not to oppress Catholics.

In 1673 the tortuous politics of King Charles II provoked a fresh outbreak of persecution. Archbishop Talbot was banished and the Archbishop of Tuam fled to Spain; at first Oliver was not interfered with, but he went into hiding with Dr Brennan, Bishop of Waterford, who was in 1676 advanced to the see of Cashel. These two were in continual danger of arrest and lived under circumstances of grinding physical hardship and penury, carrying on their pastoral work to the best of their ability. It was made even more difficult for Oliver by the enmity of a section of schismatic or quasi-schismatic Catholics.

In 1678 the Oates Plot was launched. The panic which it caused in England had its repercussions in Ireland, where an order of expulsion was made against all Catholic bishops and regular priests, and people were officially encouraged by proclamation to 'make any further discovery of the horrid popish plot . Lord Shaftesbury's agent, Hetherington, MacMoyer, an expelled Franciscan, and Murphy, an excommunicated secular priest, informed against Oliver in London, and the lord lieutenant was ordered to arrest him. On December 6, 1679, he was shut up in Dublin Castle: here he was able to help his old opponent, Dr Talbot, on his death-bed, for the archbishop of Dublin had been allowed to return to Ireland, but was arrested for complicity in the 'popish plot', although a dying man. Oliver Plunket was put on trial at Dundalk for conspiring against the state by plotting to bring 20,000 French soldiers into the country and levying a tax on his clergy to support 70,000 armed men for rebellion. For two days no witnesses turned up for the prosecution, and on the third day only MacMoyer, who was drunk, and asked for a remand until the other witnesses could be procured. It was obvious to Shaftesbury that the archbishop would never be convicted on so absurd an indictment in Ireland; he was therefore removed to Newgate prison in London.

At the first trial the grand jury found no true bill; he was not released, but it was adjourned till June 1681. There is a doubt if the court had jurisdiction over the Irishman, and the second trial was conducted with only a semblance of justice, so that Lord Campbell, writing of the judge, Sir Francis Pemberton, calls it 'a disgrace to himself and country': the jury found the accused guilty of high treason; and judgement was reserved. It was pronounced a week later, and the Primate of All Ireland was condemned to be hanged, disembowelled and quartered.

The execution took place on Friday, July 1 (o.s.), 1681; there was a huge crowd at Tyburn to whom the martyr protested his innocence of treason and his loyalty to the king, praying for him and for his own enemies. He was dead before he was cut down from the scaffold. The mutilated body was buried in the churchyard of St Giles-in-the-Fields, whence it was taken to the English Benedictine abbey of Lamspring in Westphalia in 1684; two hundred years later the relics were translated to Downside Abbey, where they are now enshrined; the martyr's head is preserved in St Peter's church at Drogheda. Oliver Plunket was beatified in 1920 and canonized in 1975.

2 : ST OTTO, BISHOP OF BAMBERG (A.D. 1139)

OTTO belonged to the family of Mistelbach in Swabia, and while still young was ordained priest and entered the service of the Emperor Henry IV, by whom he was chosen in due course to be chancellor. In the struggle between the Holy See and the emperor, Henry set up an antipope; Otto laboured to bring him to repentance and submission, and refused to approve his schism or other crimes, while supporting his politics in so far as they were lawful. When the emperor nominated him bishop of Bamberg in 1102 he refused to be consecrated until some years later when he was able to go to Rome and receive episcopal orders from Pope Paschal II himself. Under the succeeding emperor Otto worked to heal the breach with the Holy See and the harms which it produced, for Henry V altered his own policy of conciliation and followed that of his father. Yet Otto always enjoyed the trust of both parties, and amid all his political activities he discharged his episcopal duties with the greatest care, established many monasteries and other religious foundations, and led an exemplary private life.

Boleslaus III of Poland, having conquered part of Pomerania; entreated St Otto to undertake a mission in that country. The bishop in 1124 took with him a number of priests and catechists and went to eastern Pomerania: over 20,000 persons are said to have been baptized. He returned to Bamberg for Easter the following year, having appointed clergy to attend to the converts and finish the work he had begun. The towns of Stettin and Julin having relapsed into paganism, Otto again went to Pomerania in 1128, brought those cities back to the faith, and through hardships and dangers carried the light of the gospel into other remote places. He returned again to the care of his own flock, amidst which he died on June 30, 1139. He was canonized fifty years later.

3 : ST THOMAS, APOSTLE (FIRST CENTURY)

ST THOMAS was a Jew and probably a Galilean of humble birth, but we are not told that he was a fisherman or the circumstances in which our Lord made him an apostle. His name is Syriac, and means the 'twin'; Didymus, as we know he was also called, is the Greek equivalent. This apostle is especially remembered for his incredulity after our Lord had suffered, risen from the dead, and on the same day appeared to His disciples to convince them of the truth of His resurrection. Thomas was not then with them and refused to believe their report that He was truly risen: 'Except I shall see in His hands the print of the nails, and put my finger in the place of the nails, and put my hand into His side, I will not believe.' Eight days later, when they were all together and the doors shut, the risen Christ was suddenly in the midst of them, greeting them: 'Peace be to you.' Then He turned to Thomas and said, 'Put in thy finger hither, and see my hands; and bring hither thy hand and put it into my side. And be not faithless, but believing.' And Thomas fell at His feet, exclaiming, 'My Lord and my God! ' Jesus answered, 'Because thou hast seen me, Thomas, thou hast believed. Blessed are they that have not seen, and have believed.'

As with the other apostles, there are traditions, of great unreliability, about his missionary activities after the descent of the Holy Ghost at Pentecost. Eusebius states that he sent St Thaddeus (Addai; August 5) to Edessa to baptize King Abgar, and the field of his own ministry is assigned to Parthia and 'the Medes, Persians, Carmanians, Hyrcanians, Bactrians and other nations in those parts'. But the most persistent tradition is that which says that he preached the gospel in India. This is supported from several seemingly independent sources, of which the chief is the *Acta Thomae*, a document dating apparently from the first quarter of the third century. The story told by these *acta* is as follows: When the Apostles at Jerusalem divided the countries of the world for their labours, India fell to the lot of Judas Thomas (so he is often called in Syriac legends). He was unwilling to go, pleading lack of strength and that a Hebrew could not teach Indians, and even a vision of our Lord could not alter his resolution. Thereupon Christ appeared to a merchant named Abban, the representative of Gundafor, a Parthian king who ruled over part of India, and sold Thomas to him as a slave for his master. When he understood what had taken place, Thomas said, 'As thou wilt, Lord, so be it', and embarked with Abban, having only his purchase price, twenty pieces of silver, which Christ had given to him.

Abban and Thomas came to Gundafor's court in India and when n the king asked the apostle's trade he replied, 'I am a carpenter and builder. I can make yokes and ploughs and ox-goads, oars for boats and masts for ships; and I can build in stone, tombs and monuments and palaces for kings.' So Gundafor ordered him to build a palace. Gundafor went on a journey, and in his absence Thomas did no building but spent all the money given him for the work on the poor. And he went about the land preaching and healing and driving out evil spirits. On his return Gundafor asked to be shown his new palace. 'You cannot see it now, but only when you have left this world', replied Thomas. Whereupon the king cast him into prison and purposed to flay him alive. But just then Gundafor's brother died, and being shown in Heaven the palace that Thomas's good works had prepared for Gundafor, he was allowed to come back to earth and offer to buy it from the king for himself. Gundafor declined to sell, and in admiration released Thomas and received baptism together with his brother and many of his subjects.

It is agreed that there is no truth behind the story just outlined, though there was undoubtedly a king named Gondophernes or Guduphara, whose dominions about the year A.D. 46 included the territory of Peshawar. Unfortunately, speculation about St Thomas cannot be left there. At the other end of India from the Punjab, along what is known as the Malabar Coast, particularly in the states of Cochin and Travancore, there is a large population of native Christians who call themselves 'the Christians of St Thomas'. Their history is known in detail since the sixteenth century, but their origin has not yet been indisputably determined. There have certainly been Christians there since very early times, and in their liturgy they use forms and a language (Syriac) that undoubtedly were derived from Mesopotamia and Persia. They claim, as their name indicates, to have been originally evangelized by St Thomas in person. They have an ancient oral tradition that he landed at Cranganore on the west coast and established seven churches in Malabar; then passed eastward to the Coromandel Coast, where he was martyred, by spearing, on the 'Big Hill', eight miles from Madras; and was buried at Mylapore, now a suburb of that city. There are several medieval references to the tomb of St Thomas in India, some of which name Mylapore; and in 1522 the Portuguese discovered the alleged tomb there, with certain small relics now preserved in the cathedral of St Thomas at Mylapore. But the bulk of his reputed relics were certainly at Edessa in the fourth century, and the *Acta Thomae* relate that they were taken from India to Mesopotamia. They were later translated from Edessa to the island of Khios in the Aegean, and from thence to Ortona in the Abruzzi, where they are still venerated.

4 : ST ELIZABETH OF PORTUGAL, WIDOW (A.D. 1336)

ELIZABETH was daughter of Peter III, King of Aragon. She was born in 1271, and received the name of Elizabeth from her great-aunt, St Elizabeth of Hungary, but she is known in her own country by the Spanish form of that name, Isabella. At twelve years of age she was married to Denis, King of Portugal. He allowed her an entire liberty in her devotion, and esteemed her piety without feeling called on to imitate it. Elizabeth therefore planned for herself a regular distribution of her time. She rose early every morning, and recited Matins, Lauds and Prime before Mass; in the afternoon she had other regular devotions after Vespers. Certain hours were allotted to her domestic affairs, public business, or what she owed to others. She gave orders to have pilgrims and poor strangers provided with lodging and necessaries, and made it her business to seek out and relieve persons who were reduced to necessity. She provided marriage dowries for girls, and founded in different parts of the kingdom charitable establishments, particularly a hospital at Coîmbra, a house for penitent women at Torres Novas, and a refuge for foundlings. Nor with it all did Elizabeth neglect any of her immediate duties, especially those of respect, love and obedience to her husband, whose neglect and infidelity she bore with much patience.

St Elizabeth had two children, Alfonso, who afterwards succeeded his father, and a daughter, Constance. This son grew up very rebellious, partly due to the favour in which his father held his illegitimate sons. Twice he rose in arms and twice his mother brought about a reconciliation, riding out between the opposing forces. But evil tongues suggested to the king that she secretly favoured her son and for a time she was banished from the court. Her love for concord and qualities as a peacemaker were indeed very notable; she stopped or averted war between Ferdinand IV of Castile, and his cousin, and between that prince and her own brother, James II of Aragon.

Her husband Denis became seriously ill in 1324, and Elizabeth gave all her attention to him, scarcely ever leaving his room except to go to church. During his long illness the king gave marks of sincere sorrow for the disorders of his life, and he died at Santarem on January 6, 1325. After his burial the queen made a pilgrimage to Compostela, after which she wished to retire to a convent of Poor Clares which she had founded at Coîmbra. However, she was dissuaded, and instead she was professed in the third order of St Francis, and lived in a house which she built near to her convent, leading a life of great simplicity.

Elizabeth's death came about on July 4, 1336 at Estremoz, whither she had gone on an errand of reconciliation in spite of her age and the great heat. She was buried in the church of her monastery of Poor Clares at Coîmbra. In 1626 her cult was crowned by canonization.

5 : ST ATHANASIUS THE ATHONITE, ABBOT (c. A.D. 1000)

THE father of Mount Athos as a congeries of monasteries was Athanasius, who was born at Trebizond about the year 920, the son of an Antiochene, and baptized Abraham. He studied at Constantinople, where he became a professor. While he was teaching he met St Michael Maleinos and his nephew, Nicephorus Phocas, who as emperor was to be Abraham's patron. He received the monastic habit in St Michael's monastery at Kymina in Bithynia, taking the name of Athanasius, and lived there till about the year 958. Kymina was a *laura*, the name then reserved for monasteries wherein the monks lived in separate cells grouped more or less closely round their church. When the abbot St Michael Maleinos died Athanasius saw that he would be elected in his place; he therefore fled, and eventually found his way to Mount Athos, to void this responsibility—only to find that God was reserving for him a greater.

He disguised himself, assuming the name of Dorotheos, and hid in a cell near Karyes, but he was soon traced and found by his friend Nicephorus Phocas who was about to undertake an expedition against the Saracens. He persuaded Athanasius to come to Crete to help him organize it and to support it with his blessing and prayers. Athanasius was very unwilling but he went; the expedition was victorious, and Athanasius asked permission to return to Athos. Before he was allowed to he was forced to accept a large sum of money, with which to build a monastery. This, the first monastery proper on Athos, was begun in the spring of 961 and the church two years later; it was dedicated in honour of the All-holy Mother of God, but is now called 'of St Athanasius', or, more often, simply Laura, 'The Monastery'.

When Nicephorus Phocas became emperor, Athanasius feared that he might be called to court, so he ran away from Athos to Cyprus. Phocas again found him and told him to go back and govern his monastery in peace, giving him more money, with which was built a harbour for Athos. In adopting the *laura* system for his monks, Athanasius had deliberately reversed the policy of St Basil and St Theodore Studites and returned in a measure to the ancient monastic tradition of Egypt; his monks were to be as 'out of the world' as is possible for human beings. But in spite of this he was involved in great difficulties with the solitaries who had been on Athos long before he came and who felt, understandably, that generations of predecessors had given them a prescriptive right to have the place to themselves; they resented his coming there and building monasteries and churches and harbours, imposing rules and keeping order generally. Twice attempts were made to murder St Athanasius. Emperor John Tzimisces interfered; he confirmed the donations and rights granted by Nicephorus Phocas, forbade opposition to Athanasius, and recognized his authority over the whole of the mountain and its inhabitants. He thus became superior general over fifty-eight communities of hermits and monks, and the monasteries of Iviron, Vatopedi and Esphigmenou were founded. St Athanasius died about the year 1000, being killed with five of his monks by the falling of a keystone of the vault of the church on which they were working.

6 : ST MARIA GORETTI, VIRGIN AND MARTYR (A.D. 1902)

MARIA GORETTI was born in 1890 at Corinaldo, a village some thirty miles from Ancona, the daughter of a farm-labourer, Luigi Goretti, and his wife Assunta Carlini. They had five other children, and in 1896 the family moved to Colle Gianturco, near Galiano, and later to Ferriere di

Conca, not far from Nettuno in the Roman Campagna. Almost at once after settling down here, Luigi Goretti was stricken with malaria and died. His widow had to take up his work as best she could, but it was a hard struggle and every small coin and bit of food had to be looked at twice. Of all the children none was more cheerful and encouraging to her mother than Maria, commonly called Marietta.

On a hot afternoon in July 1902 Maria was sitting at the top of the stairs in the cottage, mending a shirt: she was not yet quite twelve years old. A cart stopped outside, and a neighbour, a young man of eighteen named Alexander, ran up the stairs. He beckoned Maria into an adjoining bedroom: she refused to go. Alexander seized hold of her, pulled her in, and shut the door.

Maria struggled and tried to call for help, but she was being half-strangled and could only protest hoarsely, gasping that she would be killed rather than submit. Whereupon Alexander half pulled her dress from her body and began striking at her blindly with a long dagger. She sank to the floor, crying out that she was being killed: Alexander plunged the dagger into her back, and ran away.

An ambulance fetched Maria to hospital, where it was seen at once that she could not possibly live. Her last hours were most touching—her concern for where her mother was going to sleep, her forgiveness of her murderer (she disclosed that she had been going in fear of him, but did not like to say anything lest she cause trouble with his family), her childlike welcoming of the holy viaticum. Some twenty-four hours after the assault, Maria Goretti died. Her mother, the parish priest of Nettuno, a Spanish noblewoman and two nuns, had watched by her bed all night.

Alexander was sentenced to thirty years' penal servitude. He was unrepentant. Then one night he had a dream in which Maria Goretti appeared gathering flowers and offering them to him. From then on he was a changed man. At the end of twenty-seven years he was released: his first act when free was to visit Maria's mother to beg her forgiveness.

Meanwhile the memory of his victim had become more and more revered. On April 27, 1947, Maria Goretti was declared blessed by Pope Pius XII. When he afterwards appeared on the balcony of St Peter's he was accompanied by Maria's mother, Assunta Goretti, then eighty-two years old, together with two of Maria's sisters and a brother. Three years later the same pope canonized Maria Goretti in the piazza of St Peter's, before the biggest crowd ever assembled for a canonization. Her murderer was still alive.

7 : ST PALLADIUS, BISHOP (A.D. 432)

ST PROSPER of Aquitaine in his chronicle tells us that when Agricola had corrupted the British Christians by Pelagian doctrine it was at the instance of the deacon Palladius that St Germanus of Auxerre was sent into Britain to combat the heresy. This was in 429. In 431 Prosper says that 'Palladius was consecrated by Pope Celestine and sent to the Irish believing in Christ, as their first bishop', and he landed at Arklow in Leinster. He met with opposition at once, but he managed to make some converts, as we learn from an ancient Life of St Patrick, and built three churches, which have been identified as Cilleen Cormac, near Dunlavin, Tigroney beside the Avoca, and Donard in the west of County Wicklow. Before the end of the year Palladius 'seeing that he could not do much good there and wishing to return to Rome, departed to the Lord in the country of the Picts. Others, however, say that he was crowned with martyrdom in Ireland'. That is to say, he crossed over into Scotland and there died. He was not a martyr and the story of his twenty-three years' mission in Scotland cannot be maintained: the early Irish writers state plainly that he died soon after leaving their country, at Fordun, near Aberdeen, where his relics were venerated in the middle ages. He was probably a Gallo-Roman or Romano-Briton.

8 : ST WITHBURGA, VIRGIN (c. A.D. 743)

SHE was the youngest of the holy daughters of Anna, King of the East Angles. Like her sisters, she devoted herself to the divine service, and led an austere life in solitude for several years at Holkham, near the sea-coast in Norfolk, where a church dedicated in her honour was afterwards built. After the death of her father she changed her dwelling to Dereham, now a market-town in Norfolk but then an obscure retired place. Withburga assembled there some devout maidens, and laid the foundation of a church and nunnery, but did not live to finish the buildings. Her death happened on March 17, 743. Her body was interred in the churchyard at East Dereham and fifty years after found incorrupt and translated into the church. In 974, Brithnoth, Abbot of Ely, removed it to Ely, and deposited it near the bodies of her two sisters. In 1106 the remains of four saints were translated into the new church and laid near the high altar. The bodies of SS. Sexburga and Ermenilda were reduced to dust, except the bones. That of St Etheldreda was entire, and that of St Withburga was not only sound but also fresh, and the limbs flexible. This is related by Thomas, monk of Ely, in his history of Ely, which he wrote the year following; he also tells us that in the place where St Withburga was first buried, in the churchyard of Dereham, a spring of clear water gushed forth: it is to this day called St Withburga's well.

9 : SS. NICHOLAS PIECK, AND HIS COMPANIONS, THE MARTYRS OF GORKUM (A.D. 1572)

NINETEEN priests and religious, taken by Calvinists in Gorkum, near Dordrecht, were hanged on account of their religion. Of these, eleven were Franciscan friars of the Observance of the convent of Gorkum, against whom were St Nicholas Pieck, the guardian, and St Jerome Weerden, vicar. With them were SS. Leonard Vechel, Nicholas Janssen and Godfrey van Duynen, secular priests, and John van Oosterwyk, a canon regular of St Augustine of great age. Vechel was the parish priest at Gorkum. To these fiteen were afterwards added St John van Hoornaer, a Dominican, who came to the assistance of his Franciscan brethren; two Premonstratensians, SS Adrian van Hilvarenbeek and James Lacops, the last of whom had been very slack in his religious observance and contumacious under reproof; and

St Andrew Wouters, a secular priest who went straight from an irregular life to imprisonment and martyrdom.

In June 1572 the anti-Spanish Calvinist forces called the *Watergeuzen*, 'Sea-Beggars', or *Gueux*, 'Ragamuffins', seized Gorkum, and from June 26 to July 5 the Franciscans and four other priests were at the mercy of the soldiers, who treated them with cruelty, partly out of contempt for their religion and partly in order to discover the whereabouts of the hidden church vessels. Word came from the admiral, Lumaye, Baron de la Marck, to bring them to Briel, where they disembarked in the early morning of the 7th and, half-naked as they were, marched to the market-place in a caricature of a religious procession, and there contemptuously ordered to sing the Litany of the Saints, which they did gladly enough. That evening and the next morning they were interrogated before the admiral and, confronted by Calvinist ministers, invited to purchase their freedom by abandoning the Catholic doctrine of the Blessed Sacrament; this they refused to do. Letters now arrived to the Baron de la Marck from the magistrates of Gorkum, complaining of the detention of the prisoners, and from the Prince of Orange, ordering that they be released; at the same time two brothers of Nicholas Pieck made personal appeal for him. The admiral said that all should at once be set free if they would abjure the primacy of the pope: again they refused, and all the efforts of his brothers could not induce Father Pieck to abandon either his faith or his religious brethren. Soon after midnight an apostate priest of Liège was sent to lead the prisoners to a deserted monastery at Ruggen, in the outskirts of Briel.

Here they were gathered in a turf-shed where were two convenient beams. At this last moment, when already Father Pieck had been flung off the ladder, speaking words of encouragement, the courage of some failed them. All nineteen were hanged, St James Lacops from a ladder, the rest from the beams; one, St Antony van Willehad, was ninety years old. Their bodies were ignominiously cast into two ditches and there lay till 1616, when, during a truce between Spain and the United Provinces, they were dug up and the remains translated to the Franciscan church in Brussels. The martyrs of Gorkum were canonized in 1867.

10 : SS. ANTONY AND THEODOSIUS PECHERSKY, ABBOTS
OF THE CAVES OF KIEV (A.D. 1073 AND 1074)

ANTONY was born in 983 at Lubech, near Chernigov, and early in life made an experiment at living as a solitary after the pattern of the Egyptian anchorites; but he soon realized that one must be trained for that life as for any other, and he went on pilgrimage to Mount Athos, where he became a hermit attached to the monastery of Esphigmenou. After some years there his abbot bade him return to his own land. Antony did as he was told, but finding insufficient peace and solitude in the prince-founded monasteries, after the strictness of Athos, he took up his abode in a cave in a wooded cliff beside the river Dnieper at Kiev.

People came to consult him and ask his blessing. Some of these visitors stayed on with him, the first being the monk Nikon, who was a priest; and after a time there were other aspirants, who dug caves for themselves and larger ones to serve as chapel and dining-room. Unlike the other abbots of that time, St Antony accepted anybody who showed the right dispositions, rich or poor, free men or serfs, with the result that the community outgrew its accommodation. Prince Syaslav offered to give them the land on the hill above their caves, and here the monks built of wood a monastery and a church, dedicated in honour of the Falling-asleep of the All-holy Mother of God.

St Antony had early given up the direction of the community to one Barlaam and, disturbed by strife among the nobles of Kiev, he retired after a while to Chernigov and established another monastery there. But he eventually came back to the Pecherskaya Lavra and died in his cave there in 1073; he was ninety years old.

Forty years before there had come to Pechersk a certain Theodosius, and he it was rather than the severe and solitude-loving Antony who first struck the Russian imagination. He was the son of well-to-do parents, and as a young man had put on serf's clothes and joined the labourers in his father's fields. Later, in the face of blows and attempts to shut him up, Theodosius apprenticed himself to a baker and learned how to make the bread for the Holy Mysteries, and then about 1032 he joined the monks at the Caves of Kiev.

St Theodosius soon succeeded Barlaam as abbot, and he was the real organizer of the monastery, who gave direction to the first generations of Russian monks. He completed and enlarged the buildings and put the community under the discipline and rule given by St Theodore to the 'Studion'. Emphasis was put, not on personal sanctification solely by means of prayer and mortification, but on the necessity of the corporal works of mercy and on the need of identifying oneself with all the suffering children of Christ. He followed both the liturgical prescriptions and the social activities of the Studites: a hospital for the sick and disabled and a hostel for travellers were established at the monastery, and every Saturday a cartload of food was sent to the city jails. His monks played a part in the evangelization of Kiev and he took part in the general life of the country, with the result that his influence was not confined to his community but was felt all over Varangian Russia: he was able to defend the rights of the poor and oppressed and to protest to his face when Svyatoslav drove his own brother from the throne of Kiev. Moreover, to Theodosius may be traced the beginnings of the institution of *staretz*, 'spiritual directors', so characteristic of Russian religious life; he encouraged the lay people of Kiev, without distinction of sex or age or rank, to come to him with their problems and difficulties, and we are told of a man and wife, John and Mary, of whom he was particularly fond, 'because they loved God and loved one another'. He emphasized, too, the importance of community life and the holding of all things in common, nevertheless, there must also be times of solitude and retirement (as during Lent). Theodosius thus sought to harmonize the contemplative and the active life, just as he sought to harmonize the needs of men as they are with the call to bring about the kingdom of God on earth. In all these things he was following the Palestinian tradition and the spirit of St Basil, father of Eastern monks. Even when he had all the responsibility of ruling a large community and caring for the welfare of numerous spiritual children, St Theodosius still did his share of the ordinary daily work, whether in the fields or in the house.

St Theodosius celebrated the Easter of 1074 with his brethren as usual, and a week later he was dead. At his own wish he was buried in one of the caves that formed the original monastery, but in 1091 his body was translated to the principal church and in 1108 he was canonized by the bishops of the Kiev province—the second Russian canonization and the first of the 'very-like ones', that is, Christlike monks.

11 : ST BENEDICT, ABBOT, PATRIARCH OF WESTERN MONKS (c. A.D. 547)

BENEDICT was of good birth, and was born and brought up at the ancient Sabine town of Nursia (Norcia). He was sent to Rome for his 'liberal education', being accompanied by a 'nurse', probably to act as a housekeeper. He was then in his early teens, or perhaps a little older. But Benedict, revolted by the licentiousness of his companions in the city made up his mind to leave Rome. He made his escape without telling anyone of his plans excepting his nurse, who accompanied him. They made their way to the village of Enfide in the mountains thirty miles from Rome. What was the length of his stay we do not know, but it was sufficient to enable him to determine his next step. Absence from the temptations of Rome, he soon realized, was not enough; God was calling him to be a solitary and to abandon the world.

In search of complete solitude Benedict started forth once more, alone, and climbed further among the hills until he reached a place now known as Subiaco. In this wild and rocky country he came upon a monk called Romanus, to whom he opened his heart, explaining his intention of leading the life of a hermit. Romanus assisted the young man, clothing him with a sheepskin habit and leading him to a cave in the mountain. In this desolate cavern Benedict spent the next three years of his life, unknown to all except Romanus, who kept his secret and daily brought bread for the young recluse, who drew it up in a basket let down by a rope over the rock.

Disciples began to gather about him, attracted by his sanctity and by his miraculous powers, seculars fleeing from the world as well as solitaries who lived dispersed among the mountains. He therefore settled all who would obey him in twelve wood-built monasteries of twelve monks, each with its prior. He himself exercised the supreme direction over all from where he lived with certain monks whom he wished to train with special care. We do not know how long the saint remained at Subiaco, but he stayed long enough to establish his monasteries on a firm and permanent basis. His departure was sudden.

Having set all things in order, he withdrew from Subiaco to the territory of Monte Cassino. It is a solitary elevation on the boundaries of the Campania, commanding on three sides narrow valleys running up towards the mountains, and on the fourth, as far as the Mediterranean, an undulating plain which had once been rich and fertile, but having fallen out of cultivation owing to repeated irruptions of the barbarians, it had become marshy and malarious. Upon the site of a big temple he built two chapels, and round about these sanctuaries there rose little by little the great building which was destined to become the most famous abbey the world has ever known, the foundation of which is likely to have been laid by St Benedict in the year 530 or thereabouts.

It is probable that Benedict, who was now in middle age, again spent some time as a hermit; but disciples soon flocked to Monte Cassino too. Profiting no doubt by the experience gained at Subiaco, he no longer placed them in separate houses but gathered them together in one establishment, ruled over by a prior and deans under his general supervision. It almost immediately became necessary to add guest-chambers, for Monte Cassino, unlike Subiaco, was easily accessible from Rome and Capua. Not only laymen but dignitaries of the Church came to confer with the holy founder, whose reputation for sanctity, wisdom and miracles became widespread. It is almost certainly at this period that he composed his Rule.

The holy abbot, far from confining his ministrations to those who would follow his rule, extended his solicitude to the population of the surrounding country: he cured their sick, relieved the distressed, distributed alms and food to the poor, and is said to have raised the dead on more than one occasion. The great saint who had foretold so many other things was also forewarned of his own approaching death. He notified it to his disciples and six days before the end bade them dig his grave. As soon as this had been done he was stricken with fever, and on the last day he received the Body and Blood of the Lord. Then, while the loving hands of the brethren were supporting his weak limbs, he uttered a few final words of prayer and died—standing on his feet in the chapel, with his hands uplifted towards heaven.

12 : ST JOHN GUALBERT, ABBOT, FOUNDER OF THE VALLOMBRO-SAN BENEDICTINES (A.D. 1073)

ST JOHN GUALBERT was born at Florence towards the end of the tenth century, the son of a nobleman. Hugh, his elder and only brother, was murdered by a man reputed to be his friend, and John conceived it to be his duty to avenge his brother. One day he came upon the murderer in so narrow a passage that it was impossible for either to avoid the other. John drew his sword and advanced upon the defenceless man, who fell upon his knees, his arms crossed on his breast. The remembrance of Christ, who prayed for His murderers on the cross seized the heart of the young man; he put up his sword, embraced his enemy, and they parted in peace.

John went on his way till he came to the monastery of San Miniato, where, going into the church, he offered up his prayers before a crucifix. And as he continued his prayer the crucifix miraculously bowed its head, as it were to give a token how acceptable were the sacrifice of his revenge and his sincere repentance. Divine grace so took possession of his heart that he went to the abbot and asked to be admitted to the religious habit. The abbot was apprehensive of his father's displeasure; but after a few days John cut off his hair himself, and put on a habit which he borrowed. John devoted himself to his new state in the dispositions of a true penitent, so that he became entirely a new man.

When the abbot of San Miniato died John, apparently on account of a scandal concerning the abbatial succession, left the house with one companion in quest of a closer solitude. He paid a visit to the hermitage of Camoldoli, and while there decided to make a new foundation of his own. This he did in a pleasant place near Fiesole, called Vallis Umbrosa, where with his companions he built a small monastery of timber and mud walls and formed a little community serving God according to the primitive austere rule and spirit of St Benedict. The abbess of Sant' Ellero gave them ground on which to build. The saint added to the original Rule of St Benedict certain constitutions, one of which was the provision of *conversi*, lay-brothers, and the abolition of manual work for choir-monks. Vallombrosa was perhaps the first monastery in which the institution of *conversi* appeared. The life of this congregation was one of great austerity, and for some time it flourished and established other houses.

St John Gualbert feared no less the danger of too great lenience and forbearance than of harshness, and was a true imitator of both the mildness and zeal of Moses, whom the Holy Ghost calls 'a man exceeding meek above all men that dwelt upon earth'. His humbleness would not allow him to receive even minor orders; he was zealous for poverty, and would not allow any of his monasteries to be built on a costly or imposing scale, thinking such edifices not agreeable to a spirit of poverty. His kindness to the poor was not less active than his love for poverty. He would have no poor person sent from his door without an alms, and often emptied the stores of his monasteries in relieving them. Pope St Leo IX went to Passignano on purpose to converse with him and Stephen X had the greatest esteem for him. Pope Alexander II testified that the whole country where he lived owed to his zeal the extinction of simony, for John's enthusiasm for the purely contemplative life did not prevent him and his monks from taking an active part in putting down that disorder, which was rife at the time.

St John Gualbert died on July 12, 1073, the only certain date in his history, being eighty or more years old. Pope Celestine III enrolled him among the saints in 1193.

13 : ST HENRY THE EMPEROR, (A.D. 1024)

ST HENRY II was son of Henry, Duke of Bavaria, and Gisela of Burgundy, and was born in 972. He was educated by St Wolfgang, Bishop of Ratisbon, and in 995 succeeded his father in the duchy of Bavaria; in 1002, upon the death of his cousin Otto III, he was chosen emperor. He knew the end for which alone he was exalted by God to the highest temporal dignity, and worked his hardest to promote the peace and happiness of his realm. Nevertheless, Henry at times made use of the Church for politcal ends, in accordance with the imperial policy of his predecessor Otto the Great. He refused his support to ecclesiastical aggrandizement in temporal concerns, while maintaining the Church's proper authority; but some of his politics look equivocal when examined from the point of view of the welfare of Christendom.

He had to engage in numerous wars for the defence and consolidation of the empire, as for example in Italy, before he could receive that crown;

Arduin of Ivrea had had himself crowned king at Milan, so the emperor crossed the Alps and drove him out. In 1014 he went in triumph to Rome, where he was crowned emperor by Pope Benedict VIII. Henry munificently repaired and restored the episcopal sees of Hildesheim, Magdeburg, Strasburg and Meersburg, and made benefactions to the churches of Aachen, Basle and others.

In 1006 Henry founded the see of Bamberg and built a great cathedral there, in order to solidify German power among the Wends. In this he was opposed by the bishops of Würzburg and Eichstätt, whose dioceses were thus dismembered, but Pope John XIX approved, and Benedict VIII consecrated the cathedral in 1020. Henry also built and endowed a monastery at Bamberg, and made foundations in several other places, that the divine honour and the relief of the poor might be provided for to the end of time. In 1021 the emperor again came to Italy, on an expedition against the Greeks in Apulia; on his way back he was taken ill at Monte Cassino, where he was said to have been miraculously cured at the intercession of St Benedict, but he contracted a lameness which never left him.

Henry identified himself in time with those ideas of ecclesiastical reform which radiated from the great monastery of Cluny, and in support of them he even opposed himself to his kinsman, friend, and former chaplain, Aribo, whom he had appointed archbishop of Mainz and who in synod had condemned appeals to Rome without episcopal permission. Accounts of his ascetic practices do not entirely accord with what is known of his character and life; Henry was one of the great rulers of the Holy Roman Empire, and triumphed precisely as a Christian statesman and soldier, whose ways were, in the nature of things, not those of the cloister.

What we know of him is mostly a matter of general history: he clearly promoted ecclesiastical reform, taking great care about episcopal appointments and supporting such great monks as St Odilo of Cluny and Richard of Saint-Vanne. St Henry was canonized by Eugenius III in 1146, and Pius X declared him the patron of Benedictine oblates.

14 : ST CAMILLUS DE LELLIS, FOUNDER OF THE MINISTERS OF THE SICK (A.D. 1614)

CAMILLUS DE LELLIS was born in 1550 at Bocchianico in the Abruzzi, when his mother was nearly sixty. He grew to be a very big man—6 feet 6 inches tall and the rest in proportion—and when he was seventeen he went off with his father to fight with the Venetians against the Turks; but soon he had contracted that painful and repulsive disease in his leg that was to afflict him for the rest of his life. In 1571 he was admitted to the San Giacomo hospital for incurables at Rome, as a patient and servant; after nine months he was dismissed, for his quarrelsomeness among other things, and he returned to active service in the Turkish war. Though Camillus habitually referred to himself as a great sinner, his worst disorder was an addiction to gambling. In the autumn of 1574 he gambled away his savings, his arms, everything down to the proverbial shirt, which was stripped off his back in the streets of Naples.

The indigence to which he had reduced himself, and the memory of a vow he had made in a fit of remorse to join the Franciscans, caused him to accept work as a labourer on the new Capuchin buildings at Manfredonia, and there a moving exhortation which the guardian of the friars one day made him completed his conversion. Ruminating on it as he rode upon his business, he at length fell on his knees, and with tears deplored his past unthinking life, and cried to Heaven for mercy. This happened on Candlemas day in the year 1575, the twenty-fifth of his age. He entered the novitiate of the Capuchins, but could not be admitted to profession of account of the disease in his leg. He therefore returned to the hospital of San Giacomo and devoted himself to the service of the sick. The administrators, having been witnesses to his charity and ability, after some time appointed him superintendent of the hospital.

Camillus, grieving to see the unscrupulousness and slackness of hired servants in attending the sick, formed a project of associating for that office some of the attendants who desired to devote themselves to it out of a motive of charity. He found several persons so disposed, but met with great obstacles in the execution of his design, particularly from that jealousy and suspicion that are so often provoked by disinterested reformers. To make himself more useful in spiritually assisting the sick, he resolved, with the approval of his confessor, St Philip Neri, to receive holy orders, and was ordained by the vicegerent of Rome, Thomas Goldwell, Bishop of St Asaph, the exiled last bishop of the old English hierarchy. A certain gentleman of Rome named Fermo Calvi gave him an annuity as his title of ordination. Camillus decided to sever connection with San Giacomo and start on his own, though to do so was contrary to the advice of St Philip; so with two companions he laid the foundations of his congregation: he prescribed certain short rules, and they went every day to the great hospital of the Holy Spirit where they served the sick with affection and diligence.

In 1585 he hired a larger house, and the success of his undertaking encouraged him to extend his activities: so he ordained that the members of his congregation should bind themsleves to serve persons infected with the plague, prisoners, and those who lie dying in private houses; later, in 1595 and 1601, some of his religious were sent with the troops fighting in Hungary and Croatia, thus forming the first recorded 'military field ambulance'.

In 1588 Camillus was invited to Naples, and with twelve companions founded there a new house. Certain galleys having the plague on board were forbidden to enter the harbour, so the Ministers of the Sick (the name they took) went on board, and attended them: two of their number died of the pestilence, the first martyrs of charity in this institute. In 1591 Gregory XIV erected this congregation into a religious order, for perpetually serving the sick. The founder was, as has already been said, himself afflicted with many corporal sufferings: the disease in his leg for forty-six years; a rupture for thirty-eight years; two sores in the sole of one of his feet, which gave him great pain; and, for a long time before he died, a distaste for food and inability to retain it. Under this complication of infirmities he would not suffer anyone to wait on him, but sent all his brethren to serve others. St Camillus saw the foundation altogether of fifteen houses of his brothers and eight hospitals, and Almighty God acknowledged his zeal and selflessness by the spirit of prophecy and the gift of miracles, and by many heavenly communications and favours.

The saint laid down the canonical leadership of his order in 1607. But he assisted at the general chapter in Rome in 1613, and after it, with the new superior general, visited the houses, giving them his last exhortations. At Genoa he was extremely ill; he recovered so as to be able to finish the visitation of his hospitals, but soon relapsed, and his life was now despaired of. He received viaticum from the hands of Cardinal Ginnasi, and when he received the last anointing he made a moving exhortation to his brethren; he expired on July 14, 1614, being sixty-four years old. St Camillus de Lellis was canonized in 1746, and was, with St John-of-God, declared patron of the sick by Pope Leo XIII, and of nurses and nursing associations by Pope Pius XI.

15 : ST BONAVENTURE, CARDINAL-BISHOP OF ALBANO, DOCTOR OF THE CHURCH (A.D. 1274)

OF the youth of this greatest successor of St Francis of Assisi nothing is known beyond the facts that he was born at Bagnorea, near Viterbo, in the year 1221, the son of John Fidanza and Mary Ritella. He was clothed in the order of Friars Minor and studied at the University of Paris under an Englishman, Alexander of Hales, 'the Unanswerable Doctor'; Bonaventure, who was to become known as the Seraphic Doctor, himself taught theology and Holy Scripture there from 1248 to 1257.

Bonaventure was called by his priestly obligations to labour for the salvation of his neighbour, and to this he devoted himself with enthusiasm. He preached to the people with an energy which kindled a flame in the hearts of those that heard him. While at the University of Paris he produced one of the best-known of his written works, the *Commentary on the Sentences* of Peter Lombard, which covers the whole field of scholastic theology. The years of his public lecturing at Paris were greatly disturbed, however, by the attack made on the mendicant friars by the other professors at the university. Jealousy of their pastoral and academical success and the standing reproof to worldliness and ease of the friars' lives were in part behind this attempt to get them excluded from the schools. The leader of the secular party was William of Saint-Amour, who made a bitter onslaught on the mendicants in a book called *The Perils of the Last Times*, and other writings. Bonaventure, who had to suspend lecturing for a time, replied in a treatise on evangelical poverty, named *Concerning the Poverty of Christ*. The pope, Alexander IV, appointed a commission of cardinals to go into the matter at Anagni, and on their findings ordered Saint-Amour's book to be burnt, vindicated and reinstated the friars, and ordered the offenders to withdraw their attack. A year later, in 1257, St Bonaventure and St Thomas Aquinas received the degree of doctor of theology together.

For Blessed Isabella, St Louis IX's sister, and her nunnery of Poor Clares at Longchamps, St Bonaventure wrote *Concerning Perfection of Life*. Other mystical works of his are the *Soliloquy* and *Concerning the Threefold Way*.

In 1257 Bonaventure was chosen minister general of the Friars Minor. He was not yet thirty-six years old, and the order was torn by dissensions, some of the friars being for an inflexible severity, others demanding certain mitigations of the rule; between the two extremes were a number of other interpretations. Some of the extreme rigorists, called Spirituals, had even fallen into error and disobedience, and thus given a handle to the friars' opponents in the Paris dispute. The new minister general wrote a letter to his provincials in which he made it clear that he required a disciplined observance of the rule, involving a reformation of the relaxed, but giving no countenance to the excesses of the Spirituals. At Narbonne in 1260, the first of the five general chapters which he held, he produced a set of constitutions on the rule, which were adopted and had a permanent effect on Franciscan life, but they failed to pacify the excessive rigorists. At the request of the friars assembled in this chapter, he undertook to write the life of St Francis, which he compiled with a spirit which shows him to have been filled with the virtues of the founder whose life he wrote. He governed his order for seventeen years and has been justly called its second founder.

In 1265 Pope Clement IV nominated St Bonaventure to be archbishop of York in succession to Geoffrey of Ludham; he induced the pope to accept his refusal, but in 1273 Gregory X created him cardinal-bishop of Albano. Gregory X also ordered him to prepare the matters to be dealt with in the general council which he had called to meet at Lyons for the reunion of the Greeks, the Emperor Michael Palaeologus having made proposals to Pope Clement IV for union. All the best theologians were sent for: St Thomas Aquinas died on the way. St Bonaventure was the outstanding figure in this great assembly.

He arrived with the pope some months before it began, and between the second and third sessions he held his last general chapter of his order, in which he abdicated the office of minister general. When the Greek delegates arrived he conferred with them, and the reunion with Rome was duly effected. In thanksgiving the pope sang Mass on the feast of SS. Peter and Paul, and the epistle, gospel and creed were sung first in Latin then in Greek; St Bonaventure preached. But amidst all this triumph, on the night of July 14–15, the Seraphic Doctor died.

He was declared a doctor of the Church in 1588, having been canonized in 1482.

16 : ST FULRAD, ABBOT (A.D. 784)

ST FULRAD was born in Alsace, where he founded three monasteries, Lièvre and Saint-Hippolyte and Salone, which were afterwards affiliated to Saint-Denis near Paris, and in 750 he was elected abbot of that house. In this office his sanctity and talents had full scope to make themselves felt, and they were recognized by his sovereigns with the added honours and responsibilities that they put upon him; he was a royal councillor and the archchaplain (that is, head of the court clergy) under Pepin, Carloman and Charlemagne, and in these capacities he received the trust of popes and princes and did great service to church and state.

In 750 he was appointed with St Burchard of Würzburg to go to Rome to lay before Pope St Zachary the question of the succession to the throne of the Franks, and brought back a reply favourable to Pepin, who accordingly became king of the Franks and promised to support the pope against the Lombards.

In 756 St Fulrad was Pepin's representative for the handing over to the Holy See of the exarchate of Ravenna and the duchy of the Pentapolis, which the king had taken by force of arms from the Lombard Aistulf (who had wrongfully seized them from their Byzantine governors); St Fulrad solemnly laid the deed of gift, with the keys of the cities, on the altar of St Peter. Thus he was closely connected with the early development of the papal states and with the shifting of the dependence of the Apostolic See for temporal support from the Byzantine emperor to the Frankish sovereigns. Among the saint's benefactions to his own monastery, of which his holy life and paternal government were the chiefest, was the enshrining of the reputed relics of St Vitus, the fourth-century martyr, which he brought from Italy; in the next century they were given to the abbey of Corvey. St Fulrad died, full of years and diversified labours for the Lord, in 784.

17 : SS. CLEMENT OF OKHRIDA, AND HIS COMPANIONS, THE SEVEN APOSTLES OF BULGARIA (NINTH-TENTH CENTURY)

IN or about the year 865 the ruler of the Bulgars, Khan Boris I, moved principally by political motives, accepted Christianity from Constantinople and imposed it on his nobles and people. This revived the old disagreement between Rome and Constantinople about patriarchal jurisdiction in Illyricum and the Balkans; it was aggravated by Boris whose policies were directed towards having a national church independent of either. When in 869 Pope Adrian II had appointed St Methodius archbishop over Moravia and Pannonia he had deliberately extended his jurisdiction to the very borders of Bulgaria, not, as Pope John VIII later explained to Boris, because the religion of Rome and Constantinople was not one and the same, but because, he said, the Byzantines were inclined to separation and schism. Methodius in fact had to keep an eye on the Bulgars, most of whom were still heathen; and for this reason he and his brother St Cyril (February 14) are reckoned the first two of their seven apostles. But it does not seem that either of them actually ever preached among the Bulgars.

After the death of St Methodius violent and cruel persecution by Svatopluk and his archbishop, Wiching, drove his principal followers into exile from Moravia. Among them was ST GORAZD, whom Methodius had designated as his successor; it is uncertain what became of him, but he is reputed to have been a great missionary, and relics supposed to be his are venerated at Berat in modern Albania. Others were welcomed to Bulgaria by Boris, who saw in them a valuable help for his own plans; they evangelized many of the people, and are held in memory as ST CLEMENT, ST NAHUM, ST SABAS and ST ANGELARIUS.

Of these Clement, probably a Slav from southern Macedonia, was clearly the most important, and much apostolic and educational work is attributed to him. Under the khan Simeon he became bishop at a place (Velitsa) which very likely was close to Okhrida where he established a monastery: later he was regarded as the founder of that primatial see, which was to be very important in subsequent history, and as the first man of Slav race to receive the episcopate.

Clement died at Okhrida in the year 916. Some say that his colleague St Nahum succeeded him as bishop; he was a convert of Cyril and Methodius in Moravia, helping them with their translations and accompanying them to Rome, and he is venerated in Russia as well as Bulgaria as a wonder-worker.

18 : ST BRUNO, BISHOP OF SEGNI (A.D. 1123)

B RUNO was of the family of the lords of Asti in Piedmont, and born near that city. He made his studies in the university of Bologna, and was made a canon of Siena. He was called to Rome and there, in the council of 1079, he defended the doctrine of the Church concerning the Blessed Sacrament against Berengarius of Tours; Pope Gregory VII nominated him bishop of Segni in the following year, Bruno's humbleness prompting him to refuse a cardinalate. Bruno served his flock with unwearied zeal; he was a personal friend of St Gregory and entered with fearless enthusiasm into all his projects for the reform of the Church, suffering imprisonment for three months at the hands of Count Ainulf, a partisan of the Emperor Henry IV. He went with Urban II into France in 1095, and assisted at the Council of Clermont-Ferrand, and returning into Italy he continued to labour for the sanctification of his flock till, not being able any longer to resist his inclination for solitude and retirement, and still persecuted by Ainulf, he withdrew to Monte Cassino and received the monastic habit. The people of Segni demanded him back; but the abbot of Monte Cassino prevailed upon the pope to allow his retreat, but not the resignation of his see. In 1107 he was elected abbot of the monastery.

Bruno by his writings laboured to support ecclesiastical discipline and to extirpate simony. This abuse, together with that of lay investiture to ecclesiastical offices, he looked upon as a main source of the disorders in the church. He indeed took it upon himself to rebuke Pope Paschal II, who had been persuaded by the emperor elect, Henry V, to make concessions in the matter of ecclesiastical privileges and investiture in Germany. The pope retorted by ordering Bruno to resign his abbacy and return to his bishopric, and was at once obeyed. He continued faithfully in the discharge of his duties and in writing, especially commentaries on the Holy Scriptures, until his death in 1123. He was the greatest scriptural commentator of his age, but in theology he maintained the erroneous view that the sacraments administered by bishops or priests who had been guilty of simony were invalid. Bruno was canonized in 1183.

19 : ST MACRINA THE YOUNGER, VIRGIN (A.D. 379)

M ACRINA was the eldest of ten children of St Basil the Elder and St Emmelia, and was born at Caesarea in Cappadocia about the year 330. She was brought up with particular care by her mother, who both taught her to read and exercised vigilance over how she used that accomplishment. At twelve years old she was betrothed, but after the sudden death of the young man she refused all other suitors, and was a great assistant to her mother in educating her younger brothers and sisters. St Basil the Great, St Peter of Sebastea, St Gregory of Nyssa and the rest learned from her contempt of the world, dread of its dangers, and application to prayer and the word of God; Basil, in particular, we are told, came back from the schools a very conceited young man, and his sister taught him humility; while to Peter, the youngest she was 'father, teacher, guide, mother, giver of good advice', for his father died just as he was born. Basil the younger then established his mother and Macrina on an estate by the river Iris in Pontus, and there they were joined by other women in an ascetic communal life.

After the death of St Emmelia, Macrina disposed of all that was left of their estate in favour of the poor, and lived on what she earned by the labour of her hands. Her brother Basil died in the beginning of the year 379, and she herself fell ill nine months after. St Gregory of Nyssa, making her a visit after eight years' absence, found her sick, lying on two boards for her bed. He was exceedingly comforted by her cheerfulness and encouragement, and impressed by the fervour of love with which she prepared herself for death. She died very happily at the hour of the lighting of lamps. Such was her poverty that nothing was found to cover her body when it was carried to the grave but her old hood and coarse veil; St Gregory therefore provided a special linen rove. Araxius, bishop of the place, and St Gregory, with two priests, themselves carried the bier in the funeral procession, choirs singing psalms all the way to the place of burial; but the press of the crowd and lamentations of the people, especially of some of the women, much disturbed the solemnity of the chant.

20 : ST VULMAR, ABBOT (c. A.D. 700)

ST VULMAR or Wulmar, whom the Roman Martyrology calls a man of wonderful holiness, was born in the territory of Boulogne in Picardy. He was married, but having been separated by force from his wife, he entered the abbey of Hautmont in Hainault, where he was employed to keep the cattle and to hew wood for the community. He was distinguished for his eminent spirit of prayer, and was promoted to the priesthood. He after obtained leave to live alone in a hermitage near Mount Cassel for some years, and then founded near Calais the abbey of Samer, corruptly so called for Saint-Vulmar; this monastery existed until the French Revolution. St Vulmar also founded a nunnery at Wierre-aux-Bois, a mile from his own monastery. Caedwalla, King of the West Saxons, passing that way in 688 on his journey to Rome to receive baptism, conferred on the abbey an alms towards carrying on the foundation. St Vulmar was glorified by miracles, and his relics were conveyed to Boulogne, and from thence to the abbey of St Peter at Ghent.

21 : ST LAURENCE OF BRINDISI, (A.D. 1619)

CESARE DE ROSSI was born at Brindisi in the kingdom of Naples in 1559, of a Venetian family of good standing. He was educated first by the Conventual Franciscans in his birthplace and then by his uncle in the college of St Mark at Venice. When he was sixteen he received the Capuchin Franciscan habit at Verona, taking the name of Laurence. He made his philosophical and theological studies at the University of Padua, displaying a marvellous gift for languages: he learned Greek, Hebrew, German, Bohemian, French and Spanish, and had an extraordinary knowledge of the text of the Bible. While still a deacon he preached a Lenten course of sermons, and after his ordination preached with great fruit in Padua, Verona, Vicenza and other towns of northern Italy. In 1596 he went to fill the office of definitor general of his order in Rome, and was charged by Pope Clement VIII to work for the conversion of the Jews. In this he had considerable success, his knowledge of Hebrew being a valuable adjunct to his learning and holy life. He was sent with Bd Benedict of Urbino into Germany to establish the Capuchins there as a bulwark against Lutheranism; they began this work by nursing those sick of the plague, and before they left they had founded friaries at Prague, Vienna and Gorizea, which developed into the provinces of Bohemia, Austria and Styria. At the chapter of 1602 he was elected minister general of the Capuchins, and administered his charge with both vigour and charity, setting out at once on a visitation of the provinces. But when his term of office was up, in 1605, he refused to accept re-election.

While still vicar general Laurence had been sent by the emperor, Rudolf II, to enlist the help of the German princes against the Turks who were threatening the whole of Hungary. He was successful in his mission, an army was got together, and Laurence was appointed chaplain general of the forces. He even fulfilled in some respects the duties of chief-of-staff as well: before the battle of Szekes-Fehervar in 1601 the friar was consulted by the generals; he advised assault, gave a rousing address to the troops, and himself rode before the army—armed with a crucifix. The crushing defeat of the Turks was attributed to St Laurence.

Having spent some time preaching and reconciling heretics in Germany he was commissioned by the emperor to induce Philip III of Spain to join the Catholic League, and took the opportunity to found a house of Capuchins in Madrid. Then he was sent to Munich as nuncio of the Holy See at the court of Maximilian of Bavaria, head of the League; from here he administered two provinces of his order and continued his work of pacification and conversion. After settling two more royal quarrels he retired in 1618 to the friary at Caserta, hoping there to be free from exterior distractions. But the chief men of Naples came to Laurence and complained of the tyranny of the Spanish viceroy, the Duke of Osuna; they feared a rising of the people; would he go to the court of King Philip and put their case before him? The saint was still not very old, but he was worn out and he was ill; he predicted that if he went he would never return. He set out. When at last he arrived in Madrid the king was not there: he had gone to Lisbon. So Laurence followed him across Spain and Portugal in the heat of summer. He used all his eloquence and power of persuasion on behalf of the Neapolitans, and gained his point; the Duke of Osuna should be recalled.

Then Laurence returned to his lodging, and there, on his birthday, July 22, in the year 1619, he died. He was buried in the cemetery of the Poor Clares at Villafranca, and was beatified in 1783. He was canonized in 1881.

221

THE LIVES OF THE SAINTS

22 : S.S. PHILIP EVANS AND JOHN LLOYD, MARTYRS (A.D. 1679)

PHILIP EVANS was born at Monmouth in 1645, was educated at
Saint-Omer, and joined the Society of Jesus at the age of twenty. In 1675
he was ordained at Liège and sent to South Wales. He was soon well known
for his zeal, but no active notice was taken by the authorities until the scare
of Oates's plot, when in the November of 1678 John Arnold, of Llanvihangel
Court near Abergavenny, a justice of the peace and hunter of priests, offered
a reward of £200 for his arrest. Father Evans refused to leave his flock, and
early in December was caught at the house of Christopher Turberville at
Sker in Glamorgan. He refused the oath and was confined alone in an
underground dungeon in Cardiff Castle. Two or three weeks afterwards he
was joined by Mr John Lloyd, a secular priest, who had been taken at
Penlline in Glamorgan. He was a Breconshire man, who had taken the
missionary oath at Valladolid in 1649 and been sent to minister in his own
country.

After five months the two prisoners were brought up for trial at the
shire-hall in Cardiff, charged not with complicity in the plot but as priests
who had come unlawfully into the realm. It had been difficult to collect
witnesses against them, and they were condemned and sentenced by Mr
Justice Owen Wynne principally on the evidence of two poor women who
were suborned to say that they had seen Father Evans celebrating Mass. On
their return to prison they were better treated and allowed a good deal of
liberty, so that when the under-sheriff came on July 21 to announce that
their execution was fixed for the morrow, Father Evans was playing a game
of tennis and would not return to his cell till he had finished it. Part of his few
remaining hours of life he spent playing on the harp and talking to the
numerous people who came to say farewell to himself and Mr Lloyd when
the news got around. The execution took place on Gallows Field (at the
north-eastern end of what is now Richmond Road, Cardiff). St Philip died
first, after having addressed the people in Welsh and English, and saying
'Adieu, Mr Lloyd, though for a little time, for we shall shortly meet again', to
St John, who made only a very brief speech because, as he said, 'I never was
a good speaker in my life'.

23 : ST BRIDGET, WIDOW, FOUNDRESS OF THE ORDER OF THE MOST HOLY SAVIOUR (A.D. 1373)

ST BIRGITTA, more commonly called Bridget, was daughter of Birger,
governor of Upland, the principal province of Sweden, and his second
wife, Ingeborg, daughter to the governor of East Gothland. Ingeborg, who
had several other children, died about the year 1315, some twelve years after
the birth of Bridget, who thenceforward was brought up by an aunt at
Aspenäs on Lake Sommen. Before she was fourteen, Bridget married Ulf
Gudmarsson, who was himself only eighteen, and the marriage subsisted
happily for twenty-eight years. They had eight children, four boys and four
girls, of whom one is venerated as St Catherine of Sweden. For some years
Bridget led the life of a feudal lady on her husband's estate at Ulfasa, with
the difference that she cultivated the friendship of a number of learned and
virtuous men.

222

About the year 1335 St Bridget was summoned to the court of the young king of Sweden, Magnus II, to be principal lady-in-waiting to his newly-wedded queen, Blanche of Namur. Magnus was weak and tended to be wicked; Blanche was good-willed but irresponsible and luxury-loving. The saint bent all her energies to developing the better side of the queen's character and to establishing an influence for good over both of them.

The personal revelations which later were to make St Bridget so famous were already supporting her, and concerned matters so far apart as the necessity of washing and terms for peace between England and France. However the court did not seem susceptible to these influences: 'What was the Lady Bridget dreaming about last night?' became a byword. And St Bridget had troubles of her own. Her eldest daughter had married a riotous noble whom his mother-in-law refers to as 'the Brigand'; and about 1340 the youngest son, Gudmar, died. St Bridget thereupon made a pilgrimage to the shrine of St Olaf of Norway at Trondhjem, and on her return made a further attempt to curb the excesses of Magnus and Blanche. Meeting with no more success than before, she got leave of absence from the court, and with Ulf went on pilgrimage to Compostela. On the way back Ulf was taken ill at Arras, where he received the last sacraments. Bridget spared neither pains nor prayers for his recovery, and he was in fact restored again to health, so husband and wife vowed henceforward to devote their lives to God in religious houses. But, apparently before this resolution could take effect, Ulf died in 1344, at the monastery of Alvastra of the Cistercian Order.

St Bridget continued to live at Alvastra for four years, having taken upon herself the state of a penitent. Her visions and revelations now became so insistent that she was alarmed, fearing to be deluded by the Devil or by her own imagination. But a thrice-repeated vision told her to submit them to Master Matthias, a canon of Linköping and a priest of experience and learning, and he pronounced them to be of God. From now to her death she communicated them as they occurred to Peter, prior at Alvastra, who wrote them down in Latin. Those of this period culminated in a command of our Lord to go to the royal court and warn King Magnus of the judgement of God on his sins. She did so, and included the queen, the nobles and the bishops in her denunciation. For a time Magnus mended his ways, and liberally endowed the monastery which St Bridget now, in consequence of a further vision, planned to found at Vadstena, on Lake Vättern.

In this house St Bridget provided for sixty nuns, and in a separate enclosure monks, to the number of thirteen priests, in honour of the twelve Apostles and St Paul, four deacons, representing the Doctors of the Church, and eight choir-brothers not in orders, making the number of our Lord's apostles and disciples, eighty-five, in all. She prescribed them certain particular constitutions which are said to have been dictated to her by our Saviour in a vision.

In this institute, as in the Order of Fontevrault, the men were subject to the abbess of the nuns in temporals, but in spirituals the women were subject to the superior of the monks, because the order was principally instituted for women and the men were admitted only to afford them spiritual ministrations. The convents of the men and women were separated but had the same church, in which the nuns' choir was above in a gallery, so they could not even see one another. There are now no men in the Order of the Most Holy Saviour, or Bridgettines as they are commonly called, and where formerly there were seventy houses of nuns there are today but about a dozen. All surplus income had every year to be given to the poor, and ostentatious buildings were forbidden; but each religious could have as many books for study as he or she pleased.

In 1349, in spite of the Black Death that was ravaging Europe, she decided to go to popeless Rome for the year of jubilee in 1350. With her confessor, Peter of Skeninge and others, she embarked at Stralsund, amid the tears of the people who were never to see her again: for at Rome she settled down, to work among the people and for the return of the popes to their City. Among the places particularly associated with St Bridget in Rome are the churches of St Paul's-outside- the-Walls and San Francesco a Ripa. In the first is the most beautiful crucifix of Cavallini before which she prayed, which is said to have spoken to her, and in the second she had a vision of St Francis, who said to her, 'Come, eat and drink with me in my cell'. She took this to be an invitation to go to Assisi, which she accordingly did. Later she made a tour of shrines in Italy which lasted for two years.

The saint's prophecies and revelations had reference to most of the burning political and religious questions of her time, both of Sweden and Rome. She prophesied that pope and emperor would shortly meet amicably in Rome (which Bd Urban V and Charles IV did in 1368), and the using of her by factions did somewhat to abate her popularity among the Romans. Her prophecies that their iniquities would be visited with condign punishments had the same effect, and several times her ardour drew down persecution and slander upon her. On the other hand, she was not sparing of her criticisms, and did not fear to denounce even a pope.

In 1371, in consequence of another vision, St Bridget embarked on the last of her journeys, a pilgrimage to the Holy Places, taking with her St Catherine, her daughter, her sons Charles and Birger, Alphonsus of Vadaterra and others. The expedition started inauspiciously, for at Naples Charles got himself entangled with Queen Joanna I, of unenviable reputation. Although his wife was still alive in Sweden, and her third husband in Spain, Joanna wanted to marry him, and he was far from unwilling. His mother was horror-stricken, and set herself to ceaseless prayer for the resolution of the difficulty. Charles was struck down by a fever, and after a fortnight's illness died in the arms of his mother. He was, with St Catherine, her favourite child, and Bridget after his funeral went on in deepest grief to Palestine. Here, after being nearly drowned in a wreck off Jaffa, her progress through the Holy Places was a succession of visions of the events that had happened there and other heavenly consolations. The party arrived back in Rome in March 1373. Bridget had been ailing for some months, and now she got weaker every day till, having received the last sacraments from her faithful friend, Peter of Alvastra, she died on July 23 in her seventy-first year.

St Bridget was canonized in 1391 and is the patron saint of the kingdom of Sweden.

24 : ST CHRISTINA THE ASTONISHING, VIRGIN (A.D. 1224)

CHRISTINA was born at Brusthem in the diocese of Liège, in 1150, and at the age of fifteen was left an orphan, with two elder sisters. When she was about twenty-two Christina had a seizure, was assumed to be dead, and in due course was carried in an open coffin to the church, where a Mass of requiem was begun. Suddenly, after the *Agnus Dei*, Christina sat up, soared to the beams of the roof, and there perched herself. Everyone fled from the church except her elder sister, who, though thoroughly frightened, gave a good example of recollection to the others by stopping till the end of Mass. The priest then made Christina come down (it was said that she had taken refuge up there because she could not bear the smell of sinful human bodies). She averred that she had actually been dead; that she had gone down to Hell and there recognized many friends, and to Purgatory, where she had seen more friends, and then to Heaven.

This was only the beginning of a series of hardly less incredible occurrences. Christina fled into remote places, climbed trees and towers and rocks, and crawled into ovens, to escape from the smell of humans. She would handle fire with impunity and, in the coldest weather, dash into the river, or into a mill-race and be carried unharmed under the wheel. She prayed balancing herself on the top of a hurdle or curled up on the ground in such a way that she looked like a ball. Not unnaturally, everyone thought she was mad or 'full of devils', and attempts were made to confine her, but she always broke loose. Eventually she was caught by a man who had to give her a violent blow on the leg to do it, and it was thought her leg was broken. She was therefore taken to the house of a surgeon in Liège, who put splints on the limb and chained her to a pillar for safety. She escaped in the night. On one occasion when a priest, not knowing her and frightened by her appearance, had refused to give her communion, she rushed wildly through the streets, jumped into the Meuse, and swam away. She lived by begging, dressed in rags, and behaved in a terrifying manner.

The last years of her life Christina passed in the convent of St Catherine at Saint-Trond, and there she died at the age of seventy-four. Even while she lived there were some who regarded her with great respect. Louis, Count of Looz, treated her as a friend, welcoming her to his castle, accepting her rebukes, and on his deathbed insisting on manifesting his conscience to her. Bd Mary of Oignies had regard for her, the prioress of St Catherine's praised her obedience, and St Lutgardis sought her advice.

25 : ST JAMES THE GREATER, APOSTLE (A.D. 44)

ST JAMES, the brother of St John Evangelist, son of Zebedee, was called the Greater to distinguish him from the other apostle of the same name, surnamed the Less because he was the younger. St James the Greater was by birth a Galilean, and by trade a fisherman with his father and brother, living probably at Bethsaida, where St Peter also dwelt at that time. Jesus walking by the lake of Genesareth saw Peter and Andrew fishing, and He called them to come after Him, promising to make them fishers of men. Going a little farther on the shore, He saw two other brothers, James and John, in a ship, with Zebedee their father, mending their nets, and He also called them; they left their nets and their father and followed Him.

St James was present with his brother St John and St Peter at the cure of Peter's mother-in-law, and the raising of the daughter of Jairus from the dead, and in the same year Jesus formed the company of His apostles, into which He adopted James and John. He gave these two the surname of Boanerges, or 'Sons of Thunder', seemingly on account of an impetuous spirit and fiery temper. Those apostles who from time to time acted impetuously, and had to be rebuked, were the very ones whom our Lord turned to on special occasions. Peter, this James and John alone were admitted to be spectators of His glorious transfiguration, and they alone were taken to the innermost recesses of Gethsemani on the night of agony and bloody sweat at the beginning of His passion.

Where St James preached and spread the gospel after the Lord's ascension we have no account from the writers of the first ages of Christianity. According to the tradition of Spain, he made an evangelizing visit to that country, but the earliest known reference to this is only in the later part of the seventh century, and then in an oriental, not a Spanish source. St James was the first among the apostles who had the honour to follow his divine Master by martyrdom, which he suffered at Jerusalem under King Herod Agrippa I, who inaugurated a persecution of Christians in order to please the Jews.

He was buried at Jerusalem, but, again according to the tradition of Spain, dating from about 830, the body was translated first to Iria Flavia, now El Padron, in Galicia, and then to Compostela, where during the middle ages the shrine of Santiago became one of the greatest of all Christian shrines. The relics still rest in the cathedral and were referred to as authentic in a bull of Pope Leo XIII in 1884.

26 : ST BARTHOLOMEA CAPITANIO, VIRGIN, CO-FOUNDRESS
OF THE SISTERS OF CHARITY OF LOVERE (A.D. 1833)

BARTHOLOMEA was born at Lovere in the Brescian Alps, not far from Castiglione, the ancestral home of the Gonzagas. She acquired nothing of piety from her father, a rough corn-factor, who was given to heavy drinking. Her mother, on the other hand, was a most exemplary Christian woman, and the child learnt from her and from the nuns whose school she attended to put God before everything else and to aim at a high standard of perfection. She could not obtain her parents' leave to become a nun, so after making, with her director's sanction, a vow of perpetual chastity, she devoted herself to the work of education, obtaining an elementary teacher's diploma. In this way she set about consecrating her life to the apostolate of the young, and organized a guild or sodality of St Aloysius, which, spreading to other districts, produced marvellous effects.

Seeing the need of creating some kind of religious institute to perpetuate the good she had most at heart, St Bartholomea joined forces with another earnest worker of the same district, Catherine Gerosa (now, in virtue of the name she took in religion, known as St Vincentia Gerosa), a woman twenty years her senior. Catherine's main interest was in nursing and relieving the sick poor, for whom she had already founded a hospital, taking the heaviest burdens upon herself. But now both activities, of teaching and nursing, were combined, and to facilitate matters it was decided at the suggestion of ecclesiastical authority that the two friends should adopt the rule of the Sisters of Charity of St Vincent de Paul. So a new institute was begun which took the name of 'Suore della carità', and which, being encouraged by the bishop from the first, eventually obtained papal approval: the congregation is now widely diffused.

St Bartholomea never spared herself; her endless correspondence and outside activities left her no moment of leisure, and though for four months before the end she obeyed her doctor, who prohibited the writing of letters, she was already far gone in consumption, and the relief came too late. She died aged twenty-six on July 26, 1833, and was canonized in 1950.

27 : ST THEOBALD OF MARLY, ABBOT (A.D. 1247)

THIS monk, the great ornament of the illustrious family of Montmorency in France, was born in the castle of Marly. His father, Bouchard de Montmorency, gave him an education suitable to his birth, trained him for arms, and sent him for a time to the court of King Philip Augustus II. But Theobald manifested a strong inclination to a state of retirement; he spent a great part of his time in prayer, and resorted often to the church of the nunnery called Port Royal, which had been founded in 1204 by the wife of Matthew de Montmorency, and on which his father Bouchard had bestowed so many estates that he was regarded as a second founder. Theobald took the Cistercian habit at Vaux-de-Cernay in 1220, and was chosen abbot in 1235. He lived in the midst of his brethren as the servant of every one, and surpassed all others in his love of poverty, silence and prayer. He was known to and much venerated by St Louis. Theobald died on December 8, 1247.

28 : ST SAMSON, BISHOP OF DOL (c. A.D. 565)

ST SAMSON was born about the year 485, his father, Amon, being of the Welsh province of Dyfed, and his mother, Anna, from Gwent, he being a 'child of promise' after his parents' long childlessness. Out of gratitude the child was, at the age of five years, dedicated to God in the monastery founded and governed by St Illtud at Llantwit in Glamorgan. The young Samson was most virtuous in his life, quick in his studies, and austere in his monastic observance, so he was early made deacon and priest by St Dyfrig (Dubricius). Samson obtained the abbot's permission to go to an island where was a small community governed by one Piro. This island is usually identified with Caldey (Ynys Byr), off the coast of Pembrokeshire.

His father being, as he supposed, near death, sent for Samson to administer the last rites. At first he was unwilling to go out into the world, but Piro rebuked him and appointed a deacon to bear him company, and when he had ministered the sacraments to his father, the man recovered. Whereupon Amon and his wife wished to retire from the world, and when provision had been made for her, Samson with his father and his uncle

Umbrafel and the deacon returned to the island. Shortly afterwards Piro died and Samson was made abbot in his stead. In this office, while himself being regarded as a hermit, he brought the monks gently into better discipline, and also made a journey to Ireland; a monastery which was there confided to him he put in charge of Umbrafel. But on his return he refused to continue as abbot and retired, with Amon and two others, to somewhere near the river Severn and there they lived as hermits.

But his peace was soon disturbed. He was made abbot of the monastery and was consecrated bishop by St Dubricius. Soon after, on Easter eve, he had a vision in which he was told to go beyond the seas. Accordingly he went into Cornwall, with his companions, and landed at or near Padstow. He proceeded towards the monastery called Docco (now Saint Kew), and when the monks heard of his approach they sent one of their number, the most prudent and a man with the gift of prophecy, Winiau, to meet him. This was not, however, the sign of an eager welcome, for when St Samson proposed to stay at the monastery for a little, Winiau tactfully intimated that it was not convenient.

Samson took his words as an indication from God, and went on across Cornwall, travelling by means of a chariot he had brought from Ireland. Going through the district of Trigg he converted a number of idol-worshippers by restoring miraculously a boy who had been thrown from a horse; he founded a church at Southill and another at Golant, coming by way of the Fowey river to its mouth, whence he took ship to Brittany, leaving his father in charge of a monastery at Southill. It is possible that before leaving Cornwall, where he must have spent a considerable time, he visited the Scilly Islands, for one of them is named after him.

Of Samson's work in Brittany his biographers speak most of his miracles; he made missionary journeys in all directions, including the Channel Islands, where a town on Guernsey bears his name, and founded two monasteries, one for himself at Dol and another at Pental in Normandy. He helped to restore to Brittany its rightful prince, Judual, against his rival Conmor in the year 555. Upon visiting Paris Samson attracted the favourable notice of King Childebert, who is said to have nominated him bishop of Dol, and he is probably the 'Samson, peccator, Episcopus' who signed the acts of the Council of Paris in 557; but Dol was not a regular episcopal see until the ninth century. St Samson died peacefully among his monks about the year 565.

29 : ST OLAF OF NORWAY, MARTYR (A.D. 1030)

OLAF was the son of Harold Grenske, a lord in Norway, and after eight years of piracy and fighting succeeded to his father in 1015 at the age of twenty, at a time when most of Norway was in the hands of the Danes and Swedes. These parts he conquered and then set about the subjection of the realm to Christ, for he himself had already been baptized at Rouen by Archbishop Robert; the work had been begun, but had not made much real progress, by Haakon the Good and by Olaf Tryggvason, whose methods of evangelization seem to have been preposterous and wicked. In 1013 Olaf Haraldsson had sailed to England and assisted King Ethelred against the

Danes, and he now turned to that country for help in his more peaceable task. He brought over from England a number of priests and monks, one of whom, Grimkel, was chosen bishop of Nidaros, his capital. Olaf relied much on the advice of this prelate, and by his counsel published many good enactments and abolished ancient laws and customs contrary to the gospel. Unfortunately, like St Vladimir of Russia and other princes he used force without compunction. To his enemies he was merciless, added to which some of his legislation and political objects were not everywhere approved. Therefore many rose in arms, and, with the assistance of Canute, King of England and Denmark, defeated and expelled him. St Olaf fled, but returned with a few Swedish troops to recover his kingdom; he was slain by his rebellious and infidel subjects in a battle fought at Stiklestad, on July 29, 1030.

The king's body was buried in a steep sandbank by the river Nid, where he had fallen; here a spring gushed out whose waters became credited with healing power and the bishop, Grimkel, in the following year ordered that he was to be there venerated as a marytr and a chapel built over the place. In 1075 the chapel was replaced by a bishop's church, dedicated to Christ and St Olaf, which in time became the metropolitan cathedral of Nidaros (Trondhjem).

30 : ST PETER CHRYSOLOGUS, ARCHBISHOP OF RAVENNA, DOCTOR OF THE CHURCH (c. A.D. 450)

ST PETER was a native of Imola, a town in eastern Emilia. He was taught the sacred sciences and ordained deacon by Cornelius, bishop of that city, of whom he speaks with veneration and gratitude. Archbishop John of Ravenna dying about the year 433, St Peter became archbishop in his stead. The Emperor Valentinian III and his mother, Galla Placidia, then resided in that city, and St Peter enjoyed their regard and confidence, as well as the trust of the successor of Sixtus, St Leo the Great.

At the town of Classis, then the port of Ravenna, St Peter built a baptistery, and a church dedicated in honour of St Andrew. We have many of his discourses still extant: they are all very short, for he was afraid of fatiguing the attention of his hearers, but the matter of the discourses of St Peter Chrysologus caused him to be declared a doctor of the Church by Pope Benedict XIII in 1729. St Peter is said to have preached with such vehemence that he sometimes became speechless from excitement. In 448 St Peter received St Germanus of Auxerre with great honour at Ravenna, and after his death there on July 31 officiated at his funeral and kept his hood and sackcloth shirt as relics. St Peter Chrysologus did not long survive him. Being forewarned of approaching death, he returned to Imola, and there died on December 2, probably in 450.

31 : ST IGNATIUS OF LOYOLA, FOUNDER OF THE SOCIETY OF JESUS (A.D. 1556)

ST IGNATIUS was born, probably in 1491, in the castle of Loyola at Azpeitia, in Guipuzcoa, a part of Biscay that reaches to the Pyrenees. His father, Don Beltran, was lord of Oñaz and Loyola, head of one of the most ancient and noble families of that country, and his mother, Marina Saenz de Licona y Balda, was not less illustrious. They had three daughters and eight sons, and Ignatius (he was christened Inigo) was the youngest child.

His short military career came to an abrupt end on May 20, 1521 when, in the defence of Pamplona, a cannon ball broke his right shin and tore open the left calf. At his fall the Spanish garrison surrendered. The French then sent him in a litter to the castle of Loyola. His broken leg had been badly set, and the surgeons therefore thought it necessary to break it again, which he suffered without any apparent concern; but he limped for the rest of his life.

While he was confined to his bed, finding the time tedious, Ignatius called for some book of romances. None being found, a book of the life of our Saviour and another of legends of the saints were brought him. He read them first only to pass away the time, but afterward began to relish them and to spend whole days in reading them. Taking at last a firm resolution to imitate the saints at least in some respects, he began to treat his body with all the rigour it was able to bear, and spent his retired hours in weeping for his sins. He went on pilgrimage to the shrine of our Lady at Montserrat, and resolved thenceforward to lead a life of penance. Near Montserrat is the small town of Manresa, and here he stayed, sometimes with the Dominican friars, sometimes in a paupers' hospice; and there was a cave in a neighbouring hill whither he might retire for prayer and penance. So he lived for nearly a year. During this time he began to note down material for what was to become the book of his *Spiritual Exercises*.

In February 1523, Ignatius started on his journey to the Holy Land; begging his way, he took ship from Barcelona, spent Easter at Rome, sailed from Venice to Cyprus, and thence to Jaffa. He went by donkey from thence to Jerusalem, with the firm intention of staying there. But the Franciscan guardian of the Holy Places commanded him to leave Palestine, lest his attempts to convert Moslems should cause him to be kidnapped and held to ransom. He returned to Spain in 1524; and he now set himself to study.

He began at Barcelona with Latin grammar, being assisted by the charities of a pious lady of that city, called Isabel Roser: he was then thirty-three years old. After studying two years at Barcelona he went to the University of Alcala, where he attended lectures in logic, physics and divinity. He lodged at a hospice, lived by begging, and wore a coarse grey habit. He catechized children, held assemblies of devotion in the hospice, and by his mild reprehensions converted many loose livers. Those were the days of strange cults in Spain, and Ignatius was accused to the bishop's vicar general, who confined him to prison two-and- forty days. He declared him innocent of any fault at the end of it; but forbade him and his companions to wear any singular dress, or to give any instructions in religious matters for three years. So he migrated with his three fellows to Salamanca, where he was exposed again to suspicions of introducing dangerous doctrines, and the inquisitors imprisoned him; but after three weeks declared him innocent.

Recovering his liberty again, he resolved to leave Spain, and in the middle of winter travelled on foot to Paris, where he arrived in the beginning of February 1528. He spent two years improving himself in Latin; in vacation time he went into Flanders, and once into England, to procure help from the

Spanish merchants settled there, from whom and from some friends at Barcelona he received support. He studied philosophy three years and a half in the college of St Barbara, where he induced many of his fellow-students to spend the Sundays and holy days in prayer, and to apply themselves more fervently to good works. In 1534 the middle-aged student—he was forty-three—graduated as master of arts of Paris.

At that time six students in divinity associated themselves with Ignatius in his spiritual exercises. They were Peter Favre, a Savoyard; Francis Xavier, a Basque like Ignatius; Laynez and Salmeron, both fine scholars; Simon Rodriguez, a Portuguese; and Nicholas Bobadilla. These made all together a vow to observe poverty and chastity and to go to preach the gospel in Palestine, or if they could not go thither to offer themselves to the pope to be employed in the the service of God in what manner he should judge best. They pronounced this vow in a chapel on Montmartre, after they had all received holy communion from Peter Favre, who had been lately ordained priest. This was on the feast of the Assumption, 1534, Ignatius returned home in spring 1535, and was joyfully received in Guipuzcoa, where, however, he refused to go to the castle of Loyola, taking up his quarters in the poor-house of Azpeitia.

Two years later they all met in Venice, but it was impossible to find a ship to sail to Palestine. Ignatius's companions (now numbering ten) therefore went to Rome, where Pope Paul III received them well, and granted them an indult that those who were not priests might receive holy orders from what bishop they pleased. They were accordingly ordained and then retired into a cottage near Vicenza to prepare themselves for the holy ministry of the altar.

There being no likelihood of their being able soon to go to the Holy Land, it was at length resolved that Ignatius, Favre and Laynez should go to Rome and offer the services of all to the pope, and they agreed that if anyone asked what their association was they might answer, 'the Company of Jesus', because they were united to fight against falsehood and vice under the standard of Christ. On his road to Rome, praying in a little chapel at La Storta, Ignatius saw our Lord loaded with a heavy cross, and he heard the words 'I will be favourable to you at Rome'. Paul III appointed Favre to teach in the Sapienza and Laynez to explain the Holy Scriptures; Ignatius laboured by means of his spiritual exercises and instructions to reform the manners of the people and the others were likewise employed in the city—that none of them yet spoke Italian properly did not deter them.

It was now proposed to form a religious order. It was resolved, first, besides the vows of poverty and chastity already made by them, to add a third of obedience, to appoint a superior general whom all should be bound to obey, subject entirely to the Holy See. They likewise determined to prescribe a fourth vow, of going wherever the pope should send them for the salvation of souls. It was agreed that the celebration of the Divine Office in choir (as distinct from the obligatory private recitation) should be no part of their duties. The cardinals appointed by the pope to examine this new order at first opposed it, but after a year changed their opinions, and Paul III approved it by a bull, dated September 27, 1540. Ignatius was chosen the first general superior, but only acquiesced in obedience to his confessor. He entered upon his office on Easter-day, 1541, and the members all made their religious vows in the basilica of St Paul-outside-the-Walls a few days later. For the rest of his life Ignatius lived in Rome, tied there by the immense work of directing the activities of the order which he ruled till his death. Among the establishments which he made there, he founded a house for the reception of converted Jews during the time of their instruction, and another for penitents from among women of disorderly life. St Francis Borgia in 1550 gave a considerable sum towards building the Roman College for the Jesuits; St Ignatius made this the model of all his other colleges and took care that it should be supplied with able masters and all possible helps for the advancement of learning. He also directed the foundation of the German College in Rome, originally intended for scholars from all countries seriously affected by Protestantism. Other universities, seminaries and colleges were established in other places; but the work of education for which the Jesuits are so famous was a development that only came by degrees, though well established before the founder's death. One of the most famous and fruitful works of St Ignatius was the book of his *Spiritual Exercises*, begun at Manresa and first published in Rome in 1548 with papal approval.

In the fifteen years that he directed his order St Ignatius saw it grow from ten members to one thousand, in nine countries and provinces of Europe, in India and in Brazil. And in those fifteen years he had been ill fifteen times, so that the sixteenth time caused no unusual alarm. But it was the last. He died suddenly, so unexpectedly that he did not receive the last sacraments, early in the morning of July 31, 1556. He was canonized in 1622, and by Pope Pius XI he was declared the heavenly patron of spiritual exercises and retreats.

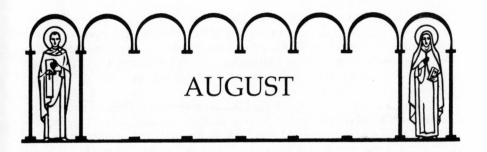

AUGUST

1 : ST PETER JULIAN EYMARD, FOUNDER OF THE PRIESTS OF THE BLESSED SACRAMENT (A.D. 1868)

ST PETER JULIAN was born in 1811 at La Mure d'Isère, a small town in the diocese of Grenoble. His father was a cutler, and Peter Julian worked at his father's trade, and in an oil-press, until he was eighteen; in his spare hours he studied Latin and had some instruction from a priest at Grenoble for whom he worked for a time, and in 1831 he went to the seminary of Grenoble. He was ordained there in 1834 and for the five following years ministered in the parishes of Chatte and Monteynard. What they thought of him there was expressed in the words of his bishop, Mgr de Bruillard, when the Abbé Eymard asked for permission to join the Marists. After his novitiate he was made spiritual director of the junior seminary at Belley, and in 1845 provincial of his congregation at Lyons.

In 1851 Father Eymard made a pilgrimage to Notre-Dame de Fourvières: 'One idea haunted me, and it was this: that Jesus in the Blessed Sacrament had no religious institute to glorify His mystery of love, whose only object was entire consecration to Its service..There ought to be one . . . . I promised Mary to devote myself to this end. It was still all very vague, and I had no idea of leaving the society . . . . What hours I spent there! ' His superiors advised him to defer his plans till they were more mature, and he spent four years at La Seyne. During this time he received encouragement from Pope Pius IX and from the Ven. John Colin, founder of the Marists, and he determined to sacrifice his vocation with the Society of Mary and to devote himself to a new society. In 1856, with the approval of the Marist superior general, he submitted his scheme for an institute of priest-adorers of the Blessed Sacrament to Mgr de Sibour, Archbishop of Paris, and at the end of twelve anxious days it was approved. Mgr de Sibour put a house at his disposal, wherein Father Eymard took up his residence with one companion, and on January 6, 1857, the Blessed Sacrament was exposed in its chapel for the first time, and Father Eymard preached to a large assembly.

The first members of the Congregation of Priests of the Most Blessed Sacrament were Father de Cuers and Father Champion, and they began with exposition three times a week. Vocations were slow: many were called but few chosen; and the difficulties were great. They had to leave their first house, and in 1858 they obtained a small chapel in the Faubourg Saint-

Jacques, where during nine years the grace of God was poured out so abundantly that Father Eymard called it the 'chapel of miracles'. In the following year Pope Pius IX gave the congregation a laudatory brief and a second house was opened, at Marseilles, and in 1862 a third, at Angers. By this time there were enough members to establish a regular novitiate, and the congregation rapidly expanded.

In 1858 Father Eymard established the Servants of the Blessed Sacrament, sisters who are also engaged in perpetual adoration and spreading the love of our Lord; and he founded the Priests' Eucharistic League. But Father Eymard did not confine his labours to the clergy and religious: in his Work for Poor Adults he put before his congregation the necessity for preparing for first communion all adults who are no longer of an age to attend the parish catechism classes, or who are unable to go to these classes, and he also organized the Archconfraternity of the Blessed Scarament; he also wrote a number of books on the Eucharist which have been translated into several languages.

Of the difficulties which beset St Peter Julian in making his new foundation one of the most trying was the adverse criticism he was subjected to at its very inception, because he had left the Society of Mary, and detractors of the work were not wanting when it was started. There were other grave difficulties and disappointments, but in spite of all the congregation was approved by the Holy See, as has been said, in his lifetime, and was finally confirmed *in perpetuum* in 1895.

During the last four years of his life St Peter Julian suffered from rheumatic gout and insomnia, and his sufferings were added to by saddening difficulties. In July 1868 he broke down and his doctor ordered him to leave Paris at once. On the 21st he left Grenoble by coach for La Mure; it was very hot and he arrived in a state of collapse and partial paralysis. On August 1 he died. Miracles took place at his tomb before the end of that year, and in 1925 Peter Julian Eymard was beatified. He was canonized in 1962 during the Second Vatican Council.

2 : ST EUSEBIUS, BISHOP OF VERCELLI (A.D. 371)

ST EUSEBIUS was born in the isle of Sardinia, where his father is said to have died in chains for the faith. His mother, when left a widow, took him and a daughter, both in their infancy, to Rome, where Eusebius was brought up and ordained lector. He was called to Vercelli, in Piedmont, and served that church with such distinction that he was chosen to govern it by the clergy and people. He is the first bishop of Vercelli whose name we know. St Ambrose assures us that he was the first who in the West united the monastic discipline with the clerical, living himself with some of his clergy a common life in community.

In 354 Pope Liberius deputed St Eusebius, with Lucifer of Cagliari, to beg the Emperor Constantius to assemble a council to try and end the trouble between Catholics and Arians. Constantius agreed, and a council met at Milan in 355. Eusebius, seeing things would be carried by force through the power of the Arians, though the Catholic prelates were more numerous, refused to go to it till he was pressed by Constantius himself. When the bishops were called on to sign a condemnation of St Athanasius that had been drawn up, Eusebius refused, and instead laid the Nicene creed on the table and insisted on all signing that before the case of St Athanasius should be considered. Great tumult and confusion followed. Eventually the emperor sent for St Eusebius, St Dionysius of Milan and Lucifer of Cagliari, and pressed them to condemn Athanasius. They insisted upon his innocence and that he could not be condemned without being heard, and urged that secular force might not be used to influence ecclesiastical decisions. The emperor stormed and threatened to put them to death, but was content to banish them. The first place of exile of St Eusebius was Scythopolis (Beisan) in Palestine, where he was put in charge of the Arian bishop, Patrophilus.

He was lodged at first with St Joseph of Palestine (the only orthodox household in the town), and was comforted by the visits of St Epiphanius and others, and by the arrival of the deputies of his church of Vercelli with money for his subsistence. But his patience was to be exercised by great trials. Count Joseph died, and the Arians insulted the bishop, dragged him through the streets half naked, and shut him up in a little room, where he was pestered for four days to make him conform. Eusebius undertook a sort of 'hunger-strike', and after he had remained four days without food the Arians sent him back to his lodging. Three weeks afterwards they came again, broke into the house, and dragged him away. They rifled his goods, plundered his provisions, and drove away his attendants. Later he was removed from Scythopolis into Cappadocia, and some time afterwards into the Upper Thebaid in Egypt.

When Constantius died towards the end of the year 361, Julian gave leave to the banished prelates to return to their sees, and St Eusebius came to Alexandria to concert measures with St Athanasius for applying proper remedies to the evils of the Church. He took part in a council there, and then went on to Antioch to put into effect the wish of the council that St Meletius should there be recognized as bishop and the Eustathian schism healed. But he found it widened by Lucifer of Cagliari.

Unable to do any good at Antioch, St Eusebius travelled over the East and through Illyricum, confirming in the faith those who were wavering and bringing back many that were gone astray. In Italy St Hilary of Poitiers and St Eusebius met, and were employed together in opposing the arianizing Auxentius of Milan. Vercelli, on the return of its bishop after so long an absence, 'laid aside her garments of mourning', as St Jerome says, but of the last years of St Eusebius nothing is known. He died on August 1.

3 : ST WALTHEOF or WALTHEN, ABBOT OF MELROSE (c. A.D. 1160)

WALTHEOF was second son of Simon, Earl of Huntingdon, and Matilda or Maud, daughter to Judith, the niece of William the Conqueror. His elder bróther was called Simon, and in their childhood it was the pastime of this Simon to build castles and play at soldiers, but Waltheof's to build churches and monasteries of stones and wood. When grown up, the elder inherited his father's martial disposition together with his title; but Waltheof had a strong inclination for the religious life and was mild and peace-loving. Their mother Maud, after the death of her first husband, was given in marriage by King Henry I to St David I, King of Scotland, and Waltheof followed his mother to that court, where he formed an intimate friendship with St Aelred, who was master of the royal household at that time.

Soon after he decided to become a religious. He left Scotland, and made his profession among the regular canons of St Augustine in their monastery at Nostell, near Pontefract in Yorkshire. He was soon after chosen prior of Kirkham, in the same county, and, realizing the obligations he now lay under for the sanctification of others as well as for his own, he redoubled his austerity and regularity of observance.

Waltheof, impressed by the life and vigour of the Cistercian monks, became anxious to join them; naturally he was encouraged by the advice of his friend St Aelred, then abbot of Rievaulx, and accordingly he took the habit at Wardon in Bedfordshire. Waltheof found Cistercian life excessively severe, yet, only four years after profession, he was chosen abbot of Melrose, recently founded on the banks of the Tweed by King David. Whenever he fell into the smallest failing by inadvertence Waltheof immediately had recourse to confession, a practice of perfection which the confessors found rather trying, as one of them admitted to Jordan, the saint's biographer. In 1154 Waltheof was chosen archbishop of Saint Andrews; but he prevailed on St Aelred to oppose the election and not to oblige him to accept it.

St Waltheof died at a great age on August 3, about 1160.

4 : ST JOHN VIANNEY, (A.D. 1859)

THE world into which John Mary Vianney was born, at Dardilly, near Lyons, on May 8, 1786, was a disturbed one. When he was three the French Revolution began and two years later Dardilly found itself saddled with a 'constitutional priest', so the little John and his parents had to assist in secret at the Mass of any fugitive loyal priest who came to the neighbourhood. While the Terror was going on, no less at Lyons than at Paris and elsewhere, he was learning to be a herd-boy, shepherding the cattle and sheep of Matthew Vianney's farm in the meadows on either side of the little river Planches. He made his first communion, in secret, when he was thirteen, and very shortly after Mass could be offered again in public at Dardilly. Five years later he broached to his father his project of becoming a priest. But it was not until he was twenty that John Mary could get permission to leave home for the neighbouring village of Ecully, where the Abbé Balley had established a 'presbytery-school'.

His studies were a source of great trouble to him; he had little natural aptitude and his only schooling had been a brief period at the village school opened at Dardilly when he was nine. Through his name not having been entered on the roll of exempt ecclesiastical students, John Mary Vianney was conscripted for the army; he had to report at the depot in Lyons on October 26, 1809. Two days later he was taken ill and sent to hospital, and his draft for the army in Spain left without him. On January 5, being barely convalescent, he was ordered to report at Roanne for another draft on the morrow, and, having gone into a church to pray, arrived only after it had gone. However, he set out to catch up the draft at Renaison, having still no military acoutrements but his knapsack.

While he was resting at the approach to the mountains of Le Forez a stranger suddenly appeared, picked up the knapsack, and peremptorily ordered him to follow; he presently found himself in a hut near the remote mountain village of Les Noës. He now learned that the stranger was a deserter from the army, and that many more such were hiding in the woods and hills around. John saw at once that his situation was compromising, and reported himself to the mayor of the commune. M. Fayot was an humane official and a sensible man; he pointed out to John that he was already technically a deserter, and that of two evils the lesser was to remain in refuge where he was; and found him a lodging in the house of his own cousin. His hiding-place was in a stable under a hay-loft. For fourteen months John Mary was at Les Noës. Several times he was nearly taken by gendarmes, once feeling the point of a sword between his ribs as it was thrust about in the hay of the loft. In March 1810 the emperor, on the occasion of his marriage with the Archduchess Marie-Louise, had proclaimed an amnesty for all defaulters, and early in the following year, on his brother volunteering to join up before his time as a substitute, John Mary was able to return home, a free man.

In 1811 he received the tonsure and at the end of the following year was sent for a year's philosophy to the *petit séminaire* at Verrières. He plodded on humbly and doggedly, and in the autumn of 1813 went to the *grand séminaire* at Lyons. Here John Mary made no headway at all. At the end of the first term he left the seminary to be coached privately by M. Balley at Ecully, and after three months presented himself for examination. On July 2, 1814, John Mary Vianney received the minor orders and subdiaconate. He returned to Ecully to continue his studies with M. Balley, and in June 1815 he received the diaconate (five days after the battle of Waterloo), and on August 12 the priesthood. He offered his first Mass the following day, and was appointed curate to M. Balley, to whose clear-sightedness and perseverance is due, under God, the fact that St John Mary Vianney ever attained to the priesthood.

In 1817, to the infinite sorrow of his pupil, M. Balley died, and early in the following year the Abbé Vianney was made parish-priest of Ars-en-Dombes, a remote and neglected place of 230 souls. When he had personally visited every household under his care and provided a regular catechism-class for the children, he set to work in earnest to make a real conversion of Ars, by the confessional, and by laboriously and carefully prepared sermons which he delivered naturally, but not quietly. He waged relentless war against blasphemy, profanity and obscentiy, and was not afraid to utter from the pulpit the words and expressions that offended God, so there should be no mistake as to what he was talking about. For eight years and more he struggled for a proper observance of Sunday: not merely to get everybody to Mass and Vespers, but to abolish work which at times was done on Sunday without a shadow of necessity. Above all he set his face against dancing, maintaining that it was of necessity an occasion of sin to those who took part, and even to those who only looked on; to those who took part in it, whether publicly or privately, he was merciless: they must give it up entirely and keep to their resolution, or absolution was refused them. M. le Curé waged this battle, and the associated engagement of modesty in clothes, for twenty-five years; but he won in the end.

In 1824 there was opened at Ars by the enterprise of the curé a free school for girls, run by Catherine Lassagne and Benedicta Lardet, two young women of the village whom he had sent away to a convent to be trained. From this school sprang, some three years later, the famous institution of *La Providence*, a shelter for orphans and other homeless or deserted children, neither babies on the one hand nor adolescent girls on the other being turned away. Another of the astonishing circumstances of the Abbé Vianney's incumbency of Ars was its becoming a place of pilgrimage even during his lifetime: and that not to the shrine of 'his dear little St Philomena', which he had set up, but to himself. People from afar began to consult him so early as 1827; from 1830 to 1845 the daily visitors averaged over three hundred; at Lyons a special booking-office was opened for Ars, and 8-day return tickets issued—one could hardly hope to get a word with the *curé* in less. For him this meant not less than eleven or twelve hours every day in the confessional in winter, and anything up to sixteen in summer; nor was he content with that: for the last fifteen years of his life he gave an instruction every day in the church at eleven o'clock.

It is not surprising that as time went on M. Vianney longed more and more for solitude and quiet. But there is more to it than that: every one of his forty-one years at Ars was spent there against his own will; all the time he had to fight his personal predilection for the life of a Carthusian or Cistercian. He left the village three times, 'ran away' in fact, and in 1843, after a grave illness, it needed the diplomacy of the bishop to get him to return.

In 1852 Mgr Chalandon, Bishop of Belley, made M. Vianney an honorary canon of the chapter; he was invested almost by force and never again put on his *mozzetta*, which indeed he sold for fifty francs which he required for some charitable purpose. Three years later he was made a knight of the Imperial Order of the Legion of Honour. But with this he positively refused to be invested, and no persuasion could induce him to have the imperial cross pinned to his cassock, even for a moment. In 1853 M. Vianney made his last attempt at flight from Ars. It is a moving story, of the old and worn-out priest cajoled back to his presbytery on behalf of the numerous poor sinners who were unable to do without him.

It is not impossible that Bishop Chalandon should have been mistaken in not allowing him to resign his cure. But such a possibility was not one which M. Vianney would entertain; he devoted himself to his ministry more assiduously than ever. In the year 1858–9 over 100,000 pilgrims visited Ars; the *curé* was now a very old man of seventy-three, and the strain was too much. On July 18 he knew the end was at hand, and on July 29 he lay down on his bed for the last time. On August 3 the Bishop of Belley arrived in haste, and at two o'clock in the morning of August 4, amid a storm of thunder and lightning, the earthly life of the Curé of Ars came to a gentle end.

St John Mary Baptist Vianney was canonized by Pius XI in 1925. The same pope made him principal patron-saint of the parochial clergy throughout the world in 1929.

5 : SS. ADDAI AND MARI, BISHOPS (C. A.D. 180?)

THERE is evidence of a Christian colony at Edessa in the second century, but it was probably not till the coming of the Sassanid dynasty that the faith began to spread from there over Mesopotamia, Adiabene and Persia. Local ecclesiastical tradition, however, attributes their evangelization to the apostle St Thomas, and more particularly to St Addai, St Aggai and St Mari. The story of how they came to Edessa, combined from the narratives of Eusebius and of a Syriac document called *The Doctrine of Addai* (written c. 400), is as follows.

At the time when our Lord was still incarnate upon earth there reigned in Osroene a king called Abgar the Black, who lived at Edessa. He suffered from some incurable disease and, having heard of the miracles of healing of our Lord, he sent to Him a letter by the hand of his secretary, Hannan. In it he addresses Christ as 'the good Physician' and asks Him to come to Edessa and heal him. Hannan found our Lord in the house of Gamaliel, and He replied to Abgar that, 'I am about to return to my Father, all for which I was sent into the world being finished. But when I shall have ascended to Him I will send one of my disciples, who shall heal you of your sickness and bring you and yours to eternal life.' According to Eusebius our Lord wrote out this message Himself and it was accordingly greatly reverenced throughout Christendom during the middle ages. The Syriac document states that Hannan also brought back to Abgar a portrait of our Lord which he had painted (later, 'not-made-by-human-hands'), and which as the Holy Mandylion is famous in Christian iconography.

After the Ascension, the apostle Thomas accordingly sent one of the seventy-two disciples, Addai (Thaddeus), to the court of King Abgar. He lodged at the house of a Jew, Tobias, and when he was brought before the king he healed him of his disease, and spoke to him of the faith of Christ. Addai converted Abgar and multitudes of his people, among others the royal jeweller, Aggai, whom he made bishop and his successor, and Palut, whom he ordained priest on his death-bed. In due course St Aggai was martyred and Palut had to go to Antioch to be consecrated by Serapion, who in his turn had been made bishop by Pope St Zephyrinus at Rome. Quite apart from any other consideration, this last statement throws the whole of the legend into confusion, for it is known that there was a Serapion, Bishop of Antioch, who was at least contemporary with St Zephyrinus, and was, moreover, contemporary with another Abgar, who was a Christian king of Edessa between about 179 and 213, and probably the first; so Serapion could not have consecrated a convert of one of the Seventy-two.

The most, then, that can be said of St Addai is that he was perhaps a missionary in Edessa, before the end of the second century. St Mari is an even less satisfactory person, for there are serious doubts of his existence at all. According to his late 'acts' he was a disciple of St Addai, who sent him to Nisibis; he preached there and took up the work of Jonas the prophet at

Ninive, then he went down the Tigris, until he began 'to smell the smell of the apostle Thomas', and died near Seleucia-Ctesiphon, after consecrating as its bishop Papa bar Aggai, another certainly historical personage, the first katholikos of the East Syrian churches—but at the beginning of the fourth century. Wherever he went St Mari made numerous converts, destroyed temples, built churches and founded monasteries, on a scale familiar in spurious legends but rarely, if ever, found in sober history. Nevertheless, SS. Addai and Mari, nebulous as they now are, have from early ages been venerated as the evangelists of the lands around the Tigris and Euphrates, and still are by their successors, the Catholic Chaldeans and the Nestorians of Iraq and Kurdistan.

6 : ST HORMISDAS, POPE (A.D. 523)

HORMISDAS, a Campanian by birth, was a widower and a deacon of the Roman church, whose son St Silverius was also to become pope. He earned the high regard of St Ennodius, Bishop of Pavia, who prophesied that this deacon would one day be pope. Two days after the death of St Symmachus in 514 the prediction was fulfilled. Practically the whole of the pontificate of St Hormisdas was devoted to dealing with the delicate and complex situation brought about in the East by the Acacian schism, caused by the attempt of Acacius of Constantinople to placate the monophysites; and to this pope belongs the honour of having brought it to an end by means of the confession of faith that bears his name, the Formula of Hormisdas.

Nothing is recorded of the less public life of St Hormisdas, but it is clear that he was able and sagacious, and a man of peace: he severely rebuked some African monks for their quarrelsomeness. His last days were made happy by the cessation of the Vandal persecution in Africa.

7 : ST CAJETAN, CO-FOUNDER OF THE THEATINE CLERKS REGULAR (A.D. 1547)

ST CAJETAN (Gaetano) was son of Caspar, Count of Thiene, and Mary di Porto, of the nobility of Vicenza, where he was born in 1480. Two years later his father was killed, fighting for the Venetians against King Ferdinand of Naples. Cajetan went for four years to Padua University where he distinguished himself in theology, and took the degree of doctor in civil and canon law in 1504. He then returned to his native town, of which he was made a senator, and in pursuance of his resolve to serve God as a priest he received the tonsure. In 1506 he went to Rome. Soon after his arrival Pope Julius II conferred on him the office of protonotary, with a benefice attached. On the death of Julius II in 1513 Cajetan refused his successor's request to continue in his office, and devoted three years to preparing himself for the priesthood: he was ordained in 1516, being thirty-three years old, and returned to Vicenza in 1518.

Cajetan had re-founded a confraternity in Rome, called 'of the Divine Love', which was an association of zealous and devout clerics who devoted themselves to labour with all their power to promote God's honour and the welfare of souls. At Vicenza he now entered himself in the Oratory of St

Jerome, which was instituted upon the plan of that of the Divine Love but consisted only of men in the lowest stations of life. This circumstance gave great offence to his friends, who thought it a reflection on the honour of his family. He persisted, however, and sought out the sick and the poor over the whole town, served them, and cared for those who suffered from the most loathsome diseases in the hospital of the incurables, the revenues of which he greatly increased. He founded a similar oratory at Verona, and then went in 1520 to Venice and, taking up his lodgings in the new hospital of that city, pursued his former manner of life there. He remained in Venice three years, and introduced exposition of the Blessed Sacrament in that city, as well as continuing the promotion of frequent communion.

The state of Christendom at this time shocked and distressed Cajetan, and in 1523 he went back to Rome to confer with his friends of the Oratory of Divine Love. They agreed that little could be done otherwise than by reviving in the clergy the spirit and zeal of those holy pastors who first planted the faith, and a plan was formed for instituting an order of regular clergy upon the model of the lives of the Apostles. The first associates of St Cajetan in this design were John Peter Caraffa, afterwards pope under the name of Paul IV but at that time bishop of Theate (Chieti); Paul Consiglieri, of the family of Ghislieri; and Boniface da Colle, a gentleman of Milan. The institute was approved by Clement VII, and Caraffa was chosen the first provost general. From his episcopal name of Theatensis these clerks regular came to be distinguished from others as Theatines. On September 14, 1524 the four original members made their profession in St Peter's in the presence of a papal delegate.

The success of the new congregation was not immediate, and in 1527, when it still numbered only a dozen members, a calamity happened which might well have put an end to it. The army of the Emperor Charles V sacked Rome: the Theatines' house was nearly demolished, and the inmates had to escape to Venice. Caraffa's term as superior expired in 1530, and St Cajetan was chosen in his place. At the end of the three years of office, Caraffa was made superior a second time, and Cajetan was sent to Verona, where both the clergy and laity were opposing the reformation of discipline which their bishop was endeavouring to introduce among them. Shortly after, he was called to Naples to establish the clerks regular there. A general improvement was the fruit of his example, preaching and labours.

During the last years of his life he established with Bd John Marinoni the benevolent pawnshops (*montes pietatis*) sanctioned some time before by the Fifth Lateran Council. Worn out with trying to appease civil strife in Naples, and disappointed by the suspension of the Council of Trent from which he hoped so much for the Church's good, St Cajetan had to take to his bed in the summer of 1547. The end came on Sunday, August 7. Many miracles wrought by his intercession were approved at Rome after a rigorous scrutiny, and he was canonized in 1671.

8 : ST DOMINIC, FOUNDER OF THE ORDER OF PREACHERS (A.D. 1221)

ST DOMINIC was born soon after 1170 at Calaruega in Castile. Practically nothing is known with certainty of his father Felix, though he is said to have been of the Guzmán family; his wife was Bd Joan of Aza. When he was fourteen years old he left the care of his uncle, who was the archpriest of Gumiel d'Izan, and was entered at the school of Palencia. While still a student he was made a canon of the cathedral of Osma, and after his ordination he took up his duties there. The chapter lived a community life under the Rule of St Augustine, and their regularity of observance was such as to provide an admirable school for the young priest. When Diego d'Azevedo became bishop of Osma about 1201 he succeeded him as prior of the chapter. He was then thirty-one years old, and had been leading this contemplative life for six or seven years; it at last came to an end, and Dominic began his work in the world in unexpected fashion in 1204.

In that year Alfonso IX, King of Castile, chose the bishop of Osma to go as ambassador to Denmark to negotiate a marriage for his son. The bishop took Dominic with him. On their way they passed through Languedoc, which was then filled with the heresy of the Albigenses. He in whose house they lodged at Toulouse professed it. St Dominic spent the whole night in discussion with him, and the man abjured his errors. It is generally supposed that from this moment Dominic knew what work God required of him. Their embassy fulfilled, Bishop Diego and Dominic went to Rome to ask of Pope Innocent III leave to go to preach the gospel in Russia. The pope exhorted them to oppose a heresy which threatened the Church at home. On their return they made a visit to Cîteaux, whose monks were the officially appointed organizers and preachers against the Albigenses, and at Montpellier they met the Abbot of Cîteaux, together with two monks, Peter of Castelnau and Raoul of Fontefroide, who had been in charge of the missions in Languedoc. St Dominic and the Bishop of Osma invited these preachers to follow more closely the example of their opponents: to give up travelling with horses and retinues and staying at the best inns, with servants to wait on them. Then, when they had shown themselves worthy of being listened to, to use persuasion and peaceful discussion, rather than threats and overbearingness.

A series of conferences was held with the heretics; they influenced some of the rank and file, but had little effect on the leaders. Soon Bishop Diego returned to Osma, leaving his companion in France. But before he went St Dominic had already taken that step which was the first in the definite foundation of his order, by which the tide of Albigensianism began to be stayed. On the feast of St Mary Magdalen in 1206 he had a sign from Heaven, and in consequence of it within six months he had founded at Prouille, near Fanjeaux, a monastery to shelter nine nuns, all of whom were converts from the heresy. Nearby was a house for his helpers, and thus St Dominic began to provide for a supply of trained and virtuous preachers, for a shelter for converted women, for the education of girls, and for a permanent house of prayer.

St Dominic spent nearly ten years preaching in Languedoc as leader, though with no canonical status, of a small band of special preachers. All this time he had worn the habit of a regular canon of St Augustine, and followed that rule. But he earnestly desired to revive an apostolic spirit in the ministers of the altar. He projected a body of religious men not like the monks who were contemplatives and not necessarily priests, but who to contemplation should join a close application to sacred studies and all the functions of a pastoral life, expecially that of preaching. In order that he might have means at his disposal Fulk of Toulouse in 1214 gave him an endowment and extended his episcopal approval to the embryonic order in the following year. A few months later Dominic accompanied Fulk to the Fourth Lateran Council.

Pope Innocent III received the saint with great kindness and gave his approbation of the nunnery of Prouille. He gave a guarded approval by word of mouth, bidding the founder return to his brethren and select which of the already approved rules they would follow. They met at Prouille in August 1216, and after consultation with his sixteen colleagues, of whom eight were Frenchmen, seven Spaniards, and one Englishman (Brother Laurence), he made choice of the Rule of St Augustine. St Dominic added certain particular constitutions, some borrowed from the Order of Prémontré. Pope Innocent III died on July 18, 1216, and Honorius III was chosen in his place. This change retarded St Dominic's second journey to Rome; and in the meantime he finished his first friary, at Toulouse, to which the bishop gave the church of St Romain, wherein the first community of Dominicans assembled and began common life under vows.

St Dominic arrived at Rome again in October 1216, and Honorius III confirmed his order and its constitutions the same year. On August 13, 1217, the Friars Preachers met under their leader at Prouille. He instructed them on their method of preaching and teaching and exhorted them to unremitting study. Then, on the feast of the Assumption, to the surprise of all, for heresy was again gaining ground in all the neighbourhood, St Dominic broke up his band of friars and dispersed them in all directions. Four were sent to Spain, seven to Paris, two returned to Toulouse, two remained at Prouille, and the founder himself in the following December went back to Rome.

On his arrival in Rome the pope gave him the church of St Sixtus (San Sisto Vecchio), and while making a foundation there the saint lectured on theology, and preached in St Peter's with such eloquence as to draw the attention of the whole city. At this time a large number of nuns lived in Rome without keeping enclosure, and almost without regularity, some dispersed in small monasteries, others in the houses of their parents or friends. Pope Innocent III had made several attempts to assemble all such nuns into one enclosed house, but had not been able, with all his authority, to compass it. Honorius III committed the management of this reformation to St Dominic, who successfully carried it out. He gave the nuns his own monastery of St Sixtus, which was built and then ready to receive them, and which Innocent III had formerly offered them; and he received for his friars a house of the Savelli, on the Aventine, with the church of St Sabina.

A foundation having been successfully made by Friar Matthew of France at the University of Paris, St Dominic sent some brethren to the University of Bologna, where, under the guidance of Bd Reginald of Orleans, one of the most famous of Dominican establishments was set on foot. In 1218–19 the founder journeyed in Spain, France and Italy, establishing friaries in each country, and arrived at Bologna about the end of summer 1219, which city he made his ordinary residence to the end of his life. In 1220 Pope Honorius

III confirmed Dominic's title and office as master general, and at Pentecost was held the first general chapter of the order, at Bologna, at which were drawn up the final constitutions which made the organization of the Friars Preachers.

This was the discipline and strength that was behind the rapid spread of his order; by the second general chapter in 1221 it had some sixty friaries divided into eight provinces; friars had already got to Poland, Scandinavia and Palestine, and Brother Gilbert with twelve others had established monasteries in Canterbury, London and Oxford. After the second general chapter Dominic visited Cardinal Ugolino at Venice. On his return he was ill, and he was taken to a country place for the better air. But he knew he was dying. To his brethren he spoke more at length on the subject of poverty, and then at his request was carried back to Bologna that he might be buried 'under the feet of his brethren'. Gathered round him, they said the prayers for the dying; at the *Subvenite* St Dominic repeated those great words, and died. It was the evening of August 6, 1221; he was about fifty-two years old.

9 : ST OSWALD OF NORTHUMBRIA, MARTYR (A.D. 642)

AFTER the death of King St Edwin in the year 633 in battle against Penda and Cadwallon, Oswald, nephew of Edwin, prepared to regain possession of both parts of Northumbria; he had received Christianity with his whole heart and, far from forsaking Christ as his unhappy brothers had done to court the favour of his subjects, he wished to bring them to the spiritual kingdom of divine grace. While Cadwallon ravaged the Northumbrian provinces, Oswald assembled what troops he was able, and marched confidently, though with a small force, against his enemy. In 634 battle was joined some three miles south of Hexham, near Rowley Burn. The evening before the engagement, the king caused a great wooden cross to be made, and he held it up whilst the hole dug in the earth to plant it in was filled up round the foot. When it was fixed, St Oswald cried out to his army (in which only a handful of individuals were Christians), 'Let us now kneel down, and together pray to the almighty and only true God that He will mercifully defend us from our enemy; for He knows that we fight in defence of our lives and country'. All the soldiers did as he commanded, and that same night Oswald had a vision wherein St Columba of Iona appeared to stretch his cloak over his sleeping troops and to promise them victory on the morrow. And so it fell out: the superior forces of Cadwallon were routed and himself killed in the battle.

St Oswald immediately set himself to restore good order throughout his dominions, and to plant in them the faith of Christ. Naturally enough he looked not to Canterbury but to Scotland, where he had received the faith himself, for help in this task. St Aidan, a native of Ireland and a monk of Iona, was chosen and he by his mildness repaired the mischief done by another monk, sent before him, whose harshness had alienated many from the gospel which he professed to preach. The king bestowed on Aidan the isle of Lindisfarne for his episcopal see, and, before the bishop could sufficiently speak the English language, he would himself be his interpreter and explain his sermons and instructions to the people. The kingdom of

Northumberland then extended as far as the Firth of Forth, and so great was his power that the other kings of England recognized in him some sort of nominal overlordship (*bretwalda*), so that St Adamnan, in his life of St Columba, styles him 'Emperor of all Britain'.

St Oswald married Cyneburga, daughter of Cynegils, the first Christian king of Wessex; he stood sponsor for him at his baptism. They had one child, a son, Ethelwald, who became king of Deira and was little credit to his father.

When St Oswald had reigned some years war broke out with the pagan Penda of Mercia. Penda again allied himself with the Welsh and the struggle lasted until a decisive battle was fought at Maserfield (probably Oswestry in Shropshire). St Oswald met him with an inferior force, and was killed in the battle. When he saw himself surrounded with his enemies, he offered his last prayer for the souls of his soldiers, and it became a proverb: 'O God, be merciful to their souls, as said Oswald when he fell.' He was slain in the thirty-eighth year of his age, on August 5, 642.

10 : ST LAURENCE, MARTYR (A.D. 258)

THE Emperor Valerian in 257 published his edicts against Christians and Pope St Sixtus, the second of that name, was apprehended the year following and put to death; on the fourth day after the faithful deacon Laurence followed him to martyrdom. That is all that is known for certain of the life and death of St Laurence, but Christian peity has adopted and consecrated as its own the details supplied by St Ambrose, the poet Prudentius, and others. According to these traditions, as Pope St Sixtus was led to execution, his deacon Laurence followed him weeping, and said to him, 'Father, where are you going without your deacon?' The pope answered, 'I do not leave you, my son. You shall follow me in three days.'

During this interval Laurence went all over the city, seeking out the poor who were supported by the Church. On the third day he gathered together a great number of them, then he went to the prefect and invited him to come and see the treasure of the Church. The prefect, astonished to see such an assembly of misery and misfortune, turned to the deacon with threatening looks, asked him what all this meant, and where the treasures were which he had promised to show him. St Laurence answered, 'What are you displeased at? These *are* the treasure of the Church.' The prefect's anger was redoubled, then he had a great gridiron made ready, and glowing coals put under it, that the martyr might be slowly burnt. Laurence was stripped and bound upon this iron bed over the slow fire, which roasted his flesh by little and little. Having suffered a long time, he turned to the judge and said with a cheerful smile, 'Let my body be turned; one side is broiled enough'. When the executioner had turned him, he said, 'It is cooked enough, you may eat'. Then, having prayed for the conversion of the city of Rome that the faith of Christ might spread thence throughout the world, St Laurence gave up the ghost.

He has been one of the most venerated martyrs of the Roman church since the fourth century. He was certainly buried in the cemetery of Cyriaca *in agro Verano* on the Via Tiburtina, where Constantine built the first chapel on the site of what is now the church of St Laurence-outside-the-Walls, the fifth patriarchal basilica of the city.

11 : ST CLARE, VIRGIN, FOUNDRESS OF THE POOR CLARES OR MINORESSES (A.D. 1253)

CLARE was born about the year 1193. Her mother was Ortolana di Fiumi and her father Faverone Offreduccio, and she had a younger sister, Agnes, and another, Beatrice, but of her childhood, adolescence and home-life there are no certain facts. When she was eighteen St Francis came to preach the Lenten sermons at the church of San Giorgio in Assisi; his words fired her, she sought him out secretly, and he strengthened her nascent desire to leave all things for Christ. On Palm Sunday in the year 1212 Clare attended at the cathedral of Assisi for the blessing of palms; when all the rest went up to the altar-rails to receive their branch of olive a sudden shyness kept her in her place, which the bishop seeing, he went from the altar down to her and gave her the branch. In the evening she ran away from home and went a mile out of the town to the Portiuncula, where St Francis lived with his little community. He and his brethren met her at the door of the chapel of our Lady of the Angels with lighted tapers in their hands, and before the altar she put off her fine clothes, and St Francis cut off her hair, and gave her his penitential habit, which was a tunic of sackcloth tied about her with a cord. The holy father not having yet any nunnery of his own, placed her for the present in the Benedictine convent of St Paul near Bastia, where she was affectionately received.

No sooner was her action made public but her friends and relations came in a body to draw her out of her retreat. St Francis soon after removed her to another nunnery, that of Sant' Angelo di Panzo. There her sister Agnes joined her, which drew on them both a fresh persecution. Agnes's constancy proved at last victorious, and St Francis gave her also the habit, though she was only fifteen years of age. Eventually St Francis placed them in a poor house continguous to the church of San Damiano, on the outskirts of Assisi, and appointed Clare the superior. She was later joined by her mother and others, among whom three were of the illustrious family of the Ubaldini in Florence.

St Clare saw founded within a few years monasteries of her nuns at several places in Italy, France and Germany. Bd Agnes, daughter to the King of Bohemia, founded a nunnery of the order in Prague, in which she took the habit. St Clare and her community had neither stockings, shoes, sandals nor any other covering on their feet; they slept on the ground, observed perpetual abstinence from meat, and never spoke but when they were obliged by necessity and charity. St Francis wished that his order should never possess any rents or other property even in common, subsisting on daily contributions, and St Clare possessed this spirit in perfection. Pope Gregory IX desired to mitigate this part of her rule, and offered to settle a yearly revenue on the Poor Ladies of San Damiano; but she persuaded him to leave her order in its first rigorous establishment. Gregory accordingly granted in 1228 the *Privilegium paupertatis*, that they might not be constrained by anyone to accept possessions. The convents of Perugia and

AUGUST

Florence also received this privilege, but others thought it more prudent to accept a mitigation. After the death of Gregory IX (who as Cardinal Ugolino had drawn up the first written rule for the Poor Ladies of San Damiano), Innocent IV in 1247 published another recension of the rule which in some respects brought it nearer to Franciscan than to Benedictine observance, but which permitted the holding of property in common; he wrote that he did not wish to force this rule on any community unwilling to accept it. St Clare was unwilling, and she set to work to draw up a rule which should unequivocally provide that the sisters possess no property, either as individuals or as a community. It was not until two days before she died that this rule was approved for the convent of San Damiano by Pope Innocent IV.

From the time when she was appointed abbess, much against her will, by St Francis in 1215, St Clare governed the convent for forty years. Thomas of Celano, who often heard St Francis warning his followers to avoid any injudicious association with the Poor Ladies, states categorically that St Clare never left the walls of San Damiano. Unhappily even during her life, and for long after her death at intervals, there was disagreement between the Poor Clares and the Friars Minor as to the relations of the two orders: the observant Clares maintaining that the friars were under obligation to serve them in things both spiritual and temporal.

St Clare bore years of sickness with sublime patience, and at last in 1253 the long-drawn-out agony began. Twice during its course she was visited by Pope Innocent IV, who gave her absolution. She died the day after the feast of St Laurence, the forty-second year after her religious profession, and the sixtieth of her age. She was buried on the day following, on which the Church keeps her festival. Pope Alexander IV canonized her at Anagni in 1255.

12 : SS. PORCARIUS, AND HIS COMPANIONS, MARTYRS (c. A.D. 732)

AT the beginning of the fifth century the great abbey of Lérins was founded on an island off the coast of Provence now known after the founder as Saint-Honorat, opposite Cannes. By the eighth century the community numbered over five hundred monks, novices, *alumni* and familiars, and about the year 732 the head of this great body, Abbot Porcarius, was warned by an angel that they were threatened by a descent of barbarians from the sea. The medieval account calls these marauders Saracens, that is, probably Moors from Spain or North Africa. Porcarius at once sent off to a place of safety all for whom there was room on ship-board, namely, the *alumni* or boys being educated in the monastery, and thirty-six of the younger religious, and gathered together the remainder of his community and prepared them for death, exhorting them to suffer bravely for the faith of Christ. The pirates landed, broke into the abbey, and slaughtered every one of its inmates with the exception of four, whom they carried off as slaves. St Porcarius and his monks are mentioned in the Roman Martyrology and their feast is kept in the diocese of Fréjus, but the story is not wanting in difficulties.

13 : ST MAXIMUS THE CONFESSOR, ABBOT (A.D. 662)

MAXIMUS was born about the year 580 and belonged to Constantinople; when he grew up he was placed at the imperial court and became the principal secretary of the Emperor Heraclius. But after a time he resigned this post and became a monk at Chrysopolis (now known as Scutari); there he was elected abbot and wrote some of his mystical treatises. On the death in 638 of St Sophronius, Patriarch of Jerusalem, who had been a hermit and whom Maximus calls his master, father and teacher, Maximus took his place as the champion of orthodoxy against the Monothelitism (the attribution of only one, a divine, will to our Lord) of the Emperor Heraclius and his successor Constans II. He defended the memory of Pope Honorius from the charge of having held that heresy, and condemned Pyrrhus, who had been exiled from the see of Constantinople.

In 645 Gregory, the governor of the African province and a friend of Maximus, arranged a public disputation between the saint and Pyrrhus, as the result of which Pyrrhus went to Rome to abjure his monothelite heresy. Three years later the Emperor Constans II issued a decree in favour of Monothelitism, called the *Typos*, and St Maximus was in Rome at the time of the council summoned by Pope St Martin I at which this document was condemned. In 653 the pope was dragged from Rome by the imperial exarch, banished to the Chersonese, and there bullied and starved to death, the last martyred pope. St Maximus remained in Rome until, having argued against the *Typos* before an imperial legate, he too was seized, being now an old man of seventy-five, and carried off to Constantinople. He was put on trial on a charge of conspiring against the empire and sentenced to banishment at Bizya, in Thrace, where he suffered greatly from cold, hunger and neglect. After some months a commission was sent to interview him, headed by Theodosius, Bishop of Caesarea in Bithynia. Maximus so eloquently demonstrated to them the two natures in Christ that Theodosius was convinced, gave the confessor money and some clothes. St Maximus was then removed to a monastery at Rhegium, and there arrived another deputation, offering him honours from the emperor if he would accept the *Typos*. Maximus remained firm; he was struck and spat upon, his few possessions were taken away from him, and the next day he was taken to Perberis, where his two friends and supporters, Anastasius the Abbot and Anastasius the Apocrisiarius, were already in captivity.

Here they remained in great hardship and distress for six years, and then were brought back to Constantinople to appear before a tribunal. All three were condemned, and with them the memory of St Martin I and St Sophronius, and they were sentenced to be scourged, to be deprived of their tongues and their right hands, thus mutilated to be pilloried in each of the twelve quarters of the city, and to be imprisoned for life. St Maximus survived only a few weeks, after a terrible journey to Skhemaris, near Batum on the Black Sea. This great confessor of the faith and mystical religious writer suffered thus in his eighty-second year.

14 : ST MARCELLUS, BISHOP OF APAMAEA, MARTYR (C. A.D. 389)

IN 380 Theodosius the Great and the co-emperor, Gratian, issued a decree that all their subjects were to profess the faith of the bishops of Rome and Alexandria. Eight years later he sent an officer into Egypt, Syria, and Asia Minor, whose duty it was to enforce an edict that all pagan temples were to be destroyed; this violent policy was carried out very roughly and not unnaturally aroused the anger and resentment of the pagans. When the imperial prefect arrived at Apamaea in Syria he set his soldiers to work to pull down the temple of Zeus there, but it was a large building and well built and the soldiers, being inexpert at systematic demolition, made little progress. The bishop of the place was one Marcellus; he told the prefect to take off his men to their next job and in his absence means would be sought efficiently to destroy the temple. The very next day a navvy came to the bishop and said that, if he would pay him double wages, he could do the work himself. St Marcellus agreed, and the man proceeded to demolish the temple by the simple device of undermining some of the supporting columns, holding up the foundations with timber, and then burning it away.

Marcellus proceeded to have other temples dealt with in this manner, until he went to one in a certain unidentified place; this building was stoutly defended by those who worshipped in it, and the bishop had 'to take up a position some way from the scene of conflict, out of the reach of the arrows, for he suffered from gout and so was not able either to fight or to run away'. But while he was watching from this point of vantage, some of the pagans seized him, and put him to death by throwing him into the flames. The sons of St Marcellus (he had been married) afterwards wanted to take vengeance on his murderers, but the council of the province forbade them, saying they should rather rejoice that God had accounted their father worthy to die in His cause.

15 : THE BLESSED VIRGIN MARY, ON THE FEAST OF HER ASSUMPTION INTO HEAVEN (FIRST CENTURY)

MARY is the mother of Jesus, Jesus is God, therefore she is the Mother of God; the denial of this was condemned by the third general council at Ephesus in 431. Both before and after her miraculous child-bearing she was a virgin and so remained all her days, according to the unanimous and perpetual tradition and teaching of the Church. That she remained for her whole life absolutely sinless is affirmed by the Council of Trent. As the 'second Eve' Mary is the spiritual mother of all living, and veneration is due to her with an honour above that accorded to all other saints; but to give divine worship to her would be idolatry, for Mary is a creature, like the rest of human-kind, and all her dignity comes from God.

It has been for ages the explicit belief of the Church that the body of the Blessed Virgin was preserved from corruption and taken into Heaven and re-united to her soul, by an unique anticipation of the general resurrection. This preservation from corruption and assumption to glory was a privilege which seems due to that body which was never defiled by sin. Whether or

249

not our Lady died is not certain; but it is generally held that she did in fact die before her glorious assumption, some conjecture at Ephesus but others think rather at Jerusalem. But did this feast commemorate only the assumption of her soul, and not of her body as well, its object would still be the same. For, as we honour the departure of other saints out of this world, so we have great reason to rejoice and praise God on this day when the Mother of Christ entered into the possession of those joys which He had prepared for her.

At the time that Alban Butler wrote, belief in our Lady's bodily assumption to Heaven was still, in the words of Pope Benedict XIV, a probable opinion the denial of which would be impious and blasphemous; and so it remained for another two hundred years. Then, in 1950, after taking counsel with the whole Church through her bishops, Pope Pius XII solemnly declared this doctrine to be divinely revealed and an article of faith. In the bull *Munificentissimus Deus* he declared that:

he remarkable unanimity of the Catholic episcopacy and faithful in the matter of the definibility of our Lady's bodily assumption into Heaven as a dogma of faith showed us that the ordinary teaching authority of the Church and the belief of the faithful which it sustains and directs were in accord, and thereby proved with infallible certainty that that privilege is a truth revealed by God and is contained in the divine deposit which Christ entrusted to His bride the Church, to be guarded faithfully and declared with infallible certainty.

And on November 1, the feast of All Saints, the pope promulgated the bull publicly in the square before St Peter's basilica at Rome, defining the doctrine in the following terms:

Having repeatedly raised prayers of urgent supplication to God and having called upon the light of the Spirit of Truth—to the glory of Almighty God, who has bestowed His signal favours on Mary; in honour of His Son, deathless King of all the ages and conqueror of sin and death; to the increase of the glory of the same exalted Mother: and to the joy and exultation of the whole Church: By the authority of our Lord Jesus Christ, by that of the blessed apostles Peter and Paul, and by our own authority, We pronounce, declare and define to be divinely revealed the dogma that the immaculate Mother of God, the Ever-virgin Mary, was on the completion of her earthly life assumed body and soul into the glory of Heaven.

To discuss in brief space the introduction and development of our Lady's Assumption feast would not be easy. Three points seem clear. First that the building of churches in veneration of Mary, the *Theotokos*, Mother of God, inevitably brought in its train the celebration of some sort of dedication feast. That such churches dedicated to our Lady existed both in Ephesus and at Rome in the first half of the fifth century is certain, and some scholars think it probable that 'a commemoration of the ever-virgin Mary, Mother of God' was known at Antioch as early as A.D. 370. Secondly, in such a commemoration or annual feast of the Blessed Virgin no stress was at first laid upon the manner of her departure from this world. In her case, as in the case of the martyrs and other saints, it was simply the heavenly 'birthday' (*natalis*) which was originally honoured, and the festival was spoken of indifferently either as the 'birthday' or the 'falling-asleep' (*dormitio*), the 'passing away' (*transitus*), the 'deposition', or the 'assumption'. Thirdly, according to an apocryphal but ancient belief, the Blessed Virgin actually died on the anniversary of her Son's birth, *i.e.* on Christmas day. As this day was consecrated to the veneration of the Son, any distinctive commemoration of the Mother had to be postponed. In some parts of the world this separate feast was assigned to the winter season. Thus we know from St Gregory of Tours (*c*. 580) that a great feast in Mary's honour was then kept in Gaul in the middle of January. But it is equally certain that in Syria there was a summer feast on the fifth day of the month Ab, roughly August. This, with some fluctuations, was also adopted in the West, and in England St Aldhelm (*c*. 690) speaks plainly of our Lady's 'birthday' being kept in the middle of August.

16 : ST STEPHEN OF HUNGARY, (A.D. 1038)

GEZA, duke of the Magyars, saw the political necessity of Christianity to Hungary and (encouraged by St Adalbert of Prague) he was baptized and a number of his nobles followed his example. But it was largely a conversion of expediency, and the Christianity of the converts was largely nominal. An exception to this was Geza's son, Vaik, who had been baptized at the same time as his father and been given the name of Stephen (Istvan); he was then only about ten. In the year 995, when he was twenty, he married Gisela, sister of Henry, Duke of Bavaria, better known as the Emperor St Henry II, and two years later he succeeded his father as governor of the Magyars.

Stephen was soon engaged in wars with rival tribal leaders and others; and when he had consolidated his position he sent St Astrik, whom he designed to be the first archbishop, to Rome to obtain Pope Silvester II's approval for a proper ecclesiastical organization for his country; and at the same time to ask his Holiness to confer upon him the title of king. Silvester was disposed to grant his request, and prepared a royal crown to send him with his blessing, acting no doubt in concert with political representations from the Emperor Otto III who was then in Rome. At the same time the pope confirmed the religious foundations which the prince had made and the elections of bishops. St Stephen went to meet his ambassador upon his return and listened, standing with great respect, to the pope's bulls whilst they were read. The same prelate who had brought the crown from Rome crowned him king with great solemnity in the year 1001.

King Stephen established episcopal sees only gradually, as Magyar clergy became available; Vesprem is the first of which there is reliable record, but within some years Esztergom was founded and became the primatial see. At Szekesfehervar he built a church in honour of the Mother of God, in which the kings of Hungary were afterwards both crowned and buried; This city St Stephen made his usual residence. He also completed the foundation of the great monastery of St Martin, begun by his father.

For the support of the churches and their pastors and the relief of the poor throughout his dominions he commanded tithes to be paid. Every tenth town had to build a church and support a priest; the king himself furnished the churches. He abolished customs derived from the former religion and repressed blasphemy, murder, theft, adultery and other public crimes. He commanded all persons to marry except religious and church-men, and forbade all marriages of Christians with idolators.

The example of his virtue was a most powerful sermon to those who came under his influence, and it was exemplified in his son, Bd Emeric, to whom St Stephen's code of laws was inscribed. These laws he caused to be promulgated throughout his dominions, and they were well suited to a fierce and rough people newly converted to Christianity. He abolished tribal divisions and divided the land into 'counties', with a system of governors and magistrates. Thus, and by means of a limited application of feudal ideas, making the nobles vassals of the crown, he welded the Magyars into a unity; and by retaining direct control over the common people he prevented undue accumulation of power into the hands of the lords. St Stephen was indeed the founder and architect of the independent realm of Hungary.

As the years passed, Stephen wanted to entrust a greater part in the government to his only son, but in 1031 Emeric was killed while hunting. The death of Emeric left him without an heir and the last years of his life were embittered by family disputes about the succession, with which he had to cope while suffering continually from painful illness. He eventually died, aged sixty-three, on the feast of the Assumption 1038, and was buried beside Bd Emeric at Szekesfehervar.

17 : ST CLARE OF MONTEFALCO, VIRGIN (A.D. 1308)

The community of pious young women, living penitentially in hermit-ages under the direction of her sister Joan, to which Clare belonged for fifteen years, consisted of secular tertiaries of St Francis: but when they wished to adopt a regular conventual life the bishop of Spoleto gave them the Augustinian rule. Their convent, of the Holy Cross, was erected in 1290 and, her sister dying, St Clare much against her will was elected abbess. A number of miracles were attributed to her, frequent ecstasies, and super-natural gifts, which she utilized for the good of those outside her convent as well as those within. St Clare had a very great devotion to the passion of our Lord. She once said to a sister, 'If you seek the cross of Christ, take my heart; there you will find the suffering Lord'. These words were taken literally, and when her heart was examined after death in 1308 an image of the cross was said to have been found imprinted on it.

Apart from her faithful observance and the austerity of her penance, St Clare is alleged to have been honoured by three divine favours of exceptional interest. First, the marvellous incorruption of her remains. Secondly, the cross and other instruments of the Passion formed solidly within her heart in some fibrous tissue, just referred to. Thirdly, the alleged liquefaction and ebullition of her blood. St Clare of Montefalco was canonized in 1881.

18 : ST HELEN, WIDOW (c. A.D. 330)

S T HELEN was born, so far as can be ascertained, at Drepanum in Bithynia, perhaps the daughter of an inn-keeper. Somewhere about 270 the Roman general Constantius Chlorus met her there and, in spite of her humble birth, married her; but when he was made *caesar*, he was persuaded to divorce her and marry Theodora, the stepdaughter of the Emperor Maximian. Some years earlier Helen had given birth at Naissus (Nish in Serbia) to Constantine the Great, who had a deep regard and affection for his mother, and afterwards conferred on her the title of 'Nobilissima Femina', changing the name of her birth-place to Helenopolis.

Constantius Chlorus lived for fourteen years after the repudiation of St Helen, and when he died in 306 their son Constantine was proclaimed *caesar* by his troops at York, and eighteen months later emperor. He entered Rome after the battle of the Milvian Bridge on October 28, 312, and by the Edict of Milan early in the following year Christianity was tolerated throughout the empire. It appears from Eusebius that St Helen was converted only at this time, when she was about sixty-three years old. She made use of the treasures of the empire in liberal alms, and was the mother of the indigent and distressed. She built numerous churches, and when after his victory over Licinius in 324 Constantine became master of the East, the noble lady went to Palestine to venerate the places made sacred by the bodily presence of our Lord.

After Golgotha and the holy sepulchre had been laid bare by the removal of the terrace and temple of Venus with which the Emperor Hadrian had over-built them, Constantine wrote to St Macarius, Bishop of Jerusalem, ordering a church to be built. St Helen, then fourscore years of age, took the charge on herself to see this work executed, desiring at the same time to discover the sacred cross on which our Redeemer died. The finding of three crosses in a rock-cistern just to the east of Calvary is celebrated on May 3.

Whether or not she actually took an active part in the finding of the cross, it is beyond dispute that Helen's last days were spent in Palestine. Eusebius, reports that she built two basilicas, the *Eleona* on the Mount of Olives and one at Bethlehem. The latest coins which, by order of her son, bore her name, Flavia Julia Helena, were minted in 330, which presumably was the year of her death. This occurred apparently somewhere in the East, and her body was taken to Rome.

19 : ST JOHN EUDES, FOUNDER OF THE CONGREGATIONS OF JESUS AND MARY AND OF OUR LADY OF CHARITY OF THE REFUGE (A.D. 1680)

I N the second half of the sixteenth century there lived at Ri, in Normandy, a certain Isaac Eudes. He was a yeoman farmer, and he married Martha Corbin; when after two years they had no children the couple made a pilgrimage to a neighbouring shrine of our Lady, and nine months later a boy was born to them; subsequently they had five more children. The first-born was baptized John, and when he was fourteen he was sent by his parents to the Jesuit college at Caen. They wished him to marry and carry on his father's estate; but John had taken a private vow of celibacy and in 1621 he received minor orders and returned to Caen to study theology, with the idea of enrolling himself among the parochial clergy. But he decided to offer himself to the Congregation of the Oratory of France, which had been founded in 1611 by M. (afterwards Cardinal) Pierre de Bérulle, and was accepted by the superior general at Paris early in 1623. He made so great an impression upon Bérulle that he permitted him to preach while yet in minor orders. After a year at Paris John Eudes was sent to Aubervilliers to be under the instruction of Charles de Condren.

Two years later a virulent epidemic of plague broke out in Normandy and St John volunteered to go and work among the sufferers of his own countryside. Father Eudes spent two months ministering spiritually and medically to the sick, dying and endangered. He was then sent to the Oratory of Caen, where he remained quietly till a visitation of plague to that city in 1631 called him out again; during that time, in order to avoid the danger of infecting his brethren, he lived in a large cask in the middle of a field, receiving his food daily from a nearby convent. For the following ten years St John was chiefly engaged in giving missions and incidentally gaining much experience for the work which he was afterwards to undertake.

Among the matters that troubled St John during the course of his mission was the difficult position of women and girls who were reclaimed by God's grace from a disorderly life. For a time he tried to deal with the problem by finding for these penitents temporary homes with religious people, but this arrangement was soon seen to be inadequate. A certain woman of humble origin, Madeleine Lamy, who had taken charge of several of these girls, strongly realized the unsatisfactoriness of the position and wanted St John to make some more permanent provision. In 1641 a house was rented as a refuge for penitent women until honest work could be found for them. But he soon saw that it was necessary for the work to be in the hands of a religious congregation and offered it to the Visitandines of Caen, who accepted it.

In 1643 Father Eudes, after much prayer, consideration and consultation with his superiors and high ecclesiastics, severed his connection with the Oratorians. He had learnt in the course of his missions that the clergy needed reform even more than their flocks, and became convinced that the first necessity was to establish seminaries, and that until this was done the Congregation of the Oratory could not hope to have its full effect. His views were shared by Father de Condren, who had become superior general, but his successor Father Bourgoing would not countenance the plan of a seminary in connection with the Oratory of Caen. Father Eudes then formed the project of a new congregation of secular priests whose object should be the formation of a zealous and virtuous parochial clergy by the conduct of seminaries, and such a congregation was founded at Caen on the feast of the Annunciation, 1643. It was called the Congregation of Jesus and Mary and was modelled on that of the Oratory, consisting of secular priests who were not bound by vows; the first members were St John Eudes and five others, and they were consecrated to 'the Most Holy Trinity as the first principle and last end of priestly dignity and holiness'. The badge by which they were to be distinguished was the hearts of Jesus and Mary regarded as mystically one, symbolizing the eternal love of Jesus. The new venture met with immediate criticism and opposition, particularly from the Jansenists and from the French Oratorians; and when in 1646 Father Eudes sent Father Maunoury to Rome to try and get papal approval for his foundation the opposition was so strong that he was unsuccessful.

In 1650 the bishop of Courtances invited St John to set up a seminary in that city and in the following year he was invited by M. Olier to give a ten weeks' mission at the parish-church of Saint-Sulpice in Paris. During the course of it news was brought that the sisters at the refuge in Caen, having separated from the Visitandines, were recognized by the bishop of Bayeux as a separate congregation, under the name of the Sisters of Our Lady of Charity of the Refuge. St John founded a seminary at Lisieux in 1653 and another at Rouen in 1659, and he then went to Rome, where he made personal representations for the formal approbation of his work; but even saints do not do everything properly and herein Father Eudes failed, in part through his own disregard for prudence and tact. But a year after his return, in 1666, the Refuge sisters by a bull of Pope Alexander VII were erected as a recognized institute to labour for the reclamation of unchaste women and to care for penitents from among them. This work begun by Father Eudes and the devoted Madeleine Lamy had then been going on for thirty years. St John continued to give long and successful missions and founded two more seminaries, at Evreux in 1666 and at Rennes in 1670.

In the latter year he published a book entitled *The Devotion to the Adorable Heart of Jesus*; he had already given a feast of the Holy Heart of Mary to his congregation, and in this book was included a proper Mass and Office of the Sacred Heart of Jesus. On August 31, 1670, this feast was first observed in the seminary chapel at Rennes, and other dioceses took it up. In 1674, the year before St Margaret Mary's 'great revelation', Pope Clement X issued six briefs of indulgences for the confraternities of the Hearts of Jesus and Mary erected in Eudist seminaries.

During the last years of his life St John spent much time on his treatise *The Admirable Heart of the Most Holy Mother of God*, at which he had been working for many years and which he finished less than a month before his death. His last mission had been at Saint-Lô in 1675, where in the wintry weather he had preached in the open *palce* nearly every day for nine weeks; from this ordeal the old man never properly recovered and his days of active work were practically ended. He died on August 19, 1680, was canonized in 1925, and in 1928 his feast was added to the general calendar of the Western church.

20 : ST BERNARD, ABBOT OF CLAIRVAUX, DOCTOR OF THE CHURCH (A.D. 1153)

ST BERNARD was the third son of Tescelin Sorrel, a Burgundian noble, and Aleth, who was daughter of Bernard, lord of Montbard. He was born in 1090 at Fontaines, a castle near Dijon, a lordship belonging to his father. His parents had seven children, namely, Bd Guy, Bd Gerard, St Bernard, Bd Humbeline, Andrew, Bartholomew and Bd Nivard. They were all well educated, and learned Latin and verse-making before the sons were applied to military exercise and feats of arms; but Bernard was sent to Châtillon on the Seine, to pursue a complete course of studies in a college of secular canons.

Bernard made his appearance in the world with all the advantages and talents which can make it attractive to a young man, but he presently began to think of forsaking the world and the pursuit of letters and of going to Cîteaux, where only a few years before SS. Robert, Alberic and Stephen Harding had established the first monastery of that strict interpretation of the Benedictine rule, called after it 'Cistercian'. His friends endeavoured to dissuade him from it; but he not only remained firm-he enlisted four of his brothers as well, and an uncle. Hugh of Mâcon (who afterward founded the monastery of Pontigny, and died bishop of Auxerre), an intimate friend, wept bitterly at the thought of separation, but by two interviews was induced to become his companion. Nor were these the only ones who, with apparently no previous thought of the religious life, suddenly decided to leave the world for the austere life of Cîteaux. Bernard induced in all thirty-one men to follow him-he who himself had been uncertain of his call only a few weeks before.

They assembled at Châtillon, and the company arrived at Cîteaux about Easter in 1112. The abbot, the English St Stephen, who had not had a novice for several years, received them with open arms. St Bernard was then twenty-two years old. After three years the abbot, seeing the great progress which Bernard had made and his extraordinary abilities, ordered him to go with twelve monks to found a new house in the diocese of Langres in Champagne. They walked in procession, singing psalms, with their new abbot at their head, and settled in a place called the Valley of Wormwood, surrounded by a forest. These thirteen monks grubbed up a sufficient area and, with the assistance of the bishop and the people of the country, built themselves a house. This young colony lived through a period of extreme and grinding hardship. The land was poor and their bread was of coarse barley; boiled beech leaves were sometimes served up instead of vegetables. Bernard at first was so severe in his discipline, coming down upon the smallest distractions and least transgressions of his brethren, whether in confession or in chapter, that although his monks behaved with the utmost humility and obedience they began to be discouraged, which made the abbot sensible of his fault. He condemned himself for it to a long silence. At length he resumed his preaching, and provided that meals should be more regular, though the food was still of the coarsest. The reputation of the house and of the holiness of its abbot soon became so great that the number of monks had risen to a hundred and thirty; and the name of the valley was changed to Clairvaux, because it was situated right in the eye of the sun. Bernard's aged father Tescelin and the young Nivard followed him in 1117, and received the habit at his hands. The first four daughter-houses of Cîteaux became each a mother-house to others, and Clairvaux had the most numerous offspring, including Rievaulx and, in a sense, Fountains in England.

Notwithstanding St Bernard's love of retirement, obedience and the Church's needs frequently drew him from his cell. So great was the reputation of his character and powers that princes desired to have their differences determined by him and bishops regarded his decisions with the greatest respect, referring to him important affairs of their churches. The popes looked upon his advice as the greatest support of the Holy See.

After the disputed papal election of 1130 the cause of Pope Innocent II took St Bernard up and down France, Germany and Italy. On one of his returns to Clairvaux he took with him a new postulant, a canon of Pisa, Peter Bernard Paganelli, who was to become a beatified pope as Eugenius III; for the present he was put to stoke the fire in the monastery calefactory. After the general acknowledgement of Innocent II Bernard was present at the tenth general council in Rome, the second of the Lateran, and it was at this pe.iod that he first met St Malachy of Armagh; the ensuing friendship between the two lasted until Malachy's death in Bernard's arms nine years later. All this time Bernard had continued diligently to preach to his monks whenever he was able, notably those famous discourses on the Song of Songs. In 1140 he preached for the first time in a public pulpit, primarily to the students of Paris.

Probably about the beginning of the year 1142 the first Cistercian foundation was made in Ireland, from Clairvaux, where St Malachy had put some young Irishmen with St Bernard to be trained. The abbey was called Mellifont, in county Louth, and within ten years of its foundation six daughter-houses had been planted out. At the same time Bernard was busied in the affair of the disputed succession to the see of York, set out in the account of St William of York (June 8), in the course of which Pope Innocent II died. His third successor, within eighteen months, was the Cistercian abbot of Tre Fontane, that Peter Bernard of Pisa to whom reference has been made, known to history as Bd Eugenius III.

In the meantime the Albigensian heresy and its social and moral implications had been making alarming progress in the south of France. St Bernard had already been called on to deal with a similar sect in Cologne, and in 1145 the papal legate Cardinal Alberic, asked him to go to Languedoc. Bernard was ill and weak and hardly able to make the journey, but he obeyed. He preached against the heresy throughout Languedoc; its supporters were stubborn and violent, especially at Toulouse and Albi, but in a very short time he had restored the country to orthodoxy and returned to Clairvaux. But he left too soon, the restoration was more apparent than real, and twenty-five years later Albigensianism had a stronger hold than ever. Then came St Dominic.

On Christmas-day, 1144, the Seljuk Turks had captured Edessa, centre of one of the four principalities of the Latin kingdom of Jerusalem, and appeals for help were at once sent to Europe, for the whole position was in danger. Pope Eugenius commissioned St Bernard to preach a crusade. He began at Vézelay on Palm Sunday 1146, when Queen Eleanor and many nobles were the first to take the cross, and were followed by such large numbers of people, moved by the monk's burning words, that the supply of badges was exhausted and he had to tear strips from his habit to make others. When he had roused France, he wrote letters to the rulers and peoples of western and central Europe, and then went in person into Germany. The Emperor Conrad III took the cross from him, and set out with an army in the May of

1147, followed by Louis of France. But this, the second, crusade was a miserable failure; Conrad's forces were cut to pieces in Asia Minor and Louis did not get beyond laying siege to Damascus.

Early in the year 1153 St Bernard entered on his last illness. For a time he mended a little in the spring, and was called on for the last time to leave Clairvaux.

The inhabitants of Metz having been attacked by the duke of Lorraine, they were vehemently bent on revenge. To prevent the shedding of more blood the archbishop of Trier went to Clairvaux, and implored Bernard to journey to Metz in order to reconcile the parties that were at variance. At this call of charity he forgot his infirmity and made his way into Lorraine, where he prevailed on both sides to lay aside their arms and accept a treaty which he drew up.

God took him to Himself, on August 20, 1153; he was sixty-three years old, had been abbot for about thirty-eight, and sixty-eight monasteries had been founded from Clairvaux—Bernard may indeed be counted among the founders of the Cistercian Order, who brought it out of obscurity into the centre of western Christendom. He was canonized in 1174, and in 1830 formally declared a doctor of the Church: *Doctor mellifluus*, the Honey-sweet Doctor,'as he is now universally called.

21 : ST PIUS X, POPE (A.D. 1914)

THAT distinguished historian of earlier popes, Baron von Pastor, has written of Pope Pius X: 'He was one of those chosen few men whose personality is irresistible. Everyone was moved by his simplicity and his angelic kindness. Yet it was something more that carried him into all hearts: and that "something" is best defined by saying that all who were ever admitted to his presence had a deep conviction of being face to face with a saint. And the more one knows about him the stronger this conviction becomes'.

Pius X was born in 1835, son of the municipal messenger and postman of the big village of Riese in Venetia, and was then known as Giuseppe Sarto; he was the second of ten children, and the circumstances of the family were very poor. Young Joseph went to the local elementary school, from thence, through the encouragement of his parish priest, to the 'grammar school' at Castelfranco, and then by bursary to the seminary at Padua. He was ordained priest at the age of twentyewnt-three, and for seventeen years gave himself wholeheartedly to the pastoral ministry; then he became a canon of Treviso, and in 1884 bishop of Mantua. In 1892 Pope Leo XIII appointed Mgr Sarto cardinal-priest and promoted him to the metropolitan see of Venice, which carries with it the honorary title of patriarch.

On the death of Leo XIII in 1903 it was generally believed that Cardinal Rampolla del Tindaro would succeed him, and the first three ballots of the conclave so far bore this out that Cardinal Puzyna, Archbishop of Cracow, communicated to the electors the formal veto against Rampolla of the Emperor Francis Joseph of Austria. There was a profound sensation, and the cardinals solemnly protested against the interference: but Rampolla withdrew his candidature with great dignity, and after four more ballots Cardinal Sarto was elected.

One of the new pope's earliest acts, by the constitution 'Commissum nobis', was to put an end once and for all to any right of the civil power to interfere in a papal election, by veto or in any other way. His way of dealing with the most critical situation that soon arose in France was more direct and not less effective than ordinary diplomatic methods. After a number of incidents, the French government in 1905 denounced the concordat of 1801, decreed the separation of church and state, and entered on a campaign against the Church. For dealing with ecclesiastical property it proposed an organization called *associations cultuelles*, to which many prominent French Catholics wanted to give a trial; but, Pope Pius in two strong and dignified pronouncements condemned the law of separation and forbade the *associations*.

The name of Pius X is associated with the purging of the Church of Modernism. A decree of the Holy Office in 1907 condemned certain writers and propositions, and it was soon followed by the encyclical letter 'Pascendi dominici gregis', wherein the dangerous tendencies were set out, examined, and condemned. Strong disciplinary measures were also taken.

In his first encyclical letter Pius X had announced his aim to be to 'renew all things in Christ', and nothing was better calculated to do that than his decrees concerning the sacrament of the Eucharist. These formally recommended daily communion when possible, directed that children should be allowed to approach the altar upon attaining the use of reason, and facilitated the communion of the sick. He also strongly urged daily reading of the Bible—but here the pope's words did not receive so much heed. In 1903 he issued an instruction on church music which struck at current abuses and aimed at the restoration of congregational singing of the Roman plainchant. He encouraged the work of the commission for the codifying of canon law, and was responsible for a thorough reorganization of the tribunals, offices and congregations of the Holy See. Pius also set up a commission for the revision and correction of the Vulgate text of the Bible, and in 1909 founded the Biblical Institute for scriptural studies in charge of the Society of Jesus.

On June 24, 1914, the Holy See signed a concordat with Serbia; four days later the Archduke Franz Ferdinand and his wife were assassinated at Sarajevo; by the midnight of August 4 Germany, France, Austria, Russia, Great Britain, Serbia, Belgium were at war: it was the eleventh anniversary of the pope's election. The outbreak of the war killed him. After a few days' illness he developed bronchitis on August 19: next day he was dead.

The pontificate of Pius X had not been a quiet one, and the pope had been resolute in his policies. If he had no enemies he had many critics, inside the Church as well as outside. But now the voice was unanimous. In 1923 the cardinals in curia decreed that his cause be introduced, and in 1954 Pope Pius XII solemnly canonized his predecessor before a vast multitude in St Peter's Square at Rome—the first canonized pope since Pius V in 1672.

22 : ST SIGFRID, ABBOT OF WEARMOUTH (A.D. 690)

WHILE St Benedict Biscop was away on his fifth visit to Rome his coadjutor abbot at Wearmouth, St Esterwine, died, and the monks, together with St Ceolfrid, coadjutor abbot of Jarrow, elected in his place the deacon Sigfrid.

On Sigfrid's promotion and St Benedict's return to his monasteries both saints were stricken with sickness and had to take to their beds; they knew that death was upon them and wished for a last conference about one another's welfare and that of their monks. Sigfrid therefore was carried on a stretcher to Benedict's cell and laid on his bed, but they were too weak even to embrace one another unaided. After consultation with Sigfrid, Benedict sent to Ceolfrid and, with the approval of all, appointed him abbot of both monasteries, that so peace, unity and concord might be preserved. Two months later St Sigfrid died. He was buried in the abbey-church of St Peter beside his master, St Benedict, and his predecessor, St Esterwine.

23 : ST ROSE OF LIMA, VIRGIN (A.D. 1617)

SHE was of Spanish extraction, born at Lima, the capital of Peru, in 1586, her parents, Caspar de Flores and Maria del Oliva, being decent folk of moderate means. She was christened Isabel but was commonly called Rose, and she was confirmed by St Toribio, Archbishop of Lima, in that name only. When she was grown up, she seems to have taken St Catherine of Siena for her model, in spite of the objections and ridicule of her parents and friends. Hearing others frequently commend her beauty, and fearing lest it should be an occasion of temptation to anyone, she used to rub her face with pepper, in order to disfigure her skin with blotches. A woman happening one day to admire the fineness of the skin of her hands and her shapely fingers, she rubbed them with lime, and in consequence was unable to dress herself for a month. By these and other even more surprising austerities she armed herself against external dangers and against the insurgence of her own senses.

Her parents having been reduced to straitened circumstances by an unsuccessful mining venture, Rose by working all day in the garden and late at night with her needle relieved their necessities. These employments were agreeable to her, and she probably would never have entertained any thoughts of a different life if her parents had not tried to induce her to marry. She had to struggle with them over this for ten years, and to strengthen herself in her resolution she took a vow of virginity. Then, having joined the third order of St Dominic, she chose for her dwelling a little hut in the garden, where she became practically a recluse. She wore upon her head a thin circlet of silver, studded on the inside with little sharp prickles, like a crown of thorns.

God favoured St Rose with many great graces, but she also suffered during fifteen years persecution from her friends and others, and the even more severe trial of interior desolation and anguish in her soul. The last three years of her life were spent under the roof of Don Gonzalo de Massa, a government official, and his wife, who was fond of Rose. In their house she was stricken by her last illness, and under long and painful sickness it was her prayer, 'Lord, increase my sufferings, and with them increase thy love in my heart'. She died on August 24, 1617, thirty-one years old. The chapter, senate, and other honourable corporations of the city carried her body by turns to the grave. She was canonized by Pope Clement X in 1671, being the first canonized saint of the New World.

24 : ST AUDOENUS, OR OUEN, BISHOP OF ROUEN (A.D. 684)

ST OUEN (Dado) was born at Sancy, near Soissons, about 600, of a Frankish family, his father being St Authaire. While he and his brother Ado were still children, living at Ussy-sur-Marne, their father entertained the exiled St Columban in his house. The brothers were educated well and when they were of sufficient age were put at the court of King Clotaire II, where Ouen became one of a group of remarkable young men which included St Eligius, St Wandrille and St Didier of Cahors. Ouen was in great favour with the king and with his son and successor, Dagobert I, who made him his referendary or chancellor; in this office Ouen steadily opposed the prevalent simony. He obtained of the king a grant of a piece of land situated in the forest of Brie where, in 636, he erected a monastery, called at present Rebais. By the advice of St Faro, Bishop of Meaux, he sent for Aile, a disciple of St Columban from Luxeuil, and had him appointed the first abbot. St Ouen would have retired himself to Rebais, but Dagobert and his nobles could not be induced to give their consent.

When Dagobert died in 639, Clovis II, his son and successor, testified the same esteem for St Ouen, and kept him in the office of referendary. At length Clovis was prevailed upon to give Ouen leave to receive ordination from Dieudonné, Bishop of Mâcon, and he was shortly after elected bishop of Rouen; at the same time his friend St Eligius was chosen bishop of Noyon. They took a considerable time to prepare themselves for this dignity, by retreat, fasting and prayer, and received the episcopal consecration together at Rheims in 641.

St Ouen in this new office increased his humility, austerities and charities. He encouraged learning by the foundation of monasteries, and sent missionaries to those parts of his diocese that were still pagan; nor did he slacken his efforts for extirpating simony and other abuses. He was a trusted adviser of King Thierry III and upheld the policy of Ebroin, the mayor of the palace, to such a degree that he was, perhaps inculpably, involved in Ebroin's ill-treatment of St Leger and of St Philibert. Returning from a political mission to Cologne, St Ouen went to Clichy, and there fell ill and died, on August 24, 684.

25 : ST LOUIS OF FRANCE, (A.D. 1270)

LOUIS was son of Louis VIII and was eight years old when the death of his grandfather, Philip II Augustus, put his father in possession of the crown of France. He was born at Poissy on April 25, 1214. His mother was Blanche, daughter of Alfonso of Castile and Eleanor of England, and to her care and attention in the education of St Louis we are indebted, under God, for the great example of his virtues.

King Louis VIII died on November 7, 1226, and Queen Blanche was declared regent for her son, who was then only twelve years old. The whole time of the king's minority was disturbed by ambitious barons, but Blanche by several alliances and by her courage and diligence overcame them in the field and forced their submission. Louis was merciful even to rebels, and by his readiness to receive any proposals of agreement gave the proof that he neither sought revenge nor conquests. Never had any man a greater love for the Church, or a greater veneration for its ministers. Yet this was not blind; for he opposed the injustices of bishops.

When he was nineteen Louis IX married Margaret, the eldest daughter of Raymund Berenger, Count of Provence, whose second daughter, Eleanor, was married to Henry III, King of England; his third, Sanchia, to his brother Richard of Cornwall; and Beatrice; the youngest, to Charles, brother to St Louis. The marriage was blessed with a happy union of hearts and eleven children, five sons, six daughters. In 1235, having come of age, St Louis took the government of his kingdom into his own hands. But he continued to show the greatest deference to his mother, and to profit by her c counsel, though Blanche was inclined to be jealous of and unkind to her daughter-in-law. The first of many religious foundations for which Louis was responsible was the abbey of Royaumont. In 1239 Baldwin II, the Latin emperor at Constantinople, made St Louis (in gratitude for his largesse to the Christians in Palestine and other parts of the East) a present of the Crown of Thorns, which was then in the hands of the Venetians as a pledge for a loan of money to Baldwin, which Louis had to discharge. He sent two Dominican friars to bring this treasure to France, and met it himself beyond Sens, attended by his whole court. To house it he pulled down his chapel of St Nicholas and built the *Sainte Chapelle*, which is now empty of its relic. He brought the Carthusians to Paris and endowed them with the palace of Vauvert, and helped his mother in the foundation of the convent of Maubuisson.

Several ordinances of this prince show us how much he applied himself to see justice well administered. In succeeding reigns, whenever complaints were raised among the people, the cry of those dissatisfied was to demand that abuses should be reformed and justice impartially administered as was done in the reign of St Louis. In 1230 he forbade all manner of usury, and restrained the Jews in particular from practising it. He published a law commanding all who should be guilty of blasphemy to be branded, and thus punished a rich and important citizen of Paris; to some who murmured at this severity he said that he would undergo that punishment himself if thus he might put a stop to the crime. He protected vassals from oppressive lords, and when a Flemish count had hanged three children for hunting rabbits in his woods, had him imprisoned and tried, not by his peers as he demanded, but by the ordinary judges, who condemned him to death. He afterwards spared his life, but subjected him to a fine which deprived him of the greater part of his estates. This money the king ordered to be expended on religious and charitable works.

Hugh of Lusignan, Count of La Marche, made trouble soon after the king's majority. Hugh's wife, Isabel, was the widow of King John and mother of Henry III of England, who came over to support his stepfather. St Louis defeated King Henry III (who was never born to be a soldier) at Taillebourg in 1242. Henry fled to Bordeaux and the next year returned to England, having made a truce with the French. Seventeen years later Louis concluded another treaty with Henry III. By it he yielded to England the Limousin and Périgord, King Henry renouncing on his side all pretensions to Normandy, Anjou, Maine, Touraine and Poitou.

After an illness in 1244 Louis determined to undertake a crusade in the East. At the thirteenth general council at Lyons in 1245 all benefices were taxed a twentieth of their income for three years for the relief of the Holy Land (the English representatives strongly protested against this), and this gave encouragement to the crusaders. In 1248 Louis sailed for Cyprus, where he was joined by William Longsword, Earl of Salisbury, and two hundred English knights. The objective was Egypt. Damietta, in the delta of the Nile, was easily taken and St Louis made a solemn entry into the city, not with the pomp of a conqueror but with the humility of a truly Christian prince, walking barefoot with the queen, the princes his brothers and other great lords, preceded by the papal legate.

The crusaders could not follow up their advantage, and it was not till six months had passed that they advanced to attack the Saracens, who were on the other side of the river. Then followed another six months of desultory fighting, in which the crusaders lost many by battle and sickness, until in April 1250 St Louis himself was taken prisoner, and his army routed with frightful slaughter. During his captivity the king recited the Divine Office every day with two chaplains just as if he had been in perfect health in his own palace, and to the insults that were sometimes offered him he opposed an air of majesty and authority which kept his guards in awe. The sultan at that time was overthrown by the Mamluk emirs, and these eventually released the king and the other prisoners.

St Louis then sailed to Palestine with the remainder of his army. There he remained until 1254, visiting all the holy places he could, encouraging the Christians, and strengthening the defences of the Latin Kingdom. Then, news being brought to him of the death of his mother, who was regent in his absence, he returned to France. He had been away almost six years, but he was oppressed by the memory of the distresses of the Christians in the East and he continued to wear the cross on his clothes to show that he intended to return to their assistance. People were not surprised when in 1267 he announced another crusade: nor were they pleased.

The king embarked with his army at Aigues-Mortes on July 1, 1270; when the fleet was over against Cagliari in Sardinia it was resolved to proceed to Tunis, where soon after landing the king himself and his eldest son Philip both sickened with typhus. It was soon seen that Louis was dying. He gave his last instructions to his sons and to his daughter, the queen of Navarre, and composed himself for death. On August 24, which was Sunday, he received the last sacraments, and called for the Greek ambassadors, whom he strongly urged to reunion with the Roman Church. He lost his speech the next day from nine till twelve o'clock; then, recovering it, he repeated aloud the words of the psalmist, 'Lord, I will enter into thine house; I will worship in thy holy temple, and will give glory to thy name'. He spoke again at three in the afternoon, 'Into thy hands I commend my soul', and immediately after breathed his last. His bones and heart were taken back to France and enshrined in the abbey-church of St Denis, whence they were scattered at the Revolution; he was canonized in 1297.

26 : ST ELIZABETH BICHIER DES AGES, VIRGIN, CO-FOUNDRESS OF THE DAUGHTERS OF THE CROSS OR SISTERS OF ST ANDREW (A.D. 1838)

THIS holy woman was born at the Château des Ages, at Le Blanc, between Poitiers and Bourges, in the year 1773. Her father was Antony Bichier, lord of the manor of Ages and a public official, and her mother Mary Augier de Moussac, whose father also held public office. The child was christened Jean Elizabeth Mary Lucy, and was commonly called by her second name. Little is known of her childhood, except that when she was ten she was sent for schooling to a convent at Poitiers. Her maternal uncle, the Abbé de Moussac, was vicar general at Poitiers, and the superioress of the convent was a relative and Elizabeth seems to have been very happy there. Her favourite game was building sandcastles.

When Elizabeth was nineteen her father died, and a few weeks later, in February 1792, the National Assembly issued a decree against the property of those citizens, the *émigrés*, who had left France in face of the revolution. Her eldest brother was among these *émigrés* and, her mother being old and ill, Elizabeth took on herself the job of looking after his interests. She asked the Abbé de Moussac to instruct her in the law of property and in the keeping of accounts, studies which did not come easy to her but which she was to find again useful later on, and she undertook the defence of her brother and the whole family in a long law case that was eventually decided in their favour.

In 1796 she and her mother left the Château des Ages and went to live at La Guimetière, on the outskirts of Béthines in Poitou. The local parish was in a bad way as a result of the revolution, so every night Elizabeth used to collect the farmers and their wives at La Guimetière for prayers and hymns and spiritual reading. And then she first heard of a priest in a parish twenty-five miles away who was grappling with a similar situation, and had reopened his church in a barn. It was the Abbé Fournet at Maillé, now known as St Andrew Fournet (May 13).

Elizabeth made her way to Maillé, and the two at once took to one another. She became a frequent visitor to the barn at Petits Marsillys, and Abbé Fournet devised for her a rule of life, at the same time discouraging her suggestions of joining the Trappistines. And so she went on repairing the ravages of religious discord in Béthines, helped by her uncle and her new friend, visiting the sick and needy, and teaching the smaller children.

St Andrew Fournet had had it in his mind for some time that that part of the country needed a small community of nuns to care for the sick and to teach the girls, especially in the rural districts, and that Miss Bichier should be in charge of it. Her reaction to the proposal was that she had never even been a novice, much less a mother superior; and as this was undeniable St

Andrew sent her off to do a year's novitiate with the Carmelite nuns in Poitiers. But, perhaps because he thought she might never come out again, Abbé Fournet soon transferred her to the Society of Providence. Meanwhile he set about forming a community at La Guimetière, consisting of Madeleine Moreau, Mary Anne Guillon and two other young women, and when she had been away hardly six months Elizabeth Bichier was called back to take charge in spite of her protests. As La Guimetière was so far from Maillé, in May 1806 they moved into the Château de Molante, which was quite close. Here they began to teach the children, to give shelter and care to the aged and sick, and to make reparation for the outrages of the revolution against Christ in the Blessed Sacrament.

At first neither St Andrew nor St Elizabeth had in mind anything more than a small local congregation. The foundation members made temporary vows early in 1807, and then looked around for a suitable established congregation to which they could affiliate themselves. But by the end of 1811 it was clear that they would have to stand on their own feet, and they moved into a bigger house, Rochefort, in Maillé itself, for they already numbered twenty-five sisters. Five years later their rule was approved by the diocesan authorities of Poitiers, with the name of Daughters of the Cross.

During 1819–20 thirteen new convents were opened. The civil authorities were in favour of small convents dotted about the countryside, their inmates working among the people, and between 1821 and 1825 the Daughters of the Cross opened some fifteen houses in a dozen dioceses. Then the bishop of Bayonne invited them to the Midi, and they spread to Béarn, the Basque country, Gascony and Languedoc. Altogether by 1830 they had over sixty convents, and Sister Elizabeth's record of travelling challenged that of St Teresa herself. When the Basque house of Igon was opened, the spiritual director appointed was a young curate named Garicoïts: we now know him as St Michael Garicoïts (May 14).

In the autumn of 1836 St Elizabeth's health began seriously to fail. In the spring of 1838 her condition became alarming: she suffered constant and acute pain, and was subject to fits of delirium. Then, after ten days of agony borne with heroic patience, she died peacefully in the evening of August 26. St Elizabeth Bichier des Ages was canonized in 1947.

27 : ST CAESARIUS, BISHOP OF ARLES (A.D. 543)

ST CAESARIUS was born in 470, in the territory of Chalon on the Saône, of a Gallo-Roman family. At eighteen years of age he asked that he might enter the service of the Church. This he did, but two years after Caesarius withdrew to the monastery of Lérins. He was glad to be at liberty to give himself entirely to contemplation and penance; but his health gave way and he was sent to Arles to recover. Here his scruples about the use of pagan authors for study by Christian clerics drew the attention of the bishop, Eonus, to him; they were kinsmen, and Eonus was sufficiently attracted by the young man to write to the abbot of Lérins asking that he might be released for the episcopal service. Caesarius was then ordained deacon and priest, and put by Eonus in charge of a neighbouring monastery whose discipline was very relaxed. He gave these monks a rule, governed them for three years, and in spite of his youth and inexperience made them a model body of religious. The bishop of Arles on his death-bed recommended him for his successor. He was then thirty-three years old, and he presided over that church forty years.

Among the first things he did was to regulate the singing of the Divine Office, which he ordered to be celebrated publicly every day as was done in other neighbouring churches; and he did not scruple to modify the office to encourage the attendance of lay people. He established a monastery to give a more permanent home to the maidens and widows of southern Gaul who wished to give themselves to God. Caesarius drew up a rule for these women, who were one of the principal preoccupations of his life; in it he put strong emphasis on stability and the completeness and permanence of enclosure. He also drew up a rule for men on the same lines, which he imposed throughout his diocese, whence it spread further. St Caesarius was promoted to the see of Arles when it had just succeeded in maintaining its extensive jurisdiction against the bishop of Vienne, and he found himself metropolitan of many suffragan sees. As such he presided over several synods, of which the most important was that at Orange in 529.·

The city of Arles was at that time subject to Alaric II, King of the Visigoths. It was suggested to this prince that the bishop, being born a subject of the king of Burgundy, did all that lay in his power to bring the territory of Arles under his dominion. This was untrue, but he recalled him from exile and condemned his accuser to be stoned, but pardoned him at the intercession of Caesarius.

After the death of the king of the Visigoths, Theodoric the Ostrogoth, King of Italy, seized those dominions in Languedoc, and St Caesarius was apprehended and brought under guard to Ravenna. When the saint came into the king's presence and saluted him, Theodoric, seeing his venerable aspect and intrepid air, rose and returned his courtesy. He then spoke kindly with the bishop on the state of his city. He went on to Rome, where Pope St Symmachus confirmed the metropolitan rights of Arles, recognized him as apostolic delegate in Gaul, and conferred the *pallium*, which St Caesarius is said to have been the first bishop in western Europe to receive.

St Caesarius returned to Arles in 514 and continued to watch over and instruct his people for many years. When the city was taken by the Franks in 536 he retired somewhat from public life and spent much time at the convent of St John. He made a will in favour of those nuns, and in his seventy-third year began to prepare finally for death which he knew to be near. He died on the eve of the feast of St Augustine in 543.

28 : ST AUGUSTINE, BISHOP OF HIPPO, DOCTOR OF THE CHURCH (A.D. 430)

ST AUGUSTINE, who used commonly to be called Austin in English, was born on November 13 in the year 354 at Tagaste, a small town of Numidia in north Africa, not far from Hippo, but at some distance from the sea, which he had never seen till he was grown up. His parents were of good position, but not rich; his father, Patricius, was an idolater, and of a violent disposition; but through the example and prudent conduct of St Monica, his wife, he was baptized a little before his death. She bore him several children; St Augustine speaks of his brother Navigius, who left a family behind him, and of a sister who died a dedicated virgin. As a child Monica had instructed him in the Christian religion and taught him to pray; falling dangerously ill, he desired baptism and his mother got everything ready for it: but he suddenly grew better, and it was put off.

Augustine went to Carthage towards the end of the year 370, in the beginning of his seventeenth year. There he took a foremost place in the school of rhetoric and applied himself to his studies with eagerness and pleasure. Soon he entered into relations with a woman, irregular but stable, to whom he remained faithful until he sent her from him at Milan in 385; she bore him a son, Adeodatus, in 372. His father, Patricius, died in 371; but Augustine still continued at Carthage and, by reading the *Hortensius* of Cicero, his mind was turned from rhetoric to philosophy. Then he fell into the error of the Manichees, who sought to solve the problem of evil by teaching a metaphysical and religious dualism, according to which there are two eternal first principles, God, the cause of all good, and matter, the cause of all evil. Meeting the leading Manichean teacher, Faustus, however, he began to be disillusioned about that sect, and in 383 departed to Rome, secretly, lest his mother should prevent him. He opened a school of rhetoric there, but finding the scholars were accustomed frequently to change their masters in order to cheat them of their fees he applied for and received a post as master of rhetoric in Milan. Here he was well received and the bishop, St Ambrose, gave him marks of respect. Augustine was very desirous of knowing him, not as a teacher of the truth, but as a person of great learning and reputation. He often went to his sermons, not so much with any expectations of profiting by them as to gratify his curiosity and to enjoy the eloquence; but he found the discourses more learned than those of the heretic Faustus, and they began to make an impression; at the same time as he read Plato and Plotinus.

St Monica, having followed him to Milan, wished to see him married, and the mother of Adeodatus returned to Africa; leaving the boy behind; but neither marriage nor single continence followed. And so the struggle, spiritual, moral, intellectual, went on. He had been greatly impressed by hearing the conversion of the Roman neo-Platonist professor, Victorinus, related by St Simplician; and soon after Pontitian, an African, came to visit Augustine and his friend Alipius. Finding a book of St Paul's epistles lying on the table, he took occasion to speak of the life of St Antony, and was surprised to find that his name was unknown to them. Pontitian then went on to speak of two men who had been suddenly turned to the service of God by reading a life of St Antony. Directly Pontitian had gone, he got up and went into the garden. Augustine was torn between chastity and the seductive memory of his former sins, and going alone further into the garden he threw himself on the ground under a tree, crying out, 'How long, O Lord? Wilt thou be angry for ever? Remember not my past iniquities! '

As he spoke he heard as it were the voice of a child singing from a neighbouring house, which frequently repeated these words, *Tolle lege! Tolle lege!* 'Take up and read! Take up and read! ' He returned to where Alipius was sitting with the book of St Paul's epistles, opened it, and read in silence the words on which he first cast his eyes: 'Not in rioting and drunkenness; not in chambering and impurities; not in contention and envy; but put ye on the Lord Jesus Christ, and make not provision for the flesh in its concupiscences.' He shut the book, and told Alipius what had passed. Alipius asked to see the passage he had read, and found the next words to be: 'Him that is weak in faith, take unto you'; which he applied to himself, and joined his friend in his resolution. They immediately went in and told St Monica, who rejoiced and praised God, 'who is able to do all things more abundantly than we desire or understand'. This was in September 386, and Augustine was thirty-two.

He at once gave up his school and retired to a country house at Cassiciacum, near Milan, which his friend Verecundus lent to him, he was accompanied by his mother Monica, his brother Navigius, his son Adeodatus, St Alipius, and several other friends, and they lived a community life together. From the conversations which took place during these seven months St Augustine drew up his three dialogues, *Against the Academicians*, *Of the Happy Life* and *Of Order*.

St Augustine was baptized by St Ambrose on Easter-eve in 387, together with Alipius and his dearly loved son Adeodatus, who was about fifteen years of age and was to die not long afterwards. In the autumn he resolved to return to Africa. Accordingly he went to Ostia with his mother and several friends, and there St Monica died in November 387. He returned for a short while to Rome, and went on to Africa in September 388, where he hastened with his friends to his house at Tagaste. There he lived almost three years, serving God in fasting, prayer, good works, meditating upon His law and instructing others by his discourses and books. All things were in common and were distributed according to everyone's needs; St Augustine himself reserved nothing which he could call his own. He had no idea of becoming a priest, but in 391 he was ordained as an assistant to Valerius, Bishop of Hippo. So Augustine had to move to that city; and in a house adjoining the church he established a sort of monastery, modelled on his household at Tagaste, living there with St Alipius, St Evodius, St Possidius, and others. During these early days he vigorously opposed the Manicheans and the beginnings of Donatism, as well as effecting such domestic reforms as the abolition of feasting in the chapels of the martyrs and of family fights as a public amusement.

In 395 he was consecrated bishop as coadjutor to Valerius, and succeeded him in the see of Hippo on his death soon after. Augustine established regular and common life in his episcopal residence, and required all the priests, deacons, and subdeacons that lived with him to renounce property and to follow the rule he established there. Throughout his thirty-five years as bishop of Hippo St Augustine had to defend the Catholic faith against one heresy or another. He was obliged in 405 to invoke the civil power to restrain the Donatists about Hippo from the outrages which they perpetrated, and in the same year the Emperor Honorius published severe laws against them. Augustine at first disapproved such masures, though afterwards changed his opinion, except that he would not countenance a death-penalty. A great conference between the two parties at Carthage in 411 marked the beginning of the decline of these heretics, but almost at once the Pelagian controversy began.

Pelagius rejected the doctrine of original sin and taught that baptism was simply a title of admission to Heaven, and that grace is not necessary to salvation. In 411 he left Rome for Africa with his friend Caelestius, and during that year their doctrines were for the first time condemned by a synod at Carthage. St Augustine was not at this council, but from that time he began to oppose these errors in his sermons and letters. When Rome was plundered by Alaric the Goth in 410 the pagans renewed their attack on the Christian religion, to which they imputed the calamities of the empire. To answer their slanders, St Augustine began his great work *Of the City of God* in 413, though he only finished it in 426, the work of his which is the most widely read after his *Confessions*. In the *Confessions* St. Augustine, with the most sincere humility and contrition, lays open the errors of his conduct; in his seventy-second year he began to do the like for his judgement. In this work, his *Retractions*, he reviewed his writings, which were very numerous, and corrected with candour and severity the mistakes he ahd made, without seeking the least gloss or excuse to extenuate them.

Augustine's last years were full of turmoil. Count Boniface, who had been the imperial general in Africa, having justly incurred the suspicion of the regent Placidia and being in disgrace, incited Genseric, King of the Vandals, to invade the African provinces. The Vandals appeared before Hippo about the end of May 430, and the siege continued fourteen months. In the third month St Augustine was seized with a fever. The strength of his body daily and hourly declined, yet his senses and intellectual faculties continued sound to the last, and he calmly resigned his spirit into the hadns of God on August 28, 430, after having lived seventy-six years and spent almost forty of them in the labours of the ministry.

29 : ST MEDERICUS, OR MERRY, ABBOT (*c.* A.D. 700)

HE was born at Autun, in the seventh century, and when still very young he entered a local monastery, probably St Martin's in Autun. In that monastery then lived fifty-four fervent monks, whose penitential and regular lives were an object of edification to the whole country.

Being chosen abbot much against his own inclination, Merry pointed out to his brethren the narrow path of true virtue by example, walking before them in every duty, and the reputation of his sanctity drew the eyes of all men upon him. The distractions which continual consultations from all parts gave him, and a fear of falling into vanity, made him resign his office and retire into a forest four miles from Autun, where he lay hid for some time. He earned himself all necessaries of life by the labour of his hands. The place of his retreat at length becoming public, and being struck down by sickness, he was obliged to return to the monastery. After having edified his brethren and strengthened them in religious perfection, he again left them in old age in order to make a pilgrimage to the shrine of St Germanus of Paris (also a native of Autun) in that city. There with one companion, St Frou or Frodulf, he chose his abode in a small cell adjoining a chapel dedicated in honour of St Peter, in the north suburb of the city; and, after two years and nine months during which he bore with patience a painful lingering illness, he died happily about the year 700.

30 : ST PAMMACHIUS, (A.D. 410)

HE belonged to the house of the Furii and was a senator; in 385 he married Paulina, the second daughter of St Paula, a great friend of St Jerome. Pammachius was probably one of the religious men who denounced to Pope St Siricius a certain Jovinain, who maintained among other errors that all sins and their punishments are equal; he certainly sent copies of the heretic's writings to Jerome, who replied to them in a long treatise. This reply did not meet with the entire approval of St Pammachius: he found its language too strong (a failing to which Jerome was very inclined) and that it contained exaggerated praise of virginity and depreciation of marriage; so he wrote and told him so, and St Jerome replied in two letters, thanking him for his interest and defending what he had written.

In 397 the wife of St Pammachius died, and Pammachius devoted the rest of his life to study and works of charity. Together with St Fabiola he built at Porto a large hospice to shelter pilgrims coming to Rome, especially the poor and the sick; Pammachius and Fabiola spent much time there personally looking after their guests.

St Pammachius was greatly disturbed by the bitter controversy between Jerome and Rufinus; he wrote to him urging that he should undertake the translation of Origen's *De principiis*, and gave Jerome very useful help in his controversial writings: but abate the imprudence of expression of much of them he could not. He also wrote to the people living on his estates in Numidia urging them to abandon the Donatist schism and return to the Church, and this action drew a letter of thanks from St Augustine at Hippo in 401. Pammachius had a church in his house on the Coelian hill, consequently called *titulus Pammachii*: its site is now occupied by the Passionist church of SS. Giovanni e Paolo, beneath which remains of the original house have been found. St Pammachius died in 410 at the time Alaric and the Goths captured Rome.

31 : ST AIDAN, BISHOP OF LINDISFARNE (A.D. 651)

AIDAN was a native of Ireland, and is said to have been a disciple of St Senan on Scattery Island, but nothing else is known with certainty of his early life, before he became a monk of Iona. He was well received by King Oswald, who bestowed on him for his episcopal seat the isle of Lindisfarne. By his actions he showed that he neither sought nor loved the things of this world; the presents which were made him by the king, or by the other rich men, he distributed among the poor. He rarely would go to the king's table, and never without taking with him one or two of his clergy, and always afterwards made haste away to get on with his work.

The centre of St Aidan's activity was the island of Lindisfarne, now generally called Holy Isle, off the coast of Northumberland, between Berwick and Bamburgh. Here he had his see and established a monastery under the Rule of St Columcille; it has not improperly been called the English Iona, for from it the paganism of Northumbria was gradually dispelled and barbarian customs undermined. St Aidan took to this monastery twelve English boys to be brought up there, and he was indefatigable in caring for the welfare of children and of slaves, for the manumission of many of whom he paid from alms bestowed on him. The great king St Oswald assisted his bishop in every possible way, as did St Oswin his successor, and when in 651 Oswin was murdered at Gilling, Aidan survived him only eleven days. He died at the royal castle at Bamburgh, which he used as a mission centre, leaning against a wall of the church where a tent had been set up to shelter him. He was first buried in the cemetery of Lindisfarne, but when the new church of St Peter was built there his body was translated into the sanctuary.

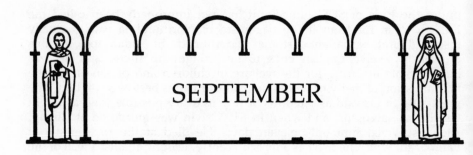

SEPTEMBER

1 : ST DRITHELM, (c. A.D. 700)

DRITHELM was a householder in Northumbria and a person of virtuous life, father of a God-fearing family. Somewhere about the year 693 he was seized with an illness and one evening appeared to be dead, but the next morning he suddenly sat up, to the fear of those mourning around his body, who all fled except his wife. To her he said: 'Be not afraid, for I am now truly risen from death and allowed again to live among men. But hereafter I am not to live as I have been wont but rather in a very different manner.' He then went to pray in the church of the village and afterwards returned to his house where he made a division of his goods, one-third to his wife, one-third to his children, and the remaining third to the poor. He then made his way to King Aldfrith and told him his story, and at the king's request St Ethelwald, who was then abbot of Melrose, tonsured Drithelm and admitted him among his monks. Of the things which Drithelm had seen 'he would not tell to tepid persons and such as lived negligently, but only to those who, being feared with the dread of Hell or delighted with the hope of heavenly joys, would make use of his words to advance in religion'.

St Drithelm lived for the rest of his days in a cell on the banks of the Tweed, into the freezing waters of which he would sometimes cast himself by way of penance, and stand reciting his office with ice floating around him. At which some would say: 'It is wonderful, Brother Drithelm, that you can stand such cold.' And he would reply simply, 'I have seen greater cold.' Or if they said, 'It is strange how you can endure such hardship', he would answer, 'I have seen greater hardship'. He continued to mortify his body till the day of his death and forwarded the salvation of many by his words and example.

2 : ST WILLIAM, BISHOP OF ROSKILDE (c. A.D. 1070)

WILLIAM was an English priest, chaplain to King Canute. In one of the voyages which that prince made from England to Denmark, William was so moved with compassion at the sight of the ignorance, idolatry and superstition in which so many of the Danes lived that he decided to stay behind to preach Christ and His gospel. He later was advanced to the episcopal see of Roskilde in the island of Zealand. Most of the things related of St William have reference to his unwearying efforts to reform the behaviour of King Sweyn Estridsen. This prince having once caused some persons to be put to death not only without trial but also within the bounds of a church, the saint met him at the church door the next day and, holding out his pastoral staff, forbade him to enter the house of God till his hands were cleansed from the blood he had unjustly spilt: and seeing some of the courtiers draw their swords, he presented his neck, saying he was ready to die in defence of the Church of God. Sweyn publicly confessed his crime, and later gave some land to the church of Roskilde as a peace offering.

For some years the saint and the penitent concurred to promote the cause of religion. Upon the death of the king his body was temporarily buried in the abbey he had founded at Ringsted, till the cathedral of Roskilde should be ready for its reception. At the same time a tomb was prepared there for St William, and it is said that, while Sweyn's body was being conveyed from Ringsted to Roskilde, St William came out to meet it and himself died at its approach, so that the two friends were borne together to burial.

3 : ST GREGORY THE GREAT, POPE, DOCTOR OF THE CHURCH (A.D. 604)

POPE GREGORY I, most justly called 'the Great', and the first pope who had been a monk, was elected to the apostolic chair when Italy was in a terrible condition after the struggle between the Ostrogoths and the Emperor Justinian, which ended with the defeat and death of Totila in 562. The state of Rome itself was deplorable: it had been sacked four times within a century and a half, and conquered four times in twenty years, but no one restored the damage done by pillage, fire and earthquake.

The saint's family, one of the few patrician families left in the city, was distinguished also for its piety, having given to the Church two popes, Agapitus I and Felix III, Gregory's great-great-grandfather. Little is known of Gordian, Gregory's father, except that he was a *regionarius*—whatever that might be—and that he owned large estates in Sicily as well as a house on the Coelian Hill; his wife Silvia is named as a saint in the Roman Martyrology. Gregory appears to have received the best education obtainable at that time in Rome, and to have taken up the career of a public official. At the age of about thirty we find him exercising the highest civil office in Rome—that of prefect of the city. Faithfully and honourably though Gregory fulfilled his duties, at length he resolved to retire from the world and to devote himself to the service of God alone. He was one of the richest men in Rome, but he gave up all, retiring into his own house on the Clivus Scauri, which he turned into a monastery and which he placed under the patronage of St Andrew and in the charge of a monk called Valentius.

It was not likely that a man of St Gregory's talents and prestige would be left long in obscurity at such a time, and we find him ordained seventh deacon of the Roman church, and then sent as papal *apocrisiarius* or ambassador at the Byzantine court. He had the great disadvantage of knowing no Greek, and more and more he lived a monastic life with several of the monks of St Andrew's who had accompanied him. Most of the dates in St Gregory's life are uncertain but it was probably about the beginning of the year 586 that he was recalled to Rome by Pelagius II. He immediately settled down again, deacon of Rome though he was, in his monastery of St Andrew, of which he soon became abbot; and it seems that it is to this period we must refer the celebrated story told by the Venerable Bede on the strength of an old English tradition.

St Gregory, it appears, was one day walking through the market when he noticed three golden-haired, fair-complexioned boys exposed for sale and inquired their nationality. 'They are Angles or Angli', was the reply. 'They are well named,' said the saint, 'for they have angelic faces and it becomes such to be companions with the angels in heaven.' Learning that they were pagans, he asked what province they came from. 'Deira.' 'De ira!' exclaimed St Gregory. 'Yes, verily they shall be saved from God's ire and called to the mercy of Christ. What is the name of the king of that country?' 'Aella.' 'Then must Alleluia be sung in Aella's land.' So greatly was he impressed by their beauty and by pity for their ignorance of Christ that he resolved to preach the gospel himself in Britain, and started off with several of his monks. However, when the people of Rome heard of their departure they raised such an outcry that Pope Pelagius sent envoys to recall them to Rome.

A terrible inundation of the Tiber was followed by another and an exceptionally severe outbreak of the plague: Rome was again decimated, and in January 590 Pelagius died of the dread disease. The people unanimously chose Gregory as the new pope, and to obtain by penitence the cessation of the plague he ordered a great processional litany through the streets of Rome. From seven churches in the city proceeded seven columns of people, who met at St Mary Major.

A correspondence with John, Archbishop of Ravenna, who had modestly censured him for trying to avoid office, led to Gregory's writing the *Regula Pastoralis*, a book on the office of a bishop. In it he regards the bishop as first and foremost a physician of souls whose chief duties are preaching and the enforcement of discipline. The work met with immediate success, and the Emperor Maurice had it translated into Greek by Anastasius, Patriarch of Antioch. Later St Augustine took it to England, where 300 years later it was translated by King Alfred, and at the councils summoned by Charlemagne the study of the book was enjoined on bishops, who were to have a copy delivered to them at their consecration.

In his instructions to his vicar in Sicily and to the overseers of his patrimony generally, Gregory constantly urged liberal treatment of his vassals and farmers and ordered that money should be advanced to those in difficulties. Large sums were spent in ransoming captives from the Lombards, and we find him commending the bishop of Fano for breaking up and selling church plate for that object and advising another prelate to do the same. In view of a threatened corn shortage he filled the granaries of Rome, and a regular list was kept of the poor to whom grants were periodically made. St Gregory's sense of justice showed itself also in his enlightened treatment of the Jews, whom he would not allow to be oppressed or deprived of their synagogues. He declared that they must not be coerced but must be won by meekness and charity, and when the Jews of Cagliari in Sardinia complained that their synagogue had been seized by a converted

Jew who had turned it into a church, he ordered the building to be restored to its former owners.

From the very outset of his pontificate the saint was called upon to face the aggressions of the Lombards, who from Pavia, Spoleto and Benevento made incursions into other parts of Italy. No help was obtainable from Constantinople or from the exarch at Ravenna, and it fell upon Gregory, the one strong man, not only to organize the defences of Rome, but also to lend assistance to other cities. When in 593 Agilulf with a Lombard army appeared before the walls of Rome Gregory induced him to withdraw his army and leave the city in peace. For nine years he strove in vain to bring about a settlement between the Byzantine emperor and the Lombards; Gregory then proceeded on his own account to negotiate a treaty with King Agilulf, obtaining a special truce for Rome and the surrounding districts.

Of all his religious work in the West that which lay closest to Gregory's heart was the conversion of England, and the success which crowned his efforts in that direction was to him the greatest triumph of his life. The pope's first action was to order the purchase of some English slaves, boys of about seventeen or eighteen, in order to educate them in a monastery for the service of God. Still, it was not to them that he intended primarily to entrust the work of conversion. From his own monastery of St Andrew he selected a band of forty missionaries whom he sent forth under the leadership of Augustine.

During nearly the whole of his pontificate St Gregory was engaged in conflicts with Constantinople—sometimes with the emperor, sometimes with the patriarch, occasionally with both. He protested constantly against the exactions of Byzantine officials whose extortions reduced the Italian people to despair, and remonstrated with the emperor against an imperial edict which prohibited soldiers from becoming monks. With John the Faster, Patriarch of Constantinople, he had an acrimonious correspondence over the title of Oecumenical or Universal which that hierarch had assumed. It seemed to savour of arrogance, and Gregory resented it. For his own part, though one of the most strenuous upholders of the papal dignity, he preferred to call himself by the proudly humble title of *Servus servorum Dei*—Servant of the servants of God. Almost his last action was to send a warm winter cloak to a poor bishop who suffered from the cold. Gregory was buried in St Peter's, and as the epitaph on his tomb expresses it, 'after having confirmed all his actions to his doctrines, the great consul of God went to enjoy eternal triumphs'.

4 : ST ROSE OF VITERBO, VIRGIN (A.D. 1252 ?)

WHEN Frederick II was excommunicated for the second time by Pope Gregory IX the emperor set out to conquer the papal states, and in 1240 he occupied Viterbo in the Romagna. A few years previously there had been born in this city, to parents of lowly station, a girl child, who was christened Rose.

During an illness when she was eight years old Rose is said to have had a vision or dream of our Lady, who told her that she was to be clothed in the habit of St Francis, but that she was to continue to live at home and to set a good example to her neighbours by both word and work. Rose soon recovered her health, received the dress of a lay penitent in due course, and began when she was about twelve years old to preach up and down the streets, upbraiding the people for their supineness in submitting to Frederick. Crowds would gather outside her house to get a glimpse of her, till her father became frightened, and forbade her to show herself in public; if she disobeyed she would be beaten. At the instance of their parish priest her father withdrew his prohibition and for about two years the pope's cause continued to be preached in public by this young girl. Then the partisans of the emperor became alarmed and clamoured that Rose should be put to death as a danger to the state. The *podestà* of the city would not hear of this: he was a just man, and moreover he feared the people; but instead he passed a sentence of banishment against St Rose and her parents. They took refuge at Soriano, and here, in the beginning of December 1250, St Rose is said to have announced the approaching death of the Emperor Frederick II. He in fact died in Apulia on the 13th of the month; the papal party thereupon got the upper hand in Viterbo, and St Rose returned.

She now went to the convent of St Mary of the Roses at Viterbo and asked to be received as a postulant. The abbess refused, for want of a dowry. Her parish priest, however, took it upon himself to open a chapel close by the convent, with a house attached wherein St Rose and a few companions might lead a religious life; but the nuns got an order from Pope Innocent IV for it to be closed, on the ground that they had the privilege of having no other community of women within a given distance of their own. St Rose therefore returned to her parents' house, where she died on March 6 1252, about the age of seventeen. She was buried in the church of Santa Maria in Podio, but her body was on September 4 in 1258 translated to the church of the convent of St Mary of the Roses, as she had foretold.

Immediately after her death Pope Innocent IV ordered an inquiry into her virtues but St Rose's canonization was not achieved until 1457.

5 : ST LAURENCE GIUSTINIANI, PATRIARCH OF VENICE (A.D. 1455)

ST LAURENCE was born at Venice in 1381. His father, Bernard Giustiniani, was of illustrious rank among the nobility of the commonwealth and his mother was not less noble. She was early left a widow with a number of young children, and she devoted herself altogether to the upbringing of her children, to works of charity, and the exercise of virtue. In Laurence she discovered even from the cradle an uncommon docility and generosity of soul; and when he was nineteen he was called by God to consecrate himself to His service. He addressed himself for advice to his uncle, a holy priest called Marino Querini, who was a canon of St George's chapter, established in a little isle called Alga, a mile from Venice. Don Querini advised him first to make trial of himself at home, and represented to him on one side honours, riches and worldly pleasures, and on the other the hardships of poverty, fasting and self-denial. His mother, fearing lest his mortifications should damage his health, tried to divert him from that course, and proposed a marriage to him. He replied by retiring to the chapter of St George in Alga, and was admitted to the community.

St Laurence was promoted to the priesthood in 1406, and the fruit of his spirit of prayer and penitence was a wonderful experimental knowledge of spiritual things and of the paths of interior virtue, and great light and prudence in the direction of souls. The tears which he shed whilst he offered the sacrifice of the Mass strongly affected all the assistants and awakened their faith; and he often experienced raptures at prayer, especially in celebrating Mass one Christmas night. Soon after his ordination he was made provost of St George's, and the most sincere humility was the first thing in which he grounded his religious disciples.

In 1433 Pope Eugenius IV appointed St Laurence to the bishopric of Castello, a diocese which included part of Venice. He tried hard to avoid this dignity and responsibility, and he took possession of his cathedral-church so privately that his own friends knew nothing of the matter till the ceremony was over. He remitted nothing of the austerities which he had practised in the cloister, and from his prayer drew a light, courage and vigour which directed and animated him in his whole conduct; he pacified dissensions in the state and governed a diocese in most difficult times with as much ease as if it had been a single well-regulated convent. The flock loved and respected so holy and tender a pastor. When any private persons opposed his religious reforms he overcame them by meekness and patience. Under his rule the face of his whole diocese was changed. Crowds every day resorted to Laurence's residence for advice, comfort or alms; his gate and purse were always open to the poor. He gave alms more willingly in bread and clothes than in money, which might be ill spent; when he gave cash it was always in small sums. He employed married women to find out and relieve the bashful poor or persons of family in decayed circumstances.

The popes of his time held St Laurence in great veneration. Eugenius IV, meeting him once at Bologna, saluted him with the words, 'Welcome, ornament of bishops!' His successor, Nicholas V, equally esteemed him and when in 1451 he suppressed the see of Castello and transferred that of Grado to Venice, he named St Laurence as the new patriarch. The senate of the republic, always jealous of its prerogatives and liberty, made difficulties lest his authority should trespass upon their jurisdiction. Whilst this was being debated in the senate-house, St Laurence asked an audience of the assembly, before which he declared his desire rather to resign a charge for which he was unfit and which he had borne against his will eighteen years, than to feel his burden increased by this additional dignity. His bearing so strongly affected the whole senate that the doge himself asked him not to entertain such a thought or to raise any obstacle to the pope's decree, and he was supported by the whole house. St Laurence therefore accepted the new office and dignity, and for the few years during which he survived to administer it he continually increased the reputation for goodness and charity which he had earned as bishop of Castello.

St Laurence left some valuable ascetical writings; he was seventy-four years old when he wrote his last work, entitled *The Degrees of Perfection*, and he had just finished it when he was seized with a sharp fever. His servants prepared a bed for him, at which the true imitator of Christ was troubled and could not be contented till he was laid on his straw. During the two days that he lived after receiving the last anointing many of the city came in turn according to their different rank to receive his blessing. He insisted on having the beggars admitted, and gave to each class a short instruction.

St Laurence died on January 8, 1455, but his feast is kept on this date whereon he received episcopal consecration. He was canonized in 1690.

6 : ST BEGA, OR BEE, VIRGIN (SEVENTH CENTURY)

SHE is the heroine of a legend which makes her the daughter of an Irish king, sought in marriage by a son of the king of Norway. She had, however, vowed herself a virgin to Christ, and had been given by an angel a bracelet marked with a cross as a token of her heavenly betrothal. The day before she was to be given to the prince, while her suitor and her father were revelling in the hall, she escaped with the help of this bracelet and, seated on a clod of earth, was navigated across the sea and landed safely on the coast of Cumberland. For a time she lived as an anchoress, and the sea-gulls, guillemots and gannets brought food for her sustenance; but human marauders were less kind, and she was advised by the king of Northumbria, St Oswald, to become a nun. She therefore received the veil from St Aidan and established a monastery at St Bees (Copeland) which afterwards became a cell of the Benedictine abbey of St Mary at York.

Whatever background of truth there may be in the legend of St Bega, she was venerated in Northumbria. The promontory on which she lived is named St Bee's Head after her, and she was the patroness of the people of the neighbourhood, ground down between the exactions of their lords and the raids of the border Scots. They claimed even to possess her miraculous bracelet, and treasured equally the stories of how St Bega in her earthly life had been devoted to the poor and oppressed and had cooked, washed and mended for the workmen who built her monastery.

7 : ST CLODOALD, OR CLOUD, (c. A.D. 560)

ON the death of Clovis, King of the Franks, in the year 511 his kingdom was divided between his four sons, of whom the second was Clodomir. Thirteen years later he was killed fighting against his cousin, Gondomar, King of Burgundy (he had first murdered St Sigismund of Burgundy, whom the Roman Martyrology calls a martyr), leaving three sons to share his dominions. The youngest of these sons of Clodomir was St Clodoald, a name more familiar to English people under its French form of Cloud from the town of Saint-Cloud near Versailles.

The three boys were brought up by their grandmother St Clotilda, widow of Clovis, who lavished much care and affection on them in her home at Paris, while their kingdom was administered by their uncle Childebert. When Cloud was eight years old, Childebert entered into a plot with his brother, Clotaire of Soissons, to get rid of these boys and partition their kingdom. A familiar of Childebert was sent to Clotilda asking her to choose whether the three boys should be put to death or forcibly tonsured and shut up in monasteries. He so twisted the reply of the distracted queen that she was made to appear to choose their death, whereupon Clotaire seized the eldest boy, Theodoald, and stabbed him. The second, Gunther, fled in terror to his uncle Childebert, whose heart was so softened by fear and sickened at the brutal killing that he tried to protect him. But Clotaire did not approve of such faintheartedness, dragged Gunther from Childebert's arms and killed him too. Cloud escaped, and was taken for safety into Provence or elsewhere.

Childebert and Clotaire shared the fruits of their crime, and Cloud made no attempt to recover his kingdom when he came of age. He had seen quite enough of the politics of the world, and voluntarily hid himself in a hermit's cell. After some time he put himself under the discipline of St Severinus, a recluse who lived near Paris, and he afterwards went to Nogent on the Seine and had his hermitage where is now Saint-Cloud. St Cloud was indefatigable in instructing the people of the neighbouring country, and ended his days at Nogent about the year 560 when he was some thirty-six years old.

8 : ST CORBINIAN, BISHOP (A.D. 725)

THIS early apostle of Bavaria was born at Châtres, near Melun, in France. He was baptized Waldegiso after his father, but his mother afterwards changed his name to Corbinian, after herself. He lived as a recluse for fourteen years in a cell which he built near a chapel in the same place. The fame of his sanctity, which was increased by the occurrence of several miracles and the prudence of the advice which he gave in spiritual matters, made his name famous, and he admitted several persons to form themselves into a religious community under his discipline. The distraction which this gave him made him think of seeking some new place where he might live in obscurity, and he determined to go to Rome. Pope St Gregory II sent Corbinian, who may already have been a bishop, to preach in Bavaria, where he put himself under the protection of Duke Grimoald. After having much increased the number of the Christians, he fixed his headquarters at Freising, in Upper Bavaria, which, however did not become a regular episcopal see till St Boniface made it such in 739.

St Corbinian discovered that his patron Grimoald, though a Christian, had defied the discipline of the Church by marrying his brother's widow, Biltrudis. Corbinian refused to have anything to do with the duke until they separated. But the lady Biltrudis was not at all satisfied and pursued Corbinian with persecution in the hope that he would allow her to be reinstated; she abused him as a foreign interloper, specifically, a British bishop—which of course he was not. At length she even conspired to have him murdered. The saint took refuge at Meran, and remained in semi-exile until Grimoald (who had rejoined the lady) was killed in battle shortly after and Biltrudis was carried off by the Franks. He was then recalled by Grimoald's successor, and continued his missionary work throughout Bavaria. Corbinian was buried at a monastery he had founded at Obermais, at Meran, but his body was brought to Freising in 765 by Aribo, his second successor and biographer.

9 : ST PETER CLAVER, (A.D. 1654)

HE was born at Verdu, in Catalonia, about 1581, and as he showed fine qualities of mind and spirit was destined for the Church and sent to study at the University of Barcelona. Here he graduated with distinction and, after receiving minor orders, determined to offer himself to the Society of Jesus. He was received into the novitiate of Tarragona at the age of twenty, and was sent to the college of Montesione at Palma, in Majorca. Here he met St Alphonsus Rodriguez, who was porter in the college, though with a reputation far above his humble office.

In after years St Peter Claver said that St Alphonsus had actually foretold to him that he would go and the very place wherein he would work. Moved by the fervour of these exhortations Peter Claver approached his provincial, offering himself for the West Indies, and was told that his vocation would be decided in due course by his superiors. He was sent to Barcelona for his theology and after two years was, at his further request, chosen to represent the province of Aragon on the mission of Spanish Jesuits being sent to New Granada. He left Spain for ever in April 1610, and after a wearisome voyage landed with his companions at Cartagena, in what is now the republic of Colombia. Thence he went to the Jesuit house of Santa Fé to complete his theological studies, and was employed as well as sacristan, porter, infirmarian and cook, and was sent for his tertianship to the new house of the Society at Tunja. He returned to Cartagena in 1615 and was there ordained priest.

By this time the slave trade had been established in the Americas for nearly a hundred years, and the port of Cartagena was one of its principal centres, being conveniently situated as a clearing-house. The trade had recently been given a considerable impetus, for the local Indians were not physically fitted to work in the gold and silver mines, and there was a big demand for Negroes from Angola and the Congo.

At the time of Father Claver's ordination the leader of the work among the Negroes was Father Alfonso de Sandoval, a great Jesuit missionary who spent y forty years in the service of the slaves, and after working under him Peter Claver declared himself 'the slave of the Negroes for ever'. Although by nature shy and without self-confidence he threw himself into the work with method and organization. He enlisted bands of assistants, whether by money, goods or services, and as soon as a slave-ship entered the port he went to wait on its living freight. The slaves were disembarked and shut up in the yards. Into these yards or sheds St Peter Claver plunged, with medicines and food, bread, brandy, lemons, tobacco to distribute among the Negroes, some of whom were too frightened, others too ill, to accept them. 'We must speak to them with our hands, before we try to speak to them with our lips', Claver would say. When he came upon any who were dying he baptized them, and then sought out all babies born on the voyage that he might baptize them. He had a band of seven interpreters, one of whom spoke four Negro dialects, and with their help he taught the slaves and prepared them for baptism, not only in groups but individually; for they were too backward and slow and the language difficulty too great for him to make himself understood otherwise. He made use of pictures, showing our

Lord suffering on the cross for them; above all he tried to instil in them some degree of self-respect, to give them at least some idea that as redeemed human beings they had dignity and worth, even if as slaves they were outcast and despised.

It is estimated that in forty years St Peter Claver instructed and baptized over 300,000 slaves. When there was time and opportunity he took the same trouble to teach them how properly to use the sacrament of penance, and in one year is said to have heard the confessions of more than five thousand. Every spring after Easter Peter would make a tour of those plantations nearer Cartagena in order to see how they Negroes were getting on. He was not always well received. The masters complained that he wasted the slaves' time with his preaching, praying and hymn-singing; their wives complained that after the Negroes had been to Mass it was impossible to enter the church; and when they misbehaved Father Claver was blamed. But he was not deterred, not even when the ecclesiastical authorities lent too willing an ear to the complaints of his critics.

Many of the stories both of the heroism and of the miraculous powers of St Peter Claver concern his nursing of sick and diseased Negroes, in circumstances often that no one else, black or white, could face, but he found time to care for other sufferers besides slaves. There were two hospitals in Catagena, one for general cases, served by the Brothers of St John-of-God; this was St Sebastian's; and another, of St Lazarus, for lepers and those suffering from the complaint called 'St Antony's Fire'. Both these he visited every week, waiting on the patients in their material needs and bringing hardened sinners to penitence. He also exercised an apostolate among the Protestant traders, sailors and others whom he found therein, and brought about the conversion of an Anglican dignitary, represented to be an archdeacon of London, whom he met when visiting prisoners-of-war on a ship in the harbour.

His country missions in the spring, during which he refused as much as possible the hospitality of the planters and owners and lodged in the quarters of the slaves, were succeeded in the autumn by a mission among the traders and seamen, who landed at Cartagena in great numbers at that season and further increased the vice and disorder of the port. Sometimes St Peter would spend almost the whole day in the great square of the city, where the four principal streets met, preaching to all who would stop to listen. He became the apostle of Cartagena as well as of the Negroes, and in so huge a work was aided by God with those gifts that particularly pertain to apostles, of miracles, of prophecy, and of reading hearts.

In the year 1650 St Peter Claver went to preach the jubilee among the Negroes along the coast, but sickness attacked his emaciated and weakened body, and he was recalled to the residence at Cartagena. But here a virulent epidemic had begun to show itself, and one of the first to be attacked among the Jesuits was the debilitated missionary, so that his death seemed at hand. After receiving the last sacraments he recovered, but he was a broken man. For the rest of his life pain hardly left him, and a trembling in his limbs made it impossible for him to celebrate Mass. He perforce became almost entirely inactive, but would sometimes hear confessions, especially of his dear friend Doña Isabella de Urbina, who had always generously supported his work with her money. Otherwise he remained in his cell, not only inactive but even forgotten and neglected; the numbers in the house were much reduced, and those who remained were fully occupied in coping with the confusion and duties imposed by the spreading plague, but even so their indifference to the saint is surprising. Doña Isabella and her sister remained faithful to him; doubtless his old helper, Brother Nicholas Gonzalez, visited him when he could.

In the summer of 1654 Father Diego Ramirez Fariña arrived in Cartagena from Spain with a commission from the king to work among the Negroes. St Peter Claver was overjoyed and dragged himself from his bed to greet his successor. He shortly afterward heard the confession of Doña Isabella, and told her it was for the last time, and on September 6, after assisting at Mass and receiving communion, he said to Nicholas Gonzalez, 'I am going to die'. That same evening he was taken very ill and became comatose. The rumour of his approaching end spread round the city, everyone suddenly remembered the saint again, and numbers came to kiss his hands before it was too late; his cell was stripped of everything that could be carried off as a relic. St Peter Claver never fully recovered consciousness, and died two days later on the birthday of our Lady, September 8, 1654. The civil authorities who had looked askance at his solicitude for mere Negro slaves, and the clergy, who had called his zeal indiscreet and his energy wasted, now vied with one another to honour his memory.

St Peter Claver was never again forgotten and his fame spread throughout the world: he was canonized at the same time as his friend St Alphonsus Rodriguez in 1888, and he was declared by Pope Leo XIII patron of all missionary enterprises among Negroes.

10 : ST NICHOLAS OF TOLENTINO, (A.D. 1305)

THIS saint received his surname from the town which was his residence for the most considerable part of his life, and in which he died. He was a native of Sant' Angelo, a town near Fermo in the March of Ancona, and was born in the year 1245. His father lived many years in happiness with his wife, but when both had reached middle age they were still childless. Nicholas was the fruit of their prayers and a pilgrimage to the shrine of St Nicholas at Bari, in which his mother especially had earnestly begged of God a son who should faithfully serve Him. At his baptism he received the name of his patron.

While still a boy he received minor orders, and was presented to a canonry in the collegiate church of St Saviour at Sant' Angelo; and there were not wanting those who were willing to use their influence for his promotion within the ranks of the secular clergy. Nicholas, however, aspired to a state which would allow him to consecrate his whole time and thoughts directly to God, and it happened that he one day went into the Augustinian church and heard a friar preaching on the text: 'Love not the world, nor the things which are in the world . . . . The world passeth away . . . . ' This sermon finally determined him absolutely to join the order of that preacher. This he did so soon as his age would allow, and he was accepted by the Augustinian friars at Sant' Angelo. He went through his novitiate under the direction of the preacher himself, Father Reginald, and made his profession before he had completed his eighteenth year.

Friar Nicholas was sent to San Ginesio for his theology, and he was entrusted with the daily distribution of food to the poor at the monastery gate. He made so free with the resources of the house that the procurator complained and reported him to the prior. About 1270 he was ordained priest at Cingoli, and in that place he became famous among the people, particularly on account of his healing of a blind woman. But he did not stay there long, for during four years he was continually moving from one to another of the friaries and missions of his order. For a short time he was novice-master at Sant' Elpidio, where there was a large community which included two friars who are venerated as *beati* among the Augustinians today, Angelo of Furcio and Angelo of Foligno. While visiting a relative who was prior of a monastery near Fermo, Nicholas was tempted by an invitation to make a long stay in the monastery, but while praying in the church he seemed to hear a voice directing him: 'To Tolentino, to Tolentino. Persevere there.' Shortly after to Tolentino he was sent, and stopped there for the remaining thirty years of his life.

This town had suffered much in the strife of Guelf and Ghibelline, and civil discord had had its usual effects of wild fanaticism, schism and reckless wickedness. A campaign of street-preaching was necessary, and to this new work St Nicholas was put. He was an immediate success. He went about the slums of Tolentino, comforting the dying, waiting on (and sometimes miraculously curing) the sick and bed-ridden, watching over the children, appealing to the criminals, composing quarrels and estrangements: one woman gave evidence in the cause of his canonization that he had entirely won over and reformed her husband who for long had treated her with shameful cruelty.

The final illness of St Nicholas lasted nearly a year, and in the last months he got up from bed only once, to absolve a penitent who he knew intended to conceal a grievous sin from any priest but himself. The end came quietly on September 10, 1305.

11 : ST PAPHNUTIUS, BISHOP (c. A.D. 350?)

THE holy confessor Paphnutius was an Egyptian who, after having spent several years in the desert under the direction of the great St Antony, was made bishop in the Upper Thebaid. He was one of those confessors who under the Emperor Maximinus lost the right eye, were hamstrung in one leg, and were afterwards sent to work in the mines. Peace being restored to the Church, Paphnutius returned to his flock, bearing all the rest of his life the glorious marks of his sufferings for the name of his crucified Master. He was one of the most zealous in defending the Catholic faith against the Arian heresy and for his holiness, and as one who had confessed the faith before persecutors and under torments, was an outstanding figure of the first general council of the Church, held at Nicaea in the year 325.

St Paphnutius remained always in close union with St Athanasius and the other orthodox prelates. He and other Egyptian bishops accompanied their holy patriarch to the Council of Tyre in 335, where they found the greater part of the members who composed that assembly to be professed Arians. Paphnutius, seeing Maximus, Bishop of Jerusalem, among them and full of concern to find a prelate who had suffered in the last persecution in such bad company, took him by the hand, led him out, and told him that he could not bear that anyone who bore the same marks as himself in defence of the faith should be led away and imposed upon by persons who were resolved to condemn the most strenuous asserter of its fundamental article. Maximus was overcome by the saint's appeal and let himself be led to a seat among the Supporters of St Athanasius, whom he never afterwards deserted.

St Paphnutius is sometimes called 'the Great' to distinguish him from other saints of the same name; the year of his death is not known.

12 : ST GUY OF ANDERLECHT, (c. A.D. 1012)

ST GUY (Guidon), called the Poor Man of Anderlecht, was born in the country near Brussels, of poor parents, but both virtuous and happy. They were not able to give their son a school education, but instead they were diligent in instructing him early in the Christian faith and the practices of our holy religion. St Augustine says that God ranks among the reprobate, not only those who shall have received their comfort on earth, but also those who shall have grieved to be deprived of it. This was what Guy dreaded. In order to preserve himself from it he never ceased to beg of God the grace to love the state of poverty in which divine providence had placed him, and to bear all its hardships with joy. The charity which Guy had for his neighbour was no less active. He divided his pittance with the poor, and often fed them whilst he fasted himself.

When he grew up St Guy wandered about for a time, until one day he came to the church of our Lady at Laeken, near Brussels, whose priest was struck with the piety and willingness of the man, and retained him in the service of his church as sacristan. Guy accepted the offer with pleasure; and the cleanliness and good order that appeared in everything under his direction struck all that came to that church. But Guy, like other simple folk before and since, was induced by a merchant of Brussels to invest his small savings in a commercial venture, with the unusual motive of having more at his disposal to relieve the poor.

The ship carrying their goods was lost in going out of harbour, and Guy, whose place in the church of Laeken had upon his leaving been given to another, was left destitute. He saw his mistake in following his own ideas and in forsaking secure and humble employment to embark, though with good intention, on the affairs of the world, and he blamed himself for the false step he had taken.

In reparation for his folly Guy made a pilgrimage on foot first to Rome and then on to Jerusalem, and visited all the most celebrated shrines in that part of the Christian world. After seven years' absence he again reached Belgium, where he made his way to Anderlecht, dying from exhaustion and illness brought on by the fatigue of his journeys and other hardships. Shortly after he was received into the hospital of Anderlecht he yielded up his soul to God.

13 : ST JOHN CHRYSOSTOM, ARCHBISHOP OF CONSTANTINOPLE AND DOCTOR OF THE CHURCH (A.D. 407)

THIS incomparable teacher, on account of his eloquence, obtained after his death the surname of Chrysostom, or Golden Mouth. He was born about the year 347 at Antioch in Syria, the only son of Secundus, commander of the imperial troops. His mother, Anthusa, left a widow at twenty, divided her time between the care of her family and her exercises of devotion. She provided for her son the ablest masters which the empire at that time afforded. Eloquence was esteemed the highest accomplishment, and John studied that art under Libanius, the most famous orator of the age.

According to a common custom of those days young John was not baptized till he was over twenty years old, being at the time a law student. Soon after, together with his friends Basil, Theodore (afterwards bishop of Mopsuestia) and others, he attended a sort of school for monks, where they studied under Diodorus of Tarsus; and in 374 he joined one of the loosely-knit communities of hermits among the mountains south of Antioch. He afterwards wrote a vivid account of their austerities and trials. He passed four years under the direction of a veteran Syrian monk, and afterwards two years in a cave as a solitary. The dampness of this abode brought on a dangerous illness, and for the recovery of his health he was obliged to return into the city in 381. He was ordained deacon by St Meletius that very year, and received the priesthood from Bishop Flavian in 386, who at the same time constituted him his preacher, John being then about forty. He discharged the duties of the office for twelve years, supporting during that time a heavy load of responsibility as the aged bishop's deputy.

Nectarius, Archbishop of Contantinople, dying in 397, the Emperor Arcadius, at the suggestion of Eutropius, his chamberlain, resolved to procure the election of John to the see of that city. He therefore despatched an order to the count of the East, enjoining him to send John to Constantinople, but to do so without making the news public, lest his intended removal should cause a sedition. Theophilus, Archbishop of Alexandria, a man of proud and turbulent spirit, had come to Constantinople to recommend a nominee of his own for the vacancy; but he had to desist from his intrigues, and John was consecrated by him on February 26 in 398.

When regulating his domestic concerns, the saint cut down the expenses which his predecessors had considered necessary to maintain their dignity, and these sums he applied to the relief of the poor and supported many hospitals. The next thing he took in hand was the reformation of his clergy. This he forwarded by zealous exhortations and by disciplinary enactments, which, while very necessary, seem in their severity to have been lacking in tact. But to give these his endeavours their due force, he lived himself as an exact model of what he inculcated on others. The immodesty of women in their dress aroused him to indignation, and he showed how false and absurd was their excuse in saying that they meant no harm. By his zeal and eloquence St John tamed many sinners, converting, moreover many idolaters and heretics.

Not all Chrysostom's opponents were blameworthy men: there were undoubtedly good and earnest Christians amongst those who disagreed with him—he who became St Cyril of Alexandria among them. His principal ecclesiastical adversary was Archbishop Theophilus of Alexandria, already mentioned, who had several greivances against his brother of Constantinople. A no less dangerous enemy was the empress Eudoxia. John was accused of referring to her as 'Jezebel', and when he had preached a sermon against the profligacy and vanity of so many women it was represented by some as an attack levelled at the empress. Knowing the sense of grievance entertained by Theophilus, Eudoxia, to be revenged for the supposed affront to herself, conspired with him to bring about Chrysostom's deposition. Theophilus landed at Constantinople in June 403, with several Egyptian bishops; he refused to see or lodge with John; and got together a cabal of thirty-six bishops in a house at Chalcedon called The Oak. They proceeded to a sentence of deposition against him, which they sent to the Emperor Arcadius, accusing him at the same time of treason, apparently in having called the empress 'Jezebel'. Thereupon the emperor issued an order for his banishment.

For three days Constantinople was in an uproar, and Chrysostom delivered a vigorous manifesto from his pulpit. Then he surrendered himself, unknown to the people, and an official conducted him to Praenetum in Bithynia. But his first exile was short. The city was slightly shaken by an earthquake. This terrified the superstitious Eudoxia, and she implored Arcadius to recall John; she got leave to send a letter the same day, asking him to return and protesting her own innocence of his banishment. All the city went out to meet him, and the Bosphorus blazed with torches. Theophilus and his party fled by night.

But the fair weather did not last long. A silver statue of the empress having been erected before the great church of the Holy Wisdom, the dedication of it was celebrated with public games which, besides disturbing the liturgy, were an occasion of disorder, impropriety and superstition. Chrysostom fearing lest his silence should be construed as an approbation of the abuse, spoke loudly against it with his usual freedom and courage. The vanity of the Empress Eudoxia made her take the affront to herself, and his enemies were invited back. Theophilus sent three deputies. This second cabal appealed to certain canons of an Arian council of Antioch, made to exclude St Athanasius, by which it was ordained that no bishop who had been deposed by a synod should return to his see till he was restored by another synod. Arcadius sent John an order to withdraw.

Chrysostom was suffered to remain at Constantinople two months after Easter. On the Thursday after Pentecost the emperor sent an order for his banishment. The holy man bade adieu to the faithful bishops, and took his leave of St Olympias and the other deaconesses, who were overwhelmed with grief. He then left the church by stealth to prevent a sedition, and was conducted into Bithynia, arriving at Nicaea on June 20 404. The Emperor Arcadius chose Cucusus, a little place in the Taurus mountains of Armenia, for St John's exile. He set out from Nicaea in July, and suffered very great hardships from the heat, fatigue and the brutality of his guards. After a seventy days' journey he arrived at Cucusus where the good bishop of the place vied with his people in showing him every mark of kindness and respect.

Meanwhile Pope Innocent and the Emperor Honorius sent five bishops to Constantinople to arrange for a council, requiring that in the meantime Chrysostom should be restored to his see. But the deputies were cast into prison in Thrace, for the party of Theophilus (Eudoxia had died in childbed in October) saw that if a council were held they would inevitably be condemned. They also got an order from Arcadius that John should be taken farther away, to Pityus at the eastern end of the Black Sea, and two officers were sent to convey him thither. They had often to travel in scorching heat, from which the now aged Chrysostom suffered intensely; and in the wettest weather they forced him out of doors and on his way. When they reached Comana in Cappadocia he was very ill, yet he was hurried a further five or six miles to the chapel of St Basiliscus.

The next day, exhausted and ill, John begged that he might stay there a little longer. No attention was paid; but when they had gone four miles, seeing that he seemed to be dying, they brought him back to the chapel. There the clergy changed his clothes, putting white garments on him, and he received the Holy Mysteries. A few hours later St John Chrysostom uttered his last words, 'Glory be to God for all things', and gave up his soul to God. It was Holy Cross day, September 14, 407.

14 : ST NOTBURGA, VIRGIN (C. A.D. 1313)

NOTBURGA was the daughter of a peasant, and at the age of eighteen entered the service of Count Henry of Rattenberg and was employed in the kitchen. There was a good deal of food left over from the tables of this feudal establishment, and Notburga used to take it to one of the side doors of the castle and give it away to the poor people who daily waited there. Not content with this, she would even stint her own meals to increase the portion of the poor. When County Henry's mother died, his wife, the Countess Ottila, looked less favourably on the charity of the kitchen-maid, and gave orders that the broken food was to go into the pigbuckets as heretofore, and be fed to the swine. For a time Notburga did as she was told, and gave to the poor only what she could save from her own food and drink, but she soon began secretly to continue her old practice, till one day her mistress caught her at it and she was dismissed.

Count Henry in the meantime had been suffering considerably in the strife between the count of Tirol and the duke of Bavaria, and St Notburga's biographer, who wrote in the seventeenth century, says that Henry attributed all his misfortunes to the meanness of his wife, lately dead, and the consequent dismissal of Notburga. So, when he married a second time and somebody was required to manage the household, Notburga was installed as housekeeper and lived a happy and holy life at Rattenberg for the rest of her days. Before she died she particularly recommended her beloved poor to her master, and asked him to lay her body on a farm-wagon and bury it wherever the oxen should finally rest. This was done, and after a journey of which the usual miraculous accompaniments are recorded, the oxen brought the burden to a halt before the door of the church of St Rupert at Eben. Here accordingly St Notburga was buried.

15 : ST CATHERINE OF GENOA, WIDOW (A.D. 1510)

THE Fieschi were a great Guelf family of Liguria, with a long and distinguished history. In 1234 it gave to the Church the vigorous Pope Innocent IV, and in 1276 his nephew, who ruled for a few weeks as Adrian V. By the middle of the fifteenth century it had reached the height of its power and splendour in Liguria, Piedmont and Lombardy; one member was a cardinal, and another, James, descended from the brother of Innocent IV, was viceroy of Naples for King René of Anjou. This James Fieschi was married to a Genoese lady, Francesca di Negro, and to them was born at Genoa in the year 1447 the fifth and last of their children, Caterinetta, now always called Catherine.

From the age of thirteen Catherine was undoubtedly strongly attracted to the religious life. Her sister was already a canoness regular and the chaplain of her convent was Catherine's confessor, so she asked him if she also could take the habit. In consultation with the nuns he put her off on account of her youth, and about the same time Catherine's father died. Then, at the age of sixteen, she was married.

The star of the Ghibelline family of the Adorni was in decline, and by an alliance with the powerful Fieschi they hoped to restore the fortunes of their house. The Fieschi were willing enough, and Catherine was their victim. Her bridegroom was Julian Adorno, a young man with too poor a character to bring any good out of his marriage as a marriage. Catherine was beautiful in person (as may be seen from her portraits), of great intelligence and sensibility, and deeply religious; of an intense temperament, without humour or wit. Julian was of very different fibre, incapable of appreciating his wife. He was, on his own admission, unfaithful to her; for the rest, he was pleasure-loving to an inordinate degree, undisciplined, hot-tempered and spendthrift. He was hardly ever at home, and for the first five years, of her married life Catherine lived in solitude and moped amid vain regrets. Then for another five she tried what consolations could be found in the gaieties and recreations of her world, and was little less sad and desperate than before.

She had, however, never lost trust in God, or at least so much of it as was implied in the continued practice of her religion, and on the eve of the feast of St Benedict in 1473 she asked that saint, 'St Benedict, pray to God that He make me stay three months sick in bed'. Two days later she was kneeling for a blessing before the chaplain at her sister's convent when she was suddenly overcome by a great love of God and realization of her own unworthiness. Within the next day or two she had a vision of our Lord carrying His cross which caused her to cry out, 'O Love, if it be necessary I am ready to confess my sins in public!' Then she made a general confession of her whole life with such sorrow 'as to pierce her soul'. On the feast of the Annunciation she received holy communion, the first time with fervour for ten years, and shortly after became a daily communicant, so remaining for the rest of her life.

At about this time his luxury and extravagance had brought Julian to the verge of ruin, and his wife's prayers, added to his misfortunes, brought about a reformation in his life. They moved from their *palazzo* into a small house, much more humble and in a poorer quarter than was necessary; agreed to live together in continence; and devoted themselves to the care of the sick in the hospital of Pammatone. Associated with them was a cousin of Catherine, Tommasina Fieschi, who after her widowhood became first a canoness and then a Dominican nun. This went on for six years until in 1479 the couple went to live in the hospital itself, of which eleven years later she was appointed matron. She proved as capable an administrator as she was a devoted nurse, especially during the plague of 1493, when four-fifths of those who remained in the city died. In 1496 Catherine's own health broke down and she had to resign the control of the hospital, though still living within the building, and in the following year her husband died after a painful illness.

From the year 1473 on St Catherine without intermission led a most intense spiritual life combined with unwearying activity on behalf of the sick and sad, not only in the hospital but throughout Genoa. The life of St Catherine has been taken as the text of a most searching work on the mystical element in religion yet she also kept the hospital accounts without ever being a farthing out and was so concerned for the right disposition of property that she made four wills with several codicils.

Catherine suffered from ill health for some years and had to give up not only her extraordinary fasts, but even to a certain extent those of the Church, and at length in 1507 her health gave way completely. She rapidly got worse, and for the last months of her life suffered great agony; among the physicians who attended her was John-Baptist Boerio, who had been the principal doctor of King Henry VII of England. On September 13, 1510, she was in a high fever and delirium, and died at dawn of the 15th.

She was beatified in 1737, and Benedict XIV added her name to the Roman Martyrology, with the title of saint.

16 : ST CYPRIAN, BISHOP OF CARTHAGE, MARTYR (A.D. 258)

CAECILIUS CYPRIANUS, popularly known as Thascius, and was born about the year 200, probably at Carthage; certainly he was, according to St Jerome, a native of Proconsular Africa. Very little is known of his pre-Christian life; he was a public orator, teacher of rhetoric, and pleader in the courts, and engaged to the full in the life of Carthage, both public and social. God's instrument of his conversion, somewhere about middle age, was an old priest, Caecilian, and Cyprian ever after reverenced him as his father and guardian angel. Caecilian, in turn, had the greatest confidence in his virtue and on his death-bed recommended his wife and children to Cyprian's care and protection. A complete change came over Cyprian's life. Before his baptism he made a vow of perfect chastity, which greatly astonished the Carthaginians and drew even from his biographer St Pontius the exclamation, 'Who ever saw such a miracle! '

With the study of the Holy Scriptures St Cyprian joined that of their best expositors, and in a short time became acquainted with the works of the greatest religious writers: he particularly delighted in the writings of his countryman Tertullian. Cyprian was soon made priest, and in 248 he was designated for the bishopric of Carthage. At first he refused and sought to fly, but finding it in vain he yielded and was consecrated.

The Church continued to enjoy peace for about a year after St Cyprian's promotion to the see of Carthage, till the Emperor Decius began his reign by raising a persecution. Years of quietness and prosperity had had a weakening effect among the Christians, and when the edict reached Carthage there was a stampede to the capitol to register apostasies with the magistrates, amid cries of 'Cyprian to the lions! ' from the pagan mob. The bishop was proscribed, and his goods ordered to be forfeited, but Cyprian had already retired to a hiding-place, a proceeding which brought upon him much adverse criticism both from Rome and in Africa. He felt put on his defence, and set out justifying reasons for his action in several letters to the clergy.

During the absence of St Cyprian a priest who had opposed his episcropal election, named Novatus, went into open schism. Some among the lapsed, and confessors who were displeased at St Cyprian's discipline towards the former, adhered to him, for Novatus received, without any canonical penance, all apostates who desired to return to the communion of the Church. St Cyprian denounced Novatus, and at a council convened at Carthage when the persecution slackened he read a treatise on the unity of the Church.

The leaders of the schismatics were excommunicated, and Novatus departed to Rome to help stir up trouble there, where Novatian had set himself up as antipope. Cyprian recognized Cornelius as the true pope and was active in his support both in Italy and Africa during the ensuing schism; with St Dionysius, Bishop of Alexandria, he rallied the bishops of the East to Cornelius, making it clear to them that to adhere to a false bishop of Rome was to be out of communion with the Church. In connexion with these disturbances he added to his treatise on Unity one on the question of the Lapsed.

St Cyprian complains in many parts of his works that the peace which the Church had enjoyed enervated in some Christians the watchfulness and spirit of their profession, and had opened a door to many converts who had no true spirit of faith, and many lacked courage to stand the trial. These, whether apostates who had sacrificed to idols or *libellaticii* who, without sacrificing, had purchased for money certificates that they *had* offered sacrifice, were the lapsed (*lapsi*), concerning the treatment of whom so great a controversy raged during and after the Decian persecution: on the side of excessive lenience Novatus went into schism, while Novatian's severity crystallized into the heresy that the Church cannot absolve an apostate at all. At this time those guilty of less heinous sins than apostasy were not admitted to assist at the holy Mysteries before they had gone through a rigorous course of public penance, consisting of four degrees and of several years' continuance. Relaxations of these penances were granted on certain extraordinary occasions, and it was also customary to grant 'indulgences' to penitents who received a recommendation from some martyr going to execution, or from some confessor in prison for the faith, containing a request on their behalf, which the bishop and his clergy examined and often ratified. In St Cyprian's time this custom degenerated in Africa into an abuse, by the number of such *libelli martyrum*, and their often being given in too vague or peremptory terms, and without examination or discernment.

Cyprian condemned these abuses severely, but though it would appear that he himself tended to severity he in fact pursued a middle way, and in practice was considerate and lenient. After he had consulted the Roman clergy he insisted that his episcopal rulings must be followed without question until the whole matter could be brought up for discussion by all the African bishops and priests. This was eventually done in 251, at the council at Carthage mentioned above, and it was decided that, whereas *libellaticii* might be restored after terms of penance varying in length according to the case, *sacrificati* could receive communion only at death. But in the following year the persecution of Gallus and Volusian began, and another African council decreed that 'all the penitents who professed themselves ready to enter the list afresh, there to abide the utmost heat of battle and manfully to fight for the name of the Lord and for their own salvation, should receive the peace of the Church'.

Between the years 252 and 254 Carthage was visited by a terrible plague, of the ravages of which St Pontius has left a vivid description. Cyprian organized the Christians of the city and spoke to them strongly on the duty of mercy and charity, teaching them that they ought to extend their care not only to their own people, but also to their enemies and persecutors. To comfort and fortify his flock during the plague, Cyprian wrote his treatise *De mortalitate*.

Whereas St Cyprian so strongly supported Pope St Cornelius, in the closing years of his life he was moved to oppose Pope St Stephen I in the matter of baptism conferred by heretics and schismatics—he and the other African bishops refused to recognize its validity. Though Cyprian published a treatise on the goodness of patience, he displayed considerable warmth during this controversy, an excess for which, as St Augustine says, he atoned by his glorious martyrdom. For in August 257 was promulgated the first edict of Valerian's persecution, which forbade all assemblies of Christians and which required bishops, priests and deacons to take part in official worship under pain of exile, and on August 30 the bishop of Carthage was brought before the proconsul. Paternus ordered him into exile, but when Galerius replaced him as proconsul Cyprian was recalled from exile and again put on trial. Once more, however, he refused to offer sacrifice to the pagan gods, and on this occasion he was sentenced to death by beheading. The sentence was carried out immediately. It was September 14, A.D. 258.

17 : ST HILDEGARD, VIRGIN (A.D. 1179)

S HE was born in the year 1098 at Böckelheim, on the Nahe, and when she was eight years old her parents confided her to the care of Bd Jutta, sister to Count Meginhard of Spanheim, who was living as a recluse in a cottage adjoining the church of the abbey founded by St Disibod on the Diessenberg close by her home. The child was sickly, but she continued her education, learning to read and sing Latin and other things appertaining to a nun. By the time Hildegard was old enough to receive the veil of a nun the hermitage of Bd Jutta had had become a community, following the Rule of St Benedict. She was clothed when she was fifteen and continued for another seventeen years to lead an uneventful life. In 1136 Bd Jutta died, and Hildegard became prioress in her place.

Revelations and visions now pressed more and more upon her. There was a continual interior urging that she should write them down, but she feared what people would say, their mockery, and her own inadequate Latin. At last she opened her heart fully to her confessor, the monk Godfrey, and authorized him to refer the matter to his abbot, Conon, who after careful consideration ordered Hildegard to write down some of the things she said God had made known to her. They dealt with such matters as the charity of Christ and the continuance of the kingdom of God, the holy angels, the Devil and Hell. These writings Conon submitted to the archbishop of Mainz, who examined them with his theologians and gave a favourable verdict. The abbot then appointed a monk named Volmar to act as secretary to Hildegard, and she at once began the dictation of her principal work, which she called *Scivias*, for *Nosce vias [Domini]*.

This book took ten years to complete, and consists of twenty-six visions dealing with the relations between God and man by the Creation, the Redemption and the Church, mixed with apocalyptic prophecies, warnings, and praises expressed in symbolical fashion. She reiterated time and again that she saw these things in vision, and they were the inspiration of all her active work. In 1147 the pope, Bd Eugenius III, came to Trier and the archbishop of Mainz referred st Hildegard's writings to him. Eugenius appointed a commission to examine both them and her, and on reciving a favourable report he read and discussed the writings himself with his advisers, including St Bernard of Clairvaux, who wished him to approve the visions as genuine. The pope then wrote to Hildegard expressing wonder and happiness at the favours granted her by Heaven, and warning her against pride; authorizing her to publish, with prudence, whatever the Holy Spirit told her to publish; and exhorting her to live with her sisters in the place she had seen in vision in faithful observance of the Rule of St Benedict. St Hildegard wrote a long letter in reply, full of parabolic allusions to the troubles of the times and warning Eugenius against the ambitions of his own household.

The place to which Bd Eugenius referred was the new home which Hildegard had chosen for her community, which had outgrown its accommodation at the Diessenberg. The migration was stoutly opposed by the monks of St Disibod's, whose abbey owed much of its importance to the neighbouring convent, with its relics of Bd Jutta and the growing reputation of Hildegard. The abbot acccused her of acting from pride, but she claimed that God had revealed to her that she should move her nuns and the place to which they should go. This was the Rupertsberg, an exposed and unfertile hill above the Rhine, near Bingen. The move was made some time between 1147 and 1150, the nuns exchanging their house on the vine-clad Diessenberg for a dilapidated church and unfinished buildings in a deserted spot.

The energy of St Hildegard was responsible for the building of a large and convenient monastery, 'with water piped to all the offices', we are told, which housed a community of fifty nuns. For the recreation of these the versatility of Hildegard provided a large number of new hymns, canticles and anthems, of which she wrote both the words and the music, and a sort of morality play, or sacred cantata, called *Ordo Virtutum,* and for reading in the chapter-house and refectory she composed fifty allegorical homilies. From the Rupertsberg St Hildegard conducted a voluminous correspondence, and nearly three hundred of her letters have been printed, though doubt has been thrown on the authenticity of some of them and of the letters she received. Her letters are full prophecies and warnings, and they soon made her notorious. On the one hand people of all kinds came from all parts to consult her; on the other she was denounced as a fraud, a sorceress, a demoniac. Though her meaning was often wrapped up in difficult symbolism, she always made it quite clear when she was reproving, which she most frequently found occasion to do.

In spite of all her work and continual sickness the activities of St Hildegard were not confined to her convent, and between 1152 and 1162 she made numerous journeys in the Rhineland. She founded a daughter-house at Eibingen, near Rudesheim, and did not hesitate roundly to rebuke the monks and nuns of those monasteries whose discipline she saw to be relaxed; indeed, her expeditions were rather in the nature of the progress of an 'abbess visitor'. At Cologne, Trier, and elsewhere, she addressed herself to selected representatives of the clergy, imparting to them the divine warnings she had received, and exhorted bishops and lay folk with equal ease and straightforwardness.

During the last year of her life St Hildegard was in great trouble on account of a young man who, having been at one time excommunicated, died and was buried in the cemetery at St Rupert's. The vicar general of Mainz ordered that the body be removed. St Hildegard refused, on the grounds that the man had received the last sacraments and that she had been favoured with a vision justifying her action. Thereupon the church was put under an interdict; and Hildegard wrote to the chapter of Mainz a long letter about sacred music—'A half-forgotten memory of a primitive state which we have lost since Eden'—'symbol of the harmony which Satan has broken, which helps man to build a bridge of holiness between this world and the World of all Beauty and Music. Those therefore who, without a good reason, impose silence on churches in which singing in God's honour is wont to be heard, will not deserve to hear the glorious choir of angels that praises the Lord in Heaven'. Apparently she was doubtful of the effect of her touching eloquence on the canons of Mainz, for at the same time she wrote very energetically to the archbishop himself who was in Italy. He thereupon removed the interdict, but, in spite of a promise, he did not fulfil Hildegard's other request, to leave fighting and intriguing and come and govern his diocese. St Hildegard was now broken by infirmity and mortifications, she could not stand upright, and had to be carried from place to place. But the broken instrument, in the phrase of her friend and chaplain, Martin Guibert, still gave out melody; to the last she was at the disposition of everybody, giving advice to those that sought it, answering perplexing questions, writing, instructing her nuns, encouraging the sinners who came to her, never at rest. She survived her trouble with the chapter of Mainz a very little time, and died peacefully on September 17, 1179. The process of her canonization was twice undertaken. It was never achieved, but she is named as a saint in the Roman Martyrology.

18 : ST JOSEPH OF CUPERTINO, (A.D. 1663)

JOSEPH DESA was born June 17, 1603, at Cupertino, a small village between Brindisi and Otranto. His parents were so poor that Joseph himself was born in a shed at the back of the house: his father, a carpenter, was unable to pay his debts and the home was being sold up. His childhood was unhappy. His widowed mother looked on him as a nuisance and a burden, and treated him with great severity, and he developed an extreme absentmindedness and inertia. He would forget his meals, and when reminded of them say simply, 'I forgot', and wander open-mouthed in an aimless way about the village so that he earned the nick-name of 'Boccaperta', the gaper. He had a hot temper, which made him more unpopular, but was exemplary and even precocious in his religious duties. When the time came for him to try and earn his own living, Joseph was bound apprentice to a shoemaker, which trade he applied himself to for some time, but without any success. When he was seventeen he presented himself to be received amongst the Conventual Franciscans, but they refused to have him. Then he went to the Capuchins, and they took him as a lay brother; but after eight months he was dismissed as unequal to the duties of the order.

Joseph then turned for help to a wealthy uncle, who curtly refused to aid an obvious good-for-nothing, and the young man returned home in despair and misery. His mother was not at all pleased to see him on her hands again and used her influence with her brother, a Conventual Franciscan, to have him accepted by the friars of his order at Grottella as a servant. He was given a tertiary habit and put to work in the stables. A change then seems to have come over Joseph; he was more successful in his duties, and his humility, his sweetness, his love of mortification and penance gained him so much regard that in 1625 it was resolved he should be admitted amongst the religious of the choir, that he might qualify himself for holy orders. Joseph therefore began his novitiate, and his virtues rendered him an object of admiration; but his lack of progress in studies was also remarked.

After having received the priesthood in 1628 he passed five years without tasting bread or wine, and the herbs he ate on Fridays were so distasteful that only himself could use them. His fast in Lent was so rigorous that he took no nourishment except on Thursdays and Sundays, and he spent the hours devoted to manual work in those simple household and routine duties which he knew were, humanly speaking, all he was fitted to undertake. From the time of his ordination St Joseph's life was one long succession of ecstasies, miracles of healing and supernatural happenings on a scale not paralleled in the reasonably authenticated life of any other saint.

During the seventeen years he remained at Grottella over seventy occasions are recorded of his levitation, the most marvellous being when the friars were building a calvary. The middle cross of the group was thirty-six feet high and correspondingly heavy, defying the efforts of ten men to lift it. St Joseph is said to have 'flown' seventy yards from the door of the house to the cross, picked it up in his arms 'as if it were a straw', and deposited it in its place. This staggering feat is not attested by an eye-witness, and, in common with most of his earlier marvels, was recorded only after his death, when plenty of time had elapsed in which events could be exaggerated and legends arise. But, whatever their exact nature and extent, the daily life of St Joseph was surrounded by such disturbing phenomena that for thirty-five years he was not allowed to celebrate Mass in public, to keep choir, to take his meals with his brethren, or to attend processions and other public functions.

There were not wanting persons to whom these manifestations were an offence, and when St Joseph attracted crowds about him as he travelled in the province of Bari, he was denounced. The vicar general carried the complaint to the inquisitors of Naples, and Joseph was ordered to appear. The heads of his accusation being examined, the inquisitors could find nothing worthy of censure, but did not discharge him; instead they sent him to Rome to his minister general, who received him at first with harshness, but he became impressed by St Joseph's innocent and humble bearing and he took him to see the pope, Urban VIII. The saint went into ecstasy at the sight of the vicar of Christ, and Urban declared that if Joseph should die before himself he would give evidence of the miracle to which he had been a witness. It was decided to send Joseph to Assisi, where again he was treated by his superiors with considerable severity, they at least pretending to regard him as a hypocrite. He arrived at Assisi in 1639, and remained there thirteen years. At first he suffered many trials, both interior and exterior. God seemed to have abandoned him; his religious exercises were accompanied with a spiritual dryness that afflicted him exceedingly and terrible temptations cast him into so deep a melancholy that he scarce dare lift up his eyes. The minister general, being informed, called him to Rome, and having kept him there three weeks he sent him back to Assisi. The saint on his way to Rome experienced a return of those heavenly consolations which had been withdrawn from him.

In 1653, for reasons which are not known, the Inquisition of Perugia was instructed to remove St Joseph from the care of his own order and put him in charge of Capuchins at a lonely friary among the hills of Pietrarossa, where he was to live in the strictest seclusion. In effect, he had gone to prison. He was not allowed to leave the convent enclosure, to speak to anyone but the friars, to write or to receive letters; he was completely cut off from the world. But soon his whereabouts were discovered and pilgrims flocked to the place; whereupon he was spirited away to lead the same sort of life with the Capuchins of Fossombrone. The rest of his life was spent like this. When in 1655 the chapter general of the Conventual Franciscans asked for the return of their saint to Assisi, Pope Alexander VII replied that one St Francis at Assisi was enough, but in 1657 he was allowed to go to the Conventual house at Osimo. Here the seclusion was, however, even more strict, and only selected religious were allowed to visit him in his cell. But all this time, and till the end, supernatural manifestations were his daily portion: he was in effect deserted by man but God was ever more clearly with him. He fell sick on August 10, 1663, and knew that his end was at hand; five weeks later he died, at the age of sixty. He was canonized in 1767.

19 : ST EMILY DE RODAT, VIRGIN, FOUNDRESS OF THE CON-
GREGATION OF THE HOLY FAMILY OF VILLEFRANCHE (A.D. 1852)

FACING the plateau on which stands the ancient city of Rodez in the south of France is a handsome manor-house called Druelle, and it was here that Marie Guillemette (Wilhelmina) Emilie de Rodat was born in 1787. When she was only eighteen months old Emily was taken to live with her maternal grandmother in the Château of Ginals, on a hill outside Villefranche-de-Rouergue. Emily was certainly what would be called a pious child, and a cousin who tried to kiss her received an impressively heavy smack. When she was sixteen she began to see something of life in society, and her devotion cooled a little: she found her confessor over-strict, and sought another; and she made her prayers as short as possible. The vigilant grandmother did not fail to notice this and, as she rejected the company of 'nuns and pious females' in Villefranche, Emily had to go back to Ginals, where her parents were now living. But here she gradually realized where her happiness and duty really lay, and from about Corpus Christi 1804, when she underwent a sudden and definitive spiritual experience, she never looked back.

In the following year, when she was eighteen, Emily returned to Villefranche to help the nuns at the establishment, Maison Saint-Cyr, where she had herself been to school. She had charge of the children's recreation, prepared them for first communion, and taught them geography. But the important thing that happened was her meeting with the Abbé Marty, the spiritual director of the establishment. Three times during her eleven years at the Maison Saint-Cyr Emily left, with his permission, to try elsewhere: at Figeac with the Ladies of Nevers, at Cahors with the Picpus Sisters' at Moissac with the Sisters of Mercy; each time she was disappointed and restless, and came back to Villefranche reproaching herself for instability.

Then one day in the spring of 1815 Emily de Rodat, calling on a sick woman, found a number of the neighbours there; they were discussing the near impossibility of getting schooling for their children because they had no money for it. Within a few weeks Emily had started teaching in her own room at the Maison Saint-Cyr.

It was only a small room, but somehow she got forty children into it, as well as three young women to help her with the teaching. This was the beginning of what was to become the Congregation of the Holy Family, and there was the usual opposition. But, with the quiet encouragement of the Abbé Marty, Emily went ahead, rented premises on her own, and in May 1816 her free school was started. Meanwhile the community at the Maison Saint-Cyr was breaking up, and less than eighteen months after leaving it Sister Emily (who had now taken public vows) returned to take possession of that house, with eight other sisters and a hundred pupils.

Two years later Sister Emily was able to buy better buildings but there soon followed a disaster that threatened to put an end to the growing community. Starting with Sister Eleanor Dutriac there was a series of deaths that physicians were unable properly to account for and which the famous priest Mgr Alexander von Hohenlohe attributed to diabolic influence. Sister Emily was inclined to take this as a sign that she was not called to make a foundation, and she seriously thought of uniting hei community with the Daughters of Mary, newly established by Adèle de Batz de Trenquelléon. This probably would have happened but that the Villefranche sisters refused any mother superior but Emily de Rodat, and so the installation in the new house was carried through; in the autumn of 1820 perpetual vows were taken, and the habit adopted of which the distinguishing feature was the transparent edge of the veil covering the upper part of the face.

During the next seven years Mother Emily suffered cruelly in body, firstly from cancerous growths in the nose and then from a complaint which left her with permanent and incurable noises in the ears. It was this ill-health that led to the establishment of the first daughter house, at Aubin, whither Mother Emily had gone to consult a doctor. There was now added to Mother Emily's physical ill-health a prolonged and severe 'dark night of the soul', but she continued to expand her congregation and to make further foundations (there were thirty-eight of them before her death). To teaching were added sick-nursing and other good works, and the strain on the sisters' resources was often considerable; but Mother Emily always had complete faith that the needs of their poor would be met, and so they were, sometimes by a multiplication of resources both of money and goods that had every mark of the miraculous.

In 1843 the sisters at Villefranche began to visit the prison, with encouraging results, and two years later there was an important development when their first 'rescue-home' for women was opened. And then there was what Mgr Gély called 'l'Hôtel des Invalides', a place of retirement for aged religious, to which was added a novitiate house and another for orphans. But with all these and other developments the enclosed sisters of the congregation were not neglected. Mother Emily never lost an opportunity to open a cloistered convent, seeing in the two branches a personification of Martha and Mary.

In 1835 the Abbé Marty died. He had not always seen eye-to-eye with Mother Emily, nor had she always dissembled her disagreement but affection, respect and common purpose had bound them together, and not the least thing that Mother Emily owed to the Abbé Marty was a deep appreciation of the abiding presence of the Holy Spirit and His significance for Christians. Mother Emily outlived her old friend by seventeen years.

In April 1852 a cancerous growth appeared in her left eye. She resigned the government of the congregation into the hands of Mother Foy, leaving herself, as she said, nothing else to do but to suffer. Among the things she thought of was the Confraternity of the Holy Childhood and its work for abandoned babies in China: 'Keep up interest in that among the children, and teach them to love it', she said to her daughters. 'The wall is crumbling', she told them in the evening of September 18; and on the following day it fell, to be rebuilt in the streets of the heavenly Jerusalem where play those children to whom she had devoted her earthly life. Emily de Rodat was canonized in 1950.

20 : ST VINCENT MADELGARIUS, ABBOT (C. A.D. 687)

HE was born about the year 615, and became the husband of St Waldetrudis (April 9). They had four children all venerated as saints, namely Landericus or Landry, Madelberta, Aldetrudis and Dentelinus. About 653 his wife became a nun, and Madelgarius took the Benedictine habit and the name of Vincent in the monastery of Hautmont, which he founded. He later established another abbey on his estate at Soignies, where he died.

21 : ST MICHAEL OF CHERNIGOV AND ST THEODORE, MARTYRS (A.D. 1246)

THE Church in Russia had no martyrs, properly speaking, before the Tartar invasions of the thirteenth century. The number who then gave their lives for Christ was very large, and the first to receive both popular and liturgical veneration were those among them who were also nobles and military leaders against the barbarian invaders. Outstanding in popularity among these was Michael, Duke of Chernigov.

The first we hear of him is unpromising. He showed cowardice in face of the enemy and fled from Kiev, abandoning the city to the Tartars. But then, hoping to attract their violence to himself and distract it from the people, he returned of his own will and made his way into the camp of the Horde. Their leader, Bati, tried to persuade Michael to treachery, making great promises if he would only make an act of idolatrous worship. St Michael refused: he was not willing to be a Christian only in name. His friends then formed a plan for his escape from the camp, but this also he refused, lest they should suffer Bati's reprisals. So the Tartars tortured and then beheaded him, on September 20, 1246, and there suffered with him one of his nobles, St Theodore.

22 : ST THOMAS OF VILLANOVA, ARCHBISHOP OF VALENCIA (A.D. 1555)

ST THOMAS was born at Fuentellana in Castile in 1488, but received his surname from Villanueva de los Infantes' a town where he was brought up. His parents were also originally of Villanueva; the father was a miller; their state was not affluent, but solid, and their charitable disposition was the most valuable part of their son's inheritance. At the age of sixteen he was sent to the University of Alcalá, and he pursued his studies there with success; he became master of arts and licentiate in theology and, after ten years at Alcalá, was made professor of philosophy in that city, being then twenty-six years old; among those who attended his lectures was the famous Dominic Soto.

In 1516 Thomas joined the Augustinian friars at Salamanca, and in 1518 he was promoted to priestly orders, employed in preaching, and teaching a course of divinity in his convent. He was exceptionally clear-headed, with a firm and solid judgement, but had always to cope with absent-mindedness and a poor memory. He was afterwards prior in several places, and was particularly solicitous for those friars who were sick.

When Don George of Austria resigned the archbishopric of Valencia, the emperor thought of not offering St Thomas this see because he knew how grievous a trial it would be to him. He therefore, it is said, ordered his secretary to draw up a letter of nomination in favour of a certain religious of the Order of St Jerome. Afterwards finding that the secretary had put down the name of Brother Thomas of Villanova, he asked the reason. The secretary answered that he thought he had heard his name, but would rectify the mistake. 'By no means', said Charles. 'This has happened by a particular providence of God. Let us therefore follow His will.' So he signed the appointment for St Thomas and it was forthwith sent to Valladolid, where he was prior. The saint used all means possible to excuse himself, but had to accept the appointment and was consecrated at Valladolid. Thomas set out very early next morning for Valencia. Upon his arrival at Valencia he retired to an Augustinian friary where he spent several days in penance and prayer to beg the grace of God by which he might be enabled worthily to acquit himself of his charge. He took possession of his cathedral on the first day of the year 1545 amidst the rejoicings of the people.

St Thomas discharged all the duties of a good pastor and visited the churches of his diocese, preaching everywhere in the towns and villages with zeal and affection. He assembled a provincial council (the first for many years) wherein with the help of his fellow bishops he made ordinances to abolish the abuses he had taken notice of in his visitation of his clergy. To effect that of his own chapter cost him much difficulty and time. There came to St Thomas's door every day several hundred poor people, and each of them received an alms, which was ordinarily a meal with a cup of wine and a piece of money. He took destitute orphans under his particular care, and for the eleven years that he was archbishop not one poor maiden was married who was not helped by his charity. When in 1550 pirates had plundered a coast town in his diocese the archbishop immediately sent four thousand ducats and cloth worth as much more to furnish the inhabitants with necessaries and to ransom the captives.

St Thomas wished to help the *nuevos Cristianos* or *Moriscos*, Moors who were converted to Christianity but whose conversion was often unreal or who lapsed into apostasy and so were brought under the brutal jurisdiction of the Spanish Inquisition. He was never able to achieve much for them in his large diocese, but he induced the emperor to provide a fund to support special priests for work among them and himself founded a college for the children of the newly converted. He also founded a college for poor scholars at his old university at Alcalá, and then, having scruples at having expended money outside his own diocese, he endowed another at Valencia.

It is not known for certain why St Thomas did not attend the Council of Trent; he was represented thereat by the bishop of Huesca, and most of the Castilian bishops consulted him before they left. He impressed on them that it was at least as necessary for the council to legislate for an internal reformation in the Church as against the Lutheran heresy, and made two interesting suggestions neither of which was in fact acted upon. One was that all benefices having the cure of souls should be filled by incumbents native of the place, so far as possible and providing they were well qualified, especially in rural districts; the other was that the ancient canon which forbade the translation of a bishop from one see to another should be re-enforced. The idea of the union of a bishop with his see as with a bride was always present to the saint, and he lived in perpetual concern for the proper discharge of his own episcopal duties.

He was seized by *angina pectoris* in August 1555. Having commanded all the money then in his possession to be distributed among the poor, he ordered all goods to be given to the rector of his college, except the bed on which he lay; he gave this bed to the gaoler for the use of prisoners, but borrowed it of him till such time as he should no longer require it. On September 8 the end was at hand. He ordered Mass to be offered in his presence, and after the consecration recited the psalm *In te, Domine, speravi:* after the priest's communion he said that verse, 'Into thy hands, O Lord, I commend my spirit', at which words he rendered his soul into the hands of God, in the sixty-seventh year of his age. He was buried, according to his desire, in the church of the Austin friars at Valencia; and he was canonized in 1658.

23 : ST ADAMNAN, OR EUNAN, ABBOT OF IONA (A.D. 704)

HE was born about the year 624 at Drumhome in the county of Donegal. He entered a monastery which had been founded there. Afterwards, following the steps of his holy kinsman Columba, he retired to the monastery of Iona, of which he became ninth abbot in the year 679. On the death of Oswy, King of Northumbria, his son Aldfrith had had to fly from the usurper Egfrith, and had taken shelter at Iona, where he met Adamnan. When in 686, Aldfrith being then on his throne, someone was required to go on behalf of the Irish to the Northumbrians to negotiate for the release of some captives, it was therefore natural that St Adamnan should be chosen for the mission. He succeeded, and while he was in England again in 688 he visited the monasteries of Wearmouth and Jarrow, and was seen by the young Bede, who was then a boy of thirteen. The important result of this visit was that, by the persuasion of St Ceolfrith, he laid aside the custom of his predecessors and conformed on the time of celebrating Easter. Upon his return home he used his utmost endeavours to guide his monks at Iona into the same practice, but without success.

After his failure to convert his monks from Celtic to Roman customs, St Adamnan spent a good deal of time in Ireland. At the Council of Birr he was instrumental in persuading the assembly that women should not take part in warfare and that they and their children should be neither killed nor taken as prisoners; this decision was called Adamnan's Law after him. All the time he was zealously propagating the observance of the true Easter, which was accepted nearly wherever he went, except where the influence of Columban monasteries was strong, and notably in his own Iona. After St Columba Adamnan was Iona's most accomplished scholar. He himself refers to the writing-tablets, the pens and *stili* and ink-horns, in the monastic scriptorium, and of these he made full use himself. His own name is remembered for, more than anything, his Life of St Columba, one of the most important hagiographical documents in existence and the most complete biography of the early middle ages. He wrote it in Latin at the request of his brethren. In the latter part of the seventh century a Frankish bishop called Arculf went on pilgrimage to Jerusalem, and on the way back his ship was driven by contrary winds to the western coast of Britain. Arculf found himself at Iona, where he was warmly received by Adamnan and gave a long account to the monks of all he had seen in the East. St Adamnan wrote this narrative down, and so composed his other well-known work, *De locis sanctis*. This book was presented by Adamnan to King Aldfrith.

He died on September 23, 704.

24 : ST GERARD, BISHOP OF CSANAD, MARTYR (A.D. 1046)

ST GERARD, sometimes surnamed Sagredo, the apostle of a large district in Hungary, was a Venetian, born about the beginning of the eleventh century. At an early age he consecrated himself to the service of God in the Benedictine monastery of San Giorgio Maggiore at Venice, but after some time left it to undertake a pilgrimage to Jerusalem. While passing through Hungary he became known to the king, St Stephen, who made him tutor to his son, Bd Emeric, and Gerard began as well to preach with success. When St Stephen established the episcopal see of Csanad he appointed Gerard to be its first bishop. The greater part of the people were heathen, but St Gerard laboured among them with much fruit.

King Stephen seconded the zeal of the good bishop so long as he lived, but on his death in 1038 the realm was plunged into anarchy by competing claimants to the crown, and a revolt against Christianity began. Things went from bad to worse, and eventually, when celebrating Mass at a little place on the Danube called Giod, Gerard had prevision that he would on that day receive the crown of martyrdom. His party arrived at Buda and were going to cross the river, when they were set upon by some soldiers under the command of an obstinate upholder of idolatry and enemy of the memory of King St Stephen. They attacked St Gerard with a shower of stones, overturned his conveyance, and dragged him to the ground. Whilst in their hands the saint raised himself on his knees and prayed with St Stephen, 'Lord, lay not this sin to their charge. They know not what they do.' He had scarcely spoken these words when he was run through the body with a lance; the insurgents then hauled him to the edge of a cliff called the Blocksberg, on which they were, and dashed his body headlong into the Danube below. It was September 24, 1046.

25 : ST ALBERT, PATRIARCH OF JERUSALEM (A.D. 1214)

WHEN the Latin kingdom of Jerusalem was set up in 1099 by the crusaders under Godfrey de Bouillon, the Greek hierarchs were driven from their principal sees and churches and replaced by bishops from the West, whose only subjects were in the ranks of the crusaders themselves. Thus there came to be a Latin patriarch in Jerusalem, and it must be regretfully recorded that most of the prelates who held this office in crusading times were as equivocal in character as they were in position.

When therefore the Patriarch Michael died in the year 1203 the canons regular of the Holy Sepulchre, supported by King Amaury II de Lusignan, petitioned Pope Innocent III to send to succeed him a prelate whose holiness and abilities were well known even in Palestine. This was Albert, Bishop of Vercelli. He belonged to a distinguished family of Parma, and after brilliant theological and legal studies had become a canon regular in the abbey of the Holy Cross at Mortara in Lombardy. When he was about thirty-five years old, namely in 1184, he was made bishop of Bobbio and almost at once translated to Vercelli. His diplomatic ability and trustworthiness caused him to be chosen as a mediator between Pope Clement III and Frederick Barbarossa. By Innocent III he was made legate in the north of Italy, and in that capacity he brought about peace between Parma and Piacenza in 1199. Innocent did not want to spare him for Jerusalem, but approved the choice of the canons; he invested him with the *pallium* and created him his legate in Palestine, and in 1205 St Albert set out.

Already in 1187 the Saracens had retaken Jerusalem, and the see of the Latin patriarch had been moved to Akka (Ptolemais), where the Frankish king had set up his court. At Akka accordingly St Albert established himself, and set out to gain the respect and trust not only of Christians but of the Moslems as well, which his predecessors had conspicuously failed to do. As patriarch and legate he took a foremost part in the ecclesiastical and civil politics of the Levant, but Albert is best remembered now for a quite different work. Between 1205 and 1210 St Brocard, prior of the hermits living on Mount Carmel, asked him to embody the life they were leading in a rule for the observance of himself and his subjects. This St Albert did in a document of sixteen very short and definite 'chapters'. His rule was confirmed by Pope Honorius III in 1226, and modified by Innocent IV twenty years later. Whoever may have been the founder of the Carmelite Order, there is no doubt that St Albert of Jerusalem, an Augustinian canon, was its first legislator.

Innocent III summoned St Albert to the forthcoming council of the Lateran; but he did not live to be present at that great assembly, which opened in November 1215. For twelve months he faithfully supported the pope's hopeless efforts to get back Jerusalem, and then his life was suddenly and violently cut short. He had found it necessary to depose from his office the master of the Hospital of the Holy Ghost at Akka, and the man was nursing his resentment. On the feast of the Exaltation of the Cross in 1214 St Albert officiated at a procession in the church of the Holy Cross at Akka, and in the course of it he was attacked and stabbed to death by the deposed hospitaller.

26 : ST TERESA COUDERC, VIRGIN, CO-FOUNDRESS OF THE CONGREGATION OF OUR LADY OF THE RETREAT IN THE CENACLE (A.D. 1885)

IN the year 1824 the Reverend J. P. E. Terme and other priests were sent by their bishop to La Louvesc, in the Vivarais in south-eastern France, to do missionary work among the peasants and to look after the pilgrim shrine of St John Francis Regis. It was soon found urgently necessary to open a hostel for women pilgrims; and to look after this hostel Father Terme turned to a community of sisters whom he had established to teach in his former parish of Aps. Three young women were accordingly sent to La Louvesc in 1827, among them Sister Teresa Couderc. Sister Teresa, born in 1805 and christened Mary Victoria, came of good farming stock at Sablières, and had been one of the first members of the community at Aps.

When she was only twenty-three, Father Terme made her superioress at La Louvesc, where under considerable difficulties (especially from the climate which, at 4000 feet up, is fierce in winter) the community was already showing signs of growth. The year after that came its turning-point. Father Terme went to a retreat at a Jesuit house near Le Puy: and on his return he announced that the Daughters of St Regis (as they were then called) should add to their work the giving of retreats for women. This was at that time a most remarkable innovation; it was an immediate success, especially among the countrywomen, and in years to come it was to spread across the world. But meanwhile, on December 12, 1834, Father Terme died.

The shrine and parish of La Louvesc had recently been taken over by the Jesuit fathers. With their advice it was decided to separate the work of school-teaching from that of retreats. Twelve carefully-chosen sisters were therefore withdrawn from the Daughters of St Regis, and, with Mother Teresa Couderc at their head, installed at La Louvesc, under the direction of Father Rigaud, S.J.. The giving of retreats according to the method of St Ignatius went ahead, and a new house and church for the convent soon became necessary. But the source on which reliance had been put to meet these and other expenses suddenly failed, and the community was left with very large debts and nothing to pay them with. Mother Teresa blamed herself—quite unnecessarily—for what had happened, and in 1838 she resigned her office as superioress. Thereupon the bishop of Viviers named in her place a wealthy widow who had been in the community less than a month.

Thus began a long, complex and not always edifying story, which is a matter of the history and development of the Society of the Cenacle (as it was soon to be known) rather than of its holy foundress. Mother Teresa was sent to make a new foundation at Lyons, in most difficult conditions; but she more and more dropped into obscurity. It was nearly twenty years before Mgr Guibert, bishop of Viviers, declared once and for all that the founder of the Cenacle was Father John Terme and the foundress Mother Teresa Couderc, and nobody else; and at that time she was sent to the Paris convent as temporary superioress at a moment of crisis. Then she sank into the background again, so the Cardinal Lavigerie on a visit to the nuns, at once detecting holiness in her face, had to ask who was the one that had been *left out*.

St Teresa Couderc was a foundress, yet for well over half of her eighty years her life was a hidden one, forwarding the work of her foundation in hiding as it were, with her prayers, her penances, her humiliations. Towards the end of her life Mother Teresa's health began to fail badly, and for the last nine months she suffered terribly in body. At Fourvière on September 26, 1885, Mary Victoria Couderc, Mother Teresa, died. In 1951 she was beatified, and canonized in 1970.

27 : ST VINCENT DE PAUL, FOUNDER OF THE CONGREGATION OF THE MISSION AND THE SISTERS OF CHARITY (A.D. 1660)

ST VINCENT DE PAUL was a native of Pouy, a village near Dax, in Gascony. His parents occupied a very small farm, upon the produce of which they brought up a family of four sons and two daughters, Vincent being their third child. His father placed him under the care of the Cordeliers (Franciscan Recollects) at Dax. Vincent finished his studies at the university of Toulouse, and in 1600 was ordained priest at the age of twenty. His ambition was to be comfortably off. He was already one of the chaplains of Queen Margaret of Valois and, according to the custom of the age, he was receiving the income of a small abbey. He went to lodge with a friend in Paris. And there it was that we first hear of a change in him. His friend was robbed of four hundred crowns. He charged Vincent with the theft, thinking it could be nobody else; Vincent calmly denied the fact. He bore this slander for six months, when the true thief confessed.

At Paris Vincent became acquainted with the holy priest Peter de Bérulle, afterwards cardinal. Bérulle conceived a great esteem for Vincent and prevailed with him to become tutor to the children of Philip de Gondi, Count of Joigny. Mme de Gondi was attracted by Vincent, and chose him for her spiritual director and confessor.

In the year 1617, whilst they were at a country seat at Folleville, Monsieur Vincent was sent for to hear the confession of a peasant who lay dangerously ill. He discovered that all the former confessions of the penitent had been sacrilegious, and the man declared before many persons and the Countess of Joigny herself, that he would have been eternally lost if he had not spoken to Monsieur Vincent. The good lady was struck with horror to hear of such past sacrileges. To Vincent himself also appears to have come at that moment an enlightening as to the terrible spiritual state of the peasantry of France. Mme de Gondi had no difficulty in persuading him to preach in the church of Folleville, and fully to instruct the people in the duty of repentance and confession of sins. He did so; and such crowds flocked to him to make general confessions that he was obliged to call the Jesuits of Amiens to his assistance.

With the help of Father de Bérulle, St Vincent left the house of the countess in 1617 to become pastor of Châtillon-les-Dombes. He there converted the notorious Count de Rougemont and many others from their scandalous lives. But he soon returned to Paris, and began work among the galley-slaves who were confined in the Conciergerie. He was officially appointed chaplain to the galleys (of which Philip de Gondi was general), and in 1622 gave a mission for the convicts in them at Bordeaux.

Mme de Gondi now offered him an endowment to found a perpetual mission among the common people in the place and manner he should think fit, but nothing at first came of it, for Vincent was too humble to regard himself as fit to undertake the work. She induced her husband to concur with her in establishing a company of missionaries to assist their tenants, and the people of the countryside in general. This project they proposed to their brother, who was archbishop of Paris, and he gave the Collège des Bons Enfants for the reception of the new community. Its members were to renounce ecclesiastical preferment, to devote themselves to the smaller towns and villages, and to live from a common fund. St Vincent took possession of this house in April 1625.

Vincent attended the countess till her death, which happened only two months later; he then joined his new congregation. In 1633 the prior of the canons regular of St Victor gave to this institute the priory of Saint-Lazare, which was made the chief house of the congregation, and from it the Fathers of the Mission are often called Lazarists, but sometimes Vincentians, after their founder. They are a congregation of secular priests, who make four simple vows of poverty, chastity, obedience and stability. They are employed in missions, especially among country people, and undertake the direction of diocesan and other seminaries; they now have colleges and missions in all parts of the world. St Vincent lived to see twenty-five houses founded in France, Piedmont, Poland and other places, including Madagascar. For this purpose he also established confraternities of charity (the first had been at Châtillon) to attend poor sick persons in each parish, and from them, with the help of St Louise de Marillac, sprang the institute of Sisters of Charity. He invoked the assistance of the wealthy women of Paris and banded them together as the Ladies of Charity to collect funds for and assist in his good works. He procured and directed the foundation of several hospitals for the sick, foundlings, and the aged, and at Marseilles the hospital for the galley-slaves, which, however, was never finished. All these establishments he settled under excellent regulations, and found for them large sums of money.

During the wars in Lorraine, being informed of the miseries to which those provinces were reduced, St Vincent collected alms in Paris, which were sent there to the amount of thousands of pounds. He sent his missionaries to the poor and suffering in Poland, Ireland, Scotland, the Hebrides, and uring his own life over 1200 Christian slaves were ransomed in North Africa, and many others succoured. He was sent for by King Louis XIII as he lay dying, and was in high favour with the queen regent, Anne of Austria, who consulted him in ecclesiastical affairs and in the collation of benefices; during the affair of the Fronde he in vain tried to persuade her to give up her minister Mazarin in the interests of her people. It was largely due to Monsieur Vincent that English Benedictine nuns from Ghent were allowed to open a house at Boulogne in 1652.

Towards the end of his life he suffered much from serious ill-health. In the autumn of 1660 he died calmly in his chair, on September 27, being fourscore years old. Monsieur Vincent, the peasant priest, was canonized by Pope Clement XII, in 1737, and by Pope Leo XIII he was proclaimed patron of all charitable societies, outstanding among which is the society that bears his name and is infused by his spirit, founded by Frederic Ozanam in Paris in 1833.

28 : ST WENCESLAUS OF BOHEMIA, MARTYR (A.D. 929)

THE baptism of the ruler of Bohemia, Borivoy, and his wife St Ludmila was not followed by the conversion of all their subjects, and many of the powerful Czech families were strongly opposed to the new religion. From the year 915 Duke Borivoy's son Ratislav governed the whole country. He married a nominally Christian woman, Drahomira, daughter of the chief of the Veletians, a Slav tribe from the north, and they had two sons, Wenceslaus (Vaclav), born in 907 near Prague, and Boleslaus. St Ludmila, who was still living, arranged that the upbringing of the elder might be entrusted to her, and she undertook with the utmost care to form his heart to the love of God. Ludmila joined with herself in this task a priest, her chaplain Paul, who had been a personal disciple of St Methodius and had baptized Wenceslaus. He was still young when his father was killed fighting against the Magyars, and his mother Drahomira assumed the government, pursuing an anti-Christian or 'secularist' policy.

St Ludmila, afflicted at the public disorders and full of concern for the interest of religion, which she and her consort had established with so much difficulty, showed Wenceslaus the necessity of taking the reins of government into his own hands. Fearing what might happen, two nobles went to Ludmila's castle at Tetin and there strangled her, so that, deprived of her support, Wenceslaus should not undertake the government of his people. But it turned out otherwise: other interests drove Drahomira out, and proclaimed Wenceslaus. He straightway announced that he would support God's law and His Church, punish murder severely, and endeavour to rule with justice and mercy. His mother had been banished to Budech, so he recalled her to the court, and there is no evidence that for the future she ever opposed Wenceslaus.

The political policy of St Wenceslaus was to cultivate friendly relations with Germany, and he preserved the unity of his country by acknowledging King Henry I as his over-lord, about the year 926, seeing in him the legitimate successor of Charlemagne. This policy, and the severity with which he checked oppression and other disorders in the nobility, raised a party against him, especially among those who resented the influence of the clergy in the counsels of Wenceslaus. Then, when the young duke married and had a son, his jealous brother Boleslaus lost his chance of the succession, and he threw in his lot with the malcontents.

In September 929 Wenceslaus was invited by Boleslaus to go to Stara Boleslav to celebrate the feast of its patron saints Cosmas and Damian. On the evening of the festival Wenceslaus proposed a toast, said his prayers, and went to bed. Early the next morning, as Wenceslaus made his way to Mass, he met Boleslaus and stopped to thank him for his hospitality. 'Yesterday', was the reply, 'I did my best to serve you fittingly, but this must be my service to-day', and he struck him. The brothers closed and struggled; whereupon friends of Boleslaus ran up and killed Wenseslaus, who murmured as he fell at the chapel door, 'Brother, may God forgive you'.

At once the young prince was acclaimed by the people as a martyr.

29 : SS. RHIPSIME, GAIANA, AND THEIR COMPANIONS, VIRGINS AND MARTYRS (c. A.D. 312?)

ALTHOUGH these maidens, apparently the protomartyrs of the Armenian church, are mentioned in the Roman Martyrology on this date as suffering under King Tiridates, nothing at all is known of their history or the circumstances of their passion. They are referred to in the legend of St

Gregory the Enlightener, and may have been put to death during the persecution which preceded the baptism of Tiridates and his family by Gregory, but more likely later: their *acta* is a romance.

These legends tell us that Rhipsime (Hrip'sime) was a maiden of noble birth, one of a community of consecrated virgins at Rome presided over by Gaiana. The Emperor Diocletian, having made up his mind to marry, sent a painter around Rome to paint the portraits of all those ladies who seemed to him eligible, and he did his work with such thoroughness that he penetrated into the house of Gaiana and made likenesses of some of her Christian maidens. When Diocletian examined the portraits his choice fell on Rhipsime, and she was informed of the honour that had befallen her. It was not at all to her liking, and Gaiana was so afraid of what the emperor might do that she summoned her charges at once from Rome, went aboard ship, and proceeded to Alexandria. From thence they made their way through the Holy Land to Armenia, where they settled down at the royal capital, Varlarshapat, and earned their living by weaving. The great beauty of Rhipsime soon attracted attention, but the noise of it apparently reached back to Rome before it came to the ears of King Tiridates, for Diocletian wrote asking him to kill Gaiana and send Rhipsime back—unless he would like to keep her for himself. Tiridates thereupon sent a deputation to fetch her to his palace with great magnificence, but when it arrived at the convent Rhipsime prayed for deliverance, and so fierce a thunderstorm at once broke out that the horses of the courtiers and their riders were scattered in confusion. When Tiridates heard this and that the girl refused to come he ordered her to be brought by force, and when she was led into his presence he was so attracted by her beauty that he at once tried to embrace her. Rhipsime not only resisted but threw the king ignominiously to the floor, so that in a rage he ordered her to prison. But she escaped and returned to her companions during the night.

At morning when they found her gone the king sent soldiers after her with orders that she was to die, and all the other maidens with her. St Rhipsime was roasted alive and torn limb from limb, and St Gaiana and the others to the number of thirty-five likewise were brutally slain. St Mariamne was dragged to death from a bed of sickness, but one, St Nino, escaped and became the apostle of Georgia in the Caucasus. This massacre took place on October 5.

30 : ST JEROME, DOCTOR OF THE CHURCH (A.D. 420)

JEROME (EUSEBIUS HIERONYMUS SOPHRONIUS), the father of the Church most learned in the Sacred Scriptures, was born about the year 342 at Stridon, a small town upon the confines of Pannonia, Dalmatia and Italy, near Aquileia. His father took great care to have his son instructed in religion and in the first principles of letters at home and afterwards sent him to Rome. Jerome had there for tutor the famous pagan grammarian Donatus. He became master of the Latin and Greek tongues (his native language was Illyrian), read the best writers in both languages with great application, and made progress in oratory; but being left without a guide under the discipline of a heathen master he forgot some of the piety which had been instilled into him in his childhood. Jerome went out of this school free indeed from gross vices, but a stranger to a Christian spirit and enslaved to vanity and other weaknesses, as he afterward confessed and bitterly lamented. On the other hand he was baptized there. After some three years in Rome he determined to travel in order to improve his studies and, with his friend Bonosus, he went to Trier. Here it was that the religious spirit with which he was so deeply imbued was awakened, and his heart was entirely converted to God.

In 370 Jerome settled down for a time at Aquileia, where the bishop, St Valerian, had attracted so many good men that its clergy were famous all over the Western church. With many of these St Jerome became friendly, and their names appear in his writings.

Already he was beginning to provoke strong opposition, and after two or three years an unspecified conflict broke up the group. Jerome decided to withdraw into some distant country. Bonosus, who had been the companion of his studies and his travels from childhood, went to live on a desert island in the Adriatic. Jerome himself happened to meet a well-known priest of Antioch, Evagrius, at Aquileia, which turned his mind towards the East. With his friends Innocent, Heliodorus and Hylas (a freed slave of St Melania) he determined to go thither.

St Jerome arrived in Antioch in 374 and made some stay there. Innocent and Hylas were struck down by illness and died, and Jerome too sickened. In a letter to St Eustochium he relates that in the heat of fever he fell into a delirium in which he seemed to himself to be arraigned before the judgement-seat of Christ. Being asked who he was, he answered that he was a Christian. 'Thou liest', was the reply, 'Thou art a Ciceronian: for where thy treasure is, there is thy heart also.' This experience had a deep effect on him which was deepened by his meeting with St Malchus. As a result, St Jerome withdrew into the wilderness of Chalcis, a barren land to the south-east of Antioch, where he spent four years alone. He suffered much from ill health, and even more from strong temptations of the flesh.

The church of Antioch was at this time disturbed by doctrinal and disciplinary disputes. The monks of the desert of Chalcis vehemently took sides in these disputes and wanted St Jerome to do the same and to pronounce on the matters at issue. He preferred to stand aloof and be left to himself, but he wrote to Damasus, who had been raised to the papal chair in 366. However, not receiving a speedy answer he sent another letter on the same subject. The answer of Damasus is not extant: but it is certain that he and the West acknowledged Paulinus as bishop of Antioch, and St Jerome received from his hands the order of priesthood when he finally left the desert of Chalcis. Jerome had no wish to be ordained (he never celebrated the eucharist) and he only consented on the condition that he should not be obliged to serve that or any other church by his ministry: his vocation was to be a monk or recluse. Soon after he went to Constantinople to study the Scriptures under St Gregory Nazianzen. Upon St Gregory's leaving Constantinople in 382, St Jerome went to Rome with Paulinus of Antioch and St Epiphanius to attend a council which Damasus held about the schism at Antioch. When the council was over, Pope Damasus detained him and employed him as his secretary; Jerome, indeed, claimed that he spoke through the mouth of Damasus.

Side by side with this official activity he was engaged in fostering and directing the marvellous flowering of asceticism which was taking place among some of the noble ladies of Rome. But when St Damasus died in 384, and his protection was consequently withdrawn from his secretary, St Jerome found himself in a very difficult position. In the preceding two years, while impressing all Rome by his personal holiness, learning and honesty, he had also contrived to get himself widely disliked; on the one hand by pagans whom he had fiercely condemned and on the other by people who were offended by the saint's harsh outspokenness and sarcastic wit. It cannot be matter of surprise that, however justified his indignation was, his manner of expressing it aroused resentment. His own reputation was attacked with similar vigour; even his simplicity, his walk and smile, the expression of his countenance were found fault with. Neither did the severe virtue of the ladies that were under his direction nor the reservedness of his own behaviour protect him from calumny: scandalous gossip was circulated about his relations with St Paula. He was properly indignant and decided to return to the East, there to seek a quiet retreat. He embarked at Porto in August 385.

At Antioch nine months later he was joined by Paula, Eustochium and the other Roman religious women who had resolved to exile themselves with him in the Holy Land. Soon after arriving at Jerusalem they went to Egypt, to consult with the monks of Nitria, as well as with Didymus, a famous blind teacher in the school of Alexandria. With the help of Paula's generosity a monastery for men was built near the basilica of the Nativity at Bethlehem, together with buildings for three communities of women. St Jerome himself lived and worked in a large rock-hewn cell near to our Saviour's birthplace, and opened a free school, as well as a hospice.

Here at last were some years of peace. But Jerome could not stand aside and be mute when Christian truth was threatened. At Rome he had composed his book against Helvidius on the perpetual virginity of the Blessed Virgin Mary, Helvidius having maintained that Mary had other children, by St Joseph, after the birth of Christ. This and certain associated errors were again put forward by one Jovinian. St Paula's son-in-law, St Pammachius, and other laymen were scandalized at his new doctrines, and sent his writings to St Jerome who in 393 wrote two books against Jovinian. In the first he shows the excellence of virginity embraced for the sake of virtue, which had been denied by Jovinian, and in the second confutes his other errors. This treatise was written in Jerome's characteristically strong style and certain expressions in it seemed to some persons in Rome harsh and derogatory from the honour due to matrimony; St Pammachius informed St Jerome of the offence which he and many others took at them. Thereupon Jerome wrote his Apology to Pammachius, sometimes called his third book against Jovinian, in a tone that can hardly have given his critics satisfaction. A few years later he had to turn his attention to Vigilantius—Dormantius, sleepy, he calls him—a Gallo-Roman priest who both decried celibacy and condemned the veneration of relics, calling those who paid it idolaters and worshippers of ashes.

From 395 to 400 St Jerome was engaged in a war against Origenism, which unhappily involved a breach of his twenty-five years friendship with

Rufinus. Few writers made more use of Origen's works and no one seemed a greater admirer of his erudition than St Jerome; but finding in the East that some had been seduced into grievous errors by the authority of his name and some of his writings he joined St Epiphanius in warmly opposing the spreading evil. Rufinus, who then lived in a monastery at Jerusalem, had translated many of Origen's works into Latin and was an enthusiastic upholder of his authority.

St Augustine was distressed by the resulting quarrel, which, however, he the more easily understood because he himself became involved in a long controversy with St Jerome arising out of the exegesis of the second chapter of St Paul's epistle to the Galatians. By his first letters he had unintentionally provoked Jerome, and had to use considerable charitable tact to soothe his easily wounded susceptibilities.

Nothing has rendered the name of St Jerome so famous as his critical labours on the Holy Scriptures. While in Rome under Pope St Damasus he had revised the gospels and the psalms in the Old Latin version followed by the rest of the New Testament. His new translation from the Hebrew of most of the books of the Old Testament was the work of his years of retreat at Bethlehem, which he undertook at the earnest entreaties of many devout and illustrious friends, and in view of the preference of the original to any version however venerable. He did not translate the books in order, but began by the books of Kings, and took the rest in hand at different times. The psalms he revised again, with the aid of Origen's *Hexapla* and the Hebrew text.

In the year 404 a great blow fell on St Jerome in the death of St Paula and a few years later in the sacking of Rome by Alaric; many refugees fled into the East. Again towards the end of his life he was obliged to interrupt his studies by an incursion of barbarians, and some time after by the violence and persecution of the Pelagians who sent a troop of ruffians to Bethlehem to assault the monks and nuns who lived there under the direction of St Jerome, who had opposed them. Some were beaten, and a deacon was killed, and they set fire to the monasteries. In the following year St Eustochium died and Jerome himself soon followed her: worn out with penance and work his sight and voice failing, his body like a shadow, he died peacefully on September 30, 420. He was buried under the church of the Nativity close to Paula and Eustochium, but his body was removed long after and now lies somewhere in St Mary Major's at Rome.

OCTOBER

1 : ST TERESA OF LISIEUX, VIRGIN (A.D. 1897)

THE parents of the saint-to-be were Louis Martin, a watchmaker of Alençon, son of an officer in the armies of Napoleon I, and Azélie-Marie Guérin, a maker of point d' Alençon in the same town, whose father had been a gendarme at Saint-Denis near Séez. Five of the children born to them survived to maturity, of whom Teresa was the youngest. She was born on January 2, 1873, and baptized Marie- Françoise-Thérèse. Her childhood was happy and ordinary. She had a quick intelligence and an open and impressionable mind. In 1877 Mrs Martin died, and Mr Martin sold his business at Alençon and went to live at Lisieux (Calvados), where his children might be under the eye of their aunt, Mrs Guérin. Mr Martin had a particular affection for Teresa, but it was an older sister, Mary, who ran the household and the eldest, Pauline, who made herself responsible for the religious upbringing of her sisters.

When Teresa was nine this Pauline entered the Carmel at Lisieux and Teresa began to be drawn in the same direction. When Teresa was nearly fourteen her sister Mary joined Pauline in the Carmel and on Christmas eve of the same year Teresa underwent an experience which she ever after referred to as her conversion. Characteristically, the occasion of this sudden accession of strength was a remark of her father about her child-like addiction to Christmas observances, not intended for her ears at all.

During the next year Teresa told her father her wish to become a Carmelite, and Mr Martin agreed; but both the Carmelite authorities and the bishop of Bayeux refused to hear of it on account of her lack of age. A few months later she was in Rome with her father and a French pilgrimage on the occasion of the secerdotal jubilee of Pope Leo XIII. At the public audience, when her turn came to kneel for the pope's blessing, Teresa boldly broke the rule of silence on such occasions and asked him, 'In honour of your jubilee, allow me to enter Carmel at fifteen'. Leo was clearly impressed by her appearance and manner, but he upheld the decision of the immediate superiors.

At the end of the year the bishop, Mgr Hugonin, gave his permission, and on April 9, 1888, Teresa Martin entered the Carmel at Lisieux whither her two sisters had preceded her. In 1889 the three sisters in blood and in Carmel sustained a sad blow when their beloved father's mind gave way following two paralytic attacks and he had to be removed to a private asylum, where he remained for three years. But 'the three years of my father's martyrdom', wrote St Teresa, 'seem to me the dearest and most fruitful of our life. I would not exchange them for the most sublime ecstasies.' She was professed on September 8, 1890.

One of the principal duties of a Carmelite nun is to pray for priests, a duty which St Teresa discharged with great fervour at all times; and she never ceased in particular to pray for the good estate of the celebrated ex-Carmelite Hyacinth Loyson, who had apostatized from the faith. Although she was delicate she carried out all the practices of the austere Carmelite rule from the first, except that she was not allowed to fast. The autobiography which St Teresa wrote at the command of her prioress, *L'histoire d'une âme*, is an unique and engaging document, written with a delightful clarity and freshness, full of surprising turns of phrase, bits of unexpected knowledge and unconscious self-revelation, and, above all, of deep spiritual wisdom and beauty.

In 1893 Sister Teresa was appointed to assist the novice mistress and was in fact mistress in all but name. In 1894 Mr Martin died and soon after Céline, who had been looking after him, made the fourth Martin sister in the Lisieux Carmel. Eighteen months later, during the night between Maundy Thursday and Good Friday, St Teresa heard, 'as it were, a far-off murmur announcing the coming of the Bridegroom': it was a haemorrhage at the mouth. At the time she was inclined to respond to the appeal of the Carmelites at Hanoi in Indo-China, who wished to have her, but her disease took a turn for the worse and the last eighteen months of her life was a time of bodily suffering and spiritual trials. In June 1897 she was removed to the infirmary of the convent and never left it again; from August 16 on she could no longer receive holy communion because of frequent sickness. On September 30, with words of divine love on her lips, Sister Teresa of Lisieux died. She was beatified by Pope Pius XI in 1923, and in 1925 the same pope declared Teresa-of-the-Child-Jesus s to have been a saint. In 1927 she was named the heavenly patroness of all foreign missions, with St Francis Xavier, and of all works for Russia.

2 : THE GUARDIAN ANGELS

FROM early times liturgical honour was paid to all angels in the office of the dedication of the church of St Michael the Archangel *in Via Salaria* on September 29, and in the oldest extant Roman sacramentary, called Leonine, the prayers for the feast make indirect reference to them as individual guardians. A votive Mass, *Missa ad suffragia angelorum postulanda*, has been in use at least from the time of Alcuin—he died in 804—who refers to the subject twice in his letters. Whether the practice of celebrating such a Mass originated in England is not clear, but we find Alcuin's text in the Leofric Missal of the early tenth century. This votive Mass of the Angels was commonly allotted to the second day of the week (Monday), as for example in the Westminster Missal, written about the year 1375. In Spain it became customary to honour the Guardian Angels not only of persons, but of cities and provinces. An office of this sort was composed for Valencia in 1411.

Outside of Spain, Francis of Estaint, Bishop of Rodex, obtained from Pope Leo X a bull in 1518 which approved a special office for an annual commemoration of the Guardian Angels on March 1. In England also there seems to have been much devotion to them. Herbert Losinga, Bishop of Norwich, who died in 1119, speaks eloquently on the subject; and the well-known invocation beginning *Angele Dei qui custos es mei* is apparently traceable to the verse-writer Reginald of Canterbury, at about the same period. Pope Paul V authorized a special Mass and Office and at the request of Ferdinand II of Austria granted the feast to the whole empire. Pope Clement X extended it to the Western church at large as of obligation in 1670 and fixed it for the present date, being the first free day after the feast of St Michael.

3 : ST THOMAS CANTELUPE, BISHOP OF HEREFORD (A.D. 1282)

THE father of St Thomas was steward of Henry III's household, and his mother, Millicent de Gournay, dowager Countess of Evreux and Gloucester. His parents had four other sons and three daughters, towards whom Thomas was not very friendly when he grew up. He was born about the year 1218 at Hambleden, near Great Marlow, and his education was entrusted to his uncle Walter, Bishop of Worcester, who sent Thomas to Oxford when he was nineteen; but he did not stay there long, going on to Paris with his brother Hugh. The young patricians lived in considerable state, and in 1245 accompanied their father, who was one of the English envoys, to the thirteenth general council, at Lyons. Here Thomas was probably ordained, and received from Pope Innocent IV dispensation to hold a plurality of benefices, a permission of which he afterwards freely availed himself.

After reading civil law at Orleans, Thomas returned to Paris, and after getting his licence he came back to Oxford to lecture there in canon law; in 1262 he was chosen chancellor of the university. Thomas was always noted for his charity to poor students; he was also a strict disciplinarian. There were large numbers of undergraduates in residence; they were allowed to carry arms and were divided into opposing camps of northerners and southerners. Thomas had an armoury of weapons, confiscated for misuse. When Prince Edward camped near the city and the whole university was 'gated', the young gentlemen burned down the provost's house, wounded many of the townspeople, and emptied the mayor's cellar (he was a vintner). Unlike his grandfather, who had been a strong supporter of King John, Thomas the Chancellor was with the barons against Henry III, and was one of those sent to plead their cause before St Louis at Amiens in 1264. After the defeat of the king at Lewes, Thomas was appointed chancellor of the kingdom. His prudence, courage, scrupulous justice, and disregard of human respect and of the least bribe which could be offered him completed the character of an accomplished magistrate. But he did not hold office long, being dismissed after the death of Simon de Montfort at Evesham. Thomas was then about forty-seven years old and he retired to Paris.

Thomas came back to Oxford after some years, was perhaps re-appointed chancellor there, and took his D.D. in the church of the Dominicans: on which occasion Robert Kilwardby, then archbishop elect of Canterbury, declared in his public oration that the candidate had lived without reproach. But he continued to demonstrate that pluralism is not necessarily inconsistent with high character, for in addition to being archdeacon of Stafford and precentor of York he held four canonries and seven or eight parochial livings, especially in Herefordshire. These he administered by vicars, and he was in the habit of making unannounced visits to see how the souls and bodies of their flocks were being cared for. In 1275 he was chosen bishop of Hereford, and consecrated in Christ Church at Canterbury. On that occasion St Thomas commented on the fact that his episcopal brethren from across the Welsh border were not present; he was not pleased.

Owing to the civil wars and the pusillanimity of his two predecessors the large and wealthy diocese of Hereford was in a bad state when St Thomas came to govern it. One after another he met, defied and overcame the lords, spiritual and temporal, who encroached on its rights and possessions.

Among the numerous habits and traits of St Thomas recorded in the process of his canonization is that when he travelled in his diocese he asked every child he met if he had been confirmed, and if not the bishop at once supplied the omission. Public sinners he rebuked and excommunicated, equally publicly, particularly those who in high places set a bad example to those below them. Pluralism without the proper dispensation he would not permit, and among those whom he deprived of benefices in his diocese were the dean of Saint Paul's and the archdeacons of Northampton and Salop.

Unhappily, during the last years of his life there was dissension between St Thomas and John Peckham, Archbishop of Canterbury, first on some general questions of jurisdiction and then on particular cases arising in the diocese of Hereford. In a synod held at Reading in 1279 St Thomas was leader of the aggrieved suffragans, and in due course Rome gave them the reliefs they asked; but in his personal dispute he was excommunicated by the metropolitan. Some bishops refused to publish the sentence, and St Thomas publicly announced his appeal to Pope Martin IV, whom he set out to see in person. Some of Peckham's letters to his procurators at Rome are extant, but in spite of their fulminations St Thomas was very kindly received by the pope at Orvieto. Pending the consideration of his cause he withdrew to Montefiascone, but the fatigues and heat of the journey had been too much for him and he was taken mortally sick. Commending his soul to God, St Thomas died on August 25, 1282, and was buried at Orvieto; soon his relics were conveyed to Hereford, where his shrine in the cathedral became the most frequented in the west of England.

4 : ST FRANCIS OF ASSISI, FOUNDER OF THE FRIARS MINOR (A.D. 1226)

ST FRANCIS was born at Assisi in Umbria in 1181 or 1182. His father, Peter Bernadone, was a merchant, and his mother was called Pica. Much of Peter's trade was with France, and his son having been born while he was absent in that country, they called him *Francesco*, 'the Frenchman', though the name of John had been given him at his baptism. In his youth he was devoted to the ideas of romantic chivalry propagated by the troubadours; he had plenty of money and spent it lavishly, even ostentatiously. He was uninterested alike in his father's business and in formal learning.

When he was about twenty, strife broke out between the cities of Perugia and Assisi, and Francis was carried away prisoner by the Perugians. This he bore a whole year with cheerfulness and good temper. But as soon as he was released he was struck down by a long and dangerous sickness. On his recovery he determined to join the forces of Walter de Brienne, who was fighting in southern Italy. He bought himself expensive equipment and handsome outfit, but as he rode out one day in a new suit, meeting a gentleman reduced to poverty and very ill-clad, he was touched with compassion and changed clothes with him. At Spoleto he was taken ill again, and as he lay there a heavenly voice seemed to tell him to turn back, 'to serve the master rather than the man'. Francis obeyed. At first he returned to his old life, but more quietly and with less enjoyment. Then, riding one day in the plain of Assisi, he met a leper, whose sores were so loathsome that at the sight of them he was struck with horror. But he dismounted, and as the leper stretched out his hand to receive an alms, Francis, whilst he bestowed it, kissed the man.

Henceforward he often visited the hospitals and served the sick, and gave to the poor sometimes his clothes and sometimes money. One day as he was praying in the church of St Damian, outside the walls of Assisi, he seemed to hear a voice coming from the crucifix, which said to him three times, 'Francis, go and repair my house, which you see is falling down'. The saint, seeing that church was old and ready to fall, thought our Lord commanded him to repair that. He therefore went home, and in the simplicity of his heart took a horseload of cloth out of his father's warehouse and sold it, with the horse. The price he brought to the poor priest of St Damian's, asking to be allowed to stay with him. The priest consented, but would not take the money, which Francis therefore left on a window-sill. His father, hearing what had been done, came in great indignation to St Damian's, but Francis had hid himself. After some days spent in prayer and fasting, he appeared again, though so disfigured and ill-clad that people pelted him and called him mad. Bernardone, more annoyed than ever, carried him home, beat him unmercifully (Francis was about twenty-five), put fetters on his feet, and locked him up, till his mother set him at liberty while his father was out. Francis returned to St Damian's. His father, following him thither, hit him about the head and insisted that he should either return home or renounce all his share in his inheritance and return the purchase-price of the goods he had taken. Francis had no objection to being disinherited, but said that the other money now belonged to God and the poor. He was therefore summoned before Guido, Bishop of Assisi, who told him to return it and have trust in God. Francis did as he was told and, with his usual literalness, added, 'The clothes I wear are also his. I'll give them back.' He suited the action to the word, stripped himself of his clothes, and gave them to his father. The dress of a labourer, a servant of the bishop, was found, and Francis received this first alms with many thanks, made a cross on the garment with chalk, and put it on.

Francis went in search of shelter, singing the divine praises. He met a band of robbers, who asked him who he was. He answered, 'I am the herald of the great King'. They beat him and threw him into a ditch full of snow. He went on singing the praises of God. He passed by a monastery, and there received alms and a job of work as an unknown poor man. In the city of Gubbio, one who knew him took him into his house, and gave him a tunic, belt and shoes, such as pilgrims wore, which were decent though poor and shabby. These he wore two years, and he walked with a staff in his hand like a hermit. He then returned to San Damiano at Assisi. For the repair of the church he gathered alms and begged in Assisi, where all had known him rich, bearing with joy the railleries and contempt with which he was treated by some. For the building he himself carried stones and served the masons and helped put the church in order. He next did the same for an old church which was dedicated in honour of St Peter. After this he went to a little chapel called Portiuncula, belonging to the abbey of Benedictine monks on Monte Subasio, who gave it that name probably because it was built on so small a parcel of land. It stands in a plain two miles from Assisi, and was at that time forsaken and ruinous. The place appealed to St Francis, and he was delighted with the title which the church bore, it being dedicated in honour of our Lady of the Angels. He repaired it, and fixed his abode by it. Here, on the feast of St Matthias in the year 1209, his way of life was shown to St Francis. In those days the gospel of the Mass on this feast was Matt. x 7–19: 'And going, preach saying: The kingdom of Heaven is at hand . . . Freely have you received, freely give . . . . Do not possess gold . . . nor two coats nor shoes nor a staff . . . . Behold I send you as sheep in the midst of wolves . . . .' The words went straight to his heart and, applying them literally to himself, he gave away his shoes, staff and girdle, and left himself with one poor coat, which he girt about him with a cord. This was the dress which he gave to his friars the year following: the undyed woollen dress of the shepherds and peasants in those parts.

Many began to admire Francis, and some desired to be his companions and disciples. The first of these was Bernard da Quintavalle, a rich tradesman of Assisi. Bernard sold all his effects and divided the sum among the poor. Peter of Cattaneo, a canon of the cathedral of Assisi, desired to be admitted with him, and Francis 'gave his habit' to them both together on April 16, 1209. The third to join them was the famous Brother Giles, a person of great simplicity and spiritual wisdom. When his followers had increased to a dozen, Francis drew up a short informal rule consisting chiefly of the gospel counsels of perfection. This he took to Rome in 1210 for the pope's approbation. Innocent III afterwards told his nphew, from whom St Bonaventure heard it, that in a dream he saw a palm tree growing up at his feet, and in another he saw St Francis propping up the Lateran church, which seemed ready to fall. He therefore sent for St Francis, and approved his rule, but only by word of mouth, tonsuring him and his companions and giving them a general commission to preach repentance.

St Francis and his companions now lived together in a little cottage at Rivo Torto, outside the gates of Assisi, whence they sometimes went into the country to preach. After a time they had trouble with a peasant who wanted the cottage for the use of his donkey. Francis went off to see the abbot of Monte Subasio. The abbot, in 1212, handed over the Portiuncula chapel to St Francis, upon condition that it should always continue the head church of his order. Round about the chapel the brothers built themselves huts of wood and clay. St Francis would not suffer any property to be vested in his order, or in any community or convent of it; he called the spirit of holy poverty the foundation of the order, and in his dress, in everything that he used, and in all his actions he showed the reality of his love for it. He never proceeded in holy orders beyond the diaconate, not daring to be ordained priest.

In the autumn of 1212 Francis, not content with all that he did and suffered for souls in Italy, resolved to go and preach to the Moslems. He embarked with one companion at Ancona for Syria, but they were driven straight on to the coast of Dalmatia and wrecked. The two friars could get no further and, having no money for their passage, travelled back to Ancona as stowaways. After preaching for a year in central Italy, during which the lord of Chiusi put at the disposal of the Franciscans as a place of retreat Mount Alvernia (La Verna) in the Tuscan Apennines, St Francis made another attempt to reach the Moslems; this time in Morocco by way of Spain. But again he was disappointed in his object, for somewhere in Spain he was taken ill, and when he recovered he returned into Italy, where again he laboured strenuously to advance the glory of God among all Christian people.

Out of humility St Francis gave to his order the name of Friars Minor, desiring that his brethren should really be below their fellows and seek the last and lowest places. Many cities were anxious to have the brothers in their midst, and small communities of them sprang up throughout Umbria, Tuscany, Lombardy and Ancona. In 1216 Francis is said to have begged from Pope Honorius III the Portiuncula indulgence, or pardon of Assisi; and in the following year he was in Rome, where he probably met his fellow friar St Dominic, who had been preaching faith and penance in southern France while Francis was still a 'young man about town' in Assisi. St Francis also wanted to preach in France, but was dissuaded by Cardinal Ugolino (afterwards Pope Gregory IX); so he sent instead Brother Pacifico and Brother Agnello, who was afterwards to bring the Franciscans to England. The development of the brotherhood was considerably influenced by the good and prudent Ugolino. The members were so numerous that some organization and systematic control was imperatively necessary. The order was therefore divided into provinces, each in charge of a minister to whom was committed 'the care of the souls of the brethren, and should anyone be lost through the minister's fault and bad example, that minister will have to give an account before our Lord Jesus Christ'. The friars now extended beyond the Alps, missions being sent to Spain, Germany and Hungary.

The first general chapter was held at the Portiuncula at Pentecost in 1217; and in 1219 was held the chapter called 'of Mats', because of the number of huts of wattles and matting hastily put up to shelter the brethren: there were said to be five thousand of them present. St Francis sent some of his friars from this chapter to Tunis and Morocco, reserving to himself the Saracens of Egypt and Syria. Innocent III's appeal at the Lateran Council in 1215 for a new crusade had resulted only in a desultory attempt to bolster up the Latin kingdom in the East: Francis would wield the sword of the word of God.

He set sail with twelve friars from Ancona in June 1219, and came to Damietta on the Nile delta, before which the crusaders were sitting in siege.

Francis was profoundly shocked by the dissoluteness and self-seeking of the soldiers of the Cross. Burning with zeal for the conversion of the Saracens, he desired to pass to their camp, though he was warned that there was a price on the head of every Christian. Permission was given him by the papal legate and he went with Brother Illuminato crying out, 'Sultan! Sultan! ' Being brought before Malek al-Kamil and asked his errand, he said boldly, 'I am sent not by men but by the most high God, to show you and your people the way of salvation by announcing to you the truths of the gospel'. Discussion followed, and other audiences. The sultan was somewhat moved and invited him to stay with him.

After some days Malek al-Kamil sent Francis back to the camp before Damietta. Disappointed that he could do so little either with the crusaders or their opponents, St Francis returned to Akka, whence he visited the Holy Places. Then summoned by an urgent message of distress, he returned to Italy.

Francis found that in his absence his two vicars, Matthew of Narni and Gregory of Naples, had introduced certain innovations whose tendency was to bring the Franciscans into line with the other religious orders and to confine their proper spirit within the more rigid framework of monastic observance and prescribed asceticism. With the sisters at San Damiano this had taken the form of regular constitutions, drawn up on the Benedictine model by Cardinal Ugolino. When St Francis arrived at Bologna he was amazed and grieved to find his brethren there housed in a fine convent: he refused to enter it, and lodged with the Friars Preachers, from whence he sent for the guardian of his brethren, upbraided him and ordered the friars to leave that house. St Francis saw these events as a betrayal: it was a crisis that might transform or destroy his followers. He went to the Holy See, and obtained from Honorius III the appointment of Cardinal Ugolino as official protector and adviser to the Franciscans, for he was a man who believed in St Francis and his ideas while being at the same time an experienced man of affairs. Then he set himself to revise the rule, and summoned another general chapter, which met at the Portiuncula in 1221. To this assembly he presented the revised rule, which abated nothing of the poverty, humbleness and evangelical freedom which characterized the life he had always set before them: it was Francis's challenge to the dissidents and legalists who now, beneath the surface, were definitely threatening the peaceful development of the Franciscans. Chief among them was Brother Elias of Cortona, who, as vicar of St Francis, who had resigned active direction of the order, was in effect minister general of the brethren; but he did not dare too openly to oppose himself to the founder whom he sincerely respected.

At the end of two years, throughout which he had to face the growing tendency to break away from his ideas and to expand in directions which seemed to him to compromise the Franciscan vocation, Francis once again revised his rule. This done, he handed it to Brother Elias for communication to the ministers. It was promptly lost, and St Francis had again to dictate it to Brother Leo, amid the protests of many of the brethren who maintained that the forbiddance of holding corporate property was impracticable. In the form in which it was eventually approved by Pope Honorius III in 1223, it represented substantially the spirit and manner of life for which St Francis had stood from the moment that he cast off his fine clothes in the bishop's court at Assisi. About two years earlier St Francis and Cardinal Ugolino may have drawn up a rule for the fraternity of lay people who associated themselves with the Friars Minor in the spririt of Francis's 'Letter to all Christians', written in the early years of his mission—the Franciscan tertiaries of today.

St Francis spent the Christmas of 1223 at Grecchio in the valley of Rieti where, he told his friend John da Vellita, 'I would make a memorial of that Child who was born in Bethlehem and in some sort behold with bodily eyes the hardships of His infant state, lying on hay in a manger with the ox and the ass standing by'. Accordingly a 'crib' was set up at the hermitage, and the peasants crowded to the midnight Mass, at which Francis served as deacon and preached on the Christmas mystery. The custom of making a crib was probably not unknown before this time, but this use of it by St Francis is said to have begun its subsequent popularity. He remained for some months at Grecchio in prayer and quietness, and the graces which he received from God in contemplation he was careful to conceal from men.

Towards the festival of the Assumption in 1224, St Francis retired to Mount Alvernia and there made a little cell. He kept Leo with him, but forbade any other person to come to him before the feast of St Michael. It was here on or about Holy Cross day 1224, that the miracle of the *stigmata* happened. Having been thus marked with the signs of our Lord's passion, Francis tried to conceal this favour of Heaven from the eyes of men, and for this purpose he ever after covered his hands with his habit, and wore shoes and stockings on his feet.

The two years that remained of his life were years of suffering and of happiness in God. His health was getting worse, the *stigmata* were a source of physical pain and weakness, and his sight was failing. He got so bad that in the summer of 1225 Cardinal Ugolino and the vicar Elias obliged him to put himself in the hands of the pope's physicians at Rieti. He complied with simplicity, and on his way thither paid his last visit to St Clare at San Damiano. Here, almost maddened with pain and discomfort, he made the 'Canticle of Brother Sun', which he set to a tune and taught the brethren to sing. He went to Monte Rainerio to undergo the agonizing treatment prescribed, and got but temporary relief. He was taken to Siena to see other physicians, but he was dying.

Then he went to Assisi and was lodged in the bishop's house. The doctors there, pressed to speak the truth, told him he could not live beyond a few weeks. 'Welcome, Sister Death!' he exclaimed, and asked to be taken to the Portiuncula. As they came on the way to a hill in sight of Assisi he asked for the stretcher to be put down, and turning his blind eyes towards the town called down the blessing of God upon it and upon his brethren. Then they carried him on to the Portiuncula. When he knew the end was close at hand, Francis asked that they would send to Rome for the Lady Giacoma di Settesoli, who had often befriended him, and ask her to come, bringing with her candles and a grey gown for his burial, and some of the cake that he liked so well. But the lady arrived before the messenger started.

He sent a last message to St Clare and her nuns, and bade his brethren sing the verse of the song he had made to the Sun which praises Death. Then he called for bread and broke it and to each one present gave a piece in token of mutual love and peace, saying, 'I have done my part; may Christ teach you to do yours'. He was laid on the ground and covered with an old habit, which the guardian lent him. He exhorted his brethren to the love of God, of poverty, and of the gospel 'before all other ordinances', and gave his blessing to all his disciples, the absent as well as those that were present. The passion of our Lord in the gospel of St John was read aloud, and in the evening of Saturday, October 3, 1226, St Francis died.

He had asked to be buried in the criminals' cemetery on the Colle d'Inferno, but the next day his body was taken in solemn procession to the church of St George in Assisi. Here it remained until two years after his canonization when, in 1230, it was secretly removed to the great basilica built by Brother Elias.

5 : ST FLORA OF BEAULIEU, VIRGIN (A.D. 1347)

THE 'Hospitalieres', nuns of the Order of St John of Jerusalem, had a flourishing priory known as Beaulieu, between Figeac and the shrine of Rocamadour. Here about the year 1324 entered a very devout novice of good family, who is now venerated as St Flora. If we can trust the biography in the form we have it, she had passed a most inncoent childhood, had resisted all her parents' attempts to find her a husband, but on dedicating herself to God at Beaulieu she was overwhelmed by every species of spiritual trial. She seems, in consequence, to have fallen into a state of intense depression which showed itself in her countenance and behaviour to a degree which the other sisters found intensely irritating.

In all this time, obtaining help occasionally from some visiting confessor who seemed to understand her state, she was growing dearer to God and in the end was privileged to enjoy many unusual mystical favours. It is alleged that one year on the feast of All Saints she fell into an ecstasy in which she continued without taking any nourishment at all until St Cecilia's day, three weeks later. Again, we hear of a fragment of the Blessed Sacrament being brought to her by an angel from a church eight miles away. Many instances were apparently reported of her inexplicable or prophetic knowledge of matters of which she could not naturally have learnt anything. She died in 1347 at the age of thirty-eight, and many miracles are believed to have been worked at her tomb.

6 ST BRUNO, FOUNDER OF THE CARTHUSIAN ORDER (A.D. 1101)

BRUNO came of a good family and was born at Cologne about the year 1030. While still young he left home to finish his education at the cathedral school of Rheims, and returned to Cologne where he was ordained and was given a canonry in the collegiate church of St Cunibert (he may have held this even before he went to Rheims). In 1056 he was invited to go back to his school as professor of grammar and theology. Many eminent scholars in philosophy and divinity did him honour by their proficiency and abilities, and carried his reputation into distant parts; among these, Eudes de Châtillon became afterwards a beatified pope under the name of Urban II.

He taught in and maintained the reputation of the school of Rheims for eighteen years, when he was appointed chancellor of the diocese by Manasses, a man whose life made him unfit to be in holy orders at all, much less an archbishop. Bruno soon learned the truth about him, and Hugh of St Dié, the pope's legate, summoned Manasses to appear at a council at Autun in 1076, and upon his refusing to obey declared him suspended. St Bruno, another Manasses, the provost, and Pontius, a canon of Rheims, accused him in this council, and Bruno behaved with so much prudence and dignity, that the legate, writing to the pope, extolled his virtue and wisdom. Manasses, exasperated against the three canons who had appeared against him, caused their houses to be broken open and plundered, and sold their prebends. The persecuted priests took refuge in the castle of Ebles de Roucy, and remained there till the simoniacal archbishop, by deceiving Pope St Gregory VII (no easy matter), had been restored to his see, when Bruno went to Cologne.

Some time before, Bruno had come to a decision to abandon the active ecclesiastical life. He forsook the world in a time of flattering prosperity, when he enjoyed in it riches, honour and the favour of men, and when the church of Rheims was ready to choose him archbishop. He resigned his benefice and renounced whatever held him in the world, and persuaded some of his friends to accompany him into solitude. They first put themselves under the direction of St Robert, abbot of Molesmes (who was afterwards to help found Citeaux), and lived in a hermitage at Sèche-Fontaine near by. In this solitude Bruno, with an earnest desire for true perfection in virtue, considered with himself and deliberated with his companions what it was best for them to do. He decided to apply to St Hugh, bishop of Grenoble, who was a person well qualified to assist him; moreover, he was told that in the diocese of Grenoble there were woods and deserts most suitable to his desire of finding perfect solitude. Six of those who had accompanied him in his retreat attended him, including Landuin, who afterwards succeeded him as prior of the Grande Chartreuse.

St Bruno and these six arrived at Grenoble about midsummer in 1084, and came before St Hugh, begging some place where they might serve God, remote from worldly affairs and without being burdensome to men. Hugh embraced them very lovingly and assigned them the desert of Chartreuse for their retreat, promising his utmost assistance to establish them there. St Bruno accepted the offer with joy, St Hugh made over to them all the rights he had in that forest, and they had some spiritual tie with the abbot of Chaise-Dieu in Auvergne. Bruno and his companions immediately built an oratory there, and small cells at a little distance one from the other, like the ancient *lauras* of Palestine. Such was the origin of the order of the Carthusians, which took its name from this desert of Chartreuse.

St Hugh forbade any woman to go into their lands or any person to fish, hunt or drive cattle that way. The monks first built a church on a summit and cells near it, in which they lived two together in each cell (soon after, alone), meeting in church at Matins and Vespers; other hours they recited in their cells. They never took two meals in a day except on the great festivals, on which they ate together in a refectory. On other days they ate in their cells as hermits. Everything amongst them was extremely poor: even in their church they would have no gold or silver, except a silver chalice. Labour succeeded prayer. It was a chief work to copy books, by which they endeavoured to earn their subsistence, and, if all else was poor, the library was rich. The soil of their mountains was poor and its climate hard, so they had few cornfields, but they bred cattle. Their manner of life they followed without any written rule, though they conformed to that of St Benedict in some points which were compatible with an eremitical life. St Bruno made his disciples fervent observers of the customs and practices he had established, which Guigo, fifth prior of the Chartreuse, drew up in writing in 1127. Guigo made many changes in the rule, and his *Consetudines* remained its foundation.

St Hugh became so great an admirer of Bruno that he took him for his spiritual father, and without regard to the difficulty of the way often went from Grenoble to the Chartreuse to enjoy his conversation and improve himself by his advice and example. But his fame went beyond Grenoble and reached the ears of Eudes de Châtillon, his former pupil and now Pope Urban II. Hearing of the holy life which he led, and being from his own personal acquaintance fully convinced of his great prudence and learning, the pope sent him an order to come to Rome that he might assist him by his counsels in the government of the Church. Bruno could have scarcely met with a more severe trial of his obedience or made a greater sacrifice. Nevertheless he set out early in 1090, having nominated Landuin prior at the Chartreuse. The departure of the saint was an inexpressible grief to his disciples, and some of them went away. The rest, with Landuin, followed their master to Rome, but they were prevailed upon by Bruno to return to their former habitation, of which the monks of Chaise-Dieu had taken charge upon their leaving. They recovered their former cells, which were restored to them by the abbot of Chaise-Dieu.

St Bruno, meanwhile, had permission to occupy a hermitage among the ruins of the baths of Diocletian, where he would be close at hand when required by the pope. Exactly what part he played in the papal activities of the time we do not know. Work formerly attributed to him is now recognized as having been done by his namesake, St Bruno of Segni, but he certainly helped in the preparation of various synods in which Bd Urban aimed at the reformation of the clergy. Soon Urban pressed him to accept the archbishopric of Reggio in Calabria, but the saint excused himself with so great earnestness, and redoubled his importunities for the liberty of living in solitude, that the pope at length consented that he might retire into some wilderness in Calabria where he would be at hand, but not to the Chartreuse—that was too far off. Count Roger, brother of Robert Guiscard, gave him the beautiful and fertile valley of La Torre, in the diocese of Squillace, where he settled with some new disciples whom he had gained in Rome. Here he betook himself to a solitary life with more joy and fervour than ever.

In the year 1099 Landuin, prior of the Chartreuse, went into Calabria to consult St Bruno about the form of living which he had instituted, for the monks were desirous not to depart from the spirit and rule of their master. Bruno wrote them a letter full of tender charity and the spirit of God: in it he instructed them in all the practices of solitary life, solved the difficulties which they proposed to him, comforted them in their troubles, and encouraged them to perseverance. In his two Calabrian hermitages, St Mary's and St Stephen's, Bruno fostered that spirit which guided the monks of the Grande Chartreuse, and on its temporal side he was generously helped by Count Roger, with whom he formed a close friendship.

His last sickness came upon him towards the end of September 1101, and when he saw death near he gathered him monks about his bed, and in their presence made a public confession of his life and a profession of faith, which his disciples set down and preserved. He resigned his soul to God on Sunday, October 6, 1101. St Bruno has never been formally canonized, the Carthusians being averse from all occasions of publicity; but in 1514 they obtained leave from Pope Leo X to keep his feast, and in 1674 Clement X extended it to the whole Western church.

7 : ST OSITH, VIRGIN AND MARTYR (c. A.D. 700)

ACCORDING to her legend St Osith was the daughter of a Mercian chief, Frithwald, and his wife Wilburga, said to have been a daughter of Penda of Mercia. She was brought up in a nunnery, perhaps at Aylesbury, and wished herself to become a nun; but her parents affianced her to Sighere, king of the East Saxons. If this be the Sighere mentioned by St Bede, he apostatized from the faith during a pestilence about 665, but was, presumably, reconciled by the bishop Jaruman. This man had a passion for hunting, and when after the wedding he attempted to embrace his wife, against her will, his attention was distracted to a stray stag: he went off in pursuit, and on his return he found his bride had gone. She made her way to the East Anglian bishops, Acca of Dunwich and Bedwin of Elmham, and Sighere, realizing that it was better to have no wife than an unwilling one, let them clothe her with the religious habit. He himself gave to St Osith some land at a place called Chich, on a creek of the Colne between Brightlingsea and Clacton, and here she established her monastery. She governed it for some years with prudence and holiness, but it was situated in a dangerous place and disaster soon overtook it. In a piratical raid the marauders tried to carry St Osith off, and when she fiercely resisted they smote off her head.

The body of St Osith was taken to Aylesbury, but afterwards brought back to Chich, where a priory of Austin canons under her invocation was established in the twelfth century. Near it grew up the present village of Saint Osith, and the memory of the martyred abbess is preserved in several other local place-names, St Osith Creek, St Osith Marsh, St Osith Wick, and St Osith's Well.

8 : ST KEYNE, VIRGIN (SIXTH CENTURY?)

THE account of her given in her *vita*, edited by John of Tynemouth in the fourteenth century probably from an earlier and longer life, is as follows. The father of the blessed Keyne was King Brychan Brycheiniog, who had twelve sons and twelve daughters. Keyne grew into a very beautiful young woman, but resolutely refused all suitors and took a vow of virginity; therefore she was called in Welsh *Cain Wyry*, Keyne the Maiden. Then she resolved to become a solitary and, crossing the Severn, she took up her abode in the forests on the left bank. She lived there for years, making many journeys and founding oratories, till at St Michael's Mount she met her nephew St Cadoc, who persuaded her (with the help of an angel) to return to Wales. 'She made for herself a habitation in a certain hillock at the roots of a certain great mountain', and there caused a healing well to spring up. Just before her death she told Cadoc that that place would fall into the hands of a sinful race, whom she would root out and lead thither other men, who would find her forgotten tomb, 'and in this place the name of the Lord shall be blessed for ever'.

9 : ST LOUIS BERTRAND, (A.D. 1581)

LUIS BERTRÁN was born at Valencia in Spain in 1526. He was related through his father to St Vincent Ferrer and was baptized at the same font as that saint had been 175 years before. The celebrated Father John Mico, who had been brought up a shepherd in the mountains, gave the Dominican habit to young Bertrand when he was eighteen. Sacerdotal ordination was given to him by the archbishop of Valencia, St Thomas of Villanova, in 1547. Louis was made master of novices five years after profession, and discharged that office for periods which totalled thirty years. He was very severe and strict, but both by his example and words taught them sincerely and perfectly to renounce the world and to unite their souls to God.

In 1557 a pestilence raged in Valencia and the saint knew no danger and spared no pains in comforting and assisting the sick. He about this time made the acquaintance of St Teresa, who wrote and asked his advice about her projected convent of reformed Carmelites.

In 1562 St Louis left Spain to preach the gospel to the Indians in America, and landed at Cartagena in New Granada (Columbia). He spoke only Spanish and had to use an interpreter, but the gifts of tongues, of prophecy and of miracles were conferred by Heaven on this apostle, the bull of his canonization tells us. In the isthmus of Panama and the province of Cartagena, in the space of three years, he converted to Christ many thousand souls. The baptismal registers of Tubera, in St Louis's own handwriting, show that all the inhabitants of that place were converted, and he had a like success at Cipacoa. The people of Paluato were more difficult, but in his next mission, among the inhabitants of the mountains of Santa Marta, he is said to have baptized about fifteen thousand persons; and also a tribe of fifteen hundred Indians who, having changed their minds, had followed him thither from Paluato. He visited the Caribs of the Leeward Islands, San Thomé in the Virgin Islands, and San Vincente in the Windwards, and then returned to Columbia. He was pierced to the quick to see the avarice and cruelty of the Spanish adventurers in the Indies and not to be able to find any means of putting a stop to those evils. He was desirous to seek redress in Spain, and about that time he was recalled thither, thus ending a marvellous mission of six years. St Louis arrived at Seville in 1569, whence he returned to Valencia. He trained up many excellent preachers, who succeeded him in the ministry of the word. The first lesson he gave them was that humble and fervent prayer must always be the principal preparation of the preacher: for words without works never have power to touch or change hearts.

The two last years of his life he was afflicted with painful illness; in 1580 he went to preach in the cathedral at Valencia, where he was carried from the pulpit to his bed, from which he never rose again, dying eighteen months later on October 9, 1581, being fifty-five years old. St Louis Bertrand, who is the principal patron of Colombia, was canonized in 1671.

10 : ST FRANCIS BORGIA, (A.D. 1572)

THE family of Borja was one of the most noble of the kingdom of Aragon, but it was not till the fifteenth century that it became known outside Spain, when from 1455 to 1458 Alphonsus Borgia was pope under the name of Callistus III. At the end of that century there was another Borgia pope, Alexander VI, who at the time of his elevation to the papacy was the father of four children. As a provision for his son, Peter, he bought the dukedom of Gandia in Spain, and on Peter's death bestowed it upon another son, John. John was murdered soon after his marriage, and his son, the third duke of Gandia, married the daughter of a natural son of King Ferdinand V of Aragon. Of this union was born at Gandia in the year 1510 Francisco de Borja y Aragon, now known to us as St Francis Borgia, great-grandson of a pope and of a king and cousin of the Emperor Charles V. At the age of eighteen, his education completed, young Francis was received at the imperial court. At Alcalá de Henares Francis was impressed by the appearance of a man whom he saw being taken to the prison of the Inquisition. That man was Ignatius Loyola.

In the following year Francis Borgia, having been created marquis of Lombay, married Eleanor de Castro, and ten years later Charles V made him viceroy of Catalonia, whose capital was Barcelona. He devoted as much time to prayer as he could without prejudice to public affairs or the needs of his growing family, and the frequency of his sacramental communions caused comment, mostly unfavourable. In 1543 St Francis became duke of Gandia by the death of his father, whereupon he retired with his family to his estates, following on the refusal of King John of Portugal to recognize him as master of the household to Prince Philip of Spain, who was about to marry the king's daughter. This was a definite check to the public career of Francis Borgia and he proceeded to interest himself in more personal affairs. He fortified Gandia that it might not be exposed to the Moors and pirates from Barbary, built a convent for the Dominicans at Lombay, and repaired the hospital.

This happy and peaceful life at Gandia was brought suddenly to an end by the death in 1546 of Doña Eleanor. They had eight children, of whom the youngest was eight at his mother's death. Shortly afterwards Bd Peter Favre paid a brief visit to Gandia, and he left for Rome bearing a message to St Ignatius Loyola that Francis Borgia had resolved to ask to be received into the Society of Jesus—he had in fact made a vow to do so. St Ignatius advised the duke to defer the execution of his design till he had settled his children and finished the foundations he had begun, telling him in the meantime to study theology at Gandia in the university he had inaugurated there and to take the degree of doctor; he was, moreover, to take every precaution to prevent this astonishing piece of news from being prematurely divulged. Francis obeyed but was troubled in the following year by being summoned to assist at the *cortes* of Aragon. He therefore wrote to St Ignatius and as a consequence was allowed to make his profession privately. Three years were enough to see his children properly established and on August 31, 1550, St Francis Borgia set out for Rome. He was forty years old.

After less than four months in Rome, Francis went back to Spain, and retired to a hermitage at Oñate, near Loyola. Here he received the emperor's permission to make over his titles and estates to his son Charles, whereupon he shaved his head and beard, assumed clerical dress, and was ordained priest in Whitsun week, 1551. 'A duke turned Jesuit' was the sensation of the day, and when Francis celebrated his first public Mass, for assistance at which the pope granted a plenary indulgence, the crowd at Vergara was so great that the altar had to be set up in the open air. Directly after his ordination he was allowed to preach throughout Guipùzcoa, and he went through the villages with a bell, calling the children to catechism, instructing and preaching. But within the house the superior treated Father Francis with such severity as he deemed the previous exalted position of his subject required.

St Francis's corporal mortifications after his 'conversion' became excessive: he was an exceedingly fat man, and his girth decreased very notably; his excesses were now curbed by religious obedience, but he was ingenious in the devising of physical discomforts. In after years he was of the opinion that he had been imprudent in his ways of mortifying his body, especially before he became a Jesuit. He left Oñate for several months to preach in other parts of Spain. Much success attended his labours and he was one of the first to recognize the greatness of the Carmelite nun of Avila, Teresa. After doing wonders in Castile and Andalusia, he seemed to surpass himself in Portugal, and in 1554 St Ignatius made him commissary general of the Society of Jesus in Spain, an office which he discharged at times with something of the autocracy of a distinguished nobleman.

During his years as commissary general St Francis Borgia was practically the founder of the Society in Spain, establishing in a short time houses and colleges at a score of places. But he did not neglect the immediate care of those whom he had left behind him in the world. He soothed and made sweet the last moments of the queen dowager, Joanna, who fifty years before had gone mad at the death of her husband and had shown a special aversion from the clergy. In the next year, soon after the death of St Ignatius, the Emperor Charles V abdicated, and sent for St Francis to visit him at Yuste. Charles had been prepossessed against the Society of Jesus and expressed his surprise that Francis should have preferred it to so many older orders. The saint removed his prejudices.

St Francis was no friend of the Inquisition, nor that body of him; and King Philip II listened to the calumnies which jealousy was raising against Francis. He remained on the work of the Society in Portugal till 1561, and was then summoned to Rome by Pope Pius IV, at the instance of the Jesuit general, Father Laynez. St Francis was most warmly received in Rome and among those who regularly attended his sermons were Cardinal Charles Borromeo and Cardinal Ghislieri, afterwards St Pius V. Becoming acquainted with the work of the headquarters of the Jesuits, he filled high offices, and on the death of Father Laynez in 1565 was elected father general. During seven years he promoted the work of the Society of Jesus in all parts of the world. St Francis's first care was to establish a properly regulated novitiate in Rome and to provide for the same in the provinces. When he first came to the city fifteen years before he had shown a strong interest in the project of a Roman college, and had given a large sum of money. He now concerned himself personally in the direction of the college and the arrangement of its curriculum. In effect he was the founder of this college, but he always refused the title, which is given to Pope Gregory XIII who re-established it as the Gregorian University. St Francis also built the church of Sant' Andrea on the Quirinal, with the adjoining residence, to house the novitiate, began the Gesù, and enlarged and improved the German college.

Pope St Pius V had confidence in the Society of Jesus and a great trust and admiration for its general, so that he could proceed freely with the projects he had at heart. St Francis provided for the extension of the Society of Jesus across the Alps, and established the province of Poland. He used his influence with the French court to obtain a more favourable reception for the Jesuits in France, where he was able to set up colleges. And he was engrossed by the foreign missions: those of the East Indies and the Far East were reformed and those of the Americas begun. St Francis published a new edition of the rules of the Society and drew up regulations and directions for those members who were engaged in special work of various kinds. Nor was St Francis so immersed in the responsibilities of his office that he had no time to spare for matters outside. This was shown when in 1566 a pestilence made great havoc in Rome, on which occasion he raised alms for the relief of the poor, and commissioned the fathers of his order, two and two, to attend the sick in all parts of the city, with imminent danger to their own lives.

In the year 1571 the pope sent Cardinal Bonelli on an embassy to Spain, Portugal and France, and St Francis accompanied him. Though politically not a great success, it was a personal triumph for the Jesuit. Everywhere crowds clamoured 'to see the saint' and to hear him preach, old animosities were forgotten, and King Philip received him as gladly as did his people. But the fatigues entailed were too much for St Francis. He had been for some time in bad health; his infirmities, inclination to retirement, and a deep sense of the weight of his post had worn him out, and at Ferrara on his return Duke Alfonso, who was his cousin, sent him from thence to Rome in a litter. He lived for two days only after his arrival. By his brother Thomas he sent his blessing to all his children and grandchildren, and as their names were rehearsed to him he prayed for each one. When he had lost his speech a painter was, with peculiar insensibility, introduced to his bedside. Francis saw him, expressed his displeasure with his dying hands and eyes, and turned away his face so that nothing could be done. He died at the midnight of September 30-October 1, 1572.

11 : ST MARY SOLEDAD, VIRGIN, FOUNDRESS OF THE HANDMAIDS OF MARY SERVING THE SICK (A.D. 1887)

THE parents of Mary Soledad were Francis Torres and Antonia Acosta, an exemplary couple living obscurely by a little business in Madrid; she was the second of five children, born in 1826, and was christened Emanuela. For a time it looked as if she would join the Dominican nuns, whose convent she frequented, but she was content to wait for a more clear indication of what was required of her.

This eventually came from the Chamberi quarter of Madrid, where the vicar was a Servite tertiary named Michael Martinez y Sanz, who had long been worried by the neglected state of so many of the sick in his parish. In 1851 he gathered together seven women to devote themselves to their service in a religious community. The last of them was twenty-five-year-old Emanuela Torres-Acosta, who took at her clothing the name Mary Soledad, Spanish for *Desolata*, 'alone and grief-stricken', a token of her love for our Lady of Sorrows.

Five years after the foundation Don Michael took half of the members with him to make a separate foundation in Fernando Po; six were left in Madrid, with Sister Mary Soledad as superioress. For a moment the little group was threatened with dissolution by episcopal authority. But with the help of a new director, Father Gabino Sanchez, an Augustinian friar, it was able to struggle on; and through the enterprise of Mother Mary support was obtained from the queen and from the local authorities. The turning-point came in 1861, when the rule of the Handmaids of Mary received diocesan approval and another Augustinian, Father Angelo Barra, was appointed director. Beginning with the taking-over of an institution for young delinquents in Madrid, several new foundations were made, and in the cholera epidemic of 1865 all eyes were turned to the selfless work of Mother Mary Soledad and her nuns. A few years later there was a secession of some members to another congregation, with the usual complaints and accusations from which mother-foundresses have to suffer. Heaven's reply was the first foundation overseas, at Santiago in Cuba in 1875. From that time on there was an accelerated spreading of the houses and hospitals of the congregation in every province of Spain, culminating in 1878 in the taking-over of the ancient hospital of St Charles in the Escorial itself.

The work involved and the increasing commitments continued to the end of Mother Mary's life, the last ten years of which were happily serene. Towards the end of September 1887, however, she was taken ill.

Mother Mary Soledad was beatified in 1950 and canonized twenty years later.

12 : ST WILFRID, BISHOP OF YORK (A.D. 709)

HE was born in 634, son of a Northumbrian thegn. His mother died when he was a child, and the unkindness of his stepmother made him seek the court of Oswy, King of Northumbria, when he was thirteen. He was befriended by Queen Eanfleda, who sent him to the monastery of Lindisfarne that he might be trained in the study of the sacred sciences. A desire of greater improvement than he could attain to in that house, where he perceived the Celtic discipline that was practised to be imperfect, gave rise to a project of travelling into France and Italy. He made some stay at Canterbury, where he studied the Roman discipline under St Honorius, and learned the psalter according to the Roman version, instead of that which he had used before. In 654 St Benet Biscop, his countryman, passed through Kent on his first journey to Rome; and St Wilfrid, who had set out with the same object, crossed the sea with him.

At Lyons Wilfrid was detained a whole year by St Anne mund, bishop of that city, who took so great a liking to him that he offered him his niece in marriage, and promised him a considerable position; but the youth continued steadfast in the resolution he had taken to devote himself to God. At Rome he put himself under Boniface the archdeacon, a pious and learned man; he was secretary to Pope St Martin, and took much delight in instructing young Wilfrid. After this, Wilfrid returned to Lyons. He stayed three years there and received the tonsure after the Roman manner, thus adopting an outward and visible sign of his dissent from Celtic customs. St Annemund desired to make him his heir, but his own life was suddenly cut short by murder, and Wilfrid himself was spared only because he was a foreigner. He returned to England, where King Alcfrith of Deira, hearing that Wilfrid had been instructed in the discipline of the Roman church, asked him to instruct him and his people accordingly. Alcfrith had recently founded a monastery at Ripon and peopled it with monks from Melrose, among whom was St Cuthbert. These the king required to abandon their Celtic usages, whereupon the abbot Eata, Cuthbert and others, elected to return to Melrose. So St Wilfrid was made abbot of Ripon, where he introduced the Rule of St Benedict, and shortly after he was ordained priest by St Agilbert, the Frankish bishop of the West Saxons.

Wilfrid used all his influence to win over the clergy of the north to Roman ways. The principal trouble was that they followed another calculation of Easter; and King Oswy and his Queen Eanfleda, who came from Kent, sometimes kept Lent and Easter at different times in the same court. To put an end to this dispute, in 663 a conference was held in the monastery of St Hilda at Whitby, before Oswy and Alcfrith. The pro-Roman party triumphed, and Bishop Colman of Lindisfarne retired to Iona. Tuda was consecrated bishop of the Northumbrians in his room, but soon after died, and Alcfrith desired to have his own priest, Wilfrid, placed in the episcopal see. Wilfrid, quite unjustifiably, looked on the noncomforming northern bishops as schismatics, and so went to France to receive consecration, at Compiègne, at the hands of his old friend St Agilbert, who had returned to his native country. He was then in his thirtieth year. For some reason St Wilfrid did not come back at once, and when he did was delayed by shipwreck. In the meantime King Oswy sent St Chad, Abbot of Lastingham, south, where he was consecrated by Wine, Bishop of the West Saxons, and then appointed him to be bishop at York. Wilfrid on his return to England would not dispute the election of St Chad, but retired to Ripon monastery. He was often called into Mercia by King Wulfhere to ordain, and at the invitation of King Egbert he went to Kent for the same purpose. On his return he brought with him a monk named Eddius Stephanus, who became his friend and biographer.

In 669 St Theodore, the newly appointed archbishop of Canterbury, in his visitation found the election of St Chad to have been irregular, and removed him, and at the same time put St Wilfrid in possession of the see of York. With the help of Eddius, who had been precentor at Canterbury, he established in all the churches of the north the use of Roman chant, he restored the cathedral at York, and discharged all his episcopal duties in a most exemplary way. He made visitations of his large diocese on foot, and was deeply beloved and respected by all his people—but not by his prince, Egfrith, who had succeeded Oswy. Egrith had in 659 married St Etheldreda, daughter of King Anna of the East Angles. For ten years she refused to consummate her marriage, and when he had appealed to the bishop, Wilfrid had taken Etheldreda's part and helped her to leave her husband's house and become a nun at Coldingham. In these circumstances Egfrith, not without reason, thought he had a grievance against the bishop, and had no intention of letting his resentment remain inactive. When therefore there was indication that St Theodore wanted as metropolitan to subdivide the great diocese of the Northumbrians, he encouraged the project, and moreover slandered St Wilfrid's administration and demanded his deposition. Theodore appears to have listened to Egfrith, the diocese of York was divided, and Theodore consecrated three bishops in Wilfrid's own cathedral. Wilfrid protested, and in 677 or 678 appealed to the judgement of the Holy See—the first example of such an appeal in the history of the Church in England. He set out for Rome, and being driven by contrary winds upon the coast of Friesland, during that winter and the following spring he stayed there and converted and baptized many. Thus he began that harvest which St Willibrord and others afterwards carried on.

After a stay in France, St Wilfrid reached Rome late in 679, and found Pope St Agatho already apprised of what had passed in England by a monk whom Theodore had despatched with letters. To discuss this cause the pope assembled a synod in the Lateran, which decided that Wilfrid was to be restored to his see, and that he himself should choose coadjutors or suffragans to assist him. St Wilfrid stayed over four months at Rome, and assisted at the Lateran council which condemned the monothelite heresy. When he arrived in England, he went to King Egfrith and showed him the decrees of the pope. The prince cried out that they had been obtained by bribery, and commanded Wilfrid to be taken to prison, where he was detained nine months. He then went by way of Wessex into Sussex. Here Wilfrid was among the still pagan South Saxons, but their King Ethelwalh, who had been lately baptized in Mercia, received him with open arms. The saint by his preaching converted nearly the whole people, and extended his activities to the Isle of Wight. In Sussex he freed 250 slaves, men and women.

The king gave him land at Selsey, whereon he established a monastery; this place became an episcopal see, which was afterwards removed to Chichester. St Wilfrid chiefly resided in the peninsula of Selsey, and conducted his missions from thence for five years till, upon the death of King Egfrith, St Theodore, who was very old and ill, sent to him requesting that he would meet him at London with St Erconwald, bishop of the city. He confessed to them all the actions of his life, and said to St Wilfrid, 'The greatest remorse that I feel is that I consented to your losing your see without any fault committed on your part'.

Accordingly, St Theodore wrote to Egfrith's successor, Aldfrith, to Ethelred, King of the Mercians, to St Elfleda, who had succeeded St Hilda in the abbey of Whitby, and others. Aldfrith recalled the bishop towards the end of the year 685, and restored to him his monastery of Ripon. How the complicated position in the north then developed is not altogether clear. But within five years there was disagreement between Aldfrith and Wilfrid, and he was again banished, in 691. He then retired to Ethelred of Mercia, who entreated him to take care of the vacant see of Lichfield, which he administered for some years. The new archbishop of Canterbury, St Berhtwald, was not sympathetic to St Wilfrid, and in 703 he called a synod which decreed, at the instigation of Aldfrith, that Wilfrid should resign his bishopric and retire to his abbey of Ripon. Wilfrid vindicated all he had done for the Church in the north in an impassioned speech, and again appealed to the Holy See. The synod broke up, and he started on his third journey to Rome. He was in his seventieth year.

St Wilfrid's opponents also sent representatives to Rome and many sessions were held over a period of four months to examine the cause. John VI finally sent letters to the kings of Mercia and Northumbria, charging Archbishop Berhtwald to call a synod which should do him justice: in default of which he ordered the parties to make their personal appearance at Rome. St Wilfrid on his return found that King Aldfrith still made difficulties; but he died in 705, and in his last sickness repented of the injustice he had done to St Wilfrid, as his sister St Elfleda gave testimony. Restitution, therefore, was agreed to. St Wilfrid, having vindicated the canons and the authority of the Holy See, consented to a compromise: he took possession of the diocese of Hexham, but chiefly resided in his monastery of Ripon, leaving York to St John of Beverley.

In 709 St Wilfrid made a visitation of the monasteries in Mercia of which he had been the founder, and he died at one of these, at Oundle in Northamptonshire, having divided his goods between his monasteries, churches and the former companions of his exile. His body was buried in his church of St Peter at Ripon.

13 : ST EDWARD THE CONFESSOR, (A.D. 1066)

EDWARD was the son of Ethelred the Redeless by his Norman wife Emma, and during the Danish supremacy was sent to Normandy for safety, with his brother Alfred, when he was ten years old. Alfred came to England in 1036 but was seized and mutilated, and died by the brutality of Earl Godwin. Thus Edward did not set foot again in his native land until he was called to be king in 1042: he was then forty years old. Two years later he married Edith, the daughter of Godwin. It is traditionally claimed as an aspect of Edward's sanctity that, for love of God and greater perfection, he lived with his wife in absolute continence. The fact is not certain, nor, if it were so, is his motive certain either.

Godwin was the chief opponent of a certain Norman influence which had its centre at the royal court and made itself felt in appointments to bishoprics and offices as well as in lesser matters. After a series of 'incidents', things came to a crisis and Godwin and his family were banished; even his daughter, Edward's queen, was confined to a convent for a time. In the same year, 1051, William of Normandy visited the English court, and it can hardly be doubted that Edward then offered him the succession to the crown. It was not many months before Godwin returned, and as both sides were averse from a civil war the king restored him, and the council 'outlawed all Frenchmen'. The Norman archbishop of Canterbury had another bishop fled overseas.

The king's religious and just administration caused him to reign in the hearts of his people. The love, harmony and agreement seen in retrospect between him and the great council of the nation became the traditional measure of the people's desires in all succeeding reigns. He was generous to the poor and strangers, especially if they were from abroad, and a great encourager of monks. His favourite diversions were hunting and hawking, at which he would go out for days on end, but even then never omitted to be present at Mass every morning. In appearance he was tall and well built, with a ruddy face and white hair and beard.

During his exile in Normandy St Edward had made a vow to go on pilgrimage to St Peter's tomb at Rome if God should be pleased to put an end to the misfortunes of his family. When he was settled on the throne he held a council, in which he declared the obligation he lay under. The assembly commended his devotion, but represented that the kingdom would be left exposed to domestic divisions and to foreign enemies. The king was moved by their reasons, and consented that the matter should be referred to Pope St Leo IX. He, considering the impossibility of the king's leaving his dominions, dispensed his vow upon condition that by way of commutation he should give to the poor the sum he would have expended in his journey and should build or repair and endow a monastery in honour of St Peter. King Edward selected for his benefaction an abbey already existing close to London, in a spot called Thorney. He rebuilt and endowed it in a magnificent manner out of his own patrimony, and obtained of Pope Nicholas II ample exemptions and privileges for it. From its situation it had come to be called West Minster in distinction from the church of St Paul in the east of the city.

The last year of St Edward's life was disturbed by troubles between the Northumbrians and their earl, Tostig Godwinsson, whom eventually the king was constrained to banish. At the end of the year, when the nobles of the realm were gathered at the court for Christmas, the new choir of Westminster abbey-church was consecrated with great solemnity, on Holy Innocents' day, 1065. St Edward was too ill to be present; he died a week later and was buried in his abbey.

14 : ST CALLISTUS, or CALIXTUS, I, POPE AND MARTYR (c. A.D. 222)

IT is unfortunate that most of what is known of St Callistus I is derived from an unfriendly source. The story of Hippolytus is that, when a young slave, Callistus was put in charge of a bank by his master, a Christian named Carpophorus, and lost the money deposited with him by other Christians. He fled from Rome but was caught at Porto, after jumping into the sea in trying to escape, and was sentenced to the slave's punishment at the mill, a horrible penalty. From this he was released at the request of the creditors, who thought he might be able to recover some of the money, but was rearrested on a charge of brawling in a synagogue—presumably he had tried to collect debts owing by Jews and had carried his importunities into their place of worship. He was sentenced to work in the mines of Sardinia, and here he was when the Christians there were released at the instance of Marcia, a mistress of the Emperor Commodus.

When St Zephyrinus became pope about the year 199 he made Callistus, who was now enfranchised, superintendent of the public Christian burial-ground on the Via Appia, which is to this day called the cemetery of St Callistus: in a part of it known as the papal crypt all the popes from Zephyrinus to Eutychian were buried, except Cornelius and Callistus himself. He is said to have extended and unified the cemetery, bringing the isolated private portions into communal possession, perhaps the first property in land held by the Church. Zephyrinus also ordained Callistus deacon, and he became the pope's friend and counsellor.

After Callistus himself became pope by the election of a majority of the Roman clergy and people, he was bitterly attacked by St Hippolytus (who was the choice of a faction for the papal chair) both on doctrinal and disciplinary grounds, especially when, expressly basing himself on the power of binding and loosing, he admitted to communion those who had done public penance for murder, adultery and fornication. The critics of the pope were rigorists, and St Hippolytus is found complaining that St Callistus had ruled that commission of mortal sin was not in itself sufficient reason for deposing a bishop; that he had admitted the twice or thrice married to the clergy; that he recognized as legitimate marriage between free women and slaves, contrary to Roman civil law: matters of discipline, for his action in which, and for his opposition to his own theological views, Hippolytus calls Callistus a heretic—but he no longer speaks against his personal character.

Although he did not live at a time of persecution there is reason to think that St Callistus I was martyred, perhaps during a popular rising; but his *acta*, which allege that he was flung down a well, have no authority. He was buried on the Aurelian Way. The chapel of St Callistus *in Trastevere* is possibly the successor of one built by the pope on a piece of ground adjudged to the Christians by Alexander Severus as against some inn-keepers: the emperor declared that any religious rites were better than a tavern.

15 : ST TERESA OF AVILA, VIRGIN, FOUNDRESS OF THE DISCALCED CARMELITES (A.D. 1582)

ST TERESA was born at or near Avila in Castile on March 28, 1515, and when only seven took great pleasure in the lives of the saints, in which she spent much time with a brother called Rodrigo, who was near the same age. The martyrs seemed to them to have bought Heaven very cheaply by their torments, and they resolved to go into the country of the Moors, in hopes of dying for their faith. They set out secretly, praying as they went that they might lay down their lives for Christ. But when they had got as far as Adaja they were met by an uncle, and brought back to their frightened mother, who reprimanded them; whereupon Rodrigo laid all the blame on his sister.

Teresa and the same little brother then wanted to become hermits at home, and built themselves hermitages with piles of stones in the garden, but could never finish them. Teresa sought to be much alone, and had in her room a picture of our Saviour discoursing with the Samaritan woman at the well, before which she often repeated the words, 'Lord, give me of that water that I may not thirst'. Her mother died when she was fourteen, and the change in Teresa was sufficiently noticeable to disturb the mind of her father. He placed his daughter, who was then fifteen, with a convent of Augustinian nuns in Avila where many young women of her rank were educated.

After a year and a half spent in this convent Teresa fell sick, and her father took her home, where she began to deliberate seriously about undertaking the religious life. She told her father that she wished to become a nun, but he would not give his consent: after his death she might dispose of herself as she pleased. Fearing she might relapse, though she felt a severe interior conflict in leaving her father, she went secretly to the convent of the Incarnation of the Carmelite nuns outside Avila, where her great friend, Sister Jane Suarez, lived. She was then twenty years old and, the step being taken, Don Alonso ceased to oppose it. A year later she was professed. An illness, which seized her before her profession, increased very much after it, and her father got her removed out of her convent. Sister Jane Suarez bore her company, and she remained in the hands of physicians. Their treatment only made her worse (she seems to have been suffering from malignant malaria), and she could take no rest day or night. The doctors gave her up, and she got worse and worse. Under these afflictions she was helped by the prayer which she had then begun to use. Her devout uncle Peter had put into her hands a little book of Father Francis de Osuna, called the *Third Spiritual Alphabet*. Taking this book for her guide she applied herself to mental prayer, but for want of an experienced instructor she made little solid progress. But after three years' suffering Teresa was restored to bodily health.

By an irregular custom of her convent quite common in those days, visitors of all kinds were freely received and mixed with, and Teresa spent much time conversing in the parlour of the monastery. She began to neglect mental prayer, and persuaded herself that this was a part of humility, as her unrecollected life rendered her unworthy to converse so much or so familiarly with God. She also said to herself that there could be no danger or sin in what so many others, more virtuous than she, did; and for her neglect of meditation she alleged the infirmities to which she was subject.

When her father died his confessor, a Dominican friar, pointed out to Teresa the dangerous state she was in. At his insistence she returned to the practice of private prayer and never again abandoned it. But she had not yet the courage to follow God perfectly, or entirely to renounce dissipating her time and gifts. Becoming more and more convinced of her own unworthiness, she had recourse to the two great penitents, St Mary Magdalen and St Augustine, and with them were associated two events decisive in fixing her will upon the pursuit of religious perfection. One was the reading of St Augustine's *Confessions:* the other was a movement to penitence before a picture of our suffering Lord, in which 'I felt St Mary Magdalen come to my assistance . . . from that day I have gone on improving much ever since in my spiritual life'.

After she had finally withdrawn herself from the pleasures of social intercourse and other occasions of dissipation and faults St Teresa was very frequently favoured by God with the prayer of quiet, and also with that of union, which latter sometimes continued a long time with great increase of joy and love, and God began to visit her with intellectual visions and interior communications. The warning of certain women who had been miserably duped by imagination and the Devil much impressed her and, though she was persuaded her graces were from God, she was perplexed, and consulted so many persons that, though binding them to secrecy, the affair was divulged abroad, to her mortification and confusion. One to whom she spoke was Francis de Salsedo, a married man who was an example of virtue to the whole town. He introduced to her Dr Daza, a learned and virtuous priest, who judged her to be deluded by the Devil, saying that such divine favours were not consistent with a life so full of imperfections as she claimed hers to be. Teresa was alarmed and not satisfied, and Don Francis (to whom the saint says she owed her salvation and her comfort) bade her not to be discouraged. He recommended that she should consult one of the fathers of the newly-formed Society of Jesus, to whom she made a general confession in which, with her sins, she gave him an account of her manner of prayer and her extraordinary favours. The father assured her these were divine graces, but told her she had neglected to lay the true foundation of an interior life. On his advice, though he judged her experiences in prayer to be from God, she endeavoured for two months to resist and reject them. But her resistance was in vain.

Another Jesuit, Father Balthasar Alvarez, told her she would do well to beg of God that He would direct her to do what was most pleasing to Him, and for that purpose to recite every day the *Veni Creator Spiritus*. She did so, and one day whilst she was saying that hymn she was seized with a rapture, in which she heard these words spoken to her within her soul, 'I will not have you hold conversation with men, but with angels'. The saint afterwards had frequent experience of such interior speeches and explains how they are even more distinct and clear than those which men hear with their bodily ears, and how they are also operative, producing in the soul the strongest impressions and sentiments of virtue, and filling her with an assurance of their truth, with joy and with peace. Whilst Father Alvarez was her director she suffered grievous persecutions for three years.

In 1557 St Peter of Alcantara came to Avila, and of course visited the now famous, or notorious, Carmelite. He declared that nothing appeared to him more evident than that her soul was conducted by the Spirit of God; but he foretold that she was not come to an end of her persecutions and sufferings. If the various proofs by which it pleased God to try Teresa served to purify her virtue, the heavenly communications with which she was favoured served to humble and fortify her soul, to give her a strong disrelish of the things of this life, and to fire her with the desire of possessing God. In raptures she was sometimes lifted in the air, of which she gives a careful description, and adds that God 'seems not content with drawing the soul to Himself, but He must needs draw up the very body too, even whilst it is mortal and compounded of so unclean a clay as we have made it by our sins'.

During this time took place such extraordinary manifestations as spiritual espousals, mystical marriage, and the piercing (*transverberatio*) of the saint's heart. Her response to this remarkable happening was in the following year (1560) to make a vow that she would in everything do always that which seemed to be the most perfect and best pleasing to God.

The necessity of the spirit of prayer, the way it is practised, and the nature of its fruits are set out incomparably in her writings. These works were written during the years in which she was actively engaged in the most difficult business of founding convents of reformed Carmelite nuns and thus, quite apart from their nature and contents, are significant of St Teresa's vigour, industry and power of recollection. She wrote the *Way of Perfection* for the direction of her nuns, and the book of *Foundations* for their edification and encouragement, but the *Interior Castle* may be said to have been written for the instruction of the Church.

The Carmelite nuns, and indeed those of other orders as well, were very much relaxed from their early austerity and enthusiasm in sixteenth-century Spain. We have seen how the parlour at Avila was a sort of social centre for the ladies and gentlemen of the town, and that the nuns went out of their enclosure on the slightest pretext: those who wanted an easy and sheltered life without responsibilites could find it in a convent. The size of the communities was both a cause and an effect of this mitigation: there were 140 nuns in the convent at Avila. This state of things was so taken for granted that when a Carmelite of the Incarnation house at Avila, her niece, began to talk of the possibility of the foundation of a small community bound to a more perfect way of life the idea struck St Teresa not as a very natural one but as an inspiration from Heaven. She had been a nun for 25 years: she now determined to undertake the establishment of such a reformed convent, and received a promise of immediate help from a wealthy widow, Doña Guiomar de Ulloa. The project was approved by St Peter of Alcantara, St Louis Bertrand, and the Bishop of Avila, and Teresa procured the licence and approbation of Father Gregory Fernandez, prior provincial of the Carmelites; but no sooner had the project taken shape than he was obliged by the objections which were raised to recall his licence. A storm fell upon Teresa through the violent opposition which was made by her fellow nuns, the nobility, the magistrates and the people. Father Ibañez, a

Dominican, secretly encouraged her, and assisted Doña Guiomar to pursue the enterprise, together with Doña Juana de Ahumada, a married sister of the saint, who began with her husband to build a new convent at Avila in 1561, but in such a manner that the world took it for a house intended for herself and her family.

Eventually a brief arrived from Rome authorizing the establishment of the new convent. St Peter of Alcantara, Don Francis de Salsedo and Dr Daza had persuaded the bishop to concur, the new monastery of St Joseph was set up by his authority, and on St Bartholomew's day in 1562 was made subject to him, Mass being celebrated in the chapel and the saint's niece and three other novices taking the habit. Hereupon great excitement broke out in the town. The people of Avila looked on the new foundation as uncalled for, were nervous of suspicious novelties, and feared that an unendowed convent would be too heavy a burden on the town. The mayor and magistrates would have had the new monastery demolished, had not Father Bañez, also a Dominican, dissuaded them from so hasty a resolution. Amidst slanders and persecution the saint remained calm, recommending to God His own work, and was comforted by our Lord in a vision. In the meantime Francis de Salsedo and other friends of the new establishment deputed a priest to go before the royal council to plead for the convent, the two Dominicans, Ibañez and Bañez, reasoned with the bishop and the provincial, the public clamour abated, and at the end of four months Father Angel sent Teresa to the new convent, whither she was followed by four other nuns from the old house.

Strict enclosure was established with almost perpetual silence, and the most austere poverty, at first without any settled revenues; the nuns wore habits of coarse serge, sandals instead of shoes (whence they are called 'discalced'), and were bound to perpetual abstinence. At first St Teresa would not admit more than thirteen nuns to a community, but in those which should be founded with revenues, and not to subsist solely on alms, she afterwards allowed twenty-one. The prior general of the Carmelites, John Baptist Rubeo (Rossi), came to Avila in 1567, and was charmed with the foundress and the wise regulations of the house. He gave St Teresa full authority to found other convents upon the same plan, in spite of the fact that St Joseph's had been established without his knowledge or leave, and she even received from him a licence for the foundation of two houses of reformed friars ('Contemplative Carmelites') in Castile. St Teresa passed five years in her convent of St Joseph with thirteen nuns.

In August 1567 she went to Medina del Campo and, having conquered many difficulties, founded there a second convent. The Countess de la Cerda earnestly desired to found a convent of this order at her town of Malagon, and Teresa went to see her about it, incidentally paying a visit to Madrid which she describes as 'boring'. When this convent was safely launched she went to Valladolid and there founded another. St Teresa made her next foundation at Toledo. At Medina del Campo she had met with two Carmelite friars who were desirous to embrace her reform, Antony-of-Jesus (de Heredia), then prior there, and John Yepes (afterwards John-of-the-Cross). As soon, therefore, as an opportunity offered itself she founded a convent for men at a village called Duruelo in 1568, and in 1569 a second at

Pastrana, both in extreme poverty and austerity. After these two foundations St Teresa left to St John-of-the-Cross the care of all other foundations
that should be made for men. At Pastrana she also established a nunnery.
When Don Ruy Gomez de Silva, who had founded these houses at Pastrana,
died, his widow wished to make her religious profession there, but claimed
many exemptions and would still maintain the dignity of princess. Teresa,
finding she could not be brought to the humility of her profession, ordered
the nuns, lest relaxations should be introduced, to leave that house to her
and retire to a new one in Segovia. In 1570 St Teresa founded a convent at
Salamanca.

At this time Pope St Pius V appointed visitors apostolic to inquire into
relaxations in religious orders with a view to reform, and he named a
well-known Dominican, Peter Fernandez, to be visitor to the Carmelites of
Castile. At Avila he not surprisingly found great fault with the convent of
the Incarnation, and to remedy its abuses he sent for St Teresa and told her
she was to take charge of it as prioress. It was doubly distasteful to her to be
separated from her own daughters and to be put from outside at the head of
a house which opposed her activities with jealousy and warmth. The nuns at
first refused to obey her; some of them went into hysterics at the very idea.
She told them that she came not to coerce or instruct but to serve, and to
learn from the least among them.

The prior general, Father Rubeo, who had hitherto favoured St Teresa,
now sided with the objectors and upheld a general chapter at Plasencia
which passed several decrees gravely restricting the reform. The new
nuncio apostolic, Philip de Sega, dismissed Father Gracián from his office of
visitor to the Discalced Carmelites, and St John-of-the-Cross Cross was
imprisoned in a monastery; St Teresa herself was told to choose one of her
convents to which to retire and to abstain from further foundations. While
recommending her undertaking to God, she did not disdain to avail herself
of the help of her friends in the world. These interested the king, Philip II, on
her behalf, and he warmly espoused her cause. The nuncio was called before
him and sternly rebuked for his activities against the discalced friars and
nuns, and in 1580 an order was obtained at Rome to exempt the Reformed
from the jurisdiction of the mitigated Carmelites, so that each should have
their own provincial. Father Garcián was elected for the Reformed.

St Teresa was certainly endowed with great natural talents. The sweetness of her temperament, the affectionate tenderness of her heart, and the
liveliness of her wit and imagination, poised by an uncommon maturity of
judgement and what we should now call psychological insight, gained the
respect of all and the love of most. The quality of St Teresa is seen very
clearly in her selection of novices for the new foundations. Her first
requirement, even before any promise of a considerable degree of piety, was
intelligence. A person can train herself to piety, but more hardly to
intelligence, by which quality she meant neither cleverness nor imagination,
but a power of good judgement.

By the time of the separation between the two observances of the
Carmelite Order in 1580 St Teresa was sixty-five years old and quite broken
in health. During her last two years she saw her final foundations, making
seventeen in all. The last foundation, at Burgos, was made under difficul-

ties, and when it was achieved in July 1582 St Teresa wished to return to Avila, but was induced to set out for Alba de Tormes, where the Duchess Maria Henriquez was expecting her. Bd Anne-of-St- Bartholomew describes the journey, not properly prepared for and the foundress so ill that she fainted on the road; one night they could get no food but a few figs, and when they arrived at Alba St Teresa went straight to bed. Three days later she said to Bd Anne, 'At last, my daughter, the hour of death has come'. St Teresa-of-Jesus died in the arms of Bd Anne at nine in the evening of October 4, 1582.

The very next day the Gregorian reform of the kalendar came into force and ten days were dropped, so that it was accounted October 15, the date on which her feast was ultimately fixed. Her body was buried at Alba de Tormes, and there it remains. She was canonized in 1622, and declared a Doctor of the Church in 1970.

16 : ST MARGARET-MARY, VIRGIN (A.D. 1690)

SHE was born in 1647 at Janots, the eastern quarter of L'Hautecour, a small town in Burgundy. Her father was a notary of some distinction, whose wife bore him seven children, of whom Margaret was the fifth. When she was about eight her father died and she was sent to school with the Poor Clares at Charolles; she was at once attracted by what she could see and understand of the life of the nuns, and they on their side were so impressed by Margaret's piety that she was allowed to make her first communion when she was nine. Two years later she was afflicted by a painful rheumatic affection that kept her to her bed till she was fifteen, and in the course of it she was taken back to her home at L'Hautecour. Her father's house was now occupied by several other members of the family as well, and one sister and her husband had taken all domestic and business authority out of the hands of the widow Alacoque. She and Margaret were treated almost as servants, and she recovered from her sickness only to be confronted by this persecution of her mother. When she was twenty, pressure was put on her to marry, but, fortified by a vision of our Lord, she firmly refused. Not till she was twenty-two did she receive the sacrament of confirmation (it was then that she took the name of Mary), and thus armed she was able to withstand the final opposition of her family. Her brother Chrysostom furnished her dowry, and in June 1671 she entered the Visitation convent at Paray-le-Monial.

From that time 'my divine Master urged me incessantly to ask for humiliations and mortifications'. They came unsought when she was appointed to assist in the infirmary. The infirmarian, Sister Catherine Marest, was temperamentally very different from her assistant: active, energetic, efficient, while Margaret-Mary was quiet, slow and clumsy. During these two and a half years our Lord continually made Himself sensibly present to Margaret-Mary, often crowned with thorns, and on December 27, 1673, her devotion to His passion was rewarded with the first of the revelations.

She was kneeling alone at the *grille* before the Blessed Sacrament exposed on the altar, and all at once she felt herself, as she says, 'invested' by the divine Presence, and heard our Lord inviting her to take the place which St John (it was his feast) had occupied at the Last Supper. He then went on speaking, 'in so plain and effective a manner as to leave no room for doubt, such were the results that this grace produced in me, who am always afraid of deceiving myself about what I assert to take place interiorly'. He told her that the love of His heart must needs spread and manifest itself to men by means of her, and that He would reveal the treasures of its graces through her, His chosen instrument and the disciple of His Sacred Heart. During a period of eighteen months our Lord continued to appear to Margaret-Mary at intervals, explaining and amplifying the first revelation. He told her that His heart was to be honoured under the form of a heart of flesh, represented in a way now familiar to Catholics throughout the world, and that, in consideration of the coldness and rebuffs given to Him by mankind in return for all His eagerness to do them good, she should make up for their ingratitude so far as she was able. This was to be done by frequent loving communion, especially on the first Friday of each month and by an hour's vigil every Thursday night in memory of His agony and desertion in Gethsemane—practices which Catholics have made their own in the devotions of the Nine Fridays and the Holy Hour. After a long interval a final revelation was made within the octave of Corpus Christi in 1675, when our Lord said to St Margaret-Mary, 'Behold the heart which has so much loved men that it has spared nothing, even exhausting and consuming itself in testimony of its love. Instead of gratitude I receive from most only indifference, by irreverence and sacrilege and the coldness and scorn that men have for me in the sacrament of love.' Then He asked that a feast of reparation be instituted for the Friday after the octave of Corpus Christi (now the feast of the Sacred Heart).

When she carried the matter to her superior, Mother de Saumaise, she 'mortified and humiliated her with all her might, and allowed her to do none of the things that our Lord had asked of her, treating contemptuously all that the poor sister had said'. She was seriously over-wrought by all that had happened, was taken ill, and her life was in danger. Mother de Saumaise was looking for a sign to guide her in dealing with Sister Alacoque, and said to her, 'If God cures you, I shall take it as a proof that all you experience comes from Him, and I will allow you to do what our Lord wishes in honour of His Sacred Heart'. St Margaret-Mary prayed accordingly, she at once recovered, and Mother de Saumaise fulfilled her promise. But there was a minority in the community definitely hostile to their sister and her spiritual experiences, and the superior ordered her to set them out for the opinion of certain theologians. These diagnosed them as delusions, and recommended that the visionary should take more food. Our Lord, however, had promised that an understanding director should come to St Margaret-Mary, and when Claud La Colombière arrived as confessor extraordinary to the nuns she knew at once that he was the man. He did not stay at Paray long, but long enough to be convinced of the genuineness of Margaret-Mary's experiences, to gain a deep respect and affection for her, and sincerely to adopt the teaching of the Sacred Heart while confirming the saint herself in it. Soon after Claud left for England.

During the rule of Mother Greyfié, who succeeded Mother de Saumaise, St Margaret-Mary alternately received great graces and underwent great trials, both interiorly and from her fellow-creatures. She was tempted to despair, vainglory and self-indulgence, and had a good deal of sickness. In 1681 Claud La Colombière came to Paray for the good of his health, and died there in February of the following year. Two years later Mother Melin, who had known Margaret-Mary during all her religious life, was elected superior at Paray and she appointed the saint as her assistant, with the approval of the chapter. From henceforth any remaining opposition ceased, or at least was silenced. The secret of her divine revelations was made known to the community in a rather dramatic (and for her embarrassing) way, being read out, presumably by accident, in the refectory in the course of a book written by Claud La Colombière.

St Margaret-Mary was also made mistress of the novices, with such success that professed nuns would ask leave to attend her conferences. Her secret being now known, she was less reticent in encouraging devotion to the Sacred Heart, and inculcated it among her novices, who privately observed the feast in 1685. In the following year the family of a dismissed novice caused trouble by denouncing the novice mistress as an impostor and unorthodox innovator, and for a time some of the old feeling was raised against her in the convent, but it soon subsided and on June 21 the whole house privately celebrated the feast so far as they were able. Two years later a chapel was built at Paray in honour of the Sacred Heart, and the devotion began to be accepted in other convents of the Visitandines, and to be propagated here and there throughout France.

While serving a second term as assistant superior St Margaret-Mary was taken ill in October 1690. She asked for the last sacraments, saying, 'I need nothing but God, and to lose myself in the heart of Jesus'. The priest came and began to administer the last rites; at the fourth anointing, of the lips, she died. St Margaret-Mary Alacoque was canonized in 1920.

17 : ST IGNATIUS, BISHOP OF ANTIOCH, MARTYR (c. A.D. 107)

ST IGNATIUS, surnamed Theophorus or God-bearer, was possibly a convert and a disciple of St John the Evangelist, but we know little that is reliable concerning his earlier history. He seems to have taken charge of the church at Antioch about the year 69, and was condemned to death during Trajan's persecution.

Having prayed for the Church and commended it with tears to God, Ignatius joyfully submitted his limbs to the fetters and was hurried away by the soldiers to be taken to Rome. At Seleucia, a seaport about sixteen miles from Antioch, they boarded a ship which, for some reason unknown to us, was to coast along the southern and western shores of Asia Minor, instead of proceeding at once to Italy. The numerous stoppages, however, gave the saint opportunities of confirming in the faith the various churches near the coast of Asia Minor. At Smyrna, he had the joy of meeting his former fellow disciple St Polycarp, and hither came also Bishop Onesimus at the head of a deputation from Ephesus, Bishop Damas with envoys from Magnesia, and Bishop Polybius from Tralles. One of the deputies, Burrhus, was so useful that St Ignatius asked the Ephesians to allow him to stay with him as a companion. From Smyrna, the saint wrote four letters: to the Ephesians, to the churches of Magnesia and Tralles and to the Christians in Rome.

The guards were in a hurry to leave Smyrna in order that they might reach Rome before the games were over—for illustrious victims of venerable appearance were always a great attraction in the amphitheatre—and Ignatius himself gladly acquiesced. They next sailed to Troas, where they learnt that peace had been restored to the church at Antioch. At Troas he wrote three more letters: to the Philadelphians, to the Smyrnaeans, and to St Polycarp.

As the saint approached Rome, the faithful are said to have come out to meet him, rejoicing at his presence in their midst but grieving that they were to lose him so soon. As he had anticipated, they were desirous of taking steps to obtain his release, but he entreated them not to hinder him from going to the Lord. Then, kneeling down with the brethren, he prayed for the Church, for the cessation of persecution, and for charity and unanimity among the faithful. According to legend he arrived in Rome on December 20, the last day of the public games, and was brought before the prefect of the city, to whom the emperor's letter was delivered. In due course the soldiers hurried him off to the amphitheatre, and we are told that two fierce lions were let out upon him, who devoured him immediately, leaving nothing but the larger bones.

18 : ST LUKE, EVANGELIST (FIRST CENTURY)

WE learn from St Paul that St Luke was a gentile, for he is not named among those of his helpers whom Paul mentions as Jews (Col. iv 10–11); that he was a fellow worker with the apostle, 'Mark, Aristarchus, Demas and Luke, who share my labours'; and that he was a medical man, 'Luke, the beloved physician' (or 'the beloved Luke, the physician'), who doubtless had the care of Paul's much-tried health.

The first time in the history of the mission of St Paul that Luke speaks in his own name in the first person is when the apostle sailed from Troas into Macedonia (Acts xvi 10). Before this he had doubtless been for some time a disciple of St Paul, and from this time seems never to have left him, unless by his order for the service of the churches he had planted; he was certainly with him not only during the first but also during the second imprisonment in Rome. According to Eusebius, Luke's home was at Antioch, and he was almost certainly a Greek; and his journeyings and tribulations with St Paul are, of course, set out by Luke himself in the Acts of the Apostles.

Luke was with St Paul in his last days: after writing those famous words to Timothy, 'The time of my dissolution is at hand. I have fought a good fight: I have finished my course: I have kept the faith . . . ', the apostle goes on to say, 'Only Luke is with me'. Of what happened to St Luke after St Paul's martyrdom we have no certain knowledge: the later statements about him are impossible to reconcile. But according to a fairly early and widespread tradition he was unmarried, wrote his gospel in Greece, and died at the age of 84 in Boeotia.

19 : THE MARTYRS OF NORTH AMERICA, (A.D. 1642–1649)

BY the wish of the French King Henry IV, in 1608 two Jesuits, Peter Biard and Ennemond Massé, sailed from Europe, and on their arrival in Acadia (Nova Scotia) began work among the Souriquois Indians at Port Royal (now Annapolis). Their first task was to learn the language. Massé went into the woods to live with these nomad tribes and to pick up what he could of their speech, while Biard stayed at the settlement and bribed with food and sweets the few Indians who remained, in order to induce them to teach him the words he required. After a year they were able to draw up a catechism and to begin to teach.

By the time the missionaries were joined by fresh colonists and by two more Jesuit priests, as well as by a lay-brother, the work of evangelization seemed well inaugurated. But in 1613 a raid was made from the sea by the piratical English captain of a merchant vessel, who descended with his crew on the unfortunate inhabitants, pillaged the settlement, and set adrift fifteen of the colony, including Massé. He then sailed back to Virginia with Biard and Quentin on board. Eventually the missionaries found their way back to France, but their work of preaching the gospel was brought to a standstill.

In the meantime Samuel Champlain, governor of New France, was continually imploring that good religious should be sent out, and in 1615 several Franciscans arrived at Tadroussac. They laboured heroically, but finding that they could not obtain enough men or enough money to convert the Indians, they invited the Jesuits to come to their assistance. In 1625 three priests of the Society of Jesus landed in Quebec in time to meet the Indian traders who had just murdered the friar Vial and his catechist and had thrown them into that part of the rapids which is still known as Sault-au-Récollet. Of the three new-comers one was Massé, returning to his former labours, but the two others, Brébeuf and Charles Lalemant, were new to the work.

As Brébeuf was unable to trust himself at once to the Hurons he wintered with the Algonquins, learning their speech and their customs under conditions of appalling discomfort and occasionally of hunger. The following year he went with a Franciscan and a fellow Jesuit to the Huron country. The Jesuits settled at Tod's Point, but Brébeuf's companions were soon recalled and Brébeuf was left alone with the Hurons, whose habit of living, less migratory than that of other tribes, gave the missionaries a better prospect of evangelizing them. During that period however, he failed to make a single convert among them, but his stay was cut short. The colony was in distress: the English closed the St Lawrence to all relief from France and obliged Champlain to surrender. Colonists and missionaries were forced to return to their own country, and Canada became, for the first time and for a short period, a British colony. Before long the indefatigable Champlain brought the matter to the law courts in London, and was able to prove so conclusively that the seizure of the colony was unjust that in 1632 Canada reverted to France.

The Franciscans were immediately invited to return, but they had not enough men, and the Jesuits took up the work of evangelization once more. Father Le Jeune, who was placed in charge of the mission, came to New France in 1632, Antony Daniel soon followed, and in 1633 Brébeuf and

Massé arrived with Champlain, the governor. Le Jeune conceived the plan of keeping the entire nation informed of the actual conditions in Canada by a series of graphic descriptions, beginning with his own personal experiences on the voyage and his first impressions of the Indians. The earliest reports were written and despatched to France within two months and were published at the end of the year. These missives, known as 'The Jesuit Relations', continued to pass from New to Old France almost without interruption, and often embodied the letters of other Jesuits, such as Brébeuf and Perrault. They awakened interest not only in France but in all Europe.

When the Hurons came to Quebec for their annual market they were delighted to meet Brébeuf and to be addressed by him in their own language. They wished him to go back with them, and he was eager to do so, but they were frightened at the last moment by an Ottawa chieftain, and for the time refused. The following year, however, when they came again, they agreed to take Brébeuf, Daniel and another priest named Darost, and after a most uncomfortable journey in which they were robbed and abandoned by their guides, the three Jesuits reached their destination, where the Hurons built a hut for them. Brébeuf gave his companions lessons in Huron, and Daniel, who proved himself an apt pupil, could soon lead the children in chanting the Lord's Prayer when Brébeuf held assemblies in his cabin.

It was resolved to establish a seminary at Quebec for Indians, and Daniel started back with two or three children to found the new institution which became the centre of the missionaries' hopes. For a short time Brébeuf was again alone among the Hurons and he then wrote for those who were to come to the Huron mission an instruction which afterwards became famous.

In 1636 arrived five more Jesuits, two of whom were destined to be numbered among the martyrs—Jogues, who was to become the apostle of a new Indian nation, and Garnier. Isaac Jogues had been born at Orléans, and after entering the Jesuit novitiate at Rouen at the age of seventeen had sstudied at the royal college of La Flèche, which Descartes considered one of the first schools of Europe. After his ordination he was appointed to Canada and sailed with the governor of New France, Huault de Montmagny. Charles Garnier was a Parisian, educated at the Clermont college. At nineteen he became a Jesuit, and after his ordination in 1635 he volunteered for the Canadian mission. He sailed with Jogues in 1636. Garnier was then thirty years of age, Jogues was twenty-nine.

While Brébeuf was alone with the Hurons he had gone through the excitement of a threatened invasion by their bitter enemies the Iroquois, and had to witness the horrible sight of an Iroquois tortured to death. He could do nothing to avert this; but, as he had baptized the captive shortly before, he was determined to stand by to encourage him.

Five of the new-comers went almost at once to join Father de Brébeuf. and Jogues, who had not been intended at first for the Huron mission, followed a few months later. A second mission was established at Teanaustaye, and Lalemant was appointed in charge of both stations, whilst Brébeuf at his own wish undertook the care of a new location, called Sainte-Marie, at some distance from the Indian villages. This settlement acted as a central bureau for missions and as a headquarters for priests and their attendants, as well as for the Frenchmen who served as labourers or soldiers. A hospital and a fort were erected and a cemetery established, and for five years the pioneers worked perseveringly, often undertaking long and perilous expeditions to other tribes—to the Petun or Tobacco Indians, the Ojibways, and to the Neuters north of Lake Erie—by whom they were more often than not very badly received. The first adult to be baptized (in 1637) was followed by over eighty, two years later, and by sixty in 1641. It did not seem much, but it proved that genuine conversion was possible.

In 1642 the Huron country was in great distress: harvests were poor, sickness abounded, and clothing was scarce. Quebec was the only source of supplies, and Jogues was chosen to lead an expedition. It reached its objective safely and started back well supplied with goods for the mission, but the Iroquois, the bitter enemies of the Hurons, and the fiercest of all Indian tribes, were on the war-path and ambushed the returning expedition. The story of the ill-treatment and torture of the captives cannot here be told. Suffice it to say that Jogues and his assistant René Goupil, besides being beaten to the ground and assailed several times with knotted sticks and fists, had their hair, beards and nails torn off and their forefingers bitten through.

The first of all the martyrs to suffer death was Goupil, who was tomahawked on September 29, 1642, for having made the sign of the cross on the brow of some children. This René Goupil was a remarkable man. He had tried hard to be a Jesuit and had even entered the novitiate, but his health forced him to give up the attempt. He then studied sugery and found his way to Canada, where he offered his services to the missionaries, whose fortitude he emulated.

Jogues remained a slave among the Mohawks, one of the Iroquois tribes, who, however, had decided to kill him. He owed his escape to the Dutch, who, ever since they had heard of the sufferings he and his friends were enduring, had been trying to obtain his release. Through the efforts of the governor of Fort Orange and of the governor of New Netherlands he was taken on board a vessel and, by way of England, got back to France, where his arrival roused the keenest interest. But early in 1644 Jogues was again at sea on his way back to New France. Arriving at Montreal, then recently founded, he began to work among the Indians of that neighbourhood, pending the time when he could return to the Hurons, a journey which was becoming yearly more perilous because Iroquois Indians were everywhere along the route. Unexpectedly the Iroquois sent an embassy to Three Rivers to sue for peace: Jogues, who was present at the conference, noticed that no representative came from the chief village, Ossernenon. Moreover, it was clear to him that the Iroquois only desired peace with the French—not with the Hurons. However, it was considered desirable to send a deputation from New France to meet the Iroquois chiefs at Ossernenon, and Jogues was selected as ambassador, together with John Bourdon, who represented the government of the colony.

They went by the route of Lake Champlain and Lake George, and after spending a week in confirming the pact they returned to Quebec, Jogues leaving behind a box of religious articles because he was resolved later to return to the Mohawks as a missionary, and was glad to be relieved of one of his packages. This box proved the immediate cause of his martyrdom. The

Mohawks had had a bad crop, and soon after Jogues's departure an epidemic broke out which they attributed to a devil concealed in the box. So when they heard that Jogues was paying a third visit to their villages, they waylaid, stripped and ill-treated him and his companion Lalande. Some of them treacherously invited Jogues to a meal on the evening of October 18 and tomahawked him as he was entering the cabin. His head they cut off and placed on a pole facing the route by which he had come. The following day his companion Lalande and the Huron guide were likewise toma- hawked and beheaded, their bodies being afterwards thrown into the river. John Lalande was, like René Goupil, a *donné* or oblate of the mission. The martyrdom of Jogues sealed the fate of the Hurons, who were gradually becoming Christian, and with a period of peace the whole tribe would have been converted. But the Iroquois were unremitting in their hostilities. They began to attack and pillage the Huron villages, sparing no one, and on July 4, 1648, they appeared at Teanaustaye, just as Daniel had finished celebrating Mass. He went forth alone to meet the enemy. They surrounded him on all sides, covering him with arrows till he fell dead, pierced through the breast. They stripped him and threw his body into the church, which they set on fire.

Within a year, on March 16, 1649, the Iroquois attacked the village at which Brébeuf and Lalemant were stationed. The torture of these two missionaries was as atrocious as anything recorded in history. At the height of the torments Father Lalemant raised his eyes to Heaven and invoked God's aid, whilst Father de Brébeuf set his face like a rock as though insensible to the pain. Then, like one recovering consciousness, he preached to his persecutors and to the Christian captives until the savages gagged his mouth, cut off his nose, tore off his lips, and then, in derision of baptism, deluged him and his companion martyrs with boiling water. Finally, large pieces of flesh were cut out of the bodies of both the priests and roasted by the Indians, who tore out their hearts before their death by means of an opening above the breast, feasting on them and on their blood, which they drank while it was still warm.

Before the end of the year 1649 the Iroquois had penetrated as far as the Tobacco nation, where Father Garnier had founded a mission in 1641 and where the Jesuits now had two stations. The inhabitants of the village of Saint-Jean, hearing that the enemy was approaching, sent out their men to meet the attackers, who, however, took a roundabout way and arrived at the gates unexpectedly. An orgy of incredible cruelty followed, in the midst of which Garnier, the only priest in the mission, hastened from place to place, giving absolution to the Christians and baptizing the children and catechu- mens, totally unmindful of his own fate. While thus employed he was shot down by the musket of an Iroquois. He strove to reach a dying man whom he thought he could help, but after three attempts he collapsed, and subsequently received his death-blow from a hatchet which penetrated to the brain.

Father Noel Chabanel, the missionary companion of Garnier, was immediately recalled. He had started on his way back with some Christian Hurons when they heard the cries of the Iroquois returning from Saint-Jean. The father urged his followers to escape, but was too much exhausted to keep up with them. His fate was long uncertain, but a Huron apostate eventually admitted having killed the holy man out of hatred of the Christian faith.

These martyrs of North America, *viz*. SS. John de Brébeuf, Isaac Jogues, Antony Daniel, Gabrial Lalemand, Charles Garnier, Noel Chabanel, René Goupil and John Lalande, were canonized in 1930.

20 : ST BERTILLA BOSCARDIN, VIRGIN (A.D. 1922)

BERTILLA was born into a poor peasant family in 1888 at Brendola, between Vicenza and Verona, was christened Anne Frances, and was called Annetta. Her father, Angelo Boscardin, a jealous man, was given to drink and accordingly there were rows and violence in the home—as Boscardin confessed in giving evidence for his daughter's beatification. Annetta went spasmodically to the village school, but had also from an early age to work in the house and as a domestic servant nearby. When a local priest, Don Capovilla, recognized in her a religious vocation, her pastor, the Archpriest Gresele, laughed at the idea. Nevertheless, since, as he said, the girl could at any rate peel potatoes, Don Gresele proposed her to a convent, which refused to receiver receive her. However, when she was sixteen Annetta was accepted by the Sisters of St Dorothy at Vicenza, and given the name Bertilla, after the abbess of Chelles. 'I can't do anything', she said to the novice-mistress, 'I'm a poor thing, a goose. Teach me. I want to become a saint.'

For a year Sister Bertilla worked in the scullery, the bakehouse and the laundry, and then was sent to learn nursing at Treviso, where the Sisters of St Dorothy had charge of the municipal hospital. But the local superioress used her as a kitchen-maid, and she remained among the pots and pans till after her profession in 1907, when she was promoted to help in the children's diphtheria ward. From then on Bertilla was the devoted servant of the sick; but she soon became sick herself, and for the last twelve years of her life was in constant and severe pain from an internal malady that surgery failed to cure and which eventually killed her.

Early in 1915 the Treviso hospital was taken over for troops, and when two years later the disaster of Caporetto drove the Italians back to the Piave it was in the front line. When during air-raids some of the sisters were helpless with fear, Bertilla—no less frightened—saying her rosary, busied herself taking coffee and marsala to the patients who could not be moved to the basement. She was among those soon evacuated to a military hospital at Viggiù, near Como, and here it was that she came under the admiring notice of the chaplain Peter Savoldelli and of the officer Mario Lameri. The superioress, however, like other local superiors before her, failed to understand and appreciate Sister Bertilla: she thought she was overworking herself and getting too attached to her patients. And so Bertilla was banished to the laundry: here she remained uncomplainingly for four months, till she was rescued by the mother general, a remarkable woman named Azelia Farinea, who withdrew her from Viggiù. After the armistice she returned to the hospital at Treviso and was put in charge of the children's isolation ward.

THE LIVES OF THE SAINTS

Sister Bertilla's health had been getting worse and worse, and three years later a serious surgical operation was indicated. It was done; but after three days, on October 20, 1922, Sister Bertilla died. Crowds flocked to her first grave at Treviso and to her tomb at Vicenza; miracles of healing were attributed to her intercession in Heaven; and in 1952 Bd Bertilla was beatified, in the presence of members of her family and patients whom she had nursed. She was canonized in 1961.

21 : ST HILARION, ABBOT (c. A.D. 371)

HILARION was born in a village called Tabatha, to the south of Gaza, his parents being idolaters. He was sent by them to Alexandria to study, where, being brought to the knowledge of the Christian faith, he was baptized when he was about fifteen. Having heard of St Antony, he went into the desert to see him, and stayed with him two months, observing his manner of life. But Hilarion found the desert only less distracting than the town, and, not being able to bear the concourse of those who resorted to Antony to be healed of diseases or delivered from devils, and being desirous to begin to serve God in perfect solitude, he returned into his own country. Finding his father and mother both dead, he gave part of his goods to his brethren and the rest to the poor, reserving nothing for himself (for he was mindful of Ananias and Sapphira, says St Jerome). He retired into the desert seven miles from Majuma, towards Egypt, between the seashore on one side and a swamp on the other. His clothing consisted only of a sackcloth shirt, a leather tunic which St Antony gave him, and an ordinary short cloak. He never changed a tunic till it was worn out and never washed the sackcloth which he had once put on.

For years together his food was fifteen figs a day, which he never took till sunset. His occupation was tilling the earth and, in imitation of the Egyptian monks, making baskets, whereby he provided himself with the necessaries of life. During the first years he had no other shelter than woven reeds and rushes. Afterwards he built himself a cell, which was still to be seen in St Jerome's time; it was four feet broad and five in height, and a little longer than his body, like a tomb rather than a house. Soon he found that figs alone were insufficient to support life properly and permitted himself to eat as well vegetables, bread and oil.

St Hilarion was informed by revelation in 356 of the death of St Antony. He was then about sixty-five years old, and had been long afflicted at the number of people, especially women, who crowded to him; moreover, the charge of his disciples was a great burden. So he resolved to leave Palestine, and the people assembled in great numbers to stop him. He told them he would neither eat nor drink till they let him go; and seeing him pass seven days without taking anything, they left him. He then chose some monks who were able to walk without eating till after sunset, and with them he travelled into Egypt and at length came to St Antony's mountain, near the Red Sea, where they found two monks who had been his disciples. On the top of the mountain (to which the ascent was very difficult, twisting like a vine) they found two cells to which St Antony often retired to avoid visitors and even his own disciples; St Hilarion asked to see the place where he was buried. They led him aside, but they said that St Antony had given strict charge that his grave should be concealed, lest a certain rich man in that country should carry the body away and build a church for it.

St Hilarion returned to Aphroditopolis (Atfiah), and thence went into a neighbouring desert and gave himself with more earnestness than ever to abstinence and silence. Finding himself too popular also in that place, Hilarion spent a year in an oasis of the western desert. But finding that he was too well known ever to lie concealed in Egypt, he determined to seek some remote island and embarked with one companion for Sicily. From Cape Passaro they travelled twenty miles up the country and stopped in an unfrequented place. St Hesychius, the saint's disciple, sought him in the East and through Greece when, at Modon in Peloponnesus, he heard from a Jewish pedlar that a prophet had appeared in Sicily who wrought many miracles. He arrived at Passaro and, inquiring for the holy man at the first village, found that everybody knew him: he was not more distinguished by his miracles than by his disinterestedness, for he could never be induced to accept anything from anyone.

He found that St Hilarion wanted to go into some country where not even his language should be understood, and so Heyschius took him to Epidaurus in Dalmatia (Ragusa). Miracles again defeated the saint's design of living unknown. St Hilarion, troubled over what he should do or whither he should turn, going alone over the world in his imagination, mourned that though his tongue was silent yet his miracles spoke. At last he fled away in the night in a small vessel to Cyprus. Arrived there, he settled at a place two miles from Paphos. He had not been there long when his identity was discovered, so he went a dozen miles inland to an inaccessible but pleasant place, where he at last found peace and quietness. Here after a few years Hilarion died at the age of eighty; among those who visited him in his last illness was St Epiphanius, Bishop of Salamis, who afterwards wrote about his life to St Jerome. He was buried near Paphos, but St Hesychius secretly removed the body to the saint's old home at Majuma.

22 : SS. PHILIP, BISHOP OF HERACLEA, AND HIS COMPANIONS, MARTYRS (A.D. 304)

PHILIP, Bishop of Heraclea, the metropolis of Thrace, was a martyr of Christ in the persecution of Diocletian. Having discharged every duty of a faithful minister as deacon and priest, he was raised to the episcopal dignity and governed that church with virtue and prudence when it was shaken by persecution. To extend and perpetuate the work of God he trained many disciples in sacred learning and solid piety. Two of the most eminent among them had the happiness to be companions of his martyrdom, namely, Severus, a priest, and Hermes, a deacon, who was formerly the first magistrate of the city, but after he was engaged in the ministry earned his livelihood with his hands, and brought up his son to do the same. When Diocletian's first edicts against the Christians were issued, many advised the bishop to leave the city; but he would not stir, continuing to exhort the brethren to constancy and patience. Aristomachus, an officer, came by the governor's order to seal up the door of the church. Philip said to him, 'Do you imagine that God dwells within walls, and not rather in the hearts of men?' and continued to hold his assembly outside. The next day officers came and set their seal upon the sacred vessels and books. The faithful who beheld this were much grieved; but the bishop stood leaning against the door of the church, encouraged them with burning words, and refused to leave his post.

Afterwards the governor, Bassus, finding Philip and many of his flock keeping the Lord's Day assembled before the church, gave orders that they should be brought before him. Bassus said, 'You know that the emperor has forbidden your assemblies. Give up to me the vessels of gold and silver which you use and the books which you read.' The bishop answered, 'The vessels we will give you, for it is not by precious metal but by charity that God is honoured. But the sacred books it becomes neither you to demand nor me to surrender.' The governor ordered executioners to be called, and commanded one among them to torture Philip, who bore his torments with invincible courage. Hermes told the governor that it was not in his power to destroy the word of God, even though he should take away all the writings in which the true doctrine is contained, and in reply Bassus had him scourged. After this he was taken with Publius, the governor's assistant, to the place where the sacred writings and plate were hid. Publius would have taken away some of the vessels, but being hindered by Hermes he gave him such a blow on the face that blood flowed. The governor was provoked at Publius for this action, and ordered the wound to be dressed. He then ordered Philip and the other prisoners to be brought to the market-place, and the church roof to be stripped. In the meantime soldiers burned the sacred writings, the flames mounting so high as to frighten the bystanders. Bassus pressed the bishop to sacrifice to the gods, to the emperors and to the fortune of the city. Pointing at a large and beautiful statue of Hercules, he bid him just to touch it: Philip replied by expounding the value of graven images to stone-carvers but their helplessness to worshippers. Then, turning to Hermes, Bassus asked if he, at least, would sacrifice. 'I will not', replied Hermes, 'I am a Christian.' Bassus asked, 'If we can persuade Philip to offer sacrifice, will you follow his example?' Hermes answered he would not; neither could they persuade Philip. After many useless threats and pressing them to sacrifice at least to the emperors, Bassus ordered them to be carried to prison.

Bassus went out of office at the end of his term and Justin succeeded him. The Christians were much disappointed at this change: for Bassus often yielded to reason and his wife had for some time been a Christian herself; but Justin was a violent man. Zoilus, the magistrate of the city, brought Philip before him, and Justin pressed him to sacrifice and threatened him with torture. The bishop replied, 'You may torment, but will not conquer me; no power can induce me to sacrifice'. Then Justin told the soldiers to tie his feet and drag him along. They dashed him against the stones so roughly that he was torn and bruised all over, and the Christians carried him in their arms when he was brought back to his dungeon.

The persecutors had long been in quest of the priest Severus, who had hidden himself. He at length surrendered and was committed to prison. Hermes was firm in his examination before Justin, and was treated in the same manner. The three martyrs were kept imprisoned for seven months and then removed to Adrianople, where they were confined in a private house till the arrival of the governor. The next day, holding his court at the Baths, Justin had Philip brought before him and beaten till his flesh was a pulp. Hermes was next examined. He persisted in his profession, and was sent back to prison, where the martyrs joyfully gave thanks to Jesus Christ for this beginning of their victory. Three days after this, Justin brought them again before his tribunal, and having in vain pressed Philip to obey the emperors, said to Hermes, 'If the approach of death makes this man think life not worth preserving, do not you be insensible to its blessings. Offer sacrifice.' Hermes replied by denouncing idolatry. Having then consulted his assessor and others, Justin pronounced sentence: 'We order Philip and Hermes who, despising the commands of the emperor, have rendered themselves unworthy of the name and rights of Roman citizens, to be burned, that others may learn to obey.'

They went joyfully to the stake. Philip's feet were so mutilated that he could not walk, and had to be carried. At the place of punishment the executioners, according to custom, covered Philip's feet and legs with earth up to the knees, and tied his hands behind his back. They likewise made Hermes go down into the ditch. Before the executioners lighted the fire Hermes called Velogius, a Christian, and said to him, 'I implore you, by our Saviour Jesus Christ, tell my son Philip from me to restore whatever was committed to my charge, that I may incur no fault'. Then his hands were tied, and fire was set to the pile. The martyrs praised and gave thanks to God as long as they were able to speak. Their bodies were found entire. Justin ordered them to be thrown into the river, but some citizens of Adrianople went in boats with nets, and fished them out. Severus the priest, who had been left alone in prison, when he was informed of their martyrdom, rejoiced at their glory, and earnestly besought God not to think him unworthy to partake in it, since he had confessed His name with them. He was heard, and suffered martyrdom the day following.

23 : ST JOHN OF CAPISTRANO, (A.D. 1456)

JOHN was born in 1386. From early youth the boy's talents made him conspicuous. He studied law at Perugia with such success that in 1412 he was appointed governor of that city and married the daughter of one of the principal inhabitants. During hostilities between Perugia and the Malatestas he was imprisoned, and this was the occasion of his resolution to change his way of life and become a religious. How he got over the difficulty of his marriage is not altogether clear. But it is said that he rode through Perugia on a donkey with his face to the tail and with a hugh paper hat on his head upon which all his worst sins were plainly written. He was pelted by the children and covered with filth, and in this guise presented himself to ask admission into the noviceship of the Friars Minor. At that date, 1416, he was thirty years old.

In 1420 John was raised to the priesthood. Meanwhile he made extraordinary progress in his theological studies, leading at the same time a life of extreme austerity, in which he tramped the roads barefoot without sandals, gave only three or four hours to sleep and wore a hair-shirt continually. In his studies he had St James of the Marches as a fellow learner, and for a master St Bernardino of Siena, for whom he conceived the deepest veneration and affection. Very soon John's exceptional gifts of oratory made themselves perceptible.

But the work of preaching and the conversion of souls by no means absorbed all the saint's attention. There is no occasion to make reference here in any detail to the domestic embarrassments which had beset the Order of St Francis since the death of their Seraphic Founder. But all these difficulties required adjustment, and Capistran, working in harmony with St Bernardino of Siena, was called upon to bear a large share in this burden. Further, he was keenly interested in that reform of the Franciscan nuns which owed its chief inspiration to St Colette, and in the tertiaries of the order.

When the Emperor Frederick III, finding that the religious faith of the countries under his suzerainty was suffering grievously from the activities of heretical sectaries, appealed to Pope Nicholas V for help, St John Capistran was sent as commissary and inquisitor general, and he set out for Vienna in 1451 with twelve of his Franciscan brethren to assist him. John's work as inquisitor and his dealings with the Hussites and other Bohemian heretics have been severely criticized. His zeal was of the kind that scars and consumes, though he was merciful to the submissive and repentant, and he was before his time in his attitude to witchcraft and the use of torture.

It was the capture of Constantinople by the Turks which brought this spiritual campaign to an end. Capistran was called upon to rally the defenders of the West and to preach a crusade. His earlier efforts in Bavaria, and even in Austria, met with little response, and early in 1456 the situation became desperate. St John wore himself out in preaching and exhorting the Hungarian people in order to raise an army which could meet the threatened danger, and himself led to Belgrade the troops he had been able to recruit. Very soon the Turks were in position and the siege began. Animated by the prayers and the heroic example in the field of Capistran the garrison in the end gained an overwhelming victory. The siege was abandoned, and western Europe for the time was saved. But the infection bred by thousands of corpses which lay unburied round the city cost the life a month or two later of Capistran. He died most peacefully at Villach on October 23, 1456, and was canonized in 1724.

24 : ST ANTONY CLARET, ARCHBISHOP OF SANTIAGO DE CUBA, FOUNDER OF THE MISSIONARY SONS OF THE IMMACULATE HEART OF MARY (A.D. 1870)

BORN in 1807 at Sallent in the north of Spain, Antony practised his father's trade of cloth-weaving, and in his spare time learned Latin and printing. When he was twenty-two he entered the seminary at Vich, where he was ordained priest in 1835. After a few years he again began to entertain the idea of a Barthusian vocation, but as that seemed to be beyond his physical strength, he proceeded to Rome and eventually entered the Jesuit noviciate with the idea of consecrating his life to the foreign missions. Here, however, his health broke down, and he was advised by the Jesuit father general to return to Spain and busy himself with the evangelization of his countrymen. This course he adopted and for ten years he was engaged in giving missions and retreats throughout Catalonia; he was associated with Bd Joachima de Mas in the establishment of the Carmelites of Charity. His zeal inspired other priests to join in the same work, and in 1849 he was mainly instrumental in founding the congregation of Missionary Sons of the Immaculate Heart of Mary. The institute, commonly known by his name as 'The Charetians', has spread and flourished, not only in Spain, but in the Americas and beyond.

Almost immediately after this great work had been inaugurated, Father Claret was appointed archbishop of Santiago de Cuba. The task was one of exceptional difficulty, in which his efforts to bring about much-needed reforms were resisted. Several attempts were made upon his life, and in one instance a serious wound was inflicted by an assassin infuriated by the loss of his mistress who had been won back to an honest life. In 1857 St Antony returned to Spain to become confessor to Queen Isabella II. He resigned his Cuban archbishopric, but avoided residence at the court for any longer than his official duties required, devoting himself to missionary work and the diffusion of good literature, especially in his native Catalan.

In the course of his life St Antony is said to have preached 10,000 sermons and to have published 200 books or pamphlets for the instruction and edification of clergy and people. While rector of the Escorial he established a science laboratory, a museum of natural history, schools of music and languages, and other foundations. His continual union with God was rewarded by many supernatural graces not only in the way of ecstasies and the gift of prophecy, but also by the miraculous cure of bodily diseases.

Political conditions in Spain and the queen's attitude towards the Holy See made St Antony's position very difficult, and in the revolution of 1868 he was exiled together with the queen. He then went to Rome, where he made his influence felt in promoting the definition of papal infallibility. An attempt was made to bring him back to Spain, but it failed; a fatal illness came upon him in France, and he went to his reward in the Cistercian monastery of Fontfroide, near Narbonne, on October 24, 1870. He was canonized in 1950.

25 : ST GAUDENTIUS, BISHOP OF BRESCIA (c. A.D. 410)

GAUDENTIUS seems to have been educated under St Philastrius, Bishop of Brescia, whom he styles his 'father'. His reputation was very high and he travelled to Jerusalem, partly on pilgrimage and partly hoping by his absence to be forgotten at home. During his absence St Philastrius died, and the clergy and people of Brescia chose Gaudentius for their bishop: he was consecrated by St Ambrose about the year 387.

The church of Brescia soon found how great a treasure it possessed in so holy a pastor. A certain nobleman named Benevolus, who had been disgraced by the Empress Justina because he refused to draw up an edict in favour of the Arians, had retired to Brescia, and being hindered by sickness from attending the Easter sermons of Gaudentius, requested that he would commit them to writing for his use. By this means were preserved ten out of the twenty-one sermons of the saint which are extant.

In 405, St Gaudentius was deputed with two others by Pope St Innocent I and the Emperor Honorius to go into the East to defend the cause of St John Chrysostom before Arcadius, for which Chrysostom sent him a letter of thanks. The deputies were ill received, and imprisoned in Thrace; their papers were forcibly taken from them, and bribes were offered if they would declare themselves in communion with the bishop who had supplanted St John Chrysostom. They eventually arrived back safely in Italy, though it is supposed their enemies intended them to be cast away at sea, for they were put on a most unseaworthy vessel. St Gaudentius seems to have died about the year 410.

26 : ST CEDD, BISHOP OF THE EAST SAXONS (A.D. 664)

ST CEDD was the brother of St Chad and long served God in the monastery of Lindisfarne. When Peada, King of the Middle Angles, became a Christian at the court of his father-in-law, Oswy of Northumbria, in 653, being baptized by St Finan of Lindisfarne, four priests were sent to preach the gospel to his people. Of these St Cedd was one. After labouring there for a time he was called to a new harvest. Sigebert, King of the East Saxons, was also persuaded to renounce heathenism and was baptized by St Finan, whereupon Cedd was called out of the midlands and sent with another priest into Essex. They travelled throughout the province to examine the situation, and then St Cedd revisited Lindisfarne to confer with Finan, who consecrated him bishop for the East Saxons. He returned among them to continue the work he had begun, building churches and ordaining priests and deacons.

Two monasteries were founded by St Cedd, which seem to have been destroyed by the Danes later and never restored. The first, where remains of Cedd's church still exist, was at Bradwell-on-Sea (Ythancaestir, Othona); the other was at Tilbury. His visits to his native Northumbria were the occasion of a third foundation. Ethelwald, King of Deira, gave him a tract of land for a monastery in an inaccessible spot among the fells of Yorkshire. Here Cedd spent forty days in fasting and prayer, to consecrate the place to God according to the custom of Lindisfarne, derived from St Columba. This monastery, founded in 658, was called Laestingaeu, which has been identified with Lastingham in the North Riding; and it also came to be destroyed by the Danes.

In 664 St Cedd was present at the Synod of Whitby, being one of those who agreed to observe Easter by the Roman computation. Very soon after this he died at Lastingham during a great pestilence. At the news of his death thirty of his religious brethren among the East Saxons came to Lastingham to consecrate their lives where their holy father had ended his. But they too were carried off by the same pestilence, all except one boy, who was afterwards found not to have been baptized: he lived to become a priest and zealous missionary. Florence of Worcester tells us that St Cedd died on October 26, 664.

27 : ST FRUMENTIUS, BISHOP OF AKUSM (c. A.D. 380)

SOMEWHERE about the year 330 a philosopher of Tyre, named Mero-pius, undertook a voyage to the coasts of Arabia. He took with him two young men, Frumentius and Aedesius, with whose education he was entrusted. In the course of their voyage homeward the vessel touched at a certain port of Ethiopia. The natives fell out with some of the sailors, attacked them, and put the whole crew and all the passengers to the sword, except the two boys, who were studying their lessons under a tree at some distance. When they were found they were carried to the king, who resided at Aksum in Tigre country. He was attracted by the bearing and knowledge of the young Christians, and not long after made Aedesius his cupbearer and Frumentius, who was the elder, his secretary. This prince on his death-bed thanked them for their services and, in recompense, gave them their liberty. The queen, who was left regent for her eldest son, entreated them to remain and assist her, which they did.

Frumentius had the principal management of affairs and induced several Christian merchants who traded there to settle in the country. He procured them privileges and all conveniences for religious worship. When the young king came of age and, with his brother, took the reins of government into his own hands, the Tyrians resigned their posts, though he urged them to stay. Aedesius went back to Tyre, where he was ordained priest and told his adventures to Rufinus, who incorporated them in his *Church History*. But Frumentius, having nothing so much at heart as the conversion of the whole nation, took the route to Alexandria, and entreated the bishop, St Athanasius, to send some pastor to that country. Whereupon Athanasius ordained Frumentius himself bishop of the Ethiopians, judging no one more proper to finish the work which he had begun.

The consecration of St Frumentius took place probably just before the year 340 or just after 346 (or perhaps c. 355–356). He went back to Aksum and gained numbers to the faith by his preaching and miracles; the two royal brothers are said to have themselves received baptism. But the conversion even of the Aksumite kingdom was far from completed during the lifetime of St Frumentius. After his death he was called *Abuna*, 'Our father', and *Aba salama*, 'Father of peace', and *abuna* is still the title of the primate of the Church of Ethiopia.

28 : SS. SIMON AND JUDE, OR THADDEUS, APOSTLES (FIRST CENTURY)

ST SIMON is surnamed the Cananean or Zelotes in the Holy Scriptures, words which both mean 'the Zealous'. Some have mistakenly thought that the first of these names was meant to imply that St Simon was born at Cana in Galilee. The name refers to his zeal for the Jewish law before his call, and does not necessarily mean that he was one of that particular party among the Jews called Zealots. No mention of him appears in the gospels beyond that he was chosen among the apostles. Western tradition recognized in the Roman liturgy is that, after preaching in Egypt, he joined St Jude from Mesopotamia and that they went as missionaries for some years to Persia, suffering martyrdom there.

The apostle Jude (Judas), also called Thaddeus (or Lebbeus), 'the brother of James', is usually regarded as the brother of St James the Less. It is not known when and by what means he became a disciple of Christ, nothing having been said of him in the gospels before we find him enumerated among the apostles. The history of St Jude after our Lord's ascension and the descent of the Holy Spirit is as unknown as that of St Simon. Jude's name is borne by one of the canonical epistles, which has much in common with the second epistle of St Peter.

29 : ST THEUDERIUS, OR CHEF, ABBOT (c. A.D.575)

ST THEUDERIUS was born at Arcisia (Saint-Chef-d'Arcisse) in Dauphiné. Having exercised himself in monastic life at Lérins and been ordained priest by St Caesarius at Arles, he returned to his own country; and, being joined by several disciples, built for them first cells and afterwards a monastery near the city of Vienne. It was anciently a custom here that some monk of whose sanctity the people entertained a high opinion was chosen voluntarily to lead the life of a recluse; St Theuderius was asked to undertake this penitential state, which obligation he willingly took upon himself, and discharged with much fervour at the church of St Laurence during the last twelve years of his life. An extraordinary gift of miracles made his name famous. He died about the year 575.

30 : ST ALPHONSUS RODRIGUEZ, (A.D. 1617)

DIEGO RODRIGUEZ was a well-to-do wool-merchant in Segovia, and Alphonsus, born about 1533, was his third child in a big family. When Bd Peter Favre and another Jesuit came to preach a mission at Segovia they stayed with Diego, and at the end accepted his offer of a few days' holiday at his country house. Young Alphonsus, then about ten, went with them and was prepared for his first communion by Bd Peter. When he was fourteen he was sent with his elder brother to study under the Jesuits at Alcala, but before the first year was out their father died, and it was decided that Alphonsus must go into the business, which his mother was going to carry on. She retired and left him in sole charge when he was twenty-three, and three years later he married a girl called Maria Suarez.

The business had been doing badly and his wife's dowry did not do much to improve it; Alphonsus was not an incapable business man, but times were hard. Then he lost his little daughter, and, after a long illness following the birth of a boy, his wife too. Two years later his mother died, and this succession of misfortunes and losses made Alphonsus give very serious thought to what God was calling him to do in the world. He began to realize that he was meant to be something different from the numerous commercial men who led exemplary but unheroic lives in Segovia. He sold his business and went to live with his two maiden sisters. These two, Antonia and Juliana, were a pious couple and taught their brother the rudiments of mental prayer, so that he was soon meditating two hours every morning and evening on the mysteries of the rosary. After some years his son died, and he now contemplated, not for the first time, the possibility of becoming a religious and applied to the Jesuits at Segovia. They unhesitatingly refused him: he was nearly forty, his health was not good, and he had not finished an education good enough to make him fit for sacerdotal studies. Undaunted, he went off to see his old friend Father Louis Santander, s.j., at Valencia. Father Santander recommended him to get ordained as soon as possible, and as a first step to learn Latin. So he put himself to school with the little boys. As he had given nearly all his money to his sisters and to the poor before leaving Segovia, he had to take a post as a servant and supplement his earnings by begging to support himself.

In 1571 the Jesuit provincial, over-ruling his official consultors, accepted Alphonsus Rodriguez as a lay-brother, or temporal coadjutor, as such is called in the Society. Six months later he was sent from Spain to the College of Montesione in the island of Majorca, and soon after his arrival was made hall-porter. St Alphonsus carried out the duties of this post till he became too old and infirm. Every minute left free by his work and what it entailed was given to prayer, but though he achieved a marvellous habitual recollection and union with God his spiritual path was far from an easy one. Especially in his later years he suffered from long periods of desolation and aridity, but he never despaired, carrying out every duty with exact regularity, knowing that in God's own time he would be seized again in an ecstasy of love and spiritual delight. Priests who had known him for forty years used to say that they had never noticed a word or action of Brother Alphonsus which could justly receive adverse criticism. In 1585, when he was fifty-four years old, he made his final vows, which he used to renew every day at Mass.

At Montesione, in addition to the students, there was a constant coming and going of clergy of all sorts, of nobles and professional men and members of their families having business with the Jesuit fathers, of the poor wanting help and merchants and tradesmen from Palma wanting orders. All these people got to know, to respect and to love Brother Alphonsus, and his reputation was known far beyond the boundaries of the college. The most famous of his 'pupils' was St Peter Claver, who was studying at the college in 1605.

In May of 1617 the rector of Montesione, Father Julian, was down with rheumatic fever, and asked for the prayers of St Alphonsus. He spent the night interceding for him, and in the morning Father Julian was able to celebrate Mass. In October Alphonsus knew that his end was at hand, and after receiving holy communion on October 29 all pain of mind and body ceased. He lay as it were in an unbroken ecstasy until, at midnight of October 31, a terrible agony began. At the end of half an hour composure returned, he looked around lovingly at his brethren, kissed the crucifix, uttered the Holy Name in a loud voice, and died. He was canonized in 1888 with St Peter Claver.

31 : ST WOLFGANG, BISHOP OF REGENSBURG (A.D. 994)

S T WOLFGANG came of a Swabian family and was born about the year 930. In his youth he was sent to the abbey of Reichenau, on an island in

Lake Constance, which was at that time a flourishing school of learning; here he became friendly with a young nobleman called Henry, brother to Poppo, Bishop of Würzburg, who had set up a school in that city. This Henry persuaded Wolfgang to bear him company to this new school at Würzburg, where the ability of the young Swabian soon provoked jealousy as well as admiration.

In 956 Henry was elected archbishop of Trier, and took Wolfgang with him, making him a teacher in the cathedral school. At Trier he came under the influence of the reforming monk Ramuold, and entered wholeheartedly into Henry's efforts for the improvement of religion in his diocese. Upon the death of the archbishop in 964 Wolfgang became a Benedictine in the monastery of Einsiedeln, governed at that time by Gregory, an Englishman. The abbot soon found the reputation of Wolfgang to be less than his merit, and appointed him director of the school of the monastery. St Ulric, Bishop of Augsburg, now ordained St Wolfgang priest; and with his ordination he received an apostolic missionary spirit, and was sent to preach the gospel to the Magyars in Pannonia. The results of this undertaking did not correspond to his zeal, and he was recommended to the Emperor Otto II as a person qualified to fill the see of Regensburg (Ratisbon) which was then vacant. He was conducted to the emperor at Frankfurt, who gave him the investiture of the temporalities, though Wolfgang entreated him to allow him to return to his monastery. Being sent back to Regensburgh, at Christmas 972 he was consecrated.

St Wolfgang never quitted the monastic habit, and practised all the austerities of conventual life when in the episcopal dignity. The first thing he did after regulation of his own household was to settle a thorough reformation among all his clergy, and in all the monasteries of his diocese, especially two disorderly nunneries. One of the sources of revenue of the see was the abbey of St Emmeram at Regensburg, which the bishops held *in commendam*, with the usual bad results. Wolfgang restored its autonomy and called Ramuold from Trier to be its abbot.

The territory of Behemia being part of his vast diocese, he gave up a part of it for a bishopric in that country, the see being set up at Prague. Henry, Duke of Bavaria, held St Wolfgang in the highest veneration, and entrusted to him the education of his son Henry, afterwards emperor and canonized saint. Wolfgang was taken ill while travelling down the Danube into Lower Austria and died at a little place called Puppingen, not far from Linz. He was canonized in 1052.

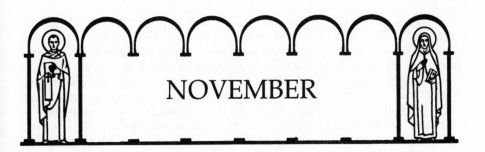

NOVEMBER

1 : ALL SAINTS

THERE are considerable indications of the celebration in quite early times of a collective feast of the martyrs—martyrs in those days being alone reckoned as saints. Although certain passages which have been appealed to in Tertullian and in St Gregory of Nyssa's Life of St Gregory Thaumaturgus are too vague to be of much service, we are on firmer ground when, in the *Misibene Hymnus* of St Ephraem (d. *cF46 373*), *we find mention of a feast kept in honour of 'the martyrs of all the earth'. This was apparently fixed for May 13, a fact which suggests the intervention of some oriental influence in the choice of precisely May 13 for the dedication of the Pantheon in Rome, mentioned below. Throughout the Syrian church in general, however, we know that already in 411, or earlier, a feast of 'all the martyrs' was celebrated on the Friday of Easter week, for the Syriac Short Martyrology* expressly records this. Easter Friday is still thus distinguished by the Catholics of the Chaldean rite and by the Nestorians. On the other hand the Byzantine churches kept and still keep a feast of all the saints on the Sunday after Pentecost, our Trinity Sunday; Chrysostom at Constantinople tells his hearers, in a sermon entitled 'A Panegyric of all the Martyrs that have suffered throughout the world', that seven days have hardly passed since the feast of Pentecost.

How the celebration of All Saints began in the West still remains somewhat of a problem. In both the *Félire* of Oengus and the Martyrology of Tallaght we find on April 17 a commemoration of all the martyrs, and on April 20 a feast 'of all the Saints of the whole of Europe': as the Tallaght text phrases it, this day is the 'communis sollemnitas omnium sanctorum et virginum Hiberniae et Britanniae et totius Europea'. Turning to England, we note that the primitive text of Bede's Martyrology contained no mention of All Saints, but in copies dating from the close of the eighth century or the beginning of the ninth, we find on November 1 the entry: 'Natale sancti Caesarii et festivitas omnium sanctorum.' Dom Quentin has suggested that the idea that Pope St Boniface IV intended by the dedication of the Pantheon (in honour of our Lady and all martyrs, on May 13, *c* 609; still commemorated in the Roman Martyrology) to establish something in the nature of a feast of All Saints may have been deduced by Ado and others from a phrase used by Bede, who has spoken of this dedication both in his *Ecclesiastical History* and in his *On the Calculation of Time*. Bede says—what was not stated in the *Liber*

Pontificalis which he had before him—that the pope designed that 'the memory of all the saints might in future be honoured in the place which had formerly been devoted to the worship, not of gods, but of demons'. In any case it is certain that Alcuin in the year 800 was in the habit of keeping the *solemnitas sanctissima* of All Saints on November 1, with a previous three days' fast. He knew that his friend Arno, Bishop of Salzburg, shared his interest in the festival, since Arno had a short time before presided over a Bavarian council which included that day in its list of holy days. We also hear of a certain Cathwulf who about the year 775 besought Charlemagne to institute a feast, with a fasting vigil preceding, 'in honour of the Trinity, the Unity, the angels and all the saints'. In the calendar in Bodley MS. Digby 63, ninth century, northern English, All Saints is marked on November 1 as a principal feast. Rome seems finally to have adopted that date under Gallican influence.

2 : ST MARCIAN, (*c.* A.D. 387)

THE city of Cyrrhus in Syria was the birthplace of St Marcian; his father was a patrician. Marcian himself retired into the desert of Chalcis, between Antioch and the Euphrates. He chose in it the most remote part and shut himself up in a small enclosure. He built himself a cell so narrow and low that he could neither stand nor lie in it without bending his body. Notwithstanding his care to live unknown to men, the reputation of his holiness spread abroad and he was prevailed upon to admit two first disciples, Eusebius and Agapitus. In time St Marcian had a considerable body of followers, over whom he appointed Eusebius abbot.

St Marcian wrought several miracles and was greatly humiliated by the reputation of a wonder-worker which consequently attached to him. He would not listen to requests for any miraculous intercession, and when a certain hermit came on behalf of a man of Beroea to get some oil blessed for his sick daughter, St Marcian refusd peremptorily. But at the same hour the girl recovered. Marcian lived to a considerable age, and during his last years was troubled by the indecent importunity of those who looked forward to having the custody of his dead body. Several people went so far as to build chapels in different places wherein to bury it, among them being his nephew Alipius. St Marcian therefore made Eusebius promise to bury him secretly. This accordingly was done and it was not till fifty years after the saint's death that the place of burial was disclosed, when the relics were solemnly translated and became an object of pilgrimage.

3 : ST MARTIN DE PORRES, (A.D. 1639)

HE was born in Lima in Peru in 1579, the natural child of John de Porres (Porras), a Spanish knight, and a coloured freed-woman from Panama, Anna by baptism. Young Martin inherited the features and dark complexion of his mother, which was a matter of vexation to the noble Porres, who nevertheless acknowledged the boy and his sister as his children, but eventually left Martin to the care of his mother. When he was twelve she apprenticed him to a barber-surgeon; but three years later, having received the habit of the third order of St Dominic, he was admitted to the Rosary convent of the Friars Preachers at Lima, eventually becoming a professed lay-brother.

Martin extended his care of the sick to those of the city, and was instrumental in establishing an orphanage and foundling-hospital, with other charitable institutions attached; he was given the office of distributing the convent's daily alms of food to the poor (which he is said sometimes to have increased miraculously); and he took upon himself to care for the slaves who were brought to Peru from Africa.

Brother Martin's charity embraced the lower animals (which seems to have surprised the Spaniards) and even vermin, excusing the depredations of rats and mice on the ground that the poor little things were insufficiently fed, and he kept a 'cats' and dogs' home' at his sister's house.

St Martin's protégé, Juan Vasquez Parra, shows the lay-brother as eminently practical in his charities, using carefully and methodically the money and goods he collected, raising a dowry for his niece in three days (at the same time getting as much and more for the poor), putting up the banns, showing Parra how to sow camomile in the well-manured hoof-prints of cattle, buying a Negro servant to work in the laundry, looking after those who needed blankets, shirts, candles, sweets, miracles or prayers—the procurator apparently both of the priory and the public.

St Martin was a close friend of St Rose of Lima as well as of Bd John Massias, who was a lay-brother at the Dominican priory of St Mary Magdalen in the same town. Martin was at the Rosary priory, and he died there on November 3, 1639: he was carried to his grave by prelates and noblemen. He was beatified in 1837, after long delays, and canonized on May 6, 1962. He is patron of social justice.

4 : ST CHARLES BORROMEO, ARCHBISHOP OF MILAN AND CARDINAL (A.D. 1584)

HE was an aristocrat by birth, his father being Count Gilbert Borromeo, himself a man of talent and sanctity. His mother, Margaret, was a Medici, whose younger brother became Pope Pius IV. Charles, the second of two sons in a family of six, was born in the castle of Arona on Lake Maggiore on October 2, 1538, and from his earliest years showed himself to be of a grave and devout disposition. At the age of twelve he received the clerical tonsure, and his uncle, Julius Caesar Borromeo, resigned to him the rich Benedictine abbey of SS. Gratinian and Felinus, at Arona, which had been long enjoyed by members of his family *in commendam*.

Charles learned Latin at Milan and was afterwards sent to the university of Pavia, where he studied under Francis Alciati, who was later promoted cardinal by St Charles's interest. On account of an impediment in his speech and a lack of brilliance he was esteemed slow, yet he made good progress. Count Gilbert made his son a strictly limited allowance from the income of his abbey, and we learn from his letters that young Charles was continually short of cash, owing to the necessity in his position of keeping up a household. It was not till after the death of both his parents that he took his doctor's degree, in his twenty-second year. He then returned to Milan, where he soon after received news that his uncle, Cardinal de Medici, was chosen pope, in 1559, at the conclave held after the death of Paul IV.

Early in 1560 the new pope created his nephew cardinal-deacon and on February 8 following nominated him administrator of the vacant see of Milan. Pius IV, however, detained him at Rome and intrusted him with many duties. In quick succession Charles was named legate of Bologna, Romagna and the March of Ancona, and protector of Portugal, the Low Countries, the Catholic cantons of Switzerland, and the orders of St Francis, the Carmelites, the Knights of Malta, and others. The recipient of all these honours and responsibilities was not yet twenty-three years old and only in minor orders. He still found time to look after his family affairs, and took recreation in music and physical exercise. He was a patron of learning, and promoted it among the clergy; and, among other establishments for this end, having also in view the amenities of the pope's court, he instituted in the Vatican a literary academy of clergy and laymen, some of whose conferences and studies appear among the saint's works as *Noctes Vaticanae*. He judged it so far necessary to conform to the custom of the renaissance papal court as to have a magnificent palace, to keep a large household and a table suitable to his secular rank, and to give entertainments. He had provided for the diocese of Milan, for its government and the remedying of its disorders, in the best manner he was able, but the command of the pope by which he was obliged to attend in Rome did not make him entirely easy on that head.

Pope Pius IV had announced soon after his election his intention of reassembling the council of Trent, which had been suspended in 1552. St Charles used all his influence and energy to bring this about, amid the most difficult and adverse ecclesiastical and political conditions. He was successful, and in January 1562 the council was reopened. But as much work, diplomacy and vigilance were required of Charles during the two years it sat as the negotiation for its assembly. Several times it nearly broke up with its work unfinished, but St Charles's never-failing attention and his support of the papal legates kept it together, and in nine sessions and numerous meetings for discussion many of the most important dogmatic and disciplinary decrees of the great reforming council were passed. To the efforts of St Charles more than of any other single man this result was due; he was the master-mind and the ruling spirit of the third and last period of the Council of Trent.

During its assembly Count Frederick Borromeo died, so that St Charles found himself the head of this noble family. Many took it for granted that he would leave the clerical state and marry. But Charles resigned his family position to his uncle Julius and received the priesthood in 1563. Two months later he was consecrated bishop.

He was not allowed to go to his diocese, and, in addition to his other duties, he had to supervise the drawing-up of the Catechism of the Council of Trent and the reform of liturgical books and church-music; to his commission we owe the composition of Palestrina's mass called 'Papae Marcelli'. Milan had been without a resident bishop for eighty years, and was in a deplorable state. St Charles's vicar there had done his best to carry out a programme of reform, assisted by a number of Jesuits specially sent, but he was far from successful and at length St Charles was given permission to go and hold a provincial council and make a visitation.

Ten suffragans attended the provincial council, and the excellence of its regulations for the observance of the decrees of the Council of Trent for the discipline and training of the clergy, the celebration of divine service, the administration of the sacraments, the giving of catechism on Sundays, and many other points, caused the pope to write to St Charles a letter of congratulation. But while discharging legatine duties in Tuscany he was summoned to Rome to assist Pius IV on his death-bed, where St Philip Neri was also present. The new pope, St Pius V, induced St Charles to stay on at Rome for a time in the same offices which he had discharged under his predecessor. But Charles saw the opportunity for which he had been waiting, and pressed his return to his people with such zeal that the pope presently dismissed him with his blessing.

St Charles arrived at Milan in April 1566 and went vigorously to work for the reformation of his diocese. He began by the regulation of his household then, he sold plate and other effects to the value of thirty thousand crowns, and applied the whole sum for the relief of distressed families. His almoner was ordered to give the poor two hundred crowns a month, besides whatever extra sums he should call upon the stewards for, which were very many. His liberality appears too in many monuments, and his help to the English College at Douai was such that Cardinal Allen called St Charles its founder. He arranged retreats for his clergy and himself went into retreat twice a year. It was his rule to confess himself every morning before celebrating Mass. His ordinary confessor was Dr Griffith Roberts, of the diocese of Bangor, author of a famous Welsh grammar. St Charles appointed another Welshman, Dr Owen Lewis (afterwards a bishop in Calabria), to be one of his vicars general, and he always had with him a little picture of St John Fisher. He had a great regard for the Church's liturgy, and never said any prayer or carried out any religious rite with haste.

St Charles, in provincial councils, diocesan synods and by many pastoral instructions, made regulations for the reform both of clergy and people which pastors have ever since regarded as a model and studied to emulate. He was one of the foremost of the great pastoral theologians who arose in the Church to remedy the disorders engendered by the decay of medieval life. Partly by tender entreaties and zealous remonstrances and partly by inflexible firmness in the execution of these decrees, without favour, distinction of persons or regard to rank or pretended privileges, the saint in time overcame the obstinate and broke down difficulties which would have daunted the most courageous. St Charles directed that children in particular should be properly instructed in Christian doctrine. Not content with enjoining parish-priests to give public catechism every Sunday and holy-day, he established the Confraternity of Christian Doctrine, whose schools are said to have numbered 740, with 3000 catechists and 40,000 pupils.

But the saint's reforms were far from being well received everywhere, and some were carried through only in the face of violent and unscrupulous opposition. The religious order called Humiliati having been reduced to a few members, but having many monasteries and great possessions, had submitted to reform at the hands of the archbishop. But the submission was unwilling and only apparent. They tried to annul the regulations which had been made. When they failed three priors of the order hatched a plot to assassinate St Charles. One of the Humiliati themselves, a priest called Jerome Donati Farina, agreed to do the deed for forty gold pieces, which sum was raised by selling the ornaments from a church. On October 26, 1569, Farina posted himself at the door of the chapel in the archbishop's house, whilst St Charles was at evening prayers with his household. An anthem by Orlando di Lasso was being sung, and at the words 'It is time therefore that I return to Him that sent me', Charles being on his knees before the altar, the assassin discharged a gun at him. Farina made good his escape during the ensuing confusion, and St Charles, imagining himself mortally wounded, commended himself to God. But it was found that the bullet had only struck his clothes in the back, raising a bruise, and fallen harmlessly to the floor. After a solemn thanksgiving and procession, he shut himself up for some days in a Carthusian monastery to consecrate his life anew to God.

St Charles then returned to the three valleys of his diocese in the Alps; and took that opportunity of visiting each of the Catholic cantons, wherein he converted a number of Zwinglians and restored discipline in the monasteries. The harvest having failed, Milan was afflicted the following year with a great famine. St Charles by his care and appeals procured supplies for the relief of the poor, and himself fed 3000 people daily for three months. He had been very unwell for some time and at doctors' orders he modified his way of life, but without getting any relief. After visiting Rome for the conclave which elected Pope Gregory XIII he returned to his normal habits, and soon recovered his health.

During his episcopate of eighteen years he held five provincial councils and eleven diocesan synods. He was indefatigable in parochial visitations. The archdiocese of Milan owed three seminaries to the zeal of St Charles, for the requirements of three different classes of clerical student, and everywhere he urged that the Tridentine directions for sacerdotal training should be put into effect. In 1575 he went to Rome to gain the jubilee indulgence and in the following year published it at Milan. Huge crowds of penitents and others flocked to the city, and they brought with them the plague, which broke out with great virulence.

The governor fled and many of the rest of the nobility left the town. St Charles gave himself up completely to the care of the stricken. The number of priests of his own clergy to attend the sick not being sufficient, he assembled the superiors of the religious communities and begged their help. The effect of this appeal was that a number of religious at once volunteered, and were lodged by Charles in his own house. He then wrote to the governor, Don Antony de Guzman, upbraiding him for his cowardice, and induced him and other magistrates to return to their posts and try to cope with the disaster. The hospital of St Gregory was entirely inadequate, overflowing with dead, dying, sick and suspects, having nobody to care for them. The sight of their terrible state reduced St Charles to tears, but he had to send for priests and lay helpers to the Alpine valleys, for at first the Milanese clergy would not go near the place. With the coming of the plague commerce was at an end and want began. It is said that food had to be found daily for sixty or seventy thousand persons. St Charles literally exhausted all his resources in relief and incurred large debts on behalf of the sufferers. He even made use of the coloured fabrics that hung up from his house to the cathedral during processions, having it made up into clothes for the needy. Empty houses for the sick were taken outside the walls and temporary shelters built, lay helpers were organized for the clergy, and a score of altars set up in the streets so that the sick could assist at public worship from their windows. But the archbishop was not content with prayer and penance, organization and distribution; he personally ministered to the dying, waited on the sick and helped those in want. The pestilence lasted with varying degrees of intensity from the summer of 1576 until the beginning of 1578. Even during its continuance the magistrates of Milan tried to make mischief between St Charles and the pope. It is possible that some of their complaints were not altogether ill-founded, but the matters complained of were ultimately due to their own supineness and inefficiency. When it was over St Charles wanted to reorganize his cathedral chapter on a basis of common life, and it was the canons' refusal which finally decided him to organize his Oblates of St Ambrose.

In the spring of 1580 he entertained at Milan for a week a dozen young Englishmen, who were going on the English mission, and one of them preached before him. This was St Ralph Sherwin, who in some eighteen months' time was to give his life for the faith at Tyburn. In the same way he met his fellow martyr, St Edmund Campion, and talked with him. A little later in the same year St Charles met St Aloysius Gonzaga, then twelve years old, to whom he gave his first communion. At this time he was doing much travelling and the strain of work and worry was beginning to tell on him; moreover, he curtailed his sleep too much and Pope Gregory personally had to warn him not to overdo his Lenten fasting. At the end of 1583 he was sent as visitor apostolic to Switzerland, and in the Grisons he had to deal not only with Protestantism but with an outbreak of alleged witchcraft and sorcery.

During 1584 St Charles's health got worse and, after arranging for the establishment of a convalescent home in Milan, he went iCckkll in October to Monte Varallo to make his annual retreat, having with him Father Adorno, S.J. He had clearly foretold to several persons that he should not remain long with them, and on October 24 he was taken ill. On October 29 he started off for Milan, where he arrived on All Souls', having celebrated Mass for the last time on the previous day at his birth-place, Arona. He went straight to bed and asked for the last sacraments, and after receiving them died quietly in the first part of the night between November 3 and 4. He was only forty-six years old.

5 : ST BERTILLA, VIRGIN (A.D. 705?)

ST BERTILLA (Bertila is the more correct form) was born in the territory of Soissons. As she grew up she learned the deceits of the world, and earnestly desired to renounce it. She was encouraged by St Ouen, Bishop of Rouen, and her parents sent her to Jouarre, a monastery near Meaux, founded not long before under the Rule of St Columban. St Bertilla was received with joy in this community and trained up in the strictest practice of monastic perfection.

When St Bathildis, the English wife of Clovis II, refounded the abbey of Chelles, she asked the abbess of Jouane to furnish this community with a small colony of her most experienced and virtuous nuns. Bertilla was sent at the head of this company, and was appointed first abbess of Chelles. The reputation of the saint and the discipline which she established in this house attracted a number of foreign vocations, among them Hereswitha, widow of Ethelhere, King of the East Angles and sister to St Hilda. The widowed Queen Bathildis herself, as soon as her son Clotaire was of age to govern, retired hither. She took the religious habit from the hands of St Bertilla c. 665 and obeyed her as if she had been the last sister in the house, rather than its sovereign and foundress. In her old age, far from abating her fervour, St Bertilla strove to redouble it both in her penances and in her devotions, and she died beloved by all, after having governed Chelles for forty-six years.

6 : ST ILLTUD, OR ILLTYD, ABBOT (SIXTH CENTURY)

THE first information we have about Illtud, one of the most celebrated of the Welsh saints, is in the perhaps early seventh-century Life of St Samson. Here it is said that he was a disciple of St Germanus (of Auxerre), who ordained him priest, and that he presided over the monastic school at Llantwit in Glamorgan; much stress is laid on his learning and wisdom. There are further references in the ninth-century Life of St Paul Aurelian: there it is stated that the saint's monastery was established on a certain island 'within the borders of Dyfed, called Pyr', which is usually identified with Caldey, off Tenby.

The only Life we have of St Illtud himself is a Latin composition dating from about 1140. This tells us that his father was a Briton who lived in Letavia with his wife: it has been suggested that Letavia here really means a district in central Brecknock rather than Brittany. When he grew up Illtud went by water to visit 'his cousin King Arthur', and married a lady called Trynihid. Leaving Arthur, he entered the military service of a chieftain in Glamorgan, whence he is sometimes called Illtud the Knight. The story goes that he was startled into taking up the monastic life by a hunting accident in which some of his friends lost their lives, and that he was recommended to leave the world by St Cadoc (who was hardly born at this time). Illtud went to live with Trynihid in a reed hut by the river Nadafan, but was warned by an angel, in peculiar circumstances, to leave his wife. This he did, very roughly, early in the morning, and went to St Dubricius to receive the tonsure of a monk. Then he made his abode by a stream called the Hodnant, and lived austerely there as a solitary until disciples began to flock around. They flourished materially and spiritually, their land was good and they worked hard, and St Illtud's monastery became the first great monastic school of Wales, known as Llanilltud Fawr (now Llantwit Major in Glamorgan).

When Illtud was driven from his monastery by the oppression of a local chieftain he had to take refuge for a time in a cave by the river Ewenny, where he was fed from Heaven; their lands were threatened by the collapse of the sea-wall, which the monks built up again, but finally it had to be made good miraculously by the saint. He is said to have gone with corn-ships to relieve a famine in Brittany, and places and churches bearing his name are found there as well as many in Wales. The Life states that in his old age Illtud again crossed the sea, and died at Dol; but the Life of Samson gives a moving account of his last days at Llantwit.

7 : ST WILLIBRORD, BISHOP OF UTRECHT (A.D. 739)

ST WILLIBRORD was born in Northumbria in the year 658, and placed before he was seven years old in the monastery of Ripon, which was at that time governed by St Wilfrid. In his twentieth year he went over to Ireland, where he joined St Egbert and St Wigbert who had gone thither to study in the monastic schools and lead a more perfect life among their monks. In their company he spent twelve years in the study of the sacred sciences. St Egbert was anxious to preach the gospel in northern Germany but was prevented, and his companion Wigbert came back to Ireland after spending two fruitless years on this mission. Thereupon Willibrord, who was then thirty-one, and had been ordained priest a year before, expressed a desire to be allowed to undertake this laborious and dangerous task, and was accordingly sent out with eleven other monks, Englishmen, among whom was St Swithbert.

They landed in 690 at the mouth of the Rhine, made their way to Utrecht, and then to the court of Pepin of Herstal, who encouraged them to preach in Lower Friesland, between the Meuse and the sea, which he had conquered from the heathen Radbod. Willibrord set out for Rome and cast himself at the feet of Pope St Sergius I, begging his authority to preach the gospel to idolatrous nations. The pope granted him ample jurisdiction and gave him relics for the consecration of churches. He then returned and with his companions preached the gospel with success in that part of Friesland that had been conquered by the Franks. St Swithbert was consecrated as bishop by St Wilfrid in England, but perhaps Pepin did not approve of this, for Swithbert soon went off up the Rhine to preach to the Boructvari; and Pepin soon sent St Willbrord to Rome, with letters of recommendation that he might be ordained bishop. Pope Sergius received him with honour, changed his name to Clement and ordained him bishop of the Frisians in St Cecilia's basilica on her feast-day in the year 695. St Willibrord stayed only fourteen days in Rome and, coming back to Utrecht, built there the church of our Saviour, in which he fixed his see. Some years after his consecration, assisted by the liberality of Pepin and the abbess St Irmina, he founded the abbey of Echternach in Luxemburg, which soon became an important centre of his influence.

Willibrord extended his labours into Upper Friesland, which still obeyed Radbod, and penetrated into Denmark, but with no more success than to purchase thirty young Danish boys, whom he instructed, baptized and brought back with him. In his return, according to Alcuin, he was driven by stress of weather upon the island of Heligoland, revered as a holy place by the Danes and Frisians, where one of Willibrord's company was sacrificed to the superstition of the people and died a martyr for Jesus Christ. The saint, upon leaving Heligoland, went ashore on Walcheren and his charity and patience made considerable conquests to the Christian religion there. He overthrew and destroyed an idol, whereupon he was attacked by its outraged priest who tried to kill the missionary, but he escaped and returned in safety to Utrecht. In 714 Charles Martel's son Pepin the Short, afterwards king of the Franks, was born, and baptized by St Willibrord.

In 715 Radbod regained the parts of Frisia he had lost, and undid much of Willibrord's work, destroying the churches, killing missionaries and inducing many apostasies. For a time Willibrord retired, but after the death of Radbod in 719 he was at full liberty to preach in every part of the country. He was joined in his apostolical labours by St Boniface, who spent three years in Friesland before he went into Germany. By the prayers and labours of this apostle and his colleagues the faith was planted in many parts of Holland, Zeeland, and the Netherlands, whither St Amand and St Lebwin had never penetrated; and the Frisians, till then a rough and barbarous people, became more civilized and virtuous. He is commonly called the Apostle of the Frisians, a title to which he has every claim.

It had always been St Willibrord's habit to go from time to time to his monastery at Echternach for periods of retreat, and in his old age he made it his place of permanent retirement. There he died at the age of eighty-one on November 7, 739, and was buried in the abbey church, which has ever since been a place of pilgrimage.

8 : ST GODFREY, BISHOP OF AMIENS (A.D. 1115)

AT the age of five Godfrey was entrusted to the care of the abbot of Mont-Saint-Quentin and, having in due course decided to become a monk, he was ordained priest. He was chosen abbot of Nogent, in Champagne, a house whose community was reduced to half a dozen monks, whose discipline was, like their buildings, neglected and dilapidated. Under his direction this house began again to flourish; but when in consequence of this the archbishop of Rheims and his council pressed the saint to take upon him the government of the great abbey of Saint-Remi, he started up in the assembly and alleged contrary canons with vehemence, adding, 'God forbid I should ever desert a poor bride by preferring a rich one! ' Nevertheless, in 1104 he was appointed bishop of Amiens. His residence was truly the house of a disciple of Christ, for he never allowed himself to forget that he was a monk. He lived in the simplest fashion, and when he thought the cook was treating him too well he took the best food from the kitchen and gave it away to the poor and sick.

But in his episcopal capacity St Godfrey was unbending, severe, yet inflexibly just. He had a bitter struggle in his own diocese against simony and for the celibacy of the clergy, in the course of which it is said an attempt was made on his life by a disgruntled woman. His rigid discipline made him very unpopular among the less worthy, and he became so discouraged that he wanted to resign and join the Carthusians. St Godfrey's severity seems in some things to have been excessive, e.g., he forbade the eating of meat on Sundays in Lent. He set out in November 1115 to discuss affairs with his metropolitan and died on the way at Soissons, where he was buried.

9 : ST BENEN, OR BENIGNUS, BISHOP (A.D. 467)

WHILST St Patrick was on his way to Tara from Saul it is said he passed some days at the house of a chieftain named Sechnan, in Meath. This man and his family were converted by the teaching of Patrick, and the gospel made a particular impression on his son Benen (latinized as Benignus). The boy, we are told, would scatter flowers over Patrick as he slept, and when the apostle would continue his journey clung to his feet and implored to be allowed to go too. So he was taken, and became Patrick's dearest disciple and eventually his successor. St Benen was noted for gentleness and charm of disposition and for his good singing, wherefore he was known as 'Patrick's psalmodist'. The first evangelization of Clare and Kerry is attributed to him, and from thence he went north into Connaught. It is also claimed that St Patrick founded a church at Drumlease, in Kilmore diocese, of which Benen was given charge, and that he ruled it for twenty years. It seems certain that Benen was St Patrick's right-hand man, their names are coupled in the composition of the code of law called *Senchus Mor*, and after Patrick's death he became the chief bishop of the Irish church.

William of Malmesbury relates that St Benen resigned his office in the year 460, and came to Glastonbury, where he found St Patrick, who had preceded him thither. His old master sent him out to live as a hermit, telling him to build his cell at the spot where his staff should burst into leaf and bud. This happened at a swampy place called Feringmere, and there St Benen died and was buried, till in 1091 his relics were removed to Glastonbury Abbey. No doubt somebody's relics were translated on that occasion, but there is no truth in the legend of the association of St Patrick and St Benen with Glastonbury.

10 : ST LEO THE GREAT, POPE AND DOCTOR OF THE CHURCH (A.D. 461)

ST LEO'S family was probably Tuscan, but he seems to have been born in Rome, as he always speaks of it as his 'patria'. Of his early years and of the date of his ordination to the priesthood there are no records. It is clear from his writings that he received a good education, although it did not include Greek. We hear of him first as deacon under St Celestine I and then under Sixtus III, occupying a position so important that St Cyril wrote directly to him, and Cassian dedicated to him his treatise against Nestorius. Moreover, in 440, when the quarrels between the two imperial generals, Aetius and Albinus, threatened to leave Gaul at the mercy of the barbarians, Leo was sent to make peace between them. At the time of the death of Sixtus III he was still in Gaul, whither a deputation was sent to announce to him his election to the chair of St Peter.

Immediately after his consecration on September 29, 440, he began to display his exceptional powers as a pastor and ruler. Preaching was at that time mainly confined to bishops, and he set about it systematically, instructing the faithful of Rome whom he purposed to make a pattern for other churches. In the ninety-six genuine sermons which have come down to us, we find him laying stress on alms-giving and other social aspects of Christian life, as well as expounding Catholic doctrines—especially that of the Incarnation. Some idea of the extraordinary vigilance of the holy pontiff over the Church and its necessities in every part of the empire can be gathered from the 143 letters written by him, and the 30 letters written to him, which have fortunately been preserved. In these and in all Leo's pronouncements, couched in authoritative and almost stern language, there is no personal note, no uncertainty: it is not the man who seems to speak, but the successor of Peter.

But as pontiff of the Universal Church, he found himself called upon to deal with difficulties in the East far greater than any which had hitherto met him in the West. In the year 448, he received a letter from a Constantinopolitan abbot, called Eutyches, complaining of a revival of the Nestorian heresy. St Leo replied in guarded terms, promising to make inquiries. The next year came another communication from Eutyches, duplicates of which were sent to the patriarchs of Alexandria and Jerusalem. In this he protested against a sentence of excommunication which had been passed upon him by St Flavian, Patriarch of Constantinople, at the instance of Eusebius of Dorylaeum, and asked to be reinstated. The appeal was supported by a letter from the Emperor Theodosius II. As no official notice of the proceedings at Constantinople had reached Rome, Leo wrote to St Flavian, who sent a report of the synod at which Eutyches had been sentenced. From this it was abundantly clear that he had fallen into the error of denying the two natures of Christ—a heresy the reverse of Nestorianism. A council was now summoned at Ephesus by the Emperor Theodosius, ostensibly to inquire into the matter, but it was packed with the friends of Eutyches, and presided over by one of his strongest supporters, Dioscorus, Patriarch of Alexandria. This gathering, nicknamed 'The Robber Synod', acquitted Eutyches and condemned St Flavian, who was moreover subjected to such physical violence that he died soon after.

Two years later, under the Emperor Marcian, a general council was held at Chalcedon. Six hundred bishops or more were present, and St Leo was represented by his legates. In this assembly the memory of St Flavian was vindicated and Dioscorus was declared excommunicated and deposed. On June 13, 449, St Leo had written to St Flavian a doctrinal letter in which he had clearly set out the Catholic faith with regard to the natures of our Lord, steering clear of the errors of Nestorianism and Eutychianism. This pronouncement, which has become famous as 'The Dogmatic Letter' or 'The Tome of St Leo', had been suppressed by Dioscorus, but was read by the legates to the Council of Chalcedon. 'Peter has spoken by Leo!' exclaimed the assembled bishops, when they had heard this lucid explanation of the two-fold nature of Christ, which has become for all subsequent ages the Church's official teaching.

Meanwhile Attila with his Huns in 452 entered Italy, burning Aquileia and filling the country with blood and desolation. After sacking Milan and razing Pavia, he set out with his army to assault the capital. Upheld as usual by the sense of his sacred office, and without a moment's hesitation, Leo started out from the capital, accompanied by Avienus the consul, Trigetius the governor of the city, and some of his priests, and came face to face with the invaders on the site of the present town of Peschiera. The pope and his clergy interviewed the dreaded foe and induced him to retire and to accept an annual tribute instead of entering the holy city. Rome was freed for the moment, but not for long. Three years later, the Vandal Genseric (Gaiseric) appeared with an army before its walls, now almost defenceless. This time St Leo's intervention was not so successful, but he obtained from the barbarian chief an undertaking to be satisfied with pillaging the city and to restrain his troops from slaughter and incendiarism. The Vandals withdrew after fifteen days, taking back to Africa many captives as well as immense booty.

St Leo immediately set about the task of repairing the damage and of finding a remedy for the evils caused by the barbarians. He sent priests to minister to the captives in Africa and alms to assist them. He also replaced, as far as he could, the vessels and ornaments of the devastated churches. It was characteristic of his trust in God that he was never discouraged, and that he maintained an unruffled equanimity even in the most difficult moments. In the twenty-one years of his pontificate he had won the love and veneration of rich and poor, emperors and barbarians, clergy and lay folk alike. He died on November 10, 461, and his relics are preserved in the Vatican basilica.

11 : ST MARTIN, BISHOP OF TOURS (A.D. 397)

THE great St Martin was a native of Sabaria, a town of Pannonia. From thence his parents, who were pagans, had to remove to Pavia in Italy, for his father was an officer in the army, who had risen from the ranks. At the age of fifteen he was, as the son of a veteran, forced into the army against his will and for some years, though not yet formally a Christian, he lived more like a monk than a soldier. It was while stationed at Amiens that is said to have occurred the incident which tradition and image have made famous. One day in a very hard winter, during a severe frost, he met at the gate of the city a poor man, almost naked, trembling and shaking with cold, and begging alms of those that passed by. Martin, seeing those that went before take no notice, cut his cloak into two pieces, gave one to the beggar and wrapped himself in the other half. That night Martin in his sleep saw Jesus Christ, dressed in that half of the garment which he had given away, and heard Jesus say, 'Martin, yet a catechumen, has covered me with this garment'. His disciple and biographer Sulpicius Severus states that he had become a catechumen on his own initiative at the age of ten, and that as a consequence of this vision he 'flew to be baptized'. Martin did not at once leave the army, and when he was about twenty there was a barbarian invasion of Gaul. With his comrades he appeared before Julian Caesar to receive a war-bounty, and Martin refused to accept it. 'Hitherto', he said to Julian, 'I have served you as a soldier; let me now serve Christ. Give the bounty to these others who are going to fight, but I am a soldier of Christ and it is not lawful for me to fight.' Julian stormed and accused Martin of cowardice, who retorted that he was prepared to stand in the battle-line unarmed the next day and to advance alone against the enemy in the name of Christ. He was thrust into prison, but the conclusion of an armistice stopped further developments and Martin was soon after discharged. He went to Poitiers, where St Hilary was bishop, and this doctor of the Church gladly received the young 'conscientious objector' among his disciples.

Martin had in a dream a call to visit his home. He went into Pannonia, and converted his mother and others; but his father remained in his infidelity. In Illyricum he opposed the Arians with so much zeal that he was publicly scourged and had to leave the country. In Italy he heard that the church of Gaul also was oppressed by those heretics and St Hilary banished, so he remained at Milan. But Auxentius, the Arian bishop, soon drove him away. He then retired with a priest to the island of Gallinaria in the gulf of Genoa, and remained there till St Hilary was allowed to return to Poitiers in 360. It being Martin's earnest desire to pursue his vocation in solitude, St Hilary gave him a piece of land, now called Ligugé, where he was soon joined by a number of other hermits. This community—traditionally the first monastic community founded in Gaul—grew into a great monastery which continued till the year 1607, and was revived by the Solesmes Benedictines in 1852. St Martin lived here for ten years, directing his disciples and preaching throughout the countryside, where many miracles were attributed to him. About 371 the people of Tours demanded Martin for their bishop. He was unwilling to accept the office, so a stratagem was made use of to call him to the city to visit a sick person, where he was conveyed to the church. Some of the neighbouring bishops, called to assist at the election, urged that the meanness of his appearance and his unkempt air showed him to be unfit for such a dignity. But such objections were overcome by the acclamations of the local clergy and people.

St Martin continued the same manner of life. He lived at first in a cell near the church, but not being able to endure the interruptions of the many visitors he retired from the city to where was soon the famous abbey at Marmoutier. The place was then a desert, enclosed by a steep cliff on one side and by a tributary of the river Loire on the other; but he had here in a short time eighty monks, with many persons of rank amongst them. A very great decrease of paganism in the district of Tours and all that part of Gaul was the fruit of the piety, miracles and zealous instruction of St Martin. Every year St Martin visited each of his outlying 'parishes', travelling on foot, on a donkey, or by boat. According to his biographer he extended his apostolate from Touraine to Chartres, Paris, Autun, Sens and Vienne, where he cured St Paulinus of Nola of an eye trouble.

Whilst St Martin was spreading the kingdom of Jesus Christ, the churches in Spain and Gaul were disturbed by the Priscillianists, a gnostic-manichean sect named after their leader. Priscillian appealed to the Emperor Maximus from a synod held at Bordeaux in 384, but Ithacius, Bishop of Ossanova, attacked him furiously and urged the emperor to put him to death. Neither St Ambrose at Milan nor St Martin would countenance Ithacius or those who supported him, because they wanted to put heretics to death and allowed the emperor's jurisdiction in an ecclesiastical matter. Martin begged Maximus not to spill the blood of the guilty, saying it was sufficient that they be declared heretics and excommunicated by the bishops. Ithacius, far from listening to his advice, presumed to accuse him of the heresy involved, as he generally did those whose lives were too ascetic for his taste, says Sulpicius Severus. Maximus, out of regard to St Martin's remonstrances, promised that the blood of the accused should not be spilt. But after the saint had left

Trier, the emperor was prevailed upon, and committed the case of the Priscillianists to the prefect Evodius. He found Priscillian and others guilty of certain charges, and they were beheaded. St Martin came back to Trier to intercede both for the Spanish Priscillianists, who were threatened with a bloody persecution, and for two adherents of the late emperor, Gratian; he found himself in a very difficult position, in which he seemed to be justified in maintaining communion with the party of Ithacius, which he did: but he was afterwards greatly troubled in conscience as to whether he had been too complaisant in this matter.

He was at a remote part of his diocese when his last sickness came on him. He died on November 8, 397, today being the day of his burial at Tours, where his successor St Britius built a chapel over his grave, which was later replaced by a magnificent basilica.

12 : ST JOSAPHAT, ARCHBISHOP OF POLOTSK, MARTYR (A.D. 1623)

IN the month of October 1595, at Brest-Litovsk in Lithuania the Orthodox metropolitan of Kiev and five bishops, representing millions of Ruthenians (today called Byelorussians and Ukrainians), decided to seek communion with the Holy See. The controversies which followed this event were disfigured by deplorable excesses and violence, and the great upholder of Christian unity whose feast is kept today was called on to shed his blood for the cause, whence he is venerated as the protomartyr of the reunion of Christendom.

At the time of the Union of Brest he was still a boy, having been born at Vladimir in Volhynia in 1580 or 1584, and baptized John. His father, a Catholic, was a burgess of a good family called Kunsevich, who sent John to school in his native town and then apprenticed him to a merchant of Vilna. John was not particularly interested in trade, and employed his spare time in mastering Church Slavonic in order that he might assist more intelligently at divine worship and recite some of the long Byzantine office every day; and he got to know Peter Arcudius, who was then the rector of the oriental college at Vilna, and two Jesuits, Valentine Fabricius and Gregory Gruzevsky, who took an interest in him and gave him every encouragement. John decided to be a monk and in 1604 entered the monastery of the Holy Trinity at Vilna. He induced to join him there Joseph Benjamin Rutsky, a learned convert from Calvinism who had been ordered by Pope Clement VIII to join the Byzantine rite against his personal wishes, and together the two young monks concerted schemes for promoting union and reforming Ruthenian monastic observance.

John Kunsevich, who had now taken the name of Josaphat, was ordained deacon and priest and speedily had a great reputation as a preacher, especially on behalf of reunion with Rome. He led a most austere personal life and added to a careful observance of the austerities of eastern monastic life such extreme voluntary mortifications that he was often remonstrated with by the most ascetic. Meanwhile, the abbot of Holy Trinity having developed separatist views, Rutsky was promoted in his place and the monastery was soon full, so Father Josaphat was taken away from his study of the Eastern fathers to help in the foundation of new houses in Poland. In 1614 Rutsky was made metropolitan of Kiev and Josaphat succeeded him as abbot at Vilna. When the new metropolitan went to take possession of his cathedral Josaphat accompanied him and took the opportunity of visiting the great monastery of The Caves at Kiev. The community of two hundred monks was relaxed, and they threatened to throw the Catholic reformer into the river Dnieper. He was not successful in his efforts to bring them to unity, but his personality and exhortations brought about a somewhat changed attitude and a notable increase of good-will.

The archbishop of Polotsk at this time was a very old man and a favourer of the dissidents, and in 1617 Abbot Josaphat was ordained bishop of Vitebsk with right of succession to Polotsk. A few months later the old archbishop died and Josaphat was confronted with an eparchy which was as large in extent as it was degraded in life. The more religious people were inclined to schism through fear of arbitary Roman interference with their worship and customs; churches were in ruins and benefices in the hands of laymen; many of the secular clergy had been married two and three times and the monks were decadent. Josaphat sent for some of his brethren from Vilna to help him and got to work. He held synods in the central towns, published a catechism and imposed its use, issued rules of conduct for the clergy, and fought the interference of the 'squires' in the affairs of the local churches, at the same time setting a personal example of assiduous instructing and preaching, administration of the sacraments and visiting of the poor, the sick, prisoners and the most remote hamlets. By 1620 the eparchy was practically solidly Catholic, order had been restored, and the example of a few good men had brought about a real concern for Christian life.

But in that year a dissident hierarchy of bishops was set up in the territory affected by the Union of Brest, side by side with the Catholic one; and one Meletius Smotritsky was sent as archbishop to Polotsk, who began with great vigour to undo the work of the Catholic archbishop. He spread a report that St Josaphat had 'turned Latin', that all his flock would have to do the same, and that Catholicism was not the traditional Christianity of the Ruthenian people. St Josaphat was at Warsaw when this began and on his return he found that, though his episcopal city was firm for him, some other parts of the eparchy had begun to waver; a monk called Silvester had managed to draw nearly all the people of Vitebsk, Mogilev and Orcha to the side of Smotritsky. The nobility and many of the people adhered strongly to the union, but St Josaphat could do little with these three towns; and not only at Vitebsk but even at Vilna, when the proclamation of the King of Poland that Josaphat was the only legitimate archbishop of Polotsk was publicly read in his presence, there were riots and the life of St Josaphat was threatened.

Leo Sapieha, the chancellor of Lithuania and a Catholic, was fearful of the possible political results of the general unrest, and lent too willing an ear to the heated charges of dissidents outside of Poland that Josaphat had caused it by his policy. Accordingly in 1622 Sapieha wrote accusing him of violence in the maintenance of the union, of putting the kingdom in peril from the Zaporozhsky Cossacks by making discord among the people, of forcibly shutting-up non-Catholic churches, and so on. These and similar accusations were made in general terms, and their unjustifiability was amply demonstrated by contemporary *ad hoc* testimony from both sides: the only actual fact of the sort is the admitted one that Josaphat invoked the aid of the civil power to recover the church at Mogilev from the dissidents. Thus the archbishop had to face misunderstanding, misrepresentation and opposition from Catholics as well. He continued doggedly and fearlessly on his way and, Vitebsk continuing to be a hot-bed of trouble, he determined in October 1623 to go there in person again. He could neither be dissuaded nor would he take a military escort.

Smotritsky was fomenting agitation, his object doubtless being no worse than to drive his rival from the diocese. But his followers got out of hand, and a plot was laid to murder St Josaphat on November 12. A priest named Elias was put up to go into the courtyard of the archbishop's house and to use insulting words to his servants about their master and their religion, and after several complaints St Josaphat gave permission for him to be seized if it happened again. On the morning of November 12, as the archbishop came to the church for the office of Daybreak, he was met by Elias, who began to abuse him to his face; he therefore allowed his deacon to have the man taken and shut up in a room of the house. This was just what his enemies were waiting for: the bells of the town-hall were rung and a mob assembled, demanding the release of Elias and the punishment of the archbishop. After office St Josaphat returned to his house unharmed and let Elias go with a warning, but the people broke in, calling for their victim and striking his attendants. St Josaphat went out to them. Amid cries of 'Kill the papist! ' he was brained with a halberd and pierced by a bullet. The mangled body was dragged out and contemptuously cast into the river Dvina.

St Josaphat Kunsevich was canonized in 1867, the first saint of the Eastern churches to be formally canonized after process in the Congregation of Sacred Rites.

13 : ST FRANCES XAVIER CABRINI, VIRGIN, FOUNDRESS OF
THE MISSIONARY SISTERS OF THE SACRED HEART (A.D. 1917)

AUGUSTINE CABRINI owned and farmed land around Sant' Angelo Lodigiano, between Pavia and Lodi; his wife, Stella Oldini was a Milanese; and they had thirteen children, of whom the youngest was born on, July 15, 1850, and christened Maria Francesca (later she was to add Saverio to the second name, which is what Xavier becomes in Italian). Frances came particularly under the strict care of her sister Rosa, who had been a school-teacher and had not escaped all the dangers of that profession. But the child profited by Rosa's teaching, and family reading aloud from the 'Annals of the Propagation of the Faith' inspired her with an early determination to go to the foreign missions. Her parents however, had decided on Frances being a school-teacher, and when old enough she was sent to a convent boarding-school at Arluno. She duly passed her examinations when she was eighteen, but then in 1870 she lost both her parents.

During the two years that followed she lived on quietly with Rosa, her unassuming goodness making a deep impression on all who knew her. Then she sought admittance to the religious congregation at whose school she had been, and was refused on the ground of poor health; she tried another—with the same result. But the priest in whose school she was teaching at Vidardo had his eye on her. In 1874 this Don Serrati was appointed provost of the collegiate church at Codogno, and found in his new parish a small orphanage, called the House of Providence, whose state left much to be desired. It was managed, or rather mismanaged, by its eccentric foundress, Antonia Tondini, and two other women. The Bishop of Lodi and Mgr Serrati invited Frances Cabrini to help in this institution and to try to turn its staff into a religious community, and with considerable unwillingness she agreed.

Antonia Tondini had consented to her coming, but instead of co-operation gave her only obstruction and abuse. Frances stuck to it, however, obtained several recruits, and with seven of them in 1877 took her first vows. At the same time the bishop put her in charge as superioress. This made matters much worse. Sister Tondini's behaviour was such that it became an open scandal—indeed, she seems to have become somewhat insane. But for another three years Sister Cabrini and her faithful followers persevered in their efforts till the bishop himself gave up hope. He sent for Sister Cabrini and said to her, 'You want to be a missionary sister. Now is the time. I don't know any institute of missionary sisters, so found one yourself.'

There was an old, disused and forgotten Franciscan friary at Codogno. Into this Mother Cabrini and her seven faithful followers moved, and as soon as they were fairly settled in she set herself to draw up a rule for the community. Its work was to be principally the Christian education of girls, and its name The Missionary Sisters of the Sacred Heart. During the same year these constitutions were approved by the bishop of Lodi; within two years the first daughter house was opened, at Grumello, and soon there was another, at Milan. The general progress of the congregation and the trust of Mother Cabrini were such that in 1887 she went to Rome to ask the Holy See's approbation of her little congregation and permission to open a house in Rome. Influential efforts were made to dissuade her from this enterprise—seven years' trial was far too little: and the first interview with the cardinal vicar of the City, Parocchi, confirmed the prudence of her advisers. But only the first. The cardinal was won over; Mother Cabrini was asked to open not one but two houses in Rome, a free school and a children's home, and the decree of first approval of the Missionary Sisters of the Scared Heart was issued within a few months.

The bishop of Piacenza, Mgr Scalabrini, who had established the Society of St Charles to work among Italian immigrants in America, suggested to Frances Cabrini that she should go out there to help the work of those priests. She would not entertain the idea. The archbishop of New York, Mgr Corrigan, sent her a formal invitation. She determined to consult the pope himself. And Leo XIII said, 'Not to the East, but to the West'. When a child Frances Cabrini once fell into a river, and ever afterwards she had a fear of water. She now, with six of her sisters, set out on the first of many voyages across the Atlantic; and on March 31, 1889, they landed in New York.

The sister's reception in New York was hardly encouraging. They had been asked to organize an orphanage for Italian children and to take charge of an elementary school: but on arrival, though warmly welcomed, they found no home ready for them, and had to spend the first night at least in lodgings that were filthy and verminous. And when Mother Cabrini met Archbishop Corrigan she learned that, owing to disagreements between himself and the benefactress concerned, the orphanage scheme had fallen through, and the school consisted of pupils but no habitable building. The archbishop wound up by telling her that he could see nothing for it but that the sisters should go back to Italy. To which St Frances replied with characteristic firmness and definiteness, 'No, Monsignor, not that. The pope sent me here, and here I must stay'. Within a few weeks she had made friends with the benefactress, Countess Cesnola, reconciled her with Mgr Corrigan, found a house for the sisters, and made a start with the orphanage on a modest scale. By July 1889 she was able to revisit Italy, taking with her the first two Italo-American recruits to her congregation.

Nine months later she returned to America with reinforcements to take over West Park, on the Hudson river, from the Society of Jesus. The growing orphanage was transferred to this house, which also became the mother house and novitiate of the congregation in the United States. Its work was prospering, both among immigrants in North America and among the people at home in Italy, and soon Mother Cabrini had to make a trying journey to Managua in Nicaragua where, in difficult and sometimes dangerous circumstances, she took over an orphanage and opened a boarding-school. On her way back she visited New Orleans at the request of its archbishop, the revered Francis Janssens. The upshot was that she was able to make a foundation in New Orleans.

That Frances Cabrini was an extraordinarily able woman needs no demonstration: her works speak for her. She was slow in learning English and never lost her accent; but this apparently was no handicap. In only one direction did her tact fail, and that was in relation to non-Catholic Christians. She met such in America for the first time in her life and it took her a long time to recognize their good faith and to appreciate their good lives. It is obvious that Mother Cabrini was a born ruler, and she was as strict as she was just. Sometimes she seems to have been too strict, and not to have seen where her inflexibility was leading. It is not clear, for instance, how she thought she was upholding sexual morality when she refused to take illegitimate children in her fee-paying schools: it would appear to be a gesture that penalized only the innocent. But love ruled all, and her strictness was no deterrent to the affection she gave and received.

The year 1892, fourth centenary of the discovery of the New World, was also marked by the birth of one of the best-known of St Frances's undertakings, the Columbus Hospital in New York. Then, after a visit to Italy, where she saw the start of a 'summer house' near Rome and a students' hostel at Genoa, she had to go to Costa Rica, Panama, Chile, across the Andes into Brazil, and so to Buenos Aires. In Buenos Aires she opened a high-school for girls. After another voyage to Italy, where she had to cope with a long lawsuit in the ecclesiastical courts and face riots in Milan, she went to France and made there her first European foundations outside Italy; and the autumn of 1898 saw her in England. Mgr (later Cardinal) Bourne, then Bishop of Southwark, had already met St Frances at Codogno and asked her to open a convent in his diocese, but no foundation was made at this time.

And so it went on for another dozen years. Her love for all the children of God took her back and forth over the western hemisphere from Rio to Rome, from Sydenham to Seattle; by the time the constitutions of the Missionary Sisters of the Sacred Heart were finally approved in 1907 the eight members of 1880 had increased to over a thousand, in eight countries; St Frances had made more than fifty foundations, responsible for free-schools and high-schools and hospitals and other establishments, no longer working in America for Italian immigrants alone—did not the prisoners in Sing-Sing send her an illuminated address at the congregation's jubilee? Of the later foundations only two can be named here: the great Columbus Hospital at Chicago and, in 1902, the school at Brockley, now at Honor Oak.

From 1911 Mother Cabrini's health was failing: she was then sixty-one and physically worn out. But it was not till six years later that she was seen to be failing alarmingly. And then the end came with extreme suddenness. No one was present when St Frances Xavier Cabrini died in the convent at Chicago on December 22, 1917. She was canonized in 1946, the first citizen of that country to be canonized.

14 : ST LAURENCE O'TOOLE, ARCHBISHOP OF DUBLIN (A.D. 1180)

LORCAN UA TUATHAIL was born in 1128, probably near Castledermot in co. Kildare, son of Murtagh, chieftain of the Murrays. When Laurence O'Toole (as his name is commonly anglicized) was ten years old, the king of Leinster, Dermot McMurrogh, made a raid on his neighbour's territory, and Murtagh was forced to deliver up his son as a hostage. For two years Laurence was badly treated, in a stony and barren region near Ferns, till his father heard of it and by threats of reprisals forced Dermot to give the boy up to the bishop of Glendalough.

Laurence when twenty-five years old was chosen abbot of Glendalough and soon after avoided episcopal dignity only by alleging the canons that require in a bishop thirty years of age. He governed his community with virtue and prudence, and in a great famine which raged during the first four months of his administration was the saviour of the countryside by his boundless charities. Outside the ecclesiastical enclosure he had to cope with the outlaws and robbers who infested the Wicklow hills, and within it there were false brethren, who could not bear the regularity of his conduct and the zeal with which he condemned their disorders, and attacked his reputation by slander, to which he opposed no other arms than silence and patience. In 1161 died Gregory, the first archbishop of Dublin. Laurence was elected in his place, and consecrated in Holy Trinity (later Christ Church) cathedral by Gelasius, archbishop of Armagh. This was significant of the new unity of the Irish church since the Synod of Kells in 1152, before which the bishops of

Dublin had depended on Canterbury. But the new state of affairs was not fully to outlast St Laurence's own lifetime.

His first care was to reform his clergy and to furnish his church with worthy ministers. He bound the canons of his cathedral to receive the rule of the regular canons of Arrouaise, an abbey which was founded in the diocese of Arras in 1090 and had such reputation for sanctity and discipline that it became the pattern of numerous other houses. Laurence himself took the religious habit, ate with the religious in the refectory, observed their hours of silence and assisted with them at the midnight office. Every day he entertained at table thirty poor persons, and often many more, besides those which he maintained in private houses. All found him a father both in their temporal and spiritual necessities, and he was indefatigable in preaching and the due ordering of public worship.

The enormities of Dermot McMurrogh caused him at length to be driven from Ireland, and in order to regain his position he asked the help of Henry II of England, who was only too glad to permit any of his nobles to join an expedition. The chief of these volunteers was Richard de Clare, Earl of Pembroke ('Strongbow'), who in 1170 landed at Waterford, overran part of Leinster, and marched on Dublin. St Laurence was sent to negotiate with the invaders, but during the discussions Dermot's Anglo-Norman allies seized the city and gave themselves over to massacre and rapine. Laurence returned to succour the sufferers and defend the survivors, and to be a centre of strength in the new danger. Dermot died in his moment of success, and Strongbow claimed Leinster, as Dermot's heir and husband of his daughter Eva (who was St Laurence's niece). Thereupon King Henry recalled his vassal to England, the Irish united under the high king, Rory O'Conor, and Strongbow shut himself up in Dublin. Again Laurence conducted negotiations: they failed, but Strongbow made a sudden rally of desperation and unexpectedly routed the Irish forces.

Henry now went to Ireland, himself and in 1171 received at Dublin the submission of all the Irish chiefs, except those of Connaught, Tyrconnel and Tyrone. In the following year he convened a synod at Cashel. Here, provision was made for clerical discipline, the English form of the Roman liturgy (*i.e.* the use of Sarum) was adopted, and Pope Alexander III was asked to confirm their decisions, which in due course he did. St Laurence concurred in the synodal proceedings, and from that time on was in frequent request as a go-between and peacemaker between King Henry and the Irish princes. In 1175 he travelled to Windsor and successfully negotiated a treaty between the English sovereign and the high king, Rory O'Conor.

The third general council of the Lateran was held at Rome in 1179, and St Laurence went to Rome, with five other Irish bishops. Before they were allowed to leave England, King Henry extracted an oath that they would make no representations to the Holy See likely to prejudice his position in Ireland. Laurence explained to Alexander the state of the Irish church, and begged that effectual remedies might be applied to many disorders in the country and care taken for preserving the liberties of its church. The pope was pleased with his proposals, confirmed all the rights of his see, adding to them jurisdiction over five suffragan dioceses, and appointed him his legate in Ireland. As soon as the saint was returned home he began vigorously to execute his legatine powers. But King Henry was nervous at the authority which had been given Laurence in Rome; and accordingly when in 1180 the archbishop had met him in England to negotiate further on behalf of Rory O'Conor, the king afterwards forbade him to return home. After waiting for three weeks at Abingdon Laurence determined again to seek Henry, who was in Normandy. He got a passage across the Channel and landed near Le Tréport, at a spot still called Saint-Laurent. The king gave him permission to go back to Ireland, but on the way he was taken very ill. As he approached the abbey of the canons regular of St Victor at Eu, he murmured, 'Haec requies mea in saeculum saeculi': St Laurence was ready for death.

St Laurence O'Toole died on Friday, November 14, 1180, and he was canonized in 1225.

15 : ST ALBERT THE GREAT, BISHOP OF REGENSBURG, DOCTOR OF THE CHURCH (A.D. 1280)

HE was a Swabian by descent, born of the family of Bollstädt at the castle of Lauingen on the Danube in 1206. Little is known of his youth or the age at which he went to the University of Padua, but in 1222 Bd Jordan of Saxony, second master general of the Friars Preachers, wrote from that city that he had received ten postulants for the order. One of them was Albert, whose uncle in Padua had tried to keep him away from the Dominican church, but had failed before the influence of Bd Jordan. When he heard that his son was clothed as a mendicant the Count of Bollstädt was most indignant, and there was talk of retrieving him by force, but nothing came of it for Albert was discreetly removed to another friary. This was probably Cologne, where he was teaching in 1228; afterwards he supervised the studies and taught at Hildesheim, Freiburg-im-Breisgau, Regensburg, Strasburg and back again at Cologne. He was instructed to go to Paris and he was there some years, lecturing under a master until he himself took his master's degree. At the end of this time the Dominicans decided to open four new *studia generalia*, and in 1248 St Albert was sent to be regent of that at Cologne, where until 1252 he had among his students a young friar called Thomas Aquinas.

The writings of St Albert fill thirty-eight quarto volumes in print. He was an authority on physics, geography, astronomy, minerology, alchemy (*i.e.* chemistry) and biology, so that it is not surprising that legends grew up that he had and used magical powers. He wrote a treatise on botany and another on human and animal physiology. But his principal fame as a doctor resides not in these achievements, but in the fact that, realizing the autonomy of philosophy and seeing the use that could be made of philosophy of Aristotle in ordering the science of theology, he re-wrote the works of the philosopher so as to make them acceptable to Christian critics, and by the application of Aristotelean methods and principles to the study of theology inaugurated (with the Englishman Alexander of Hales) the scholastic system which was to be brought to prefection by his pupil St Thomas Aquinas. In 1254 he was made prior provincial of his order in Germany. Two years later he attended in that capacity the chapter general in Paris which forbade Friars Preachers at the universities to be called 'master' or 'doctor', or anything but their right name.

Albert went to Italy to defend the mendicant orders against the attacks being made on them at Paris and elsewhere, especially as voiced by William of Saint-Amour in a tract 'on the Dangers of these Present Times'. While he was in Rome, St Albert filled the office of master of the sacred place (*i.e.* the pope's personal theologian and canonist, always a Dominican friar) and preached in the churches of the City. In 1260 he received an order from the Holy See to undertake the government of the diocese of Regensburg.

He was bishop for under two years, Pope Urban IV then accepting his resignation. St Albert returned to the *studium* at Cologne. But the next year he was called away again, this time to help the Franciscan Berthold of Ratisbon to preach the crusade in Germany. This over, he went back again to Cologne and taught and wrote there in peace till 1274, when he was bidden to attend the fourteenth general council at Lyons.

St Albert probably made his last public appearance three years later, when some of the writings of St Thomas were seriously attacked by Stephen Tempier, Bishop of Paris, and other theologians. He hurried to Paris to defend the teaching of his dead disciple, teaching that was in great measure his own as well; he challenged the university to examine himself personally upon it, but he could not avert the local condemnation of certain points. In 1278, during a lecture, his memory suddenly failed. The loss of memory became acute, the strength of his mind failed, and after two years St Albert died, peacefully and without illness, sitting in his chair among his brethren at Cologne, on November 15, 1280.

16 : ST MARGARET OF SCOTLAND, MATRON (A.D. 1093)

MARGARET was a daughter of Edward d'Outremer ('The Exile'), next of kin to Edward the Confessor, and sister to Edgar the Atheling, who took refuge from William the Conqueror at the court of King Malcolm Canmore in Scotland. There Margaret, as beautiful as she was good and accomplished, captivated Malcolm, and they were married at the castle of Dunfermline in the year 1070, she being then twenty-four years of age. Margaret, through the great influence she acquired over her husband, softened his temper, polished his manners, and rendered him one of the most virtuous kings who have ever occupied the Scottish throne.

What she did for her husband Margaret also did in a great measure for her adopted country, promoting the arts of civilization and encouraging education and religion. St Margaret made it her constant effort to obtain good priests and teachers for all parts of the country, and formed a kind of embroidery guild among the ladies of the court to provide vestments and church furniture. With her husband she founded several churches, notably that of the Holy Trinity at Dunfermline.

God blessed the couple with a family of six sons and two daughters, and their mother brought them up with the utmost care, herself instructing them in the Christian faith and superintending their studies. The daughter Matilda afterwards married Henry I of England and was known as Good Queen Maud, whilst three of the sons, Edgar, Alexander and David, successively occupied the Scottish throne, the last name being revered as a saint. St Margaret's private life was most austere: she ate sparingly, and in order to obtain time for her devotions she permitted herself very little sleep. Every year she kept two Lents, the one at the proper season, the other before Christmas. At these times she always rose at midnight and went to the church for Matins, the king often sharing her vigil. On her return she washed the feet of six poor persons and gave them alms.

In 1093 King William Rufus surprised Alnwick castle, putting its garrison to the sword. King Malcolm in the ensuing hostilities was killed by treachery, and his son Edward was also slain. St Margaret at this time was lying on her death-bed. She died four days after her husband, on November 16, 1093, being in her forty-seventh year, and was buried in the church of the abbey of Dunfermline which she and her husband had founded. St Margaret was canonized in 1250 and was named patroness of Scotland in 1673.

17 : ST ELIZABETH OF HUNGARY, WIDOW (A.D. 1231)

IT is related by Dietrich of Apolda in his life of this saint that on an evening in the summer of the year 1207 the minnesinger Klingsohr from Transylvania announced to the Landgrave Herman of Thuringia that that night a daughter had been born to the king of Hungary, who should be exalted in holiness and become the wife of Herman's son; and that in fact at that time the child Elizabeth was born, in Pressburg (Bratislava) or Saros-Patak, to Andrew II of Hungary and his wife, Gertrude of Andechs-Meran. Such an alliance had substantial political advantages to recommend it, and the baby Elizabeth was promised to Herman's eldest son. At about four years of age she was brought to the Thuringian court at the castle of the Wartburg, near Eisenach, there to be brought up with her future husband. In 1221, Louis being now twenty-one and landgrave in his father's place, and Elizabeth fourteen, their marriage was solemnized. They had three children, Herman, who was born in 1222 and died when he was nineteen, Sophia, who became duchess of Brabant, and Bd Gertrude of Aldenburg. Louis, unlike some husbands of saints, put no obstacles in the way of his wife's charity, her simple and mortified life, and her long prayers.

The castle of the Wartburg was built on a steep rock, which the infirm and weak were not able to climb. St Elizabeth therefore built a hospital at the foot of the rock for their reception, where she often fed them with her own hands, made their beds, and attended them even in the heat of summer when the place seemed insupportable. Helpless children, especially orphans, were provided for at her expense. She was the foundress of another hospital in which twenty-eight persons were constantly relieved, and she fed nine hundred daily at her gate, besides numbers in different parts of the dominions, so that the revenue in her hands was truly the patrimony of the distressed.

At this time strenuous efforts were being made to launch another crusade, and Louis of Thuringia took the cross. On St John the Baptist's day he parted from St Elizabeth and went to join the Emperor Frederick II in Apulia; on September 11 following he was dead of the plague at Otranto. The news did not reach Germany until October, just after the birth of Elizabeth's second daughter.

What happened next is a matter of some uncertainty. According to the testimony of one of her ladies-in-waiting, Isentrude, St Elizabeth's brother-in-law, Henry, who was regent for her infant son, drove her and her children and two attendants from the Wartburg during that same winter that he might seize power himself; and there are shocking particulars of the hardship and contempt which she suffered until she was fetched away from Eisenach by her aunt, Matilda, Abbess of Kitzingen. It is alternatively claimed that she was dispossessed of her dower-house at Marburg, in Hesse, or even that she left the Wartburg of her own free will. From Kitzingen she visited her uncle, Eckembert, Bishop of Bamberg, who put his castle of Pottenstein at her disposal, whither she went with her son Herman and the baby, leaving the little Sophia with the nuns of Kitzingen. Eckembert had ambitious plans for another marriage for Elizabeth, but she refused to listen to them: before his departure on the crusade she and her husband had exchanged promises never to marry again. Early in 1228 the body of Louis was brought home and solemnly buried in the abbey church at Reinhardsbrunn; provision was made for Elizabeth by her relatives; and on Good Friday in the church of the Franciscan friars at Eisenach she formally renounced the world, later taking the unbleached gown and cord which was the habit of the third order of St Francis.

An influential part was played in all these developments by Master Conrad of Marburg, who henceforward was the determining influence in St Elizabeth's life. This priest had played a considerable part therein for some time, having succeeded the Franciscan Father Rodinger as her confessor in 1225. From the Friars Minor St Elizabeth had acquired a love of poverty which she could put into action only to a limited extent all the time she was landgravine of Thuringia. Now, her children having been provided for, she went to Marburg, but was forced to leave there and lived for a time in a cottage at Wehrda, by the side of the River Lahn. Then she built a small house just outside Marburg and attached to it a hospice for the relief of the sick, the aged and the poor, to whose service she entirely devoted herself.

In some respects Conrad acted as a prudent and necessary brake on her enthusiasm at this time: he would not allow her to beg from door to door or to divest herself definitely of all her goods or to give more than a certain amount at a time in alms or to risk infection from leprosy and other diseases. In such matters he acted with care and wisdom. But for her devoted waiting-women he substituted two who reported to him on her words and actions when these infringed his detailed commands in the smallest degree. He punished her with slaps in the face and blows with a 'long, thick rod' whose marks remained for three weeks.

Conrad's policy of breaking rather than directing the will was not completely successful. With reference to him and his disciplinary methods St Elizabeth compares herself to sedge in a stream during flood-time: the water bears it down flat, but when the rains have gone it springs up again, straight, strong and unhurt.

One day a Magyar noble arrived at Marburg and asked to be directed to the residence of his sovereign's daughter, of whose troubles he had been informed. Arrived at the hospital, he saw Elizabeth in her plain grey gown, sitting at her spinning-wheel. He would have taken her back to the court of Hungary, but Elizabeth would not go. Her children, her poor, the grave of her husband were all in Thuringia, and she would stay there for the rest of her life. It was not for long. St Elizabeth died in the evening of November 17, 1231, being then not yet twenty-four years old.

18 : ST ODO OF CLUNY, ABBOT (A.D. 942)

HE was brought up in the family of Fulk II, Count of Anjou, and afterwards in that of William, Duke of Aquitaine, who founded the abbey of Cluny. At nineteen Odo received the tonsure, and was instituted to a canonry in St Martin's church at Tours, and he spent some years studying in Paris. Here he gave much time to music, an enthusiasm which was shared by his master, Remigius of Auxerre. One day, in reading the Rule of St Benedict, Odo was shocked to see how much his life fell short of the rules of perfection there laid down, and he determined to embrace the monastic state. He some time after went to the monastery of Baume-les-Messieurs in the diocese of Besançon, where the abbot, Berno, admitted him to the habit in 909. When he was about forty-eight, St Odo was appointed to succeed St Berno as abbot of Cluny. Odo ruled there with a rod of iron, and would intimidate refractory monks with stories yet more terrific than his own discipline.

In 936 St Odo made his first visit to Rome, called thither by Pope Leo VII. The city was being beseiged by Hugh of Provence, who called himself king of Italy and who had considerable respect for St Odo, and it was to try to conclude a peace between him and Alberic, 'Patrician of the Romans', that Odo had been summoned. His first, temporary success was the negotiation of a marriage between Alberic and Hugh's daughter. At the abbey of St Paul-outside-the-Walls he 'regulated the spiritual life of the monastery in an apostolical way and by his words kindled faith, piety and love of truth in all hearts'. The spirit of Cluny had been carried beyond the borders of France, and the influence of St Odo was felt in the monasteries of Monte Cassino, Pavia, Naples, Salerno and elsewhere in Italy.

Twice more within six years Odo had to go to Rome to try and keep the peace between Hugh and Alberic for the distracted pope, and on each occasion he extended the sphere of his reforming zeal. Meanwhile in France the work went on, secular nobles handing over to him monasteries over which they had exercised an uncanonical control and superiors inviting him to visit their abbeys and prescribe for their communities.

In the year 942 St Odo went to Rome for the last time, and on his return called at the monastery of St Julian at Tours. After assisting at the solemnities of the feast of his patron, St Martin, he took to his bed, and died on November 18.

19 : ST NERSES I, KATHOLIKOS OF THE ARMENIANS, MARTYR
(c. A.D. 373)

THIS bishop, the first of several Armenian saints of his name, was a strong reformer and began the work which was carried on by his son St Isaac. He was brought up at Caesarea in Cappadocia, where he married. After the death of his wife he became an official at the court of the Armenian king, Arshak, received holy orders, and in 363 was made chief bishop of Armenia, much against his will. At Caesarea he had come under the influence of St Basil, and accordingly about the year 365 he convened the first national synod at Astishat, in order to bring better discipline and efficiency to his church.

He encouraged monasticism, established hospitals, and promulgated canonical legislation imitated from the Greeks. This embroiled him with the king, and worse followed when Arshak murdered his wife, Olympia. St Nerses condemned him and refused to attend the court, whereupon he was banished and another bishop intruded in his office. Arshak was killed in battle with the Persians shortly after and St Nerses returned, only to find that the new king, Pap, was even worse than his predecessor. His life was so atrocious that St Nerses refused him entrance to the church until he mended his ways. Pap meditated revenge. Pretending penitence he invited Nerses to dine at his table, and there poisoned him.

20 : ST EDMUND THE MARTYR, (A.D. 870)

ON Christmas Day, 855, the nobles and clergy of Norfolk, assembled at Attleborough, acknowledged as their king Edmund, a youth of fourteen, who in the following year was accepted by Suffolk as well. He is said to have been as talented and successful as a ruler as he was virtuous as a man, learning the Psalter by heart in order that he might join in the Church's worship.

Then came the biggest Danish invasion that had yet been. 'In the year 866,' says the *Anglo-Saxon Chronicle*, 'a great army [of Danes] came to the land of the Angle kin and took up winter quarters among the East Angles, and there they were provided with horses. And the East Angles made peace with them.' Then the invaders crossed the Humber and took York, and marched south into Mercia as far as Nottingham, plundering, burning and enslaving as they went. In 870 the host rode across Mercia into East Anglia, and took up winter quarters at Thetford. 'And that winter Edmund fought against them, and the Danish men got the victory and slew the king, and subdued all that land and destroyed all the monasteries that they came to.'

That brief and unadorned statement tells us all that is historically certain about the death of St Edmund. The other traditions are summed up by Alban Butler as follows. The king met a part of the Danes' army near Thetford, and discomfited them. But seeing them soon after reinforced he retired towards his castle of Framlingham in Suffolk. The barbarian leader, Ingvar, had sent him proposals which the saint rejected. In his flight he was overtaken and surrounded at Hoxne, upon the Waveney (alternatively, he allowed himself to be taken in the church). Terms were again offered him prejudicial to religion and to his people, which he refused, declaring that religion was dearer to him than his life, which he would never purchase by offending God. Ingvar had him tied to a tree and torn with whips. Then his tormentors shot at him with arrows. At last Ingvar cut his bonds, dragged him from the tree to which he was nailed by the arrows, and his head was hacked off.

The body of the king was buried at Hoxne, and about the year 903 translated to Beodricsworth, the town now known as Bury St Edmund's (*i.e.* St Edmund's Borough).

21 : ST ALBERT OF LOUVAIN, BISHOP OF LIÈGE, MARTYR
   (A.D. 1192)

ALBERT of Louvain was born about the year 1166, son of Godfrey III, Duke of Brabant, and his wife Margaret of Limburg, and was brought up in his father's castle on that hill of Louvain which is now called Mont-César. Albert was early destined for the clerical state and while still a school-boy of twelve was made a canon of Liège, but when he was twenty-one he renounced his benefice and asked Baldwin V, Count of Hainault (his own bitter enemy), to receive him as a knight. Baldwin agreed, and attached him to his own entourage. When a few months later the papal legate, Cardinal Henry of Albano, preached the crusade in Liège among those who 'took the cross' was Albert—but he at the same time rejoined the ranks of the clergy and received back his canonry. The inner history of this curious episode is not known, but certainly Albert never went to the East, either as a soldier or churchman, and in the following year he was archdeacon of Brabant. Other dignities followed, but, though he was archdeacon and provost by office, Albert was still only subdeacon by orders.

In 1191 the bishop of Liège died and two candidates were put forward to fill the vacancy: both were named Albert, both were archdeacons, and neither of them was a priest. Albert of Rethel was a deacon, cousin of Baldwin of Hainault, and uncle of the Empress Constance, wife of Henry VI. But there was no doubt that Albert of Louvain was the more suitable candidate and the chapter appointed him by an overwhelming majority. Thereupon Albert of Rethel appealed to his relative the emperor, who was an enemy of Albert of Louvain's brother, Henry of Brabant, and the cause was appointed to be heard at Worms. St Albert was supported by practically all the clergy of Liège, Albert of Rethel by his minority of canons, but the emperor would pronounce in favour of neither of them. He announced that he had disposed of the see of Liège to Lothaire, provost of Bonn, whom he had just made imperial chancellor in return for three thousand marks. St Albert quietly told Henry that his own election was canonically valid, rebuked the interference with the Church's liberties, and gave notice of his appeal to the Holy See. He set out for Rome in person and, as the emperor was trying to intercept him, travelled by a devious route and disguised as a servant. Pope Celestine III after due deliberation pronounced the election of St Albert to be valid and confirmed it.

On his return, however, Albert was unable to take possession of his see, held by the intruded Lothaire, and Archbishop Bruno of Cologne would not ordain and consecrate him for fear of the emperor. Pope Celestine had foreseen this and had authorized Archbishop William of Rheims to carry out these duties and St Albert was made priest and bishop at Rheims. At the same time news was brought that the Emperor Henry was in Liège, vowing to exterminate Albert and his followers. Albert's uncle would have set off at once with a following of nobles to assert his nephew's rights, but St Albert had a better idea of the duties of a Christian and preferred to remain in exile rather than to precipitate war. The emperor meanwhile took strong measures with the faithful clergy of Liège, forced the submission of Albert's supporters, and left the city for Maestricht, where a further plot was hatched. On November 24, 1192, when St Albert had been nearly ten weeks at Rheims, he went on a visit to the abbey of Saint-Remi, outside the walls. In a narrow part of the way German knights set upon and murdered him. The whole city was horrified, and Albert was buried with honour in the cathedral.

22 : ST CECILIA, OR CECILY, VIRGIN AND MARTYR (DATE UNKNOWN)

HER 'acts' state that Cecilia was a patrician girl of Rome and that she was brought up a Christian. She wore a coarse garment beneath the clothes of her rank, fasted from food several days a week, and determined to remain a maiden for the love of God. But her father had other views, and gave her in marriage to a young patrician named Valerian. On the day of the marriage, when they retired to their room, she took her courage in both hands and said to her husband gently, 'I have a secret to tell you. You must know that I have an angel of God watching over me. If you touch me in the way of marriage he will be angry and you will suffer; but if you respect my maidenhood he will love you as he loves me.' 'Show me this angel,' Valerian replied.

Cecilia said, 'If you believe in the living and one true God and receive the water of baptism, then you shall see the angel'. Valerian agreed and was sent to find Bishop Urban. He was received with joy and baptized. Then he returned to Cecilia, and found standing by her side an angel, who put upon the head of each a chaplet of roses and lilies. Then appeared his brother, Tiburtius. He, too, was offered a deathless crown if he would renounce his false gods. Cecilia talked long to him, until he was convinced by what she told him of Jesus, and he, too, was baptized.

From that time forth the two young men gave themselves up to good works. Because of their zeal in burying the bodies of martyrs they were both arrested. Almachius, the prefect before whom they were brought, began to cross-examine them. Almachius told him to tell the court if he would sacrifice to the gods and go forth free. Tiburtius and Valerian both replied: 'No, not to the gods, but to the one God to whom we offer sacrifice daily.' The prefect asked whether Jupiter were the name of their god. 'No, indeed', said Valerian.

Valerian rejoiced when they were delivered over to be scourged. Even then the prefect was disposed to allow them a respite in which to reconsider their refusal, but his assessor assured him that they would only use the time to distribute their possessions, thus preventing the state from confiscating their property. They were accordingly condemned to death and were beheaded in a place called Pagus Triopius, four miles from Rome. With them perished one of the officials, a man called Maximus, who had declared himself a Christian after witnessing their fortitude.

Cecilia gave burial to the three bodies, and then she in turn was called upon to repudiate her faith. Instead she converted those who came to induce her to sacrifice; and when Pope Urban visited her at home he baptized over 400 persons there: one of them, Gordian, a man of rank, established a church in her house, which Urban later dedicated in her name. When she was eventually brought into court, Almachius argued with Cecilia at some length, and was not a little provoked by her attitude. At length she was sentenced to be suffocated to death in the bathroom of her own house. But though the furnace was fed with seven times its normal amount of fuel, Cecilia remained for a day and a night without receiving any harm, and a soldier was sent to behead her. He struck at her neck three times, and then left her lying. She was not dead and lingered three days, during which the Christians flocked to her side and she formally made over her house to Urban and committed her household to his care. She was buried next to the papal crypt in the catacomb of St Callistus.

This well-known story, familiar to and loved by Christians for many ages, dates back to about the end of the fifth century, but unfortunately can by no means be regarded as trustworthy or even founded upon authentic materials. No mention is made of a Roman virgin martyr named Cecilia in the period immediately following the persecutions. There is no reference to her in the poems of Damasus or Prudentius, in the writings of Jerome or Ambrose, and her name does not occur in the *Depositio martyrum* (fourth century). Moreover, what was later called the *titulus Sanctae Caeciliae* was originally known simply as the *titulus Caeciliae, i.e.* the church founded by a lady named Cecilia.

Today perhaps St Cecilia is most generally known as the patron-saint of music and musicians. At her wedding, the *acta* tell us, while the musicians played, Cecilia sang to the Lord in her heart.

23 : ST COLUMBAN, ABBOT OF LUXEUIL AND BOBBIO (A.D. 615)

COLUMBAN was born in west Leinster and had a good education, which was interrupted when he was a young man by a sharp struggle with the insurgent flesh. He asked the advice of a religious woman who had lived solitary from the world for years, and she told him to flee the temptation even to the extent of leaving the land of his birth. Columban heard her words as more than just sensible counsel to a youth distracted by an ordinary trial of adolescence; it was to him a call to renounce the world, definitely to choose the cloistered rather than secular life. He left his mother, grievously against her will, and fled to Sinell, a monk who lived on Cluain Inis, an island in Lough Erne, and from thence in time he went on to the great monastic seat of learning at Bangor, opposite Carrickfergus on Belfast Lough. How long he lived here is not known; Jonas speaks of 'many years', and he was probably about forty-five when he obtained St Comgall's permission to leave the monastery and adventure in foreign lands. With twelve companions Columban passed over into Gaul, where barbarian invasions, civil strife and clerical slackness had reduced religion to a low ebb.

The Irish monks at once set about preaching to the people by showing an example of charity, penance and devotion, and their reputation reached the king of Burgundy, Guntramnus, who *c*. 590 offered St Columban ground for building at Annegray in the mountains of the Vosges, which became his first monastery. This house soon became too small to contain the numbers that desired to live under the discipline of the saint. He therefore built a second monastery called Luxeuil, not far from the former, and a third, which an account of its springs was called Fontes, now Fontaine. These, with Bobbio later, were the foundations of Columban himself; his followers established numerous monasteries in France, Germany, Switzerland and Italy, centres of religion and industry in Europe throughout the dark ages. St Columban lays down for the foundation of his rule the love of God and of our neighbour, as a general precept upon which the superstructure of all the rest is raised. After the rule follows a penitential, containing prescriptions of penances to be imposed upon monks for every fault, however light. It is in the harshness of its discipline, characteristics of much Celtic Christianity, the imposition of fasts on bread and water, and beatings, for the smallest transgressions, and the great length of the Divine Office (there was a maximum of seventy-five psalms a day in winter), that the Rule of St Columban most obviously differs from that of St Benedict. In austerity the Celtic monks rivalled those of the East.

After the Columban monks had pursued their strenuous life in peace for twelve years a certain hostility manifested itself among the Frankish bishops, and St Columban was summoned before a synod to give an account of his Celtic usages (computation of Easter, etc.). He refused to go. As the bishops pressed him he appealed to the Holy See, and addressed letters to two popes in which he protests the orthodoxy of himself and his monks, explains the Irish customs, and asks that they be confirmed. He writes freely and respectfully apologises for seeming to argue with the Supreme Pontiff.

But soon Columban was involved in worse trouble. King Theodoric II of Burgundy had respect for St Columban and the abbot reproved him for keeping concubines instead of marrying a queen. His grandmother, Queen Brunhilda, who had been regent, fearing lest a queen should ruin her power, was much provoked against Columban. Her resentment was increased by his refusing to bless at her request the king's four natural children. Columban also denied her entrance into his monastery, as he did to all women and even to lay men, and this, being contrary to Frankish custom, Brunhilda made a pretext for stirring up Theodoric against Columban. The upshot was that he was in 610 ordered to be deported to Ireland, with all his Irish brethren but none others: there may probably be seen the hidden influence of Frankish court bishops behind all this. At Nantes he wrote a famous letter to the monks left at Luxeuil, and then embarked. But the ship at once met bad weather and ran aground, and the next we hear of Columban is that he made his way through Paris and Meaux to the court of Theodebert II of Austrasia at Metz, by whom he was well received. Under his protection he went with some of his disciples to preach to pagans near the lake of Zurich, but the zeal of the missionaries was not well received and they went on to the neighbourhood of Lake Constance, to a fruitful pleasant valley amidst the mountains (now Bregenz), where they found an abandoned oratory dedicated in honour of St Aurelia, near which they built themselves cells. But here too the vigorous methods of some of the missionaries (especially of St Gall) provoked the people against them, and danger arose as well from another quarter. Austrasia and Burgundy were at war, and Theodebert, being defeated, was delivered up by his own men and sent by his brother Theodoric to their grandmother Brunhilda.

St Columban, seeing his enemy was master of the country where he lived and that he could no longer remain there with safety, went across the Alps (he was about seventy years old by now) and came to Milan, where he met with a kind reception from the Arian Agilulf, King of the Lombards, and his wife Theodelinda. He at once began to oppose the Arians, against whom he wrote a treatise, and became involved in the affair of the Three Chapters (writings which were condemned by the fifth general council at Constantinople as favouring Nestorianism). The bishops of Istria and some of Lombardy defended these writings with such warmth as to break off communion with the pope, and the king and queen induced St Columban to write very outspokenly to Pope St Boniface IV in defence of them, urging him to take steps that orthodoxy might prevail. The subject at issue was one upon which St Columban was badly informed indeed; on the other hand, he makes clear his burning desire for unity in the faith and his own intense devotion to the Holy See.

Agilulf gave to Columban a ruined church and some land at Ebovium (Bobbio), in a valley of the Appenines between Genoa and Piacenza, and here he began the establishment of the abbey of St Peter. In spite of his age he himself was active in the work of building, but for the rest Columban now wanted only retirement to prepare for death. When he had visited King Clotaire II of Neustria on his way back from Nantes he had prophesied the fall of Theodoric within three years. This had been verified: Theodoric was dead, old Brunhilda brutally murdered, and Clotaire was master of Austrasia and Burgundy as well. He remembered the prophecy of St Columban, and invited him to come back to France. He would not go, but asked the king to look kindly on the monks of Luxeuil. Soon after, on November 23 in 615, St Columban died.

24 : ST COLMAN OF CLOYNE, BISHOP (SIXTH CENTURY)

COLMAN OF CLOYNE was son of Lenin, born in Munster near the beginning of the sixth century. He was a poet of great skill and became royal bard (that is, chronicler and genealogist as well as poet laureate) at Cashel. He was nearly fifty years old before he became a Christian, and the circumstances of his conversion are said to have been as follows. St Brendan came to Cashel to help in the settlement of a dispute about the succession, and while he was there the grave and relics of St Ailbhe were found. Colman took part in this discovery, and St Brendan observed that hands that had been hallowed by the touch of such holy remains should not remain the hands of a pagan. So the bard was baptized by Brendan, and received from him the name of Colman. In the Life of St Columba of Terryglass we hear that the boy Columba was given to the care of this Colman, who taught him to read. Having been ordained priest and afterwards consecrated bishop, St Colman preached in Limerick and the eastern parts of Cork, where he was granted land for a church at Cloyne, of which he is venerated as the first bishop.

25 : ST MOSES, MARTYR (A.D. 251)

MOSES, perhaps of Jewish origin, was a priest at Rome and leader of a group of clergy who, according to St Cyprian, were the first confessors in the Decian persecution. They exchanged letters of encouragement with St Cypian and the clergy of Carthage, and withdrew themselves from communion with Novatian, the danger of whose rigorism St Moses perceived. After he had been in prison with his companions for eleven months and eleven days, that is to say, about January 1, 251, Moses died and was accounted a martyr.

26 : ST SILVESTER GOZZOLINI, ABBOT, FOUNDER OF THE SILVESTRINE BENEDICTINES (A.D. 1267)

THE Gozzolini were a noble family of Osimo, where St Silvester was born in 1177. He was sent to read law at Bologna and Padua, but soon abandoned his legal studies for theology and the Holy Scriptures, greatly to the anger of his father, who is said to have refused to speak to him for ten years on that account. Silvester was presented to a canonry at Osimo, where he laboured until his zeal involved him in difficulties with his bishop. This prelate was a man of disedifying life, and Silvester took it upon himself to rebuke him, respectfully but firmly. The bishop threatened to relieve the saint of his benefice, which would not have troubled him much for he had long been strongly drawn to the contemplative life.

In 1227, being fifty years old, St Silvester resigned his rich benefice and retired to a lonely spot some thirty miles from Osimo, where he lived in great poverty and discomfort till the lord of the place gave him a better hermitage. But this proved to be too damp, and he moved to Grotta Fucile where he stayed, living an extremely penitential life, till 1231, when he decided to establish a monastery for the disciples who now surrounded him. This he did at Monte Fano, near Fabriano, building it partly from the ruins of a pagan temple.

St Silvester chose for his monks the Rule of St Benedict in its most austere interpretation. He governed his congregation with great wisdom and holiness for thirty-six years and, when he died at the age of ninety, eleven monasteries, either new or reformed, recognized his leadership.

27 : ST VIRGIL, BISHOP OF SALZBURG (A.D. 784)

ST VIRGIL was an Irishman, Feargal or Ferghil by name, and in the *Annals of the Four Masters* and the *Annals of Ulster* he is identified with an abbot of

Aghaboe. About the year 743 he started out on a pilgrimage to the Holy Land, but after spending two years in France got no further than Bavaria. Here Duke Odilo appointed him abbot of St Peter's at Salzburg and administrator of the diocese. St Virgil had a bishop, and Irishman like himself, to perform episcopal acts, reserving to himself the office of preaching and ruling, till he was compelled by his colleagues to receive episcopal consecration. In the course of his duties he came across a priest who was so ignorant of Latin that he did not pronounce the words of baptism properly. St Virgil decided that as the error was an accidental one of language, baptisms that this priest had administered were valid and need not be repeated. St Boniface, then archbishop of Mainz, strongly disapproved of the verdict, and appeal was made to Pope St Zachary. He confirmed the ruling of Virgil, and expressed surprise that Boniface had questioned it.

Some time after this incident, Virgil was denounced to the Holy See, again by St Boniface, for teaching that—if his doctrine be accurately represented—there is beneath the earth another world and other men and also a sun and a moon. Zachary answered that this was a 'perverse and wicked doctrine, offensive alike to God and to his own soul': and that if it were proved that Virgil did hold it he should be excommunicated by a synod. There is evidence for supposing that Virgil was tried, condemned and made to retract; but he must have satisfied his critics for about 767 (or earlier) he was consecrated bishop.

St Virgil rebuilt the cathedral of Salzburg on a grand scale, and translated thereto the body of St Rupert, founder of the see. He baptized at Salzburg two successive Slav dukes of Carinthis, and at their request sent thither four preachers under the bishop St Modestus; other missionaries followed. Virgil himself preached in Carinthis as far as the borders of Hungary, where the Drava falls into the Danube. Soon after his return home he was taken ill, and cheerfully departed to the Lord on November 27, 784.

28 : ST CATHERINE LABOURÉ, VIRGIN (A.D. 1876)

ZOE LABOURÉ was the daughter of a yeoman-farmer at Fain-les-Moutiers in the Côte d'Or, where she was born in 1806. She was the only one of a large family not to go to school and did not learn to read and write. Her mother died when Zoé was eight, and when her elder sister, Louisa, left home to become a Sister of Charity the duties of housekeeper and helper to her father devolved upon her. From the age of fourteen or so she also heard a call to the religious life, and after some opposition M. Labouré allowed her to join the Sisters of Charity of St Vincent de Paul at Châtillon-sur-Seine in 1830. She took the name of Catherine, and after her postulancy was sent to the convent in the rue du Bac at Paris, where she arrived four days before the translation of the relics of St Vincent from Notre-Dame to the Lazarist church in the rue de Sèvres. On the evening of the day of those festivities began the series of visions which were to make the name of Catherine Labouré famous. The first of the three principal ones took place three months later, on the night of July 18, when at about 11.30p.m. she was woken up suddenly by the appearance of a 'shining child', who led her down to the sisters' chapel. There our Lady appeared and talked with her for over two hours, telling her that she would have to undertake a difficult task.

On November 27 following, our Lady appeared to Sister Catherine in the same chapel, in the form of a picture and as it were standing on a globe with shafts of light streaming from her hands towards it, surrounded by the words: 'O Mary, conceived free from sin, pray for us who turn to thee!' Then the picture turned about, and Sister Catherine saw on the reverse side a capital M, with a cross above it and two hearts, one thorn-crowned and the other pierced with a sword, below. And she seemed to herself to hear a voice telling her to have a medal struck representing these things, and promising that all who wore it with devotion should receive great graces by the intercession of the Mother of God. This or a similar vision was repeated in the following month and on several other occasions up to September 1831.

Sister Catherine confided in her confessor, M. Aladel, and he, after making very careful investigations, was given permission by the archbishop of Paris, Mgr de Quélen, to have a medal struck. In June 1832 the first 1500 were issued—the medal now known to Catholics throughout the world as 'miraculous'. In 1836, the archbishop of Paris instituted a canonical inquiry into the alleged visions before which, however, Sister Catherine could not be induced to appear. The precautions she had taken to keep herself unknown, the promise she had wrung from M. Aladel not to tell anybody who she was, the secrecy she had kept towards everyone except her confessor, her constant unwillingness to appear before an ecclesiastical authority, account for this inquiry not being extended to the young sister herself. The tribunal decided in favour of the authenticity of the visions, taking into consideration the circumstances, the character of the sister concerned, and the prudence and level-headedness of M. Aladel. The popularity of the medal increased daily, especially after the conversion of Alphonse Ratisbonne in 1842. He was a Jew from Alsace who, having reluctantly agreed to wear the medal, received a vision of our Lady in that form in the church of Sant' Andrea delle Frate at Rome, whereupon he became a Christian and was later a priest and founder of a religious congregation, the Fathers and Sisters of Zion.

This vision of Ratisbonne also was the subject of a canonical inquiry, and the reports of this and of the archbishop of Paris's were extensively used in the process of beatification of Catherine Labouré, of whose personal life very little is recorded. Her superiors speak of her as 'rather insignificant', 'matter-of-fact and unexcitable', 'cold, almost apathetic'. From 1831 until her death on December 31, 1876, she lived unobtrusively among the community at Enghien-Reuilly, as portress, in charge of the poultry, and looking after the aged who were supported in the hospice. Not until eight months before her death did she speak to anyone except her confessor of the extraordinary graces she had received, and then she revealed them only to her superior, Sister Dufé.

St Catherine Labouré was canonized in 1947.

29 : ST RADBOD, BISHOP OF UTRECHT (A.D. 918)

RADBOD, the last pagan king of the Frisians (who said he preferred to be in Hell with his ancestors rather than in Heaven without them), was great-grandfather of this saint, whose father was a Frank. The young Radbod received his first schooling under the tuition of Gunther, Bishop of Cologne, his maternal uncle. Little is known of St Radbod's life, but he wrote hymns and an office of St Martin, an eclogue and sermon on St Lebwin, a hymn on St Swithbert and other poems which are extant. In a short chronicle which he compiled he says, under the year 900, 'I Radbod, a sinner, have been taken, though unworthy, into the company of the ministers of the church of Utrecht; with whom I pray that I may attain to eternal life'.

Before the end of that year he was chosen bishop of that church, when he put on the monastic habit, his predecessors having been monks because the church of Utrecht had been founded by priests of the monastic order. After he had received the episcopal consecration he never tasted meat, often fasted two or three days together, and was renowned for his kindness to the poor. During a Danish invasion St Radbod removed his see to Deventer, and there died in peace.

30 : ST CUTHBERT MAYNE, MARTYR (A.D. 1577)

THE English College at Douai was founded in 1568 and in the early days of the penal laws a legal distinction was made between those priests trained in this and other seminaries abroad and those 'Marian priests' who had been ordained in England. The first 'seminary priest' to pay for his mission with his life was Cuthbert Mayne. He was a Devon man, born at Youlston, near Barnstaple, in 1544, and brought up a Protestant by his uncle, a schismatic priest. He went to Barnstaple Grammar School and at eighteen or nineteen was ordained a minister, with neither inclination nor preparation. His uncle then sent him to Oxford, where at St John's College he got to know Dr Gregory Martin and Edmund Campion, who was still a Protestant, and he was soon inwardly persuaded of the truth of Catholicism; but he held back for fear of losing his appointments and falling into poverty. When Martin and Campion had gone over to Douai they wrote several times to Mayne urging him to join them, and in 1570, soon after he had taken his M.A., one of these letters fell into the hands of the bishop of London, who sent a pursuivant to Oxford to arrest all those named therein. Mayne was away at the time, and this narrow escape decided him: he abjured Protestantism and in 1573 was accepted at Douai. During the next three years he was ordained priest and took his bachelor's degree in theology, and in April 1576 was sent back to England with St John Payne. Mayne was the fifteenth missionary priest sent out from Douai.

He took up residence at the mansion of Francis Tregian at Golden in the parish of Probus in Cornwall, where he passed as the estate-steward. Few particulars are known of his ministry from this centre, but suspicions were excited and a year later the high sheriff, Richard Grenville, searched Tregian's house. Mayne was found to have an *agnus Dei* round his neck, and was accordingly arrested, together with Mr Tregian. Cuthbert was carried by the sheriff from one gentleman's house to another till they came to Launceston, where he was confined in a filthy cell of the prison, chained to the bedpost. At the Michaelmas assizes he was indicted for having obtained from Rome and published at Golden a 'faculty containing matter of absolution' of the Queen's subjects (actually they had found a printed announcement, from Douai, of the jubilee indulgence of 1575, two years out of date); for having taught, in Launceston jail, the ecclesiastical power of the Bishop of Rome (on the uncertain evidence of three illiterate witnesses); that he had brought into the kingdom and delivered to Mr Tregian 'a vain and superstitious thing, commonly called an *agnus Dei*' (no evidence was offered of importation or delivery); and for having celebrated Mass (on the strength of finding a misal, chalice and vestments at Golden). All these things contrary to statutes of 1 and 13 Elizabeth.

On the direction of Mr Justice Manwood (and after prolonged consultation with Mr Sheriff Grenville) the jury found a verdict of guilt; Cuthbert was sentenced to death, and three of the four gentlemen and their three yeomen, charged with him as abettors, to perpetual imprisonment and forfeiture. But the second judge, Mr Justice Jeffrey, had qualms about these proceedings and procured a reconsideration of the case by the whole judicial bench, at Serjeants' Inn. These judges could not agree and, though the weight of opinion favoured Jeffrey's opinion, the Privy Council directed that the conviction should stand as a warning to priests coming from beyond the seas. The day before his execution Cuthbert was offered his liberty if he would swear to the queen's ecclesiastical supremacy. He asked for a Bible, kissed it, and said, 'The queen neither ever was nor is nor ever shall be the head of the Church of England'. He was drawn to Launceston market-place on a sledge, but was not allowed to address the crowd from the scaffold. When invited to implicate Mr Tregian and his brother-in-law, Sir John Arundell, Mayne replied, 'I know nothing of them except that they are good and pious men; and of the things laid to my charge no one but myself has any knowledge'. He was cut down alive but was probably unconscious before the butchery of disembowelling began. He was canonized in 1970 as one of the Forty Martyrs.

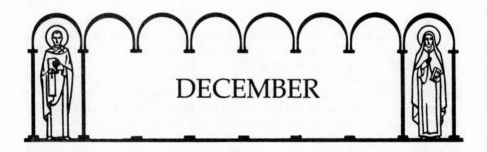

DECEMBER

1 : ST EDMUND CAMPION, MARTYR (A.D. 1581)

EDMUND CAMPION, senior, was a bookseller in the city of London, Edmund junior was born about 1540. When fifteen he was given a scholarship in St John's College, Oxford, then newly founded by Sir Thomas White. Two years later Campion was appointed a junior fellow, and he made a great reputation as an orator; he was chosen to speak at the re-burial of Lady Amy Dudley (Robsart), at the funeral of Sir Thomas White, and before Elizabeth when she visited Oxford in 1566. His talents and personality earned him the goodwill and patronage of the queen, of Cecil and of Leicester; to the last-named he dedicated his *History of Ireland*, and Cecil later referred to him as 'one of the diamonds of England'. He had taken the oath of royal supremacy and was persuaded to receive the diaconate of the Anglican Church. But the taking of orders in a church about which he was doubtful began to trouble him and, at the end of his term as junior proctor of the university in 1569 he went to Dublin, where an attempt was being made to revive its university. While there he wrote a short history of the country.

After the publication of Pope St Pius's bull against Elizabeth, he was in danger as a suspected person. In 1571 he returned to England in disguise, was present at the trial of Bd John Storey in Westminster Hall, and then made for Douai. He was stopped on the way for having no passport, but was allowed to escape on giving up his luggage and money. Campion took his B.D. and was ordained subdeacon at Douai, and then, in 1573, went to Rome and was admitted to the Society of Jesus. As there was yet no English province he was sent to that of Bohemia, and after his novitiate at Brno went to the college of Prague to teach.

In view of the great success of the Society among the Protestants of Germany, Bohemia and Poland, Dr Allen persuaded Pope Gregory XIII to send some Jesuits to England, and at the end of 1579 Father Edmund Campion and Father Robert Persons were chosen.

The Jesuits were not welcomed by all the Catholics, many of whom feared what new troubles the arrival of representatives of the redoubtable Society might bring on their heads. Their coming was known to the government, and they soon had to leave London, Campion going to work in Berkshire, Oxfordshire and Northamptonshire, where he made some notable converts.

After meeting Persons in London, where persecution was very hot, he went to Lancashire, where he preached almost daily and with conspicuous success, pursued always by spies and several times nearly taken. All this time he was writing a Latin treatise, which was called *Decem Rationes* because in it he expounded ten reasons why he had challenged the most learned Portestants openly to discuss religion with him. The greatest difficulty was found in getting this work printed, but eventually it was achieved on a secret press at the house of Dame Cecilia Stonor, in Stonor Park, Berkshire, and on 'Commemoration', June 27, 1581, four hundred copies of it were found distributed on the benches of the university church at Oxford. It made a tremendous sensation, and efforts to capture the writer were redoubled.

It was judged prudent that Edmund should retire to Norfolk, and on the way he stayed at the house of Mrs. Yate at Lyford, near Wantage. On Sunday, July 16, some forty people assembled there to assist at Mass and hear him preach, but among them was a traitor. Within the next twelve hours the house was searched three times, and at the last Edmund was found with two other priests concealed above the gateway. They were taken to the Tower, from Colnbrook onward being pinioned and Edmund labelled: 'Campion, the seditious Jesuit.' After three days in the 'little-ease' he was interviewed by the Earls of Bedford and Leicester, who tried to bribe him into apostasy. Other attempts of the same sort having failed he was racked. While still broken by torture he was four times confronted by Protestant dignitaries, whose questions, objections and insults he answered with spirit and effectiveness. He was then racked again, so fiercely that when asked the next day how he felt he could reply, 'Not ill, because not at all'. On November 14 he was indicted in Westminster Hall, with Ralph Sherwin, Thomas Cottam, Luke Kirby and others, on the fabricated charge of having plotted at Rome and Rheims to raise a rebellion in England and coming into the realm for that purpose. When told to plead to the charge he was too weak to move his arms, and one of his companions, kissing his hand, held it up for him. Campion conducted the defence both of himself and the others with much ability, protesting their loyalty to the queen, demolishing the evidence, discrediting the witnesses, and showing that their only offence was their religion. The packed jury brought them in 'guilty', but it took them an hour to make up their minds to do it. Before sentence of death St Edmund addressed the court:' . . . In condemning us you condemn all your own ancestors . . . . To be condemned with these old lights—not of England only, but of the world—by their degenerate descendants is both gladness and glory to us. God lives. Posterity will live. Their judgement is not so liable to corruption as that of those who now sentence us to death.'

On December 1, a wet, muddy day, Campion, Sherwin, and Briant were drawn to Tyburn together, and there executed with the usual barbarities. On the scaffold Edmund again refused to give an opinion of the pope's bull against Elizabeth, and publicly prayed for her: 'your queen and my queen, unto whom I wish a long reign with all prosperity'. Some of the blood of this man, 'admirable, subtle, exact and of sweet disposition', splashed on to a young gentleman, one Henry Walpole, who was present: he too became a Jesuit and was canonized with him as one of the Forty Martyrs in 1970.

2 : ST CHROMATIUS, BISHOP OF AQUILEIA (c. A.D. 407)

CHROMATIUS was brought up in the city of Aquileia, of which he was probably a native, and lived there with his widowed mother (of whom St Jerome's good opinion is seen in a letter written to her in the year 374), his brother, who also became a bishop, and unmarried sisters. After his ordination to the priesthood St Chromatius took part in the synod of Aquileia against Arianism in 381, baptized Rufinus in his early manhood, and soon acquired a great reputation.

On the death of St Valerian in 388 he was elected bishop of Aquileia, and in that office became one of the most distinguished prelates of his time. He was a friend and correspondent of St Jerome (who dedicated several of his works to him), at the same time preserving his association with Rufinus, and trying to act as peace-maker and moderator in the Origenistic dispute. It was owing to the encouragement of St Chromatius that Rufinus undertook the translation of the *Ecclesiastical History* of Eusebius and other works, and at his suggestion St Ambrose commented on the prophecy of Balaam; he helped St Heliodorus of Altino to finance St Jerome's translation of the Bible. Chromatius was an energetic and valued supporter of St John Chrysostom, who had a high opinion of him; he wrote to the Emperor Honorius protesting against the persecution of Chrysostom, and Honorius forwarded the protest to his brother, Arcadius, at Constantinople. But the efforts of Chromatius were without effect. He was himself a capable commentator of the Holy Scriptures; seventeen of his treatises on parts of St Matthew's gospel are extant and a homily on the Beatitudes. St Chromatius died about the year 407.

3 : ST FRANCIS XAVIER, (A.D. 1552)

HE was born in Spanish Navarre, at the castle of Xavier, near Pamplona, in 1506 (his mother-tongue was Basque), the youngest of a large family, and he went to the University of Paris in his eighteenth year. He entered the college of St Barbara and in 1528 gained the degree of licentiate. Here it was that he met Ignatius Loyola and, though he did not at once submit himself to his influence, he was one of the band of seven, the first Jesuits, who vowed themselves to the service of God at Montmartre in 1534. With them he received the priesthood at Venice three years later and in 1540 St Ignatius appointed him to join Father Simon Rodriguez on the first missionary expedition the Society sent out, to the East Indies.

They arrived at Lisbon about the end of June, and Francis went immediately to Father Rodriguez, who was lodged in a hospital in order to attend and instruct the sick. They made this place their ordinary dwelling, but catechized and instructed in the town, and were taken up all Sundays and holidays in hearing confessions at court, for the king, John III, had a high regard for these religious; so much so that eventually Rodriguez was retained by him at Lisbon. Before he at last sailed, on his thirty-fifth birthday, April 7, 1541, the king delivered to him briefs from the pope in which Francis Xavier was constituted apostolic nuncio in the East.

There were all sorts among the ship's company and passengers; Xavier had to compose quarrels, quell complaints, check swearing and gaming, and remedy other disorders. Scurvy broke out, and there was no one but the three Jesuits to nurse the sick. It took them five months to get round the Cape of Good Hope and arrive at Mozambique, where they wintered. They continued to hug the east coast of Africa and called at Malindi and Socotra, from whence it took them two months to reach Goa, where they arrived on May 6, 1542, after a voyage of thirteen months (twice the then usual time). St Francis took up his quarters at the hospital to await the arrival of his companions, who were following in another ship.

The scandalous behaviour of the Christians in Goa was like a challenge to Francis Xavier and he opened his mission with them, instructing them in the principles of religion and forming the young to the practice of virtue. Having spent the morning in assisting and comforting the distressed in the hospitals and prisons he walked through the streets ringing a bell to summon the children and slaves to catechism. He offered Mass with lepers every Sunday, preached in public and to the Indians, and visited private houses: the sweetness of his character and his charitable concern for his neighbours were irresistible to many. For the instruction of the very ignorant or simple he versified the truths of religion to fit popular tunes, and this was so successful that the practice spread till these songs were being sung everywhere, in the streets and houses and fields and workshops.

After five months of this St Francis was told that on the Pearl Fishery coast, which extends from Cape Comorin to the isle of Manar, opposite Ceylon, there were people called Paravas, who to get the protection of the Portuguese against the Arabs and others had been baptized, but for want of instruction still retained their superstitions and vices. Xavier went to the help of these people. Under every difficulty he set himself to learn the native language and to instruct and confirm those who had been already baptized, especially concentrating on teaching the rudiments of religion to the children. Then he preached to those Paravas to whom the name of Christ was till that time unknown. So great were the multitudes he baptized that sometimes by the bare fatigue of administering the sacrament he was scarcely able to move his arms, according to the account which he gave to his brethren in Europe. The Paravas were a low-caste people, and St Francis had a different reception and very little success among the Brahmans; at the end of twelve months he had converted only one. It seems certain that at this time God wrought a number of miracles of healing through him.

St Francis, as always, came before the people as one of themselves. His food was that of the poorest, rice and water; he slept on the ground in a hut. He was able to extend his activities to Travancore; here his achievements have been rather exaggerated by some writers, but village after village received him with joy, and after baptizing the inhabitants he wrote to Father Mansilhas telling him to come and organize the converts. His difficulties were increased by the misfortunes of the Christians of Comorin and Tuticorin, who were set upon by the Badagas from the north, who robbed, massacred and carried them into slavery. Xavier is said on one occasion to have held off the raiders by facing them alone, crucifix in hand. He was again handicapped by the Portuguese, their local commandant having his own secret dealings with the Badagas.

The ruler of Jaffna, in northern Ceylon, hearing of the progress of the faith in his island of Manar, slew six hundred Christians there. The governor, Martin de Sousa, ordered an expedition to punish this massacre and it was to fit out at Negapatam, whither St Francis went to join it; but the officers were diverted from their purpose and so Francis instead made a journey on foot to the shrine of St Thomas at Mylapore, where there was a small Portuguese settlement to be visited. Many incidents are related of him during these travels, especially of his conversion of notorious sinners among the Europeans by the gentle and courteous way in which he dealt with them; other miracles too were ascribed to him.

In the spring of 1545 St Francis set out for Malacca, on the Malay peninsula, where he spent four months. He was received with great reverence and cordiality, and his efforts at reform met with some success. For the next eighteen months his movements are difficult to follow, but they were a time of great activity and interest, for he was in a largely unknown world, visiting islands, which he refers to in general as the Moluccas, not all of which are now identifiable. He preached and ministered at Amboina, Ternate, Gilolo, and other places, in some of which there were Portuguese merchants and settlements. When he got back to Malacca he passed another four months there, ministering to a very unsatisfactory flock, and then departed for India again. But before he left he heard about Japan for the first time, from Portuguese merchants and from a fugitive Japanese named Anjiro. Xavier arrived back in India in January 1548.

The next fifteen months were spent in endless travelling between Goa, Ceylon and Cape Comorin, consolidating his work (notably the 'international college' of St Paul at Goa) and preparing for an attempt on that Japan into which no European had yet penetrated. In April 1549, St Francis set out, accompanied by a Jesuit priest and a lay-brother, by Anjiro—now Paul—and by two other Japanese converts. On the feast of the Assumption following they landed in Japan, at Kagoshima on Kyushu.

At Kagoshima they were not molested, and St Francis set himself to learn Japanese. A translation was made of a simple account of Christian teaching, and recited to all who would listen. The fruit of twelve months' labour was a hundred converts, and then the authorities began to get suspicious and forbade further preaching. So, leaving Paul in charge of the neophytes, Francis decided to push on further with his other companions and went by sea to Hirado, north of Nagasaki. Before leaving Kagoshima he visited the fortress of Ichiku, where the 'baron's' wife, her steward and others accepted Christianity. To the steward's care Xavier recommended the rest at departure; and twelve years later the Jesuit lay-brother and physician, Luis de Almeida, found these isolated converts still retaining their first fervour and faithfulness. At Hirado the missionaries were well received by the ruler (*daimyô*), and they had more success in a few weeks than they had had at Kagoshima in a year. These converts St Francis left to Father de Torres and went on with Brother Fernandez and a Japanese to Yamaguchi in Honshu. Francis preached here, in public and before the *daimyô*, but the missionaries made no impression and were treated with scorn.

Xavier's objective was Miyako (Kyoto), then the chief city of Japan, and having made a month's stay at Yamaguchi and gathered small fruit of his labours except affronts, he continued his journey with his two companions. It was towards the end of December, and they suffered much on the road from heavy rains, snow and the difficult country, and did not reach their destination till February. Here Francis found that he could not procure an audience of the mikado (who in any case was but a puppet) without paying a sum of money far beyond his resources; moreover, civil strife filled the city with such tumult that he saw it to be impossible to do any good there at that time and, after a fortnight's stay, they returned to Yamaguchi. Seeing that evangelical poverty did not have the appeal in Japan that it had in India, St Francis changed his methods. Decently dressed and with his companions as attendants he presented himself before the *daimyô* as the representative of Portugal, giving him the letters and presents (a musical-box, a clock and a pair of spectacles among them) which the authorities in India had provided for the mikado. The *daimyô* received the gifts with delight, gave Francis leave to teach, and provided an empty Buddhist monastery for a residence. When thus he obtained protection, Francis preached with such fruit that he baptized many in that city.

Hearing that a Portuguese ship had arrived at Funai (Oita) in Kyushu St Francis decided to make use of it to revisit his charge in India, from whence he now hoped to extend his mission to China. Francis found that good progress had been made in India, but there were also many difficulties and abuses, both among the missionaries and the Portuguese authorities, that urgently needed his attention. These matters he dealt with, lovingly and very firmly and thoroughly. At the end of four months, on April 25, 1552, with a Jesuit priest and a scholastic, an Indian servant and a young Chinese to interpret (but he had forgotten his own language), he sailed eastward again; he was awaited at Malacca by Diogo Pereira, whom the viceroy in India had appointed ambassador to the court of China.

At Malacca St Francis had to treat about this embassy with Don Alvaro da Ataide da Gama (a son of Vasco da Gama), the maritime authority there. This Alvaro had a personal grudge against Diogo Pereira, whom he flatly refused to let sail either as envoy or as private trader. At length Don Alvaro conceded that Xavier should go to China in Pereira's ship, but without its owner; and to this Pereira most nobly agreed. When the project of the embassy thus failed Francis sent his priest companion to Japan, and eventually was left with only the Chinese youth, Antony. With him he hoped to find means to land secretly in China, the country being closed to foreigners. In the last week of August 1552 the convoy reached the desolate island of Sancian (Shang-chwan), half-a-dozen miles off the coast and a hundred miles south-west of Hong Kong.

He had with great difficulty hired a Chinese merchant to land him by night in some part of Canton, for which Xavier had engaged to pay him, and bound himself by oath that nothing should ever bring him to confess the name of him who had set him on shore. Whilst waiting for his plans to mature, Xavier fell sick and, when the Portuguese vessels were all gone except one, was reduced to extreme want. The Chinese merchant did not turn up. A fever seized the saint on November 21, and he took shelter on the ship; but the motion of the sea was too much for him, so the day following he requested that he might be set on shore again, which was done. The vessel was manned chiefly by Don Alvaro's men who, fearing to offend their master by common kindness to Xavier, left him exposed on the sands to a piercing north wind, till a friendly Portuguese merchant led him into his hut, which afforded only a very poor shelter. He lay thus in a high fever, being bled with distressing results, praying ceaselessly between spasms of delirium. He got weaker and weaker till at last, in the early morning of December 3, which fell on a Saturday, 'I [Antony] could see that he was dying and put a lighted candle in his hand. Then, with the name of Jesus on his lips, he rendered his soul to his Creator and Lord with great repose and quietude'. St Francis was only forty-six years old, of which he had passed eleven in the East. His body was laid in the earth on the Sunday evening: four people were present, the Chinese Antony, a Portuguese and two slaves.

The coffin had been packed with lime around the body in case it should later be desired to move the remains. Ten weeks and more later the grave and coffin were opened. The lime being removed from the face, it was found quite incorrupt and fresh-coloured. The body was brought to Malacca, where it was received with great honour by all, except Don Alvaro. At the end of the year it was taken away to Goa, where its continued incorruption was verified by physicians; there it still lies enshrined in the church of the Good Jesus. St Francis Xavier was canonized in 1622, at the same time as Ignatius Loyola, Teresa of Avila, Philip Neri and Isidore the Husbandman.

4 : ST JOHN DAMASCENE, DOCTOR OF THE CHURCH (c. A.D. 749)

THE Moslem rulers of Damascus, where St John was born, were not unjust to their Christian subjects, although they required them to pay a poll tax and to submit to other conditions. They allowed both Christians and Jews to occupy important posts, and in many cases to acquire great fortunes. The khalif's doctor was nearly always a Jew, whilst Christians were employed as scribes, administrators and architects. Amongst the officials at his court in 675 was a Christian called John, who held the post of chief of the revenue department—an office which seems to have become hereditary in his family. He was the father of our saint, and the surname of al-Mansur which the Arabs gave him was afterwards transferred to the son.

The younger John was born about the year 690 and was baptized in infancy. He had as a tutor a monk called Cosmas whom the Arabs had brought back from Sicily amongst other captives. John the elder had to pay a great price for him, and well he might for, if we are to believe our chronicler, 'he knew grammar and logic, as much arithmetic as Pythagoras and as much geometry as Euclid'. He taught all the sciences, but especially theology, to the younger John and also to a boy whom the elder John seems to have adopted, who also was called Cosmas, and who became a poet and a singer, subsequently accompanying his adopted brother to the monastery in which they both became monks.

In spite of his theological training St John does not seem at first to have contemplated any career except that of his father, to whose office he succeeded. Even at court he was able freely to live a Christian life, and he became remarkable there for his virtues and especially for his humility. Nevertheless, after filling his responsible post for some years, St John resigned office, and went to be a monk in the laura of St Sabas (Mar Saba) near Jerusalem.

John and Cosmas settled down amongst the brethren and occupied their spare time in writing books and composing hymns. It might have been thought that the other monks would appreciate the presence amongst them of so doughty a champion of the faith as John, but this was far from being the case. They said the newcomers were introducing disturbing elements. It was bad enough to write books, but it was even worse to compose and sing hymns, and the brethren were scandalized.

If the monks at St Sabas did not value the two friends, there were others outside who did. The patriarch of Jerusalem, John V, knew them well by reputation and wished to have them amongst his clergy. First he took Cosmas and made him bishop of Majuma, and afterwards he ordained John priest and brought him to Jerusalem. St Cosmas, we are told, ruled his flock admirably until his death, but St John soon returned to his monastery. His works in defence of ikons had become known and read everywhere, and had earned him the hatred of the persecuting emperors. If his enemies never succeeded in injuring him, it was only because he never crossed the frontier into the Roman empire. The rest of his life was spent in writing theology and poetry at St Sabas, where he died at an advanced age. He was proclaimed doctor of the Church in 1890.

5 : ST SABAS, ABBOT (A.D. 532)

S T SABAS was born at Mutalaska in Cappadocia, not far from Caesarea, in 439. His father was an officer in the army and, being obliged to go to Alexandria, took his wife with him and recommended his son Sabas, with the care of his estate, to his brother-in-law. This uncle's wife used the child so harshly that, when he was eight, he ran away to another uncle, called Gregory, brother to his father. Gregory, having the care of the child, demanded also the administration of the property. Lawsuits and animosity arose between the two uncles. Sabas, who was of a quiet disposition, was upset at these discords and ran away again, this time to a monastery near Mutalaska.

When Sabas had been ten years in this monastery he went to Jerusalem to learn from the example of the solitaries of that country. He passed the winter in a monastery governed by the holy abbot Elpidius, but his love of silence and retirement made him prefer the manner of life practised by St Euthymius, who even when a monastery was built for him refused to abandon his complete solitude. Euthymius judged him too young for an absolutely solitary life, and therefore recommended him to his monastery below the hill, about three miles distant, which was under the conduct of St Theoctistus. When he was thirty years of age he obtained leave of St Euthymius to spend five days a week in a remote cave in prayer and manual labour. He left his monastery on Sunday evening carrying bundles of palm-twigs, and came back on Saturday morning with fifty baskets which he had made, imposing upon himself a task of ten a day. After the death of Euthymius, St Sabas retired further into the desert towards Jericho. Four years he spent in this wilderness in total separation from intercourse with men, when he chose a new dwelling in a cave on the face of a cliff, at the bottom of which ran the brook Cedron.

After Sabas had lived here some time many came to him, desiring to serve God under his direction. He was at first unwilling to consent, but eventually founded a new laura. The number of his disciples increased to one hundred and fifty, but he had no priest in his community, for he thought no religious man could aspire to that dignity without presumption. This provoked some of the monks to complain to Sallust, Patriarch of Jerusalem. The bishop found their grievances groundless, except that the want of a priest was a trouble in the community. He therefore compelled Sabas to receive ordination at his hands in 491. The abbot was then fifty-three years old. The reputation of his sanctity drew persons from remote countries to his laura, and among the monks were Egyptians and Armenians, for whom special arrangements were made so that they could celebrate the offices in their own tongues. After the death of the saint's father, his mother came to Palestine and served God under his direction. With the money which she brought he built two hospitals, one for strangers and another for the sick; and also a hospital at Jericho and another monastery on a neighbouring hill. In 493 the patriarch of Jerusalem established St Sabas as archimandrite over all the monks of Palestine who lived in separate cells (hermits), and St Theodosius of Bethlehem over all who lived in community (cenobites).

St Sabas, after the example of St Euthymius, left his disciples every year, or oftener, and at least passed Lent without being seen by anyone. This was one of the things complained of by some of his monks. As they got no sympathy from the patriarch some sixty of them left the laura, and settled themselves in a ruined monastery at Thecua. When he heard they were in sore straits, St Sabas gave them supplies and repaired their church. He himself had been driven for a time from his own monastery by the factions therein, but returned at the command of St Elias, the successor of Sallust at Jerusalem.

At this time the Emperor Anastasius was supporting the Eutychian heresy, and banished many orthodox bishops. In 511 the Patriarch Elias sent St Sabas with other abbots, to endeavour to stop this persecution: Sabas was seventy years old. He stayed the winter in Constantinople, and often visited the emperor to argue against heresy. But Anastasius procured the banishment of Elias of Jerusalem and put one John into his place. St Sabas and other monks hastened to Jerusalem and persuaded the intruder at least not to repudiate the Council of Chalcedon. Sabas is said to have been with the exiled Elias at his death at Aïla on the Red Sea; in the following years he went to Caesarea, Scythopolis and other places, preaching the true faith, and bringing back many to orthodoxy and right living.

In his ninety-first year, at the request of Patriarch Peter of Jerusalem, St Sabas undertook a second journey to Constantinople, in connection with troubles arising out of the Samaritan revolt and its violent repression by the emperor. Justinian received him with honour and offered to endow his monasteries. Sabas gratefully replied that they did not need such revenues so long as the monks should faithfully serve God, but he begged a remission of taxes in favour of the people of Palestine in consideration of what they had suffered on account of the Samaritans; that he would build a hospital at Jerusalem for pilgrims and a fortress for the protection of the hermits and monks against raiders; and that he would authorize further strong measures for the putting down of the Samaritans. All these were granted.

Very shortly after his return to his laura he fell sick, and the patriarch persuaded him to let himself be taken to a neighbouring church, where he served him with his own hands. Finding his last hour approach, Sabas begged the patriarch that he might be carried back to his laura. He appointed his successor, gave him instructions, and then lay four days in silence without seeing anyone, that he might concern himself with God alone. On December 5, 532, in the evening he departed to the Lord, being ninety-four years old.

6 : ST NICHOLAS, CALLED 'OF BARI', BISHOP OF MYRA (FOURTH CENTURY)

HE is said to have been born at Patara in Lycia, a province of Asia Minor. Myra, the capital, not far from the sea, was an episcopal see, and this church falling vacant, the holy Nicholas was chosen bishop, and in that station became famous by his extraordinary piety and zeal and many astonishing miracles. The Greek histories of his life agree that he suffered imprisonment for the faith and made a glorious confession in the latter part of the persecution raised by Diocletian, and that he was present at the Council of Nicaea and there condemned Arianism. He died at Myra, and was buried in his cathedral.

This summary account tells us all that is known about the life of the famous St Nicholas, and even a little more: for his episcopate at Myra during the fourth century is really all that seems indubitably authentic. Nevertheless, the universal popularity of the saint for so many centuries requires that some account of the legends should be given here.

His parents died when he was a young man, leaving him well off, and he determined to devote his inheritance to works of charity. An opportunity soon arose. A citizen of Patara had lost all his money, and had moreover to support three daughters who could not find husbands because of their poverty; he was going to give them over to prostitution. This came to the ears of Nicholas, who thereupon took a bag of gold and, under cover of darkness, threw it in at the open window of the man's house. Here was a dowry for the eldest girl, and she was soon duly married. At intervals Nicholas did the same for the second and third; at the last time the father was on the watch, recognized his benefactor, and overwhelmed him with his gratitude. It would appear that the three purses, represented in pictures, came to be mistaken for the heads of three children, and so they gave rise to the absurd story of the children, resuscitated by the saint, who had been killed by an innkeeper and pickled in a brine-tub.

St Methodius asserts that 'thanks to the teaching of St Nicholas the metropolis of Myra alone was untouched by the filth of the Arian heresy, which it firmly rejected as death-dealing poison', but says nothing of his presence at the Council of Nicaea in 325. According to other traditions he was not only there but so far forgot himself as to give the heresiarch Arius a slap in the face. Whereupon the conciliar fathers deprived him of his episcopal insignia and committed him to prison: but our Lord and His Mother appeared there and restored to him both his liberty and his office.

The accounts are unanimous that St Nicholas died and was buried in his episcopal city of Myra, and by the time of Justinian there was a basilica built in his honour at Constantinople. When Myra and its great shrine finally passed into the hands of the Saracens, several Italian cities saw this as an opportunity to acquire the relics of St Nicholas for themselves. There was great competition for them between Venice and Bari. The last-named won, the relics were carried off under the noses of the lawful Greek custodians and their Muslim masters, and on May 9, 1087 were safely landed at Bari, a not inappropriate home seeing that Apulia in those days still had large Greek colonies. A new church was built to shelter them and Pope Urban II was present at their enshrining. Devotion to St Nicholas was known in the West long before his relics were brought to Italy, but this happening naturally greatly increased his veneration among the people, and miracles were as freely attributed to his intercession in Europe as they had been in Asia.

It is the image of St Nicholas more often than that of any other that is found on Byzantine seals; in the later middle ages nearly four hundred churches were dedicated in his honour in England alone; and he is said to have been represented by Christian artists more frequently than any saint except our Lady. St Nicholas is venerated as the patron-saint of several classes of people, especially, in the East, of sailors and, in the West, of children. The first of these patronages is probably due to the legend that, during his life-time, he appeared to storm-tossed mariners who invoked his aid off the coast of Lycia, and brought them safely to port.

The legend of the 'three children' gave rise to his patronage of children and various observances, ecclesiastical and secular, connected therewith; such were the boy-bishop and, especially in Germany, Switzerland and the Netherlands, the giving of presents in his name at Christmas time.

7 : ST AMBROSE, BISHOP OF MILAN, DOCTOR OF THE CHURCH (A.D. 397)

AT the time of Ambrose's birth at Trier, probably in 340, his father, whose name also was Ambrose, was prefect of Gaul. Ambrose senior died while his youngest child was still young, and his widow returned with her family to Rome. She took great care in the upbringing of her children, and Ambrose owed much both to her and to his sister, St Marcellina. He learned Greek, became a good poet and orator, went to the bar, and was soon taken notice of, particularly by Anicius Probus and Symmachus, the last-named being prefect of Rome and still a pagan. The other was praetorian prefect of Italy, and in his court St Ambrose pleaded causes with so much success that

Probus made choice of him to be his assessor. Then the emperor Valentinian made him governor of Liguria and Aemilia, with his residence at Milan.

Auxentius, an Arian, who had held the see of Milan for almost twenty years, died in 374. The city was distracted by party strife about the election of a new bishop, some demanding an Arian, others a Catholic. To prevent, if possible, too outrageous a disorder St Ambrose went to the church in which the assembly was held. There he made a speech to the people, exhorting them to proceed in their choice in the spirit of peace and without tumult. While he was speaking a voice cried out: 'Ambrose, bishop!' and the whole assembly took up the cry with enthusiasm. This unexpected choice astounded Ambrose, for though professedly a Christian, he was still unbaptized.

A relation of all that had passed was sent to the emperor, and Ambrose wrote also on his own behalf, asking that he might be excused. Valentinian answered that it gave him the greatest pleasure that he had chosen governors who were fit for the episcopal office; and at the same time sent an order to the *vicarius* of the province to see that the election took place. In the meantime Ambrose tried to escape, and hid himself in the house of the senator Leontius, who, when he heard the imperial decision, gave him up, and Ambrose received episcopal consecration a week later, on December 7, 374. He was about thirty-five years old.

St Ambrose was acutely conscious of his ignorance of theological science, and at once applied himself to study the Holy Scriptures and the works of religious writers, particularly Origen and St Basil. His personal life was one of simplicity and hard work; he dined only on Sundays, the feasts of certain famous martyrs, and all Saturdays, on which it was the custom at Milan never to fast (but when he was at Rome he fasted on Saturdays); he excused himself from going to banquets, and entertained others with decent frugality. Every day he offered the Holy Sacrifice for his people, and devoted himself entirely to the service of his flock, any member of which could see and speak with him at any time, so that his people loved and admired him. It was his rule never to have any hand in making matches, never to persuade anyone to serve in the army, and never recommend to places at court. Ambrose in his discourses frequently spoke in praise of the state and virtue of virginity undertaken for God's sake, and he had many consecrated virgins under his direction. At the request of his sister, St Marcellina, he collected his sermons on this subject, making thereby a famous treatise. Mothers tried to keep their daughters away from his sermons, and he was charged with trying to depopulate the empire. Wars, he said, and not maidens, are the destroyers of the human race.

The Goths having invaded Roman territories in the East, the Emperor Gratian determined to lead an army to the succour of his uncle, Valens. But in order to guard himself against Arianism, of which Valens was the protector, he asked St Ambrose for instruction against that heresy. He accordingly wrote in 377 the work entitled *To Gratian, concerning the Faith*, which he afterwards expanded. After the murder of Gratian in 383 the Empress Justina implored St Ambrose to treat with the usurper Maximus lest he attack her son, Valentinian II. He went and induced Maximus at Trier to confine himself to Gaul, Spain and Britain. This is said to have been the first occasion on which a minister of the gospel was called on to interfere in matters of high politics.

At this time certain senators at Rome attempted to restore the cult of the goddess of Victory. At their head was Quintus Aurelius Symmachus, son and successor of that prefect of the city who had patronized the young Ambrose, and an admirable scholar, statesman and orator. This man presented a request to Valentinian begging that the altar of Victory might be re-established in the senate-house; to it he ascribed the victories and prosperity of ancient Rome. It was a skilfully drawn and in some respects moving document. 'What does it matter', he asked, 'the way in which each seeks for truth? There must be more than one road to the great mystery.' The petition was particularly a covert attack on St Ambrose and he remonstrated with the emperor for not having at once consulted him, since it was a matter of religion. He then drew up a reply whose eloquence surpassed that of Symmachus. Both documents, that of Symmachus and that of Ambrose, were read before Valentinian in council. There was no discussion. Then the emperor spoke: 'My father did not take away the altar. Nor was he asked to put it back. I therefore follow him in changing nothing that was done before my time.'

The Empress Justina dared not openly espouse the interests of the Arians during the lives of her husband and of Gratian, but when the peace which St Ambrose arranged between Maximus and her son gave her an opportunity to oppose the Catholic bishop, she forgot the obligations which she had to him. When Easter was near, in 385, she induced Valentinian to demand the Portian basilica, now called St Victor's, outside Milan, for the use of the Arians, herself and many officers of the court. The saint replied that he could never give up the temple of God. By messengers Valentinian then demanded the new basilica of the Apostles; but the bishop was inflexible. Officers of the court were sent to take possession of the basilica.

Throughout these troubles, when St Ambrose had the bulk of the excited people and even of the army on his side, he was studiously careful to say or do nothing that would precipitate violence or endanger the position of the emperor and his mother. He was resolute in his refusal to give up the churches, but would not himself officiate in either for fear of creating disturbance. While he was expounding a passage of Job to the people in a chapel a party of soldiers, who had been sent to take charge of the larger basilica, came in. They had refused to obey orders and wished to pray with the Catholics. At once the people surged into the adjoining basilica, and tore down the decorations put up for the emperor's visit, giving them to the children to play with. But Ambrose did not enter the church himself until Easter day, when Valentinian had ordered the guards to be removed, upon which all joined in joy and thanksgiving.

In January of the following year Justina persuaded her son to make a law authorizing the religious assemblies of the Arians and, in effect, proscribing those of the Catholics. It forbade anyone, under pain of death, to oppose Arian assemblies, and no one could so much as present a petition against a church being yielded up to them without danger of being proscribed. St Ambrose disregarded the law, would not give up a single church, and no one dare touch him.

On Palm sunday he preached on not giving up churches, and then, fears being entertained for his life, the people barricaded themselves in the basilica with their pastor. The imperial troops surrounded the place to starve them out, but on Easter Sunday they were still there. To occupy their time Ambrose taught the people psalms and hymns composed by himself, which they sang at his direction divided into two choirs singing alternate stanzas. Then Dalmatius, a tribune, came to St Ambrose from the emperor, with an order that he should choose judges, as the Arian bishop, Auxentius, had done on his side, that his and Auxentius's cause might be tried before them; if he refused, he was forthwith to retire and yield his see to Auxentius. Ambrose wrote asking to be excused and forcibly reminding Valentinian that laymen (lay-judges had been stipulated) could not judge bishops or make ecclesiastical laws. Then he occupied his episcopal *cathedra* and related to the people all that had passed between him and Valentinian during the previous year. And in a memorable sentence he summed up the principle at stake: 'The emperor is in the Church, not over it.'

Meanwhile it became known that Maximus was preparing to invade Italy. Valentinian and Justina asked St Ambrose to venture on a second embassy to stop the march of a usurper. At Trier Maximus refused to admit him to audience except in public consistory, though he was both bishop and imperial ambassador. When, therefore, he was introduced into the consistory and Maximus rose to give him a kiss, Ambrose stood still and refused to approach to receive it. On his arrival St Ambrose had refused to hold communion with the court prelates who had connived at the execution of the heretic Priscillian, which meant with Maximus himself, and the next day he was ordered to leave Trier. He therefore returned to Milan, writing to Valentinian an account of events and advising him to be cautious how he treated with Maximus. Then Maximus suddenly marched into Italy. Leaving St Ambrose alone to meet the storm at Milan, Justina and Valentinian fled to Greece and threw themselves on the mercy of the Eastern emperor, Theodosius. He declared war on Maximus, defeated and executed him in Pannonia, and restored Valentinian to his own territories and to those of the dead usurper. But henceforward Theodosius was the real ruler of the whole empire.

As was almost inevitable, conflicts arose between Theodosius himself and Ambrose, in the first of which right does not seem to have been wholly on the side of the bishop. At Kallinikum, in Mesopotamia, Christians pulled down the synagogue. Theodosius, when informed of the affair, ordered the bishop to rebuild it. St Ambrose was appealed to, and he wrote a letter to Theodosius in which he based his protest, not on the uncertainty of the actual circumstances, but on the statement that no Christian bishop could pay for the erection of a building to be used for false worship. Theodosius disregarded the protest, and Ambrose preached against him to his face; whereupon a discussion took place between them in the church, and he would not go up to the altar to sing Mass till he had procured a promise of the revocation of the order.

In the year 390 news of a dreadful massacre committed at Thessalonica was brought to Milan. Butheric, the governor, had a charioteer put in prison for having seduced a servant in his family, and refused to release him when his appearance in the circus was demanded by the public. The people were so enraged that some officers were stoned to death and Butheric himself was slain. Theodosius ordered reprisals. While the people were assembled in the circus, soldiers surrounded it and rushed in on them. The slaughter continued for hours and seven thousand were massacred, without distinguishing age or sex or the innocent from the guilty. Ambrose took counsel with his fellow bishops. Then he wrote to Theodosius exhorting him to penance, and declaring that he neither could nor would receive his offering at the altar or celebrate the Divine Mysteries before him till that obligation was satisifed.

In the funeral oration over Theodosius, St Ambrose himself says simply that: 'He stripped himself of every sign of royalty and bewailed his sin openly in church. He, an emperor, was not ashamed to do the public penance which lesser individuals shrink from, and to the end of his life he never ceased to grieve for his error.' By this triumph of grace in Theodosius and of pastoral duty in Ambrose Christianity was vindicated as being no respecter of persons. And the emperor himself testified to the personal influence of St Ambrose. He was, he said, the only bishop he knew who was worthy of the name.

In 393 occurred the death of the young Valentinian, murdered by Arbogastes while alone among his enemies in Gaul. Arbogastes manoeuvred for the support of Ambrose for his ambitions but Ambrose left Milan before the arrival of Eugenius, the imperial nominee of Arbogastes, who now openly boasted the approaching overthrow of Christianity. St Ambrose went from city to city, strengthening the people against the invaders. Then he returned to his see and there received the letter of Theodosius announcing his victory over Arbogastes at Aquileia, the final blow to the old paganism within the empire. A few months later Theodosius himself died, in the arms of St Ambrose.

St Ambrose survived him only two years, and one of his last treatises was on the 'Goodness of Death'. His written works, mostly homiletical in origin, exegetical, theological, ascetical and poetical, were numerous; as the Roman empire declined in the West he inaugurated a new lease of life for its language, and in the service of Christianity. When he fell sick he foretold his death, but said he should live till Easter. On the day of his death he lay with his hands extended in the form of a cross for several hours, moving his lips in constant prayer. St Honoratus of Vercelli was there, resting in another room, when he seemed to hear a voice crying three times to him, 'Arise! Make haste! He is going'. He went down and gave him the Body of the Lord, and soon after St Ambrose was dead. It was Good Friday, April 4, 397, and he was about fifty-seven years old. He was buried on Easter day, and his relics rest under the high altar of his basilica, where they were buried in 835.

8 : ST ROMARIC, ABBOT (A.D. 653)

IN the account of St Amatus of Remiremont it is related how he brought about the conversion to God of a Merovingian nobleman named Romaric, who became a monk at Luxeuil; and how they afterwards went together to the estate of Romaric at Habendum in the Vosges, and established the monastery which was later known as Remiremont (*Romarici Mons*). The father of Romaric had lost his life and his lands at the hands of Queen Brunehilda, and his young son became a homeless wanderer; but at the time of his meeting St Amatus, Romaric was a person of distinction at the court of Clotaire II, with considerable property and a number of serfs. These he enfranchised, and it is said that when he was tonsured at Luxeuil several of these newly freed men presented themselves to the abbot for the same purpose. Remiremont was founded in 620 and St Amatus was its first abbot, but his duties soon devolved upon St Romaric, who at the time of his death had governed for thirty years.

Among the early recruits was the friend of Romaric, St Arnulfus of Metz, who about 629 came to end his days in a nearby hermitage. Shortly before his death St Romaric was disturbed by the news that Grimoald, the son of another old friend, Bd Pepin of Landen, was plotting to exclude the young prince Dagobert from the Austrasian throne. The aged abbot made his way to Metz, where he remonstrated with Grimoald and warned the nobles who supported him. They heard him quietly, treated him with courtesy, and sent him back to his monastery. Three days later St Romaric died.

9 : ST PETER FOURIER, CO-FOUNDER OF THE AUGUSTINIAN CANONESSES REGULAR OF OUR LADY (A.D. 1640)

PETER FOURIER was born at Mirecourt, in Lorraine, in 1565, and at the age of fifteen was sent by his father to the university directed by the Jesuits at Pont-à-Mousson, where he may have met Bd William Lacey, the future martyr, then studying there. He completed a very creditable course of studies and opened a school at his home, but he had already decided against a secular career and at the age of twenty joined the Canons Regular of St Augustine at Chaumousey. In 1589 he was ordained priest; it was not till some months later that his humility and sense of unworthiness would let him celebrate his first Mass, and then his abbot sent him back to the university for further theological study. He remained there for some years, took his doctorate, and displayed an astonishing memory. When he was recalled to his monastery he was appointed procurator and vicar of the abbey parish; he carried out his duties under most disheartening conditions, for the observance of the abbey was bad and his attempts to improve it were met with ridicule.

In 1597 he was offered the cure of souls in one of the three other parishes served by the canons, and he chose Mattaincourt, as that presented the greatest difficulties. He served his flock first by his prayers and by his example; he never forgot that he was a canon regular, subject to the vows of religion, and always lived with an austerity, poverty and simplicity befitting the monastic life; he dispensed with a fire, except for the comfort of visitors, and never refused the needy alms or advice whether spiritual or temporal. He was faced with what has been called the problem of 'leakage', and after much prayer and consideration he decided that the free education of children was a first necessity.

He first of all tackled the boys. But the time was not yet; St Peter Fourier saw at once that he had failed, wasted no more time on it, and turned his attention to four women volunteers, Alix Le Clercq, Ganthe André, Joan and Isabel de Louvroir. These he tested, put for training in the house of canonesses of Poussey in 1598, and in due course they opened a free school at Mattaincourt. The saint was a man of ideas in education and himself gave the mistresses a daily lesson in pedagogy. He required that the older girls should be taught how to draw up invoices and receipts, should be given practice in composition and in writing letters, and should be able to speak correctly. He urged that for their own good and the welfare of the state poor children as well as others should be educated in the love of God and as much as possible in everything that would help them to live with decency and dignity, and that their schooling was to cost nothing. He wrote some dialogues on the virtues and vices (with a particular eye to the shortcomings of his parishioners), which the children would recite before their elders in the church on Sunday afternoons. The new institute of nuns in 1616 received papal approval under the title of Canonesses Regular of St Augustine of the Congregation of Our Lady. In 1628 Pope Urban VIII allowed the nuns to take a fourth vow binding themselves to the *free* education of children. Father Fourier's chief partner, Alix Le Clercq, was beatified as co-foundress in 1947.

Monastic life was at a low ebb in Lorraine at that time, and in 1622, having had him appointed visitor to the canons regular by the Holy See, Mgr John de Porcelets de Maillane, Bishop of Toul, called on him to re-establish discipline in the houses of his order and to unite them all into one reformed congregation. His mission was not enthusiastically received, but in the following year the abbot of Lunéville handed over his monastery to St Peter Fourier and a handful of reformed canons. By 1629 the work was done, observance was re-established, and the canons regular of Lorraine formed into the Congregation of Our Saviour: St Peter, much against his wish, was elected their superior general in 1632.

It had been his hope that the reformed canons would undertake that work of educating boys which he had failed to establish in Mattaincourt, and they were quite willing to take it on. When therefore he sent representatives to Rome in 1627 to see about the recognition of the Congregation of Our Saviour, he told them to bring this matter up. They did, and were refused. But they did in fact do some educational work and had several colleges; and when the Jesuits were suppressed in the eighteenth century, those of Lorraine handed their colleges over to the canons regular.

St Peter Fourier was greatly attached to the house of Lorraine and Duke Charles IV, so that when in 1636 he was tendered the oath of allegiance to King Louis XIII he refused it and fled to Gray in Franche-Comté. Here in exile he spent the last four years of his life, as chaplain of a convent and teaching in the free school which he caused to be opened. He died on December 9, 1640, and was canonized in 1897.

10 : ST GREGORY III, POPE (A.D. 741)

AMONG the clergy at the funeral of Pope St Gregory II, in the year 731, there was a priest of Syrian nationality who was so well known for his holiness, learning and ability that the people spontaneously carried him off from the procession and elected him by acclamation to the vacant see; he accordingly became pope as Gregory III. He inherited from his predecessor the problem of dealing with the Emperor Leo III the Isaurian, who had begun a campaign against the veneration of holy images, and one of Gregory's first acts was to send a letter of protest. But the bearer, George, a priest, got frightened and returned to Rome without delivering it, to the indignation of the pope, who threatened to degrade him. So George set out again, but was seized by the imperial officers in Sicily and banished. Thereupon Gregory summoned a synod at Rome, where bishops, lower clergy and lay-people approved the excommunication of any who should condemn the veneration of images or destroy them. Leo retorted as some of his predecessors had done in similar circumstances: he sent ships to bring Gregory to Constantinople; but they were lost in a storm, so the emperor contented himself with seizing the papal estates in Calabria and Sicily and recognizing the jurisdiction of the patriarch of Constantinople over eastern Illyricum.

After this inauspicious beginning of his pontificate there was a period of peace, during which St Gregory rebuilt and decorated a number of churches; in particular he set up a row of pillars before the *confessio* of St Peter, with images of our Lord and the saints thereon and lamps burning around them, a mute but solid protest against Iconoclasm. He sent the *pallium* to St Boniface in Germany, and when the English missionary made his third visit to Rome, in 738, Gregory wrote an appeal to the 'Old Saxons': the letter consisted chiefly of quotations from the Bible, which perhaps were not very meaningful to its heathen recipients. It was this pope who sent the English monk St Willibald to help Boniface.

Towards the end of St Gregory's life the Lombards again threatened Rome. The pope sent a famous appeal for help to Charles Martel and the Franks of the West, rather than to the emperor in the East, but it was long before they could be induced to act. To the bishops of Tuscany Gregory wrote urging them to work for the recovery of four cities captured by the Lombards. Then on October 22, 741, Charles Martel died, and a few weeks later, on December 10, St Gregory III followed him to the grave.

11 : ST DAMASUS, POPE (A.D. 384)

POPE DAMASUS is said in the *Liber Pontificalis* to have been a Spaniard, which may be true of his extraction but he seems to have been born at Rome, where his father was a priest. Damasus himself was never married, and he became deacon in the church which his father served. When Pope Liberius died in 366, Damasus, who was then about sixty years old, was chosen bishop of Rome. His accession was far from unopposed, a minority electing another deacon, called Ursicinus or Ursinus, whom they supported with great violence. It appears that the civil power in its maintenance of Damasus used considerable cruelty. The adherents of the antipope were not easily quelled, and as late as 378 Damasus had to clear himself both before the Emperor Gratian and a Roman synod of a charge of incontinence maliciously laid against him by his enemies.

Pope St Damasus had to oppose several heresies, but in 380 Theodosius I in the East and Gratian in the West proclaimed Christianity, as professed by the bishops of Rome and Alexandria, to be the religion of the Roman state, and Gratian, on the petition of the Christian senators, supported by St Damasus, removed the altar of Victory from the senate-house and laid aside the title of Pontifex Maximus. In the following year the second ecumenical council was held, the first of Constantinople, at which the pope was represented by legates. But the action of Damasus that was most far-reaching was his patronage of St Jerome and encouragement of his biblical studies, which had their consummation in the Vulgate version of the Bible.

St Damasus is, too, specially remembered for his care for the relics and resting-places of the martyrs and for his work in the draining, opening out and adornment of the sacred catacombs and for the inscriptions which he set up therein.

St Damasus died on December 11, 384, at the age of about eighty. He had put up in the 'papal crypt' of the cemetery of St Callistus a general epitaph which ends:

> I, Damasus, wished to be buried here, but I feared
> to offend the ashes of these holy ones.

He was accordingly laid to rest with his mother and sister at a small church he had built on the Via Ardeatina; and among his epitaphs which have been preserved in writing is the one which he wrote for himself, an act of faith in Christ's resurrection and his own.

12 : ST JANE FRANCES DE CHANTAL, WIDOW,
CO-FOUNDRESS OF THE ORDER OF THE VISITATION (A.D. 1641)

THE father of St Jane de Chantal was Bénigne Frémyot, president of the *parlement* of Burgundy. M. Frémyot was left a widower whilst his children were yet in their infancy; but he took such care of their education that nothing was wanting for forming them in the practice of every religious duty and preparing them for life. Jane, who at her confirmation was called Frances, profited above the rest and was tenderly beloved by her father, who gave her in marriage when she was twenty years of age to Christopher de Rabutin, Baron de Chantal, then twenty-seven years old, an officer in the French army and an accomplished but penitent duellist; on his mother's side he was descended from Bd Humbeline, whose feast is kept on this same day. The marriage was solemnized at Dijon, and a few days after Jane Frances went with her husband to his seat at Bourbilly. She found an estate and household which since the death of her husband's mother had not been much accustomed to regularity, and the baroness made it her first care to establish order and good management. After three children had died soon after birth, they were blessed with a boy and three girls who throve.

The happiness of Bourbilly lasted only nine years. One day in 1601 M. de Chantal, in company with a friend, went out shooting; the circumstances are not known, but accidentally M. d'Aulézy shot him in the thigh. He survived nine days, during which he suffered great pain from the efforts of an unskilful surgeon and received the sacraments with edifying resignation. During the year of her mourning her father sent for her to his house at Dijon, where she lived with her children until she had to go with them to

Monthelon, near Autun, to live with the old Baron de Chantal, who was then seventy-five years of age. In 1604 St Francis de Sales came to preach the Lent at Dijon, and she went to stay with her father there that she might have the opportunity of hearing so celebrated a preacher. She recognized him as the person she had once seen in vision and knew him to be the spiritual director she had long begged of God to send her. She prevailed on St Francis after some difficulty to undertake her direction. By his advice she regulated her devotions and other exercises so as to conform herself to what she owed to the world whilst she lived in the houses of her father and father-in-law. She followed a strict rule of life, devoting much time to her children, and visited the poor that were sick in the neighbourhood and watched whole nights by those that were dying.

For some time various considerations, including the presence of Carme-lite nuns at Dijon, inclined Madame de Chantal to enter a cloister. When she had talked to St Francis about this he took some time to recommend the matter to God, and at length in 1607 he unfolded his project of forming a new establishment, a congregation of the Visitation of the Virgin Mary. St Francis having provided a house, called the Gallery House, on the edge of the lake at Annecy, he inaugurated his convent on Trinity Sunday, 1610. With St Jane Frances were clothed two other sisters, Mary Favre and Charlotte de Bréchard, and a servant, Anne Coste, and they were soon joined by ten others. So far the institute had no name, and indeed the founder had no certain idea of its scope, except that it was to be a haven for those whose health, age or other considerations debarred them from the already established orders, and that he wished the sisters to be unenclosed and so more free to undertake work for souls and bodies.

It encountered much opposition, from the usual failure of the narrow and unimaginative to understand anything new. St Francis changed the plan of the congregation so far as to make it an enclosed religious order, under the Rule of St Augustine, to which he added constitutions admirable in their wisdom and moderation. He wrote specifically for St Jane and her more experienced sisters his famous treatise *On the Love of God*.

The affairs of her children and the foundation of new convents obliged her often to leave Annecy. The year after she took the habit, upon the death of her father, she went to Dijon and stayed there some months to settle his affairs and place her son in a college. After convents had been established at Lyons, Moulins, Grenoble and Bourges, St Francis from Paris sent for Mother de Chantal to see about a foundation there, which she was able to bring about in 1619 in the face of open hostility and underhand intriguing. She governed her convent at Paris for three years, during which St Vincent de Paul directed it at the request of St Francis, and she made the acquaintance of Angélique Arnauld, abbess of Port-Royal, who failed to get permission to resign her office and join the Visitation Order.

In 1622 the death of St Francis was a grievous affliction to her, which her resignation to the divine will made her bear with unshaken constancy. In 1627 her son was killed fighting against the English and the Huguenots in the isle of Ré, in his thirty-first year, leaving his wife with a daughter not a year old, who became the celebrated Madame de Sévigné. During the following year a terrible plague ravaged France, Savoy and Piedmont, causing great suffering to several Visitation convents. When it reached Annecy St Jane Frances refused to leave the town, put all the resources of her convent at the disposal of the sick, and whipped up the local authorities to greater efforts on behalf of the sufferers. In 1632 came the news of the death of Celse-Bénigne's widow, and then of her much-loved son-in-law, Antony de Toulonjon, and of Michael Favre, the confessor of St Francis and a close and devoted friend of the Visitandines. To these bereavements were added interior anguish, darkness and spiritual dryness which she sometimes experienced to a terrible degree, as appears from several of her letters.

During the years 1635–6 St Jane Frances made a visitation of the convents of the order, which now numbered sixty-five and many of which had never seen their spiritual mother; and in 1641 she went into France on an errand of charity to Madame de Montmorency. It was her last journey. She was invited to Paris by the queen, Anne of Austria, and to her distress was treated there with great distinction and honour. On her return she fell ill on the road, in her convent at Moulins. There it was that she died on December 13, 1641, being sixty-nine years old. Her body was taken to Annecy and buried near St Francis de Sales; she was canonized in 1767.

13 : ST JUDOC, OR JOSSE, (A.D. 668)

JUDOC was a son of Juthaël, King of Armorica (Brittany), and brother of that Judicaël who has a cult in the diocese of Quimper.

About the year 636 Judoc withdrew from secular life and, it is said, was ordained priest of Ponthieu. After a pilgrimage to Rome he eventually settled as a hermit at Runiacum near the mouth of the Canche, later called after him, Saint-Josse. Here he died about the year 668. We are told that his body was not buried in the earth and that it remained incorrupt; moreover, the surprising circumstance is added that his hair, beard and nails continued to grow with such luxuriance that his successors in the hermitage had to cut them from time to time.

It is said that Charlemagne gave this hermitage at Saint-Josse-sur-Mer to Alcuin as a hospice for cross-Channel travellers, and that Alcuin sometimes stayed there. According to the tradition of the New Minster (Hyde) at Winchester, St Judoc's relics were brought there, about the year 901, and this translation was commemorated on January 9. Chaucer's *Wife of Bath* swears 'by God and by Seint Joce'.

14 : ST JOHN OF THE CROSS, DOCTOR OF THE CHURCH (A.D. 1591)

GONZALO DE YEPES belonged to a good Toledan family, but having married 'beneath him' he was disinherited and had to earn his living as a silk-weaver. On his death his wife, Catherine Alvarez, was left destitute with three children, of whom John, born at Fontiveros in Old Castile in 1542, was the youngest. He went to a poor-school at Medina del Campo and was then apprenticed to a weaver, but he showed no aptitude for the trade and was taken on as a servant by the governor of the hospital at Medina. He stopped there for seven years, already practising bodily austerities, and continuing his studies in the college of the Jesuits. At twenty-one years of age he took the religious habit among the Carmelite friars at Medina, receiving the name of John-of-St-Matthias. After his profession he asked for and was granted permission to follow the original Carmelite rule, without the mitigations approved by various popes and then accepted in all the friaries. It was John's desire to be a lay-brother, but this was refused him. He had given satisfaction in his course of theological studies, and in 1567 he was promoted to the priesthood.

St Teresa was then establishing her reformation of the Carmelites and, coming to Medina del Campo, heard of Brother John. She admired his spirit, and told him that God had called him to sanctify himself in the Order of Our Lady of Mount Carmel; that she had received authority from the prior general to found two reformed houses of men; and that he himself should be the first instrument of so great a work. Soon after the first monastery of discalced (*i.e.* barefooted) Carmelite friars was established in a small and dilapidated house at Duruelo. St John entered this new Bethlehem in a perfect spirit of sacrifice, and about two months after was joined by two others, who renewed their profession on Advent Sunday, 1568, St John taking the new religious name of John-of-the-Cross. The fame of the sanctity of this obscure house spread, and St Teresa soon established a second at Pastrana, a third at Mancera, whither she translated that from Duruelo, and in 1570 a fourth, at Alcalá, a college of the university, of which John was made rector. St John, after tasting the first joys of contemplation, found himself deprived of all sensible devotion. This spiritual dryness was followed by interior trouble of mind, scruples and a disrelish of spiritual exercises, and, while the Devil assaulted him with violent temptations, men persecuted him by calumnies. The most terrible of all these pains was that of scrupulosity and interior desolation, which he described in his book called *The Dark Night of the Soul*. This again was succeeded by another more grievous trial of spiritual darkness, accompanied with interior pain and temptations in which God seemed to have forsaken him. But in the calm which followed this terrible tempest he was wonderfully repaid with divine love and new light.

In 1571 St Teresa undertook, under obedience, the office of prioress of the unreformed convent of the Incarnation at Avila, and she sent for St John to be its spiritual director and confessor. He was sought out by seculars as well as religious, and God confirmed his ministry by evident miracles. But grave troubles were arising between the Discalced and the Mitigated Carmelites. The old friars looked on this reformation, though undertaken with the licence and approbation of the prior general given to St Teresa, as a rebellion against their order; on the other hand, some of the Discalced were tactless and exceeded their powers and rights. Moreover, confusing and contradictory policies were pursued by the prior general, the general chapter and the papal nuncios respectively. At length, in 1577, the provincial of Castile ordered St John to return to his original friary at Medina. He refused, on the ground that he held his office from the papal nuncio and not from the order. Whereupon armed men were sent, who broke open his door and carried him off. Knowing the veneration which the people of Avila had for him, they removed him to Toledo, where he was pressed to abandon the reform. When he refused he was locked up in a small cell that had practically no light.

St John's cell measured some ten feet by six, and the one window was so small and high up that he had to stand on a stool by it to see to read his office. He was bloodily beaten—he bore the marks to his dying day—publicly in chapter, by order of Jerome Tostado, vicar general of the Carmelites in Spain and a consultor of the Inquisition. St John's were all those sufferings described in St Teresa's 'Sixth Mansion'—insults, slanders, physical pain, agony of soul and temptation to give in. But, 'Do not be surprised', he said in after years, 'if I show a great love of suffering; God gave me a high idea of its value when I was in prison at Toledo'. And his immediate answer was his earliest poems, a voice crying in the wilderness.

John made his escape after nine months in prison, and fled to the reformed friary of Beas de Segura and then to the nearby hermitage of Monte Calvario; in 1579 he became head of the college at Baeza, and in 1581 he was chosen prior of Los Martires, near Granada. Though the male founder and spiritual leader of the Discalced friars he took little part during these years, when their continued existence hung in the balance, in the negotiations and events which led up to the establishment of a separate province for the Discalced in 1580. Instead he began those writings which have made him a doctor of the Church in mystical theology.

After the death of St Teresa in 1582 a disagreement within the ranks of the Discalced friars themselves became more pronounced, St John favouring the moderate policy of the prior provincial, Father Jerome Gracián, against the extremist Father Nicholas Doria, who aimed at separating the Discalced completely from the old stock. After Father Nicholas himself became provincial, the chapter made St John vicar for Andalusia and he applied himself to the correction of certain abuses, especially those arising from the necessity of religious going out of their monasteries for the purpose of preaching. It was his opinion that their vocation and life was primarily contemplative. Thus opposition was raised against him. He founded more friaries, and on the expiry of his term of office went as prior to Granada. The policy of Father Nicholas had so prospered that a chapter held at Madrid in 1588 received a brief from the Holy See authorizing a further separation of the Discalced Carmelites from the Mitigated. In spite of protests the venerable Father Jerome Gracián was deprived of all authority; Father Nicholas Doria was made vicar general; and the one province was divided into six, with a consultor for each (St John himself was one) to help him in the government of the new congregation. This innovation caused grave discontent, especially among the nuns, and the Venerable Anne-of-Jesus, then prioress at Madrid, obtained from the Holy See a brief confirming their constitutions, without reference to the vicar general. The consequent troubles were eventually composed, but at a chapter held at Whitsun 1591, St John spoke in defence both of Father Jerome Gracián and of the nuns. Father Nicholas Doria had suspected him all along of being in league with them, and he now took the opportunity of reducing St John from all offices to the status of a simple friar and sending him to the remote friary of La

Peñuela. Here he spent some months, passing his days in meditation and prayer among the mountains.

But there were those who would not leave St John alone even here. When visiting Seville as vicar provincial he had had occasion to restrict the preaching activities of two friars and to recall them to the observance of their rule. They submitted at the time, but the rebuke had rankled, and now one of them, Father Diego, who had become a consultor of the congregation, went about over the whole province making inquiries about St John's life and conduct, trumping up accusations, and boasting that he had sufficient proofs to have him expelled from the order.

John in the midst of all this was taken ill, and the provincial ordered him to leave out-of-the-way Peñuela and gave him the choice to go either to Baeza or Ubeda. The first was a convenient convent and had for prior a friend of the saint. At the other Father Francis was prior, the other person whom he had corrected with Father Diego. St John chose this house of Ubeda. The fatigue of his journey made him worse, he suffered great pain, and submitted cheerfully to several operations. But the unworthy prior treated him with inhumanity, forbade any one to see him, changed the infirmarian because he served him with tenderness, and would not allow him any but the ordinary food. The provincial did all he could for the saint, and reprimanded Father Francis so sharply that he was brought to repentance for his malice. After suffering acutely for nearly three months, St John died on December 14, 1591, still under the cloud which the ambition of Father Nicholas and the revengefulness of Father Diego had raised against him in the congregation of which he was co-founder and whose life he had been the first to take up.

15 : ST MARY DI ROSA, VIRGIN, FOUNDRESS OF THE HANDMAIDS OF CHARITY OF BRESCIA (A.D. 1855)

MARY DI ROSA (called Paula or Pauline at home), born in 1813, was sixth of the nine children of Clement di Rosa, and his wife, Countess Camilla Albani. Her childhood was uneventful, but saddened by the death of her deeply loved mother when Paula was eleven. When she was seventeen Paula left school to look after the household for her father, and he began to look around for a suitable husband for her. When he had found one, Paula was rather startled, and took her difficulties to the archpriest of the cathedral, Mgr Faustino Pinzoni, a sagacious priest who had already dealt prudently with her spiritual problems. He decided himself to see Clement di Rosa, and explained gently to him that his daughter had decided that she would never marry.

During the next ten years Paula continued to live at home, but engaging herself more and more in social good works, in which she had the worthy example of her father before her eyes. Among his properties was a textile mill at Acquafredda where a number of girls worked, and one of Paula's first undertakings was to look after the spiritual welfare of these young women; this solicitude she extended to those of Capriano, where the Rosas had a country house. Here, with the co-operation of the parish priest, she established a women's guild and arranged retreats and special missions in the parish. The cholera epidemic that devastated Brescia in 1836 gave Paula di Rosa another opportunity. She asked her father's permission to work in the hospital, and after some doubt and with considerable trepidation he agreed. The hospital welcomed Paula, who was accompanied by a widow, Gabriela Echenos-Bornati, who had already had some experience of nursing the sick, and they set an example of selfless hard work and gentle care that made a very deep impression on everybody.

In consequence Paula was asked to undertake the supervision of an institution which was a sort of workhouse for penniless and abandoned girls—a delicate and difficult post for a young woman of only twenty-four. She filled it successfully for two years, but then resigned in consequence of a difference with the trustees, who did not want the girls to lodge in the house at night. Paula herself then established a small lodging-house with room for a dozen girls to sleep, and at the same time gave her attention to a work that had been projected by her brother Philip and Mgr Pinzoni, namely, a school for deaf-and-dumb girls, on the lines of what Ludovic Pavoni was doing for boys. This school was still in its infancy when Paula handed it over to the Canossian sisters, who wished to do the same work in Brescia on a bigger scale.

All this was a really extraordinary ten-year record for a woman still under thirty and of delicate health and physique. But she had physical energy and courage – she once rescued somebody from a bolting horse and carriage in very dangerous circumstances. And her mind was quick, acute and steady. She acquired an unusual knowledge of theology, and brought to her reading the same liveliness of spirit and delicacy of perception that informed her dealings with practical affairs. Her mental ability was particularly noted when she became involved in the complexities inseparable from the establishment of a religious congregation, and she was further helped by a remarkably good memory.

This congregation began to take shape in 1840, first in the form of a religious society of which Paula was appointed superioress by the Archpriest Pinzoni. With her was associated Mrs Bornati (who indeed may be called co-foundress), and the object of the society was to look after the sick in hospitals, not simply as nurses but as giving the whole of their time and interest unreservedly to the sick and suffering. They took the name of Handmaids of Charity, and the first four members took up their residence in a dilapidated house near the hospital; these were soon joined by fifteen Tirolese, who had heard about the undertaking from a visiting missioner, and before long the community numbered thirty-two. Their work aroused admiration that was publicly expressed in the press by a local doctor, who underlined the spiritual as well as the physical activities of the handmaids.

Before long a new and more commodious house in Brescia was given to the handmaids by Clement di Rosa, and their provisional rule of life was approved by the bishop in 1843; but there was a counter-balance to these causes for rejoicing a few months later, when Gabriela Bornati died. Paula was thus deprived of her chief lieutenant, but she still had Mgr Pinzoni to advise and guide her, and the society continued to grow and to undertake the direction of new hospitals. But in the summer of 1848 death took the archpriest too, and that at a time when political upheaval was convulsing Europe and war had come to northern Italy. Paula's first response to new opportunities was to staff St Luke's military hospital, where again the handmaids had to meet the opposition of doctors who preferred secular nurses and military orderlies. Civilian victims of war and prisoners were succoured and, anticipating Florence Nightingale by several years, the Handmaids of Charity ministered to the souls and bodies of the wounded on the battlefields.

Paula aimed at a body of sisters who should combine spiritual with temporal care, lives of prayer and work. In the autumn of 1850 she set out for Rome; on October 24 she was received by the pope, Pius IX; and two months later, with most remarkable speed for Rome, the constitutions of the congregation of Handmaids of Charity of Brescia were approved. The approval of the civil power was less speedy, and it was not till the summer of 1852 that the first twenty-five sisters and their foundress made their vows, and Paula took the name of Maria Crocifissa, 'Mary of the Crucified'. There was still work to be done—a threat of cholera at Brescia, convents to be opened at Spalato in Dalmatia and near Verona. Then at Mantua she collapsed, and reached home only to say, 'Thank God He has let me get home to Brescia to die'. And die she did, very peacefully and quietly, three weeks later, on December 15, 1855.

16 : ST ADELAIDE, EMDPRESS (A.D. 999)

WHEN in the year 933 Rudolf II of Upper Burgundy concluded a treaty with Hugh of Provence in their struggle for the crown of Italy (Lombardy), one of the terms was that Rudolf's daughter, Adelaide, then a baby of two, should marry Hugh's son, Lothair. Fourteen years later her brother, Conrad of Burgundy, saw to the fulfilling of this contract, Lothair being by then nominally king of Italy, but actually in the power of Berengarius of Ivrea. One child was born of the marriage, Emma (she eventually married Lothair II of France), and in 950 Lothair of Italy died, not without strong suspicion of having been poisoned by Berengarius, who succeeded him. Berengarius then tried to make Adelaide marry his son, and on her refusal treated her with brutality and indignity, and shut her up in a castle on Lake Garda. At this time the German king, Otto the Great, was leading an army into Italy to try to reduce the north to order. He defeated Berengarius and released Adelaide; or, as it is said, she escaped from her prison and joined him. To consolidate his authority in Italy, Otto married Adelaide, who was twenty years his junior, on Christmas day 951, at Pavia. Of this union five children were born. Ludolf, Otto's son by his first wife (sister of Athelstan of England), was jealous of the influence of his stepmother and her children and became a centre of discontent and rebellion, but to the German people the gentle and gracious Adelaide soon endeared herself. In 962 Otto was crowned emperor at Rome. Nothing is heard of Adelaide for the next ten years, till in 973 her husband died and their eldest son succeeded.

Otto II soon estranged his mother and allowed himself to be turned against her by his wife, the Byzantine Theophano, and other counsellors. Adelaide left the court and went to her brother, Conrad, at Vienne. She appealed to St Majolus, abbot of Cluny, whom she had wanted to see made pope when Benedict VI was murdered in 974, and he eventually succeeded in bringing about a reconciliation; mother and son met at Pavia, and Otto asked pardon on his knees for his unkindness.

But similar trouble came when Otto died in 983. Otto III was a baby and his mother, Theophano, became regent. She had the flair for politics of the great Byzantine princesses and in this respect was more capable than her mother-in-law. Adelaide again left the court, but Theophano died suddenly in 991 and the old empress came back to be herself regent, a task now beyond her strength and peace-loving nature, though she had the assistance of St Willigis of Mainz. Throughout her life she had shown herself generous and forgiving to enemies, and amenable to the wise guidance in turn of St Adalbert of Magdeburg, St Majolus and St Odilo of Cluny. She founded and restored monasteries of monks and nuns, and urged the conversion of the Slavs, whose movements on the eastern frontier troubled her closing years before she finally returned to Burgundy. Death overtook her at a monastery of her foundation at Seltz, on the Rhine near Strasburg, on December 16, 999.

17 : ST STURMI, ABBOT (A.D. 779)

STURMI, the son of Christian parents in Bavaria, was entrusted to the care of St Boniface who left him to be educated under St Wigbert in his abbey of Fritzlar. He was there in due course ordained priest and did mission work in Westphalia for three years, after which he was allowed with two companions to lead an eremitical life in the forest at Hersfeld. This place was unprotected from the marauding Saxons, and was soon abandoned. St Boniface had found a district further south more suitable for a monastery from which the Saxons could be evangelized, and St Sturmi rode down into it on his donkey and selected a site at the junction of the Greizbach and the Fulda. In 744 the monastery of Fulda was founded, St Boniface appointing St Sturmi its first abbot. It was the favourite foundation of St Boniface, who intended it to be the pattern monastery and seminary of priests for all Germany; he used frequently to visit it to superintend its progress, and his body was buried in the abbey church.

Soon after its foundation St Sturmi went into Italy to study Benedictine observance at its fountain-head at Monte Cassino, and it seems that Pope St Zachary gave his monastery complete autonomy by withdrawing it from episcopal jurisdiction and subjecting it directly to the Holy See. The abbey of Fulda continued to prosper under St Sturmi, but he was involved in serious difficulties after the martyrdom of St Boniface, for the attitude of his successor at Mainz, St Lull, towards the monastery was very different. Lull claimed that it should be subject to him as bishop, and the ensuing struggle was long and bitter. In 763 an order was obtained from Pepin for the banishment of Sturmi, and Lull nominated a superior in his place, but the monks of Fulda refused to accept him and expelled him from the house, threatening that they would go in a body and appeal to the king. To pacify them Lull told them to choose a superior of their own, whereupon they elected a life-long disciple of Sturmi. He took a deputation of monks to court, and they were successful in inducing Pepin to recall their beloved abbot, who returned to Fulda amid great rejoicing after two years of exile.

The efforts of St Sturmi and his monks to convert the Saxons did not meet with much external success, and the wars of Pepin and Charlemagne, first punitive and then of conquest, were not calculated to recommend his religion to the heathen. When Charlemagne was recalled from Paderborn to attack the Moors in Spain, the Saxons at once rose and drove out the monks; Fulda itself was threatened. In 779, Charlemagne returned and St Sturmi accompanied him to the mobilization at Düren which preceded fresh military success against the Saxons, but he did not live to recommence his missions. He was taken ill at Fulda and, in spite of the efforts of the physician sent by Charlemagne, died on December 17, 779. The name of St Sturmi was added to the roll of saints in 1139; he is apparently the first German known to have become a Benedictine monk.

18 : ST FLANNAN, BISHOP (SEVENTH CENTURY?)

S T FLANNAN is venerated as the first bishop of Killaloe, a diocese nearly conterminous with the district of Thomond, of which his father, Turlough, was chieftain. According to his very late life, Flannan determined, in spite of the opposition of his friends and relatives, to make a pilgrimage to Rome, and he achieved the voyage in the miraculous manner common in Celtic hagiology, namely, on a floating stone. While there he was consecrated bishop by Pope John IV (d. 642).

The teaching of St Flannan caused his father in his old age to become a monk under St Colman at Lismore. Three of his sons having been killed, Turlough asked Colman for a special blessing on his family. Whereupon Colman made seven strides and said, 'From you shall seven kings spring': and so it was, all of them called Brian. Flannan was afraid that the kingship would descend to him, and that he might be ineligible for it he prayed that he should be visited with a physical deformity. Accordingly, says his biographer, 'scars and rashes and boils began to appear on his face so that it became most dreadful and repulsive'. St Flannan is supposed to have preached as well in the Western Isles: a small group off the west coast of Lewis, the Seven Hunters, is also known by his name. Several great marvels are attributed to him, as well as such Celtic practices as reciting his office immersed in icy water.

19 : ST ANASTASIUS I, POPE (A.D. 401)

S T ANASTASIUS was a Roman and the successor of St Siricius in the year 399; among his friends and admirers were St Jerome, St Augustine and St Paulinus of Nola. The first named wrote of him that he was a distinguished man, of blameless life and apostolic solicitude, whom Rome did not deserve to possess long lest the world's head be cut off while ruled by such a bishop (referring to the subsequent invasion by Alaric the Goth). St Jerome was as kind in speaking of his friends as he was merciless to his opponents, and Anastasius earned his gratitude by condemning certain writings of Origen (d. 254), about which Jerome was having a fierce controversy with Rufinus.

20 : ST DOMINIC OF SILOS, ABBOT (A.D. 1073)

DOMINIC was born at the beginning of the eleventh century at Cañas in Navarre, on the Spanish side of the Pyrenees. His people were peasants, and for a time he followed their way of life, looking after his father's flocks among the foothills of the mountains. This work encouraged his taste for solitude and quietness, and he soon became a monk at the monastery of San Millán de la Cogolla. He made great progress in his new state, was entrusted with works of reform, and became prior of his monastery. In this office he came into conflict with his sovereign, Garcia III of Navarre, because he refused to give up some possessions of the monastery which were claimed by the king. Garcia at length drove Dominic and two other monks away, and they were welcomed by Ferdinand I of Old Castile, who sent them to the monastery of St Sebastian at Silos, of which Dominic was appointed abbot. The monastery was in a remote part of the diocese of Burgos, and was in a state of extreme decay, both materially and spiritually. Under the government of St Dominic this decay was arrested, then the house began to progress, and eventually he made it one of the most famous in Spain. Many miracles were recorded of Dominic in the course of his work, and it was said that there were no diseases known to man which had not been cured by his prayers.

Dominic died on December 20, 1073.

21 : ST PETER CANISIUS, DOCTOR OF THE CHURCH (A.D. 1597)

ST PETER CANISIUS has been called the Second Apostle of Germany—St Boniface being the first—but he is also honoured as one of the creators of a Catholic press. Born in the year 1521 at Nijmegen in Holland, then a German Reichstadt in the archdiocese of Cologne, he was the eldest son of Jacob Kanis, who had been ennobled after acting as tutor to the sons of the Duke of Lorraine and who was nine times burgomaster of Nijmegen. Although Peter had the misfortune to lose his mother at an early age, his father's second wife proved an excellent stepmother, and he grew up having before his eyes the fear of God. He accuses himself of having wasted time as a boy, but in view of the fact that he took his master of arts degree at Cologne University when he was only nineteen, it is difficult to believe that he was ever really idle. To please his father, who wished him to be a lawyer, he proceeded to Louvain, where for a few months he studied canon law. Realizing, however, that he was not called to this career he refused marriage, took a vow of celibacy, and returned to Cologne to read theology.

Great interest had been aroused in the Rhineland towns by the preaching of Bd Peter Faber (Favre), the first disciple of St Ignatius; Canisius attended an Ignatian retreat which Faber gave at Mainz, and during the second week made a vow to join the new order. Admitted as a novice, he lived for some years a community life in Cologne, spending his time in prayer, in study, in visiting the sick and instructing the ignorant. He had already begun to write, his first publications having been editions of the works of St Cyril of Alexandria and St Leo the Great. After his ordination to the priesthood, he came into prominence for his preaching; and as a delegate to the Council of Trent he had attended two of its sessions, the one at Trent and the other at Bologna, when he was summoned to Rome by St Ignatius, who retained him by his side for five months. He was sent to Messina to teach in the first Jesuit school known to history, but very shortly was recalled to Rome for his solemn profession and to be given a more important charge.

The order was to return to Germany, he having been selected to go to Ingolstadt with two brother Jesuits, in response to an urgent appeal from Duke William IV of Bavaria for Catholic professors capable of counteracting the heretical teaching which was permeating the schools. Not only was Peter Canisius successful in reforming the university, of which he was made rector and afterwards vice-chancellor, but he also effected a real religious revival amongst the people by his sermons, his catechizing, and his campaign against the sale of immoral or heretical books. In 1552 the saint was withdrawn to undertake, at the request of King Ferdinand, a somewhat similar mission in Vienna. He found that great city in a worse condition than Ingolstadt. At first Peter Canisius preached to almost empty churches, partly because of the general disaffection and partly because his Rhineland German grated on the ears of the Viennese; but he found his way to the heart of the people by his indefatigable ministrations to the sick and dying during an outbreak of the plague.

The king, the nuncio, the pope himself wanted him appointed to the vacant see of Vienna, but St Ignatius could be induced only to allow him to administer the diocese for one year, and that without episcopal orders, title or emoluments. It was about this period that St Peter began work on his famous catechism, or Summary of Christian Doctrine, published in 1555; this was followed by a Shorter and a Shortest Catechism—both of which attained enormous popularity.

In Prague, to which he was sent to found a college, he was dismayed to learn that he was to be provincial of a newly-established province covering South Germany, Austria and Bohemia. In the course of his two years' residence in Prague, Peter Canisius in great measure won back the city to the faith, and he established the college on such excellent lines that even Protestants were glad to send their sons to it. In 1557 he went by special invitation to Worms to take part in a discussion between Catholic and Protestant divines, although he was firmly convinced from past experience that all such conferences on doctrine were worse than useless, the heated discussions which always took place only widening the chasm between the disputants.

Apart from the colleges he actually founded or inaugurated, he prepared the way for many others. In 1559, at the wish of King Ferdinand, he took up his residence in Augsburg, and this town continued to be his headquarters for six years. Here again the lamp of faith was rekindled by his efforts as he encouraged the faithful, reclaimed the lapsed, and converted many heretics. Amongst the works he himself produced at the time may be mentioned a selection of St Jerome's letters, a 'Manual for Catholics', a martyrology and a revision of the Augsburg Breviary. The General Prayer which he composed is still recited in Germany on Sundays. At the close of his term of office as provincial, St Peter took up his abode at Dillingen in Bavaria, where the Jesuits not only had a college of their own but also directed the university. The town had for him the additional attraction of being the favourite place of residence of Cardinal Otto Truchsess who had long been his close friend. He occupied himself mainly in teaching, in hearing confessions, and in the composition of the first of a series of books he had undertaken by order of his superiors. They were intended as a reply to a strongly anti-Catholic history of Christianity which was being published by certain Protestant writers commonly known as the Centuriators of Magdeburg. This work he continued afterwards whilst acting as court chaplain for some years at Innsbruck, and until 1577, when he was dispensed from proceeding with it on the score of his health. There seems to have been no curtailment of his activities in other directions, for we find him still preaching, giving missions, accompanying the provincial on his visitations, and even filling the post of vice-provincial.

Canisius was at Dillingen when, in the year 1580, he was instructed to go to Fribourg in Switzerland. That city, which was the capital of a Catholic canton wedged in between two powerful Protestant neighbours, had long desired a college but had been handicapped by lack of funds and other difficulties. These obstacles were surmounted within a few years by St Peter, who obtained the money, selected the site, and superintended the erection of the splendid college which developed into the present University of Fribourg. For over eight years his principal work was preaching: on Sundays and festivals he delivered sermons in the cathedral, on weekdays he visited other parts of the canton. It may confidently be asserted that to St Peter Canisius is due the credit of having retained Fribourg in the Catholic fold at a critical period of its history. Increasing bodily infirmities obliged him to give up preaching, and in 1591 a paralytic seizure brought him to the brink of the grave, but he recovered sufficiently to continue writing, with the help of a secretary, until shortly before his death, which took place on December 21, 1597.

St Peter Canisius was canonized and declared a doctor of the Church in 1925.

22 : SS. CHAEREMON, ISCHYRION, AND OTHER MARTYRS (A.D. 250)

ST DIONYSIUS OF ALEXANDRIA in his letter to Fabian of Antioch, speaking of the Egyptian Christians who suffered in the persecution under Decius, refers to the many who were driven or fled into the desert, where they perished from hunger, thirst and exposure, by wild beasts and by men as wild; many also were seized and sold into slavery, of which only some had been ransomed at the time he wrote.

He singles out for mention by name Chaeremon, a very old man and bishop of Nilopolis, who with one companion had taken refuge in the mountains of Arabia and had never been seen or heard of again; search was made by the brethren but not even their bodies were found. St Dionysius also mentions Ischyrion, who was the procurator of a magistrate in some city of Egypt, traditionally Alexandria. His master ordered him to sacrifice to the gods, but he refused and neither abuse nor threats could move him. So the enraged magistrate had him mutilated and impaled.

23 : ST JOHN OF KANTI, (A.D. 1473)

JOHN CANTIUS receives his name from his birthplace, Kanti, near Oswiecim in Poland. His parents were country folk of respectable position and, seeing that their son was as quick and intelligent as he was good, they sent him in due course to the University of Cracow. He took good degrees, was ordained priest, and appointed to a lectureship or chair in the university. He was known to lead a very strict life, and when he was warned to look after his health he replied by pointing out that the fathers of the desert were notably long-lived.

John's success as a preacher and teacher raised up envy against him, and his rivals managed to get him removed and sent as parish priest to Olkusz. St John turned to his new work with single-hearted energy, but his parishioners did not like him and he himself was afraid of the responsibilities of his position. Nevertheless he persevered for some years, and by the time he was recalled to Cracow had won his people's hearts.

St John's second appointment at the university was as professor of Sacred Scripture, and he held it to the end of his life. He left such a reputation that his doctoral gown was for long used to vest each candidate at the conferring of degrees, but his fame was not at all confined to academic circles. He was a welcome guest at the tables of the nobility, and he was known to all the poor in Cracow. His goods and money were always at their disposition. His own needs were few; he slept on the floor, never ate meat, and when he went to Rome he walked all the way and carried his luggage on his back. Several miracles were reported of St John, and when news got round the city that he was dying there was an outburst of sorrow. 'Never mind about this prison which is decaying', he said to those who were looking after him, 'but think of the soul that is going to leave it.' He died on Christmas eve, 1473, at the age of eighty-three. St John Cantius was canonized in 1767.

24 : SS. IRMINA, VIRGIN, AND ADELA, WIDOW (C. A.D. 710 AND C. 734)

ACCORDING to tradition the Princess Irmina, a daughter of St Dagobert II, was to have been married to a Count Herman. All preparations had been made for the wedding at Trier when one of the princess's officers, who was himself in love with her, inveigled Herman to a steep cliff outside the town and there threw his rival and himself over the edge. After this tragic end to her hopes Irmina obtained her father's permission to become a nun. Dagobert founded or restored for her a convent near Trier. St Irmina was a zealous supporter of the missionary labours of St Willibrord, and in 698 gave him the manor on which he founded his famous monastery of Echternach. This gift is said to have been in recognition of his having miraculously stayed an epidemic that was devastating her nunnery, and is about the only thing that seems certain concerning Irmina.

St Adela, another daughter of Dagobert II, became a nun after the death of her husband, Alberic. She is probably the widow Adula, who about 691–2 was living at Nivelles with her little son, the future father of St Gregory of Utrecht. She founded a monastery at Palatiolum, now Pfalzel, near Trier; she became its first abbess and governed it in holiness for many years. Adela seems to have been among the disciples of St Boniface, and a letter in his correspondence from Abbess Aelffled of Whitby to an Abbess Adola is addressed to her.

25 : ST ANASTASIA, MARTYR (A.D. 304?)

THE *passio* of Anastasia relates that she was the daughter of a noble Roman named Praetextatus and had St Chrysogonus for her adviser. She married a pagan, Publius, and during the persecution of Diocletian cared for the confessors of the faith in prison, whereupon her husband forbade her to leave the house. Chrysogonus having gone to Aquileia, she kept up a correspondence with him and, when Publius died on an embassy to Persia, went to Aquileia herself to succour the Christians there. After the martyrdom of SS. Agape, Chionia and Irene, Anastasia herself was arrested and brought before the prefect of Illyricum at Sirmium, being visited in prison and fed by the dead St Theodota. Then with another Christian and a number of pagan criminals she was put aboard a vessel and abandoned at sea; but Theodota appeared again and piloted it to land, and the pagans were all converted. Anastasia was taken to the island of Palmaria and put to death by being burned alive, staked to the ground with her arms and legs outstretched and the fire kindled about her; two hundred men and seventy women were martyred in various ways at the same time.

These stories are entirely apocryphal. St Anastasia has been venerated at Rome since the late fifth century, when her name was put in the canon of the Mass, but so far as is known she had nothing to do with the City. Her cult originated at Sirmium in Pannonia, where she was perhaps martyred under Diocletian, but no authentic particulars of her life and passion have come down to us.

26 : ST STEPHEN, THE FIRST MARTYR (C. A.D. 34)

THAT St Stephen was a Jew is unquestionable, and he probably was a Hellenist of the Dispersion, who spoke Greek. The name Stephen is Greek, Stephanos, and signifies 'crown'. The circumstances of his conversion to Christianity are not known. We are told of him in the book of the Acts of the Apostles when, there being numerous converts, the Hellenists murmured against the Hebrews, complaining that their widows were neglected in the daily ministration. The Apostles assembled the faithful and told them that they could not relinquish the duties of preaching and prayer to attend to the care of tables; and recommended them to choose seven men of good character, full of the Holy Ghost and wisdom, who might superintend that business. The suggestion was approved, and the people chose Stephen, 'a man full of faith and of the Holy Ghost', and Philip, Prochorus, Nicanor, Timon, Parmenas and Nicholas a proselyte of Antioch. These seven were presented to the Apostles, who praying, imposed hands upon them, and so ordained them the first deacons.

Stephen spoke with such wisdom and spirit that his hearers were unable to resist him, and a plot was laid by the elders of certain synagogues in Jerusalem. At first they undertook to dispute with Stephen; but finding themselves unequal to the task they suborned false witnesses to charge him with blasphemy against Moses and against God. The indictment was laid in the Sanhedrin, and he was dragged thither. The main point urged against him was that he affirmed that the temple would be destroyed, that the Mosaic traditions were but shadows and types no longer acceptable to God, Jesus of Nazareth having put an end to them. Leave was given him to speak, and in a long defence, set out in Acts vii 2–53, he showed that Abraham, the father and founder of their nation, was justified and received the greatest favours of God in a foreign land; that Moses was commanded to set up a tabernacle, but foretold a new law and the Messias; that Solomon built the Temple, but it was not to be imagined that God was confined in houses made by hands: the temple and the Mosaic law were temporary, and were to give place when God introduced more excellent institutions by sending the Messias himself. He ended with a stinging rebuke: 'You stiff-necked and uncircumcised in hearts and ears, you always resist the Holy Spirit; as your fathers did, so do you also. Which of the prophets have not your fathers persecuted? And they have slain them who foretold of the coming of the Just One, of whom you have been now the betrayers and murderers: who have received the law by the disposition of angels, and have not kept it.'

The whole assembly raged at Stephen, but he, being full of the Holy Spirit and looking up steadfastly to the heavens, saw them opened and beheld the glory of God and the Saviour standing at the right hand of the Father. And he said, 'Behold, I see the heavens opened, and the Son of man standing on the right hand of God'. 'And they, crying out with a loud voice, stopped their ears and with one accord ran violently upon him. And, casting him forth without the city, they stoned him; and the witnesses laid down their garments at the feet of a young man whose name was Saul. And they stoned Stephen, invoking and saying, "Lord Jesus, receive my spirit". And falling on his knees, he cried with a loud voice, saying, "Lord, lay not this sin to their charge". And when he had said this he fell asleep in the Lord.'

27 : SS. THEODORE AND THEOPHANES, (c. A.D. 841 AND 845)

THESE brothers were natives of Kerak, across the Dead Sea, formerly the land of the Moabites, from whence their parents went and settled at Jerusalem. They both in their youth became monks in the monastery of St Sabas, and by their progress in learning and virtue acquired a high reputation. The patriarch of Jerusalem obliged Theodore to receive priestly orders, and when Leo the Armenian waged war against holy images sent him to exhort the emperor not to distuub the peace of the Church. Leo had Theodore scourged, and banished him with Theophanes to an island at the mouth of the Black Sea, where they suffered much from hunger and cold.

But they were not long there before Leo died, when they returned to their monastery at Constantinople. The Emperor Theophilus, a violent iconoclast who ascended the throne in 829, caused the two brothers to be whipped and banished once more.

Two years later they were brought back to Constantinople, and when they still persisted in their refusal to communicate with the iconoclasts, Theophilus commanded twelve lines of iambic verse, composed for that purpose by a courtier, to be inscribed on their foreheads. They were laid upon benches and the letters cut or pricked upon their skin. This barbarity took a long time and was interrupted by the coming on of night, so the torture was completed the next day. Then they were again banished, this time to Apamea in Bithynia, where St Theodore died. The Emperor Theophilus died about the same time, and St Methodius was made patriarch and restored holy images in 842. St Theophanes was then honoured for his confession of the faith and made bishop of Nicaea, that he might more effectually concur in overthrowing a heresy over which he had already triumphed. He wrote a number of hymns, including one on St Theodore, and died on October 11, 845. He is distinguished by the Greeks as 'the Poet', but both brothers are commonly surnamed 'Graptoi', that is, 'the Written-on'.

28 : ST ANTONY OF LÉRINS, (c. A.D. 520)

HE was born at Valeria in Lower Pannonia during the time of the barbarian invasions, and his father dying when he was eight years old he was entrusted to the care of St Severinus, the intrepid apostle of Noricum. Antony probably lived with him in the monastery he had founded at Faviana, and as a boy saw Odoacer go by on his triumphant march to Rome. Severinus died about 482 and Antony was then taken charge of by his uncle Constantius, Bishop of Lorch in Bavaria. He became a monk, and withdrew from Noricum into Italy with the other Romans in 488. He was then about twenty. He made his way to the neighbourhood of Lake Como, and there attached himself to a priest named Marius, who directed a number of disciples there. Marius conceived a great admiration for Antony and wanted him to be ordained priest and share in his work; but Antony's vocation was for the solitary life and, leaving Marius, he joined two hermits near the tomb of St Felix at the other end of the lake. Here he lived in a cave, spending his time in prayer, study and cultivating his garden, but he was distracted by frequent visitors.

At last, despairing of finding complete solitude and fearing the respect he received would make him vain, he passed over the Alps into southern Gaul and became a monk at Lérins. St Antony died there revered for his virtues and miracles.

29 : ST THOMAS BECKET, ARCHBISHOP OF CANTERBURY, MARTYR (A.D. 1170)

THOMAS was born on St Thomas's day 1118, in the city of London, and he was sent to school with the canons regular at Merton in Surrey. When he was twenty-one he lost his mother, and soon after his father. When he was about twenty-four he obtained a post in the household of Theobald, archbishop of Canterbury. He received minor orders and was greatly favoured by Theobald, who saw to it that Thomas was provided with a number of benefices, from Beverley to Shoreham. In 1154 he was ordained deacon and the archbishop nominated him archdeacon of Canterbury, which was then the first ecclesiastical dignity in England after the bishoprics and abbacies. Theobald committed to him the management of delicate affairs, seldom did anything without his advice, and sent him several times to Rome on important missions.

We find him in 1155, at the age of thirty-six, appointed chancellor by King Henry II. His talents had full scope, for the importance of the chancellor was equalled only by that of the justiciar. Becket was a friend of Henry II, but their friendship was not confined to a common interest in affairs of state, and their personal relations at times of relaxation have been aptly described as 'frolicsome'.

Though immersion in public affairs and a secular grandeur of state was the predominating aspect of Becket's life as chancellor, it was not the only one. He was proud, irascible, violent and remained so all his life; but we also hear of 'retreats' at Merton, of taking the discipline and of prayer in the nightwatches; and his confessor during the first part of his career testified to the blamelessness of his private life under conditions of extreme danger and temptation. And if he sometimes co-operated too far in schemes of his royal master that infringed the rights of the Church, he was not afraid to withstand him in such matters as the marriage of the abbess of Romsey.

Theobald, archbishop of Canterbury, died in 1161. King Henry was then in Normandy with his chancellor, whom he had resolved to raise to that dignity. Thomas refused to acquiesce in accepting the dignity till Cardinal Henry of Pisa, legate from the Holy See, overruled his scruples. The election was made in May 1162; Prince Henry, then in London, gave his consent in his father's name; and Becket set out immediately from London to Canterbury. On Saturday in Whit-week he was ordained priest by Walter, bishop of Rochester, and on the octave of Pentecost was consecrated by Henry of Blois, bishop of Winchester.

Soon after he received the *pallium* from Pope Alexander III, and by the end of the year there was a notable change in his manner of life. Next his skin he wore a hair-shirt, and his ordinary dress was a black cassock and linen surplice, with the sacerdotal stole about his neck. By the rule of life which he laid down for himself he rose early to read the Holy Scriptures, keeping Herbert of Bosham by him that they might discuss the meaning of passages together. At nine o'clock he sang Mass, or was present when he did not celebrate himself. At ten a daily alms was distributed, and he doubled all the ordinary alms of his predecessor. He took a siesta in the afternoon, and dined at three o'clock among the guests and household in the great hall, and, instead of music, a book was read. He kept a notably good table, decently served for the sake of others, but was himself now very temperate and moderate. He visited the infirmary and the monks working in the cloister nearly every day, and sought to establish a certain monastic regularity in his own household. He took an especial care for the selection of candidates for holy orders, examining them personally, and in his judicial capacity exerted a rigorously even-handed justice.

Although the archbishop had resigned the chancellorship contrary to the wish of the king, the relations between them remained for some time pretty much as before. In spite of some differences Henry still showed him great marks of favour and seemed still to love him as he had done from their first acquaintance.

Accumulation of conflicts provoked him in October 1163 to call the bishops to a council at Westminster, at which he demanded the handing over of criminal clergy to the civil power for punishment. The bishops wavered, but St Thomas stiffened them. Then Henry required a promise of observance of his (unspecified) royal customs. St Thomas and the council agreed, but 'saving their order'. So far as the king's object was concerned this was equivalent to a refusal, and the next day he ordered Thomas to give up certain castles and honours which he had held since he was chancellor. In a stormy interview at Northampton the king in vain tried to make his old friend modify his attitude, and the trouble came to a head at the Council of Clarendon, near Salisbury, at the beginning of 1164. For a brief space St Thomas, having received little encouragement from Pope Alexander III, was very conciliatory and promised to accept the customs; but then he saw the constitutions in which were expressed the royal customs which he was to uphold. They provided *inter alia* that no prelate should leave the kingdom without the royal licence or appeal to Rome without the king's consent; no tenant-in-chief was to be excommunicated against the royal will (this had been claimed from the time of William I, but was a clear infringement of spiritual jurisdiction); the custody of vacant benefices and their revenues was to be held by the king (this abuse had been recognized during the reign of Henry I); and—what proved to be the critical point—that clerics convicted and sentenced in ecclesiastical courts should be at the disposition of the royal officers (involving a possibility of double punishment).

The archbishop was bitterly remorseful for having weakened in his opposition to the king and setting an example which the other bishops were too ready to follow. For forty days and more, while awaiting absolution and permission from the pope, he would not celebrate Mass. Henry now pursued him with persecution which culminated in a suit for 30,000 marks alleged to be owing from the time when he was chancellor. At Woodstock the king refused him audience, and Thomas twice made vain attempts to cross the Channel to put his case before the pope. Then Henry summoned a council at Northampton. It resolved itself into a concerted attack on the archbishop, in which the prelates followed in the wake of the lords. First he was condemned to a fine for contempt in not appearing at a case in the king's court when summoned; then various monetary causes were brought against him, and finally the demand to produce certain chancery-accounts. Bishop Henry of Winchester pleaded the chancellor's discharge; it was disallowed. Then he offered an *ex gratia* payment of 2000 marks of his own money; it was refused. On Tuesday, October 13, 1164, St Thomas celebrated a votive Mass of St Stephen the Protomartyr. Then, without mitre or *pallium*, but bearing his metropolitan's cross in his own hand, he went to the council-hall. The king and the barons were deliberating in an inner room. After a long delay the Earl of Leicester came out and addressed the archbishop. 'The king commands you to render your accounts. Otherwise you must hear judgement.' 'Judgement?' exclaimed St Thomas, 'I was given the church of Canterbury free from temporal obligations. I am therefore not liable and will not plead concerning them.' As Leicester turned to report this to the king, Thomas stopped him. 'Son and earl, listen: You are bound to obey God and me before your earthly king. Neither law nor reason allows children to judge their father and condemn him. Wherefore I refuse the king's judgement and yours and everybody's; under God, I will be judged by the pope alone. You, my fellow bishops, who have served man rather than God, I summon to the presence of the pope. And so, guarded by the authority of the Catholic Church and the Holy See, I go hence.' Cries of 'Traitor!' followed him as he left the hall. That night St Thomas fled from Northampton through the rain, and three weeks later secretly embarked at Sandwich.

St Thomas and his few followers landed in Flanders and, arriving at the abbey of St Bertin at Saint-Omer, sent deputies to Louis VII, King of France, who received them graciously and invited the archbishop into his dominions. The pope, Alexander III, was then at Sens. The bishops and others from King Henry arrived there and accused St Thomas before him, but left again before the archbishop reached the city. Thomas showed the pope the sixteen Constitutions of Clarendon, of which some were pronounced intolerable, and he was rebuked for ever having considered their acceptance. On the day following he confessed that he had received the see of Canterbury, though against his will, yet by an election perhaps uncanonical, and that he had acquitted himself ill in it. Wherefore he resigned his dignity into the hands of his Holiness and, taking the ring off his finger, delivered it to him and withdrew. The pope called him again and reinstated him in his dignity, with an order not to abandon it for that would be visibly to abandon the cause of God. Then Alexander recommended the exiled prelate to the abbot of Pontigny, to be entertained by him.

St Thomas regarded this monastery of the Cistercian Order as a religious retreat and school of penance for the expiation of his sins; he submitted himself to the rules of the house and was unwilling to allow any distinction in his favour. His time he passed in study, but also in writing both to his supporters and opponents letters which were increasingly unlikely to help on a peaceful settlement. King Henry meanwhile confiscated the goods of all the friends, relations and domestics of Thomas, banished them, and obliged all who were adults to go to the archbishop that the sight of their distress might move him. These exiles arrived in troops at Pontigny. When the general chapter of the Cistercians met at Cîteaux it received an intimation from the King of England that if they continued to harbour his enemy he would sequestrate their houses throughout his dominions. The abbot of Cîteaux can hardly be blamed for hinting to St Thomas that he should leave Pontigny, which he did, and was received at the abbey of St Columba, near Sens, as the guest of King Louis. Negotiations between the pope, the archbishop, and the king dragged on for nearly six years. St Thomas was named legate *a latere* for all England except York, excommunicated several of his adversaries, and was menacing as well as conciliatory, so that Pope Alexander saw fit to annul some of his sentences. King Louis of France was drawn into the struggle. In January 1169 the two kings had a conference with the archbishop at Montmirail, whereat Thomas refused to yield on two points; a similar conference in the autumn at Montmartre failed through Henry's last-minute intransigence. St Thomas prepared letters for the bishops ordering the publication of a sentence of interdict on the kingdom of England; and then suddenly, in July 1170, king and archbishop met again in Normandy and a reconciliation was at last patched up, apparently without any overt reference to the matters in dispute.

On December 1 St Thomas landed at Sandwich, and though the sheriff of Kent had tried to impede him the short journey from there to Canterbury was a triumphal progress: the way was lined with cheering people and every bell of the primatial city was ringing. But it was not peace. Those in authority were glowering, and Thomas was faced with the task of dealing with Roger de Pont-l'Evêque, archbishop of York, and the bishops who had assisted him at the coronation of Henry's son, in defiance of the right of Canterbury and perhaps of the instructions of the pope. St Thomas had sent in advance the letters of suspension of Roger and others and of excommunication of the bishops of London and Salisbury, and the three bishops together had gone over to appeal to King Henry in France; while in Kent Thomas was being subjected to insult and annoyance at the hands of Ranulf de Broc, from whom the archbishop had recently (and rather tactlessly at such a time) again demanded the restoration of Saltwood castle, a manor belonging to the see. After a week at Canterbury St Thomas visited London, where he was joyfully received, except by Henry's son, 'the young King', who refused to see him; after visiting several friends he arrived back in Canterbury on or about his fifty-second birthday. Meanwhile the three bishops had laid their complaints before the king at Bur, near Bayeux, and somebody declared aloud that there would be no peace for the realm while Becket lived. And Henry, in one of his fits of ungovernable rage, pronounced the fatal words which were interpreted by some of his hearers as a rebuke for allowing this pestilent clerk to continue to live and disturb him. At once four knights set off for England, where they made their way to the infuriated Brocs at Saltwood. Their names were Reginald Fitzurse, William de Tracy, Hugh de Morville, and Richard le Breton.

On St John's day the archbishop received a letter warning him of his danger, and all south-east Kent was in a state of suppressed ferment and ominous expectation. In the afternoon of December 29 the knights from France came to him. There was an interview, in which several demands were made, particularly that St Thomas should remove the censures on the three bishops; it began quietly and ended angrily, the knights departing with threats and oaths. A few minutes later, shouting, breaking of doors and clangour of arms was heard, and St Thomas, urged and hustled by his attendants, began to move slowly towards the church, his cross carried before him.

As he entered the church armed men were seen behind in the dim light of the cloister (it was nearly dark). Monks slammed the door and bolted it, shutting out some of their brethren in the confusion. These beat loudly at the door. Becket turned round and re-opened the door himself. Then he went up the steps towards the choir. Only three were left with him, Robert, prior of Merton, William FitzStephen, and Edward Grim; the rest had fled to the crypt and elsewhere, and soon Grim alone remained. The knights, who had been joined by a subdeacon named Hugh of Horsea, ran in shouting, 'Where is Thomas the traitor?' 'Where is the archbishop?' 'Here I am', he replied, 'no traitor, but archbishop and priest of God', and came back down the steps, standing between the altars of our Lady and St Benedict.

They shouted at him to absolve the bishops. 'I cannot do other than I have done', he answered. Fitzurse's reply was to threaten him with an axe, seize his cloak and pull him towards the door. Becket snatched himself clear. Then they tried to carry him outside bodily, and he threw one of them to the ground. Fitzurse flung away his axe and drew his sword. 'You pander! ' exclaimed the archbishop, 'you owe me fealty and submission! ' 'I owe no fealty contrary to the king', Fitzurse shouted back. 'Strike! ' And he knocked off his cap. St Thomas covered his face and called aloud on God and his saints. Tracy struck a blow, which Grim intercepted with his own arm, but it grazed Thomas's head and blood ran down into his eyes. Another blow from Tracy beat him to his knees, and murmuring, 'For the name of Jesus and in defence of the Church I am willing to die', he pitched forward on to his face. Le Breton with a tremendous stroke severed his scalp, breaking his sword against the pavement, and Hugh of Horsea scattered the brains out of the skull with his sword-point. Hugh de Morville alone struck no blow. The murderers dashed away through the cloisters—the whole thing was over in ten minutes—while the great church filled with people and a thunderstorm broke overhead. The archbishop's body lay alone, stretched in the middle of the transept, and for long no one dared to touch or even go near it.

It is very doubtful how far Henry II can be held directly responsible for the murder; but the public conscience could not be satisfied by anything less than that the most powerful sovereign in Europe should undergo a public penance of a most humiliating kind. This he did in July, 1174, eighteen months after the solemn canonization of St Thomas as a martyr by Pope Alexander at Segni. On July 7, 1220, the body of St Thomas was solemnly translated from its tomb in the crypt to a shrine behind the high altar by the archbishop, Cardinal Stephen Langton, in the presence of King Henry III, Cardinal Pandulf, the papal-legate, the archbishop of Rheims, and a vast gathering.

30 : ST EGWIN, BISHOP OF WORCESTER (A.D. 717)

EGWIN, said to have been a descendant of the Mercian kings, devoted himself to God in his youth, and succeeded to the episcopal see of Worcester about 692. By his zeal and severity in reproving vice he incurred the hostility of some of his own flock, which gave him an opportunity of performing a penitential pilgrimage to Rome, to answer before the Holy See complaints that had been made against him. After his return, with the assistance of Ethelred, King of Mercia, he founded the famous abbey of Evesham, under the invocation of the Blessed Virgin.

Then, probably about 709, the bishop undertook a second journey to Rome, in the company of Kings Cenred of Mercia and Offa of the East Saxons, and we are told he received considerable privileges for his foundation from Pope Constantine; after the disturbances of the tenth century, Evesham became one of the great Benedictine houses of medieval

England. According to Florence of Worcester, St Egwin died on December 30, in 717, and was buried in the monastery of Evesham.

31 : ST SILVESTER I, POPE (A.D. 335)

THE *Liber Pontificalis* states that Silvester was the son of a Roman named Rufinus. He succeeded Miltiades in 314, less than a year after the Edict of Milan had granted freedom to Christianity, and the most significant legends about him are those which bring him into relation with the Emperor Constantine. These represent Constantine as suffering from leprosy, which, upon his conversion to Christianity, was cured by baptism received at the hands of Silvester; whereupon, in gratitude and in recognition of the vicar of Christ on earth, the emperor granted numerous rights to the pope and his successors and endowed the Church with the provinces of Italy. This story of the 'Donation of Constantine', which was embroidered and used for political and ecclesiastical ends during the Middle Ages, has long been recognized as a fabrication.

A few months after his accession St Silvester was represented at a synod convened at Arles to deal with the Donatist dispute: the bishops there commended the pope for not coming in person but instead remaining in the place 'where the Apostles daily sit in judgement'. In June 325 there assembled at Nicaea in Bithynia the first ecumenical or general council of the Church: probably over 220 bishops attended, nearly all orientals, and Silvester of Rome sent legates, two priests: a Western bishop, Hosius of Cordova, presided. The council condemned the heresy of Arius, but this was only the beginning of a devastating struggle within the Church. There is no record that St Silvester formally confirmed the signature of his legates to the acts of the council.

It is probable that it was to Silvester rather than to Miltiades that Constantine gave the palace of the Lateran, and there the pope set up his *cathedra* and established the Lateran basilica as the cathedral church of Rome. During his pontificate the emperor (who in 330 removed his capital from Rome to Byzantium) built also the first churches of St Peter on the Vatican, Holy Cross in the Sessorian palace and St Laurence outside the Walls; and the pope's name, joined with that of St Martin, is now given to the cardinalitial-titular church founded at this time near the Baths of Diocletian by a priest called Equitius. St Silvester also built a church at the cemetery of Priscilla on the Salarian way: there he was himself buried in 335; but in 761 his relics were translated by Pope Paul I to St Silvester *in Capite*, now the national church of English Catholics in Rome.

A LIST OF PATRON SAINTS
INDEX OF SAINTS

A LIST OF PATRON SAINTS

Accountants: Matthew
Actors: Genesius
Advertisers: Bernardine of Siena
Airmen: Our Lady of Loreto; Joseph of
  Cupertino
Air Travellers: Joseph of Cupertino
Altar boys: John Berchmans
Anaesthetists: René Goupil
Archers: Sebastian
Architects: Barbara
Art: Catherine of Bologna
Artists: Luke
Astronomers: Dominic
Athletes: Sebastian
Authors: Francis de Sales
Bakers: Elizabeth of Hungary
Bankers: Matthew
Barbers: Cosmas and Damian
Barren women: Antony of Padua
Basket-makers: Antony the Abbot
Beggars: Alexius; Giles
Blacksmiths: Dunstan
Blind: Raphael
Boatmen: Julian the Hospitaller
Bookbinders: Peter Celestine
Bookkeepers: Matthew
Booksellers: John of God
Boy Scouts: George
Bricklayers: Stephen
Brides: Nicholas of Myra
Broadcasters: Archangel Gabriel
Brushmakers: Antony
Builders: Vincent Ferrer
Cab drivers: Fiacre
Cabinetmakers: Anne
Cancer victims: Peregrine Laziosi
Canonists: Raymond of Peñafort
Carpenters: Joseph
Catechists: Charles Borromeo; Robert
  Bellarmine
Catholic Action: Francis of Assisi
Catholic Press: Francis de Sales
Charitable societies: Vincent de Paul
Childbirth: Gerard Majella
Children: Nicholas of Myra

Choirboys: Dominic Savio
Church, The: Joseph
Clerics: Gabriel
Comedians: Vitus
Confessors: Alphonsus Liguori; John
  Nepomucene
Convulsive children: Scholastica
Cooks: Martha
Cripples: Giles
Dancers: Vitus
Deaf: Francis de Sales
Dentists: Apollonia
Desperate situations: Jude
Dietitians (in hospitals): Martha
Domestic Animals: Antony
Druggists: Cosmas and Damian
Dyers: Maurice and Lydia
Dying: Joseph
Dysentry sufferers: Matrona
Earthquakes: Emygdius
Ecologists: Francis of Assisi
Editors: John Bosco
Emigrants: Frances Xavier Cabrini
Engineers: Ferdinand III
Epileptics: Dympna; Vitus
Expectant mothers: Gerard Majella
Eye trouble: Lucy
Falsely accused: Raymund Nonnatus
Farmers: Isidore the Farmer
Farriers: John Baptist
Fathers of families: Joseph
Firemen: Florian
Fire prevention: Catherine of Siena
First communicants: Tarcisius
Fishermen: Andrew; Peter
Florists: Thérèse of Lisieux
Foresters: John Gualbert
Founders: Barbara
Foundlings: Holy Innocents
Fullers: Anastasius the Fuller
Funeral Directors: Joseph of Arimathea
Gardeners: Adelard; Fiacre; Phocas
Girls: Agnes
Glassworkers: Luke
Goldsmiths: Dunstan

Gravediggers: Antony the Abbot
Grocers: Michael
Gunners: Barbara
Hairdressers: Martin de Porres
Headache sufferers: Teresa of Avila
Heart patients: John of God
Hospitals: Camillus de Lellis; John of God
Hotelkeepers: Amand
Housewives: Anne
Hunters: Hubert; Eustachius
Infantrymen: Maurice
Invalids: Roch
Jewellers: Eligius
Journalists: Francis de Sales
Jurists: John Capistran
Labourers: Isidore
Lawyers: Thomas More; Yves
Learning: Ambrose
Leatherworkers: Crispin and Crispinian
Librarians: Jerome
Lighthousekeepers: Dunstan; Venerius
Locksmiths: Dunstan
Lost articles: Antony of Padua
Lovers: Valentine
Maidens: Catherine of Alexandria
Mariners: Nicholas of Tolentine
Married women: Monica
Medical technicians: Albert the Great
Mentally ill: Dympna
Messengers: Gabriel
Midwives: Raymund Nonnatus
Millers: Arnulph
Missions: Francis Xavier; Thérèse of Lisieux;
  Leonard of Port Maurice (parish)
Mothers: Monica
Motorists: Christopher
Mountaineers: Bernard of Menthon
Musicians: Cecilia; Gregory the Great
Notaries: Luke; Mark
Nurses: Agatha; Camillus de Lellis; John of
  God
Nursing service: Elizabeth of Hungary
Orators: John Chrysostom
Orphans: Jerome Emiliani
Painters: Luke
Paratroopers: Michael
Parish Priests: John Vianney
Pawnbrokers: Nicholas of Myra
Pharmacists: Cosmas and Damian
Philosophers: Catherine of Alexandria; Justin
Physicians: Cosmas and Damian; Luke
Pilgrims: James
Plasterers: Bartholomew
Poets: David
Policemen: Michael
Poor: Antony of Padua
Porters: Christopher
Postal workers: Gabriel
Preachers: Catherine of Alexandria; John
  Chrysostom

Pregnant women: Gerard Majella
Priests: John Vianney
Printers: Augustine; Genesius; John of God
Prisoners: Dismas
Prisoners-of-war: Leonard
Prisons: Joseph Cafasso
Public relations: Bernardine of Siena
Radiologists: Michael
Radio workers: Gabriel
Retreats: Ignatius Loyola
Rheumatism: James the Greater
Saddlers: Crispin and Crispinian
Sailors: Brendan; Erasmus
Scholars: Brigid
Scientists: Albert the Great
Sculptors: Claude
Secretaries: Genesius
Seminarians: Charles Borromeo
Servants: Martha: Zita
Shoemakers: Crispin and Crispinian
Sick: John of God; Camillus de Lellis
Silversmiths: Andronicus; Dunstan
Singers: Cecilia; Gregory
Skaters: Lidwina
Skiers: Bernard of Menthon
Skin diseases: Marculf
Social justice: Joseph
Social workers: Louise de Marillac
Soldiers: George; Martin of Tours
Speleologists: Benedict
Stonecutters: Clement
Stonemasons: Barbara; Reinhold; Stephen
Students: Catherine of Alexandria; Thomas
  Aquinas
Surgeons: Cosmas and Damian; Luke
Swordsmiths: Maurice
Tailors: Homobonus
Tanners: Crispin and Crispinian; Simon
Tax collectors: Matthew
Teachers: Gregory the Great; John Baptist de
  la Salle
Telecommunications workers: Gabriel
Television: Clare of Assisi
Television workers: Gabriel
Theologians: Alphonsus Liguori; Augustine
Throat sufferers: Blaise
Tinworkers: Joseph of Arimathea
Travellers: Christopher
Vocations: Alphonsus
Watchmen: Peter of Alcantara
Weavers: Anastasia; Anastasius; Paul the
  Hermit
Widows: Paula
Winegrowers: Morand; Vincent
Wine merchants: Amand
Women in labour: Anne
Working men: Joseph
Writers: Francis de Sales
Yachtsmen: Adjutor
Youth: Aloysius Gonzaga

INDEX OF SAINTS

INDEX OF SAINTS

The index which follows is based upon that in the last complete edition of Butler's *Lives of the Saints*. The names of *beati*, however, have been omitted; the other entries have been up-dated to take account both of recent canonizations and also of changes in the Roman calendar (see Editor's Introduction, p. viii).

Only those saints whose names are listed below in bold type are described in the body of this book.

Blane. *See* Blaan
Blesilla   *January* 22
Bodo   *September* 22
Boethius. *See* Severinus Boethius
Bogumilus   *June* 10
Boisil. *See* Boswell
Bonaventure (doctor)   **July 15**
Bonet. *See* Bonitus
Bonfilius. *See* Founders of the Servites
Boniface I   *September* 4
Boniface IV   *May* 8
Boniface of Lausanne   **February 19**
Boniface of Mainz (or of Crediton) **June 5**
Boniface (or Bruno) of Querfurt   *June* 19
Bonitus (or Bonet)   *January* 15
Bonosus (with Maximian)   *August* 21
Boris (or Romanus)   *July* 24
Bosa   *March* 9
Boswell (or Boisil)   *February* 23
Botolph (or Botulf)   *June* 17
Botulf. *See* Botolph
Botvid   *July* 28
Braulio   **March 26**
Brendan   **May 16**
Brice (or Britius)   *November* 13
Bride. *See* Brigid
Bridget (or Birgitta)   **July 23**
Brieuc (or Briocus)   *May* 1
Brigid (or Bride)   *February* 1
Brigid (with Maura)   *July* 13
Briocus. *See* Brieuc
Brites. *See* Beatrice da Silva
Britius. *See* Brice
Brocard   *September* 2
Bruno (Carthusian)   **October 6**
Bruno of Cologne (bishop)   *October* 11
Bruno (or Boniface) of Querfurt   *June* 19
Bruno (of Segni)   **July 18**
Bruno of Würzburg   *May* 17
Budoc (or Beuzec)   *December* 9
Bulgaria, Seven Apostles of   *July* 17
Buonagiunta. *See* Founders of the Servites
Burchard of Würzburg   *October* 14
Burgundofara (or Fare)   *April* 3

C

Cadfan   *November* 1
Cadoc   *September* 23
Cadroe   *March* 6
Caedmon   *February* 11
Caedwalla   *April* 20
Caesaria   *January* 12
Caesarius (with Julian)   *November* 1
Caesarius (of Arles)   **August 27**
Caesarius of Nazianzen   *February* 25
Cagnoald. *See* Chainoaldus
Cainnech. *See* Canice

Cajetan (or Gaetano)   **August 7**
Calais. *See* Carilefus
Calepodius   *May* 10
Calixto Caravario   *February* 25
Calixtus. *See* Callistus
Callistus (or Calixtus) I   **October 14**
Calocerus (martyr). *See* Faustinus and
Jovita
Calocerus (with Parthenius)   *May* 19
Camerinus   *August* 21
Camillus de Lellis   **July 14**
Candida. *See* Wite
Candlemas   *February* 2
Canice (or Kenneth)   *October* 11
Cantianella   *May* 31
Cantianus   *May* 31
Cantius   *May* 31
Canute   *January* 19
Canute Lavard   *January* 7
Caprais. *See* Captasius
Caprasius of Agen   *October* 20
Caprasius of Lérins   *June* 1
Caradoc   *April* 14
Carannog. *See* Carantoc
Carantoc (or Carannog)   *May* 16
Carilefus (or Calais)   *July* 1
Carpus   *April* 13
Carthach. *See* Carthage
Carthage (or Carthach)   *May* 14
Casimir   **March 4**
Caspar del Bufalo   **January 2**
Cassian. *See* John Cassian
Cassian of Imola   *August* 13
Cassian of Tangier   *December* 3
Cassius of Narni   *June* 29
Castor of Apt   *September* 2
Castulus of Rome   *March* 26
Castus (with Aemilius)   *May* 22
Catald (or Cathal)   *May* 10
Cathal. *See* Catald
Catherine Labouré   **November 28**
Catherine dei Ricci   **February 13**
Catherine of Bologna   *March* 9
Catherine of Genoa   **September 15**
Catherine of Palma   *April* 1
Catherine of Siena   **April 29**
Catherine of Vadstena   *March* 24
Ceadda. *See* Chad
Ceallach. *See* Celsus of Armagh
Cecilia (or Cecily)   **November 22**
Cecilius   *June* 3
Cecily. *See* Cecilia
Cedd   **October 26**
Celestine I   *April* 6
Celestine V. *See* Peter Moreone
Celsus (with Nazarius)   *July* 28
Celsus (or Ceallach) of Armagh   *April* 7
Ceolfrid   *September* 25
Ceolwulf   *January* 15

Cérase. *See* Ceratius	
Ceratius (or Cérase)	*June* 6
Cerbonius	*October* 10
Cerneuf. *See* Serenus the Gardener	
Chad (or Ceadda)	**March 2**
Chaeremon	**December 22**
Chainoaldus (or Cagnoald)	*September* 6
Charity (with Faith)	*August* 1
Charles Borromeo	**November 4**
Charles Garnier. *See* **Martyrs of North**	
America	**October 19**
Charles Lwanga	**June 3**
Charles of Sezze	*January* 19
Chef. *See* Theuderius Chelidonius	*March* 3
Chionia	*April* 3
Christians. *See* Nino	
Christina of Bolsena	*July* 24
Christina the Astonishing	**July 24**
Christmas	*December* 25
Christopher	*July* 25
Chrodegang of Metz	*March* 6
Chromatius	**December 2**
Chrysanthus (with Daria)	*October* 25
Chrysogonus	*November* 24
Ciaran. *See* Kieran	
Circumcision of Our Lord, The	*January* 1
Cisellus	*August* 21
Clare (of Assisi)	**August 11**
Clare of Montefalco	**August 17**
Clarus (abbot)	*January* 1
Clarus (martyr)	*November* 4
Claud of Besançon	*June* 6
Claudia	*August* 7
Claudius (with Asterius)	*August* 23
Claudius (with Hilaria)	*December* 3
Clement (with Agathangelus)	*January* 23
Clement I (pope)	*November* 23
Clement Hofbauer	*March* 15
Clement of Okhrida	**July 17**
Cleopatra	*October* 19
Clodoald (Cloud)	*September* 7
Clodulf. *See* Cloud of Metz	
Clotilda	*June* 3
Cloud (or Clodoald)	**September 7**
Cloud of Metz	*June* 8
Cadratus of Corinth	*March* 10
Coemgen. *See* Kevin	
Colette	**March 6**
Colman of Cloyne	**November 24**
Colman of Dromore	*June* 7
Colman of Lann Elo	*September* 26
Colman of Kilmacduagh	*October* 29
Colman of Lindisfarne	*February* 18
Colmcille. *See* Columba of Iona	
Coloman	*October* 13
Columba of Cordova	*September* 17
Columba of Iona	*June* 9
Columba of Sens	*December* 31
Columban	**November 23**

Comgall	*May* 11
Comgan	*October* 13
Conan of Man	*January* 26
Concordius of Spoleto	*January* 1
Condedus	*October* 21
Conlaed. *See* Conleth	
Conleth (or Conlaed)	*May* 10
Conrad of Constance	*November* 26
Conrad of Parzham	*April* 21
Conrad of Piacenza	*February* 19
Conran	*February* 14
Constantine (with Theodore)	*September* 19
Constantine of Cornwall	*March* 11
Contardo	*April* 16
Convoyon	*January* 5
Corbinian	**September 8**
Corentin (or Cury)	*December* 12
Cornelius (pope)	*September* 16
Cosmas (with Damian)	*September* 26
Crispin (with Crispinian)	*October* 25
Crispin of Viterbo	*May* 19
Crispina	*December* 5
Crispinian	*October* 25
Cronan of Roscrea	*April* 28
Cronion	*February* 27
Cross, Exaltation of the	*September* 14
Cross, Finding of the	*May* 3
Crowned Martyrs, The Four	*November* 8
Cuby. *See* Cybi	
Cumian the Tall	*November* 12
Cunegund (empress)	**March 3**
Cungar	*November* 27
Cunibert	*November* 12
Cury. *See* Corentin	
Cuthbert	**March 20**
Cuthbert Mayne	**November 30**
Cuthburga	*September* 3
Cuthman	*February* 8
Cybard. *See* Eparchius	
Cybi	*November* 8
Cyneburga	*March* 6
Cyneswide	*March* 6
Cyprian	**September 16**
Cyprian (with Felix)	*October* 12
Cyran (or Sigiramnus)	*December* 5
Cyriacus (or Judas Quiriacus)	*May* 4
Cyriacus (with Largus)	*August* 8
Cyricus (or Quiricus)	*June* 16
Cyril (with Anastasia)	*October* 28
Cyril (with Methodius)	**February 14**
Cyril (of Alexandria)	**June 27**
Cyril of Caesarea	*May* 29
Cyril of Constantinople	*March* 6
Cyril of Heliopolis	*March* 29
Cyril of Jerusalem	**March 18**
Cyril of Turov	*April* 28
Cyrus (with John)	*January* 31

Egbert	*April* 24	Ermenilda. *See* Ermengild	
Egwin	**December 30**	Erminold	*January* 6
Eiluned. *See* Aled		Eskil	*June* 12
Elesbaan	*October* 24	Esterwine	*March* 7
Eleusippus	*January* 17	Ethbin	*October* 19
Eleutherius (with Dionysius)	*October* 9	Ethelbert (martyr)	*May* 20
Eleutherius (abbot)	*September* 6	Ethelbert of Kent	*February* 25
Eleutherius (martyr)	*April* 18	Ethelburga (or Aubierge)	*July* 7
Eleutherius of Nicomedia	*October* 2	Ethelburga of Barking	*October* 12
Eleutherius of Tournai	*February* 20	Ethelburga of Lyminge	*April* 5
Elfleda	*February* 8	Etheldreda (or Audrey)	*June* 23
Elias (martyr)	*February* 16	Ethelnoth	*October* 30
Elias of Jerusalem	*July* 20	Ethelwald of Lindisfarne	*February* 12
Eligius (or Eloi)	*December* 1	Ethelwald the Hermit	*March* 23
Elizabeth (with Zachary)	*November* 5	Ethelwold of Winchester	*August* 1
Elizabeth Bayley Seton	**January 4**	Eubulus	*March* 5
Elizabeth Bichier des Ages	**August 26**	Eurcherius of Lyons	*November* 16
Elizabeth of Hungary	**November 17**	Eucherius of Orleans	*February* 20
Elizabeth of Portugal	**July 4**	Eugendus (or Oyend)	*January* 1
Elizabeth of Schönau	**June 18**	Eugene (or Eoghan) of Ardstraw	*August* 23
Elmo. *See* Erasmus and Peter Gonzalez		Eugenia	*December* 25
Eloi. *See* Eligius		Eugenius I	*June* 2
Elphege. *See* Alphage		Eugenius of Carthage	*July* 13
Elzear of Sabran	*September* 27	Eugenius of Toledo	*November* 13
Emerentiana	*January* 23	Eugraphus	*December* 10
Emeterius	*March* 3	Eulalia of Mérida	*December* 10
Emilian Cucullatus	*November* 12	Eulampia	*October* 10
Emiliana	*December* 24	Eulampius	*October* 10
Emily de Rodat	**September 19**	Eulogius of Alexandria	*September* 13
Emily de Vialai	*June* 17	Eulogius of Cordova	*March* 11
Emma	*June* 30	Eunan. *See* Adamnan of Iona	
Emmeramus	*September* 22	Euphemia	*September* 16
Emygdius	*August* 9	**Euphrasia (or Eupraxia)**	**March 13**
Encratis	*April* 16	Euphrasia Pelletier	*April* 24
Enda	**March 21**	Euphrosyne	*January* 1
Eneco (or Iñigo)	**June 1**	Euphrosyne of Polotsk	*May* 23
Engelbert	*November* 7	Euplus	*August* 12
Engelmund	*June* 21	Eupraxia. *See* Euphrasia	
Ennodius	*July* 17	Eurosia	*June* 25
Eoghan. *See* Eugene		Eusebia of Hamage	*March* 16
Eparchius (or Cybard)	*July* 1	Eusebius (pope)	*August* 17
Ephraem	**June 9**	Eusebius (with Nestabus)	*September* 8
Epimachus (with Alexander)	*December* 12	Eusebius of Cremona	*March* 5
Epimachus (with Gordian)	*May* 10	Eusebius of Rome	*August* 14
Epiphanius of Pavia	*January* 21	Eusebius of Saint-Gall	*January* 31
Epiphanius of Salamis	*May* 12	Eusebius of Samosata	*June* 21
Epiphany of Our Lord, The	*January* 6	**Eusebius (of Vercelli)**	**August 2**
Epipodius	*April* 22	Eustace (with John)	*April* 14
Episteme	*November* 5	Eustace White	*December* 10
Equitius	*August* 11	Eustathius of Antioch	*July* 16
Erasmus (or Elmo)	**June 2**	Eustathius of Carrhae. *See* Eutychius	
Ercongota	*July* 7	Eustochium of Bethlehem	*September* 28
Erconwald	*May* 13	Eustorgius of Milan	*June* 6
Erembert	*May* 14	Eustratius of Sebastea	*December* 13
Erentrude	*June* 30	Euthymius the Enlightener	*May* 13
Erhard	*January* 8	**Euthymius the Great**	**January 20**
Eric of Sweden	**May 18**	Euthymius the Younger	*October* 15
Ermengard, Bd	*July* 16	Eutropius (with Tigrius)	*January* 12
Ermengild (or Ermenilda)	*February* 13	Eutropius of Orange	*May* 27

Fulbert	**April 10**
Fulgentius of Ruspe	*January* 1
Fulrad	**July 16**
Fursey	*January* 16
Fuscian	*December* 11

G

Gabriel (archangel)	*September* 29
Gabriel Lalemant. *See* **Martyrs of North**	
America	**October 19**
Gabriel Possenti	**February 27**
Gaetano. *See* Cajetan	
Gaiana	**September 29**
Galation	*November* 5
Galdinus	**April 18**
Galfrido. *See* Walfrid	
Gall (hermit)	*October* 16
Gall of Clermont	*July* 1
Galla (widow)	*October* 5
Gallicanus	*June* 25
Galmier. *See* Baldomerus	
Gatian	*December* 18
Gaucherius	*April* 9
Gaudentius (of Brescia)	**October 25**
Gaugericus (or Géry)	*August* 11
Gelasius I (pope)	*November* 21
Gemma Galgani	*April* 11
Genesius of Arles	*August* 25
Genesius of Clermont	*June* 3
Genesius the Comedian	*August* 25
Genevieve (or Genovfa)	**January 3**
Gengoul. *See* Gengulf	
Gengulf (or Gengoul)	*May* 11
Gennadius of Astorga	*May* 25
Genou. *See* Genulf	
Genovefa. *See* Genevieve	
Gentian	*December* 11
Genulf (or Genou)	*January* 17
George (martyr)	**April 23**
George (with Fronto)	*October* 25
George Mtasmindeli	*June* 27
George of Amastris	*February* 21
George the Younger	*April* 7
Gerald of Aurillac	*October* 13
Gerald of Mayo	*March* 13
Gerard Majella	*October* 16
Gerard of Brogne	*October* 3
Gerard (of Csanad)	**September 24**
Gerard of Gallinaro	*August* 11
Gerard of Sauve-Majeure	*April* 5
Gerard of Toul	*April* 23
Gerasimus (abbot)	*March* 5
Gerebernus	*May* 15
Geremarus (or Germer)	*September* 24
Gereon	*October* 10
Gerlac	*January* 5

Gerland	*February* 25
Germain. *See* Germanus of Paris	
Germaine of Pibrac	**June 15**
Germanicus	*January* 19
Germanus of Auxerre	*August* 3
Germanus of Capua	*October* 30
Germanus (of Constantinople)	**May 12**
Germanus of Granfel	*February* 21
Germanus (of Paris)	**May 28**
Germanus of Valaam	*June* 28
Germer. *See* Geremarus	
Germerius (or Germier)	*May* 16
Germier. *See* Germerius	
Geroldus	*April* 19
Gerontius of Cervia	*May* 9
Gertrude of Helfta	*November* 16
Gertrude of Nivelles	*March* 17
Gervase (with Protase)	*June* 19
Gervinus	*March* 3
Géry. *See* Gaugericus	
Getulius	*June* 10
Ghislain. *See* Gislenus	
Gibrian	*May* 8
Gilbert of Caithness	*April* 1
Gilbert of Sempringham	**February 16**
Gildas	**January 29**
Giles (or Aegidius)	*September* 1
Gislenus (or Ghislain)	*October* 9
Gleb (or David)	*July* 24
Glyceria of Heraclea	*May* 13
Goar	*July* 6
Goban	*June* 20
Godeberta	*April* 11
Godehard	**May 4**
Godeleva	*July* 6
Godfrey (of Amiens)	**November 8**
Godric	*May* 21
Goericus (or Abbo)	*September* 19
Gohard	*June* 25
Gommaire. *See* Gummarus	
Gonsalo Garcia. *See* Martyrs of Japan	
Gontran. *See* Guntramnus	
Good Thief, The (Dismas)	*March* 25
Gorazd. *See* Clement of Okhrida	
Gordian	*May* 10
Gorgonia	*December* 9
Gorgonius (martyr)	*September* 9
Gorgonius (with Peter)	*March* 12
Gothard. *See* Godehard	
Gottschalk	*June* 7
Gregory the Great	**September 3**
Gregory II	*February* 11
Gregory III	**December 10**
Gregory VII	*May* 25
Gregory Barbarigo	*June* 18
Gregory Lopez	*July* 20
Gregory Makar	*March* 16
Gregory Nazianzen	*January* 2
Gregory of Girgenti	*November* 23

John of the Goths	*June 26*
John of Kanti	**December 23**
John of Matera (or of Pulsano)	*June 20*
John of Matha	*February 8*
John of Meda	*September 26*
John of Nicomedia	*September 7*
John of Panaca	*March 19*
John of Sahagun	**June 12**
John of Vilna	*April 14*
John the Almsgiver	**January 23**
John of the Cross	**December 14**
John the Dwarf	*October 17*
John of God	**March 8**
John the Good	*January 10*
John 'of the Grating'	*February 1*
John the Iberian	*July 12*
John the Silent	**May 13**
Jonas (with Barachisius)	*March 29*
Josaphat (with Barlaam)	*November 27*
Josaphat (of Polotsk)	**November 12**
Joseph	**March 19**
the Worker	*May 1*
Joseph Barsabas	*July 20*
Joseph Cafasso	*June 23*
Joseph Calasanctius	*August 25*
Joseph Cottolengo	*April 29*
Joseph Mkasa	**June 3**
Joseph Oriol	*March 23*
Joseph Pignatelli	*November 28*
Joseph of Arimathea	*March 17*
Joseph of Cupertino	**September 18**
Joseph of Leonessa	*February 4*
Joseph of Palestine (*comes*)	*July 22*
Josepha Rossello	*December 7*
Josse. *See* Judoc	
Judas Quiriacus. *See* Cyriacus	
Jude (or Thaddeus) (apostle)	**October 28**
Judith	*June 29*
Judoc (or Josse)	**December 13**
Julia Billiart	**April 8**
Julia of Corsica	*May 22*
Julian (with Basilissa)	*January 9*
Julian (with Caesarius)	*November 1*
Julian (with Cronion)	*February 27*
Julian (with Theodulus)	*February 17*
Julian Sabas	*January 17*
Julian of Antioch	*March 16*
Julian of Brioude	*August 28*
Julian of Le Mans	*January 27*
Julian of Toledo	*March 8*
Julian the Hospitaller	*February 12*
Juliana Falconieri	**June 19**
Juliana of Cumae	*February 16*
Julitta (with Cyricus)	*June 16*
Julitta of Caesarea	*July 30*
Julius (with Aaron)	*July 3*
Julius I (pope)	*April 12*
Julius of Durostorum	*May 27*
Justa (with Rufina)	*July 19*

Justin (martyr)	*June 1*
Justin de Jacobis	*July 31*
Justina of Padua	*October 7*
Justus (with Pastor)	*August 6*
Justus of Beauvais	*October 18*
Justus of Canterbury	*November 10*
Justus of Lyons	*October 14*
Justus of Urgel	*May 28*
Jutta	*May 5*
Juvenal of Narni	*May 3*
Juventinus	*January 25*

K

Katherine. *See* Catherine	
Kenelm	*July 17*
Kenneth. *See* Canice	
Kennoch. *See* Mochoemoc	
Kentigern (or Mungo)	*January 14*
Kentigerna. *See* Fillan	
Kessog	*March 10*
Kevin (or Coemgen)	*June 3*
Keyne	**October 8**
Kieran of Clonmacnois	*September 9*
Kieran of Saighir (or of Ossory)	*March 5*
Kilian (martyr)	*July 8*

L

Ladislaus of Hungary	*June 27*
Laetus (with Donatian)	*September 6*
Laisren. *See* Laserian	
Lambert of Lyons	*April 14*
Lambert of Maestricht	*September 17*
Lambert of Venice	*May 26*
Landelinus (abbot)	*June 15*
Landericus (or Landry) of Paris	*June 10*
Landoald	*March 19*
Landry. *See* Landericus	
Largus (with Cyriacus)	*August 8*
Laserian (or Molaisse)	*April 18*
Laurence (martyr)	**August 10**
Laurence Giustiniani	**September 5**
Laurence O'Toole	**November 14**
Laurence of Brindisi	**July 21**
Laurence of Canterbury	*February 3*
Laurence of Spoleto	*February 3*
Laurentinus (with Pergentinus)	*June 3*
Laurus	*August 18*
Lazarus	*December 17*
Lazarus of Milan	*February 11*
Leander of Seville	*February 27*
Lebuin (or Liafwine)	*November 12*
Leger (or Leodegarius)	*October 2*
Lelia	*August 11*

Leo (with Paragorius)	*February* 18
Leo the Great	**November 10**
Leo II	*July* 3
Leo III	*June* 12
Leo IV	*July* 17
Leo IX	*April* 19
Leo (or Lyé) of Mantenay	*May* 25
Leobinus (or Lubin)	**March 14**
Leocadia	*December* 9
Leocritia. *See* Lucretia	
Leodegarius. *See* Leger	
Leonard Murialdo	*March* 30
Leonard of Noblac	*November* 6
Leonard of Port Maurice	*November* 26
Leonard of Vandoeuvre	*October* 15
Leonides of Alexandria	*April* 22
Leontius of Rostov	*May* 23
Leopold of Austria	*November* 15
Lésin. *See* Licinius	
Lesmes. *See* Adelelmus	
Leu. *See* Lupus of Sens	
Leufroy. *See* Leutfridus	
Leutfridus (or Leufroy)	*June* 21
Lewina	*July* 24
Lewis. *See* Louis	
Liafwine. *See* Lebuin	
Liberata. *See* Wilgefortis	
Liberatus of Capua	*August* 17
Libert. *See* Lietbertus	
Liborius	*July* 23
Licinius (or Lésin)	*February* 13
Lietbertus (or Libert)	*June* 23
Lifard. *See* Liphardus	
Limnaeus	*February* 22
Lioba	*September* 28
Liphard. *See* Liudhard	
Liphardus (or Lifard)	*June* 3
Liudhard	*May* 7
Livinus	*November* 12
Loman	*February* 17
Longinus	*March* 15
Louis of France (Louis IX)	**August 25**
Louis Bertrand	**October 9**
Louis Grignion of Montfort	*April* 28
Louis Versiglia	*February* 25
Louis of Anjou	*August* 19
Louise de Marillac	**March 15**
Loup. *See* Lupus of Troyes	
Luan. *See* Moloc	
Lubin. *See* Leobinus	
Lucian (with Marcian)	*October* 26
Lucian of Antioch	*January* 7
Lucian of Beauvais	*January* 8
Lucillian	*June* 3
Lucius ('king')	*December* 3
Lucius (with Montanus)	*February* 24
Lucius (with Ptolemaeus)	*October* 19
Lucius of Adrianople	*February* 11
Lucretia (or Leocritia)	*March* 15

Lucy (martyr)	*December* 13
Lucy Filippini	**March 25**
Ludan	*February* 12
Ludger	*March* 26
Ludmila	*September* 16
Ludolf	*March* 30
Lufthildis	*January* 23
Lughaidh. *See* Molua	
Luke (evangelist)	**October 18**
Luke Kirby	*May* 30
Luke the Younger	**February 7**
Lull	*October* 16
Lupicinus	*February* 28
Lupus (or Leu) of Sens	*September* 1
Lupus (or Loup) of Troyes	*July* 29
Lutgardis	**June 16**
Luxorius	*August* 21
Lyé. *See* Leo of Mantenay	

M

Macanisius	*September* 3
Macarius of Alexandria	*January* 2
Macarius of Ghent	*April* 10
Macarius of Jerusalem	*March* 10
Macarius the Elder	*January* 15
Macarius the Wonderworker	*April* 1
Macartan	*March* 26
Maccul *See* Maughold	
Macedonius the Barley-eater	*January* 24
Machabees, The Holy	*August* 1
Machar (or Mochumma)	*November* 12
Machutus. *See* Malo	
Macrina the Elder	*January* 14
Macrina the Younger	**July 19**
Madeleine Sophie Barat	**May 25**
Madelgaire. *See* Vincent Madelgarius	
Madelgisilus (or Maugeille)	*May* 30
Madern *See* Madron	
Madron (or Madern)	*May* 17
Maedoc. *See* Aidan of Ferns	
Maelor. *See* Maglorius	
Maelrubha. *See* Malrubius	
Mafalda	*May* 2
Magenulf (or Meinulf)	*October* 5
Magi, The	*July* 23
Maglorius (or Maelor)	*October* 24
Magnericus	*July* 25
Magnus of Orkney	*April* 16
Maharsapor	*October* 10
Maimbod	*January* 23
Majolus (or Mayeul)	*May* 11
Majoricus	*December* 6
Malachy of Armagh	*November* 3
Malchus	*October* 21
Mallonus. *See* Mellon	
Malo (or Machutus)	*November* 15

Malrubius (or Maelrubha)	*April* 21
Mamas	*August* 17
Mamertus	*May* 11
Mamilian. *See* Maximilian (martyr)	
Manechildis (or Ménéhould)	*October* 14
Manettus. *See* Founders of the Servites	
Mappalicus	*April* 17
Marcella of Rome	*January* 31
Marcellian (with Mark)	*June* 18
Marcellina	*July* 17
Marcellinus (with Peter)	*June* 2
Marcellinus of Carthage	*April* 6
Marcellinus of Embrun	*April* 20
Marcellus (with Apuleius)	*October* 8
Marcellus (with Valerian)	*September* 4
Marcellus I (pope)	*January* 16
Marcellus (of Apamea)	**August 14**
Marcellus of Paris	*November* 1
Marcellus of Tomi	*August* 27
Marcellus Akimetes	*December* 29
Marcellus the Centurion	*October* 30
Marchelm	*July* 14
Marcian (or Marian)	*April* 20
Marcian (with Lucian)	*October* 26
Marcian (with Nicander)	*June* 17
Marcian of Constantinople	*January* 10
Marcian (of Cyrrhus)	**November 2**
Marciana of Rusuccur	*January* 9
Marcoul. *See* Marculf	
Marculf (or Marcoul)	**May 1**
Margaret Bourgeoys	*January* 12
Margaret Clitherow	*March* 25
Margaret-Mary	**October 16**
Margaret Ward	*August* 30
Margaret of Cortona	**February 22**
Margaret 'of England'	*February* 3
Margaret of Hungary	*January* 26
Margaret of Scotland	**November 16**
Margaret the Barefooted	*August* 27
Margaret the Penitent. *See* Pelagia the Penitent	
Mari	**August 5**
Maria Goretti	**July 6**
Marian. *See* Marcian	
Marian (with James)	*April* 30
Mariana of Quito	*May* 26
Marina (or Margaret)	*July* 20
Marina (or Pelagia)	*February* 12
Marinus (San Marino)	*September* 4
Marinus (with Astyrius)	*March* 3
Marius (or May)	*January* 27
Marius (with Martha)	*January* 19
Mark (evangelist)	**April 25**
Mark (pope)	*October* 7
Mark (or Martin)	*October* 24
Mark (with Marcellian)	*June* 18
Mark of Arethusa	*March* 29
Maro	*February* 14
Mars. *See* Martius	

Martha	*July* 29
Martha (with Marius)	*January* 19
Martial (with Faustus)	*October* 13
Martial of Limoges	*June* 30
Martin (or Mark)	*October* 24
Martin I (pope)	*April* 13
Martin de Porres	**November 3**
Martin of Braga	*March* 20
Martin (of Tours)	**November 11**
Martin of Vertou	*October* 24
Martinian (with Maxima)	*October* 16
Martinian (with Processus)	*July* 2
Martinian the Hermit	*February* 13
Martius (or Mars)	*April* 13
Martyrius (with Sisinnius)	*May* 29
Martyrs of Arras	*June* 27
Martyrs of Compiègne, Carmelite	*July* 17
Martyrs of Crete, The Ten	*December* 23
Martyrs of Damascus	*July* 10
Martyrs under the Danes	*April* 10
Martyrs of Dorchester	*July* 4
Martyrs of Douay	*October* 29
Martyrs of Ebsdorf	*February* 2
Martyrs of England & Wales, Forty	*Oct* 25
Martyrs of Gorcum	*July* 9
Martyrs of Japan	*February* 6
Martyrs of Korea	*September* 21
Martyrs of Lithuania	*April* 14
Martyrs under the Lombards	*March* 2
Martyrs of Lyons	*June* 2
Martyrs of Mar Saba	*March* 20
Martyrs of Najran	*October* 24
Martyrs of Church of Rome, First	**June 30**
Martyrs at Nicomedia	*December* 25
Martyrs of North America	**October 19**
Martyrs of Orange	*July* 9
Martyrs of Paraguay	*November* 17
Martyrs in Persia, The CXX	*April* 6
Martyrs of the Alexandrian Plague	*Feb* 28
Martyrs of Prague, Servite	*August* 31
Martyrs of Salsette	*July* 27
Martyrs of Samosata, The Seven	*December* 9
Martyrs of Scillium	*July* 17
Martyrs of September 1792	*September* 2
Martyrs of the Serapeum	*March* 17
Martyrs of Sinai	*January* 14
Martyrs of Toulouse	*May* 29
Martyrs of Uganda	**June 3**
Martyrs of Utica	*August* 24
Martyrs of Valenciennes, Ursuline	*October* 17
Maruthas	*December* 4
Mary, The Blessed Virgin	
the Annunciation	*March* 25
her Assumption	**August 15**
her Birthday	*September* 8
her Immaculate Conception	*December* 8
her Motherhood	*January* 1
her Presentation	*November* 21
her Queenship	*August* 22

her Sorrows	*September* 15	May. *See* Marius	
her Visit to Elizabeth	*May* 31	Mayeul. *See* Majolus	
Our Lady of Lourdes	*February* 11	**Mechtildis of Edelstetten**	**May 31**
Our Lady of Mount Carmel	*July* 16	Mechtildis of Helfta	*November* 16
Our Lady of Ransom	*September* 24	Medard	*June* 8
the Holy Rosary	*October* 7	**Medericus (or Merry)**	**August 29**
Mary (martyr)	*November* 1	Méen (or Mewan)	*June* 21
Mary (with Flora)	*November* 24	Meingold	*February* 8
Mary Cleophas	*April* 9	**Meinrad**	**January 21**
Mary Desmaisières	*August* 26	Meinulf. *See* Magenulf	
Mary Frances	*October* 6	Mel	*February* 6
Mary Magdalen	*July* 22	Melaine	*November* 6
Mary Magdalen dei Pazzi	*May* 25	Melangel (or Monacella)	*May* 27
Mary Magdalen Postel	*July* 16	Melania the Younger	*December* 31
Mary Mazzarello	*May* 14	Melchiades. *See* Miltiades	
Mary Pelletier	*April* 24	Melchu	*February* 6
Mary di Rosa	**December 15**	**Meletius**	**February 12**
Mary Soledad	**October 11**	Meleusippus	*January* 17
Mary of Cerevellon	*September* 19	Meliot	*April* 1
Mary of Egypt	*April* 2	Mellitus of Canterbury	*April* 24
Maternus of Cologne	*September* 14	Mellon (or Mallonus)	*October* 22
Mathurin. *See* Maturinus		Melorus. *See* Mylor	
Matilda. *See* Mechtildis		Ménéhould. *See* Manechildis	
Matilda (widow)	*March* 14	Mannas (with Hermogenes)	*December* 10
Matrona	*March* 15	Mennas of Constantinople	*August* 25
Matthew (evangelist)	*September* 21	Mannas of Egypt	*November* 11
Matthias (apostle)	*May* 14	Menodora	*September* 10
Matthias Murumba Lwanga. *See* Charles Lwanga		Mercurius of Caesarea	*November* 25
		Meriadoc (or Meriasek)	*June* 7
Maturinus (or Mathurin)	*November* 1	Meriasek. *See* Meriadoc	
Maturus. *See* Pothinus		Merry. *See* Medericus	
Maudez. *See* Mawes		Mesrop	*February* 19
Maughold (or Maccul)	*April* 27	Messalina. *See* Felician of Foligno	
Maugille. *See* Madelgisilus		**Methodius (with Cyril)**	**February 14**
Maura (with Brigid)	*July* 13	**Methodius (of Constantinople)**	**June 14**
Maura (with Timothy)	*May* 3	Methodius of Olympus	*September* 18
Maura of Leucadia. *See* Anne (virgin)		Metrodora	*September* 10
Maura of Troyes	*September* 21	Metrophanes	*June* 4
Maurice of Agaunum	*September* 22	Meuris. *See* Nemesius	
Maurice of Carnoët	*October* 13	Mewan. *See* Méen	
Maurilius of Angers	*September* 13	Michael (archangel)	*September* 29
Mauruntius	*May* 5	**Michael Garicoïts**	**May 14**
Mawes (or Maudez)	*November* 18	Michael de Sanctis	*April* 10
Maxellendis	*November* 13	**Michael of Chernigov**	**September 21**
Maxentia of Beauvais	*November* 20	Milburga	*February* 23
Maxentius (abbot)	*June* 26	Mildgytha. *See* Milburga	
Maxima (with Martinian)	*October* 16	Mildred	*July* 13
Maximian (with Bonosus)	*August* 21	Miltiades (or Melchiades)	*December* 10
Maximilian (martyr)	*March* 12	Mirin	*September* 15
Maximilian Kolbe	*August* 14	Mochoemoc	*March* 13
Maximilian of Lorch	*October* 12	Mochta	*August* 19
Maximinus (with Juventinus)	*January* 25	Mochuda. *See* Carthage	
Maximinus of Aix	*June* 8	Mochumma. *See* Machar	
Maximinus of Trier	*May* 29	Mocius. *See* Mucius	
Maximus (with Tiburtius)	*April* 14	Modan	*February* 4
Maximus of Ephesus	*April* 30	Modoaldus	*May* 12
Maximus of Riez	*November* 27	Modomnoc	*February* 13
Maximus of Turin	*June* 25	Modwenna	*July* 6
Maximus the Confessor	**August 13**	Molaise. *See* Laserian	

Oswin	*August* 20
Osith	**October 7**
Otger	*May* 8
Otteran (or Odhran) of Iona	*October* 27
Ottilia. *See* Odilia	
Otto (of Bamberg)	**July 2**
Oudoceus. *See* Teilo	
Ouen (or Audoenus)	**August 24**
Outril. *See* Austregisilus	
Oyend. *See* Eugendus	

P

Pachomius	**May 9**
Pacifico of San Severino	*September* 24
Pacian	*March* 9
Padarn (or Patern)	*April* 15
Pair. *See* Paternus of Avranches	
Palladius (bishop in Ireland)	**July 7**
Pambo	*July* 18
Pammachius	**August 30**
Pamphilus of Caesarea	*June* 1
Pamphilus of Sulmona	*April* 28
Pancras (martyr)	*May* 12
Pancras of Taormina	*April* 3
Pantaenus	*July* 7
Pantaleon (or Panteleimon)	*July* 27
Panteleimon. *See* Pantaleon	
Paphnutius (bishop)	**September 11**
Papylus	*April* 13
Paregorius	*February* 18
Parisio	*June* 11
Parthenius (with Calocerus)	*May* 19
Paschal I (pope)	*February* 11
Paschal Baylon	**May 17**
Paschasius Radbertus	*April* 26
Pastor (with Justus)	*August* 6
Patern of Ceredigion. *See* Padarn	
Paternus of Abdinghof	*April* 10
Paternus (or Pair) of Avranches	*April* 16
Patiens of Lyons	*September* 11
Patricia	*August* 25
Patrick	**March 17**
Patroclus of Troyes	*January* 21
Paul (apostle)	*June* 29
his Conversion	**January 25**
Paul (with Thea)	*July* 25
Paul I (pope)	*June* 28
Paul Aurelian (or of Léon)	*March* 12
Paul Miki	**February 6**
Paul I of Constantinople	*June* 7
Paul IV of Constantinople	*August* 28
Paul of Cyprus	*March* 17
Paul of Latros	*December* 15
Paul of Narbonne	*March* 22
Paul of the Cross	*October* 19
Paul the Simple	*March* 7

Paula (widow)	*January* 26
Paula Frassinetti	*June* 12
Paulinus of Aquileia	*January* 28
Paulinus of Nola	*June* 22
Paulinus of Trier	*August* 31
Paulinus of York	*October* 10
Pega	*January* 8
Pelagia of Antioch	*June* 9
Pelagia of Tarsus	*Mary* 4
Pelagia (or Margaret) the Penitent	*October* 8
Pelagius of Cordova	*June* 26
Peleus	*September* 19
Peregrine Laziosi	*May* 1
Peregrine of Auxerre	*May* 16
Pergentinus	*June* 3
Perpetus (with Felicity)	*March* 7
Perpetuus of Tours	*April* 8
Peter (apostle)	**June 29**
his Chair at Antioch	*February* 22
his Chair at Rome	*January* 18
his Chair *ad Vincula*	*August* 1
Peter (with Gorgonius)	*March* 12
Peter (with Marcellinus)	*June* 2
Peter Arbues	*September* 17
Peter Balsam	*January* 3
Peter Baptist. *See* Martyrs of Japan	
Peter Canisius	**December 21**
Peter Chrysologus	**July 30**
Peter Claver	*September* 9
Peter Damian	**February 21**
Peter Julian Eymard	**August 1**
Peter Fourier	**December**
Peter Martyr (or of Verona)	*April* 20
Peter Mary Chanel	**April 28**
Peter Morrone	*May* 19
Peter Nolasco	*January* 28
Peter Orseolo	**January 10**
Peter Regalatus	*May* 13
Peter Thomas	*January* 28
Peter of Alcantara	*October* 19
Peter of Alexandria	*November* 26
Peter of Athos	*June* 12
Peter of Atroa	**January 1**
Peter of Braga	*April* 26
Peter of Cava	*March* 4
Peter of Chavanon	*September* 11
Peter of Lampsacus	*May* 15
Peter of Narbonne	*November* 14
Peter of Sebastea	*January* 9
Peter of Tarentaise	**May 8**
Petroc	*June* 4
Petronax	**May 6**
Petronilla	*May* 31
Petronius of Bologna	*October* 4
Pharaïldis	*January* 4
Philastrius	*July* 8
Phileas	*February* 4
Philemon (with Apollonius)	*March* 8
Philemon (with Apphia)	*November* 22

Rigobert	*January* 4
Riquier. *See* Richarius	
Rita of Cascia	**May 22**
Robert Bellarmine	*September* 17
Robert Lawrence	*May* 4
Robert Southwell	*February* 21
Robert of Chaise-Dieu	*April* 17
Robert of Molesmes	*April* 29
Robert of Newminster	*June* 7
Rock	*August* 17
Roderic	*March* 13
Rogatian (with Donatian)	*May* 24
Romanus (or Boris)	*July* 24
Romanus (monk)	*May* 22
Romanus (martyr)	*August* 9
Romanus	**February 28**
Romanus of Antioch	*November* 18
Romanus of Rouen	*October* 23
Romanus the Melodist	*October* 1
Romaric	**December 8**
Rombaut. *See* Rumold	
Romuald	*June* 19
Romula	*July* 23
Romulus of Fiesole	*July* 6
Ronan. *See* Rumon	
Rosalia	*September* 4
Rose of Lima	**August 23**
Rose of Viterbo	**September 4**
Rosendo. *See* Rudesind	
Ruadan	*April* 15
Ruan. *See* Rumon	
Rudesind (or Rosendo)	*March* 1
Rufina (with Justa)	*July* 19
Rufina (with Secunda)	*July* 10
Rufinus (with Valerius)	*June* 14
Rufus (with Zosimus)	*December* 18
Rumold (or Rombaut)	*July* 3
Rumon (or Ruan)	*August* 30
Rumwald	*November* 3
Rupert (with Bertha)	*May* 15
Rupert (of Salzburg)	**March 29**
Rusticus (with Dionysius)	*October* 9
Rusticus of Narbonne	*October* 26

S

Sabas (abbot)	**December 5**
Sabas the Goth	*April* 12
Sabina of Rome	*August* 29
Sabinian of Troyes	*January* 29
Sabinus of Canosa	*February* 9
Sabinus of Piacenza	*January* 17
Sabinus of Spoleto	*December* 30
Sadoth	*February* 20
Sahak. *See* Isaac	
Saire. *See* Salvius (hermit)	
Salaberga	*September* 22

Salome (with Judith)	*June* 29
Salvator of Horta	*March* 18
Salvius (or Saire), hermit	*October* 28
Salvius (or Sauve)(with Superius)	*June* 26
Salvius (or Salvy) of Albi	*September* 10
Salvius (or Sauve) of Amiens	*January* 11
Salvy. *See* Salvius of Albi	
Samonas	*November* 15
Samson of Constantinople	*June* 27
Samson of Dol	**July 28**
Sanchia of Portugal	**June 17**
Sancho. *See* Sanctius	
Sanctius (or Sancho)	*June* 5
Sanctus. *See* Pothinus	
Šapor	*November* 30
Saturninus (martyr)	*November* 29
Saturninus (with Dativus)	*February* 11
Saturninus (or Sernin) of Toulouse	*Nov* 29
Saturus (with Armogastes)	*March* 29
Satyrus of Milan	*September* 17
Sauve. *See* Salvius	
Sava	**January 14**
Savin	*October* 9
Scholastica	**February 10**
Sebald	*August* 19
Sebastian (martyr)	*January* 20
Sebbe	*September* 1
Sechnall. *See* Secundinus	
Secunda (with Rufina)	*July* 10
Secundinus (or Sechnall)	*November* 27
Seine. *See* Sequanus	
Senan of Scattery	*March* 8
Senator of Milan	*May* 28
Sennen	*July* 30
Senoch	*October* 24
Sequanus (or Seine)	*September* 19
Seraphina (or Fina)	*March* 12
Seraphino	*October* 17
Serapion of Antioch	*October* 30
Serapion of Thmuis	*March* 21
Serenicus	*May* 7
Serenus (with Serenicus)	*May* 7
Serenus (or Cerneuf) the Gardener	*February* 23
Serf (or Servanus)	*July* 1
Sergius I (pope)	*September* 8
Sergius of Radonezh	*September* 25
Sergius of Valaam	*June* 28
Sernin. *See* Saturninus of Toulouse	
Servais. *See* Servatius	
Servanus. *See* Serf	
Servatius (or Servais)	*May* 13
Servite Order, Seven Holy Founders	**Feb 17**
Servulus of Rome	*December* 23
Sethrida	*July* 7
Seurin. *See* Severinus of Bordeaux	
Seven Sleepers, The	*July* 27
Severian of Scythopolis	*February* 21
Severinus Boethius	*October* 23

T

Vedast (or Vaast)	*February* 6
Venantius Fortunatus	*December* 14
Venerius of Milan	*May* 4
Veremund (abbot)	*March* 8
Verena	*September* 1
Veronica	*July* 12
Veronica Giuliani	*July* 9
Viator. *See* Justus of Lyons	
Vicelin	*December* 12
Victor Maurus	*May* 8
Victor of Marseilles	*July* 21
Victor the Hermit	*February* 26
Victoria. *See* Saturninus, with Dativus	
Victoria (with Acisclus)	*November* 17
Victoria (with Anatolia)	*December* 23
Victorian (abbot)	*January* 12
Victorian (martyr)	*March* 23
Victoricus (with Fuscian)	*December* 11
Victorinus of Corinth	*February* 25
Victorinus of Pettau	*November* 2
Victricius	*August* 7
Vigilius of Trent	*June* 26
Vigor	*November* 1
Vincent Ferrer	**April 5**
Vincent Madelgarius	**September 20**
Vincent Pallotti	**January 22**
Vincent de Paul	**September 27**
Vincent Strambi	*September* 25
Vincent of Agen	*June* 9
Vincent of Lérins	**May 24**
Vincent of Saragossa	*January* 22
Vincentia Gerosa	*June* 4
Vincentia Lopez	*December* 26
Vincentian	*January* 2
Vindician	*March* 11
Virgil of Arles	*March* 5
Virgil (of Salzburg)	**November 27**
Vitalian (pope)	*January* 27
Vitalis (with Agricola)	*November* 4
Vitalis (with Valeria)	*April* 28
Vitonus. *See* Vanne	
Vitus (with Modestus)	*June* 15
Vladimir	*July* 15
Vodalus (or Voel)	*February* 5
Voel. *See* Vodalus	
Valusian	*January* 18
Vulflagius (or Wulphy)	*June* 7
Vulmar	**July 20**

W

Walaricus. *See* Valéry	
Walburga	*February* 25
Waldebert	*May* 2
Waldetrudis (or Waudru)	**April 9**
Walfrid (or Galfrido)	*February* 15
Walstan	*May* 30

Walter of L'Esterp	*May* 11
Walter of Pontoise	*April* 8
Walthen. *See* Waltheof	
Waltheof (or Walthen)	**August 3**
Wandregesilus. *See* Wandrille	
Wandrille (or Wandregesilus)	*July* 22
Waningus (or Vaneng)	*January* 9
Waudru. *See* Waldetrudis	
Wenceslaus of Bohemia	**September 28**
Werburga	*February* 3
Wiborada	*May* 2
Wigbert	*August* 13
Wilfrid	**October 12**
Wilfrid the Younger	*April* 29
Wilgefortis (or Liberata)	*July* 20
Willehad	*November* 8
William Firmatus	*April* 24
William of Bourges	*January* 10
William of Eskilsoë	**April 6**
William of Gellone	*May* 28
William of Maleval	*February* 10
William of Norwich	*March* 24
William of Rochester	*May* 23
William (of Roskilde)	**September 2**
William of Saint Benignus	*January* 1
William of Saint-Brieuc	*July* 29
William of Toulouse (martyr)	**May 29**
William of Vercelli (or Monte Vergine)	**June 25**
William of York (or of Thwayt)	**June 8**
Willibald	*June* 7
Willibrord	**November 7**
Willigis	*February* 23
Wiltrudis	*January* 6
Winebald	*December* 18
Winifred (or Gwenfrewi)	*November* 3
Winnoc	*November* 6
Winwaloe (or Guénolé)	*March* 3
Wiro	*May* 8
Wisdom (with Faith)	*August* 1
Wistan	*June* 1
Wite (or Candida)	*June* 1
Withburga	**July 8**
Wivina	*December* 17
Wolfgang	**October 31**
Wolfhard (or Gualfardus)	*April* 30
Woolo. *See* Gundleus	
Wulfram	*March* 20
Wulfric	**February 20**
Wulfstan	**January 19**
Wulphy. *See* Vulflagius	
Wulain	*January* 8
Wulstan. *See* Wulfatan	

X

Xystus. *See* Sixtus